ADDICTION TREATMENT

ADDICTION TREATMENT

A Strengths Perspective

SECOND EDITION

Katherine van Wormer
University of Northern Iowa

Diane Rae Davis
Eastern Washington University

BROOKS/COLE
CENGAGE Learning

Australia • Brazil • Japan • Korea • Mexico • Singapore • Spain • United Kingdom • United States

BROOKS/COLE
CENGAGE Learning-

Addiction Treatment:
A Strengths Perspective,
Second Edition
Katherine van Wormer,
Diane Rae Davis

Acquisitions Editor: Dan Alpert

Development Editor:
Tangelique Williams

Assistant Editor:
Ann Lee Richards

Editorial Assistant:
Stephanie Rue

Technology Project Manager:
Julie Aguilar

Marketing Manager:
Meghan McCullough

Marketing Assistant:
Teresa Marino

Marketing Communications
Manager: Shemika Britt

Project Manager, Editorial
Production: Christy Krueger

Creative Director: Rob Hugel

Art Director: Vernon Boes

Print Buyer: Nora Massuda

Permissions Editor:
Roberta Broyer

Production Service:
Aaron Downey/Matrix
Productions Inc.

Copy Editor: Frank Hubert

Cover Designer: Ross Carron

Cover Image: © Taylor S.
Kennedy/Getty Images

Compositor: ICC Macmillan Inc.

For product information and technology assistance, contact us at
Cengage Learning Customer & Sales Support, 1-800-354-9706

For permission to use material from this text or product, submit all requests online at **cengage.com/permissions**
Further permissions questions can be emailed to
permissionrequest@cengage.com

Library of Congress Control Number: 2007921099

ISBN-13: 978-0-495-09082-3

ISBN-10: 0-495-09082-4

Brooks/Cole
10 Davis Drive
Belmont, CA 94002-3098
USA

Cengage Learning is a leading provider of customized learning solutions with office locations around the globe, including Singapore, the United Kingdom, Australia, Mexico, Brazil, and Japan. Locate your local office at: **international.cengage.com/region**

Cengage Learning products are represented in Canada by Nelson Education, Ltd.

For your course and learning solutions, visit **academic.cengage.com**

Purchase any of our products at your local college store or at our preferred online store **www.ichapters.com**

Printed in the United States of America
4 5 6 7 11 10

To the frontline workers in the field of addiction, to the men and women for whom substance abuse treatment is not only a profession but a mission, who so often "have been there" themselves, persons who care so much that they may even burn out eventually, but who in the meantime will help save people from the demon that is addiction. We need to keep in mind that for every individual helped, one whole family is spared—from child abuse, violence, bankruptcy. Therefore, with gratitude to the professional helpers and AA/NA sponsors alike, I dedicate my contribution to this book to you.

And, in particular, to my son, Rupert van Wormer, MSW, a mental health case manager and harm reduction specialist who works with sheltered homeless drug addicts in Seattle (you can read about his work in chapter 8).
—Katherine van Wormer

To my family, who support me no matter what with their love—Zach, Andy, John, Jayne, Mike, and Donna—and to the men and women who are taking their lives back from addiction.
—Diane Rae Davis

Contents

PART 3 | THE PSYCHOLOGY OF ADDICTION 227

PART 4 | THE SOCIAL ASPECTS OF ADDICTION 377

There is nothing so practical as good theory.

—Kurt Lewin

Preface

In the 5 years since the publication of the first edition, the interest in the development and refinement of a strengths-based approach to work with addicted populations has continued to impact the field. Strengths-based practices increasingly are being adapted by mental health agencies and other fields of practice (Rapp & Goscha, 2006). Even more striking is the parallel growth and heightened attention devoted to harm reduction as a goal and as a process. Books have been published, conferences held, articles written in mainstream journals, and university courses shaped to focus on or at least incorporate principles of harm reduction. Workshops and lectures on the related principles of motivational interviewing and on treatment interventions tailored for the individual's stage of motivation to change have proliferated exponentially.

The response to the first edition of *Addiction Treatment: A Strengths Perspective,* both by readers of the book and by critics, has been gratifying. In fact, the only criticism was that the theoretical framework of harm reduction was not emphasized to a greater degree than it was. Because of the consistently positive response to the book's theme of harm reduction, in this edition we have bolstered our harm reduction emphasis both in terms of policy and practice through a motivational enhancement model.

A second development in the addiction field since the turn of this century has been further evolution in the theory and practice of treatment for persons with co-occurring disorders (having both a substance-related and serious mental disorder) (Center for Substance Abuse Treatment, 2005). Hence, this edition infuses content throughout the chapters on the treatment needs of substance using persons with mental health disorders.

War-related trauma increasingly is an issue at all treatment centers today due to the wars in Iraq and Afghanistan, especially at Veterans Administration (VA) hospitals. Facts concerning the treatment needs of returning soldiers, accordingly, have been incorporated in this text.

The criminal justice system is swelling. More than 1 million inmates incarcerated today are serving time for drug-related crimes. Substance abuse agencies and their staff are far more involved than in previous years in providing services to incarcerated men and women and to persons on probation and parole. This new edition, therefore, includes extensive material on the treatment needs of clients involved in the criminal justice system.

Is cutting down on drinking and drug use a realistic option for alcoholics/addicts? Or is total abstinence the only path to recovery? The moderation versus abstinence controversy is easily the most hotly contested issue in substance abuse treatment today. Each position has its strengths, and each carries inherent risks. Addiction counselors who help clients merely moderate their destructive behavior run the risk of giving some of their clients false hopes and setting them up for failure. Proponents of immediate and total abstinence, on the other hand, can rest assured that they will drive away the majority of people who might otherwise come to them for help. Opponents on one side or the other of this controversy are discussing the issue both behind closed doors at the treatment center and openly on TV talk shows, in newspaper editorials, and on social work and counseling LISTSERVs. This debate—moderation versus abstinence—which has been part of the European scene for decades, has now reached American shores. Unfortunately, the debate in the United States sometimes resembles a feud. How addiction treatment providers and their political allies resolve this dilemma will largely determine the shape of addiction treatment in the 21st century.

That it is no small matter is revealed, for example, in the case of Dr. Alex De Luca, the chief of an addiction treatment center in Manhattan, who earlier was forced to resign after he announced a plan to include a moderation management option for problem drinkers. "I was merely suggesting that you could engage people in a kinder, gentler manner," Dr. De Luca explained, "rather than telling them that they had to sign up for a goal achieving abstinence from the beginning" (Steinhaver, 2000, p. A26).

Addiction treatment in the United States today is at a crossroads. Increasingly, the Twelve-Step–total abstinence model and, more broadly, the disease concept are being subjected to public and professional scrutiny (see, e.g., Carroll & Miller, 2006; Mancini, Linhorst, Broderick, & Bayliff, in press; Wallace, 2005). This very questioning by commentators, and even the vociferous counterresponse by representatives of mainstream organizations, is testimony to the fact that change is in the wind. Why shouldn't counselors, as some commentators and even some substance abuse counselors are asking, be available to help people just cut down on their drinking and other drug use, protect themselves, even in small ways, from harm, and thereby enhance their motivation for change? Why not keep our treatment options open?

Granted there have been attacks on the "one-size-fits-all" approach from the beginning. What is new today is first that the attacks have been widely publicized and second that much of the questioning of the orthodox position is coming from within the treatment field itself. Additionally, some viable alternative models are being used and being used successfully. (For a German perspective on the same debate, see Koerkel, 2002.)

The favorable mass media coverage of moderation efforts, the volume of professional critiques of the disease-model premises, the slew of harm reduction workshops are all signals of impending change and a paradigm shift of sorts. Central to this shift is the realization that so many people in desperate need of treatment—with binge drinking, compulsive cocaine use, and other high-risk behaviors—will never seek help under present circumstances and that many literally will die as a result.

Hence, this book: a new book for a new day. Consistent with the strengths approach, this is not a book that lambastes, denigrates, or ridicules contributions of pioneers who have charted the course in substance abuse treatment. Indeed, many thought-provoking and volatile critiques of the addiction-as-disease model have already been written. Much that needed to be said has been said. Now is the time to move forward, to reconcile differences, and to get on with the task of helping people in the throes of addiction. So, no, this is not a book to tear down methods that have a history of success, methods in the promotion of which both authors have been personally involved. In our fascination in determining which faction is correct and who owns the soul of chemical dependence treatment—the abstinence or individual responsibility folk—we lose sight of the complete picture.

Tearing down is simple. The primary task of *Addiction Treatment* is more complicated than that; the task is to shape a text grounded in a strengths or empowerment perspective, a theoretical framework that is inclusive and holistic. We hope to achieve this task by providing a digest of the theory, facts, and guidelines necessary for direct practice in a field whose practitioners and administrators have been traditionally resistant to change.

Sociologically speaking, the addictions field is characterized by fierce loyalties and a devotion to principle not seen in any other comparable profession. Interventions flow logically from the basic premises. Two types of bias are common in the field of addictions. First is the tendency to see disease where there may be only bad habits or even emotionally dependent behavior. Second, there is the countertendency of these doctrinaire positions to see only bad habits where there is great personal pain, illness, and suffering.

The addiction-as-disease bias, a carryover from the antiprofessionalism in the alcoholism treatment field of the 1980s, demands immediate and total abstinence from all mood-altering substances, with the usual exception of tobacco. For persons with mental disorders, who often use alcohol and other drugs to relieve their symptoms, conformity to strict abstinence-only policies is extremely difficult (Mancini et al., in press). And despite the fact that

Twelve-Step groups operate on the principle that attendance is strictly voluntary and anonymous, this model requires regular attendance at meetings of an
Alcoholics Anonymous or Narcotics Anonymous type of group. Bolstered at
the societal level by government policies of zero tolerance for illegal drug use,
this treatment approach, in its attention to structure and mandates, is a natural
fit for work with criminal justice referrals. (To check out the tenets of the Twelve-
Step movement, see *Alcoholics Anonymous: The Big Book*, 2002.)

At the other extreme is the school of thought bent on tearing down the
basic precepts of the disease model. This "rational," highly critical orientation
focuses on individual responsibility for ending the bad habits that have erroneously been labeled a disease. This approach is probably as blaming in its way
as the predominant approach that it seeks to replace. Placing complete responsibility on individuals for their bad habits, this "rational" model expects
people simply to control their excessive urges. As in the era before the disease
model, emphasis is on will power and self-control; this treatment approach
(voiced most articulately by Fingarette, 1988; Peele, 2004) is reflected in government and insurance policies that deny funding for therapy altogether. People,
the reasoning goes, should be able to alter their bad habits on their own or at
least with nominal intervention.

In truth, these seemingly polarized positions have rather more in common
than their proponents would care to admit. Central to both approaches is a
moralism and even, at times, a blaming that are characteristically American.
This culturally based moralism will be explored from a historical standpoint in
chapter 2.

In contrast to the extreme positions of these rival camps of "true believ-
ers," both of whom are apt to hold their views intransigently, passionately,
against accusations from the other side, comes the harm reduction model. The
harm reduction model is a grassroots movement that originated in Europe as a
realistic response to serious public health problems, including the rapid spread
of AIDS/HIV. A holistic approach, harm reduction is client centered and
capable of absorbing elements from the disease model, depending on client
preferences as revealed through dialogue. Contrary to a popular misconception, this model does not preclude eventual abstinence for persons seeking help
with substance misuse problems. We seek, in this book, to integrate rather than
reject truths that, whether based on science or not, have been a godsend to so
many. So instead of "tossing out the baby with the bathwater," such as,
throwing out the Twelve Steps, we recognize Twelve-Step programs as a valuable contribution to individuals and society. Clearly, however, one size does
not fit all. What this text will focus on is how to skillfully help people find
the treatment they need to get well. The basic organizing framework of this
textbook—harm reduction—is consistent with the National Association of
Social Work's (NASW's) policy statement that "adopting a comprehensive
public health approach will enable social workers to focus on the prevention
and treatment of alcohol, tobacco, and other drug problems. This approach
will prevent unnecessary stigma and will combat substance-related illnesses,
disabilities and premature death" (NASW, 2000, p. 23).

ORGANIZATION AND FRAMEWORK

In common with the disease model, this text puts an emphasis on biology as a key factor in understanding the nature of addiction. It is our belief that human behavior can only be understood in terms of its biological, psychological, social, and spiritual components. The biopsychosocial framework, accordingly, has been chosen as the organizing framework for this book. *Biologically,* we will be looking at recent developments in neurobiological and pharmaceutical research related to addictive behavior. From a *psychological* standpoint, we will want to consider continuing treatment innovations and well-funded scientific research on treatment effectiveness. And *sociologically,* we share the recognition that the individual addict does not live in a vacuum but is both shaped by and a shaper of his or her social and political environment.

The organization of the book, in short, reflects the biopsychosocial roots of its subject, which is addiction. Divided into four parts, the first of which is introductory, *Addiction Treatment* includes the three core sections that cover the biology, psychology, and social aspects of addiction, respectively. The spiritual dimension is included in the psychological and social parts of the book.

STRENGTHS-BASED THERAPY

The terminology, ideology, and conceptual framework for this undertaking derive from the strengths perspective. This client-centered approach is compatible with the harm reduction model in that the overriding purpose is to help the client reduce the harm to himself or herself or others. Harm reduction therapy allows for creativity in the design of treatment strategies. Total abstinence from dangerous drug use is certainly not discouraged nor is total abstinence from alcoholic beverages by those with a genetic predisposition to get "hooked." But starting with "where the client is" rather than where we think the client should be is the basic principle underlying harm reduction. Placing faith in the client's ability to make choices is a related concept.

Our aim in writing this book is, above all, to be pragmatic. The word *pragmatic* is used here in the dual sense of being realistic and having relevance to direct practice. Of what use is theory, after all, without practical application? The focus on the strengths perspective in the treatment of addicts and alcoholics, accordingly, is not chosen because of some ideology of "looking at the bright side of things." Rather, it comes from the practical understanding that a focus on capabilities rather than defects fosters hope (where there is despair), options (where there is a perceived dead end), and increased self-efficacy (where there is a feeling of helplessness). Chapters 1, 3, and 10 will address the specifics of strengths-based therapy with addictive populations. Interventions will be directed at the individual, group, and community levels.

Social work and mental health counseling with clients suffering from alcoholism and other addictions must be performed within the constraints of political and economic realities. Economically, constraints on the form and length of treatment can be expected to continue under the dictates of managed care cost-saving restrictions. Largely because of the war on drugs, with the arrests and sentencing of so many drug users, much of treatment undoubtedly will continue to be provided under the auspices of departments of correction. In such a climate of oppression and meanspiritedness, it is imperative that those of us who are in the helping professions work through political advocacy to improve treatment offerings for some of our most vulnerable citizens and their families.

BASIC ASSUMPTIONS

Congruent with the biopsychosocial, ecosystems configuration, the perspective advanced in this book is that addiction, to be a viable concept, must be viewed interactionally. Each component of the system, in other words, is seen in constant and dynamic interaction with every other component; reality is rarely linear; cause and effect are intertwined. Related to addiction, the nature versus nurture controversy is resolved through an understanding that steers away from a dichotomized "either–or" type of logic, as seen in the pointless is it nature or nurture arguments, for example. Our preference is for logic of the "both–and" variety. Consistent with this perspective, addiction is viewed as both a biological and a psychosocial phenomenon. There is, further, a spiritual dimension as well. The simplistic, adversarial view of human phenomena leaves us with only partial truths and fierce loyalties that hinder us in our understanding of complexity. To advance knowledge, we need to hear from a multiplicity of voices. That the nature of addiction is infinitely complex will be revealed in the pages of this book. Essential to the study of addiction is a theoretical approach that is eclectic; such an approach is inclusive and broadening. One might even say that it is friendly rather than antagonistic toward diverse models.

To summarize, a major theoretical assumption of this book is that in our pursuit of knowledge concerning addiction and its treatment, our goal is to build upon the professional literature in the United States, Canada, and abroad and from old models and new models, whether psychodynamic or sociological, abstinence-based or experimental in nature. Some other basic assumptions that underlie this presentation are:

- Addiction exists along a continuum; many people may be addicted to one substance or product; one person may be addicted to multiple substances or activities involving risk (in relationships).
- Much of the criticism concerning various models of addiction (e.g., the disease model and individual responsibility theory) is valid; these models do tend to be unidimensional and narrow, but then, much of the criticism itself is unidimensional and narrow.
- There are hereditary tendencies toward addiction, but with work, these tendencies can usually be controlled.

- Better than forbidding adolescents from drinking is to have them learn moderate drinking from parents who drink moderately in the home.
- Whether or not alcoholism or addiction is regarded as a disease depends on the definition of disease; that addiction can be regarded as *like* a disease is a fact to which we can all agree.
- Involvement in mutual-help groups such as Alcoholics Anonymous can be invaluable in enhancing recovery and providing support to family members.
- When the focus is on promoting healthy lifestyles and on becoming motivated to change rather than on the substance misuse per se, many clients can be reached who would otherwise stay away.
- The war on drugs is politically and ethically misguided; issues of race, class, and gender define the parameters of this "war."
- Because there will never be a drug-free society, the only pragmatic approach is a public health or harm reduction approach.
- Addiction counselors who are themselves recovering have some advantages over counselors who "have not been there"; however, this kind of personal involvement is no more essential in this field than in related fields such as health and mental health. A continuously self-reflective stance is necessary for all counselors to be effective.
- Addictive behaviors are highly destructive to the family as a system and to each family member within that system; treatment therefore needs to include strong family counseling components.
- Professional training in counseling skills and neurobiological and psychosocial knowledge is just as essential for work in this field as it is for comparable fields of practice.
- Specialized training in substance misuse and the various addictions should be a requirement for practitioners in this field; such training should take place outside the treatment center and be scientifically based.
- Treatment must be tailored to the needs of the individual seeking help and include family and community support for recovery.
- Treatment ideally should be offered in all systems across health and human services and juvenile justice systems, not only in specialized substance abuse treatment centers.
- Treatment effectiveness is most accurately measured in terms of the reduction of harmful health-related practices rather than by total abstinence from drinking and drug use.

Addiction Treatment: A Strengths Perspective is intended for use as a primary text in courses related to substance misuse or as a secondary text in courses, graduate or undergraduate, related to health, social work, mental health, offender rehabilitation, and family counseling. Suffused with case examples and summaries of the latest scientific research, this book is directed to many types of practitioners in the addictions or related fields—from those who work with addicts and their families on a day-to-day basis to those who rarely see an addict but who are in positions of supervision, management, and policymaking related to addiction issues.

In the same way that hope is offered by counselors to even the most down-and-out addicts, we wish to offer hope (and appreciation) to the practitioners who dedicate their lives to work with those for whom other practitioners have little empathy or use. The hope that we would offer is ingrained in the strengths perspective itself. An approach that seeks resilience in clients and encourages workers to focus on possibilities rather than problems should go a long way toward preventing exhaustion and burnout in a field that is often characterized by both. The strengths perspective is not new to the chemical dependence field; in fact, as we argue in chapter 1, empowerment has been inadvertently used by caring counselors for years. What we are providing here is its formulation and, ideally, reinforcement. In any case, working with addicts on the verge of self-destruction is a tough assignment. We constantly have to remember that the phoenix rose from a pyre of ashes, not a soft pillow, and that it's in those ashes that we find the embers of hope and change. That is what this book is about.

A Word from Katherine van Wormer, MSSW, PhD, Professor of Social Work, University of Northern Iowa, Cedar Falls. Website: www.katherinevanwormer .com

Being from an alcoholic background (my father) and an alcoholic city (New Orleans), I had no desire to do substance abuse counseling initially. But then in the 1980s, equipped with a brand new degree in social work, I ventured to Washington State in search of scenery and a job. After an inauspicious beginning in community home health and hospice, I found myself working at the community alcohol center in Longview, Washington. This treatment center was fairly laid back as far as substance abuse treatment centers go. Unlike my previous job, the work was fun and highly creative, and the clients got progressively better instead of progressively worse. The 2-year outpatient program brought palpable results that were gratifying to see.

About 5 years later, I found myself in another scenic part of the world, Norway. As part of a mini-migration of Americans to Norway and Sweden to bring the Minnesota Model or Twelve-Step-based treatment, I trained counselors in group skills and actually learned the rudiments of the American disease model from a fellow American. Although the inevitable personnel crises abounded in a program that was run by ex-clients with limited periods of sobriety, I again witnessed the miracles of recovery and experienced the joy of seeing lives on the mend. In my public relations capacity, I spoke through translators to various community groups about alcoholism as a personal disease and as a family disease. Today, I coordinate the substance abuse certificate for social work students at the University of Northern Iowa. Books I have written include *Alcoholism Treatment: A Social Work Perspective* (1995) and *Introduction to Social Welfare and Social Work: The U.S. in Global Perspective* (2006), both published by Thomson Publishing Company. I have coauthored *Social Work with Lesbians, Gays, and Bisexuals: A Strengths Perspective* (2000) and *Women and the Criminal Justice System* (2007), both published by

Allyn & Bacon. My most recent book is a two-volume set, *Human Behavior and the Social Environment, Micro Level* and *Macro Level,* published by Oxford University Press (2007).

A Word from Diane Rae Davis, CSW, ACSW, PhD, Professor of Social Work, Eastern Washington University, Cheney.

It seems that my entire life has been intertwined with one addiction or another. If you looked at my genogram, you would see addiction all over it and the subsequent deaths, illnesses, and divorces that follow. You would also see pockets of recovery. My own recovery from alcoholism was a terrible struggle. It took 3 years to get clean and sober from the time I was absolutely convinced I was an alcoholic. When I finally did, I had no job, no husband, no home to live in, and a son in my care. Yet my middle-class background had protected me from many of the consequences that women who are addicted face: jail or prison, prostitution, bankruptcy, infectious disease, and so on.

During the years of my own recovery, I have witnessed hundreds of men and women recover from the direst circumstances, and I have also witnessed the death or suicide of others who didn't make it. One effect of all this history may seem contradictory. On the one hand, I have a strong conviction "never to give up" on even the worst scenarios—I have seen way too many miracles to ever "close the case" on anyone. On the other hand, I have learned the hard way the futility of hanging on to my own agenda regarding someone else's recovery. People make changes on their own timing, doing the best they can and surviving how they can. Behaviors that look like "resistance" and "noncompliance" from the outside may have completely different meanings when viewed from the inside. I have learned about "letting go." And finally, I've learned that there are many paths to recovery and that "recovery" means different things to different people. It took a while for me to give up the idea that what saved *my* life is the path for everyone. Having given that up, I find I have increased my capacity to help others. I have a profound belief in the strengths perspective and the possibilities of change. Similarly, I support the harm reduction model because of its many paths to sobriety, including abstinence, and because it honors a person's dignity by offering choices over and over again, no matter what.

Professionally, I have stayed close to the addiction field in social work practice and academic teaching, publishing, and research. In 1992, I received my PhD at the University of Texas at Austin under the mentorship of Dr. Diana DiNitto. I now teach a variety of courses at the School of Social Work and Human Services at Eastern Washington University, including A Systems Approach to Substance Misuse for MSW students. The publication of my article (with Golie Jansen) "Making Meaning of Alcoholics Anonymous" in *Social Work* (1998) allowed me to fulfill a personal mission to address the massive misunderstandings about mutual-help organizations among professional helpers. One of my most interesting research projects was "Women Who Have Taken Their Lives Back from Compulsive Gambling." This project involved an online research survey and qualitative interviews from women around the United States who are recovering from compulsive gambling. My current mission is to help bring the problems of compulsive gambling to the attention of social workers and other helping professions.

My other areas of research and publications include women's addiction and recovery, rural substance abuse treatment, ropes course treatment, harm reduction, alternative "sobriety" schools, and methadone maintenance.

NOTE

We both share responsibility for this book as a whole, and each chapter is a collaborative effort by both of us. However, the Preface, chapters 1, 2, 4, 5, 6, 7, and 9, and the Epilogue were the primary responsibility of Katherine van Wormer; chapters 3, 8, 10, 11, 12, and 13 were the primary responsibility of Diane Rae Davis.

ACKNOWLEDGMENTS

The authors' appreciation goes to the following reviewers for their helpful critiques of the manuscript:

Special thanks are extended to William Lounsbery and Karen Gohlke, who, as van Wormer's social work graduate assistants, helped with the typing and research and thus were tremendous assets to this production. Diane Rae Davis thanks her Dean, Michael Frumkin, PhD, School of Social Work and Human Services, Eastern Washington University for supporting her in completing the second edition. The authors would like to recognize Dan Alpert, the publisher's social work editor, for his personal support in directing this project; Aaron Downey, the production coordinator, for his efficiency in helping bring it to fruition; and Frank Hubert, the copy editor, whose meticulous attention to detail has improved the final product.

REFERENCES

Alcoholics Anonymous. (2002). *Alcoholics Anonymous: The big book*. Center City, MN: Hazelden.

Carroll, K. M., & Miller, W. R. (2006). Defining and addressing the problem. In W. R. Miller & K. M. Carroll (Eds.), *Rethinking substance abuse: What the science shows* (pp. 3–7). New York: Guilford Press.

Center for Substance Abuse Treatment (CSAT). (2005). *Substance abuse treatment with co-occurring disorders*. Treatment Improvement Protocol (TIP) Series, No. 42. Rockville, MD: Substance Abuse and Mental Health Services Administration.

Fingarette, H. (1988). *Heavy drinking: The myth of alcoholism as a disease*. Los Angeles: University of California Press.

Koerkel, J. (2002). Controlled drinking as a treatment goal in Germany. *Journal of Drug Issues, 31*(2), 667–689.

Mancini, M. A., Linhorst, D. M., Broderick, F., & Bayliff, S. (in press). Challenges to implementing the harm reduction approach. *Journal of Social Work Practices in the Addictions*.

National Association of Social Workers (NASW). (2000). *Social work speaks* (6th ed.). Washington, DC: Author.

Peele, S. (2004). *Seven tools to beat addiction.* New York: Three Rivers Press.

Rapp, C. A., & Goscha, R. (2006). *The strengths model: Case management with people with psychiatric disabilities* (2nd ed.). New York: Oxford University Press.

Steinhaver, J. (2000, July 11). Chief of addiction center quits over policy. *The New York Times*, p. A26.

Wallace, B. C. (2005). *Making mandated treatment work.* Lanham, MD: Jason Aronson.

Walters, G. D. (1999). *The addiction concept: Working hypothesis or self-fulfilling prophecy?* Boston: Allyn & Bacon.

INTRODUCTION

On the surface, our application of the strengths perspective to the field of addiction treatment marks a dramatic departure from the past. Our notion of reinforcing strengths in a self-directed program of harm reduction is seemingly a more extreme departure still. And yet the tone of this writing is intended to be conciliatory rather than adversarial; the focus is "building upon" rather than "tearing down."

Part I of this text, comprising chapters 1, 2, and 3, summarizes the current state of knowledge concerning the nature of addiction. A major task of the first chapter is definitional: to offer a conceptualization of addiction specific enough to be usable yet broad enough to encompass seemingly disparate behaviors such as compulsive overeating, compulsive gambling, excessive devotion to work, and out-of-control spending. Differentiating alcoholism from alcohol misuse is a related challenge. In these chapters and throughout the book, attention is paid to the biological, psychological, social, and spiritual aspects of addictive behavior.

The nature of addiction is complex. Its assessment and treatment represent such an inexact science that numerous theories exist, each one convincing in its own right, each with a school of followers, and each explaining only a part of the whole. The questions in the field run deep: What is addiction? Why are some people more addictive than others? How can addiction be controlled? Our perspectives—moralistic, scientific, and just plain oppositional—help shape our answers concerning the nature and treatment of addiction.

The nature of public policy is complex as well. Despite spending billions of dollars and arresting millions of Americans, the U.S. government has been unable to stop the flow of illegal drugs. Meanwhile, the harms associated with substance misuse—addiction, drug overdose, drug-related crime, the spread of HIV/AIDS—continue to mount. Add to this the casualties of the war on drugs—the broken families, children in foster care, lost worker productivity, homelessness, overcrowded prisons—and it's easy to see why so many of us are calling for change to reduce the social and psychological harm.

To learn where we are going, we need to look back to our cultural and historical roots. The purpose of chapter 2 is to trace the roots of today's policies concerning drug use and society's attempts to control it. Two basic themes are central to this historical review. The first theme is technology, and the second is ideology. In Prohibition, as we will see, these themes converged. (Technologies such as alcohol distillation created a climate for change in public opinion about drinking.) Other forces, such as the Puritan legacy of the New England colonies, were involved as well. That there is a new prohibition movement today in the form of a war on drugs is a major argument of this chapter. That the drugs of choice that are most harshly punished and apt to be outlawed are those associated with poor minority groups is a second major argument. Moving from the realm of historical context to an analysis of treatment designs, we examine strengths-based modalities (e.g., the harm reduction model) in chapter 3.

The nature of addiction and the history of its treatment—are among the issues tackled in the first two introductory chapters. Our journey to exploring these dimensions begins with chapter 1, The Nature of Addiction. The first task of this book, in short, is to explore the nature of addiction and its conceptualization. The second task, which is the subject of chapters 2 and 3, is to put today's conceptualizations in historical and theoretical context.

THE NATURE OF ADDICTION

CHAPTER I

INTRODUCTION

"The suffering of a soul that can suffer greatly—that and only that, is tragedy." So wrote Edith Hamilton (1948, p. 131), the foremost authority on ancient Greek culture of her day. She was talking about Greek tragedy. The hero in classical Greek tragedy possesses a tragic flaw, *hubris,* that ultimately will be his or her undoing. Today, in real life as in drama, the source of personal tragedy is often some sort of compulsion or obsession. The "fatal attraction" may involve a person, a substance, or an activity.

Thus, when we hear of the compulsive gambler who leads his or her family down the path of financial ruin, of the Internet whiz who, like the workaholic, sacrifices family life for an "affair" with Cyberspace, of the drug addict who deals drugs or prostitutes herself to support her habit, we may find in us a sense of pity and awe, the essence of all great tragedy.

The effects of addiction are everywhere and nowhere—everywhere because they are in every family and workplace, nowhere because so much of the behavior is hidden from public view. Sometimes, as with Internet gambling or pill addiction, even family members are unaware of the problem until a major crisis ensues.

In contrast to the tales of classic literature, in real life there may be a way out of the pain, a way for the individual to get beyond the tragic flaw. The way out is called *recovery.* "I'm in recovery," says the proud member of Alcoholics Anonymous (AA). Similarly, the person who has gotten some personal counseling in reducing the harm announces that now his or her own life has gotten under control.

In our jails, hospitals, women's shelters, and child welfare departments, all the places where professional counselors and social workers are employed, the impact of substance misuse and addiction is a given. Where there is assault, incest, rape, child neglect, or attempted suicide, more often than not some form of substance

3

misuse is involved. The effects may be immediate—for example, the neglectful parent so strung out on methamphetamines (meth) that he or she has lost all sense of time and all sense of responsibility. The effects may be lifelong—for example, the woman who suffered sexual abuse by a male predator early in childhood and who has taken to using prescription drugs and alcohol for self-medication, to dull a pain the cause of which may or may not be remembered.

This chapter explores the nature of addiction. Each section covers a different facet of drug and alcohol addiction, including definitional issues, an overview of the biological, psychological, and social aspects, various treatment approaches and trends, and a look at the politics of addiction. Two concepts that form a theme of this book—the biopsychosocial-spiritual model and the strengths perspective—are introduced in this chapter. Subsequent sections of the chapter present an introduction to the art and science of addiction treatment and con-temporary trends in treatment. (The intimate experience of substance misuse is shared by the addicts themselves, their children, and professionals in the field.)

WHAT IS ADDICTION?

Addiction is seen in the man in the detox unit of a hospital who is cringing from the pain of pancreatitis. He has no plans to quit drinking, his wife says. Addiction is evidenced in the two-pack-a-day smoker who coughs steadily from emphysema. Addiction is implicated in the actions of the trusted employee who was imprisoned for embezzlement; she needed more money to gamble.

The economic cost of addiction is incalculable. Certainly, billions of dollars are involved. There is the health toll of alcohol and drug misuse, the astronomical expenditures in running the war on drugs and in incarcerating the over 1 million persons whose crime was related to alcohol or some other drug. Catering to people's addictions is big business that ranges from marketing tobacco to special populations, to setting up state lotteries, to organized crime.

So, what is addiction? According to the *Dictionary of Word Origins* (Ayto, 1990), the roots of the word *addiction* are in the Latin past participle *addictus,* meaning "having given over or awarded to someone or being attached to a person or cause." The connotations were highly positive. Originally used as an adjective in English, its meaning has become increasingly negative over time.

In the substance misuse literature, addiction is variously defined as a brain disease (Leshner, 2006), a sin (Rosin, 2000), a sense of helplessness (Dodes, 2003), excessive behavior (Orford, 2001), a bad habit (Peele, 2004), a personal choice (Schaler, 1999), an expression of self-determination (Szasz, 2003), and a moral and spiritual deficiency (Dalrymple, 2006; Morell, 1996). And to William Miller (2006), addiction is fundamentally a problem of motivation. Or simply put, addiction is an addiction.

For an official definition, we first turn to the *Diagnostic and Statistical Manual of Mental Disorders, Text Revision* (*DSM–IV–TR*) (American Psychiatric Association [APA], 2000). Actually, the *DSM–IV–TR* avoids use of the term *addiction* in favor of the seemingly more scientific term *dependence.* The terms *addiction* and *substance dependence,* however, are more or less comparable. As defined by the APA, the diagnosis of substance dependence disorder requires the following: the presence of a maladaptive pattern of substance use, resulting in distress or clinically significant impairment and involving at least three of the following symptoms (all of which must occur within the same 12-month period):

- Tolerance
- Withdrawal problems
- Use of the substance longer than intended
- Unsuccessful attempts to control or reduce consumption
- Spending excessive amounts of time procuring, using the substance, or recovering from its effects
- Reduced involvement in important social, occupational, or recreational activities, and
- Continued use despite the presence of recurrent physical or psychological problems. (APA, 2000, p. 197)

Typical substances named by the APA are alcohol, other drugs, and tobacco. A separate listing of similar criteria is provided for pathological gambling, even though it is found under Impulse Control Disorders, not Dependence. To receive a diagnosis of pathological gambler, a person must satisfy five of the following ten criteria:

- Preoccupation with gambling
- Increased wagering in order to achieve the desired effect
- Restlessness or irritability when attempting to reduce or stop gambling
- Gambling as a way of escaping problems and reducing depression
- Gambling to recoup one's losses
- Lying to family members or to one's therapist about gambling
- Involvement in illegal activities to support gambling
- Jeopardizing or losing a significant relationship, job, or career or educational opportunity because of gambling
- Relying on others to provide money to relieve financial hardship caused by gambling
- Repeated unsuccessful efforts to curb or stop gambling. (APA, 2000, p. 674)

In *The Addiction Concept,* Walters (1999) notes that the criteria used by researchers for sexual addiction and eating disorders also involve the criterion clusters of progression, preoccupation, perceived loss of control, and negative long-term consequences. Walters strenuously objects to the use of such criteria and to the word *addiction* itself; he proposes an alternative concept—the lifestyle concept—that allows for an emphasis on personal choice. The lifestyle concept, however, has problems of its own, chiefly in the direction of blaming. A focus on individual responsibility in the use of mood-altering substances plays into the punitive response so much in evidence regarding drug use in U.S. society. (We delve into this matter more in a later section, Treatment Trends.)

The responsibility argument is one that Gold, Johnson, and Stennie (1997) and Joranby, Pineda, and Gold (2005) have little patience with. Eating disorders,

Box 1.1 | # A Social Work Major Working in a Casino
Julie Taylor

As gambling fever makes its way across the United States, we hear different views and opinions expressed in the media on what seems like a daily basis. Especially here in Iowa, where there is a constant controversy over issues such as the morality of gambling, how casinos affect the economy, the legality of gambling, and other pertinent issues. There are specials on television about addiction and how it has affected the Native American peoples, about the glamour and glitz of casinos, and about the money made and lost. I have talked with different customers about their winning or losing streaks. One night while I was working, I saw a middle-aged man dressed in a very nice business suit playing a $5 slot machine. He kept putting in one $100 bill after another. I counted four times that he went to either the automatic teller machine (ATM) or the credit card machine. He was losing what I call a ton of money. He literally had sweat running down his head and had a look of sheer panic on his face. He looked up at me at one point and said, "I'm dead. I am just dead." I just stood there and with a look of sorrow on my face said, "As much money as you've put in it, I can't believe it hasn't paid out yet." What I really wanted to say was, "Why don't you just go home before you lose more money?" I will never forget the look on that man's face. It was obvious to me that he had a serious gambling problem. I see a lot of this at the casino.

One thing that you hear almost nothing about is what it is like to work at a casino. That's something I can tell you about. My husband, Dave, and I have worked at our local casino (Meskwaki Bingo, Casino, & Hotel) for just about 2 years, and I can tell you that there is certainly nothing glamorous about it. It is hard work not only from a physical point of view but more so from an emotional point of view.

Let's begin with the atmosphere in which we work. Customers, unless they are "regulars," don't really realize that they are being watched the entire time they are in there. There are literally hundreds of cameras rolling 24 hours a day from every angle. As the song goes, every move we make, every step we take, every single day, every single way, I'll be watching you. Why? It's not necessarily to watch the customers as it is to watch us employees! The assumption made by owners is that every employee is a thief. There is more truth in this than I like to imagine. The slightest mistake, the smallest unexplained movement, a sneeze, scratching your head, and touching another person can draw an instant call from "upstairs" surveillance and quite possibly a write-up, suspension, or being fired on the spot if they don't like what you did or how you did it. This atmosphere pervades every moment of your working life. To say the least, it is incredibly degrading. The joke in the employee break room is that the next thing we know, there will be cameras in the restrooms. Believe it or not, at one time there were microphones placed in the ceiling tiles in the break rooms so they could record what was being said by the employees. Swear, a true story.

Speaking of degrading, imagine what it is like to have customers screaming at you, swearing at you, doing everything short of physically attacking you because they are losing money (or, for that matter, winning money) or not getting the immediate service

---

as they indicate, are not due to a lack of self-control: The close similarity in dependence on drugs and on food, which is a powerful mood-altering substance, is borne out in scientific findings about brain reward systems and neurotransmitter aberrations, as, for example, among bulimics. Classification of eating disorders as an addiction, as these authors further argue, would help in our prevention educational efforts. Many of the addictive chronic disorders, such as compulsive overeating and pathological gambling, are characterized by loss of they feel is due them. One constant at the casino is they cannot keep enough people employed to service the enormous number of customers they deal with on a daily basis. The turnover rate of employees is phenomenal. In some departments, such as the pit (this is where the card games are played), we are 60 dealers short of being full staffed. The turnover rate is more than 70% per year. I love dealing cards to people. It is fun because I enjoy interacting with people and I know that this work isn't my lifetime career. I also attend college at the University of Northern Iowa full time.

Now let us move on to some things that people may not realize about casinos. For instance, when you see pictures in movies and on television of casinos, it appears that the customers are young, excited, partying people, when in reality, most customers are elderly folks living on Social Security and pensions. It is so sad to have an elderly woman crying to you about having lost her entire Social Security check and now having to go home and explain what happened to all the money that she had in the world. It tears your heart out and at the same time makes you realize why some people feel gambling should be illegal.

Another interesting thing about the casino life is that it is much like life in a bar. The customers are the same people day after day, night after night. Sometimes you wonder if they have any other life! Their whole existence seems to be gambling. Like the bartender, we know their names, we learn their lives, we hear about their problems, their families, and their spouses. After a while I find myself offering advice just like a bartender does. (I also was a bartender for 8 years.) However, because we are employees of the casino (and you never know who is listening), we have to say stupid things like, "That machine should hit anytime now," "Keep going, it has to pay off soon," or "At least you haven't lost as much as that person has." What you really want to say is, "Don't you people have homes you can go to?" or "Do you realize how many groceries you could have bought with the money you put in there?" I talked to a lady once who told me that she brought her rent money to try and win enough to pay her rent and light bill; she lost it all and left crying!

Something I learned about casinos: Until the last 20 years or so, casinos were the major way of laundering money for the mob and for drug dealers. This was accomplished simply by buying poker chips to gamble with, or placing cash in the casino's vault, or even exchanging $100 bills for smaller ones. This actually doesn't happen as much since the change in federal law requiring casinos to report all transactions over $1,200 to the IRS.

One more tidbit of information: Slot machines at casinos actually pay out 94 to 96%. That means that the casino actually only makes about 5 or 6% profit on slot machines. That doesn't seem like a lot does it? In fact, you might consider if you're a player that this means that if you play a machine long enough, the most you could lose would be 5 to 6% of the money you put into it. That would be true if the customer knew which machines were paying off and which ones weren't. Casinos make millions off of the 6% they take in on slot machines. Can you imagine the total money spent on them to get them to pay out? It boggles the mind.

In this politically correct decade, the most horrific politically correct term ever created is the one that the gambling industry has made into an everyday word: Gaming. There is no game here. You pay and you lose; that is the game.

Printed by permission of Julie Taylor.

control, relapse, compulsiveness, and continuation despite negative consequences. Accordingly, as Gold et al. (1997) conclude, "As the well-known adage goes, if it looks like a duck, acts like a duck, it must be a duck" (p. 327). Before we progress any further into the maze of word usage, let us consider just how far into the depths of madness the addictive urge can lead us. Box 1.1, "A Social Work Major

Working in a Casino," takes us behind the scenes into a work environment that preys on the vulnerable ones—compulsive gamblers.

One unhelpful aspect of the *DSM* identified by Walters is its categorization of disease in terms of rigid dichotomies (e.g., substance dependence and substance misuse). Addiction, in fact, occurs along a continuum. Severe life-threatening dependence may be placed at one end, the misuse of substances somewhere in the center, and a use of substances without problems at the other end. Individuals or their behaviors can be placed along a continuum according to levels of misuse or addiction at various points in their lives. The *DSM–IV–TR*'s either–or categories fail to account for such dimensions of human behavior.

From a contemporary perspective, in marked contrast to the earlier view of alcohol dependence as a progressive and irreversible disease, most problem drinkers move in and out of periods of dependent drinking. From this perspective, as British social work educator Larry Harrison (1996) suggests, there are no rigid boundaries between normal and pathological populations or between common diagnostic categories. We need to keep in mind, of course, that persons who present themselves at specialist treatment agencies (often by court order, as is typical in the United States) are apt to have severe problems and represent the extreme end of the continuum.

We can take issue with the *DSM–IV–TR* for one other reason as well: the incompatibility of such labeling and diagnosis with the tenets of the strengths perspective. As the name would indicate, the *strengths perspective* is an approach geared to look for strengths rather than liabilities, not because they are "truer" but because it's more effective. Still, in the United States, mental health practitioners, rehabilitation counselors, and social workers in many fields utilize APA criteria for substance dependence as a means of justifying insurance reimbursement and vocational rehabilitation for their clients (Benshoff & Janikowski, 2000). The physical, psychological, and social aspects of dependence as spelled out in this manual can be helpful in assessment and communication among professionals and in giving testimony before the court.

So how does the diagnostic model differentiate dependence from abuse? The difference is found in the inclusion of three criteria: tolerance, withdrawal, and a pattern of compulsive use by which substance dependence is characterized. Substance abuse, in contrast, is defined in *DSM* terms as the absence of physical and psychological habituation to the substance. A problem semantically with the term *substance abuse* is that the substance is not being abused. The individual may be committing self-abuse, but the substance is merely consumed or otherwise ingested; it is hard to abuse an inanimate object after all. The terms *substance use* and *substance misuse* are more accurate and even more sensible, and they are used in this text to refer more specifically to general and harmful drug use, respectively. The terms *substance abuse treatment* and *substance abuse counseling* are used because of their familiarity rather than any descriptive accuracy.

For everyday social usage, Moncher, Schinke, and Holden (1992) prefer the flexibility of the word *addiction* in place of *DSM*'s substance dependence.

The concept of addiction, they believe, is more compatible with the biopsychosocial model, which attends to the *subjective* compulsion to continue the behavior pattern. Addiction can be defined as a pattern of compulsive substance use or behavior. *The Social Work Dictionary* (Barker, 2003) defines addiction as follows:

> ADDICTION: Physiological and psychological dependence on a behavior or substance. Behavioral addictions (sex, gambling, spending, obsessive internet use) and consumptive addictions (alcohol, drugs, food) often have similar etiologies, prognoses, and treatment procedures. Most professionals now use the term "substance dependence" for consumptive addictions. (p. 7)

Although the tendency is to equate addiction with loss of control, the extent to which the individual is truly beyond self-control cannot be proven but can only be inferred from external behavior. What's missing but needed, according to Howard Shaffer (1999) from the Harvard Medical School's Division on Addictions, is a "gold standard" independent of observation of the behavior (in this case, gambling) to determine an individual's level of addiction. In fact, such a standard may be around the corner. Shaffer himself cites encouraging recent brain research reflecting the impact that gambling has on the neurotransmitters in the brains of pathological gamblers. Research on biogenetic vulnerabilities in gamblers is showing promising results as well. Alan Leshner (1997), former director of the National Institute for Drug Abuse (NIDA), declares that "addiction is, at its core, a consequence of fundamental changes in brain function" (p. 46). But as he reminds us, addiction is not only a brain disease; the social and psychological pain can be overwhelming.

To understand the pain connected with addictive and compulsive behavior, one must first understand the *pleasure* side of these activities (i.e., their attractiveness). Books on treatment, whether written by scholars or by self-help authors, focus almost exclusively on the harm of substance misuse, a harm inherent in the substances themselves. Yet, according to Volpicelli and Szalavitz (2000), it is crucial to learn why substances such as alcohol and licit or illicit drugs are useful as well as attractive, and "that use itself is not always wrong or harmful, despite attempts by various factors to convince us otherwise." Alcohol, for example, when used in moderation, has many health-giving properties and, like the opiates, has been used for centuries to relieve pain. Apart from nicotine, which is highly addictive, as Volpicelli and Szalavitz, further indicate, only a small percentage of drinkers, marijuana users, or heroin users exhibit the kind of problems that would define them as abusers or addicts.

Few areas of human life exist where individual differences are more pronounced than in regard to people's taste (or distaste) for mood-altering substances, including food. Some crave uppers, ranging from caffeine to methamphetamines; others would go to incredible lengths to get hold of downers, such as alcohol and Valium. Still others use such substances to enhance their sensual pleasures, but then only occasionally. Medical science is rapidly uncovering the clues to these individual differences, clues that go beyond pharmacology or even environmental circumstances into the realm of brain chemistry. But that is the topic of another chapter.

Of all the addictions, *alcoholism* is the most studied and the most common, next to nicotine addiction. The American Medical Association (AMA) (1956) declared that alcoholism was an illness. In 1968, the AMA offered the following definition, which is still widely used:

> alcoholism is an illness characterized by preoccupation with alcohol and loss of control over its consumption such as to lead usually to intoxication if drinking is begun; by chronicity; by progression; and by tendency toward relapse. It is typically associated with physical disability and impaired emotional, occupational, and/or social adjustments as a direct consequence of persistent and excessive use of alcohol. (AMA, p. 6)

The AMA definition identifies the three basic areas of ecological concern: the physical, the psychological, and the social. Thus, it is the definition chosen for this text. The selection of the word *illness* to describe alcoholism provides a clear acknowledgment of alcoholism as a medical problem with widespread ramifications (social and moral). Illness is a nonjudgmental, non-victim-blaming term.

At the present time, on their website, the AMA (2007) "endorses the proposition that drug dependencies, including alcoholism, are diseases and that their treatment is a legitimate part of medical practice" (H-95.983). The word *disease* originally was applied to alcoholism by Jellinek (1960), who said that alcoholism was *like* a disease. It was a short road from "like a disease" to "a disease," one with vast political and medical connotations. In the United States, in recent years a trend toward the "diseasing" of behavior not ordinarily considered pathological (e.g., codependence) has been pronounced.

Simultaneously, there has been a countertrend stressing individual responsibility for a range of addictive behaviors, now labeled "bad habit." This movement away from the disease models carries some risk of "throwing the baby out with the bath water," of turning the clock back on treatment availability. Disregarding the political aspects for the moment, let us draw upon the dictionary definition of disease.

Disease

1. (Middle English) A pathological condition of a part, organ, or system of an organism resulting from various causes, such as infections, genetic defect.
2. A condition or tendency, as of society, regarded as abnormal or harmful.
3. Obsolete, lack of ease, trouble.

(*American Heritage Dictionary*, 2000, p. 517)

According to this, as in most dictionary definitions, alcoholism certainly qualifies, along with diabetes and certain heart conditions, for consideration as a disease. McNeece and DiNitto (2005), however, warn against use of the term for two reasons. The first is that it is often used as a metaphor, and very loosely at that. The second is because "if a phenomenon is a *disease* then we expect a cure in the form of a drug or other medical treatment" (p. 7). Alcohol and drug dependence are viewed by these authors as an addiction but not a disease, except when discussing the consequences of alcoholism, such as pancreatitis.

To denote the extensive pain and suffering wrought by the condition of alcoholism, we have chosen, as in the AMA definition, to favor use of the word *illness* over *disease*. Illness, to Conrad and Kern (1994), is the experience of being sick or diseased; it is a social psychological state caused by the disease. Thus, pathologists treat disease, whereas patients experience illness. The subjective level of illness, as previously suggested, makes this term more relevant to the helping professions' focus on the person in the environment and on the interaction between the person and the world outside.

Germain's description of the ecology of serious illness applies to addiction even more than to other illnesses (1984):

> Serious illness represents perceived demands that may exceed perceived resources for handling them, and so is a source of stress. The stress of illness, in turn, may lead to stress in other realms of life, especially in family, work, and community roles, thereby interfering with recovery or with management of disability. (p. 64)

The concept of addiction as an illness of body, mind, and soul is part and parcel of the biopsychosocial-spiritual understanding of this phenomenon. Through the initial act of drinking or drug ingestion, the body adapts remarkably, sometimes to the extent of permanent biochemical and psychological changes. As thought processes in the brain are altered, one's ability to adapt to stress may be weakened. Socially, the hard-drinking, drug-using life determines the company one keeps (and the company one loses); one's family members are affected in dramatic and devastating ways. The consequences of substance misuse raise stress levels; this, in combination with the physiological craving associated with heavy use, reinforces the urge to partake.

BIOPSYCHOSOCIAL-SPIRITUAL MODEL

Social work and other counseling professions conceive of addiction holistically, with attention to biological, psychological, and social components in its causation and consequences. The advantage of the biopsychosocial-spiritual model is in being able to address more than one problem at a time (G. Miller, 2005). Note that this model is a mere framework, as widely used in texts in the field to organize material. The biopsychosocial-spiritual model is atheoretical in that it doesn't explain anything, so it can be used with any philosophical approach, such as the traditional disease model or harm reduction model alike.

The pain and suffering of alcoholism and other addictions constitute the biopsychosocial reality. The *biology* of chemical use relates to the formidable hereditary components in the etiology of this illness and the physical problems that may arise with extended use. A growing literature documents the many ways in which addiction is a complex brain disease (Washton & Zweben, 2006). Predisposing characteristics such as endorphin deficiency can set the stage for future problems long before the use of any addictive substances. Thus, we hear from a man who is serving a long prison term for manslaughter following a drunken driving crash:

> My father has had a few DWI's (Driving While Intoxicated convictions), my sister one, and I've gotten two. I've never done drugs; alcohol is my drug of choice. I am also bulimic. I've struggled with my eating disorder for about eighteen years now. My problems with alcohol and bulimia along with depression just feed each other. (personal communication, June 13, 2006)

The *psychological* concept encompasses the thinking that leads to the drinking or injecting or snorting of the substance. These irrational or unhealthy thought processes may be associated with depression or anxiety, which in turn may encourage escape through drug use or other compulsive behaviors.

That the high has a psychological as well as a biological basis is revealed in this description from a male compulsive shopper (J. Anderson, 1994):

> It was like, it was almost like my heart was palpitating. . . . I couldn't wait to see what was there. It was such a sensation. In the store, the lights, the people; they were playing Christmas music. I was hyperventilating and my hands were beginning to sweat, and all of a sudden I was touching sweaters and the whole feel of it was beckoning to me. And if they had a SALE sign up, forget it; I was gone. You never know when you're going to need it. (p. 223)

Leshner (2006) concurs that the traditional dichotomization into psychological and physical addictions has been shown to be faulty. Physical dependence to a drug, he says, is not that important. Withdrawal symptoms can be offset today through medication. And the most dangerously addictive drugs—meth and crack cocaine—do not produce severe withdrawal symptoms. "What really matters most," continues Leshner (2006), "is whether or not a drug causes what we now know to be the essence of addiction, namely, the uncontrollable compulsive drug craving, seeking, and use, even in the face of negative health and social consequences" (pp. 2–3).

The *social* component in addiction relates to *where* as opposed to *why*: Where does the addictive activity take place and where is the impact felt? The peer group and family may be involved, respectively. One factor we should never lose sight of is social class. Economically disadvantaged persons are more likely to suffer alcohol-related problems, even when drinking at the same level as more economically privileged groups, because they lack the material resources and often the social supports available to others.

The *spiritual* dimension is a key component in the illness of addiction. Spirituality is crucial in recovery because it is related to one's sense of meaning and interconnectedness. A shift from negative punishing to positive forgiving views of spirituality often accompanies recovery (Neff & MacMaster, 2005). The closely related concepts of healing and forgiveness (of the self and others) enhance interpersonal relationships. A major component of the biopsychosocial-spiritual model of addiction is interactiveness. In the language of systems theory, the basic principle of interactionism is that cause and effect are intertwined. In the language of ordinary conversation, we talk of a vicious cycle. The expression "what goes around comes around" is another way of saying the same thing.

Any member of an alcoholic family becomes aware of how pain and substance misuse feed into each other until the two become almost one and the same. As suffering induces the wish to escape unpleasant feelings through the use of chemicals, this indulgence in turn leads to pain at all four levels of the biopsychosocial-spiritual model. The resultant pain exacerbates the urge to drown the feelings—physically, in the bottle.

A second major principle of interactionism concerns the overlap among the four aforementioned components. Body, mind, society, and spirituality are all furiously intertwined in the cycle that is addiction. Cocaine may be used as an upper, for example, to dull the pain of organic or situational depression. The social costs of alternatively acting depressed and engaging in illicit drug use may be enormous.

Another form of interaction that figures in addiction is that between stress and individual responses to that stress. Consider, for example, how persons under severe stress tend to use alcohol and/or tranquilizers to reduce their anxiety levels. According to a study by the National Center on Addiction and Substance Abuse (CASA) at Columbia University, substance abuse treatment admissions increased 10 to 12% nationally since the events of September 11 ("Terrorist Attacks Cause Spike," 2001). This phenomenon was reminiscent, according to the same article, of the heightened demand for treatment in Oklahoma following the Oklahoma City bombing.

Interactionism is seen most vividly in the dynamics of the family system. Much has been written about "the alcoholic family" (see chapter 9). The set of demands imposed on the family members of an alcoholic or addict can be awesome, both emotionally and financially. Each family will have its own peculiar style of adaptation and coping, whether through blaming, denial, and/or overprotecting. Because the family is a system, one member's malfunctioning throws the whole family's functioning out of whack. While the individual addict remains to some extent "out of things," family members may take the tension out on each other. (See chapter 9 for a study in addict/alcoholic family dynamics.) In personal correspondence of September 8, 2000, a woman who identifies herself only as Sue shares a childhood memory:

> During the week, he was a Grandpa/"Poppy"/teacher/best friend. On the weekends, he was this stranger who stumbled home late at night long after the corner bar had closed. And, to mollify Grandma and me, he'd carefully carry two fish fry dinners home for us. But he never understood why greasy French fries at 3 A.M. never appealed to me.
>
> After school on Friday afternoon, he volunteered to drive me to a doctor's appointment. But he had started an early weekend and so had a bottle of brandy in the car. I guess no one in the family had seen it before he left the house. We never made it to the appointment. He totaled the car on a downtown bridge. I wound up in the hospital with four fractured limbs.
>
> My father threatened to kill him; my mother threatened to leave my father for threatening her father; my grandma threatened divorce. I was crying as if my heart

would break, and Grandpa fell asleep in the hospital room visitors' lounge, oblivious to the turmoil and heart-rending aftereffects of "a few early nips."

Interactionism is a concept with special significance in a treatment book of this sort, where the focus is on effecting interpersonal change and motivation. In the chapters ahead, we will be dealing with strategies to enhance motivation. Motivation is now understood, according to Hester and Miller (2003), to be the result of an interaction between the drinker and other persons, including counselors. This means there is much the counselor can achieve through interaction to help clients move along in a health-inducing direction.

PREVALENCE OF SUBSTANCE MISUSE

Mental health professionals can expect approximately 50% of their clients to have problems stemming from their own or a family member's alcoholism (Drake & Mueser, 1996). Alcohol misuse also figures widely in family and marital counseling. Workers in child welfare observe firsthand the toll on the victims of neglect and abuse due to parental drinking problems.

The majority of addiction counselors' clients are court ordered to treatment; that is, they are persons who were convicted of drug-related crimes, or they are otherwise coerced in some way into treatment, perhaps before they make their court appearance. As Wallace (2005) suggests, in her study of mandated addictions treatment, the tremendous influx of clients from criminal justice systems referrals parallels the societal shift toward conservatism, moralism, and intolerance. Between 2004 and 2005, the numbers of male prisoners grew 1.3%, and the number of female prisoners grew 3.4% (Bureau of Justice Statistics, 2006). Of the more than 2 million people incarcerated in the United States, approximately 500,000 were sentenced for drug offenses. Diane Young (2003) reviewed the medical records of 359 mentally ill jail inmates. She found that 67% of this sample had a substance-related disorder in addition to the mental disorder.

Correctional counselors encounter the effects of drug use and dependence as a constant in their treatment of offenders. An extensive study conducted by the National Center on Addiction and Substance Abuse at Columbia University (1998) found that 80% of people behind bars were involved with alcohol and other drugs at the time their crimes were committed. A Canadian study conducted in 26 communities across Canada revealed that more than half of the people arrested for criminal offenses were under the influence of alcohol, illicit drugs, or both when the crimes were committed (Garlick, 2000).

When drug offenders reenter society after serving their lengthy sentences, they are unprepared to resume community and family life. The temptation to return to the world of drugs can be formidable. And so is the challenge facing social service providers. The need, according to O'Neil (2001), is for more extensive training of social work students in substance abuse prevention and treatment, regardless of the area of specialization they choose because addiction problems are rampant across all areas in which social services are provided.

According to a random survey of 2,000 National Association of Social Work (NASW) members, 71% of social workers had taken one or more actions with clients with substance abuse disorders in the past year (O'Neil, 2001). More specifically:

> In the past year, 43% of social workers performed screening for substance abuse; 26% diagnosed it; 19% treated primary substance abuse; 47% treated secondary substance abuse; 61% referred clients to substance abuse treatment; and 11% screened for compulsive gambling.
>
> Social workers in organizational settings reported that 28.6% of clients had substance abuse as a primary or secondary diagnosis: 9% primary and 19.6% secondary. Those in private practice saw fewer people with substance abuse problems, 19.1%, with 5.9% primary and 13.2% secondary. (p. 10)

Social work practice with alcoholics and other addicts takes place in a wide range of social work settings. Hospital social workers, for instance, encounter both the early- and late-stage effects of heavy drinking in patients. The estimate is that one hospital bed in four is occupied by a patient whose ailment is alcohol related. Alcohol misuse is the third leading cause of death, after heart disease and cancer.

THE GRIP OF ADDICTION

- "Addicted Gamers, Losing Their Way" (Richards, 2004)
- "Hooked on Tanning?" (DeNoon, 2006)
- "Shopaholics Climb on the Wagon" (Lobet, 2000)
- "Meth Abuse Cited as Top Drug Problem for Law Enforcement Agencies" (Associated Press, 2005)
- "Ex-Smokers Get Stuck on Gum" (Barker, 2000)
- "North America's First Heroin Prescription Program Introduced in Canada" (Johel, 2005)

Such are the typical headlines in any regional and national newspaper on any given day. The concern with addiction is as universal as is the battle to control it. Some stories focus on individuals, with celebrities of course drawing the most attention. Numerous articles highlighted Robert Downey Jr.'s earlier re-arrest. "If anyone ever had good reason to say no to drugs, it was surely Robert Downey, Jr." begins *Time* magazine's version (Lemonick, 2000, p. 97). This statement referred to the fact that this actor had recently completed treatment for cocaine and heroin use following an earlier arrest and had returned to a promising career, including a starring role in a Hollywood film with Julia Roberts, only to get caught possessing cocaine and speed shortly thereafter. Later, Mel Gibson similarly got into some trouble with the public when he drunkenly blurted out a series of anti-Semitic remarks (Maugh, 2006). He quickly turned himself in to a rehab center for help with his alcohol problem and probably to appease the general public.

Although the traditional psychologist might look to a pattern of self-destructiveness and the sociologist to professional stress, a multidimensional analysis would certainly take biological factors into account. Aided by powerful new diagnostic tools that can document changes in the brain as a result of drug use, researchers can now fathom the relentless craving that accompanies depletion of endorphins, or "feel-good" chemicals in the brain. The brain of the drug user is physically altered in ways that make resistance to further drug use very difficult (Leshner, 2006). More will be said about this in chapters 4 and 5.

Hereditary factors are involved in addiction as well. An anonymous male social work student shares this contradictory but revealing comment:

> Well, my Grandpa and brother are both alcoholics. Along with the rest of the family I drink, but not to that point. I believe I have a small alcohol/nicotine problem. Ever since I was 18, neither has been a big deal; now once I start drinking I really can't stop. (personal communication, August 22, 2000)

An excellent portrayal of the grip of addiction and the harrowing process of recovery is given in the 2000 Hollywood movie *28 Days*. Gwen, the alcoholic who goes into inpatient treatment to avoid a jail term for a drunken driving episode lost her mother to alcoholism as a child. In treatment, Gwen injures her ankle climbing out of a window to retrieve some pills. "The definition of insanity," says her counselor, "is repeating the same behavior over and over and getting the same results."

Perhaps the most honest representation of an addict's surrender and recovery ever put on film is in the 1988 movie *Clean and Sober* starring Michael Keaton. A cocaine-addicted real estate executive in deep financial trouble, Keaton's character hides out in a rehab center. The transformation he undergoes is moving and informative at the same time. Another noteworthy portrayal is provided in the European-produced film *Clean*. This 2004 movie depicts the emotionally charged struggle of a heroin-addicted mother to get her life and child back after serving time in a Canadian prison.

And then there is *Traffic*. Addictive behavior is woven through every generation in this powerful 2001 film portrayal of a family and other persons caught up in the war on drugs. As the leading character, played by Michael Douglas, prepares to become the nation's new drug czar, his 16-year-old daughter sinks ever more deeply into the mire of drug addiction. To learn of Johnny Cash, the legendary country music star's long struggle with addiction and related relationship issues, see *Walk the Line*, which was made available on DVD in 2006.

Marriages disrupted, kids getting into trouble, people committing illegal acts—the pattern is the same with nonsubstance addictions, sometimes called behavioral addictions, such as with compulsive gambling. Compulsive shoppers, for example, have obsessive buying urges that lead them to have closets full of never-worn clothing and then go out the next day and buy more. Medication seems to help reduce the strange cravings in many cases (J. Anderson, 1994).

Eating can present problems for persons who seem predisposed to addictive behavior. Here's how it was expressed in a speech by Wanda Haban (1999):

> I was a chronic dieter for 25 years. Today I'm eating healthy. To change habits is a forever process. My father is an alcoholic, so genetically or psychologically those

traits are instilled in me. The first drink I had I had a blackout. So I knew there was a problem there. I had hangovers, so I didn't choose that drug as my choice. I chose food as my choice. Once I eat over a certain point, I can't stop.

My ex-husband said, "Don't ever get fat." My dieting was starvation and binge-ing, yo-yo dieting. I am still obsessed with dieting.

THE STRENGTHS PERSPECTIVE

The strengths perspective, which cannot be considered a theory because it lacks explanatory power, is a way of perceiving people in their struggles to rise above difficult circumstances. In combination with the empowerment theoretical perspective, the strengths approach is the predominant approach in social work today. Positive psychology that focuses on well-being and resilience is a parallel perspective that is achieving a large following in psychology (see, e.g., Linley & Joseph, 2004). The strengths perspective is primarily a philosophy or way of interpreting information about bio-, psycho-, and social factors in people's lives (Johnson, 2004). This approach to client treatment was pioneered by the writings of Dennis Saleebey (1992) and Charles Rapp (1998) in their books *The Strengths Perspective in Social Work Practice* and *The Strengths Model: Case Management with People Suffering from Severe and Persistent Mental Illness,* respectively.

Whereas the biopsychosocial-spiritual model helps us gain understanding of the roots and intransigence of addiction, the strengths perspective is a model geared toward direct practice, which can shape our appreciation of particular treatment modalities (or aspects of these modalities) as well. This perspective represents a paradigm shift away from the treatment industry's emphasis on psychopathology, disease, and disorder, a focus on personal deficits rather than resilience. Harm reduction alone is not enough; the client caught in the mire of addiction and personal pain needs help in developing a healthy outlook on life and even a dramatically altered lifestyle.

Given the horrendous grip of addiction for certain individuals—the self-defeating behavior, guilt feelings, busted relationships—it is clear that the treatment modality used must offer hope and a way out of the morass of the addiction cycle. Hope, guidance, and relationships are three key ingredients in successful recovery. Finding a spiritual connection can help tremendously as well.

Although most recovery does not stem from formal treatment, the incentive for sobriety can very well be an outgrowth of a treatment experience. And for the family of the alcoholic or addict, family counseling can be a godsend.

The strengths approach, as its name implies, builds on clients' strengths and resources. This is "a versatile practice approach, relying heavily on ingenuity and creativity, the courage and common sense of both clients and their social workers" (Saleebey, 2006, p. 1). Traditionally, work in the substance abuse field has focused on *breaking* client resistance and denial (Rapp & Goscha, 2006). According to this more positive framework, however, client resistance and denial can be viewed as healthy, intelligent responses to a situation that might involve unwelcome court mandates and other intrusive practices.

THEMES IN RECOVERY

The strengths approach does not entail set rituals or dogma but involves certain basic principles that transcend treatment modality or style. Charles A. Rapp (1998) singles out six critical elements conducive to recovery. These are identity as a competent human being, the need for personal control or choice, the need for hope, the need for purpose, the need for a sense of achievement, and the presence of at least one key person. The experience of illness and recovery is unique to each person, but these common themes emerge in the stories of recovery. Although Rapp's focus was on mental illness, these recovery themes pertain equally well to all biochemical disorders. In the following pages, we draw on firsthand narrative accounts to illustrate each of Rapp's recovery themes.

The first critical element of recovery, which has important implications for treatment, occurs when the person moves from an all-consuming identification with the illness to a *position of managing the symptoms of the disorder*. The position is often expressed by persons who are successful in going from abusing alcohol to learning to drink moderately. As Rick Anderson (1997) states:

> My experience as an alcohol counselor and a former alcohol abuser fully supports the moderate drinking program approach. . . . Behavior management has worked best for most alcoholic abusers. We learn to be responsible, make decisions, obtain legitimate counseling, and, most important, empower ourselves. (p. 5)

Another substance abuse counselor and a strong AA proponent, Larry Heckert, similarly reveals the importance of separation of the illness and the self:

> Recovery comes through getting your priorities straight; you have to place yourself and your sobriety above everything else. Spirituality is important as well. (personal communication, December 14, 2000)

Sometimes sobriety brings with it a change in personality. Susan Cheever (1999) offers this description of her father, John Cheever, the famous writer, upon his return from treatment:

> He went from being an alcoholic with a drug problem who smoked two packs of Marlboros a day to being a man so abstemious that his principal drugs were the sugar in desserts. . . .
> Although he knew too well how easily he could slip, the change in him made it seem less likely than ever that he would. His self-pitying bombast was gone. There were apologies instead of accusations. He was a man who seemed involved with life again. (pp. 198–199)

The second theme concerns the need for personal control, or *choice*. As we hear from a former methamphetamine addict, "four years clean and sober," whose family had earlier disowned her:

> My mother took my daughter while I served the 36 days in jail. NA (Narcotics Anonymous) didn't work—all that "powerlessness" got to me. I still have a few beers—I'm cursed by my counselor for this. But by the grace of my mother and my daughter, I'm not going back. . . . Group therapy was really helpful for me. (personal communication, September 2000)

Michael Beechem (1996), a social work professor who had tried AA to no avail and then was referred by the college administrator for treatment, shares the secret of his success:

> I find myself actively engaged in the recovery process, aware of the insidious nature of alcoholism and how a small voice within me can threaten to coax me into indulging in "just one drink" to help during a stressful situation. (p. 48)

Choice is the hallmark of the harm reduction model; its task is to help clients find their own way and to carve out their own paths to sobriety. In Britain, this is the predominant model for treatment, considered to be the most effective with young persons who express willingness to work on controlling their drinking and other drug use. The focus is on prevention, not cure. In his lecture before an audience of American social work students, Philip Guy (1994) of the University of Hull in England described his counseling strategy. "I've never used total abstinence as a goal unless the client wishes," he said. "If I decide the goal, the client might as well go home. The key is choice."

The third theme, *hope,* is a quality emphasized throughout the literature on substance abuse counseling. Without hope, of course, there can be no effort on working toward a meaningful goal. At the societal level, as Saleebey (2006) informs us, the strengths-based counselor's goal is forever searching the environment for forces that enhance human possibilities and resiliencies. Rather than focusing on problems, your eye turns toward possibility. "Like social caretaking and social work, the strengths perspective is about the revolutionary possibility of hope: hope realized through the strengthened sinew of social relationships in family, neighborhood, community, culture, and country" (Saleebey, 2006, p. 20). Saleebey stresses the power that stems from membership in community organizations. Membership in mutual support groups such as AA offers hope to alcoholics through the fellowship of shared experience. Sayings such as "I can't do it alone, but together we can" reinforce the strength of mutual help.

A sense of *purpose* is the next critical ingredient in recovery. Many of van Wormer's clients expressed a sense of purpose or meaning, saying, in essence, "Now I know this all happened for a reason. So I could help people who are going through the same thing." The Twelfth Step of AA involves taking the message of what has been learned to others. As people hear personal stories from others who have achieved sobriety and a happy outlook on life, they too may think change is possible.

Spirituality is a cornerstone of the many mutual-support groups, a connection with a Higher Power that gives life meaning. Pat Coughlin, a substance abuse counselor from Marshalltown, Iowa, who once suffered from multiple drug addictions (including meth and cocaine), describes the change that came over his life following a bar fight. In inpatient treatment for the third time, Coughlin says:

> I knew the game, knew it wouldn't work. I had a spiritual awakening. I got on my knees and prayed, and things began to change. I felt God was answering my prayers.

Exactly what I prayed for came to be in the form of my 6-months stay at the Recovery House. There I formed the habit of attending AA, the habit of praying, and work with a personal sponsor. Then after 9 months sober, I started college. (speech, November 28, 2000)

A *sense of achievement* is a healthy counterpart to wrestling with the feelings of grief and loss that accompany the early period of recovery. Common types of achievement listed by Rapp (1998) are helping others, personal success at work, and self-expression through hobbies and/or the arts. In reflecting on his life, Coughlin, the speaker in the preceding passage, described how his sister, so estranged from him in the past, now has turned to requesting help with her daughter who has started to drink. "To go from a drug-dealing nothing to being called to help with a drinking child—that is the miracle of AA, the power of The Program."

The final element in recovery delineated by Rapp is *the presence of at least one person*—a friend, professional helper, teacher, or family member. This element parallels the focus on relationship in all client-centered therapies (see Carl Rogers, 1931, for the classical formulation). Genuineness, empathy, and nonpossessive warmth are the key components of the effective therapeutic relationship. Through warmth (and caring), many a tough-minded personal spokesperson from AA or NA or GA (Gamblers Anonymous) has guided the seemingly most recalcitrant addict through the rough periods of early sobriety. Whatever the personal style of the helper, it is the sincerity and caring that are key. Witness this account from Tinia Holder, at the time of writing an inmate at the federal prison at Danbury, Connecticut. Here she comments on the help she received from a dedicated psychologist:

They have yet to financially fund the Bridge Program for substance abuse treatment. Dr. Onorato is the sole staff who renders countless hours trying to assist with the plight of abused women. He always treats each of us as individuals. He is a kind soul. Without him, I firmly believe that I would have ended my own life. I have learned a great deal from the trauma program. Dr. Onorato, through his hours of counseling, has shown me that I am a strong, capable woman who is realizing that I don't have just arms and legs but that I am able to run and fight, give and take. I can reclaim all the pieces of myself that had been stolen by stronger, cruel people who did whatever they wanted. I have learned that I have not only a voice, but a strong voice that can shout the word NO! (personal communication, July 7, 1998)

Central to all these stories of recovery is the theme of personal empowerment. Both harm reduction and mutual-help programs are based on a voluntary commitment to change. The greatest weakness of The Program—its dogmatism—is possibly also its greatest strength. The Program gives people who are highly vulnerable and clutching for support something concrete, something more faith based than scientific, to latch on to. One is hard put to fault the kind of personal support that so many recovering alcoholics and other drug addicts have derived from what is commonly referred to as The Program (see chapter 12 on mutual-help groups for an in-depth analysis).

For effective work with so-called dually diagnosed clients or, as we prefer to refer to them, persons with co-occurring disorders, those with both substance use and mental health problems, Mancini, Linhorst, Broderick, and Bayliff (in press) recommend an approach that is highly flexible and consumer centered. Many persons with co-occurring disorders are unable to negotiate the demands of highly structured, abstinence-only programs, a fact that results in low retention rates in such programs. Harm reduction approaches are therefore essential for persons of such high vulnerability. Still, more than half of persons who have both a mental and a substance use disorder don't receive any treatment (Center for Substance Abuse Treatment [CSAT], 2005). Of those who do get treatment, most receive mental health treatment only, and only a fraction receive integrated treatment geared to their special needs.

Within this context, the work of clinicians such as Catherine Crisp (2005) is rare (see also Box 8.1 in Chapter 8). Crisp differentiates chemical dependence theory, which takes "a hard-lined approach," from mental illness theory, which stresses client nurturance. The following passage describes the approach that she has found most effective for working with clients with co-occurring disorders:

> Much of the work I do with clients individually is based on a strengths perspective and motivational therapy techniques. Many clients have tried and failed many times in their sobriety and have little hope in their ability to recover from their addiction. I attempt to educate them about the process of relapse, help them identify individual strengths and resources that may be helpful in their recovery, confront them on their denial, and assist them in understanding elements of their substance abuse and their mental illness or depression. The most valuable thing I think I offer clients is a belief that if they are willing to do the work, they can recover. I let them know that they have the abilities to recover, but ultimately, they must complete the task themselves. (Crisp, 2005, p. 207)

FINDING THE STRENGTHS IN DIVERGENT MODELS

The strengths perspective is essentially an approach rather than a well-integrated therapy or, as Saleebey (2006) describes it, an approach to practice that directs us to "an appreciation of the assets of individuals, families, and communities" (p. 10). Because this is basically a focus, an outlook, there is no reason we cannot apply it to the macrolevel as well and look to the positives with an attitude of appreciation rather than devaluation.

As recreational therapist Angie Woods states concerning practices at her Iowa agency:

> The newer models are beginning to be utilized, especially with populations requiring special needs. Harm reduction models are being utilized primarily with the dually diagnosed because of the increased recidivism rate with this population. Confrontation and the breaking of denial are slowly being replaced by interventions designed to assist the consumer to evaluate behavior associated with chemical usage. Change, however, is a slow process. Some professionals are reluctant to truly embrace harm reduction as the goal of abstinence is clung to as the best solution. (personal communication, July 10, 2006)

In light of policy changes allowing increasing flexibility in the provision of treatment, the time is ripe for a comprehensive approach to the field of addiction treatment. This approach is about the acceptance of differences rather than one that takes sides among the various camps. As a highly adaptable and effective approach, the strengths perspective can serve to shape our conceptualization of client-centered policies, such as drug courts that favor treatment over punishment. This perspective also leads us to an appreciation for the high-quality work done by men and women whose devotion to their multiply addicted clients is almost heroic, as well as to an appreciation for the many effective treatment strategies being used. Instead of asking the question "What is wrong with this or that approach?" a framework based on strengths seeks to find the strong points in diverse frameworks such as the Twelve-Step approach and the harm reduction alternative. For an unabashedly negative point of view, consider the title of Peele and Bufe's best-selling 2000 book, *Resisting 12-Step Coercion: How to Fight Forced Participation in AA, NA, or 12-Step Treatment.*

Granted, Peele and Bufe's attack is directed more at the courts for coercing individuals in trouble with the law into attending such groups and at Twelve-Step-based treatment programs than it is against the "once proudly voluntaristic religions' healing programs" (p. 14). Even nonaddictive drug users (of illegal drugs), as Peele and Bufe suggest, are being forced to say in treatment that they are "powerless" over the substance in question. This requirement is made in the belief that "according to drug war dogma there is no such thing as, for instance, moderate marijuana use" (p. 28).

Peele and Bufe's points are well taken; *Resisting 12-Step Coercion* is well documented and thought provoking. Missing in all its 200-plus pages, however, is any acknowledgment for a program that has clearly saved so many lives. We who know firsthand of a number of seeming miracles of recovery from membership in a mutual-help group such as AA or from participation in a professionally run Minnesota Model program regret this omission.

Today, there are more than 2 million members of AA worldwide; AA is the most prominent of the Twelve-Step groups (Lampman, 2004). Some 90% of residential and outpatient treatment programs in the United States draw directly on its principles. The Minnesota Model is defined by one of its founders in these terms:

> What we have done is successfully integrate the spiritual philosophy of Alcoholics Anonymous into the professional treatment program. And in doing this, something profound has happened. It seems that all we have done is to humanize our programs with the interpersonal mutuality found in most Alcoholics Anonymous relationships. (D. Anderson, 1981, p. 29)

In this text, we refer to this model as the *traditional disease model*.

If anything, the critics of harm reduction are more vociferous than are the critics of the Minnesota Model. Let us consider what happened when the first program to be shown on a major U.S. television network to question the lack of alternatives to treatment in the United States was broadcast. "Drinking: Are You in Control?" aired in May 2000 on ABC's *20/20* to present alternatives to the Twelve-Step total abstinence approach. From the start, the reaction in the press and on the Internet was palpable. For example, here's how Bob Eck addressed subscribers to the NASW-ATOD section LISTSERV:

> To mislead thousands of actively using alcoholics and addicts that it is indeed possible for them to "control drink" or use again is cruel, and then to attempt to support that opinion by the use of some unknown, backyard research on some chimps is truly an attempt to put one over on all of us. It looks like it worked, because I am sure there are those out there who will latch onto any potentially good reason to return to using their drug of choice. Believe me folks, there is no such thing as controlled use for the chemically dependent. The chemically abusive? Possibly so, but be careful here also. Go to the *DSM–IV* for the definition of the difference. Every so often someone comes along with this theory and some people line up behind the pied piper. Not possible, folks. (personal communication, June 16, 2000)

In fact, studies reveal the effectiveness of both traditional disease-model-based treatment and motivational enhancement therapy, the therapy favored in harm reduction programs (see Hester & Miller, 2003; Project MATCH Research Group, 1997). Bob Eck does have a point, however. Moderate drinking is a possibility for some but not for all. The difficulty is in identifying who will be able to adopt this strategy.

A primary purpose of this text is to explore such dilemmas, adopt a wider vision, and find even more ways to help individuals who want to reduce risks, improve their health, and/or stop practicing their addiction. As a starting point, let us explore the harm reduction model in greater depth.

HARM REDUCTION AND THE STRENGTHS APPROACH

Consider the following scenarios:

- Street social workers distribute literature on safe sex and drug treatment in a notoriously crime-ridden neighborhood.
- A social worker receives training in drug screening to volunteer his or her services at a first-aid station at a secretly located rave; the drug screening is to protect youth from taking Ecstasy pills laced with life-threatening adulterants.
- A worker at a women's shelter helps clients develop a personal safety plan for themselves and their children, but she does not counsel them to leave their violent relationships.
- A college program to prevent binge drinking targets youth with problems and works with them to reduce their alcohol consumption and decrease the risks associated with intoxication.
- A school social worker conducts an after school group to help kids with gender identity issues talk through problems of internalized homophobia that might otherwise lead them to seek self-destructive channels of expression.

All of these situations are high risk for the client; yet, except for volunteering at the rave, they are typical of the ones social workers encounter regularly. Common to all these interventions is the theme of pragmatism, or helping people choose from options they are willing to take, rather than trying to push on them changes that they are unprepared to make. Harm reduction is not about doing what is best; it is about doing whatever works at whatever level makes sense to the client.

What is harm reduction? Irish social work educator Shane Butler (2002) describes it best:

> The new view of drug users as health service consumers was one which ideally saw them as having strengths and competence, and as being uniquely well placed to advise on how risk might be reduced; they were to be seen as active collaborators with healthcare professionals . . . rather than as passive recipients of services delivered by professionals, on terms dictated by professionals. (p. 190)

"Meet the client where the client is" is a popular slogan of social work practice that sums up the harm reduction philosophy. Harm reduction joins client and therapist in the realistic pursuit of survival. Typical strategies include the following:

- Helping clients substitute a less harmful drug for a life-threatening drug; a controversial example is that of Brazil, where researchers help clients overcome crack cocaine addiction by providing marijuana.
- Recruiting heroin addicts into methadone-maintenance and needle exchange programs.
- Providing women returning to their battering partners a plan for self-protection.

Social work and the harm reduction approach are a natural fit: Both start where the client is and strive to help people improve their levels of functioning. This natural affinity is widely recognized by policymakers and social workers in Europe, Australia, and Canada. In the United States, in contrast, this realization is in its infancy, at least in social work. A recent search of social work abstracts as of June 2006 revealed 25 listings for harm reduction, practically all of which appeared after 2000; Criminal Justice Abstracts contain 142 listings, and PsycInfo has 900. The latter two contain a high percentage of references before the year 2000. Although social work got a relatively late start, we can conclude there is increasing interest today in harm reduction policies and practice. In an article in the *Journal of Social Work Education,* for example, McNeece (2003) calls for immediate training of tomorrow's social workers not only to work with substance using clients but also to be effective policy advocates for harm reduction.

To further define harm reduction, we need to take into account the two aspects of the term that are often poorly differentiated in the literature: policy and practice. As *policy,* harm reduction is an outgrowth of the international public health movement, a philosophy that opposes the criminalization of drug use and views substance misuse as a public health rather than a criminal justice concern. The goal of the harm reduction movement is to reduce the harm to users and misusers and to the communities in which they live, including the harm caused by the criminalization of the substances. A pragmatic approach, harm reduction seeks to control the risks in drug-taking behavior (Brocato & Wagner, 2003). From this perspective, punitive laws against drinking by young adults under age 21 and possessing or using certain substances are opposed as a new form of Prohibition. The war on drugs is seen as exacting a toll in terms of deaths generated by the use of contaminated, unregulated chemicals; the spread of hepatitis, tuberculosis, and AIDS through the sharing of dirty needles; the social breakdown in America's inner cities; and political corruption elsewhere. In several European countries, it was the AIDS epidemic of the 1980s that catapulted harm reduction policies into prominence. Drug use was medicalized, and the behavior of drug use was closely monitored at methadone and other clinics, where a safe drug supply was provided under medical supervision. Several U.S. cities, including Baltimore, have moved in the direction of such progressive policies.

At the *practitioner* level, harm reduction is an umbrella term for a set of practical strategies based on motivational interviewing and other strengths-based approaches to help people help themselves by moving from safer use, to managed use, to abstinence, if so desired. The labeling of clients, as is the custom in mental health circles ("He has an antisocial personality," "She is borderline") or in treatment circles ("He's an alcoholic," "She has an eating disorder"), is avoided; clients provide the definition of the situation as they see it. Clients who wish it are given advice on how to reduce the harm in drug use, such as, "Don't drink on an empty stomach," or "Always make sure to use a clean needle." Most of the advice, however, is provided in a less direct fashion, such as, "Here are some options you might want to consider." Consistent with the strengths perspective, the counselor and client collaborate to consider a broad range of solutions to the client-defined problem; resources are gathered or located to meet the individual needs of the client. Above all, clients are viewed as amenable to change.

The harm reduction approach recognizes the importance of giving equal emphasis to each of the biopsychosocial and spiritual factors in drug use. In collaboration, the counselor and client consider a broad range of solutions to the consequences of drug misuse, abstinence being only one. Forcing the client to admit to a substance addiction as a way of breaking through "denial," according to proponents of this approach, can lead to resistance and a battle of wills between worker and client. When the focus of the professional relationship, however, is on promoting healthy lifestyles and on reducing problems that the client defines as important rather than on the substance use per se, many clients can be reached who would otherwise stay away (Denning, 2000; Hester & Miller, 2003; McNeece, 2003). Seeking help is rare among substance misusers until the problems are overwhelming, probably due to the stringent and off-putting requirements of traditional substance abuse treatment. All of these arguments, pragmatic as opposed to dogmatic, have been introduced to America through international conferences and exchanges. Similarly, the Twelve-Step-based treatment program has made inroads in Europe, especially in private clinics, where its success with a certain type of client—extraverted, severely addicted, structure seeking—is reminiscent of the American experience. Common to all these treatments, especially in the United States, is the recognition that problems with alcohol, other drugs, and compulsive behaviors such as gambling affect not only individuals but whole families and communities as well.

This more flexible, harm reduction approach would appear more relevant to community-based treatment and prevention work than to counseling inmates sentenced for drug violations. Yet, in Scotland unlike in the United States, the drug court system operates on harm reduction principles; success is measured in reduction in drug use and in criminal activity to support the habit (McIvor et al., 2006). In Canada too, within the correctional system no less, these pragmatic principles are being adapted to substance abuse treatment. This move parallels an advance from the old punishment paradigm into a paradigm of healing (Thomas, 2005). Although needle exchanges are not allowed in prison, bleach is made available to sanitize the needles often used in tattooing. Total abstinence is not required for postprison treatment. Inmates ready to leave the system with no parole restrictions can choose either an abstinence or a moderation goal.

EMPIRICAL RESEARCH

The substance abuse treatment field, even more than most other practice disciplines, has been characterized by an ideology and folk wisdom and occasional brilliance that would be impossible to quantify. Moreover, the gap between treatment practices that research has shown effective and what is actually done in treatment agencies is immense. Within a climate of pressure to implement evidence-based treatment practices, increase performance standards, and prove the cost effectiveness of treatment programs, access to scientifically proven studies on treatment effectiveness is vital. But how can treatment effectiveness, under the circumstances, be measured?

Understandings about how addiction is conceptualized have much to do with the treatment modalities utilized and even the professional and personal qualifications of the treatment staff. Treatment effectiveness can be measured through the evaluation of improvement in terms of reduced healthcare needs, less dependence, lowered crime rates, success in employment, and so on of a group of individuals who had major economic and social problems before treatment. When measured this way, the cost effectiveness of substance abuse treatment can be seen to pay for itself multiple times over. Keep in mind that, unlike traditional healthcare interventions that focus on one specific outcome (e.g., weight loss, reduced blood pressure), substance abuse treatment can achieve effects on a number of outcome measures, including health status, criminal behavior, family functioning, mental health, and employment (Belenko, Patapis, & French, 2005).

The California Treatment Outcome Project, a rigorously designed study of the effectiveness of alcohol abuse and other drug abuse treatment, showed that the state received a $7 return for every $1 invested, the largest savings of which were from reductions in crime (Ettner et al., 2006). More than 43 substance abuse treatment providers participated in the study. Similar reports have come from virtually every state. Sadly, according to a recent report from the Treatment Research Institute conducted by Belenko et al. (2005), of the over 26.3 million Americans needing treatment for an alcohol or other drug problem, only 26% received any treatment during the year. And only a fraction (10–15%) of the 80% of state prison inmates receive the treatment they need. The state budgets are simply too small to accommodate the need. Spending priorities, however, continue to be placed on cleaning up the wreckage of substance misuse rather than on treatment and prevention. Thirteen percent of total state budgets go to "shoveling up" the wreckage caused by substance use according to a report from the Center on Addiction and Substance Abuse (Alter, 2001). Change may be underway, however: Starting in January 2007, the federal Medicaid and Medicare programs will pay for screening and brief intervention programs for alcohol and other drug addiction (Curley, 2006).

For years, researchers have argued over what scientific research says about the various treatments and their clinical recovery rates. Because virtually all U.S. programming relies on attendance at AA or NA as a supplement to treatment, solid studies comparing the disease-model abstinence-based approach and alternative approaches without AA and NA referrals have been few and far between.

EARLIER STUDIES OF NOTE

Directed by the National Institute on Alcohol Abuse and Alcoholism, the multisite, 8-year comparison study, Project MATCH (1997), involved almost 2,000 patients in the largest trial of psychotherapies ever undertaken. The goal of this $28 million project was not to measure treatment effectiveness but rather to study which types of treatments worked for which types of people.

The three treatment designs chosen for this extensive study were based on the principles of the three most popular treatment designs: conventional Twelve-Step-based treatment, cognitive strategies, and motivational enhancement therapy (MET). One uniqueness of the interventions offered under the umbrella of Project MATCH is that all treatment was one-on-one; no group therapy was provided. Attendance at AA meetings, which was stressed more by the therapists of the traditional disease-model school, was the only group contact that clients received. Any conclusion concerning treatment outcomes, accordingly, needs to take into account that Project MATCH, in contrast to the usual treatment practice in North America, provided individually delivered counseling.

The first of three treatment philosophies employed in Project MATCH was the Twelve-Step facilitation design. Counselors using this design explained to their clients the basic principles of Alcoholics Anonymous. In short, alcoholism is a disease that is primary, progressive, chronic, and fatal if not arrested. Alcoholics need to acknowledge that they are powerless over alcohol and that only through turning to a power greater than themselves can they be restored to sanity. Recovering comes through regular attendance at mutual-help groups and through humility and surrender to a Higher Power.

Cognitively based treatment, as offered by the practitioners participating in Project MATCH, focused on relapse prevention. The underlying premise of this approach is the belief that people's cognitions, or the way they view the world, and their self-destructive behavior are intertwined. Social skills training and stress management are basic strategies used by cognitive therapists to help clients find ways of reducing stress as an alternative to alcohol misuse.

The third model selected by Project MATCH for scrutiny, MET, is the pragmatic approach most closely associated with the harm reduction model. MET is client centered; the therapist assesses the level of the client's motivation for change and never fights the client but rather rolls with resistance. MET techniques are geared to help people find their own path to change; feedback is offered by reflecting back to the client what he or she seems to be saying about the need to reduce or eliminate self-destructive behaviors.

Although Project MATCH was designed to test the general assumption that matching could improve treatment outcomes, individuals were assigned randomly to three varieties of treatment so that researchers could determine which modality worked best for whom. The results were that 1 year and 3 years after treatment, clients showed substantial improvement regardless of the modality used.

To the surprise of the research team, outcome evaluations showed that patient-treatment matching is not necessary for satisfactory results and that participants in the intensive Twelve-Step format did as well on follow-up as those in the cognitive-behavioral therapy and motivational enhancement designs. Treatments were provided over 8- and 9-week periods, with motivational therapy offered only four times and the other two designs offered for 12 sessions. All participants showed significant and sustained improvements in the increased percentage of days they remained abstinent and the decreased number of drinks per drinking day, the researchers said. However, they noted that outpatients who received the Twelve-Step facilitation program were more likely to remain completely abstinent in the year following treatment than outpatients who received the other treatments. Individuals high on religiosity and those who indicated they were seeking meaning in life generally did better with the Twelve-Step, disease-model focus, while clients with high levels of psychopathology did not do better with this approach. Clients low in motivation did best ultimately with the design geared for their level of motivation.

In aftercare subjects who were studied, less successful outcomes were associated with male gender, psychiatric problems, and peer group support for drinking. Because there was no control group deprived of treatment, generalizations concerning the efficacy of treatment cannot be made, a fact that has brought this massive project in for considerable criticism (Wallace, 2005). Another major criticism is that of selection bias in study recruitment. Clients were barred from the experimental treatment if they were dependent on heroin or cocaine, used IV drugs, were suicidal, or had acute psychoses. Since the clients that counselors typically see are not so homogeneous and carefully screened, such restrictions affect generalization of the findings (Wallace, 2005). What this extensive and long-term study does show, however, is that all three individually delivered treatment approaches are relatively comparable in their results; treatment that is not abstinence based (motivational enhancement) is as helpful in getting clients to reduce their alcohol consumption as the more intensive treatment designs. These findings provide support for the guiding principle of this book, which is to find what works in seemingly diverse treatment designs.

Keep in mind that Project MATCH was concerned with diagnosable alcohol-dependent individuals only. The treatment needs of persons with alcohol and other drug problems in general, most of whom never come to the attention of specialized treatment centers, are clearly different from the needs of chronic alcoholics and addicts coerced into treatment (CSAT, 2005). Those other more typical persons with addiction problems are often seen in general social service and counseling settings for issues such as marital conflict and employment problems. An overreliance on medical models for diagnostic criteria often misses these problem substance misusers. Certainly, the conventional techniques of "breaking down denial" and forcing such individuals to abstain totally from drinking and drug using are counterproductive. When clients who enter treatment for personal problems seemingly unrelated to substance misuse are referred to a specialized chemical dependence treatment center, they often are lost to treatment altogether. A far more effective approach is to treat them for the issue at hand but to keep the channels of communication open.

We have described Project MATCH in detail not because it provides proof of treatment effectiveness—it does not, in the absence of a control group—but because it confirms the viability of diverse approaches. This finding that clients do well when treatment is steeped in Twelve-Step principles, cognitive skills training, or an approach geared for individual motivation for change validates the basic thesis of this book—the strengths inherent in each of the various standard treatment options.

Also worth noting is the manner in which treatment effectiveness was measured by Project MATCH researchers. No longer is government-funded research using subjects' ability to obtain abstinence as the standard for recovery (as in the follow-up surveys asking, "When did you have your last drink?"). Instead, the impact of treatment strategies is now being measured in terms of improvement in drinking and drug-taking habits. Retention in treatment itself is used in some evaluations as an outcome measure of success. Harm reduction models, much more commonly used in Europe than in the United States, measure success simply by whether or not harm was reduced. For example, a person who injects heroin might be reducing the harm of becoming HIV positive by using clean syringes. Rigid adherence to the traditional, total abstinence standard in the past is one reason that the myth of treatment effectiveness persists. Box 1.2 describes a

TREATMENT EFFECTIVENESS:
DOES IMPROVEMENT COUNT?
Diane Rae Davis

I will never forget the day I first presented the results of Project MATCH to a group of first-year MSW students. I put the overheads up showing graphs of the different treatment groups and the number of days of abstinence at 6 months and 15 months. As I was describing these results, trying to make it interesting by noting how few persons maintained 100% abstinence by the end of 15 months but how many had improved in number of days of abstinence, I noticed the visible agitation of a student near the back of the room. I knew she had come to the MSW program after several years of practice in the alcohol and drug treatment field, and I wondered what in the world could be upsetting her.

I finally asked if she wanted to comment on anything. She blurted out that "improvement doesn't cut it" in treatment. The idea of presenting improvement as a "success" was totally foreign to her. In fact, she suspected the information as it was presented on the graphs might be some kind of attempt to erode the recognized standard of recovery, which is "abstinence." As she talked further, it became clear that her concern was for the clients who might hear the "improvement" message and take that as permission to relapse.

I am forever grateful to this student for launching a much deeper (than I had planned) discussion on what "recovery" means and who has the power to decide the meaning. The class concluded, as we all know in our hearts, that there is no "right" answer to these two questions. The reality is that it depends on which group is valued and powerful enough to determine goals and outcomes. The MATCH outcomes were "value-free" on the surface in that they just presented "the facts." However, by defining success as maintaining 80 to 90% days of abstinence over the follow-up period, the group of this very expensive and high-profile study in essence "legitimized" that improvement does count. At a later date, the student told me she was glad her "blinders had been taken off," although this was a painful experience. She felt more prepared to deal with the complexities and ambiguities of the treatment world that are too often presented as if all answers are known. Sometimes, my biggest job as a teacher is to instill doubt.

---

classroom discussion that contrasts the all-or-nothing approach to measuring recovery in terms of a number of criteria related to a reduction in harmful pursuits.

In summary, the standard for "what is recovery?" is beginning to change in the United States, making room for broader definitions that include such variables as improvements in health, social, and legal status. It is important to note, moreover, that recovery from alcohol dependence or other drug use most often occurs outside the confines of hospitals, substance abuse clinics, or Twelve-Step groups.

Vaillant (1983) discovered as much in his classic longitudinal study of boys growing up and growing old. Vaillant's extensive study, covering a low socioeconomic status (SES) population of males for over a 40-year period, is widely cited by supporters and detractors alike of the traditional Twelve-Step approach as the study par excellence in the literature. Tracking a large contingent of adult alcoholics identified from a community sample, Vaillant (1983) concluded that factors associated with recovery in middle age were personal will power, active church membership or other group membership such as AA, stable marital relationships, and hobbies. He found that having a relative with a drinking problem significantly increased the risk of alcohol abuse irrespective of whether the individual lived with the problem drinker. More than half of the subjects in Vaillant's inner-city sample recovered at some point in their lives. In his more recent 50-year study of the same alcoholic cohorts, Vaillant (1995) found that over a lifetime, sustained recovery requires at least two of the following experiences: some sort of compulsory supervision or a painful alcohol-related event, finding a substitute dependence such as AA, a new stable relationship, and religious conversion. We learn from Vaillant's over-the-life-course study that many people recover through maturity or by other means and that alcoholism is not always progressive and fatal as is commonly thought.

RECENT RESEARCH FINDINGS

Using a different methodology from Vaillant—interview data—Dawson et al. (2005) of the National Institute on Alcohol Abuse and Alcoholism (NIAAA) found, similarly, that about one third of the previously diagnosable alcoholics matured out of their dependence; about one sixth abstained and another sixth became moderate drinkers. The greater the amount of alcohol that was consumed, the lower was the likelihood of either type of recovery. The significance of this study was in showing that many young people mature out of alcoholism and that individuals who were diagnosable alcoholics at one period in life could indeed become moderate drinkers at a later stage.

Hester and Miller's (2003) *Handbook of Alcohol Treatment Approaches* is the best known in the alcoholism treatment field for the large-scale comparisons of treatment outcomes since their first edition was published in the 1980s. What they found was that the treatment methods with the strongest support of efficacy were virtually unknown and unused in U.S. standard practice. After their most recent review of hundreds of empirically based clinical trials, the authors reached two major conclusions: (a) there is no single superior approach to treatment for all individuals, and (b) treatment programs and systems should be constructed to include a variety of approaches inasmuch as different individuals respond best to different approaches.

Of the 47 different treatment modalities that were tested in the literature, the top scores for effectiveness were received for:

- brief intervention
- motivational enhancement
- the medications acamprosate and naltrexone
- self-control and social skills training
- aversion therapy
- cognitive therapy
- acupuncture

The lowest rankings were received from worst to least bad by:

- education tapes, lectures, and films
- confrontational counseling
- relaxation training
- Twelve-Step facilitation

We should take into account, as Hester and Miller suggest, the fact that some modalities such as brief intervention and motivational enhancement generally have been conducted with less seriously addicted populations than some of the others. The central message of this comparative study is that the modalities most often used today are those with the least evidence of effectiveness.

Burke, Arkowitz, and Menchola's (2003) meta-analysis of the efficacy of motivational interviewing clinical trials is also relevant for our purposes because their person-centered approach is the one favored in this text. Data were gathered from the literature of 30 controlled clinical trials that compared an adaptation of motivational techniques to another treatment format. The overall finding was that motivational adaptations showed equivalent benefits to other strategies but that they achieved the same results in far less time. The results were positive for problems involving alcohol, drugs, and diet but less so for smoking and HIV-risk behaviors.

Finally, Belenko et al. (2005) provide very useful information for policy-makers in their survey of evidence provided from 51 recently published and 19 unpublished cost–benefit analyses of substance abuse interventions. Readers are referred to this 68-page reprint on the Treatment Research Institute web-site. Evidence provided there confirms the cost effectiveness of drug courts (see the later section on drug courts) with typical savings of thousands of dollars per client saved over a 2-year period. The cost savings were driven largely by reductions in costs of jail, Medicaid, victim costs from crime, and drug-exposed infants. Also noteworthy were the prison treatment studies that showed greatly reduced reoffending rates.

TREATMENT TRENDS

There are more than 15,000 substance abuse facilities in the United States (Substance Abuse and Mental Health Services Administration [SAMHSA], 2004). Most treatment programs (81%) provide outpatient services only; some provide both outpatient and residential treatment. The treatment system faces many challenges that affect the utilization of services. Beyond the inadequate federal, state, and private insurance funding, high staff turnover, relatively low pay, the use of outdated techniques and attitudes are all issues that negatively impact services and in turn the attractiveness of treatment to voluntary clients (McLellan, Kleber, & Carise, 2003).

Yet even within this context, a revolution of sorts is brewing in substance abuse treatment circles; a paradigm shift is clearly under way. Bolstered by extraordinary brain research showing the physiological basis in addiction, substance abuse treatment is moving slowly toward a more scientific, empirically based approach. Much of the impetus for change admittedly is economic. After expanding wildly in the 1980s, residential Twelve-Step programs are falling on hard times; insurers and employers are seeking cheaper, less intensive alternatives (Belenko et al., 2005). There is simultaneously a trend, for prevention purposes, to treat alcohol and drug users with only mild problems (e.g., problem drinkers). Nonabstinence-based treatment programs, such as Moderation Management, which allow clients a set number of drinks, are becoming increasingly popular (Hester & Miller, 2003).

The demand for brief interventions is compatible with managed healthcare requirements in both commercial markets and public systems (Zweben & Rose, 1999). Clinicians must be innovative in treating the range of severity presented by persons with substance use problems, as Zweben and Rose suggest. The premium today is on flexibility and individualized treatment. We need to suit the treatment to the client, not force the client into a standardized world. Just as new scientific discoveries are shaping knowledge about the biology of addiction, so political developments are changing the manner in which substance abuse treatment is provided. Until recently in the United States, for example, nonabstinence treatment programs were virtually unheard of. Today, at many progressive treatment centers, never-before-questioned traditions are being turned around. Chain smoking, which was previously taken for granted in treatment circles, is now correctly regarded as an addiction not unlike any other. Clients are counseled in moderate drinking and not terminated if they can't quit taking drugs altogether at once. Meanwhile, for the first time ever, television programs on the major networks discuss moderation treatment as a viable alternative to traditional treatments requiring immediate abstinence from all mood-altering substances (and activities). The recent reporting in the mainstream media and medical journals on the practicality of a harm reduction philosophy is perhaps a harbinger of future advances.

As registered in opinion polls in recent years, public opinion is changing. An opinion poll conducted by the Pew Research Center (2001) found that most men but not women thought too many people were in jail for drug possession. About 73% of all respondents believed doctors should be allowed to prescribe marijuana for medical reasons. These figures represented increases from earlier surveys. A shift in public opinion is evidenced today against continuing prison expansion and in favor of approval for rehabilitation, education, and prevention strategies. According to a recent report conducted by Greene and Pranis (2006), four times as many Californians expressed support for reducing the prison budget and redirecting funding to education and child protective services as for emphasizing incarceration for drug offenders. Similar results are found in Kentucky and Maryland. As Maryland invests huge sums of money into drug treatment, a survey shows that most respondents in the state believe that treatment is preferred to incarceration, and 69% view treatment as more effective (L. Anderson, 2006).

In any period of paradigm change, however, there is always resistance. Some years back, this resistance was brought home to Ron Schauer, who was called to return to the directorship of an agency in Washington State after a 15-year absence. In his own words:

> My brief story back in the "field" was so surreal. People—a few talk about things that they see as cutting edge, which are things we thought, 15 years ago, were about to become commonplace: family treatment, etc., etc. But the old guard re-established control. Not unexpected in a reactionary, Puritan, and cost-cutting time. Two-year-degreed people come for much less.
>
> I was daily amazed at what my staff didn't know, think, or even see in the definition of treatment. All but three were *heavy* smokers; all had disastrous personal lives, just like in 1977, when I first began.
>
> Managed care itself is, in my view, something of an evil. Yet it has served to push CD treatment off center and demanded some innovation, even in the name of greater profits and competitiveness. (personal communication, November 8, 1998)

The fact that this poorly functioning treatment center has folded is perhaps a sign of a tightening up by external funding sources that began in the 1990s. The demise of this center (where van Wormer once worked) gives credence to the view that, as virtually all contemporary writers in this area now contend, the field is reinventing itself to meet today's needs. The new addiction therapist must be prepared to meet the needs of polydrug-addicted clients, clients with mental health and addiction problems both, and persons referred from the criminal justice system (see, e.g., Belenko et al., 2005; Springer, McNeece, & Arnold, 2003; van Wormer & Bartollas, 2007; Wallace, 2005).

Among the most significant developments in recent times are the twin movements to incarcerate and decarcerate. We are referring to the impact of America's war on drugs, a war that has been driven by moral and political rhetoric but that is clearly racist and classist in practice (see chapters 10 and 11). Despite the thrust toward rehabilitation today, many Americans still support the harsh sentencing practices. Lee and Rasinski (2006) set out to discover why.

Lee and Rasinski's empirically based research drew on a representative survey which found that one quarter of White Americans prefer drug treatment or probation for persons caught for the first time with 5 grains of cocaine. The same survey also found that those who supported a prison sentence were likely to be extremely moralistic, blaming of addicts, and unaware of racism in the United States. Racism and the tendency to blame were related to support for harsh sanctions. A conclusion we can draw from this research is that the association of a drug with a minority population leads to exaggerated fears of the drug.

With more than 2 million people incarcerated in U.S. jails and prisons and most of them with chemical dependence problems and a large minority with severe mental disorders, treatment needs are exhaustive. Research has shown that recidivism rates decline significantly when inmate treatment is provided (Belenko et al., 2005).

Far better than treatment behind bars is treatment in the community. The drug court movement, which has received considerable government support, is one of the most promising developments in recent times. This is the movement to decarcerate persons whose legal problems are related to their addictions rather than to lock them away from society.

DRUG COURTS

Drug courts began experimentally in Dade County, Florida, as an intensive, judicial-supervised, community-based treatment for felony drug defendants designed to reduce the increasing recidivism rates. A countertrend to the "lock 'em up" mentality is evidenced in the alternative-to-prison movement, which got under way in the late 1980s. This "drug court" movement created hope for thousands of people with addiction problems and their families, as well as a large market for substance abuse counselors to work with offenders in the community.

As John Walters, U.S. drug czar states: "Drug courts are one of the most significant criminal justice initiatives in the past 20 years" (2005, p. 2). As of 2006, there are 1,753 drug courts with hundreds more in the planning stages (SAMHSA, 2006a). SAMHSA's Center for Substance Abuse Treatment funds 62 drug courts that help adult and juvenile offenders stay out of prison and parents at risk of losing custody of their children break the cycle of substance dependence.

When offenders enter the program, there's an entire team working with the judge. Case managers help participants tackle other problems in their lives, including emotional and health problems. Such programs can be viewed as a feasible and more effective alternative to adversarial procedures to combat nationwide drug problems. Such programs offer extensive, long-term treatment at little cost to the offender; many opportunities exist for professionally trained counselors to find employment with such diversionary, community-based programs.

According to a recent review of the research findings on drug court effectiveness by the National Institute of Justice (2006), many drug court graduates succeed, but others who are terminated return to drug use. This report makes recommendations for improving the retention rate. These include the employment of sufficient numbers of case managers for close supervision, the hiring of more minority counselors, a curriculum built on cognitive-behavioral techniques rather than a mixed approach, and the inclusion of family members in counseling sessions.

From the liberal perspective, critics of the U.S. drug courts say they are too punitive and do not go far enough. Curley (2004) has noted a rift between less traditional treatment advocates and drug court practitioners as a result. The requirement for absolute sobriety and the punitive response to relapse as a failure prevent many participants from succeeding. The constant urinalysis testing for drug use is hardly consistent with the principles of the strengths perspective. For heroin addicts and other addicted persons, medical prescriptions for methadone and related drugs to reduce cravings are not always encouraged.

In short, drug courts are a big step forward because they stress rehabilitation over punishment and positives over negatives. The Scottish design, however, goes even further in this direction by using a harm reduction model that can succeed with more clients inasmuch as the expectations of this design are more realistic. Still, the U.S. drug court movement is a first step in the journey from imprisonment of drug offenders to harm reduction.

OTHER PROMISING INITIATIVES

Quietly, in September 2001, San Francisco became the first U.S. city to adopt harm reduction as its official policy. The new philosophy is apparent at the Department of Public Health's needle exchange sites, in a media campaign to teach any addicts how to reduce deaths from heroin overdose, and in the training of workers at dozens of agencies in harm reduction strategies (Torassa, 2001).

When the state of California passed Proposition 36 in 2000, this treatment-over-incarceration law, which sends low-level drug offenders to treatment rather than prison, was a groundbreaking initiative. Despite the fact that the program has been seriously underfunded from the beginning and its existence is seriously threatened today, a recent evaluation proves its effectiveness (*New York Times*, 2006). Based on data from nearly 130,000 individuals who participated in the program, the University of California, Los Angeles, study conducted by Longshore, Hawken, Vrada, and Anglin (2006) found that over 60,000 people completed the program by the fourth year, thereby avoiding a prison term and keeping their families intact. Over the 5-year period of the study, California saved $1.4 billion dollars. If any proof is needed that addiction treatment is both humane and cost effective for drug users, this evaluation provides it.

Restorative justice, an exciting development with its roots in the rituals of indigenous populations and Canadian Mennonites, advocates nonadversarial forms of settling disputes and strives to restore individual lawbreakers to the community rather than isolating them from it. Restorative justice, like harm reduction, is a philosophy that can encompass a wide range of treatment initiatives such as the substance abuse treatment program that is actually a high school—PEASE Academy (Peers Enjoying a Sober Education).

PEASE Academy is located in a church in Minneapolis (Riestenberg, 2003). The school has incorporated the circle process in which decisions are made by all participants and other restorative principles into its program. The circle process is used to repair harms such as angry words, bullying, or healing following a relapse by one of the students. Restorative justice and harm reduction thus come together as the circle process helps restore justice or balance to the situation (see van Wormer, 2004).

One significant change little noted in the literature or elsewhere is revealed in treatment effectiveness studies (refer back to Box 1.2). Whereas formerly the standard for a successful treatment outcome was based on total abstinence— the length of time a former client abstained from the use of all psychoactive substances—today much more flexible and realistic measures of treatment success are applied. Not surprisingly, these holistic measures of improvement in social and physical functioning are bringing much more positive results than measures recording a change from chronic binge drinking to drinking three glasses of wine a week as treatment failure. The use of an improvement standard in contemporary research is entirely consistent with the harm reduction approach and is bound to have an impact at the treatment delivery end.

To help bridge the gap between research and practice, the National Institute on Drug Abuse (NIDA) has called for grant applications to participate in clinical trials, using a variety of treatment methods, including pharmaceutical medications, methadone, maintenance, nutritional guidance, and other alternative approaches.

SAMHSA similarly provides millions of dollars in funding opportunities for the development of comprehensive drug/alcohol and mental health treatment systems and for their evaluation (SAMHSA, 2006b). Since 97% of all incarcerated offenders eventually return to their communities, and the barriers to successful reintegration into society are many, one can expect that the bulk of the funding for treatment initiatives will come from here. SAMHSA is working with the U.S. Department of Labor to meet housing and treatment in generously funded initiatives for reentry (SAMHSA, 2005).

One area of substance abuse treatment desperately in need of research is the study of effective interventions to reduce intimate partner violence committed by clients in treatment for substance abuse. Fals-Stewart and Kennedy (2005) examine studies that indicate about half of married or cohabiting substance using clients report episodes of partner aggression in the year preceding entry into treatment. Intimate partner violence research, they note, is fundamentally about harm reduction, attempting to ascertain which treatments result in the greatest reduction in partner aggression. Concerted efforts to develop and evaluate new integrated treatments that combine substance abuse treatment and batterers' education are long overdue.

In light of new developments, there is no need to abandon the disease conception of addiction or the Twelve-Step-based treatment strategies in favor of harm reduction. Clearly, those who follow the Program and abstain from alcohol or drug use reduce the harm to themselves and their families. So the apparent dichotomy between the disease model and an alternative model geared toward public health is a false one. We may all have different allegiances, but in the end, we all have the same allegiance to the pursuit of health. The basic thesis of this chapter and book, then, follows the principle of both–and, not either–or. The results of Project MATCH, the most extensive and expensive comparative research in this area performed to date, confirm the viability of three internally consistent models of treatment: the conventional Twelve-Step-based approach (albeit without the group work), cognitively oriented therapy, and motivational enhancement strategies. This last is the preferred framework for treatment offered by harm reduction proponents. From the strengths perspective, we would be remiss not to extend our appreciation and gratitude to those pioneers in the field, without whom there might be no profession known as substance abuse treatment today.

SUMMARY AND CONCLUSION

While the United States seemingly has unlimited resources for the imprisonment of drug users, managed care constraints and federal funding cutbacks have led to a shift from a clinical approach to a criminal justice approach—from a call for treatment to a call for punishment. During the first decade of the new century, however, two countertrends are evident. The first is the impetus under drug court and restorative justice initiatives for offenders to serve time in the community rather than behind bars; the second is the continuous call at the highest levels for the provision of more prevention and treatment dollars. Recent survey results show that the general public is open to a shift away from the earlier punitive stance.

In state after state, studies on the cost effectiveness of drug treatment confirm tremendous savings to taxpayers and reduced crime rates. The punitive response to substance-related problems at the federal level is countered in part by more realistic and cost-effective policies at the state level. Increasingly, treatment is seen as a cost-effective alternative to incarceration. More and more, it is realized as well that for those illicit drug users who do have to serve time in prison, prison is only a revolving door if they don't get the help they need before their release back into society. Protecting the health of the community as a whole requires protecting the health of drug users, and this requires providing adequate and diversified treatment for persons with substance abuse and dependence problems. A wide range of interventions is needed to meet the client where he or she is, at the client's individual moment of motivation.

Despite the economic constraints caused by managed care and federal cutbacks, this is an exciting time to be in the addiction treatment field. The horizons of this field have expanded considerably to include attention to a broad range of addictive problems (e.g., gambling, shopping, and sex addiction) as well as the substance dependencies (e.g., alcoholism and cocaine addiction). As we move away from the doctrinaire views that have so stifled innovation and experimentation in this field in the past, the door has opened to greater professionalism by staff and more emphasis on client self-determination and empowerment. Meanwhile, advances in the scientific study of addiction as what Leshner (2006) terms a "brain disease" continue to enrich our knowledge of addiction in the causes and consequences.

Central to sound policy and treatment is an understanding of the nature of addiction as a complex biological, psychological, and sociological phenomenon. Addiction is a personal issue, a family issue, a state policy issue, and a health issue. Recent scientific discoveries, such as information about unraveling the DNA code as a blueprint for behavior and the availability of brain scan images that can show the extent of brain damage from drugs, have important implications for the addictions field. The connection between these discoveries and one's susceptibility to substance abuse is the subject of chapters 4 and 5.

Given the creation of an array of effective behavioral and pharmacological interventions, addiction treatment can now be as effective as treatment for the long-term, relapsing illnesses, such as diabetes and hypertension, with professional treatment that is tailored to the needs of particular clients (Leshner, 2000). Promising developments in providing a gender-specific treatment curriculum for female alcoholics and addicts, such as that presented by Covington (1999), should do much to enhance treatment offerings for women. Overall, the movement away from having one and only one standardized treatment model to diverse, modified programs is the most encouraging development of all.

REFERENCES

Alter, J. (2001, February 12). The war on addiction. *Newsweek*, pp. 36–39.

American Heritage Dictionary of the English Language (4th ed.). (2000). Boston: Houghton-Mifflin.

American Medical Association (AMA). (1956). AMA history: 1941 to 1960. AMA. Retrieved June 2006 from http://ama-assn.org.

American Medical Association (AMA). (2007). Definitions: Drug dependencies. Retrieved March 2007 from http://www.ama-assn.org/ama1/pub/upload/mm/388/alcoholism_treatable.pdf.

American Psychiatric Association (2000). *Diagnostic and statistical manual of mental disorders, text revision* (4th ed.). Washington, DC: Author.

Anderson, D. (1981). *Perspectives on treatment: The Minnesota experience*. Center City, MN: Hazelden Educational Service.

Anderson, J. (1994, July 15). Shop till you drop. *Chicago Tribune*, pp. 1, 6.

Anderson, L. (2006, June 4). Survey backs drug treatment. *Baltimore Sun*. Retrieved June 2006 from http://www.soros.org/initiatives/baltimore/articles_publications/articles?keywords=anderson.

Anderson, R. (1997, September 29). [Letter to the editor]. *U.S. News & World Report*, p. 5.

Associated Press. (2005, July 6). Meth abuse cited as top drug problem for law enforcement. *Washington Post*, p. A07.

Ayto, J. (1990). *Dictionary of word origins*. New York: Little, Brown.

Barker, O. (2000, November 28). Ex-smokers get stuck on gum. *USA Today*, p. 10D.

Barker, R. (2003). *The social work dictionary*, Washington, DC: NASW Press.

Beechem, M. (1996, Spring). Chained open. *Reflections: Narratives of Professional Helping*, 2(2), 42–48.

Belenko, S., Patapis, N., & French, M. T. (2005). *The economic benefits of drug treatment: A critical review of the evidence for policy makers*. Washington, DC: National Rural Institute on Drug and Alcohol Abuse.

Benshoff, J. J., & Janikowski, T. P. (2000). *The rehabilitation model of substance abuse counseling*. Belmont, CA: Wadsworth.

Brocato, J., & Wagner, E. F. (2003). Harm reduction: A social work practice model and social justice agenda. *Health and Social Work, 28*(2), 117–124.

Bureau of Justice Statistics. (2006). *Prison and jail inmates at midyear 2005*. Washington, DC: U.S. Department of Justice.

Burke, B. L., Arkowitz, H., & Menchola, M. (2003). The efficacy of motivational interviewing: A meta-analysis of controlled clinical trials. *Journal of Consulting and Clinical Psychology, 71*(5), 843–861.

Butler, S. (2002). *Alcohol, drugs, and health promotion in modern Ireland*. Dublin: Institute of Public Administration.

Center for Substance Abuse Treatment (CSAT). (2005). *Substance abuse treatment for persons with co-occurring disorders.* Treatment Improvement Protocol (TIP) Series, No. 42. Washington, DC: Substance Abuse and Mental Health Services Administration.

Cheever, S. (1999). *Not found in a bottle: My life as a drinker.* New York: Simon & Schuster.

Conrad, P., & Kern, R. (1994). The social production of disease and illness. In P. Conrad & R. Kern (Eds.), *Sociology of health and illness* (pp. 7–9). New York: St. Martin's Press.

Coughlin, P. (2000, November 28). Presentation given at the University of Northern Iowa, Cedar Falls.

Covington, S. (1999). *Helping women recover: A program for treating substance abuse.* San Francisco: Jossey-Bass.

Crisp, C. (2005). Dual diagnosis: Substance abuse and mental health in an inpatient setting. In L. M. Grobman (Ed.), *Days in the lives of social workers* (3rd ed., pp. 205–210). Harrisburg, PA: White Hat Communications.

Curley, B. (2004, September 2). Recovery advocates, drug courts seek common ground at conference. News Feature. *Join Together Online.* Retrieved June 2006 from http://www.jointogether.org/news/features.

Curley, B. (2006, October 5). Medicaid will pay for addiction screening: Advocates seek AMA action, too. *Join Together Online.* Retrieved October 2006 from http://www.jointogether.org/news/features.

Dalrymple, T. (2006). *Romancing opiates: Pharmaceutical lies and the addiction bureaucracy.* New York: Encounter Books.

Dawson, D. A., Grant, B. F., Stinson, F. S., Chou, P. S., Huang, B., & Ruan, W. J. (2005). Recovery from *DSM–IV* alcohol dependence: United States, 2001–2002. *Addiction, 100,* 281–292.

Denning, P. (2000). *Practicing harm reduction psychotherapy: An alternative approach to addictions.* New York: Guilford Press.

DeNoon, D. (2006, March 29). Hooked on tanning? *WebMD Medical News.* Retrieved January 2007 from http://www.webmd.com/content.

Dodes, L. (2003). *The heart of addiction: A new approach to understanding and managing alcoholism & other addictive behaviors.* New York: Harper Paperbacks.

Drake, R. E., & Mueser, K. T. (1996). Alcohol-use disorders and severe mental illness. *Alcohol Health & Research World, 20*(2), 87–93.

Ettner, S. L., Huang, D., Evans, E., Ash, D. R., Hardy, M., Jourabchi, M., et al. (2006). Benefit–cost in the California treatment outcome project: Does substance abuse treatment pay for itself? *Health Services Research, 41*(1), 192–213.

Fals-Stewart, W., & Kennedy, C. (2005). Addressing intimate partner violence in substance-abuse treatment. *Journal of Substance Abuse Treatment, 29*(1), 5–17.

Garlick, R. (2000). *Action News, 10*(3). Canadian Center on Substance Abuse. Retrieved January 2007 from http://www.ccsa.ca/.

Germain, C. (1984). *Social work practices in health care: An ecological perspective.* New York: Free Press.

Gold, M. S., Johnson, C. R., & Stennie, K. (1997). Eating disorders. In J. H. Lowinson, P. Ruiz, R. Millman, & J. G. Langrod (Eds.), *Substance abuse: A comprehensive textbook* (pp. 319–337). Baltimore: Williams & Wilkins.

Greene, J., & Pranis, K. (2006). *Treatment instead of prisons.* Drug Policy Alliance. Retrieved January 2007 from http://www.drugpolicy.org.

Guy, P. (1994, September). *The British and German treatment models.* Guest lecture at the University of Northern Iowa, Cedar Falls.

Haban, W. (1999, February 9). *Eating disorders.* Oral presentation given at the University of Northern Iowa, Cedar Falls.

Hamilton, E. (1948). *The Greek way to Western civilization.* New York: Norton.

Harrison, L. (1996). Introduction. In L. Harrison (Ed.), *Alcohol problems in the community* (pp. 1–13). London: Routledge.

Hester, R. K., & Miller, W. R. (2003). *Handbook of alcoholism treatment approaches: Effective alternatives* (3rd ed.). Boston: Allyn & Bacon.

Jellinek, E. M. (1960). *The disease concept of alcoholism.* New Haven, CT: Yale Center for Alcoholic Studies.

Johel, A. (2005, March 26). North America's first heroin prescription program introduced in Canada. *World Press.* Retrieved June 2006 from http://www.worldpress.org.

Johnson, H. C. (2004). *Psyche and synapse expanding worlds: The role of neurobiology of emotions, behavior, thinking, and addiction for non-scientists* (2nd ed.). Greenfield, MA: Deerfield Valley Publishing.

Joranby, L., Pineda, K., & Gold, M. (2005). Addiction to food and brain reward systems. *Sexual Addiction and Compulsivity, 12*(2–3), 201–217.

Lampman, J. (2004, January 21). How far can 12 steps go? *Christian Science Monitor,* p. 12.

Lee, R. D., & Rasinski, K. (2006). Five grams of coke: Racism, moralism, and White public opinion on sanctions for first time possession. *International Journal of Drug Policy, 17*(3), 183–191.

Lemonick, M. D. (2000, December 11). Downey's downfall. *Time,* p. 97.

Leshner, A. I. (1997, October 3). Addiction is a brain disease, and it matters. *Science, 278,* 45–47.

Leshner, A. I. (2000, June 17). Cited in M. Massey, Seeing drugs as a choice or as a brain anomaly. *New York Times,* p. A17.

Leshner, A. I. (2006). The addiction recovery guide: Your Internet guide to drug and alcohol addiction recovery. Retrieved June 2006 from http://www.addictionrecoveryguide.com.

Linley, P. A., & Joseph, S. (Eds.). (2004). *Positive psychology in practice.* New York: Wiley.

Lobet, I. (2000, September 18). Shopaholics climb on the wagon. *U.S. News & World Report,* p. 60.

Longshore, D., Hawken, A., Vrada, D., & Anglin, M. D. (2006, April 5). *Evaluation of the substance abuse and crime prevention act: Cost analysis report.* University of California, Los Angeles. Retrieved June 2006 from http://www.uclaisap.org/prop36.

Mancini, M. A., Linhorst, D. M., Broderick, F., & Bayliff, S. (in press). Challenges to implementing the harm reduction approach. *Journal of Social Work in the Addictions.*

Maugh, T. (2006, August 1). Was it alcohol or anti-Semitism talking? Doctors disagree. *Los Angeles Times.* Retrieved January 2007 from http://www.latimes.com/news.

McIvor, G., Barnsdale, L., Eley, S., Malloch, M., Yates, R., & Brown, A. (2006). *The operation and effectiveness of the Scottish drug court pilots.* Scotland government. Retrieved June 2006 from http://www.scotland.gov.uk/publications.

McLellan, A. T., Kleber, H. D., & Carise, D. (2003). The national addiction treatment infrastructure: Can it support the public's demand for quality care? *Journal of Substance Abuse Treatment, 25,* 117–121.

McNeece, C. A. (2003). After the war on drugs is over: Implications for social work education. *Journal of Social Work Education, 39*(2), 193–212.

McNeece, C. A., & DiNitto, D. (2005). *Chemical dependency: A systems approach* (3rd ed.). Boston: Allyn & Bacon.

Miller, G. (2005). *Learning the language of addiction counseling* (2nd ed.) Hoboken, NJ: Wiley.

Miller, W. R. (2006). Motivational factors in addictive behaviors. In W. R. Miller & K. M. Carroll (Eds.), *Rethinking substance abuse: What the science shows* (pp. 136–150). New York: Guilford Press.

Moncher, M., Schinke, S., & Holden, G. (1992). Tobacco addiction: Correlates, prevention and treatment. In E. Freeman (Ed.), *The addiction process* (pp. 222–236). New York: Longman.

Morell, C. (1996). Radicalizing recovery: Addiction, spirituality, and politics. *Social Work, 41*(3), 306–312.

National Center on Addiction and Substance Abuse (CASA). (1998, January). *Behind bars: Substance abuse and America's prison population.* New York: Columbia University Press.

National Institute of Justice. (2006, June). *Drug courts: The second decade.* Washington, DC: U.S. Department of Justice.

Neff, J. A., & MacMaster, S. A. (2005). Spiritual mechanisms underlying substance abuse behavioral change in faith-based substance abuse treatment. *Journal of Social Work Practice in the Addictions, 5*(3), 33–54.

New York Times. (2006, April 10). A victory for California [Editorial]. *New York Times,* p. 22A.

O'Neil, J. V. (2001, January). Expertise in addictions said crucial. *NASW News,* p. 10.

Orford, J. (2001). *Excessive appetites: A psychological view of addictions.* (2nd ed.). Chichester, England: Wiley.

Peele, S. (2004). *Seven tools to beat addiction.* New York: Three Rivers Press.

Peele, S., & Bufe, C. (2000). *Resisting 12-Step coercion: How to fight forced participation in AA, NA, or 12-Step treatment.* Tucson, AZ: Sharp Press.

Pew Research Center. (March 21, 2001). *Interdiction and incarceration still top remedies.* Pew Research Center for the People and the Press. Retrieved June 2006 from http://people-press.org/reports.

Project MATCH Research Group. (1997, January). Matching alcoholism treatment to client heterogeneity: Project MATCH post-treatment outcomes. *Journal of Studies on Alcohol, 58,* 7–28.

Rapp, C. A. (1998). *The strengths model: Case management with people suffering from severe and persistent mental illness.* New York: Oxford University Press.

Rapp, C., & Goscha, R. J. (2006). *The strengths model: Case management with people with psychiatric disabilities* (2nd ed.). New York: Oxford University Press.

Richards, C. (2004, October 5). Addicted gamers losing their way. *Washington Post,* p. C10.

Riestenberg, N. (2003). PEASE Academy: The recovery school. Minnesota Department of Education. Retrieved June 2006 from http://education.state.mn.us/mde/.

Rogers, C. R. (1931). *Client-centered therapy.* Boston: Houghton-Mifflin.

Rosin, H. (2000, May 5). Bush puts faith in a social service rule. *Washington Post,* p. A1.

Saleebey, D. (Ed.). (1992). *The strengths perspective in social work practice.* Boston: Allyn & Bacon.

Saleebey, D. (2006). Introduction: Power to the people. In D. Saleebey (Ed.), *The strengths perspective in social work* (4th ed., pp. 1–24). Boston: Allyn & Bacon.

Shaffer, H. J. (1999). Strange bedfellows: A critical view of pathological gambling and addiction. *Addiction, 94*(10), 1445–1448.

Schaler, J. (1999). *Addiction is a choice.* Chicago: Open Court.

Shavelson, L. (2001). *Hooked: Five addicts challenge our misguided drug rehabilitation system.* New York: New Press.

Springer, D. W., McNeece, C. A., & Arnold, E. M. (2003). *Substance abuse treatment for criminal offenders: An evidence-based guide for practitioners.* Washington, DC: American Psychological Association.

Substance Abuse and Mental Health Services Administration (SAMHSA). (2004). Highlights. *National survey of substance abuse treatment services.* Rockville, MD: Author.

Substance Abuse and Mental Health Services Administration (SAMHSA). (2005). President proposes $300 million for reentry. *Addiction Technology Transfer Center Network (ATTC), 7*(2), 4.

Substance Abuse and Mental Health Services Administration (SAMHSA). (2006a). Incarceration vs. treatment. *SAMHSA News,* pp. 1–4.

Substance Abuse and Mental Health Services Administration (SAMHSA). (2006b, March/April). SAMHSA announces funding opportunities. *SAMHSA News,* p. 6.

Szasz, T. (2003). *Ceremonial chemistry: The ritual persecution of drugs, addicts, and pushers* (Rev. ed.). Syracuse, NY: Syracuse University Press.

Terrorist attacks cause spike in treatment requests. (2001, December 6). Retrieved from http://www.jointogether.org.

Thomas, G. (2005, May). Harm reduction policies and programs for persons involved in the criminal justice system. Canadian Centre on substance abuse. Retrieved June 2006 from http://www.ccsa.ca/ccsa.

Torassa, V. (2001, January 15). Changing method of treatment for drug addiction. *San Francisco Chronicle.* Retrieved January 2007 from http://www.cannabisnews.com/news/thread8324.shtml.

Vaillant, G. E. (1983). *The natural history of alcoholism.* Cambridge, MA: Harvard University Press.

Vaillant, G. E. (1995). *The natural history of alcoholism revisited.* Cambridge, MA: Harvard University Press.

van Wormer, K. (2004). *Confronting oppression, restoring justice: From policy analysis to social action.* Alexandria, VA: CSWE.

van Wormer, K., & Bartollas, C. (2007). *Women and the criminal justice system* (2nd ed.). Boston: Allyn & Bacon.

Volpicelli, J., & Szalavitz, M. (2000). *Recovery options: The complete guide.* New York: Wiley.

Wallace, B. C. (2005). *Making mandated treatment work.* Lantham, MD: Jason Aronson.

Walters, G. D. (1999). *The addiction concept: Working hypothesis or self-fulfilling prophecy?* Boston: Allyn & Bacon.

Walters, J. (2005). Cited by Huddleston, Freeman-Wilson, & Marlowe, *Painting the current picture: A national report card on drug courts.* Washington, DC: Bureau of Justice Assistance.

Washton, A. M., & Zweben, J. E. (2006). *Treating alcohol and drug problems in psychotherapy practice: Doing what works.* New York: Guilford Press.

Young, D. (2003). Co-occurring disorders among jail inmates: Bridging the treatment gap. *Journal of Social Work Practice in the Addictions, 3*(3), 63–85.

Zweben, A., & Rose, S. (1999). Innovations in treating alcohol problems. In D. Biegel & A. Blum (Eds.), *Innovations in practice and service delivery across the life span* (pp. 197–246). New York: Oxford University Press.

What experiences and history teach is this—that people and governments never have learned anything from history.

—Hegel (1837)

2 CHAPTER | HISTORICAL PERSPECTIVES

INTRODUCTION

What role do our drugs of choice play in society? In what ways has society tried to curb the use of drugs? Whether it's alcohol, nicotine, opium, or cocaine, our drugs of choice have been alternatively glorified and vilified. This chapter focuses on the history of America's, Canada's, and Europe's drug use and misuse, on economic and legal history, from the earliest days to the present time. The problems we see today are hardly new; they have existed in other forms and with other drugs throughout our history.

Before there was misuse, there was use of all kinds of intoxicants, derived mostly from plants. There has been no civilization, as Zeldin (1994) suggests, whose citizens have not tried to escape from stress or tedium to alter their consciousness, with the help of alcohol, tobacco, tea, coffee, or plants of various sorts. The Aztecs, for example, had 400 gods of drink and drunkenness to help them escape into semiconscious bliss; the cacti and mushrooms they ate gave them hallucinations and courage for battle. Every place in the world where apples, grapes, and wheat grew, there was a good chance humans discovered uses for them that went beyond mere satisfaction of hunger pangs. Since even various animals have been known to seek out fermented berries, it seems obvious that the earliest humans would have done the same. The human uniqueness comes with the rituals surrounding the use of mood-altering substances, the planning entailed in their acquisition, and ultimately, the social regulation pertaining to them.

In this chapter, we trace the use of how drugs, including alcohol, became defined and over time redefined. From evangelism to criminalization to medicalization, the road has been paved with many ill-fated attempts at social control. Starting with a look at the earliest civilizations, through the Middle Ages, to the modern world as represented by the United States and Europe

44

(each taking divergent paths), we will study the policy aspect of drug manufacture and use. In our overview, we see that at times the technological advances—the ability to distill alcohol and produce smokable cocaine, for example—have exceeded our human capacity to absorb them.

Three themes will become apparent as we survey the history of substance use and addiction in a society that Denzin (1993) terms "the alcoholic society." One theme is the *ambivalence* accorded the role of intoxicants in society and the pleasure and pain associated with their use. This theme is reflected in a combination of heavy alcohol or drug use coupled with strict social control policies.

The second major theme concerns the different reactions to the same drug over time, as when the health-inducing potion of one period of time is banned as a dangerous substance (associated with dangerous people) some years later. The road from medicalization to criminalization, as we will see, is influenced less by the chemical properties of a drug than by considerations of race, class, and gender.

Third is the fact of the rising potency of drugs that has followed whenever they have been banned. Even as the sale of alcohol was outlawed in the 1920s, the consumption of spirits replaced the consumption of beer and wine. One striking parallel today is seen in the increasing purity and potency of cocaine and heroin, drugs in themselves easier to smuggle across borders than bulky marijuana.

EARLY USE AND MISUSE OF INTOXICANTS

Historical accounts from ancient Greece and Rome and other early civilizations describe the systematic doling out of alcoholic beverages to soldiers, along with food, weapons, and other military rations (Bower, 1994). Excavations in 1996 provide evidence in the form of a yellowish residue preserved in a pottery jar for wine making by early settlers of northern Iran (McGovern, 2003). Archeologists date the pottery jar as having been produced over 7,000 years ago. Through chemical testing, archeological scientists were able to establish that a substance found only in large quantities of grapes had been preserved in the residue. Additionally, the residue contained a substance used in antiquity to keep wine from turning to vinegar. The significance is that we now know that wine was being made as early as 5000 B.C., which was about the time people were establishing their first permanent settlements and domesticating plants and animals. The fact that special wine gods were worshipped by ancient people is testimony to the special place that alcohol came to assume in early civilization. Ancient Romans had their god of drink, Bacchus, and the Greeks had their Dionysus. As we know from papyri, Egyptian doctors included beer or wine in their prescriptions. Long before vineyards flourished in Bordeaux, a sophisticated wine industry arose along the banks of the Nile (Nash, 2003). In ancient Egypt, both beer and wine were deified and offered to the gods (Hanson, 1995).

In *A History of the World in Six Glasses,* economist Tom Standage (2005) signifies each historical epoch as characterized by its signature beverage. Beer, according to Standage, was first made from fermenting grain in the Fertile Crescent. By 3000 B.C., it was used to pay wages, and later it became the main export of ancient Greece.

In China, a variety of alcoholic beverages have been used since prehistoric times and in all segments of society (Hanson, 1995). Evidence attests, as Hanson indicates, that alcohol played an important role in religious life and that the use of alcohol in moderation was the norm. In what is now Greece, wine making was commonplace. The ancient Greeks were known for the temperance of their culture, their avoidance of excess in all things, "teaching practical morality and forever emphasizing moderation" (Hamilton, 1940, p. 165). Traditional Roman values of temperance and simplicity, as Hanson indicates, resembled the Greek ways of being. Gradually, however, these values were replaced by practices related to degeneracy.

From the Old Testament of the Bible, we learn of drinking practices of the Hebrews. Abundant wine made from grapes was regarded as a blessing that could "gladden the heart of man" (Psalm 105:15, King James Version). That it also had the property to wreak some havoc is revealed in Genesis 9:20:

> And Noah began to be a husbandman, and he planted a vineyard: And he drank of the wine and was drunken; and he was uncovered within his tent.

Later, we learn that the daughters of Lot got their father drunk to continue the family line (Genesis 19:32–36). Although there is a lot of drinking mentioned in the Bible, both the Old and New Testaments condemn drunkenness. Indeed, the dangers inherent in strong drink have been known at least since biblical times. Proverbs 33:29–30 provides a strong cautionary note:

> Who hath woe? Who hath sorrow? Who hath contentions? Who hath babbling? Who hath wounds without cause? Who hath redness of eyes? They that tarry long at the wine; they that go to seek mixed wine.

Whereas the large majority of the Hebrews rejoiced in wine and used it for medicinal and nutritional purposes, wine was relegated to a sacred and symbolic role. The New Testament depicts this common association.

While the Hebrews condoned drinking but not drunkenness, a different kind of religious control was adopted later in the 7th century by Islam. The Koran simply condemned wine altogether, and an effective prohibition against all alcoholic beverages prevailed. In the Far East, India, and China, alcohol consumption was secularized and widespread (Levin, 1995).

The long road from the sacred to the profane was shortened by a 10th century discovery by Rhazes, an Arabian physician (Kinney, 2006). Actually, Rhazes was looking for a way to release the spirit of the wine. The word *alcohol* itself is derived from the Arabic *al-kuhul* (Ayto, 1990). The discovery of distilled spirits, which made possible the manufacture of much stronger alcoholic concoctions, is an instance of technology's reach exceeding its grasp. The devastation unleashed with this new development, however, did not occur suddenly but took place over centuries of use (Orford, 2001).

Originally, this distilled alcohol was used as a cosmetic to darken the eyelids and as a medicine to cure a host of ailments. Use of distilled liquors gradually become common in Europe from around the 16th century.

Self-indulgence in connection with food is demonstrated by the presence of the vomitorium in ancient Rome. The practices of feasting and drinking included vomiting so that people could keep repeating these processes. This was the forerunner of the binge–purge cycle known today as bulimia. Anorexia has its roots in holy fasting practices of the 13th century women whose self-denial provided them with praise and admiration. Some of the "holy anorexics" were canonized as saints for their troubles (Bell, 1987).

Like alcohol, the use of opium goes far back in time as well, to about 5000 B.C. (Szasz, 2003). Extracted from the white juice of certain species of poppy, opium is believed to have been used by the Sumerians, an ancient Middle Eastern people, to enhance their feelings of pleasure and by later civilizations for its medical properties.

Moving to the Americas, we find that while most of the pre-Columbian Native peoples lacked knowledge of alcohol, several of the cultures of northern Mexico and the southwestern United States consumed wine and beer. Columbus found indigenous peoples of the Caribbean drinking beer from fermented maize. Limited to communal fiestas or to prepare for war, drunkenness was negatively sanctioned and therefore not disruptive. Significantly, the alcohol content was relatively low (Collins & McNair, 2003). Hard-drinking Europeans, such as traders and soldiers, promoted alcohol use among Native Americans by making high-alcohol-content distilled liquor increasingly available to them and by using it as payment in trade and negotiations (Collins & McNair, 2003).

For more than 2,000 years, native societies have utilized various naturally occurring plants such as the "sacred" mushroom of Mexico and the peyote cactus (*Encyclopaedia Britannica*, 2005). There is evidence that a mushroom cult existed in the Mayan culture of Central America. Reports from Spanish explorers tell of the cultic use of peyote. Later, the missionaries and government agents fought hard against these practices. Peyote has been used across the centuries in religious ceremonies and is not associated with compulsive use. The peyote-using American Indians are reported to have been more successful than tribes that do not use peyote in leading productive and healthy lives (*Encyclopaedia Britannica*, 2005).

The Spaniards introduced marijuana to the New World; the word *marijuana* comes from a Spanish word meaning "a substance causing intoxication" (Benshoff & Janikowski, 2000). According to Szasz, marijuana use can be traced back to cultivation by the ancient Greeks, Persians, and Chinese. In Islamic nations, which prohibit use of alcohol, there has been much more general use of cannabis (*Encyclopaedia Britannica*, 2005). Marco Polo told sensational stories of the use of the highly potent form of cannabis known as hashish by a fanatical, brutal sect of Persians.

Cocaine use as coca leaf chewing among South American indigenous peoples dates back centuries (Benshoff & Janikowski, 2000). The Spanish conquerors made the drug available to slaves to boost their stamina. This form of cocaine use was not culturally destructive and not associated with addiction, as Benshoff and Janikowski indicate.

The history of nicotine addiction goes back to the discovery of Columbus and his men of dried tobacco leaves in Central America. It was introduced to Europe in 1493 (Szasz, 2003). By the 1600s, tobacco was a permanent European commodity and used by all social classes (Goodman, 1993).

Later, in British America, however, the liquor in exchange for furs trade was to be culturally and economically devastating to a people who, with the exception of those who lived in modern-day Mexico and the American Southwest, had no chance to develop a familiarity with alcohol's powers so in the knowing of these powers, to be able to resist them. The Catawba tribal leader's plea to the colonists to cease supplying spirits to his people is one of many Native American voices for restraint described by Peter Mancall (2004).

THE EUROPEAN CONTEXT

In the *History of Intoxication,* Norwegian author Bjorn Qviller (1996) argues that from Viking drinking guilds to wine-soaked symposia in ancient Greece, alcohol played a central role in the political life of western Europe. People drank together to knit friendships and make political allies. Not much is known about the role of alcohol in women's lives in ancient history. We do know from ancient records that women's misuse of alcohol was linked to its harmful effects on unborn children (Sandmaier, 1992).

In the days before purification, alcohol was often safer than water. Although Conrad and Schneider (1992) contend that opium held no special appeal for Europeans until the mid-1800s, Zeldin (1994) suggests that opium mixed with alcohol became the fashionable way to escape from pain and boredom during the 16th century. By 1854, opium was the most valued remedy for everyday maladies such as indigestion. In a reverse of today's war on international drug trafficking, the British began illegally smuggling opium into China in the early 18th century to exchange with Chinese traders for tea (Hamid, 1998). The opium was transported from India. Opium smoking became rampant among Chinese peasants. The Chinese were forced through a series of wars, known historically as the Opium Wars, which broke out in 1839, to keep their markets open to the opium trade (Abadinsky, 2003).

Sometimes, technological advance exceeds a people's ability to handle it. So it was with the invention of the distillation process for making alcohol stronger. And so it was with the discovery by German scientists of how to isolate cocaine from the coca bush (Benshoff & Janikowski, 2000). The process of distillation was widely used in the 15th century as a way of removing water from the fermented product, thereby increasing the concentration of alcohol (Levin, 1995). In 1575, a distillery was founded in Amsterdam, which is still in operation today. From a concoction of grains, herbs, and juniper berries, *jenever,* or gin, was produced. The availability of cheap gin, combined with the population displacement caused by industrialization and associated with the growth of an urban proletariat, contributed to an epidemic of drunkenness (Levin, 1995). The devastation was so great that a staggering infant mortality rate and child starvation rate combined to prevent a growth in population from 1700 to 1750. Public outrage at the drunken woman and neglectful mother may have reached its height, as Sandmaier (1992) indicates, during the infamous gin epidemics of London. Crimes of violence and immorality among all social classes, but most evident among the poor, gave the age a debauched character, preserved in political commentary and the early novel. Parliament, which earlier had actively promoted gin production to utilize surplus grain and to raise revenue, now passed legislation to discourage its use (Hanson, 1995). Gradually, a change in attitudes, probably related to the Industrial Revolution and the need for a hardworking, sober work force, coalesced to reduce the use of spirits considerably. The availability of higher-quality and more affordable beer was an additional factor in gin's decline.

COLONIAL AMERICA

We begin this section with a thought-provoking question, one commonly asked and best articulated by social work educator Ogden Rogers:

> Gathering people's thoughts on programs such as "Rational Recovery" or work by Stanton Peele on addictive behavior is met either by anger on one end of the pole, or marginalization-almost-without-comment at the other. Whenever I encounter so much emotion about something I want to explore dispassionately, I ask myself "why?" Why is it that the subject of "use, abuse, and addiction" raises such passions? I suspect there must be deep values and/or fears enmeshed in the fabric of the issues. In an almost "X-files" sort of way, I'm impressed with how much of the conversation about drugs is focused in extreme ways. The "solutions" end up extreme as well: abstinence philosophy about many things; incarceration of huge masses. (personal communication, June 2, 2000)

For an answer, we must look back to the holy experiment known to the world as Puritanism—that band of relatively humorless religious zealots who started things off in Massachusetts Bay. Like the very language that Americans speak, the present-day American value system is rooted in that New England experience. To Puritans who sought guidance for all daily activities in Scripture, the truth was perfectly clear: God had chosen an elite few to represent Him on Earth (Erickson, 1966).

This is not to say, however, that sexual prudery or enforced abstinence from drink was a part of the Puritan scene. What these religious dissenters did was set the tone for all that took place then and was to come later—the rigidity and punitiveness but, above all, the moralism that was to become pervasive in American life.

The history of addiction in the United States begins but does not end, therefore, with alcohol (Walters, 1999). An article in the *Chicago Tribune*

("Documentary Looks at Drinking in America," 1999) puts the American experience with mood-altering substances into perspective:

> Most students of popular culture already are well aware that cocaine began insinuating itself into our society through the use of patent medicines and soft drinks; Bayer once marketed heroin alongside its aspirin products; and military service has turned more people into smokers than Humphrey Bogart, Lauren Bacall, and Joe Camel combined. What isn't well known, however, is how much booze was imbibed by our founding fathers . . . and mothers.

More beer than water was carried on the Mayflower. The Puritans saw alcohol as a blessing from God and as a good and healthy beverage (Peele, 1989/1995). Colonial Americans of all ages drank daily; pregnant women and children, along with men, consumed a lot of beer. Punishments were reserved for drunkards who made nuisances of themselves. Still, the tavern was the center of much family, social, and economic activity.

The natives adopted the drug alcohol within their cultural context. They drank not for conviviality but to alter their mood and achieve a different state of consciousness (Murrin et al., 2001). Native Americans assumed that alcoholic drinks served the same purpose as hallucinogenic plants and tobacco and treated them in the same way. To drink small quantities was considered pointless. Europeans, as mentioned earlier, took advantage of the Native American propensity to drink to the point of insensibility and cheated them out of their furs and other goods. Heavy alcohol use for American Indians became a major cause of social problems that has continued until the present day.

With the passage of time, liquor came to be valued by the early settlers for both its high alcohol content and its shipping advantages. Besides, as we learn in *Ambitious Brew: The Story of American Beer*, growing hops and barley was too much work; it was easier to plant fruit trees and make cider or fruit liqueurs (Ogle, 2005). The Puritans regarded rum as "God's good creature." Although an occasional drunk was placed in the stocks, the tavern was the center of social, economic, and political activity (Levin, 1995).

As the colonists turned to distilling alcohol, they proved as adaptable as they had earlier in producing passable beer. Honey, corn, rye, berries, and apples were used in domestic production. A general lack of concern about alcoholism and its problems was one of the most significant features of the Colonial era (Burns, 2004). Strong drink was thought to protect against disease and be conducive to good health. Alcohol was used as a solvent, antiseptic, and of course, as a painkiller. Since good drinking water was not always available, there was some substance to this argument. And as long as the social norms were followed, drinking excesses could be tolerated. Rum, made from molasses that was imported in large quantities from Jamaica, figured prominently in the economy of the new nation. For the sake of rum, New Englanders became the bankers of the slave trade that supplied the molasses needed to produce rum (Kinney, 2006). Rum was transported abroad on the same ships that went to Africa to carry the slaves back to America. The rum was traded with Europeans for slaves. According to another version of history, however, the New Englanders' role in the business aspect of the slave trade, although prominent, was more limited than is commonly believed (Barr, 1999; Burns, 2004). The early Americans loved the rum they distilled from Jamaican molasses; they consumed it themselves and made large profits through exports (Barr, 1999). About half of the molasses brought to the New World from the West Indies went to the distilleries that produced the American national beverage (Burns, 2004).

On the home front, per capita consumption of copious amounts of alcohol was the norm among early European Americans, and alcohol was measured in barrels (Hamid, 1998). Although severe restrictions were placed on drinking by slaves, laborers digging the Erie Canal were allotted a quart of whiskey a day. When Congress passed an excise tax on whiskey in 1791, farmers and distillers staged the notorious Whiskey Rebellion, which had to be crushed with federal troops.

From 1785 to 1835, however, attitudes concerning alcohol began to change dramatically. During this period, as Peele (1989/1995) argues, drinking became a disruptive force for many Americans. As farmers turned surplus grain into whiskey, the old pattern of communal drinking began to break down; new patterns of solitary and binge drinking developed. The availability of cheap spirits, alcohol misuse, and family breakdown were all intertwined. For a dramatic description of the kind of havoc that could be wreaked on a population by access to vast quantities of rum, consider what Robert Hughes (1987) had to say of an early convict settlement in Australia:

> The most sought-after commodity of all was rum, a word which stood for spirits of all kinds. . . . In this little community (of about 10,000) nearly all the men and most of the women were addicted to alcohol. In Australia, especially between 1790 and 1820, rum became an overriding social obsession. Families were wrecked by it, ambitions destroyed, an iron chain of dependency forged. (p. 290)

Dr. Benjamin Rush, surgeon general during the American Revolution, had observed firsthand the devastation wrought by rum rations on soldiers. In his pamphlet recording his observations, Rush pinpointed the dangers of potent alcohol. Through such writings and his personal influence, Rush provided a scientific voice to the call for an end to the distillation and drinking of whiskey and other spirits. This call was echoed by concerned family members and members of the clergy, especially the descendants of Puritans, who aligned themselves with concerned citizens to condemn the wasteful behavior and debauchery that was characteristic of the day. The new focus was on saving the family (Metzger, 1988). Denning, Little, and Glickman (2004) bring our attention to two facts: (a) Rush did not declare alcohol addiction a disease but, rather, said that the signs and symptoms were like those of a disease, and (b) he advocated moderation.

Two currents of thought, the temperance and medical approaches, were inextricably interwoven in the 19th century, as in recent times. At the time, these views—one stressing evil and the other illness—appeared in opposition. While one stressed the supply side of the drug alcohol, the other focused on reducing the need for the drug. Unity came because of awareness of a major social problem and the urgent need to address it (van Wormer, 1995).

A point worth underscoring: The temperance movement was about moderation, as the word implies. It was about control of "spirits," the distilled beverages, not of beer and wine. Another point worth noting concerns African traditions. The Africans brought to America as slaves came primarily from West African cultures. These, as W. L. White (1998) indicates, had blended alcohol into economic, social, and religious customs since antiquity. Under the institution of slavery, slave masters came to promote excessive alcohol use on festive occasions such as Christmas and July 4th. But the major problem for early African Americans was the risk they faced when White people were inebriated.

In the mid-1800s, alcohol consumption was cut in half, and from then on, dependence on the bottle was a specialty of a minority (Zeldin, 1994). But then a craze developed for patent medicines with a high opiate content. Morphine, in fact, was heralded as a treatment for chronic drinking problems (Conrad & Schneider, 1992). Often prescribed to older White women of high socioeconomic class, morphine frequently resulted in iatrogenic, or medically induced, addiction.

The year 1900 marked a prohibition readers will find surprising: the prohibition of tobacco. It was illegal to sell cigarettes in 14 states, and selling a lottery ticket was a federal crime (Savage, 1999). By that year, the modern tobacco industry was already under way. A ruthless businessman of North Carolina named James Buchanan Duke successfully used a cigarette-rolling machine that made mass production possible (McGinn, 1997). A free bag of cigarettes was presented to millions of male immigrants who stepped off the boat onto U.S. soil. Many became hooked then right from the start. The Supreme Court upheld Tennessee's prohibition in the belief that cigarettes were a noxious product and because of their deleterious effects among young people. All the while, opium, morphine, and heroin were being sold over the counter. Chewing tobacco, similarly, was acceptable, presumably only for men.

Smoking opium was associated with Chinese immigrant laborers; their foreign ways were feared and resented, as was their drug use (Musto, 1999). Labor unions resented the fact that these exceptionally hardworking people were willing to work for low wages. Americans thus defamed not only the Chinese but opium as well (Szasz, 2003). The invention of the hypodermic needle and the synthesis of heroin from morphine at the end of the 19th century further exacerbated the problem (Joseph, 1995). Inevitably, there was a national outcry for legislation to curb what was seen as the moral degeneracy associated with drug use. The same xenophobia aroused by heavy drinking among the poor, Catholic, European immigrants was a factor in the outcry against narcotic use as well.

Warnings of addiction as a result of morphine use began to appear in medical textbooks around 1900. In 1909, the import of opium was banned. Opium itself then became increasingly scarce at the consumer level, and heroin, a far more potent substance, not smoked but injected, became the popular form of administration of this drug. By banning alcohol and drugs, as Gardner (2000a) informs us, governments actually pressed users toward the most dangerous method of taking it.

Meanwhile, the intolerance for smoking cigarettes began to dissolve, its popularity boosted tremendously with the free distribution of cigarettes to World War I troops in France (Fishbein & Pease, 1996). The United States, as Zeldin argues, was remarkable for the suddenness with which it moved from drug to drug, "from one escape to another" (p. 231). And when prohibition of alcohol spread throughout the country, cola drinks laced with cocaine, as Zeldin further indicates, stepped in as the savior. Cocaine, in fact, was considered the remedy for addiction to other substances. Coca-Cola contained cocaine until 1903 and, not surprisingly, was an extremely popular "pick-me-upper."

The culmination of the fear of addiction and the association of the use of narcotics with the lower classes and foreigners culminated in the Harrison Act, which became law in 1914. The Harrison Act severely restricted the amount of opioids or cocaine in any remedy sold without a prescription (Musto, 1998).

Szasz's (2003) insights are relevant here. Opium is organic, coming from the dried juice of the poppy. "No chemist, no pharmaceutical industry, no physician is needed to produce it or to administer it" (p. 65). This is the point, argues Szasz. Illicit drugs are those that can't be marketed; the medical community has embraced synthetic painkillers and mood changers instead. These drugs have become the licit or legal drug remedies. Following World War I, a sociologically interesting development took place: "America no longer spoke of the inordinate American demand for drugs but instead of the evil intentions of countries that supplied them" (Musto, 1998, pp. 59–60). This shift in attitude regarding drugs and foreign nations was to have an enormous impact on U.S. policy from then on.

Let's backtrack a moment to consider cocaine, a drug with effects that have been much more pronounced on society than the sedating opiates could ever be. Cocaine, which was particularly popular in literary and intellectual circles, was widely used for everything from sinus troubles to hysteria (Abadinsky, 2003). It began to get a bad name, however, because of its association with bizarre behavior, including violence. After the turn of the 20th century, cocaine became identified with the urban underworld, according to Abadinsky, and southern Blacks. Fear of the effects of cocaine intensified until official regulation was inevitable.

Paradoxically, after restrictive laws such as the Harrison Act were passed, doctors became reluctant to prescribe drugs to addicts, and the street cost of heroin rose from $6.50 an ounce to almost $100 an ounce (Musto, 1999). The drug problem grew more prominent, accordingly, than it had ever done before. Public fear of dope peddlers grew with the increase in arrests. The same "perverse progression" seen with other drugs that were banned was seen with cocaine (Gardner, 2000a). Fairly benign forms of consuming cocaine gave way to much more dangerous practices through drug interdiction. Addicts, as

Gardner further argues, bankrupted by the inflated cost of illegal drugs, sought out drugs that gave the most "bang for the buck" and proceeded to use those drugs in the most cost-efficient way.

Marijuana was associated with Mexican immigrants in the southwestern United States. *Marijuana* is the Mexican colloquial term for a plant that has been cultivated throughout the world and known in Central Asia and China for approximately 3,000 years (*Encyclopaedia Britannica,* 2005). Cannabis has long been considered to have medicinal value as an analgesic, anesthetic, and depressant. In the early 20th century in the United States, when anti-immigrant sentiment grew (associated with a wave of emigration to the American Southwest following the Mexican Revolution of 1910), rumors began to spread that Mexicans were distributing the "killer weed" to American schoolchildren (Schlosser, 1994). The drug was also associated with jazz musicians in New Orleans. Between 1914 and 1931, 29 states outlawed marijuana. The Marijuana Tax Act of 1937 essentially criminalized the possession of marijuana throughout the United States.

Then as now, seeking to influence international policies in other nations, the United States organized international conferences on the "drug menace." In response to this pressure, Britain passed the Dangerous Drug Act, which, like the Harrison Act, was intended to limit legal distribution of addictive drugs. Unlike in the United States, however, the new law was interpreted in favor of physicians to give them final authority in providing drugs to addicts as a legitimate form of treatment (Conrad & Schneider, 1992).

PROHIBITION OF ALCOHOL

Just as technological advances relevant to the drugs heroin and cocaine led to the creation of products that seemed beyond human capability to control their use, so it was with alcohol. The distillation process mentioned earlier carried the seeds of destruction. The temperance women, for this reason following the teachings of Dr. Rush, targeted strong liquor as the source of the evils they saw around them—chronic drunkenness, violence, and family poverty.

The temperance woman represented the Victorian ideal of purity; she fought alcohol as a rude intrusion upon the family and a threat to the family's very survival. By attacking "Demon Rum" as the root cause of family disintegration, temperance advocates viewed alcohol-related domestic problems as social problems requiring legal solutions (Rotskoff, 2004). The drunkard was scorned, and the drunkard's wife was pitied. The temperance woman was thus a crusader for traditional moral values. Yet as Sandmaier (1992) indicates, the temperance woman was in fact more radical than her image suggests. She fought against men's drunkenness and for the liberation of women from the tyranny of this form of indulgence. Eventually, this volunteer army of churchwomen led into another movement of renown, the women's suffrage movement. The two movements were interconnected in that men feared women's moral fervor and independence and that they would restrict men's drinking (Burns, 2004). As it was, however, the *men* were to outlaw the sale of alcoholic beverages themselves; only shortly thereafter did the woman win the right to vote.

To understand how the women's suffrage movement and prohibition came together, let us examine the historical record in the nation's heartland. In Iowa, the legislature's plan to make Iowa the first state to give women the right to vote was destroyed by a confluence of volatile issues, chief among which was liquor. In tracing the history of the male resistance to women's suffrage, Fruhling (1996) cites the stated fear that if women were permitted to vote, they might use that political clout to close the saloons where men squandered their time and the family's money. Iowa's native thirst, as Fruhling further indicates, grew even larger with the tide of German and Irish immigrants that began arriving in the 1840s; the neighborhood saloon was a hallowed tradition.

"The modern drunk is a 100-fold worse than the ancient drunk." So said the most renowned preacher of his day, the Reverend T. DeWitt Talmage (1887, p. 599). His comment was in reference to the process of distillation. Talmage, like other Protestants, called for the politicians of his day to take a stand "in the battle between drunkenness and sobriety, God and the devil" (p. 604).

The temperance proponents, to reduce habitual drunkenness, promoted taking an abstinence pledge. Public confession figured in the decision to take this pledge. In Ireland, a religious-based temperance movement acquired a following under the leadership of a charismatic priest, Father Matthew, who was influenced by Protestant reformers. Ireland was temporarily transformed into a nation of teetotalers during this period (Butler, 2002). (The word *teetotaler* came from the letter T for total abstinence, which was put next to a man's name on the society's rolls.) Father Matthew, whose astonishingly successful temperance crusade had swept across Ireland, converted millions of men and women to total abstinence (Townend, 2005). In a series of hundreds of emotional open-air meetings beginning in 1839, the priest addressed massive crowds for days on end until he got the people to make the sign of the cross, which was the letter T. In Scotland, the Presbyterian ministry led the way toward total abstinence, which became common among the middle classes in the early 1900s. Father Matthew's well-publicized work had a large following in North America, especially among the Irish. In Norway, strong antialcoholic measures were put into effect; distilling at home was outlawed.

In his history of the philosophy and policies of alcohol and then drug treatment in Ireland, Shane Butler (2002) recalls the story of the Irish struggle with the forces of moralism and pragmatism. The two most significant developments in Irish treatment history were (a) the introduction and the enthusiastic adoption of the disease model of AA—a model with its roots in the Protestant evangelical tradition—into Ireland, a Catholic country in the strictest sense of the word and (b) the adoption of harm reduction strategies such as needle exchange and methadone maintenance but without any large-scale adoption of harm reduction principles or philosophy. "Attitudes of staff," as Butler (2002) observes, "were still moralistic and authoritarian" (p. 190).

Accordingly, methadone and other practices appeared to become a source of conflict between service users and service providers. The lesson that we can learn from Butler's insightful analysis is the need for compatibility between society's belief system and publicly instituted policy and for underlying integration of theory and practice. One could predict that change efforts that are congruent with cultural beliefs and norms will be more readily accepted than change efforts that are culturally alien.

Once under way, the temperance movement, like any social movement, went to extremes. So what had begun as an effort to protect people from strong brew became to some extent an attack on the people themselves and on the sorts of people who were the most prone to heavy drinking—the thousands upon thousands of immigrants to the United States (Helzer & Canino, 1992). Large numbers of German immigrants consumed a tremendous amount of beer. Irish immigrants also brought their drinking habits with them. Unlike the Germans, the Irish tolerated a pattern of regular intoxication.

The Germans introduced lager beer to their adopted nation, thus providing, according to Murrin et al. (2001), a "wholesome alternative for Americans who wanted to give up spirits without joining the teetotalers" (p. 315). The Germans built old-country beer halls complete with sausage counters, group singing, and family attractions. The Irish, as Murrin et al. further note, reaffirmed their love of whiskey. The term *whiskey* is actually Gaelic meaning "water of life" (Ayto, 1990, p. 572).

The anti-immigrant and anti-Catholic nativism combined to give the temperance movement a new and fierce momentum. Saloons, which were frequented by the working class and immigrants, were feared as threats to the middle-class home and as forums for labor union organizers (Helzer & Canino, 1992). The Anti-Saloon League grew out of these sentiments and became a strong lobbying group.

Ironically, as Americans became more industrialized and disciplined, saloon life grew more civilized (Rivers, 1994). Food was now served, and women began to accompany their menfolk to these establishments. Drunkenness became socially disapproved. The shift from a temperance, controlled-use philosophy to a total-abstinence model marked a shift in public perception of alcoholism as a moral failing to that of a socially proscribed behavior (Benshoff & Janikowski, 2000).

Breweries popped up in the Midwest with the arrival of Germans, more than 2,000 of them, especially in the towns where Germans settled—Milwaukee, St. Louis, and Chicago (Ogle, 2005). Saloons opened on every corner, selling truly light American beer. Unfortunately for the beer manufacturers, the anti-drinking groups were able to take advantage of the anti-German sentiment that sprang up in connection with World War I. By the time World War I broke out, anti-German prejudice was overwhelming. The support of the corporate world, which had an interest in promoting sober worker habits and reducing spending on alcohol, was instrumental in the passage of the Eighteenth Amendment to the Constitution, establishing national Prohibition in 1919 (to begin in 1920).

Of attempts throughout the world to control the use of alcohol, the most resounding failure was that of the United States from 1920 to 1933 (*Encyclopaedia Britannica*, 2005). The American experiment with Prohibition—the "noble experiment"—gave drinking the allure of the forbidden and led to the burgeoning and glamorizing of crime, the growth of organized crime, the corruption of police and politicians, and the criminalizing of ordinary citizens.

Before Prohibition, the Kennedy family had traded in alcoholic beverages and decided to stay with what they knew best. Joseph Kennedy, father to President John Kennedy and two U.S. senators, did not sell liquor directly to consumers but to figures at the highest levels of organized crime such as Frank Costello and Lucky Luciano (Burns, 2004). Kennedy was responsible for shipping huge quantities of Canadian whiskey and scotch into the United States. In his earlier best-selling and controversial *Double Cross* (1992), Chuck Giancana, the brother of Chicago Mafia godfather Sam Giancana, gives a graphic account of the Kennedy connection and ultimate refutation of organized crime. The title, *Double Cross* refers to Attorney General Robert Kennedy's prosecution of some key Mafia leaders, a fact that, as Giancana claims, played into the assassinations of the two Kennedy brothers (see Giancana & Giancana, 1992).

As with the Harrison Act and its aftermath, previously legal activities became illegal at the stroke of a pen. And while these substances—some drugs, including alcohol—were banned, the tides had reversed. The cigarette bans were lifted. Smoking was on the road to becoming a glamorous all-American habit (Savage, 1999). Today, as Hamid (1998) suggests, Americans approve of alcohol and tobacco consumption, although these substances are no less potentially destructive than the ones they have outlawed.

Despite the restrictions on alcohol, people still drank, often consuming home-brewed alcohol that was legal, moonshine, or alcohol that was from questionable sources and likely to contain adulterants. During Prohibition, drinking patterns shifted from beer to more potent liquor because the latter was easier for bootleggers to transport (Benshoff & Janikowski, 2000). Marijuana became increasingly popular. During the 1920s, moreover, women began to drink openly. Their drinking, as Carter (1997) argues, accelerated because of the greater freedom women experienced following World War I, the right to vote, and the relaxed sexual mores of the day. Women who drank publicly, however, remained linked in the public eye to promiscuity and bad motherhood.

Prohibition proved counterproductive not only because it encouraged beer drinkers to convert to spirits but also because it made drinking synonymous with drunkenness (Barr, 1999).

With the widespread disrespect for the law that developed during Prohibition's attempt to regulate what could not be regulated, the growth of organized crime became linked with police and political corruption. Although the overall quantity of alcohol consumed did go down during this time, and the rate of cirrhosis of the liver with it, the death rate from poisoned liquor was appallingly high (Burns, 2004). Homicide rates in the large cities almost doubled.

Economic interests coupled with disillusionment combined to put an end to the "noble experiment." The Depression created a desperate need for more jobs and government revenue through taxes (Ogle, 2005). Couldn't the reestablishment of the liquor industry help in this regard? In 1933, the Eighteenth Amendment was repealed.

Today, the legacy of Prohibition remains. Age-restrictive laws have been instituted. Young people often state that for them there is no difference between drinking and taking drugs (Barr, 1999). In contrast to the United States, which passed the National Minimum Drinking Age Act in 1984, restricting drinking in public places to age 21, Canada has not raised the age, which remains at 18 or 19 depending on the province. What is surprising is the lack of controversy over the age-21 laws, even in light of the surge in binge drinking by the young. Recently, however, lawmakers in Wisconsin and New Hampshire proposed lowering the drinking age for members of the U.S. military (Curley, 2006). In the South and on many American Indian reservations, dry counties and townships still outlaw the sale of alcohol, and Sunday sales of alcohol are illegal in many places. The war against other drugs is still waged on legal fronts, sometimes by means of well-publicized semimilitary-style operations.

The United States was not the only country to experience the ramifications of a temperance movement. After World War I began, support for prohibition increased in Canada. By 1918, every Canadian province except Quebec had adopted a prohibition law. Economic incentives were influential, however, in dimming Canadian enthusiasm for the restrictions. Great profits were to be made from sales to persons south of the border. The prohibition laws in Canada were therefore rescinded in most provinces. In Ireland, due to the temperance crusade described previously, a high percentage of the Irish are teetotalers (McGoldrick, 2005). Binge drinking in Ireland is an enormous problem today, and Irish street violence has increased significantly as have alcohol-related mortality rates (Elkin, 2004).

Iceland, Norway, and Finland also outlawed the sale of alcohol for a period in the early 20th century. Until recently, Sweden and Finland had high alcohol taxes by European standards and restricted sales to state-owned shops. Now that Sweden and Finland have joined the European Union, however, the days of state-sponsored temperance are over. Because of their integration in the global market, the Nordic means of alcohol control, their traditional form of harm reduction through high taxation, is no longer working. According to media reports, Swedes drink about 20% more per year than do Norwegians, who still have a high tax but can easily drive to Sweden for cheap alcohol.

A temperance movement in the 1920s in the Soviet Union was short lived, however; the answer to the serious vodka consumption problem was sought in the socialist way of life (S. White, 1996). Communism was incompatible with alcoholism, or so it was thought. Vodka had been a significant source of government revenue since the 16th century, a resource as significant as tax collection. For a brief period in 1985 under Gorbachev, directives against the use of alcohol at public banquets and receptions were issued, the sale of alcohol to persons under age 21 was forbidden, and public drunkenness was severely punished.

In sharp contrast to the American ambivalence toward drinking and the Russian overindulgence, Italians are a national group that can be singled out for their healthy enjoyment of good wine. Unlike the Irish, who avoid eating with alcohol because food diminishes the effect, Italians tend to drink primarily when eating (McGoldrick, 2005). An Italian woman from Naples, Florida, for example, provides this description of her upbringing:

> In our large, traditional Italian family, gathering together in a large group is an event of great importance. Food, talk, and wine go hand in hand at these gatherings. Talk, of course, is the most important of these. (Contrary to what most movies depict, conversation is not necessarily loud and boisterous, and not everyone talks at once.) But talking and eating together is definitely the way to keep bonds tight. At the dinner table, there is always wine. Some people choose to have a glass, or more, and others do not. No one's behavior or attitude changes because of the wine, and the only way to discern who is or is not drinking is by looking at their glasses.
>
> It is not unusual for someone to give a sip of wine, or even a small amount in a glass, to one of their children. It's just no big deal. This is similar to when I was a pre-teen and felt privileged, and very grown up, on the occasions I was allowed to have a small cup of coffee with my mother and aunts. It wasn't the coffee; it was the conversation and the belonging! By the same token it's not just the wine. I think wine would be nothing without conversation and a sense of belonging. By "belonging," I mean simply being welcomed by loved ones, and this extends, too, to people not in our family. It is not unusual for a family member to invite a neighbor, friend, or co-worker for dinner, or even a holiday meal. We always set a few extra places at the table on Sundays or holidays—"just in case."
>
> I have talked about wine because it is the alcohol most commonly used by Italians, and it's placed on the dinner table. But I think distilled alcohol is also perceived in a similar way. My feeling, though, is that distilled alcohol is not associated with that warm leisurely experience of just sipping the wine with food and family. I think that, also in this context, the Italian people I know do not use alcohol for the mood-altering effect; they are drinking for relaxation and sociability. Another advantage of wine over distilled alcohol is that distilled alcohol doesn't taste as good (in my opinion), and surely is not credited with the health benefits of wine. When Italian immigrants were poor, they could have wine regardless of finances; my grandfather was one who had a tradition of making his own wine, and storing it in the cellar.

(Catherine Studiale Lusk, personal communication, July 7, 2005. Printed with permission.)

MARIJUANA CONTROL EFFORTS

During the 1920s and 1930s, most of the states with large Mexican populations enacted antimarijuana legislation. Because marijuana smoking was common among Mexican migrant workers and other marginalized groups, racism seemingly was the key factor in the passage of the restrictive legislation (Musto, 1998). Hysterical literature of the day portrayed the marijuana user as more or less deranged and as engaging in drug-induced acts of sadistic violence (Abadinsky, 2003). In 1937, influenced by media propaganda such as the 1936 motion picture *Reefer Madness* (a film that is a great source of amusement today), Congress passed the Marijuana Tax Act. A series of harsh antidrug laws carrying severe penalties were enacted in the 1950s.

Each of the periods following the world wars was a time of fear and suspicion leading to scapegoating. Hence, strict laws carrying mandatory sentences were passed at these times. Tolerance of addiction was then attacked, as Musto (1998) argues, as a weakness of ill-informed persons. Opposition to the harsh sentencing laws by the American Bar Association and the American Medical Association, however, remained strong. The pendulum of drug policy began to shift in peacetime, accordingly, from a law enforcement model toward a treatment model (Abadinsky, 2003). Meanwhile, drug penalties had been reduced for all drugs but especially for possession of marijuana, which had now become associated with middle-class youth. The leniency was not long lasting, however, except perhaps in California and Alaska. At the federal level, moreover, an extravagant antimarijuana advertising campaign has been sponsored by drug czar John Walters. The fight against medical marijuana providers and users by the George W. Bush administration is a serious setback to progressive policy development (Abramsky, 2003).

MODERN WAR ON DRUGS

Presidential access to the media, in conjunction with the media's capacity to make or break a politician, is a dynamic not to be overlooked in setting the stage for a mobilization of public opinion. So even though drug use was on the decline in the 1980s, political leaders moved to place illegal drugs on the public agenda (Jernigan & Dorfman, 1996).

Controlling drug use was an attractive political issue for conservatives because it drew attention to individual deviance and immorality and away from questions of economic inequality and injustice (Jensen & Gerber, 1998). The drug scare was played up in the media with an orgy of news coverage to create an image of inner-city explosion centering on crack cocaine. Public opinion changed dramatically following the barrage of news "exposés." Richard Nixon was the first American president to declare what he metaphorically called a "war on drugs," a strategy he devised to separate himself from Lyndon Johnson's liberal "war on poverty." His metaphor grew into a reality as the Reagan, Bush, and Clinton administrations poured billions of dollars into a massive military operation to fight the enemy (drug suppliers) at home and on foreign soil. The political rhetoric connecting youth, violence, minorities, and crime has persisted in the minds of Americans for two decades, largely due to the crusading efforts of the New Right (Jensen & Gerber, 1998) (see chapter 13).

Media campaigns often follow government pronouncements concerning surging drug epidemics. In the 1960s, the horror stories concerned heroin; in the 1980s, crack cocaine was the focus. Concern about crack cocaine led to the writing by Congress of the antidrug statutes of 1986 and 1988, which did everything from mandatory drug testing to funding international interdiction and domestic treatment (Stern, 2006). These statutes continue to dominate the way the federal law books address drug-related crime.

In the 1990s, the drug scare was about designer drugs such as Ecstasy and now methamphetamine (meth). Although there may be a growing problem with the drugs of the day, and the media and political campaigns against them, such assertions are often prompted by a shift in political priorities rather than an increase in drug misuse (*Encyclopaedia Britannica*, 2005).

Like its predecessor, Prohibition, America's war on drugs is directed toward the poor, especially those associated with urban social disorder. Also as with the criminalization of alcohol, criminalization of these drugs represents a desperate attempt to curb the unstoppable. Harsh laws that require lengthy minimum sentences for the possession of even small amounts of drugs have created a boom in prison construction. With 70% of the federal government's expenditure on the drug problem going to law enforcement agencies and just 30% to prevention and treatment (Drug Policy Alliance, 2003), the focus is clearly not on rehabilitation but on punishment. And like antidrug legislation in the past, much of the blame is aimed at foreign forces, namely, the drug suppliers. If the supply can be stopped, whether through the use of weaponry or economic sanctioning, so the reasoning goes, illegal drug use on the streets can be curbed. Media accounts, as Jernigan and Dorfman (1996) document, play up the "us against foreigners" theme, and the foreign governments are generally shown to lack commitment to work with the United States to eradicate the problem.

Billions of dollars have been spent in drug eradication projects in Latin America. The U.S. government poured some $4 billion over the years to fumigate coca crops and arm the military in Colombia (Stokes, 2005). Colombia is the world's leading exporter of cocaine. Because the coca fields are far apart, aerial spraying when applied to a wide surface area harms crops and all other life in the region.

One of the most disturbing aspects of the war on drugs is the undeniable racism entailed in the discrepancy between the sentences mandated for possession of the cheaper variety of cocaine (crack) and for the more expensive variety (powder cocaine). Trafficking in 500 grams of powder cocaine draws the same 5-year sentence as trafficking in 5 grams of crack—the infamous 100-to-1 ratio.

To learn the extent that race figures into antidrug legislation, a comparison can be drawn between the congressional response to the crack and meth scares. Both, according to a *Congressional Quarterly Weekly* report, have been called by members of Congress a "plague on our nation" and associated with crime and community breakdown (Stern, 2006, p. 1548). But the users of crack cocaine are predominately Black, inner-city residents, while the users of meth tend to be White, rural residents.

Meth use as of 2006 exceeded crack use as the drug of choice and was the major law enforcement problem. Yet, as lawmakers describe meth as a scourge as severe as crack, if not worse, there has been no concerted legislative effort to create a federal mandatory minimum sentence for possession. Harm reduction measures have been imposed securing restrictions on the sale of pseudoephedrine, (commonly contained in cold medication), the key ingredient in the manufacture of meth. Although no direct comparison in sentencing laws can be made since combating drugs was seen as a top political priority in the late 1980s while today attitudes have mellowed, little effort is being made to equalize the federal penalties for crack and meth. Still, Black legislators can easily detect the racism in the contrasting responses to the two drugs. "There seems to be more of an emphasis on shutting down these meth labs and trying to figure out ways to treat these addicts and get them back into the flow of society," observed Representative Elijah Cummings. "We don't get for crack or heroin that kind of support for prevention, treatment, and rehabilitation" (Stern, 2006, p. 1548).

As the war on drugs has become a war on street crimes, a bonanza for drug enforcement enterprises has been created. Seizing drug-related assets has become more rewarding to police departments than the arrest itself. The profit side of property seizures is paralleled in the prison industry, now often privatized to meet the burgeoning demand for prison cells for persons convicted of drug offenses. The present policies have an extremely negative effect on high-crime-rate areas; these policies have dramatically increased the profits of drug dealers and at the same time placed economic burdens on big cities to provide more law enforcement protection (McNeece & DiNitto, 2005).

Many strategies in the war on drugs backfire. As the supply of drugs is reduced, the street market value of the drug increases. Often, drug users turn to a cheaper, more harmful drug. Restrictions on the synthetic, psychoactive drug MDMA, or Ecstasy, are a case in point. The Drug Enforcement Administration, in reaction to researchers' experiments to determine the drug's therapeutic value, banned the drug and placed it on Schedule 1, the most severe listing in the Controlled Substances Act. This overscheduling of the drug led to a controversy, much publicity, and a resulting escalation in its use (Harris, 2004). Today, teenagers and young adults across the United States experiment with this "club drug" at rock concerts and "raves."

Abramsky (2003) is optimistic that, because of a shift in public opinion against the extremely harsh and counterproductive policies and because of the impetus of the states to adopt more cost-effective policies, true drug-law reform will gain ground. She singles out the state of Arizona where state legislators voted to limit the ability of the state police to seize the assets of persons accused of drug-related crime, to allow for judicial discretion in nonviolent drug cases, and to restore welfare benefits to former drug offenders. Michigan repealed its tough mandatory-minimum laws, and progressive sentencing reform also took place in North Dakota, Louisiana, and Indiana. These actions are in sharp contrast to the war on drugs, which is a war on minorities and poor women that continues with a vengeance in federal law making and in federal court.

One of the most positive news stories to appear lately is the Baltimore success story. In a city in which heroin and other opiate overdoses have been a major cause of death, drug-related deaths hit a 10-year low. Since 1998, $50 million has been invested (by the Open Society Institute) to expand addiction treatment and teach heroin addicts how to save each other's lives in an emergency. The results have been palpable. Heroin use is down considerably, as is cocaine use, matched by a significant decline in crime and incarceration rates (Brown, 2006).

Afghanistan's opium output in 2005 was almost 4,500 tons according to a recent report from the United Nations Office of Drugs and Crime (Zaheer, 2006). About 90% of the world's heroin comes from this war-wracked nation whose rugged terrain is ideally suited for the cultivation of opium poppy plants.

Relentless international pressure has been exerted on European as well as Latin American countries. Much of it is aimed at the United Nations World Health Organization to conform to the image of drug use as a crime problem, not a health problem, and to reinforce drug control policies (Erickson & Butters, 1998). A special report in the Canadian *Ottawa Citizen* (Gardner, 2000b) provides details of the kind of economic pressure the United States has exerted on the Canadian, European, and Australian governments to pursue a global antidrug military operation. European ideology, however, is geared toward a pragmatic, public health approach that is clearly at loggerheads with American moralism and inflexibility (see chapter 13 on public policy).

HISTORY OF ADDICTION TREATMENT

Our focus now turns from the control of drug use and sales to the treatment of individuals with substance misuse problems. In 2005, an estimated 3.9 million people aged 12 or older received some kind of treatment for a problem related to the use of alcohol or drugs (American Psychiatric Association, 2006). Of these, 1.5 million received treatment for the use of both alcohol and drugs, 700,000 received treatment for a drug problem, and 1.3 million were treated for an alcohol problem. An estimated 23.2 million people aged 12 or older needed treatment for a drug or alcohol problem last year, according to a national survey, yet only 2.3 million received care at a specialty treatment facility. Of all treatment facilities, 60% are private and nonprofit, 2.6% are private and for-profit, and the rest are operated by the county and state (Substance Abuse and Mental Health Services Administration [SAMHSA], 2004).

In any given year, about 2 to 3% of the U.S. population will have a gambling problem, but only a small fraction will seek help (National Council of Problem Gambling, 2005). Nearly 50% of all clients were in treatment for both alcohol and substance abuse and about 20% for misuse of alcohol alone (SAMHSA, 2004). A comparison between 1994 and 2004 shows that alcohol as the primary problem went from 52% to 42%, marijuana as primary from 9% to 16%, heroin from 13% to 14.2%, cocaine from 17.8% to 13.7%, and meth from 2.7% to 6.2% (SAMHSA, 2004).

Throughout most of the United States, as we have seen, religious institutions with a Protestant affiliation have viewed alcohol, gambling, and drug addiction as sinful or irresponsible behavior. Only after Philadelphia physician

Benjamin Rush authored his influential pamphlet *An Inquiry into the Effects of Ardent Spirits on the Human Mind and Body* (1785) did a paradigm shift begin to emerge (Thombs, 1999). In his notion of alcohol, especially distilled alcohol, as highly addictive and the compulsion to drink as extremely powerful in some individuals, Rush anticipated much of the modern, post-Prohibition thinking about alcoholism and other addictions. Rush was also the first American medical practitioner to recommend medical treatment for chronic "inebriates."

When Prohibition—the attempt to control the supply side of alcohol—was revealed as a dismal failure, the emphasis was taken off the production of the beverage alcohol and placed on characteristics of the individual drinker. The substance was replaced by the person (Barber, 2002). During the second half of the 19th century, there was increased medical awareness of health problems associated with alcohol misuse, accompanied by a rapid growth in the number of institutions specializing in the treatment of addiction. Indeed, as William White (1998), author of the definitive study, *Slaying the Dragon: The History of Addiction Treatment and Recovery in America,* suggests, the notion of providing care for persons afflicted with alcoholic disorders goes back to ancient Egypt. And in America, mutual-aid societies were formed, often by groups of recovering alcoholics, some as early as 1750.

With the end of Prohibition in 1933, the population at large began to move toward the view that alcoholics were sick, not sinful. In fact, the social work profession had maintained this view for some time and been actively working with alcoholics and their families from early on. Roiblatt and Dinis (2004) provide a history that is little known. Social work pioneers, as they point out, had authored legislation, established institutions for the care and control of "inebriates," and supported the temperance movement that resulted in Prohibition. Caseworkers and settlement residents such as Jane Addams, who stated her belief that alcoholism was a disease as early as 1909, remained involved with alcohol issues through the era of repeal. These social work pioneers were to see their influence wane, however, after 1935. The fields of alcoholism treatment and social work diverged during this time, as Roiblatt and Dinis suggest, due to the fact that social workers had their own priorities and for various other reasons. Accordingly, the impact of social workers in the shaping of modern alcohol policy and treatment programming from this period to the start of the 21st century was considerably less than it had been previously. Instead of turning to the social work profession for leadership in treatment development, the alcoholism treatment looked elsewhere. There were new forces afoot.

The creation of Alcoholics Anonymous was instrumental in reducing some of the stigma associated with alcoholism and in offering a highly structured program for recovery (Roizen, 2004). After the twenty-first Amendment to the Constitution was passed, a new approach to viewing the problems related to alcohol was needed. The remarkable contribution of two alcoholics, Bill W. (Bill Wilson) and Dr. Bob, was to join the new disease conception of alcoholism emerging out of academic research institutes and into a remarkable organizational network of supporters united by a set of simply formulated principles of sobriety: the Twelve Steps. Although Bill Wilson himself avoided referring to alcoholism as a disease to stay out of medical controversy, he did use terms such as malady, illness, and allergy to depict the condition of active alcoholism (Davis & Jansen, 1998). Both members of the Oxford Group, an evangelical Protestant organization, Bill W. and Dr. Bob adopted the principles of the movement and, according to Peele and Bufe (2000), who cited Bill Wilson's writings, codified the central principles into the Twelve Steps. The notions of powerlessness, seeking divine guidance, making confession and restitution, and carrying the message to other persons were among the concepts borrowed. So influential was Bill Wilson, one of the two founders of Alcoholics Anonymous (AA), that recently, he was selected by *Time* magazine as one of the 100 most influential people of the 20th century, a trailblazer who helped shape the century. "From the rubble of a wasted life, he overcame alcoholism and cofounded the Twelve-Step program that has helped millions of others do the same"—or so the *Time* article about Bill W. begins (Cheever, 1999, p. 201). Today, as the article indicates, more than 2 million members in 150 countries hold meetings in church basements, school gyms, and hospital conference rooms. Although the original members of AA created the Twelve Steps as a guide for alcoholics, other self-help programs have borrowed them and adapted them to help people struggling with eating disorders, gambling addiction, cocaine and heroin addiction, and sexual compulsions, to name a few. Publication of the book *Alcoholics Anonymous* (affectionately known as "The Big Book") in 1939 marked a milestone in substance abuse treatment history. When an article on AA appeared in the *Saturday Evening Post* in 1941, the effect was stunning (W. L. White, 1998). Growth of AA groups skyrocketed from that point on. Narcotics Anonymous (NA) was officially launched in 1949 (see chapter 12 for a detailed discussion of mutual-help groups).

Not only was the AA influence felt at the level of self-help groups, but the reduction in stigmatization of alcoholics revolutionized professional treatment as well. Keep in mind that before AA was founded, treatment for alcoholics was at a primitive level. The period is known today as the "snake pit" era of alcohol treatment (Knapp, 1997). "Inebriates," as they were called, when hospitalized, were usually locked up with the mentally ill and considered hopeless.

According to an article written anonymously by M. T. (2001), non-alcoholic addicts or alcoholics with drug problems have not been made to feel welcome by AA groups from the beginning. Because AA's set of guidelines, the Twelve Traditions, directs that the primary purpose of AA is to help the alcoholic and that the only requirement for membership is a desire to stop drinking, participants are often sanctioned for speaking of problems with other drugs. As M. T. argues, alcoholism and drug addiction are the same disease; alcoholism is not a disease separate from addiction. M. T. reports on a recent AA meeting in Wilmington, North Carolina. When an attender started sharing his problems with a prescription narcotic, he was immediately interrupted by the leader and told he could not share about drugs. Someone else was then called on. Since NA meetings are less commonly available than AA meetings, and judges often recommend addicted persons to AA, AA's nonacceptance of drug addicts is not without consequences. M. T. praises NA for its more holistic acceptability of all addicts regardless of their drug of choice and for its stress on listening for similarities rather than differences among people.

A major criticism of AA and other Twelve-Step groups is their refusal to bend with the times, even to modernize the wording of the steps and traditions. On the other hand, this weakness of AA is also, in a real sense, a strength—the strength that comes from stability and structure. Milo Mead (2005), who can recite a whole chapter of "The Big Book" with ease, explains AA from his personal experience:

> Alcohol is only mentioned one time in the 12 steps. The concept of surrender is important—to win you have to surrender; the person has to be surrendered to a power greater than the self. This is a paradox. Another paradox is the saying of AA, "The only way I can keep this (peace of mind or serenity) is to give it away." This refers to Step 12 which is to spread the message and help others find the way to sobriety.

The sense of camaraderie and acceptance that prevails at a typical AA meeting is well captured in Augusten Burroughs's (2003) personal narrative of recovery, *Dry:*

> My feeling at the end is that AA is utterly amazing. Complete strangers getting together in rooms at all hours and saying things that are so personal, so incredibly intimate. This is the kind of stuff that happens in a relationship after a few months. But people here open up right away, with everyone. It's like some sort of love affair, stripped of the courtship phase. (p. 110)

The Twelve-Step influence is pronounced, although not dominant, in Europe. Disease-model programs designed along American lines generally are relegated to the private treatment sector and can be expensive. Ireland, perhaps because of its strong religious traditionalism, has embraced the Minnesota Model, which teaches the principle of powerlessness and the need to surrender oneself to a Higher Power. Both principles are derived from the Twelve Steps of recovery. Because of the compatibility between the precepts of this program and Irish cultural norms, the Minnesota Model has come to exert a major influence on Irish services for problem drinkers (Butler, 1996; McGoldrick, 2005). The nonhiring of social workers for these programs has resulted in the exclusion of approaches such as motivational interviewing and solution-focused therapy, which as Butler notes are favored by Irish social workers. Norway, in contrast, a more secular country (although the people often find a spiritual presence in nature), officially has resisted incorporating treatment based on Twelve-Step principles in their social welfare system. And extensive media coverage of scandalous practices at one Minnesota-based treatment center did not help matters (see van Wormer, 1997). However, this model, as adapted for Norwegian consumption, thrives today in a small disease-model program in rural Norway, the only such program in that country, that receives extensive county, as opposed to private, funding. Box 2.1, presented later in the chapter, provides a rare look at this program.

JELLINEK'S PIONEERING STUDY

In many ways, Jellinek's book *The Disease Concept of Alcoholism,* written in 1960, is more progressive and up to date than much of the writing from the past two decades, much of which paradoxically cites Jellinek on the disease model. E. M. Jellinek was a statistician who conducted systematic research on male AA members. His goal was to study alcoholism in its many varieties. Jellinek's worldwide travels for the World Health Organization helped provide him with an international perspective for research that provided the basis for his typology of alcoholics.

The cultural patterns that differentiate one country from another, according to Jellinek, help account for the drinking patterns. Thus, the Italian contempt for alcohol intoxication is in contrast to the French tolerance for intoxication, accompanied by an insistence that everyone must drink. Furthermore, as Jellinek observed, the drinking patterns are to a large extent ascribable to the beverages that contain the alcohol; that is, wine or beer are associated with continual use and distilled spirits with "concentrated" consumption over short periods.

Using letters of the Greek alphabet, Jellinek singled out five "species of alcoholism" that he considered disease related:

- *Alpha alcoholism* represents an undisciplined use of alcoholic beverages. Drinking may relieve emotional disturbance, but relationship problems are caused thereby. There is psychological dependence but no progression.
- *Beta alcoholism* involves heavy drinking, causing physical complications such as gastritis and cirrhosis of the liver, yet without physical or psychological dependence on alcohol.
- *Gamma alcoholism* is characterized by increased tissue tolerance, withdrawal symptoms when drinking is discontinued, and loss of control. A marked progression occurs, with interpersonal relations impaired to the highest degree. This variety predominates in Great Britain and northern Europe. Most AA members have experienced this kind of alcoholism.
- *Delta alcoholism* is similar to gamma alcoholism but without the loss of control over the amount consumed, only an inability to abstain for even one day. There are no distressing social problems over the quantity consumed, though health problems may result. This is the predominant pattern in France.
- *Epsilon alcoholism* is periodic alcoholism. In their periodic bouts, binge drinkers suffer a great deal of physical and emotional damage.

Of all the types of alcoholism, according to Jellinek, only the Gamma and Delta varieties can be considered addictions and/or diseases. Gorski (1998) includes the Epsilon type, or binge drinking, in this category. Regardless, the significance in Jellinek's writings is his conception of varieties of alcohol problems, not of one monolithic drinking disorder. It is perhaps unfortunate that only one part of his theory has been immortalized in the form of the Jellinek curve because the curve, as designed by Maxwell Glatt, depicted only one type of alcoholism, the Gamma variety, which viewed alcoholism as primary, chronic, progressive, and if untreated, fatal. Virtually every treatment center in the United States has adopted this formulation, which is often presented to their clients in the form of a lecture. The model of gradual progression into heavier and heavier drinking and to high tolerance as well as to physical, mental, and moral destruction applies to many but not to all, and not very well to polydrug or amphetamine misusers.

The Disease Concept of Alcoholism, as W. L. White (1998) notes, remains one of the most frequently cited and least read books in the alcoholism field. If more people did read the original, it might be better known what Jellinek actually said. He never said alcoholism was a disease: What he said was that alcoholism is *like* a disease. "The problem that I had all along in the field of addiction," notes Gorski (1998), "is that most people treating alcoholics never went back to this original source document, which very clearly presented an understanding of alcoholism and divided it into five subtypes" (p. 100). Gorski wisely warns his colleagues in the field against making one of two biased overgeneralizations—thinking everyone with a drinking problem has a progressive, fatal disease requiring treatment or, conversely, throwing out the disease model altogether and seeing only alcohol problems where there may be a devastating illness.

From a sociological viewpoint, according to Barber (2002), it is interesting that the modern disease concept of addiction should have emanated from the principles of AA rather than from medical research. But when the landmark work of Jellinek began to appear, the modern disease approach to alcoholism was given a foundation for articulation by the medical profession itself.

The Disease Concept of Alcoholism, in short, had a profound impact on the state of the art in addiction treatment. This work provided just the sort of data and analysis needed at the time to convince members of Congress and the medical community alike that alcoholics are not immoral but persons with a disease (or diseaselike condition) and that, once addicted, the problem drinker is no longer able to control his or her other behavior. These basic conclusions of Jellinek's work jelled nicely with the basic premises of AA and gave the rapidly growing organization a considerable boost.

The political implications of the disease concept should not be underestimated. The assumption that alcoholism is a pathology that lies within the individual and that the pathology can be measured and treated are basic to the medical or disease model. Central to the disease concept is the notion of irreversibility by which alcoholism inevitably became a progressive disease that could be arrested but never cured. The AA view begins with a crucial distinction between the alcoholic and other types of drinkers. For the alcoholic, it is a case of "one drink, one drunk," as the saying goes (Barber, 2002). The liquor industry was amenable to this reconstruction of the alcoholism concept because only a small minority could not drink, and there was no desire here to take the alcohol away from ordinary drinkers.

When the World Health Organization acknowledged alcoholism as a medical problem in 1951 and the American Medical Association declared alcoholism an illness in 1956 and a disease in 1966, the transformation to the medicalization of alcoholism was complete. The hospital now had replaced the church and legislators as the center of social control of a newly designated disease. Rather than punitive, the social response to alcoholism had become therapeutic. The new ideology provided a rationale for costly complex medical approaches and for an extensive treatment apparatus. It absolved alcoholics of responsibility for the etiology of the disease but gave them the responsibility to seek treatment. Moreover, the disease model appealed to moderate drinkers in its implication that only alcoholics are at risk. Finally, the American disease model was promoted by the alcohol beverage industry because it removed the blame from the alcohol and its sale and distribution (Barr, 1999).

MORE RECENT DEVELOPMENTS

In 1970, the Hughes Act was passed. This act, which was named after its primary sponsor, Senator Harold Hughes, provided for major research funding by the federal government and emphasized improved services for alcoholics (McNeece & DiNitto, 2005). Known officially as the Comprehensive Alcoholism Prevention and Treatment Act, this statute created the National Institute on Alcohol Abuse and Alcoholism (NIAAA). The federal seed money spawned the growth of alcoholism treatment centers across the United States, a growth that, as W. L. White (1998) observes, was almost explosive in its intensity.

And what about treatment of other drug addictions? Public concern over drug use and dependence among returning Vietnam veterans and the whole baby boom generation led President Nixon to declare drug abuse "America's Public Enemy Number One" (cited by W. L. White, 1998, p. 266). The National Institute on Drug Abuse (NIDA) was established as a research institute, along with federally funded drug abuse treatment programs in what was to be the first national system of addictions treatment. Although alcoholism treatment centers and drug abuse treatment centers are no longer separate, NIAAA and NIDA continue as separate research entities. This artificial separation is inconsistent with modern scientific research on the brain and the nature of addiction.

When the Hazelden Treatment Center opened in Minnesota in 1949, drug and alcohol sanitaria were popularly conceived as snake pits run by quacks (Karlen, 1995). The medical profession, like the general public, had little faith that alcoholics, once hooked, could recover. As developed at Willmar State Hospital and later at Hazelden, the Minnesota Model took a multidisciplinary approach (W. L. White, 1998). From psychology, therapy was borrowed, from the clergy (usually Lutherans), spirituality, and from the mutual-help group of Alcoholics Anonymous, group-based treatment and the Twelve Steps. The integration of recovering, nonprofessionally trained counselors as a legitimate component of the alcoholism treatment team was the key innovation of this model. In the early days, there was harsh confrontation in group settings; today, the regime is a pale replica of some of the antics that went on before. Gender-specific programs are offered for men and women. The sexes are kept completely separate at all times to prevent what Norwegian Minnesota Model counselors call "abstinence romance." So much treatment takes place in the state today that Minnesota sometimes is facetiously called "the land of 10,000 treatment centers." Thousands of former clients of this and the dozens of other similar treatment centers in Minnesota, many of whom come from cities on the East and West Coasts, have stayed on in nearby Minneapolis for the group support that is provided there.

By the early 1970s, more than 30 separate agencies and departments of the federal government were involved in some aspect of substance abuse treatment. A new trend was the integration of drug treatment and alcoholism treatment, fields that had been totally separate previously. The thinking had been that these addictions were unrelated. Sometimes as a result, as White indicates, residential drug abuse treatment centers focused entirely on drinking, which left alcoholic clients open to switch to other sedatives, such as prescription medications. Awareness of the reality of cross-addiction and, later, of facts about brain chemistry of addiction-prone people encouraged a merging of the two specializations: alcoholism treatment and drug abuse treatment. With the growing use of terms such as *addiction, substance abuse,* and *chemical dependence,* the professional literature reflected this merger.

In the late 1970s, when Betty Ford went public with her alcoholism, 28 inpatient days of treatment was the norm. Insurance coverage was readily available, and mass media accounts of celebrities in recovery following treatment were positive. The cumulative effect of two decades of public education on alcoholism, coupled with growing concerns about a youthful polydrug epidemic, had borne legislative fruit (W. L. White, 1998). During this time, a parallel big business had emerged—the substance abuse treatment industry. Many faltering hospitals' finances were jacked up by filling an extensive number of hospital beds with recovering alcoholics. Beginning in the 1990s, however, third-party payers balked; many patients in need of extended treatment were now denied it. Sadly, the building of prisons to house persons in trouble because of their substance misuse seems to have become the current ideological focus.

THE ANTITREATMENT BACKLASH

In his sweeping history of addiction treatment, *Slaying the Dragon,* William White provides the best account that we have come across in the literature of the ideological and cultural backlash against addiction treatment that took place in the 1980s and 1990s. In some ways, the climate for the backlash was set under the Reagan era, when zero tolerance to drug users dominated the airwaves. In some ways, too, the new ideology was promoted at the level of popular culture. A deluge of articles and books were published at this time, including Peele's (1989/1995) *The Diseasing of America* and Fingarette's

(1988) *Heavy Drinking: The Myth of Alcoholism as a Disease*. Although these writings said a lot that needed to be said concerning the multimillion-dollar substance abuse treatment industry and the oversimplified alcoholism-as-disease model that was its raison d'être, the impact of this intellectual denigration of mainstream treatment was profound. Book reviews were exclamatory and, at times, laudatory. From the back cover of *Heavy Drinking: The Myth of Alcoholism as a Disease,* we read, for example, "Herbert Fingarette is at the forefront of a social counterrevolution that could redefine how the United States views alcoholism (*Christian Science Monitor*)."

Such a counterrevolution was evidenced in the growing number of court decisions upholding the denial of benefits on the grounds that alcoholism results not from a disease but from "willful misconduct" (W. L. White, p. 284). Moreover, in light of what the court saw as the religious aspect of AA and NA, court-mandated attendance at such meetings has been determined to be a violation of the First-Amendment requirement of separation of church and state. Uniformly, four higher courts have ruled on this matter (for details, see Peele & Bufe, 2000). This is an issue within some U.S. prisons; substance abuse counselors, accordingly, are instructed, as in Iowa and New York State, to seek alternative treatment models. Significantly, Stephanie Covington's (1999) *Helping Women Recover,* which espouses a program for use in the criminal justice system, is a multidimensional manual that is holistic in focus. The four modules of this program are devoted to work on self, relationships, sexuality, and spirituality. A holistic rather than traditional disease model is the underlying philosophy of this program.

Unfortunately, the impact of the writings of scholars such as Fingarette and Peele seems to be associated with a trend to speak of "bad habits" instead of disease and even with a shift back toward blame and stigmatization of addicts and their substances of misuse. The available funding for treatment ironically is connected to the criminal justice system rather than to medically based services. About half of all treatment facilities have managed care agreements or contracts (SAMHSA, 2004). Managed care treatment options, including generous reimbursement for inpatient and extended outpatient programs, have been severely curtailed (Wallace, 2005). Changes in healthcare coverage have put most residential programs out of reach for all but the privileged few (e.g., Senator Patrick Kennedy with his recent treatment for prescription misuse at the Mayo Clinic). The positive dimension of the rising skepticism over the dominant U.S. treatment model has been the opening of the door to alternative treatments. Typically, managed care companies accept as providers only traditional mental health professionals (Vandivort-Warren, 1996).

The impact has been positive in terms of the furthering of professionalization of the substance abuse field and the emphasis promoted by insurance companies on the use of methods proven effective. The influence of third-party payers, however, has been negative in terms of the bureaucratic restraints. In a country (alone among industrialized nations) without nationalized healthcare, comprehensive insurance coverage for alcoholism and other drug addiction treatment must be mandated for all insurance and public welfare policies. To exchange the disease model for a punitive focus on individual responsibility may be less a step forward than two steps back.

A *Washington Post* article by Rosin (2000) illustrates the point. Church-based drug treatment centers with little accountability to the state have sprung up in Texas under then-Governor Bush's experiment in social welfare reform. "Drug addiction is NOT a disease. It's a sin." So says the sign over the door of one of the new treatment centers. All the major counseling professions, including the American Counseling Association, the American Psychological Association, and the National Association of Alcoholism and Drug Abuse Counselors have gone on record to oppose public funding of faith-based substance abuse treatment. This approach is hardly the one secular critics such as Fingarette and Peele had in mind. Although religion and therapy are natural allies for an individual addict's recovery, what such fundamentalist church-centered programs as described in the article share is a focus that is not disease based, not harm reduction based, and not therapeutic.

Meanwhile, the rate of closure among U.S. substance abuse treatment facilities in the rest of the private sector is considerable, further reducing access to treatments that are already in short supply in many locales. A recent publication in the *Journal of Behavioral Health Services and Research* by Knudsen, Roman, and Ducharme (2005) bears this out. Over the period of their research on treatment offerings in a representative sample of 450 substance abuse treatment centers, 26.4% of the centers ceased to offer substance abuse treatment services. Knudsen et al. concluded that centers offering a more diversified array of services had a lower likelihood of closure. Curiously, as reported in the later article (Knudsen et al., 2005), programs that added psychiatric programming for co-occurring disorders often closed down the substance abuse portion of the treatment. This development, as the authors speculate, is probably because mental health treatment receives far better financial reimbursement than does treatment for substance-related problems. One disappointing development to Knudsen et al. (2005) is the increasing reliance on federally approved medication to reduce craving (e.g., naltrexone) with a de-emphasis on personal counseling.

A University of Georgia research team led by Roman Paul involved a 5-year investigation of the nation's private substance abuse treatment centers. The goal of this study, like that of Knudsen et al., was to more closely investigate the relationship between program diversification and treatment center. In a preliminary summary of the findings, Purdy (2002) describes treatment options that were almost unthinkable until the 1990s. Through the turbulent 1980s, treatment in Georgia was identical to treatment in California and Washington State; it was "one size fits all" for client and treatment center alike. But with threats of closure related to reduced sources of funding, the treatment centers were forced to provide a wider variety of treatments. Today, the University of Georgia researchers find that innovation is being stressed and that Twelve-Step programs are being enhanced with complementary treatments, such as acupuncture and motivational enhancement therapy. Additionally, services are expanding to treat other problems such as gambling, prescription drug, sex, and Internet addictions.

This documentation of the new directions that the substance treatment field is taking (and should take) today has important implications for counselor and social work education. A comprehensive approach is required, as is a familiarity with motivational interviewing techniques. Box 2.1 discusses substance abuse treatment based on a U.S. model but within a social welfare system that clearly deserves its ranking as number one on the UN Human Development Index (see http://hdr.undp.org).

The Introduction of Harm Reduction

The history of substance abuse treatment is still being written. During the 1980s, a grassroots movement called *harm reduction* emerged in the Netherlands and northern England; it emerged somewhat later in Australia (Inciardi & Harrison, 2000; MacCoun, 1998). The spread of AIDS at this time was seen as a bigger threat than illegal drugs, and the prospect of a plague of deaths was more compelling than addiction. The focus therefore is pragmatic: To save lives, help drug users modify their behavior. In the context of the public health crisis, harm reduction refers to strategies for drug users who are either unwilling or unable to stop using drugs (Butler, 2002). Such strategies are aimed at reducing a wide range of drug-related harms while not necessarily reducing drug use per se (Butler & Maycock, 2005). This approach is decidedly optimistic and strengths-based in its drawing on positive possibility and hope. The underlying belief in the predominant Western European approaches is that through effective therapy techniques, the counselor can help people tap into their inner strengths and natural resources.

In comparing U.S. and British approaches to drug use, remember that in Britain, the medical profession had almost unlimited freedom to prescribe morphine and heroin to addicts. This policy persisted into the 1960s (Abadinsky, 2003). A significant increase in the number of heroin users and a scandal caused by a few doctors who diverted heroin onto a black market brought inevitable restrictions. Then in 1985, the year before Nancy Reagan launched her "just say no" campaign, the British government opened a program in Liverpool in response to the AIDS epidemic and started using the term *harm reduction* (Denning, Little, & Glickman, 2004). They and other countries modeled their programming on what had been provided in the Netherlands almost a decade prior to the identification of HIV/AIDS (Butler & Maycock, 2005). With the AIDS panic, countries that originally had been skeptical began in the HIV era to show a new interest in the Dutch experience. Accordingly, the Liverpool public health department and others in northern England began offering medical care, clean drugs (methadone, morphine, or heroin), clean needles, and safe injection education to injection users. By 1989, as Denning et al. (2004) inform us, "injection drug users in New York City had an HIV infection rate of 60 percent compared to an infection rate of 0.1 percent in Liverpool" (p. 5). Today in Britain, specially licensed doctors can provide heroin or cocaine to verified addicts.

Box 2.1	ALCOHOLISM TREATMENT THRIVES IN NORWAY
	Katherine van Wormer

Imagine a treatment center with little paperwork and no insurance reimbursement forms in a country where workers get paid leave as needed, even for family sessions. Literacy is 100%, and most alcoholism is still of the "pure" variety (meaning the alcoholics rarely have other drug problems except for pill misuse). This is the reality in Norway, an American substance abuse counselor's dream. It wasn't always this way, however.

The first time I went to Norway (I worked there from 1988 to 1990), I was hired to train alcoholism counselors about the basics of the Minnesota Model. My personal reasons for going had more to do with seeing the scenery and the desire to experience firsthand a truly benevolent social welfare state. This was just as well, given the way things turned out, because the treatment center was straight out of Schaef's *The Addictive Organization.* (To learn of the bizarre goings-on there, see van Wormer, 1997.)

I was back in Norway in the summer of 1997, less than 100 miles from where I had lived and worked before. Once again, I found myself in the land of sculptured trolls and Vikings, snow-streaked mountaintops, log cabins, and pine-finished houses, purple wildflowers, perpetual summer light, and dark-green landscapes dotted with pale birch trees. And once again, I was enjoying meals of moose meat with *tyttebaer* jam and baked salmon. But I wasn't here for the scenery or the meals. This time I was here for professional reasons.

I never expected to return to Norway, much less to an alcoholism treatment center where I would teach a workshop on the nature of addiction. But here I was in the company of two of the strongest personalities from my earlier work: Randi Isdahl, now the director of the clinic she founded, and Kirsten Male, a social worker and my personal translator. Isdahl, the director of *ValdresKlinikken* (Valdres Clinic), had been the assistant director and my supervisor previously at the other clinical position she had held with the fierce loyalty of the "true believer." But one day when the owner-director's antisocial behavior became apparent to her, she simply walked out.

Following a period of utter disillusionment and depression, Isdahl saw that her only chance to help fellow alcoholics as she had been helped would be through opening her own inpatient treatment center. Following a course of training in Sweden and at Hazelden in Minnesota, Isdahl assembled a group of talented people. Together they opened Valdres Clinic, a private, nonprofit, Twelve-Step inpatient program, the first treatment center of its kind in this part of Norway. Gradually, word spread about lives that were "turned around," and credibility with the local authorities followed. Male, my translator and political ally from previous days, had, like me, been fired for revealing the truth about client and staff abuse at the first treatment center.

Now happily working at a nearby social office (the equivalent of the Department of Health and Human Services in the United States), Male was a source of support and referral to the clinic. She and Isdahl, who had been on opposite sides of the earlier staff dispute, had become friends. Finding myself in Norway again, I marveled at the growing friendship and professional growth of these two extraordinary women, whose experience with life and addiction had instilled in them an almost religious calling to serve.

I expected the treatment center to be a small replica of Hazelden transplanted among fjords and cliffs. So I was not surprised that the basic program included group therapy, lectures, films, Alcoholics Anonymous meetings, and workbook assignments tied to the

Twelve Steps of recovery. What did surprise me were certain innovations in treatment drawn not from Minnesota but from the East—from China and India.

Today, Valdres Clinic offers a comprehensive program built on the following elements:

- *From the West:* The concept of alcoholism as a disease—a personal and family disease—the treatment of which looks to extensive feeling work, communication emphasis, spirituality, and personal sharing.

- *From the East:* Detoxification of all clients, not through drugs but through acupuncture under medical supervision. This involves the application of needles to five points in the ear for 40 minutes a day in early treatment (ear points relate to the endorphins in the brain, liver, lungs, and kidneys); meditation with music; and a highly nutritious diet. (Isdahl brought these aspects of the program back from India, where she had visited an amazing treatment center for opium addicts on the upper floors of a New Delhi police station.)

- *From the welfare state:* The generous Norwegian social welfare system provides complete funding for 5 weeks of inpatient treatment, including an extensive family-week program. Aftercare is provided through the government-sponsored *Rusteam,* with its extensive network of clinics throughout the country. These state-run offices provide follow-up psychological work for trauma and mental disorders.

In the 7 years I was away, Norway's alcoholism treatment program has improved, providing enhanced funding and greater options. Meanwhile, in the United States, treatment options are dictated more by reimbursement policies than by client need, and the extravagance of the war on drugs charade ties up badly needed resources. In my return visit to Norway, I did not know how to explain what had happened to treatment in the United States in the past 7 years. I didn't even try.

References
Stenius, K. (1991, Spring). The most successful treatment model in the world: Introduction of the Minnesota Model in Nordic countries. *Contemporary Drug Problems, 18,* 151–179.

van Wormer, K. (1995). Whistleblowing against the company: A case of ethical violations at a Norwegian treatment center. *International Journal of Drug Abuse, 6*(1), 8–15.

van Wormer, K. (1997). Doing alcoholism treatment in Norway: A personal reminiscence. *Reflections, 3*(3), 67–71.

(Update, September 4, 2006: In response to my request for an update, Randi Isdahl, director of Valdres Clinic, wrote: "In 2000, the government took over the treatment which means they pay the cost. And then came new standards. Some of the private centers had to close. Today we have seven centers using the 12-Step Program; three or four of them are private. The staff includes a nurse, social worker, counselors, psychiatric nurse, psychiatrist, and doctor. Most of the counselors receive their training in the 12-Step Programming in Sweden. For the clients, the inpatient program lasts from 6 weeks to 3 months, sometimes longer; relapse prevention programming follows for 6 weekends . . . Today, we do all the drugs . . . We don't use medicine to reduce cravings, only for detox. Acupuncture helps a lot in detox.")

In the United States, about 150 needle exchange programs have been set up in urban areas (Centers for Disease Control, 2002). For political reasons, however, federal funding has repeatedly been denied. Whereas the British approach and that of Vancouver, Canada, are to provide carefully monitored doses of heroin to heroin addicts (in heroin maintenance programs), the substitution of the synthetic drug methadone for heroin is the only legal recourse on this side of the Atlantic and the 49th parallel.

With regard to alcohol use, harm reduction focuses on such preventive measures as designated driver programs and moderate versus binge drinking. One of the most significant developments in substance abuse treatments is the growing popularity of motivational therapy, an approach introduced by American psychologist William Miller and his associates to European audiences (see Miller, 1996, and chapter 3 in this text). Miller's motivational theory has been hailed as the most important advance in the treatment of addiction (Barber, 2002). Much of his theory, however, as Barber indicates, will be familiar to social workers already schooled in the nondirective counseling techniques he advocates. What is new about this philosophical approach in bringing to substance abuse treatment an entirely different way of viewing motivation? Under the traditional paradigm, according to Barber, motivation to use addictive substances or to abstain was seen as a characteristic of the user. Only when the stress had become overwhelming, when they had "hit bottom," could these motivationally deficient people seek help. Until then, there would only be denial and minimization of substance misuse.

Motivational theory de-emphasizes the use of negative labels and views substance misusers as susceptible to change as the rest of the population. Significantly, therapist characteristics and behavior are seen as playing a major role in treatment outcome. Such denial and resistance as there are, or have been in treatment, often say more about the therapist than the client and can be viewed as products of the interaction. The beauty of this approach is that it is decidedly optimistic and strengths based in drawing on positive possibility and hope. The underlying belief here is that through effective therapy techniques, the counselor can help people tap into their inner strengths and natural resources.

By itself, Miller's theory was somewhat amorphous and vague. What was required was a step-by-step protocol for the training of therapists to help elicit a readiness to change in a previously unmotivated client. The missing ingredient was supplied in the empirical work of Prochaska and DiClemente (1982). From their follow-up research with cigarette smokers who had achieved change naturally and had successfully quit on their own, these researchers were able to delineate from this research (including interviews with successful changers) key factors in the process of self-change. The idea is that we change in stages, not all at once. The path to recovery or resolution from problematic use of substances involves a series of tasks that have been identified in a sequence of stages of change (DiClemente, 2006). This model is called the *transtheoretical model* to refer to the fact that it is not derived from one particular school of thought. This transtheoretical model identified particular interventions to enhance client motivation that could be tailored to meet the client where the client was at in his or her particular stage of readiness. A form of consciousness raising to increase the user's awareness of the need for change was the recommended focus in therapy with someone who was only barely ready to contemplate change (Barber, 2002). Behavioral techniques were thought appropriate to the action stage in the change process.

Historically, this joining of motivational theory with stages-of-change intervention has provided the substance abuse treatment field with a pragmatic approach to serve as the practice component of harm reduction. Harm reduction is the goal: Motivational enhancement strategies teach the counselor how best to achieve that goal. Thus, in the interests of public health, interventions such as needle exchanges—the exchange of dirty needles for clean ones—methadone maintenance, the teaching of controlled drinking and of less harmful drug-taking practices than those the client has adopted, and above all, treatment instead of incarceration, are applied.

Immediately popular in Europe, where harsh confrontation of addicts was never popular, this client-centered approach is increasingly favored by insurance companies because of its cost effectiveness, as was revealed in Project MATCH (see chapter 1).

SUMMARY AND CONCLUSION

Professional addictions treatment arrived on the scene late. Long before there was professional treatment, there was the enjoyment of a variety of mood-altering substances. Whether deriving their pleasure from fermented fruit, coca leaves, or poppy flowers, people have always and will always seek refuge through the means available to them. In this chapter, we have seen how the drug of choice during one era was the substance most vile in the next. The way a particular drug was regarded depended on the circumstances of its use, on the political climate, and especially on what sorts of people were associated with its use (e.g., war heroes, "down-and-outs," genteel ladies). The decision pertaining to which drug or drugs to outlaw clearly had little to do with public health considerations.

In the days before water purification, alcohol was often safer than water. Although the Puritans who set up their theocracy in early America set the climate for a kind of moralism that would long outlast its religious bearings, they and their earliest descendants consumed vast quantities of beer and cider. There were few problems associated with this drinking; drunkenness was frowned upon, punished through public ridicule, and for the most part, avoided.

The switch from wine to beer to more potent liquor was associated with public drunkenness and violent behavior. In Britain, the infant mortality rate soared; on American shores, male drinking cults disrupted family life. Thus, the stage was set for a temperance movement with international consequences. Since excessive drinking in America came to be associated with newly arrived immigrant groups, a politically charged call for abstinence was in order.

Throughout this chapter, we have seen the pendulum swing from prohibition of one substance to prohibition of another. Zero tolerance of certain drugs has culminated in a war on drugs of vast proportions: A military crusade in drug-supplying countries is matched on the home front by the incarceration of more than 1 million people for drug-related crimes. Meanwhile, the sale of illegal drugs has become an underground enterprise of unbelievable proportions. Not only are individual and family economies affected but also the economies of entire nations.

Economics, too, has played a role in the sale and distribution of legal drugs. On the North American continent, as this brief historical review shows, products with addictive properties assumed great economic importance. Tobacco was a commodity that, as the early settlers realized, could sustain the economic life of a colony both in terms of exports and in the money raised from taxes. The sale and consumption of alcohol likewise played a major role in American economic history. Economics determined the manner in which alcohol was consumed, whether as wine from cultivated vines or in the form of distilled spirits, such as rum, which could be produced cheaply from molasses and transported cheaply as well. During Prohibition, the price of liquor shot up, and many working-class people could no longer afford to drink. For those who could afford to buy it, distilled alcohol became much preferred over beer. Liquor was easier to conceal, and people who were now breaking the law anyway were inclined to go all out, gulping down drink after drink with the abandon that often accompanies lawbreaking.

Besides the obvious harms caused by Prohibition, including personal and political corruption, the economic incentive to get people back to work following the Great Depression was a key factor in the legalization of alcohol. Once the distilleries and breweries were humming again, tax revenues were pouring in, and people's drinking habits could be to some extent controlled. The quality of the alcohol sold could be controlled as well. Gambling, similarly, has gone from the underground economy to being a big moneymaker for the states and Indian reservations. Some form of legalized gambling is available in all but two states in the United States (Utah and Hawaii), and in Oregon, it's the second highest source of revenue for the state budget.

Economic interests and ideology came together as the disease model began to gain currency in the public mind. Although temperance leaders had blamed both the drinker and the drug itself for drug-related problems, AA proponents later shifted the focus to *individual* susceptibilities. This shift in focus away from placing the blame on the drug alcohol was of course highly acceptable to the liquor industry. Ideologically, the strong punitive slant evidenced in the United States today has its roots in the moralism of an earlier time. The story of substance abuse treatment in this and other countries is a story of the wrestling between the forces of moralism and diseases, forces that philosophically are often hard to separate.

Starting in the 1950s, as we have seen, the treatment for alcoholism took a progressive turn in its conceptualization of addiction as a disease rather than a sin. What we now sometimes call the Minnesota Model adopted many of the precepts of Alcoholics Anonymous. Harsh confrontation of alcoholics "in denial" has given way in recent years to a more client-friendly approach. Today, Alcoholics Anonymous, Narcotics Anonymous, and family member self-help groups have brought help and guidance to millions across the world. As the addictions field has matured, it has moved away from the dogmatic authoritarianism of the early days to the use of motivational strategies geared to clients' individual needs. Still, much disagreement and confusion remain about the nature of addiction; this confusion spurs acrimonious debates about public drug control policy. Issues that need to be resolved in the future relevant to addictions treatment are inequities in the sentencing laws; the war on drugs, which has become a war on poor people of color; the need for a return to judicial discretion (as opposed to mandatory minimum sentencing of drug users); and more treatment/prevention options for people with chemical dependence problems.

The opposite of the war on drugs, which in effect is a war on people with problems, is a model to reduce harm to people and society. The war on drugs is an extension of the temperance-prohibition model in its focus on the destructive power of the agent of addiction itself. Psychodynamic approaches emphasize the self in terms of ego and memory. Moral and spiritual models all place strong emphasis on factors within the person (Miller & Hester, 2003). Biological models stress the physiological impact of the substance. Ecological approaches look toward the person-environment interaction. A hallmark of harm reduction in a strengths-based formulation is its ability to address all these components—the availability of agent, which is the drug or behavior; a recognition of individual psychological and biological differences in responding to the agent of choice; and an understanding of the person-in-environment configuration as it applies to substance abuse. A harm reduction model provides the opportunity to integrate these components, each one representing a part of the whole, into a holistic framework. The opportunity to involve social workers and other professionals schooled in motivational interviewing techniques and a harm reduction philosophy is now. We continue this discussion with a closeup analysis of a perspective that is integral to harm reduction—the strengths perspective.

REFERENCES

Abadinsky, H. (2003). *Drugs: An introduction* (5th ed.). Belmont, CA: Wadsworth.

Abramsky, S. (2003, August 18). The drug war goes up in smoke. *The Nation*, pp. 25–28.

American Psychiatric Association (2006). Few receiving treatment for substance abuse. *Psychiatric News, 41*(21), 13.

Ayto, J. (1990). *Dictionary of word origins*. New York: Arcade.

Barber, J. G. (2002). *Social work with addictions* (2nd ed.). Hampshire, England: Palgrave.

Barr, A. (1999). *Drink: A social history of America*. New York: Carroll & Graf.

Bell, R. (1987). *Holy anorexia*. Chicago: University of Chicago Press.

Benshoff, J., & Janikowski, T. (2000). *Rehabilitation model of substance abuse counseling*. Belmont, CA: Wadsworth.

Bower, B. (1994). Ancient site taps into soldiers' brew. *Science News, 146,* 390.

Brown, D. (2006, June 9). Drug-related deaths hit 10-year low in Baltimore. *Washington Post,* p. A 10.

Burns, E. (2004). *The spirits of America: The social history of alcohol.* Philadelphia: Temple University Press.

Burroughs, A. (2003). *Dry: A memoir.* New York: Picador.

Butler, S. (1996). Substance misuse and the social work ethos. *Journal of Substance Misuse, 1*(3), 149–154.

Butler, S. (2002). *Alcohol, drugs, and health promotion in modern Ireland.* Dublin: Institute of Public Administration.

Butler, S., & Maycock, P. (2005). "An Irish solution to an Irish problem": Harm reduction and ambiguity in the drug policy of the Republic of Ireland. *The International Journal of Drug Policy, 16,* 415–422.

Carter, C. S. (1997). Ladies don't: A historical perspective on attitudes toward alcoholic women. *Affilia, 12*(4), 471–485.

Centers for Disease Control. (2002). Update: Syringe exchange programs. *MMWR Weekly (Morbidity and Mortality Weekly Report), 54*(27), 673–676.

Cheever, S. (1999, June 14). Bill W.: The healer. *Time,* pp. 201–204.

Collins, R. L., & McNair, L. D. (2003). Minority women and alcohol use. National Institute on Alcohol Abuse and Alcoholism. Retrieved from http://niaaa.com/nih/gov/publications.

Conrad, P., & Schneider, J. (1992). Opiate addiction. In P. Conrad & J. Schneider (Eds.), *Deviance and medicalization: From badness to sickness* (pp. 110–144). Philadelphia: Temple University Press.

Covington, S. (1999). *Helping women recover: A program for treating substance abuse, special criminal justice edition.* San Francisco: Jossey-Bass.

Curley, B. (2006, June 14). Panel debate merits of age 21 drinking law. *Join Together Online.* Retrieved June 2006 from http://www.jointogether.org.

Davis, D. R., & Jansen, G. G. (1998). Making meaning of Alcoholics Anonymous for social workers: Myths, metaphors, and realities. *Social Work, 43*(2), 169–183.

Denning, P., Little, J., & Glickman, A. (2004). *Over the influence: The harm reduction guide for managing drugs and alcohol.* New York: Guilford Press.

Denzin, N. (1993). *The alcohol society: Addiction and recovery of the self.* Somerset, NJ: Transaction.

DiClemente, C. (2006). *Addiction and change: How addictions develop and addicted people recover.* New York: Guilford Press.

Documentary looks at drinking in America. (1999, September 13). *Waterloo-Cedar Falls Courier,* p. C8.

Drug Policy Alliance. (2003, February 12). "Fuzzy math" in new ONDCP report. Retrieved June 2006 from http://www.drugpolicy.org.

Elkin, M. (2004, March 11). Irish take a sober look at binge-drinking habits. *Christian Science Monitor,* p. 12.

Encyclopaedia Britannica. (2005). Alcohol and drug consumption. *Macropaedia* (15th ed., pp. 195–223). Chicago: Encyclopaedia Britannica.

Erickson, K. (1966). *Wayward Puritans: A study in the sociology of deviance.* New York: Wiley.

Erickson, P., & Butters, J. (1998). The emerging harm reduction movement: The de-escalation of the war on drugs? In E. L. Jensen & J. Gerber (Eds.), *The new war on drugs: Symbolic politics and criminal justice policy* (pp. 177–196). Cincinnati, OH: Anderson.

Fingarette, H. (1988). *Heavy drinking: The myth of alcoholism as a disease.* Berkeley: University of California Press.

Fishbein, D. H., & Pease, S. E. (1996). *The dynamics of drug abuse.* Boston: Allyn & Bacon.

Fruhling, L. (1996, September 29). Allow women to vote? Ha! *Des Moines Register,* pp. IOA.

Gardner, D. (2000a, September 12). Do our drug laws harm us more than help? *Ottawa Citizen.* Retrieved January 2007 from http://www.mapinc.org/drugnews/v00/n1355/a06.html?152.

Gardner, D. (2000b, September 5). As long as there is demand, there will be supply. *Ottawa Citizen.* Retrieved January 2007 from http://www.mapinc.org/drugnews/v00/n1329/a01.html?152.

Giancana, S., & Giancana, C. (1992). *Double cross.* New York: Warner.

Goodman, J. (1993). *Tobacco in history: The cultures of dependence.* New York: Routledge.

Gorski, T. T. (1998). Alcoholism should be treated as a disease. In S. Barber (Ed.), *Alcohol: Opposing viewpoints* (pp. 98–104). San Diego, CA: Greenhaven Press.

Hamid, A. (1998). *Drugs in America: Sociology, economics, and politics.* Gaithersburg, MD: Aspen.

Hamilton, E. (1940). *The Greek way to Western civilization.* New York: Norton.

Hanson, D. J. (1995). *Preventing alcohol abuse: Alcohol, culture, and control.* Westport, CT: Praeger.

Harris, G. (2004). What all social workers should know about MDMA (Ecstasy). *Journal of Social Work Practice in the Addictions, 4*(1), 23–37.

Hegel, G. W. (1837). *Philosophy of history* (Vol. 10) (J. Sibree, Trans.). New York: Dover.

Helzer, J., & Canino, G. (1992). *Alcohol in North America, Europe, and Asia.* New York: Oxford University Press.

Helsingin Sanomat. (2007, January 28). Norway wants EU to raise alcohol tax. *Helsingin Sanomat (Helsinki News).* International Foreign Edition. Retrieved January 2007 from http://www.hs.fi/english/article/Norway+wants+EU+to+raise+alcohol+tax/1135220288230.

Hughes, R. (1987). *The fatal shore: The epic of Australia's founding.* New York: Knopf.

Inciardi, J. A., & Harrison, L. D. (2000). Introduction: The concept of harm reduction. In J. A. Inciardi & L. Harrison (Eds.), *Harm reduction* (pp. vii–xviii). Thousand Oaks, CA: Sage.

Jellinek, E. M. (1960). *The disease concept of alcoholism.* New Haven, CT: Yale Center for Alcoholic Studies.

Jensen, E. L., & Gerber, J. (1998). The social construction of drug problems: A historical overview. In E. L. Jensen & J. Gerber (Eds.), *The new war on drugs: Symbolic politics and criminal justice policy* (pp. 1–23). Cincinnati, OH: Anderson.

Jernigan, D., & Dorfman, L. (1996). Visualizing America's drug problem: An ethnographic content analysis of illegal drug stories on the nightly news. *Contemporary Drug Problems, 23,* 169–195.

Joseph, H. (1995). *Medical methadone maintenance: The further concealment of a stigmatized condition.* Unpublished doctoral dissertation, City University of New York.

Karlen, N. (1995, May 28). Greetings from Minnesota. *New York Times Magazine,* pp. 32–35.

Kinney, J. (2006). Alcohol. In J. Kinney (Ed.), *Loosening the grip: A handbook of alcohol information* (8th ed., pp. 2–40). Boston: McGraw-Hill.

Knapp, C. (1997). *Drinking: A love story.* New York: Delta.

Knudsen, H. K., Roman, P. M., & Ducharme, L. J. (2005) Does service diversification embrace organizational survival? Evidence from the private substance abuse treatment system. *Journal of Behavioral Health Services and Research, 32*(3), 241–253.

Levin, J. D. (1995). *Alcoholism: A bio-psycho-social approach.* Washington, DC: Taylor & Francis.

MacCoun, R. J. (1998, November). Toward a psychology of harm reduction. *American Psychologist, 53*(11), 1199–1208.

Mancall, P. (2004). "I was addicted to drinking rum," Four centuries of alcohol consumption in Indian country. In S. Tracy & C. Acken (Eds.), *Altering American consciousness* (pp. 91–107). Amherst: University of Massachusetts Press.

McGinn, A. P. (1997, July/August). The nicotine control. *World Watch,* pp. 18–27.

McGoldrick, M. (2005). Irish families. In M. McGoldrick, J. Giordano, & N. Garcia-Preto (Eds.), *Ethnicity and family therapy* (3rd ed., pp. 595–615). New York: Guilford Press.

McGovern, P. E. (2003). *Ancient wine: The search for the origins of viniculture.* Princeton, NJ: Princeton University Press.

McNeece, C. A., & DiNitto, D. M. (2005). *Chemical dependence: A systems approach* (3rd ed.). Boston: Allyn & Bacon.

Mead, M. (2005, February 21). Presentation to social work students. University of Northern Iowa: Cedar Falls.

Metzger, L. (1988). *From denial to recovery.* San Francisco: Jossey-Bass.

Miller, W. (1996). Motivational interviewing: Research, practice, and puzzles. *Addictive Behaviors, 21*(6), 835–842.

Miller, W. R., & Hester, R. K. (2003). Treating alcohol problems: Towards an informed eclecticism. In R. K. Hester & W. R. Miller (Eds.), *Handbook of alcoholism treatment approaches: Effective alternatives* (3rd ed., pp. 1–12). Boston: Allyn & Bacon.

M. T. (2001, May 9–15). AA unmasked. *Village Voice.* Retrieved June 2006 from http://www.villagevoice.com/issues/0119/mt.php.

Murrin, J., Johnson, P., McPherson, J., Gersle, G., Rosenberg, E., & Rosenberg, N. (2001). *Liberty, equality, power: A history of the American people.* Fort Worth, TX: Harcourt, Brace, Jovanovich.

Musto, D. (1998). The American experience with stimulants and opiates. In *Perspectives in crime and justice: 1997–1998 lecture series* (pp. 51–78). Washington, DC: U.S. Department of Justice.

Musto, D. (1999). *The American disease. Origins of narcotic control* (3rd ed.). New York: Oxford University Press.

Nash, J. (2003, November 24). The first vintage. *Time,* pp. 60–61.

National Council of Problem Gambling. (2005). National problem gambling awareness week. *National News, 8*(4), 7.

Ogle, M. (2005). *Ambitious brew: The story of American beer.* New York: Harcourt.

Orford, J. (2001). *Excessive appetites: A psychological view of addictions.* New York: Wiley.

Peele, S. (1989/1995). *The diseasing of America.* Lexington, MA: Lexington Books.

Peele, S., & Bufe, C. (2000). *Resisting 12-Step coercion.* Tucson, AZ: Sharp Press.

Prochaska, J. O., & DiClemente, C. C. (1982). Transtheoretical theory: Toward a more integrative model of change. *Psychotherapy: Theory, Research and Practice, 19*, 276–278.

Purdy, J. B. (2002, Summer). Sobering times for treatment centers. *University of Georgia Research Magazine*, pp. 31–35.

Qviller, B. (1996). *Rusens historie (History of intoxication)*. Oslo: Det Norske Samlaget.

Rivers, P. C. (1994). *Alcohol and human behavior: Theory, research, and practice*. Englewood Cliffs, NJ: Prentice Hall.

Robertson, N. (1988). *Getting better: Inside Alcoholics Anonymous*. New York: Fawcett.

Roiblatt, R., & Dinis, R. (2004). The lost link: Social work in the early 20th century alcohol policy. *Social Service Review, 78*(4), 652–674.

Roizen, R. (2004). How does the nation's "alcohol problem" change from era to era? In S. Tracy & C. Acken (Eds.), *Altering American consciousness: The history of alcohol and drug use in the United States, 1800–2000* (pp. 61–87). Amherst: University of Massachusetts Press.

Rosin, H. (2000, May 5). Bush puts faith in a social service role. *Washington Post*, p. A1.

Rotskoff, L. E. (2004). Sober husbands and supportive wives: Marital dramas of alcoholism in post World War II America. In S. Tracy & C. Acker (Eds.) *Altering American consciousness: The history of alcohol and drug use in the United States, 1800–2000* (pp. 298–326). Amherst: University of Massachusetts Press.

Rush, B. (1785/1943). An inquiry into the effects of ardent spirits upon the human mind and body. Reprinted in *Quarterly Journal of Studies on Alcohol, 4* [Entire issue].

Sandmaier, M. (1992). *The invisible alcoholics: Women and alcohol* (2nd ed.). Bradenton, FL: Human Services Institution.

Savage, D. G. (1999, December 27). U.S. law has come full circle on personal vices in the last century. *Los Angeles Times*, p. 24A.

Schlosser, E. (1994, August). Reefer madness. *Atlantic Monthly, 274*(2), 45–59.

Standage, T. (2005). *A history of the world in six glasses*. New York: Walker.

Stern, S. (2006, June 5). Meth vs. crack: Different legislative approaches. *Congressional Quarterly Weekly*, p. 1548.

Stokes, D. (2005). *America's other war: Terrorizing Colombia*. New York: Zed Books.

Substance Abuse and Mental Health Services Administration (SAMHSA). (2004). Highlights. *National survey of substance abuse treatment services*. Rockville, MD: Author.

Szasz, T. (2003). *Ceremonial chemistry: The ritual persecution of drugs, addicts, and pushers* (Rev. ed.). Syracuse, NY: Syracuse University Press.

Talmage, T. D. (1887). *Live coals*. Chicago: Fairbanks and Palmer.

Thombs, D. (1999). *Introduction to addictive behaviors* (2nd ed.). New York: Guilford Press.

Townend, P. (2005). Heretical plants of Irish growth: Catholic critics of Mathewite temperance. *The Catholic Historical Review, 91*(4), 611–632.

Vandivort-Warren, R. (1996). Surviving in a managed care market. *Issues of Substance, 1*(3), 1, 3.

van Wormer, K. (1995). *Alcoholism treatment: A social work perspective*. Belmont, CA: Wadsworth.

van Wormer, K. (1997). Doing alcoholism treatment in Norway: A personal reminiscence. *Reflections: Narratives of Professional Helping, 3*(3), 37–71.

Wallace, B. C. (2005). *Making mandated addiction treatment work*. Lanham, MD: Jason Aronson.

Walters, G. D. (1999). *The addiction concept: Working hypothesis or self-fulfilling prophecy?* Boston: Allyn & Bacon.

White, S. (1996). *Russia goes dry: Alcohol, state and society*. Cambridge, England: Cambridge University Press.

White, W. L. (1998). *Slaying the dragon: The history of addiction treatment and recovery in America*. Bloomington, IL: Chestnut Health Systems.

Zaheer, K. (2006, May 24). U.N. says Afghanistan "addicted to its own opium." Reuters Foundation. Retrieved June 2006 from http://in.news.yahoo.com/060524/137/64iaj.html.

Zeldin, T. (1994). *An intimate history of humanity*. New York: HarperCollins.

We help the soul's beauty come to the surface. We polish it until it gleams.

—Rabbi Abraham J. Twersky, MD (2001)

STRENGTHS-BASED HELPING STRATEGIES

CHAPTER 3

The Rose

Andrea Davis

The queen shouts profanities as I lay her jeweled head and losing
    face upon the green felt table.
My bleeding ulcer twists and turns, flaring up with the extra acid
    from adrenaline.
I bear to admit I have lost everything I thought I won.
My back is bent, hunching me forward,
The weight is huge, larger than my being.
I am kneeling on all fours.
Crying that I might never get up.
Maybe I'll just fold beneath the weight, and let it suffocate me.
I live a life the hue of coal, dark, solid, and cold.
And I am trying to press the precious stone out of it.
Looking for something to fill the void.
Searching for the beauty within me.
Hoping for the knowledge that I am loved.
In self-defeat, self-loathing, self-destruction, I am still loved.
Life calls me on.
Today, tomorrow, forever I hope.
And in that hope I feel free.
For the gleam that speckles the inside of my dark cocoon with
    prisms of light
Shows me, I am not just the darkness, my secret life.
I am beauty.

Printed with the permission of Andrea Davis.

INTRODUCTION

Practitioners of strengths-based helping strategies fiercely adhere to the hope offered in the preceding poem by Andrea Davis that "I am not just the darkness, my secret life. / I am beauty." Strengths-based practitioners believe that no matter how dismal the circumstances, people have possibilities, resiliencies, and capacities for change and even transformation. They look for and try to nurture the "gleam" that is often hidden by misery, protective strategies, and the failure to achieve goals set by others.

Diane Rae Davis once heard a highly regarded professor in social work state emphatically that ("for your own good") you just have to "write off" anyone who has been in treatment more than five times. An alternative, strengths-based understanding is that addiction is a chronic, relapsing condition that may require extended interventions not even possible in a single episode and that there is evidence that more times in treatment are related to less use (Hser, Grella, Chou, & Anglin, 1998). "Don't give up until the miracle happens" is an AA saying that applies to clinicians as well as clients. This does not mean that you as a counselor must doggedly chase down a client and try to force your agenda for change. It does mean that you continue to focus on strengths rather than liabilities, not because they are "truer" but because it's a more effective way of helping a client find the hope, motivation, and self-efficacy necessary for making changes.

The strengths perspective in social work practice and other helping professions continues to develop conceptually. Strengths-based practice, as eloquently defined by Saleebey (2006), is a dramatic departure from conventional practice, as "a versatile practice approach, relying heavily on ingenuity and creativity. . . . Rather than focusing on problems, your eye turns toward possibility" (p. 1). Saleebey offers a "lexicon of strengths" that also serves as a statement of principles. Key concepts in the strengths lexicon are empowerment of individuals and communities; membership, or belongingness; resilience, healing, and wholeness; dialogue and collaboration; and suspension of disbelief in what the client says.

Choice is the hallmark of a strengths-based intervention. In the substance misuse arena, this means choice about the goals of the helping relationship (harm reduction, including abstinence); informed choice about a variety of treatment contexts (same gender, group, individual, day treatment, outpatient, inpatient, mutual-help groups); and informed choice about treatment methods (cognitive-behavioral, Twelve-Step approach, solution-focused, motivational interviewing, types of nicotine replacement therapy, etc.). The emphasis on choice of treatment, of course, implies that a variety of community resources *are* available to help people alleviate their troubles with substance misuse and that these treatment choices are affordable. Granted, these kinds of choices are an ideal, not a reality, in the United States, but we advocate finding ways to weave a variety of options into existing programs to the fullest extent possible.

People who use illicit drugs or are dependent on alcohol, gambling, purging, and so forth are typically marginalized in their choices about what they need or want to change and how best to accomplish it. This stance is based on the belief that such people are not capable of making a good choice and must be manipulated or coerced into doing the right thing for themselves and concerned others. Granted, it is tempting to play God, particularly with people who may have wreaked havoc on themselves and others. However, in a strengths-based approach, one concedes that it simply doesn't work. A Canadian research group has discounted claims about the effectiveness of mandated treatment as nonempirical and replete with methodological problems in a review of 850 articles on the topic (Wild, 1999). Inevitably, people seem to find a way to use and misuse alcohol and drugs, gamble, smoke, and so on, even in prison and in treatment centers, if that is their goal.

By honoring choice, a strengths-based practitioner respects the right of the individual to manage his or her own destiny and to take responsibility for his or her own actions. In the field of social work, this is called the value of "self-determination," the belief that people have a right to arrange their lives in accordance with their own preferences (National Association of Social Workers [NASW], 1996). However, the right of clients to pursue their own goals regarding their addiction, take risks or reduce harms, make mistakes, and even harm themselves in the process is not uniformly endorsed by social workers or other clinicians. Many professional social workers justify or simply "go along" with legal and agency interference to these rights because of the "risk clause;" that is, "social workers may limit clients' right to self-determination when in the social workers' professional judgment, clients' actions or potential actions pose a serious, foreseeable, and imminent risk to themselves or others" (NASW, Standard 1.02).

Chronic alcohol and drug addiction, however, is not in the same crisis category as imminent suicide. It is what the ethicist Reamer (1998) refers to as one of "the more subtle forms of self-harming behavior that pose difficult ethical dilemmas for social workers" (p. 29). He says many practitioners have "instincts to protect vulnerable people from engaging in self-destructive behavior." It is this very instinct, based on good intentions, that may be a barrier for social workers and other practitioners to honor self-determination with persons who are misusing substances or addicted.

In strengths-based interventions, we try to keep in mind that alcohol, drug use, and addiction are risky behaviors that have been occurring since ancient times. These behaviors are usually tolerated and "self-determined" in the middle and upper classes. However, if you are economically poor or a member of an oppressed minority group and live in the United States, these same behaviors can make you extremely vulnerable to incarceration. You can lose custody of your own children and have limited options for reducing the harm of your addiction. Harm reduction and strengths-based practices would extend the right of choice and self-determination to all economic and racial and ethnic groups.

Providing options is the second tenet of strengths-based approaches. It doesn't help to have the right to choose without options to choose from. If a treatment center is based solely on the abstinence-only model, there is no choice. In the same way, if a community does not provide low-cost housing or if federal government regulations prohibit public financed housing for people with drug-related convictions (see chapter 13), there is no choice. A strengths-based practitioner may have to go the extra mile to develop an extensive network of referral sources and options. Rapp (2006) examined the impact of strengths-based case management in two different research projects and found that it is imperative that case managers prepare extensive networks of referral sources that include formal service providers, informal networks, program requirements, and natural helpers.

The third basic tenet of strengths-based approaches is to *pay attention to the readiness of the clients and/or client systems to make changes* in the arena they have chosen. No longer are people assumed to be eager for the counselor to tell them what to do and labeled resistant if they are not eagerly compliant. Instead, change is seen as a process on a continuum that moves from a position of unwillingness to even consider making the change to acting on behaviors that will maintain the change. Relapse is regarded not as a personal failure but rather as an integral part of the change process.

According to Velicer (1996), the vast majority of the population for any addictive behavior are in the first two stages of change: *precontemplation* (haven't even thought about making a change) and *contemplation* (thought about it, but ambivalent). Yet almost no interventions have been systematically developed and implemented for this group in the United States. Table 3.1 presents a theoretical comparison of the basic premises of the traditional approach (primarily a medical model) with a strengths-based orientation.

In this chapter, we describe four strengths-based approaches. What these approaches have in common is that they honor the principle of client self-determination, attend to the client's stage of readiness, and focus on the resources and capabilities the client and client's family may use to further their goals. The four approaches are: (a) the practices of harm reduction, (b) motivational interviewing, (c) solution-focused interventions, and (d) narrative therapy. Although some of these practices are well entrenched outside the United States, within the United States they are typically practiced outside the addiction field or on a limited basis within the addiction field.

The last section of the chapter describes the traditional system of treatment care usually available in the United States—detoxification, treatment, and aftercare—and suggests ways to incorporate strengths-based approaches. We invite you to consider the evidence available about the effectiveness of these approaches with substance misusers and others struggling with addictive processes and compare it to the effectiveness of the disease-model approach as it is widely practiced in addiction treatment in the United States. In particular, we hope you will examine the assumption of self-determination in these strengths-based practices and decide how it matches your own values and beliefs regarding professional helping processes.

TABLE 3.1 | COMPARATIVE APPROACHES TO ADDICTION

Traditional Counseling Approach	Strengths-Based Therapy
Biological	**Biological**
Looks to the individual for specific causes of disease	Stress on multiple, interactive levels of influence
Dichotomizes reality, for example, alcoholic vs. nonalcoholic	Addiction-like behaviors seen as existing along a continuum
Psychological	**Psychological**
Problem focused	Strengths focused, looks to possibilities
Uses labels such as alcoholic, codependent	Tries to avoid use of negative labels
Assesses problems and losses	Assesses and builds on strengths
Client seen as typically resistant, in denial	Client seen as active participant in a collaborative, health-seeking effort
Client motivation unimportant	Intervention geared to level of client motivation to change
Focus to prevent slip or relapse	Focus to maintain moderation or abstinence as client wishes
Expulsion from treatment for relapse	Client self-determination stressed; meet the client where he or she is
Uses confrontation to elicit change,	Rolls with the resistance; redefines resistance as a challenge
One size fits all	Individualized treatment; stresses client choice
Social	**Social**
Encourages identity as member of self-help group	Holistic approach
Identifies pathologies from upbringing in chemically dependent home	Seeks strengths in upbringing
Looks for codependence in family members	Perceives family as potential resource

HARM REDUCTION

All programs that deal with people who are misusing substances or are addicted, including abstinence-only programs, share the goal of reducing harm caused by the addiction. Specific harm reduction strategies, which we describe in this section, refer to practices that aim at reducing drug-related harm without requiring abstinence from the drug itself (Tammi, 2004). Based on a public health model of primary, secondary, and tertiary prevention, harm reduction (at the tertiary level) attempts to alleviate the social, legal, and medical problems associated with unmanaged addiction. In so doing, it tries to limit the harms, such as infectious diseases like HIV, hepatitis, and tuberculosis, violence, criminal activity, and early death, without necessarily attempting to "cure" the addiction (Nadelmann, McNeely, & Drucker, 1997). Abstinence may be an ideal outcome for many addicted persons, but harm reduction advocates point out we are not 100% effective in convincing people to become abstinent. A review of the literature on treatment options for opioid-dependent patients by Brink and Haasen (2006) concluded that abstinence-only interventions are only effective for a select few: motivated persons with stable living conditions and social support. The Project MATCH Research Group (1997) found that only 19% of the outpatient subjects maintained complete abstinence throughout the 12-month follow-up period; however, there was substantial positive improvement. This same group abstained on average more than 80% of the days posttreatment compared with slightly more than 20% pretreatment. From a harm reduction standpoint, abstinence is viewed as *only one of several means* of improving.

Because of all the myths surrounding harm reduction practices, it may be helpful to start with what harm reduction is not. It is not:

- A conspiracy to seduce alcoholics or addicts into thinking they can use alcohol or drugs moderately, thus prolonging their agony. (Rather, the extent of a person's drug/alcohol use per se is not the focus of harm reduction—use is secondary to the risk of harms *consequent* to use.)
- A potent excuse for an alcoholic, compulsive gambler, or drug addict to continue to use alcohol or drugs or gamble. (Rather, for a person who is in the throes of addiction, the principles of harm reduction are no more potent than "today it is raining" as a reason to use alcohol, drugs, gamble, etc.)
- A foolish, dangerous model designed by academics or people who don't know anything about addiction or don't care about the consequences of not getting people to abstain from their addiction. (Harm reduction practices evolved from the demands of injection drug users for strategies to prevent the spread of HIV.)
- A misguided approach that makes it easier for addicts to keep on being addicted by furnishing shelter, food, clean needles, methadone, and even heroin to people who are addicted. (Most harm reduction programs attend first to the most pressing needs of an individual as a step in the direction of less risky use or, if appropriate, abstinence.)

Harm reduction practices can be understood by looking at how one might treat a person with diabetes. Harm reduction practitioners would not wait until the person was in a diabetic coma and brought into the hospital for treatment. Rather, they would try to educate health providers and other likely contacts about the symptoms of diabetes so people who are in harm's way can be alerted and given informed choices about different ways to proceed and the cost and benefits of such actions. Resources would be available to assist the persons in finding the right path for them, whether a different diet or insulin shots.

Families and the community at large would be educated about the typical harms of the disease, such as the emotional roller coaster that can result when the problem is ignored. People with diabetes would be encouraged to reduce the various harms of going untreated, and resources would be made available to assist them. Their choices would be respected (even if we don't agree with them), and we would expect them to take responsibility for their choices. Sound familiar? This is the way it actually works in the public health system. The harm reduction model simply applies this approach to addiction.

REDUCING BARRIERS

Harm reduction practitioners reduce barriers that make it less likely that people who are misusing alcohol/drugs or addicted will get help. Typical barriers present in many treatment programs today include program locations inaccessible to or remote from the community they are trying to target, professional staff who may be perceived as knowing little about street culture or survival rules, waiting lists for intake and treatment, financial costs, and a requirement that abstinence be the goal of treatment. Reducing barriers is critical because it is estimated that only one of six adults who are injecting drug users (IDUs) is in treatment at any given time, fewer than 10% of substance abusers receive professional treatment for alcohol or drug problems (Narrow, Regier, Rae, Manderscheid, & Locke, 1993), and only 7.2% of youth (12–17) needing alcohol treatment receive it (National Survey on Drug Use and Health, 2006). An estimated 10% of pathological gamblers identified in prevalence studies will seek treatment (Ladouceur, 2005).

By far the most controversial aspect of harm reduction strategies in the United States is promoting "low-threshold" access to services by not requiring abstinence as a precondition for receiving treatment. Marlatt (1998) says abstinence-based treatments raise a "high-threshold" barrier that does not distinguish between lighter and heavier use and degrees of harm. In addition, it promotes stigmatizing individuals who use or misuse alcohol and drugs as either "criminal/immoral addicts or victims of an incurable genetic or biological disease" (p. 55). Neither one of these options would be seen as user friendly or likely to appeal to people who first of all want help in reducing the problems associated with their addiction. Harm reduction services are offered with the fewest possible restrictions, requirements, or goal expectations and the smallest possible amount of paperwork to appeal to the widest group. For example, in a preliminary study that found some gamblers can eliminate the harms of their excessive gambling by controlling the amount of money bet and the amount of time spent gambling, the author notes that none of the participants would have been willing to engage in treatment if the requirement had been abstinence (Ladouceur, 2005).

Recruiting members of the targeted group to do community-based street outreach is a common approach to reduce barriers. For example, the Indigenous Leader Outreach Model (ILOM) used in Denver, Colorado, to reduce the spread of HIV hires and trains recovering drug users. They do this because "they have insider access to the drug-using community, they know the rules governing the social systems of the streets, and they are able to develop trusting relationships with the target population of active drug users" (Booth, Kwiatkowski, Iguchi, Pinto, & John, 1998, p. 117). Several projects and programs use active injection drug users as outreach workers, and there is growing documentation that this is effective in helping street addicts control, reduce, or stop their use of drugs (see the special issue of *Journal of Drug Issues* 25(3), 1995, on "Drug Users as Risk Reduction Agents"). In the introduction to the special issue, Broadhead (1995) notes that injection drug users have been helpful in "preparing and distributing bleach kits, recruiting users who need help, helping outreach workers learn about new drug scenes and copping areas, and vouching for outreach workers that need to be established" (p. 505).

Outreach often involves providing drug education materials telling the user how to reduce the risks associated with using drugs as well as building a relationship and providing referrals for treatment and support services. Examples of pamphlets available in English and Spanish on the Internet from the Harm Reduction Coalition include "Taking Care of Your Veins: Rotate Your Spot!" and "Avoiding Arteries and Nerves When You Want a Vein" (www.harmreduction.org).

Increasing accessibility to harm reduction aids is accomplished in a variety of creative ways, some of which may surprise the American reader. For example, in Amsterdam, police stations provide clean syringes on an exchange basis; automated syringe exchange machines are accessible 24 hours a day in many European and Australian cities; in several provinces in Canada, pharmacists are actively involved in syringe exchange programs; in the United Kingdom, Europe, and Australia, methadone is available from general practitioners as well as clinics, and some even distribute through "methadone buses" (Riley et al., 1999). Activities more common in the United States include mobile vans or street workers delivering services to parts of the community where injection drug users live or "hang out." Even in the United States, there are creative ways of improving access, such as a needle exchange program aimed at younger users in Portland, Oregon, located in a trendy café, and an outreach site in Boulder, Colorado, near a gymnasium to target steroid injectors (Peterson, Dimeff, Tapert, Stern, & Gorman, 1998).

A goal of harm reduction practitioners in the United States is to make methadone treatment and needle exchange programs more accessible. Although the United States has institutionalized methadone maintenance programs since the 1960s, the distribution of methadone is confined to specialized clinics, usually in larger cities, subject to strict federal and state regulations that require exacting compliance from clients. Needle exchange programs in the United States continue to be unfunded by federal dollars and legally harassed in many localities, despite abundant research on the positive results of these programs. Approximately 10% of IV drug users in the United States have access to needle exchange programs, and 45% of these programs operate illegally (Nadelmann et al., 1997). Unfortunately, those that are legal operate under the same type of strict guidelines that make the methadone maintenance programs user unfriendly.

Other strategies that have demonstrated effectiveness in reducing barriers include "rapid intake" (Dennis, Ingram, Burks, & Rachal, 1994), where people who want to enter treatment are no longer delayed, and lowered financial barriers, such as passing out free coupons for treatment. In a New Jersey study where coupons for free methadone treatment were passed out in the IDU community, 59% redeemed treatment coupons. Nearly 50% of these people had never been in treatment; 58% tested HIV positive (Bux, Iguchi, Lidz, Baxter, & Platt, 1993). In a random assignment study in Denver that compared free treatment to paying for treatment, 52% of the injecting drug users assigned to free treatment entered treatment compared to 32% for those who had to pay (Booth et al., 1998). In spite of this evidence, lowering financial barriers is not endorsed by professionals who believe that clients "have to pay" to receive positive benefits from programs.

Looking for larger system interventions that would help reduce the barriers for women to get help with gambling problems, the "Queen of Hearts" Australian project (Brown & Coventry, 1997) elicited suggestions from women gamblers. Their ideas include: (a) timely access to other supporting services, such as mental health and especially financial counseling; (b) access to female counselors because of the need to disclose problems such as physical, sexual, and emotional abuse; and (c) easily accessible services in downtown areas as well as rural environments where services are collocated with other supportive services to lessen stigmatization and promote referrals.

Other examples of harm reduction strategies that improve access are selling nicotine replacement therapies over the counter instead of requiring a prescription, making clean syringes and methadone available in prisons, supplying free bleach kits for cleaning injecting equipment to prevent hepatitis, providing testing for street drugs at "rave" dances, developing "tolerance zones" or "injection rooms" where drug users can get clean equipment, condoms, medical advice, and attention and even take drugs in a safe environment, and launching various websites to keep consumers informed, such as the "ravesafe" organization that started in South Africa in 1993 (www.ravesafe.org). Although many of these practices are controversial in the United States and Canada, the overall purpose of improving access to a treatment system that is not yet user friendly (some say built for providers to punish consumers) needs to be respected.

CHOOSING TO REDUCE HARM: WHO CHOOSES?

Diane Riley and her colleagues (1999), of the Canadian Centre on Substance Abuse National Working Group on Policy, raise some thought-provoking questions: What drug-related "harms" should be given priority? Is preventing HIV infection more important than eliminating dependence? Abstinence-only proponents tend to view dependence as a top priority, but many harm reduction proponents do not. Success in harm reduction terms is "any reduction in drug-related harm" (Denning, 2000, p. 37). Another critical question is who decides. In abstinence-based treatment, professionals decide the priorities to be addressed, starting with abstinence. In the harm reduction approach, the person/consumer/client decides the priorities to be addressed—that is, what harms to address and in what order.

Recognizing the importance of choice in finding one's own path, Patt Denning (2000) states that "people have the right to make their own decisions in life. . . . The fact that they may make treatment choices and life choices that conflict with my professional or personal beliefs does not relieve me of my responsibility to offer them what help I can" (p. 25). Denning is a therapist who lives in San Francisco, where, since September 2000, official city policy has required that all substance abuse and HIV/AIDS treatment providers address how they will provide harm reduction treatment options and that they develop harm reduction guidelines. As a consultant and trainer to many treatment providers, Denning (2000) acknowledges that harm reduction strategies may focus on what the user might see as more pressing problems than drug or alcohol use, such as housing, repairing broken relationships or support systems, jobs, social skills training, and psychiatric symptoms. The goals within the professional helping relationship are based on the rights of individuals to make their own choices. Consequently, cultural, racial, and ethnic differences that may influence goals are not problematic but are looked on as resources and potential supports.

In Denver, a program developed to reduce the harm of HIV transmission uses a hierarchy of behavioral options called "The Indigenous Leader Outreach Model" to describe the choices available to injecting drug users (Booth et al., 1998, p. 117):

- Quit using drugs.
- If you can't or won't stop using drugs, then stop injecting.
- If you can't or won't stop injecting, then don't share needles or syringes and other works.
- If you can't or won't stop sharing, then disinfect your needles and syringes with bleach between sharing partners.

Although reducing the probability of HIV transmission is a common goal among most treatment providers, other "harms" that are the focus of harm reduction strategies include the risks of procuring illegal drugs, such as legal consequences, incarceration, and the loss of custody of children. Larger system harms may include the alarming growth of prisons, the marginalizing of certain groups, such as "crack moms," and the large amount of national resources devoted to interdiction instead of treatment (see chapter 13 on public policy). The definition of *harms* also varies depending on the type of problem and the co-occurrence of other problems, such as mental disorders, gambling, homelessness, and domestic violence.

For example, people who are homeless and chronically alcoholic are vulnerable to serious difficulties with the police, continual health crises, and deterioration of functioning at all levels. An innovative program in Canada used the principles of harm reduction to design a shelter-based project that provided healthcare, supervision, assistance with daily living tasks, and a maximum of one standard drink of alcohol hourly on demand during waking hours (Podymow, Turnbull, Coyle, Yetisir, & Wells, 2006). Although the study had only 17 participants (mean age 51, mean duration of alcoholism 35 years), the results are encouraging from a harm reduction perspective. The number of emergency room visits and police encounters decreased significantly, hygiene improved, and participants reported less alcohol consumption.

Unfortunately, for a homeless woman with a history of substance misuse who finds a place to live through a social agency, the most immediate harm of using alcohol or drugs may be the risk of homelessness. Kate Fewel, MSW, worked in a downtown women's drop-in center in Spokane, Washington, and case-managed four homeless women (with histories of alcohol/drug misuse and/or domestic violence) in their own apartments through a neighborhood-housing program. She notes the difference between the women she worked with, who are required to maintain abstinence not only from drugs or alcohol but also from abusive relationships, and an alternative model in her same community that practices harm reduction. In her housing model, abstinence is required to encourage the women to focus on the issues that led to their homelessness. However,

> the stress level is higher because they are more immediately accountable (but not over the long run) and they are at risk of losing housing if they break the rules or get caught. In the harm reduction setting, the women may experience relapse, but not at the risk of losing their housing. Because housing is the safety net, their relapses are actually informing them and helping them solidify their foundations of recovery. For example, a woman in my program drank. I had to kick her out. However, I was able to get her in the other program (harm reduction), and even though she continued to relapse a couple of times, in the long run she was able to go to outpatient treatment, resume participation in recovery meetings, and all the things that can't happen when you are homeless. (personal communication, March 21, 2001)

Women who gamble experience their own particular harms. The Queen of Hearts Australian project (Brown & Coventry, 1997) found that women who were experiencing problems with gambling also experienced stigmatization, loneliness, oppressive role requirements as women with few opportunities to socialize without the company of men, and serious financial and emotional turmoil. Suggestions from the women gamblers for reducing harm on a larger system level include: (a) involvement of all the groups associated with gambling (including women gamblers, financial institutions, gaming operators, and government) to work on solutions, instead of leaving it up to the "victims" to cope; (b) establishing alternative recreations for women in neighborhoods; (c) decreasing the accessibility of gaming venues, removing them from shopping centers, strip malls, clubs, and hotels throughout the state; and (d) timely access to other supporting services, such as mental health and especially financial counseling.

Many of the harm reduction strategies used with tobacco addiction are initiated by people on their own, without professional help or intervention.

It is estimated that "self-change" or "natural recovery" occurs with 80 to 90% of all those who stop smoking altogether (U.S. Department of Health and Human Services, 1988). In a review of harm reduction strategies with nicotine, Baer and Murch (1998) describe several interventions that may help reduce tobacco use. These include further restrictions on the accessibility of tobacco through increased taxation and limits on advertising, offering "controlled smoking" clinics, changing the product by reducing tars and nicotine, and nicotine replacement treatments, such as nicotine gum, "patches," nasal sprays, inhalers, and lozenges. The authors note that these strategies deserve more research attention, particularly around the question of how harm reduction strategies can be integrated with smoking cessation programs.

Harm reduction strategies for alcohol misuse are based on the premise that alcohol use ranges across a continuum, starting with no consequences for use and ending with devastating consequences for use, with lots of states in between. Harm reductionists emphasize the research evidence that alcohol problems are more likely to be intermittent or discontinuous, are subject to "natural recovery" without formal intervention, just like quitting smoking, and can continue at a stable level for years at a time (Larimer et al., 1998; Sobell, Ellingstad, & Sobell, 2000; Vaillant, 1996). These conclusions are difficult to swallow for professionals who have been trained to see a "progressive, fatal, disease state" that never gets better once you have it. As Larimer and her colleagues (1998) point out, "the occurrence of even a single case of controlled drinking by an alcoholic challenges the very definition of alcoholism as a disease" (p. 75). Controversy over the research on this subject has been going on since Davies (1962) found 7 "normal" drinkers among a treated group of 93 male alcoholics in the United Kingdom. Other research that consistently replicates the finding that moderate drinking is an outcome of treatment for some alcohol-dependent clients (both in moderation treatments and abstinence treatments) has been vilified and even called "fraudulent" by people who adhere to the disease model. The review of the research by Larimer and her colleagues (pp. 81–84) led them to conclude:

1. A majority of people with drinking problems self-recover with no formal treatment.
2. Over time, rates of abstinence (compared to controlled drinking) tend to increase.
3. A choice of goals tends to result in greater treatment retention and the recruitment of a broader range of problem drinkers.
4. When given a choice, people tend to choose the goal that is most appropriate for the severity of their problems.

Harm reduction strategies for alcohol misuse and dependence primarily involve offering more choice about outcome goals (moderation training as well as abstinence training), brief interventions that focus on advice and increasing motivation to change, and brief assessments that give people the opportunity to assess harm without prescriptions for a particular treatment.

An example of strategies for reducing the harm of heavy drinking in college students at the University of Washington is the recent Lifestyles Project. In this program, a thorough assessment was offered all incoming freshmen, and 25% were identified as at risk for drinking-related problems. These students were randomly assigned to the experimental group, which received motivational interviewing (see the section on motivational interviewing) with feedback about drinking patterns and risks, or to a control group, which received only a more detailed assessment. Students in the motivational interviewing group were encouraged to evaluate their risk status and think about the possibility of behavior change. Resources were offered, but the goals about change were left to each student. Feedback reports were also sent to the students at the 6- and 12-month follow-up sessions. Results indicate that the experimental group reported significantly less drinking, consuming less on each drinking occasion, and a lower peak quantity over time (Larimer et al., 1998). Four years after the intervention, the authors still found significantly reduced negative consequences for drinking, indicating long-lasting results from a modest intervention (Baer et al., 2001).

ATTENDING TO READINESS TO CHANGE

All harm reduction strategies just described are based on a common assumption: People are ultimately capable of making an informed choice in their own best interest. The choices they make depend on their readiness to change—that is, what stage of change they are in. The stages-of-change model, sometimes referred to as the *transtheoretical model* because it relies on several theories of social psychology, was first proposed by Prochaska and DiClemente (1986). It has since been applied and adopted in many addiction treatment and other helping settings around the world.

The stages-of-change model is a circular process that includes five stages in the process of behavior change. A sixth stage, precontemplation, lies outside the wheel because the person in this stage sees no need to change or has no intention of changing behavior at this time. The "precontemplator" may be defensive or angry when confronted or even questioned about alcohol or drug problems. Once there is a glimmer in the minds of the client that a problem does exist, the person enters the circle and proceeds through each stage several times before finally achieving stable change. The stages are: (a) *precontemplation* (characterized by defensiveness about substance use), (b) *contemplation* (when the person is aware that a problem exists but is ambivalent about making a change or has anxiety about what change will mean), (c) *preparation* (when the person intends to make a change in the near future or has unsuccessfully taken action in the past year), (d) *action* (when the person takes action to change his or her behavior or environment to overcome a problem behavior, such as becoming abstinent or cutting down on drug use), (e) *maintenance* (when the person consolidates gains and works to prevent relapse), and (f) *relapse* (which may occur repeatedly and is considered a normal, inevitable part of the behavior change process) (Miller & Rollnick, 2002).

Most treatment programs and mutual-help organizations such as Alcoholics Anonymous are designed to help people who are in the action stage of change; that is, they already have a "desire to stop drinking" and are ready to take action. Regrettably, a number of studies indicate that most people start at the precontemplation or contemplation stage of change. Consequently, counselors need to know how to work with unmotivated clients who may have been forced into treatment by their families or the legal system.

Many professional counselors also assume that the person is in the action stage of change or *should be in the action stage,* given all the obvious (to the counselor or family) reasons for changing behaviors. When clients are in the precontemplative or contemplative stage, they have been labeled "unmotivated," "resistant," or "in denial." Instead of the counselor's jumping to this conclusion, Miller and Rollnick (2002) propose that these problems occur when a counselor is using strategies that don't match up with a client's current stage of readiness to change. They designed the process of "motivational interviewing," discussed later, to provide a more productive fit between counselor behavior and client reality.

Rapp, Li, Siegal, and DeLiberty (2003) found that there is little relationship between a client's initial motivation at treatment entry and outcomes 6 months later. Consequently, they recommend that paying attention to the client's immediate concerns using client-centered strengths-based practices is more helpful to treatment retention and success than assigning the label of "motivated" or "unmotivated." Harm reduction practices are designed to help people move through the stages of change at their own pace. Instead of a dualistic framework of either recovery or relapse, harm reduction practice offers a wider path that encompasses and honors all stages in the change process. The application of this model to families may require some modification, for everyone may not be in the same stage at the same time. Barbara Aranda-Naranjo, who works at the South Texas AIDS Center for Infants and Their Families in San Antonio, recommends that the stages-of-change model be explained to families in a way they can understand, as part of their right to be informed of the tools and models that practitioners use to meet their needs (Fitzgerald, Aranda-Naranjo, & Denenberg, 1996). In her clinic, the model is translated into Spanish to increase the understanding of these processes.

STRENGTHS-BASED COUNSELING MODELS

Motivational interviewing (MI), solution-focused therapy (SFT), and narrative therapy have gained recognition, built evidence of effectiveness, and increased in popularity since the mid-1980s. Although MI has roots in the addiction field, narrative and SFT have only recently been applied to addiction treatment. They all have certain similarities that are congruent with the strengths-based approach to practice. Each rests on the assumption that clients have abilities, possibilities, strengths, and competencies, no matter how dire their situations may appear, and the clinician's job is to help the client ferret these out. In the narrative approach, it may mean finding strengths in letters written by clients saying "good-bye to alcohol" (Diamond, 2000); in SFT, it might be through building an imaginary preferred future where the client can envision a place for herself (De Jong & Berg, 2002); in MI, it is the assumption that the client wants to make changes that will make his life work better (Miller & Rollnick, 2002).

Both narrative and SFT are based on postmodern or social constructionist philosophy, which views the construction of reality as the product of human interaction through language; that is, people make meaning out of their experience through discourse with others. Thus, solutions, or new ways of viewing one's experience, can emerge from therapeutic dialogue. O'Hanlon (1994) coined the term "third wave" to apply to narrative therapy, and "pre-third wave" to apply to solution-focused therapy, as a way of signaling that these approaches take a new philosophic direction, away from the pathology-focused "first wave," dominated by psychodynamic theory, and the problem-focused "second wave" of the 1950s, characterized by behavioral therapy, cognitive approaches, and family therapy. Another way of looking at this is that in the first wave approach, the problem/pathology/addiction is located within the individual; in the second wave approach, the problem is located in small, interactive systems; and in the third wave approach, the person is never the problem—the problem is the problem. In addiction, a third wave practitioner would not see the person as an "alcoholic" or an "addict" but would work hard to help the person get "unstuck" from his or her label to mobilize the person's energy and confidence to find a new life path, provided that is the direction the person wants to go. MI could also be considered a third wave approach in the rejection of diagnostic labels, the importance of a non-judgmental stance, and the use of language to reflect the client's reality (Lewis & Osborn, 2004).

All three models are anchored in change: MI helps clients move through the change process; SFC focuses on what a client will be doing differently once change occurs (Lewis & Osborn, 2004); narrative helps clients change (reauthor) a problem-saturated story to one of hope and strength.

MOTIVATIONAL INTERVIEWING

> Twenty years ago it would have been difficult to persuade me that a brief intervention of this kind could have such a potent and lasting impact on behavior. (Miller, 1996, p. 840)

The development of motivational interviewing (MI) is credited to the relentless, spirited questioning by student interns in Norway of William R. Miller as he demonstrated how he would work with clients in various settings (Miller, 1996). This kind of questioning ("Why have you taken this approach rather than another?") required Miller to "make explicit the approach I had learned from my clients" (p. 835). The result was a beginning conceptual model (Miller, 1983) that was followed by years of testing and refinements and that culminated in the text *Motivational Interviewing: Preparing People to Change Addictive Behavior* (Miller & Rollnick, 1991). Since then, MI has been adapted to create motivational enhancement therapy (MET) in Project MATCH (1997), the multisite collaborative trial of three treatments for alcoholism (see chapter 1). It has also been applied in a wide variety of settings, including child welfare (Hohman, 1998), medical practice (Knight, McGowan, & Dickens, 2006), low-income, urban, community-based organizations (Carey et al., 2000), and a number of different problem areas, such as bulimia (Treasure et al., 1999), domestic violence (Easton, Swan, & Sinha, 2000), HIV risk behavior (Carey et al., 2000), weight loss (Goldberg & Kiernan, 2005), and even breastfeeding (Wilhelm, Flanders Stepans, & Hertzog, 2006).

In the MI framework, as we have seen in previous examples, a person who is exhibiting addictive behaviors is viewed as having a diminished capacity for self-control over time, but this capacity is believed to be retrievable. Miller (1998, p. 2) notes that even extreme disease-model proponents and programs still rely on the client's "volitional abstinence" to interrupt the destructive behavior. However, in MI terms, retrieving the capacity for self-control is much more than will power or "just saying no." Motivation to change the addictive pattern comes from a combination of complex factors that includes learning, conditioning, emotion, social influences, and biology. The way out of the cycle of addictive behavior for MI proponents involves an internal accounting of suffering and negative consequences associated with the addiction and enough hope that this behavior can change.

Therefore, the goal of motivational interviewing is not to get clients to admit they have a problem or for the counselor to provide solutions to the problem. Rather, it is for the counselor to provide a mirror for the clients to "look back upon themselves" and see the costs and find within themselves the means to change it. Miller (1998, p. 6) says this kind of empathic merger with the clients' perspective and lending them a mirror to see themselves differently is "essentially a form of loving."

Motivational interviewing is defined as a "client-centered, directive method for enhancing intrinsic motivation to change by exploring and resolving ambivalence" (Miller & Rollnick, 2002, p. 25). It is directive in terms of the process and techniques of resolving client ambivalence, not directive about the outcome of the counseling. It is client centered because all the benefits and consequences of making a change are elicited from the client. Motivational interviewing assumes that the *state* of motivation may fluctuate from one time or situation to another (Miller & Rollnick, 2002). Therefore, this "state" can be influenced. By providing a safe, nonconfrontational environment, eliciting hope, and helping clients clarify their ambivalence about making a change, counselors can be helpful in "tipping the scales" in favor of readiness to make a positive change.

Motivational interviewing utilizes specific strategies to enhance motivation. The strategies are not new, but how they are used (to increase motivation, not to get answers) is new. For example, MI counselors pay a great deal of attention to eliciting the person's current level of motivation, or stage of change, instead of assuming that the person is ready to jump into action behavior. Scaling questions can be used to do this, such as the following (Rollnick, Butler, & Stott, 1997, p. 195):

1. If, on a scale of 1 to 10, 1 is not at all motivated to give up smoking and 10 is 100% motivated to give it up, what number would you give yourself at the moment?
2. If you were to decide to give up smoking now, how confident are you that you would succeed? If, on a scale of 1 to 10, 1 means that you are not at all confident and 10 means that you are 100% confident you could give it up and remain a nonsmoker, what number would you give yourself now?

These questions can help identify a person's stage of change, and the answers can also build motivation or confidence by encouraging the client to identify arguments for change. This is done by asking specific follow-up questions:

1. Why did the person score as he or she did rather than a lower number; for example, "Why did you give yourself a 4 rather than a 1?" The client will then respond with some positive reasons for being motivated or confident, such as, "I know it's bad for my lungs to keep on smoking" or "I think I've finally had enough."
2. What would have to happen for the person to move up the scale to more motivation or confidence? For example, "What does it take for your motivation (or confidence) to move one step higher from a 5 to a 6?" The client will then respond with strategies that will increase his or her motivation or confidence, such as, "I think I need to get tested for my actual lung damage so far."

These types of questions illustrate how MI techniques can help the client with his or her primary task—that is, to identify and mobilize the client's own values and goals for behavior changes. The principal obstacle to change is seen as ambivalence, and the client's other major task is to articulate and resolve that ambivalence.

Techniques for Enhancing Motivation

Motivational interviewing practitioners rely on the following general principles (Miller & Rollnick, 2002) to enhance a person's motivation to change:

1. *Express empathy.* The MI style is warm, respectful, and accepting. Irrational ideas and ambivalence about change are accepted as a normal part of human experience. The client is seen as "stuck," not pathological.
2. *Develop discrepancy.* Create and amplify the discrepancy between present behavior and important personal goals. Reflective listening and focused feedback can help to highlight discrepancies using the client's own words. For example, "On the one hand, you say it's important to you to get out of debt, but every time you gamble, you lose hundreds of dollars. Tell me about this."

3. *Avoid argumentation.* In contrast to other more traditional approaches that evolved from the Minnesota Model, MI practitioners do not try to persuade, confront, or argue to clients that they are in deep trouble and would be much better off giving up their addiction. "Breaking through denial" is seen as a tactic that is not just useless but that actually can increase the likelihood of resistance and decrease the likelihood of change. For example, when a person expresses that he or she didn't really want to come to an assessment meeting and wonders "do you think I'm alcoholic?" the MI counselor would avoid the trap of starting an argument and say something like this: "That's a term that means many things to different people. What matters, really, is that we take a good close look at what's going on here. I'd like to help you get clear on what risk you're facing, and then what, if anything, you want to do about it" (Miller & Rollnick, 2002, p. 146).

4. *Roll with resistance.* Compliance from the client is not a goal. Resistance can be redirected by the simple statement, "It's really up to you." Reluctance and ambivalence are understood to be a natural stage of the change process (contemplation stage). New perspectives are invited, but not imposed. For example, "What you do with this information is entirely up to you."

5. *Support self-efficacy.* If people have no hope for change, then regardless of how serious they perceive the problem, they will not make an effort to change. The counselor can support people's confidence that they can change by removing the false idea that the counselor will change them, by showing them the success of others, and by inviting them to choose from alternative approaches to what they've already tried. A series of relapses or treatment "failures" can be reframed as "getting closer to their goal."

Elaboration on these techniques, as well as a review of some of the verbal traps that counselors may fall into when a client is in the precontemplation or contemplation stage of change, can be found on the motivational interviewing website at www.motivationalinterview.org.

MOTIVATIONAL INTERVIEWING IN GROUP SETTINGS

A group therapy manual based on motivational interviewing has been developed by Ingersoll and Wagner (1997) for use in Virginia's public sector for polysubstance-dependent clients. Although this has not yet been empirically validated, it does offer three types of MI group formats: the single-session, four-session, and eight-session formats.

The eight-session format begins with an introduction of the purposes of the motivational group and then moves to an explanation of the stages of change, an exploration of the group members' ambivalence about substance use, assistance in developing hope, potential changes, discrepancies, an exploration of change success stories, and the development of a concrete plan for change. The authors recommend that in exploring ambivalence about substance use, employing the terms "good things" and "less good things" is helpful because it avoids developing resistance by beginning with the good things. This also reminds us that we can't assume that a less good thing is a concern for the group member, even if it is a concern for you. More information on the content and formats for the different group models can be found on the MI website at www.motivationalinterview.org/clinical/satoegroup.html.

LaBrie, Pedersen, Lamb, and Quinlan (2006) evaluated a single-session MI group intervention for college students adjudicated for violation of alcohol policy. Participants ($n = 167$) elected to attend the single session rather than be fined and put on disciplinary probation. Each group had 10 to 15 participants and met for 60–90 minutes, led by an MI-trained facilitator. During the session, participants were encouraged to express their frustrations, and the facilitator empathized with their predicament. The students were given information about campus norms regarding alcohol use and the relationship between alcohol use and other consequences such as violence and forced sex. They generated reasons for and against reducing their levels of drinking and discussed specific high-risk situations they might encounter where it might be hard to "say no" to drinking. During the discussions, the facilitator maintained a nonjudgmental stance that aided in decreasing resistance. At the end of the group, participants wrote down a behavioral goal of how they would drink in the next 30 days and shared this with the group. During the next 3 months, participants were asked to keep a daily record of their drinking and any related consequences. The authors found significant reductions in levels of drinking, alcohol-related consequences (e.g., not completing homework, fighting, missing class), and judicial recidivism at the end of the 3 months. The heaviest drinkers (males and frequent binge drinkers) achieved the biggest reductions.

RESEARCH ON THE EFFECTIVENESS OF MOTIVATIONAL INTERVIEWING

Evaluation studies of MI consistently indicate its effectiveness in reducing alcohol and other drug abuse (Carey et al., 2000; Miller, 1996; Project MATCH Research Group, 1997; Saunders, Wilkinson, & Phillips, 1995). Wilk, Jensen, and Havighurst (1997) conducted a meta-analysis of brief interventions of fewer than 60 minutes with heavy drinkers and found that those who received the intervention were about twice as likely to successfully reduce their alcohol use compared to heavy drinkers who did not receive the brief intervention. Another meta-analysis of 32 controlled studies of brief intervention for problem drinkers (Bien, Miller, & Tonigan, 1993) found that persons who received the brief intervention reduced their drinking and were abstinent at a rate comparable to more extensive treatment.

Project MATCH (1997) compared motivational enhancement therapy (4 sessions) to cognitive-behavioral coping skills therapy (12 sessions) and Twelve-Step facilitation (12 sessions). The focus of MET was to employ motivational interviewing strategies (as described earlier) to produce internal motivation for change, not to guide the client through particular steps to recovery. The results indicated little difference in outcomes by type of treatment, but overall improvements in drinking outcomes were achieved by all. In aftercare, 35% of the subjects reported continued complete abstinence throughout the 12 follow-up months; 65% slipped or relapsed during that period. For the outpatient subjects, 19% maintained complete abstinence throughout the follow-up, 46% had a heavy-drinking period, and the rest "slipped." Outpatient clients low in motivation ultimately did better in MET than in the other types. The complete therapy manual for MET procedures can be obtained for no charge from NIAAA, Project MATCH Monograph Series (Miller, Zweben, DiClemente, & Rychtarik, 1995).

Although most research on MI is conducted with adults, there is a growing body of studies that indicate this approach is successful with adolescents, who are typically a difficult population to engage (Feldstein, 2006). McCambridge and Strang (2004) found in their study that adolescent polysubstance abusers who received a MI intervention significantly decreased their use. In another large randomized controlled study of outpatient treatments for adolescents that included motivational enhancement treatment (MET), the authors found that MET was one of the three most cost-effective brief interventions (Dennis et al., 2004).

SOLUTION-FOCUSED THERAPY

The origins of solution-focused therapy are found in the work of Milton Erickson (1954), who strongly believed (a) that solving the problem was more important than finding and elaborating on the root "cause" of the problem and (b) that clients had the ability within themselves and/or their social system to bring about change. The development of the solution-focused brief therapy approach began in 1978, when Insoo Kim Berg and Steve deShazer borrowed money and put up their house for collateral to open a small brief therapy office in Milwaukee (see Berg, Background Information, on the Brief Therapy website at www.brief-therapy.org). Since then, what has been called a "different paradigm" is practiced in many different settings all over the world.

This approach treats problem gambling, substance misuse or dependence, and eating disorders using the same assumptions and techniques practiced with any other need or problem that a client may bring to the therapeutic environment. Like the feminists and narrative therapists, solution-focused practitioners would not see the particular addiction as a "unitary disease" that affected everyone alike but rather would assist the person to define his or her own conception of the problem and goals for change. In a national sample of 284 alcoholism counselors (members of the National Association of Alcoholism and Drug Abuse Counselors), Osborn (1997) found that 79% of the counselors endorsed solution-focused principles, such as identifying and using client strengths and abilities, client–counselor collaboration throughout the course of treatment, highlighting and promoting already occurring nonproblem behavior, meeting the client's goal(s), and constructing solutions rather than resolving client problems. However, the counselors identified beliefs in different conceptual frameworks: 54% agreed or strongly agreed with a psychosocial concept of alcoholism (social learning theory—alcohol dependence is understood as a continuum), and 45% agreed or strongly agreed with the tenets of a disease concept of alcoholism. These results suggest that a strong adherence to the disease concept by alcoholism counselors may not be as prevalent as some have reported and that, even when it is the dominant framework for some clinicians, it is not incompatible with practicing solution-focused treatment.

Specific techniques to find out what is important to the client might involve the "miracle question," asking for exceptions to the problem, scaling questions, and coping questions. Strengths and past successes in dealing with problems of living would be highlighted instead of deficits or "pathology." The person would be seen more as a valuable resource to form goals and find solutions than as an impaired person with poor judgment. The client's immediate goal would be accepted as a good goal, whether or not it involved quitting the addiction (De Jong & Berg, 2002).

A classic example of solution-focused therapy applied to addiction is the story of "Mr. Glue-Head" (Berg & Miller, 1992, p. 15). The subject is a young man who was ordered to treatment again because of his arrest for "sniffing glue" and public intoxication. He had a long history of arrests and treatment episodes, but nothing had changed. Using a solution-focused approach that emphasized cooperation with the client, the therapist asked what he wanted to accomplish with this referral.

"Elmer" made it very clear that discontinuing glue sniffing was not what he wanted. He only wanted to stop getting arrested. The therapist then wondered whether sniffing glue on the back porch might be an acceptable alternative to getting high on the front porch—a place, the therapist pointed out, where the police could see him easily. He readily agreed to try out the idea as "an experiment" and to return in a week to report his findings.

When Elmer returned the following week, he reported that the police never even bothered to check the back porch, even though they had driven by his home on several occasions. The only time the police had stopped was late one afternoon as he sat relaxing on the front porch, "enjoying the sunset" without the help of sniffing glue. After this experience, Elmer began sitting out on the front porch straight just for the fun of it! The result, of course, was that he did not get arrested again or referred for any more treatment. Once the arrests and referrals had stopped, Elmer began to curtail his use of inhalants on his own.

According to Berg and Miller (1992), the case example of Mr. Glue Head illustrates several main tenets of the solution-focused approach. The therapist avoided issues that had always been considered problems by the therapist and others but that were not identified as problems by Elmer. Instead, the focus was shifted to a problem that Elmer identified, "not getting arrested." By following Elmer's lead, the therapist avoided perpetuating the past nonsolutions and worked with Elmer on "doing something different."

Solution-focused therapy is based on the assumption that the future can be created and negotiated regardless of the problem. The future "is not a slave of the past events in a person's life; therefore, in spite of past traumatic events, a person can negotiate and implement many useful steps that are likely to lead him/her to a more satisfying life" (Berg, 2001, p. 4). The resources, skills, and knowledge to take such steps can be uncovered through the use of several techniques.

The miracle question is a particularly helpful technique in supporting hope that things can be different in spite of many past attempts and failures to change. This question leads the client directly into imagining, describing, creating, and embellishing on a day in the future without the burden of the particular problem that led or required the client to seek help. The question is asked deliberately and dramatically: "*Suppose* that one night, while you are sleeping tonight and the entire house is quiet, a miracle happens. The miracle is that *the problem that brought you here is solved*. However, because you are sleeping, you don't know that the miracle has happened. So, when you wake up tomorrow morning, *what will be different* that will tell you that a miracle has happened and the problem which brought you here is solved?"(DeJong & Berg, 2002, p. 85)

Through persistent questioning about what the person would be doing differently on this new, problem-free day, who would notice the difference, and what effect this would have on the person, a rich picture emerges that can provide momentum for a person to start making changes. Since the "different behaviors" are already specified in the imagined future (e.g., "I would get up in the morning feeling good, no hangover," "I would sit down and eat breakfast with my son," "I would be humming as I got him dressed for school," etc.), it's a natural progression to find out what small step the person could take in reality to reach a little bit of the "miracle picture."

For example, one of the goals of a young anorexic woman in a case described by O'Halloran (1999) was to "get taller." After learning from the dietician that her low intake of calcium was likely to impact bone growth, she began to add previously rejected foods such as cheese, yogurt, and milk back into her diet very slowly. She was able to do this because the food became "medicine," not food with calories.

Scaling questions are used in a variety of ways to help the client assess level of hope, determination, confidence, sadness, how much change has occurred, and so on, similar to the motivational interviewing scales described earlier. For example, "On a scale of 1 to 10, where 10 stands for the worst upset you have ever felt, how upset are you today? What would it take for you to move up by 1 point? When you move up by 1 point, what would your husband (friend, cat, coworker) notice that would tell him that you are doing a little bit better?"

Coping questions can be used to bring out the survival strategies of people who have been managing somehow in spite of their addictions. This is very helpful in building hope and self-efficacy, two key ingredients for change. For example, "You've been through a lot in the last month with your gambling. How in the world have you coped with so much while still holding down a job?" "What else have you managed to do in spite of your addiction?" "How did you do this?"

Solution-focused therapy (as well as narrative therapy and MI) has an unintended consequence of helping counselors feel less burned out, more optimistic, and less likely to be "captured by our clients' despair" (O'Hanlon, 1994). Besides focusing on strengths, these models recognize that if you try to sell something like abstinence to people who aren't ready or don't want it, then the counselor will be frustrated most of the time (Ross, 1997). For example, a Pregnancy Outreach Program in Prince George, British Columbia, developed solution-focused strategies for promoting tobacco reduction with disadvantaged, high-risk prenatal clients (Browne, Shultis, & Thio-Watts, 1999). As clients increased in confidence and self-efficacy scores, the counselors also experienced an increased sense of efficacy in their work. They were able to apply this approach to other areas of concern to the clients, such as diet, alcohol use, and relationship problems. The authors saw this as a way of "fostering tolerance and respect for clients' values, capabilities, circumstances, and culture" and particularly relevant to women from disadvantaged groups, who often receive discriminatory treatment from mainstream culture (p. 173).

RESEARCH ON THE EFFECTIVENESS OF SOLUTION-FOCUSED THERAPY

Rigorous research studies on the effectiveness of solution-focused therapy are scarce. On the one hand, Gingerich and Eisengart (2000) cite 15 controlled outcome studies on solution-focused brief therapy that provide preliminary support for the efficacy of this approach in a broad range of applications, but they caution that more study is needed. On the other hand, Coady, Stalker, and Levene (2000) find these same studies problematic, and they conclude that there is no empirical evidence of the superiority of solution-focused therapy. Peter De Jong and Insoo Kim Berg (2002), two major developers of this approach, conclude that "there is increasing evidence supporting the overall effectiveness and efficiency of solution-focused procedures" (p. 247).

In a review of SFT as evidence-based practice, Trepper, Dolan, McCollum, and Nelson (2006) note there is enough evidence through clinical trial studies, clinically based and quasi-experimental studies to conclude that SFT is at least as effective as other current treatment models. For some problems, it is more effective and considerably more cost-effective in achieving positive outcomes.

NARRATIVE THERAPY

Narrative therapy, like solution-focused therapy, is also premised on the innate strengths and resources people possess. However, narrative therapy pays even more attention to the patterns of meaning as reflected in life histories and as experienced within a particular culture. Narrative therapy was developed principally by the work of Michael White of Australia and David Epston of New Zealand. They in turn were inspired by anthropologist and psychologist Gregory Bateson's ideas about the "news of difference" and influenced by French historian Michel Foucault's ideas on the damaging effects of normalizing practices that undermine people's efforts to lead a life of their own making. The word *narrative* refers to the "emphasis that is placed upon the stories of people's lives and the differences that can be made through particular tellings and retellings of these stories" (Dulwich Centre, 2001).

Narrative therapy is perhaps best recognized by the practice of "externalization"—that is, linguistically separating the problem from the personal identity of the client. An "alcoholic" becomes a "person oppressed by the Alcohol Bully," or "Booze." An "addict" is a "person ground down by Meth" who works to "stand up to Cravings." "Crappy Attitude" may be working to rule a woman's life and keep her from the path to recovery. The name of the problem is decided in collaboration with the client or family and has the effect of liberating the affected person from the label to strategize how to deal with "it."

Narrative therapy tends to follow a sequence that requires intense listening and persistence by the therapist (O'Hanlon, 1994). After externalizing and naming the problem, the next task is to track the problem's effect on the client's life and the tactics the problem uses to "influence, trick, or recruit" the person. For example, "How long has Anorexia been lying to you?" is a common question that can open up the whole area of distorted perceptions around weight without requiring the person to defend herself. She can then use that defensive energy to fight the problem. Other questions to help discover the effect of the problem might include: "What has the problem gotten you to do that is against your better judgment?" or "In what kind of situations does the problem tend to take over?"

Narrative therapy, like solution-focused therapy, also uses "exception" questions but with a different emphasis. Instead of asking, "Tell me about a period when you haven't been getting drunk," a narrative therapist might ask, "So what's the longest time you've stood up to 'Booze'?" Again, the purpose is to increase hope that change is indeed possible. At this point, the narrative therapist will become intensely interested in uncovering the evidence of past competence and using these stories as evidence that the person is strong, even if the individual hasn't incorporated this view of self in the present. According to O'Hanlon (1994), this is where "the person's identity and life story begin to get rewritten. . . . This is the *narrative* part" (p. 26).

After developing this "new life story," the person is encouraged to speculate on what future developments may emerge from this reframed life and on the effects this may have on others. For example, "As you continue to stand up to Crappy Attitude, what will be different about your future?" Narrative therapists, cognizant of the social context in which problems develop, will use letters, family members, and other people who have been successful in "standing up to the problem" as witnesses to reinforce this new life path. For example, narrative therapist Steve Madigan (1994, p. 27) reports on the letter-writing campaign of the Antianorexic/antibulimic League he was facilitating in an inpatient treatment center in Vancouver, B.C. In response to a call for help from a woman in a remote area, the group decided to initiate a monthly exchange of letters with the woman, "in which group members described their experiences with anorexia and bulimia and offered strategies on how to resist everything from anorexic guilt and women's magazines to the debilitating effects of medication—what the group calls 'psychiatric' drugs" (p. 27).

Jonathon Diamond (2000) is a narrative therapist who uses therapeutic letter writing to engage the person in a spirit of collaboration, as well as highlight the construction of reality through the use of words. He often asks his clients to write "good-bye" letters to their drug of choice, not to persuade them to say "good-bye" but to give them a platform to explore the role the drug/alcohol has had in their life. Holly's Good-bye Letter to Drugs is an example:

> Dear Acid,
> I want to thank you for the great times you've given me. When there was a boring night or day, you came along and gave me some good times. You made me laugh. You put me into a different world when I really needed it. You brought me up when I was down. I like how you only cost $15 and give me an enjoyment that lasted for a while and was just so cool. It is like something I have never experienced before. I love you!!!! (Diamond, 2000, pp. 32–33).

A more traditional problem-solving counselor might seize on this opportunity to confront Holly with the dangers of ingesting acid, but Diamond approaches the letter as providing a "sense of what we were up against" and a chance to "honor the important role" that her relationship to acid has in her life (p. 33). True to the narrative approach, these types of letters allow the client some distance from the problem through externalization. It can be a beginning for both the client and therapist to assess the consequences and rewards of truly saying "good-bye" to one's addiction.

Using a narrative approach with people experiencing alcohol and drug problems might require giving up the medical metaphors so common in this field (diagnosis, assessment, treatment, recovery). Although recognizing that the medical approach has been effective for many people, narrative therapists would argue that "one size doesn't fit all" and that a useful idea is not a universal truth (Winslade & Smith, 1997). Narrative therapy offers the possibility of transforming an object of medical-psychological practice to a person who is a responsible subject through an exploration of the following issues (Winslade & Smith, 1997, p. 160):

- The many conflicting messages about alcohol that circulate in various communities
- The implication of discourses about race, gender, and class in the construction and maintenance of "alcohol problems"
- The effects of the normalization of alcohol and the effects on the people of the definitions of "normal" patterns of alcohol use
- The impact of commonly held notions, such as "alcoholic," on the counseling process itself
- The opening up of space for descriptions of self that are not subsumed by the description that "alcohol trouble" brings
- The opening up of space for the development of lifestyles that are preferred over an "alcohol lifestyle"

NARRATIVE THERAPY IN GROUP SETTINGS

Narrative therapy has a different approach when working with groups than a traditional skills (facilitator/didactic) approach because of the premise that participants are expert with knowledge, skills, and resources in their own lived experience. The work of the group consists of removing the "problem-dominated personal and cultural stories that describe the individuals as inadequate in some way . . . and allowing space for preferred alternative stories" (Silvester, 1997, p. 234). The Anti-anorexia/bulimic League in Vancouver, B.C., offers an example of how a group of young women help each other act to bolster their nonproblem identity and externalize the problem. As a group, they publicly denounce "proanorexic/probulimic" activities against women's bodies by writing letters to magazines, newspapers, and company presidents, printing stickers with the slogans "Starvation kills your appetite for Life" and "YOU are not just a body," placing them over proanorexic billboard advertising and at diet centers, and holding accountable the professional systems that marginalize women with "eating disorders" (Madigan, 1995).

RESEARCH ON THE EFFECTIVENESS OF NARRATIVE APPROACHES

Narrative approaches lack rigorous controlled studies to support any superiority in their effectiveness. It is not surprising, given its postmodern philosophy that "objective reality" is a matter of interpretation, that narrative therapists have not produced empirical methods of evaluation or empirical findings on effectiveness. True to the narrative vision, stories are used primarily as anecdotal evidence that this is a viable therapeutic approach. Evidence of effectiveness has also been gathered through qualitative participant-centered research where the clients are deemed the best judges of what is helpful about the intervention. An example of this approach is the Keeling and Bermudez (2006) study on externalizing problems through art and writing. In this project, the authors used a heuristic methodology to focus on the meanings and significance of the narrative intervention to the researcher and the participants (one of the authors participated in the intervention). Journal material from participants was decoded to develop "portraits" and themes to portray the findings instead of using just numbers. The authors conclude that the participant's experience was generally consistent with the findings of other narrative therapists in that participants came to view the problem as separate from themselves and began to author new stories with a recovered sense of agency.

In the debate about what comprises "evidence" in evidence-based practice, it is important to keep in mind that research on the outcome of psychotherapy has produced no major findings other than that, with a few exceptions (e.g., cognitive-behavioral interventions with panic and phobic disorders), there are no significant differences among the different types of therapies and that therapy is better than no therapy (Stalker, Levene, & Coady, 1999).

TRADITIONAL TREATMENT
AND STRENGTHS-BASED APPROACHES

The treatment system for persons with an alcohol or drug misuse problem is commonly conceptualized as: (a) detoxification, (b) intensive treatment, (c) residential programs, (d) outpatient services, and (e) aftercare services. Although this continuum of care is not available in many rural areas of the United States, it is usually possible to piece together all of these elements by utilizing programs from other states or metropolitan areas.

The primary purpose of detoxification services is to help the client medically stabilize and reduce or endure withdrawal symptoms that could be fatal without intervention. Commonly referred to as "detox centers," these centers may either stand alone in community-based programs or be attached to a hospital-based treatment program. Staff includes physicians and nurses for medical supervision and a variety of professional helpers to attend to other immediate needs and encourage the client to continue utilizing help. Clients in community-based detox centers are often referred by police, probation/parole officers, and mental health practitioners and are frequently from poverty or homeless situations; many are dually diagnosed. Although detox programs consistently provide safe withdrawal environments, their effectiveness in reducing drug or alcohol use can be questioned. Based on the Substance Abuse and Mental Health Services Administration's (SAMHSA) Treatment Episode Data Set (TEDS) conducted in 2000, the completion rate for detoxification episodes was 52%, and only 8% were transferred for further treatment (SAMHSA, 2006).

A strengths-based approach to detoxification services may see this as an opportunity to introduce the client to choices about how to take care of immediate needs such as housing, financial assistance, and job-related services. As discussed in chapter 8 on substance misuse with a coexisting disorder or disability, basic areas of inquiry that are consistent with harm reduction and motivation enhancement practices include finding out what stage of change the person is in, how much insight the person has about the harms and benefits of the use of alcohol/drugs, and what personal strengths and resources (past exceptions to the present troubles, important persons or family that care about the person, survival strategies, and capacities for development) might be helpful (Denning, 2000; Drake & Meuser, 2000).

In an ideal world, treatment would be a seamless process connected to detox services and aftercare. In the real world, there is usually a long waiting list for treatment programs that are often located in states or metropolitan areas far from the day-to-day lives of the clients, and aftercare services may be pasted together in the local community with whatever resources exist. Many treatment programs currently involve some combination of intensive inpatient services for up to a week, intensive outpatient services or all-day sessions for another week or two, and regular outpatient services several times a week that gradually evolve into "aftercare" appointments once a month. Based on the TEDS conducted in 2000, the overall hospital inpatient treatment completion rate was 55% compared to a 38% (alcohol) completion rate for long-term residential treatment, 67% (alcohol) for short-term residential treatment, 41% for all intensive outpatient treatment, and 34% for all outpatient treatments (SAMHSA, 2006). Inpatient treatment is still recommended for persons who live under conditions unfavorable to recovery, such as few financial resources, risky environments, or co-occurring disorders (National Institute on Alcohol Abuse and Alcoholism [NIAAA], 2000).

Residential services include halfway houses (originally designed to serve alcoholics), therapeutic communities (originally designed to serve drug addicts), and missions. These programs provide a safe environment where people practice living sober with one foot in the community.

Outpatient treatment is primarily group counseling with adjunct individual sessions, offered several times a week for a period of 8 to 12 weeks. Content may include topics similar to those with inpatient treatment, such as information on the effects of alcohol and drugs, an increasing emphasis on relapse prevention, and in the United States, an introduction to Twelve-Step programs. Given the lack of specificity about treatment modalities and a lack of research, it is difficult to evaluate the effectiveness of group treatment compared to individual treatment or to recommend one modality over another. No single approach has been found clearly superior in the treatment of alcoholism (NIAAA, 2000).

Aftercare is the final formal link between professional help and the client's recovery process, and it usually involves monthly meetings with the service provider. This phase may also involve attendance at a Twelve-Step group or other support system, such as religious counseling, and/or adjunctive services to help with other problems the client may be experiencing in early recovery. More intensive case management services may be provided to persons with coexisting mental disorders, as discussed in chapter 8. Aftercare programs may also be the mechanism for monitoring progress for mandatory court requirements.

Many strengths-based approaches are already incorporated into the existing treatment system, especially offering support and encouragement to people who may be particularly hopeless about their abilities, tolerating relapses, and turning them into learning opportunities, encouraging family and extended family support, and incorporating the clients' needs into formal treatment goals. Further steps in the direction of strengths-based practice would include a serious assessment of the stage of change the client is in when entering treatment and an effort to gear treatment strategies to the needs of that stage, offering an array of change options that include abstinence but are not limited to abstinence, and honoring the ability of the person to make choices that will eventually benefit him or her.

SUMMARY AND CONCLUSION

In this chapter, we have described four strengths-based approaches that honor the principle of client self-determination, focus on the resources, capabilities, and possibilities that the client/client system may be able to use to further client goals, and pay attention to the client's stage of readiness. The practices of harm reduction are well entrenched in addiction treatment outside the United States, but a growing number of practitioners in the United States and Canada are finding reasons to creatively incorporate harm reduction methods in a variety of settings. Motivational interviewing techniques, with the focus on readiness to change and resolving ambivalence, have become well-accepted practices in many areas of addiction treatment. The therapies of solution-focused brief interventions and narrative therapy are just beginning to be acknowledged as viable alternative conceptualizations that differ from the "problem-saturated" approach of the medical model. Both therapies offer new ways of connecting to a person experiencing problems and help us appreciate the diverse ways people develop meaning and find new life paths within their cultural, racial, and ethnic influences.

REFERENCES

Baer, J. S., Kiviahan, D. R., Blume, A. W., McKnight, P., & Marlatt, G. A. (2001). Brief intervention for heavy-drinking college students: 4-year follow-up and natural history. *American Journal of Public Health, 91*(8), 1310–1316.

Baer, J. S., & Murch, H. B. (1998). Harm reduction, nicotine, and smoking. In G. A. Marlatt (Ed.), *Harm reduction: Pragmatic strategies for managing high-risk behaviors* (pp. 122–144). New York: Guilford Press.

Berg, I. (2001). What is unique about solution-focused brief therapy? Retrieved from http://www.brief-therapy.org/insoo_essays.htm.

Berg, I., & Miller, S. (1992). *Working with the problem drinker: A solution-focused approach*. New York: Norton.

Bien, T., Miller, W., & Tonigan, J. (1993). Brief interventions for alcohol problems: A review. *Addiction, 88*(3), 315–336.

Booth, R. E., Kwiatkowski, C., Iguchi, M. Y., Pinto, F., & John, D. (1998). Facilitating treatment entry among out-of-treatment injection drug users. *Public Health Reports, 113*(1), 116–128.

Brink, W., & Haasen, C. (2006). Evidenced-based treatment of opioid-dependent patients. *Canadian Journal of Psychiatry, 51*(10), 635–646.

Broadhead, R. (1995). Introduction. Special issue of *Journal of Drug Issues, 25*(3), 505.

Brown, S., & Coventry, L. (1997). *Queen of hearts: The needs of women with gambling problems*. Sydney, Australia: Financial & Consumer Rights Council.

Browne, A., Shultis, J., & Thio-Watts, M. (1999). Solution-focused approaches to tobacco reduction with disadvantaged prenatal clients. *Journal of Community Health Nursing, 16*(3), 165–177.

Bux, D. A., Iguchi, M. Y., Lidz, V., Baxter, R. C., & Platt, J. J. (1993). Participation in a coupon distribution program for free methadone detoxification. *Hospital Community Psychiatry, 44*, 1066–1072.

Carey, M., Braaten, L., Maisto, S., Gleason, J., Forsyth, A., Durant, L., et al. (2000). Using information, motivational enhancement, and skills training to reduce the risk of HIV infection for low-income urban women: A second randomized clinical trial. *Health Psychology, 19*(1), 3–11.

Coady, N., Stalker, C., & Levene, J. (2000). A closer examination of the empirical support for claims about the effectiveness of solution-focused brief therapy: Stalker et al. respond to Gingerich. *Families in Society, 81*(2), 223–227.

Davies, D. (1962). Normal drinking in recovered alcoholics. *Quarterly Journal of Studies on Alcohol, 23,* 94–104.

De Jong, P., & Berg, I. (2002). *Interviewing for solutions* (2nd ed.). Pacific Grove, CA: Wadsworth.

Denning, P. (2000). *Practicing harm reduction psychotherapy.* New York: Guilford Press.

Dennis, M. L., Godley, S. H., Diamond, G., Tims, F. M., Babor, T., Donaldson, J., et al. (2004). The Cannibis Youth Treatment Study: Main findings from two randomized trials. *Journal of Substance Abuse Treatment, 27*(3), 197–213.

Dennis, M. L., Ingram, P. W., Burks, M. E., & Rachal, J. V. (1994). Effectiveness of streamlined admissions to methadone treatment: A simplified time series analysis. *Journal of Psychoactive Drugs, 26,* 207–216.

Diamond, J. (2000). *Narrative means to sober ends: Treating addiction and its aftermath.* New York: Guilford Press.

Drake, R., & Meuser, K. (2000). Psychosocial approaches to dual diagnosis. *Schizophrenia Bulletin, 26*(1), 105–118.

Dulwich Centre. (2001). What is narrative therapy? Retrieved from http://www .dulwichcentre.com.au/questions.html.

Easton, C., Swan, S., & Sinha, R. (2000). Motivation to change substance use among offenders of domestic violence. *Journal of Substance Abuse Treatment, 19,* 1–5.

Erikson, M. (1954). Special techniques of brief hypnotherapy. *Journal of Clinical and Experimental Hypnosis, 2,* 109–129.

Feldstein, S. W. (2006). Motivational interviewing with dually diagnosed adolescents in juvenile justice settings. *Brief Treatment and Crisis Intervention, 6*(3), 218–233.

Fitzgerald, B., Aranda-Naranjo, B., & Denenberg, R. (1996). Applying the transtheoretical and harm reduction models. *Journal of the Association of Nurses in AIDS Care, 7*(1), 33–40.

Gingerich, W., & Eisengart, S. (2000). Solution-focused brief therapy: A review of the outcome research. *Family Process, 39*(4), 477–499.

Goldberg, J., & Kiernan, M. (2005). Innovative techniques to address retention in a behavioral weight-loss trial. *Health Education Research, 20*(4), 439–446.

Hohman, M. (1998). Motivational interviewing: An intervention tool for child welfare case workers working with substance-abusing parents. *Child Welfare, 127*(3), 275–289.

Hser, Y., Grella, C., Chou, C., & Anglin, M. (1998). Relationships between drug treatment careers and outcomes: Findings from the National Drug Abuse Treatment Outcome Study. *Evaluation Review, 22*(4), 496–519.

Ingersoll, K., & Wagner, C. (1997). *Motivational enhancement groups for the Virginia Substance Abuse Treatment Outcomes Evaluation (SATOE) model: Theoretical background and clinical guidelines.* Richmond: Virginia Addiction Technology Transfer Center.

Keeling, M. L., & Bermudez, M. (2006). Externalizing problems through art and writing: Experiences of process and helpfulness. *Journal of Marital and Family Therapy, 32*(4), 405–420.

Knight, K. M., McGowan, L, & Dickens, C. (2006). A systematic review of motivational interviewing in physical health care settings. *British Journal of Health Psychology, 11*(2), 319–332.

LaBrie, J., Pedersen, E., Lamb, T., & Quinlan, T. (2006). A campus-based motivational enhancement group intervention reduces problematic drinking in freshmen male college students. *Addictive Behaviors, 47,* 267–280.

Ladouceur, R. (2005). Controlled gambling for pathological gamblers. *Journal of Gambling Studies, 21*(1), 51–59.

Larimer, M. E., Marlatt, G. A., Baer, J. S., Quigley, L. A., Blume, A. W., & Hawkins, E. H. (1998). Harm reduction for alcohol problems: Expanding access to and acceptability of prevention and treatment services. In G. A. Marlatt (Ed.), *Harm reduction: Pragmatic strategies for managing high-risk behaviors* (pp. 69–121). New York: Guilford Press.

Lewis, T., & Osborn, C. (2004). Solution-focused counseling and motivational interviewing: Consideration of confluence. *Journal of Counseling and Development, 82*(1), 38–49.

Madigan, S. (1994, November/December). Body politics. *Networker,* p. 27.

Madigan, S. (1995). *The politics of identity: Tales from the anti-anorexia/bulimia league.* Paper presented at the narrative therapy conference, Vancouver, B.C.

Marlatt, G. A. (Ed.). (1998). *Harm reduction: Pragmatic strategies for managing high-risk behaviors.* New York: Guilford Press.

McCambridge, J., & Strang, J. (2004). The efficacy of single-session motivational interviewing in reducing drug consumption and perceptions of drug-related risk and harm among young people: Results from a multi-site cluster randomized trial. *Addiction, 99,* 39–52.

Miller, W. (1983). Motivational interviewing with problem drinkers. *Behavioral Psychotherapy, 11,* 147–172.

Miller, W. R. (1996). Motivational interviewing: Research, practice, and puzzles. *Addictive Behaviors, 21*(6), 835–842.

Miller, W. R. (1998). Toward a motivational definition and understanding of addiction. *Motivational Interviewing Newsletter for Trainers, 5*(3), 2–6. Retrieved October 2006 from http://www.motivationalinterview.org/clinical/motmodel.html.

Miller, W. R., & Rollnick, S. (1991). *Motivational interviewing: Preparing people for change.* New York: Guilford Press.

Miller, W. R., & Rollnick, S. (2002). *Motivational interviewing: Preparing people for change* (2nd ed.). New York: Guilford Press.

Miller, W., Zweben, A., DiClemente, C., & Rychtarik, R. (1995). *Motivational enhancement therapy manual: A clinical research guide for therapists treating individuals with alcohol abuse and dependence* (NIH Publication No. 94-3723). Project MATCH Monograph Series, Vol. 2. Rockville, MD: National Institute on Alcohol Abuse and Alcoholism.

Nadelmann, E., McNeely, J., & Drucker, E. (1997). International perspectives. In J. Lowinson, P. Ruiz, R. Millman, & J. Langrod (Eds.), *Substance abuse: A comprehensive textbook* (3rd ed., pp. 22–39). Baltimore: Williams & Wilkins.

Narrow, W. E., Regier, D. A., Rae, D. S., Manderscheid, R. W., & Locke, B. Z. (1993). Use of services by persons with mental and addictive disorders: Findings from the National Institute of Mental Health epidemiologic catchment area program. *Archives of General Psychiatry, 50,* 95–107.

National Association of Social Workers. (1996). *Code of ethics.* Silver Spring, MD: Author.

National Institute on Alcohol Abuse and Alcoholism (NIAAA). (2000). *10th special report to the U.S. Congress on alcohol and health.* Rockville, MD: U.S. Department of Health and Human Services.

National Research Council. (1999). *Pathological gambling: A critical review.* Washington DC: National Academy Press.

National Survey on Drug Use and Health. (2006). *Substance abuse treatment need among adolescents: 2003–2004.* Office of Applied Studies, SAMHSA. Retrieved from http://www.oas.samhsa.gov.

O'Halloran, M. (1999). Family involvement in the treatment of anorexia nervosa: A solution-focused approach. *Family Journal, 7*(4), 384–389.

O'Hanlon, B. (1994, November/December). The third wave. *Networker,* pp. 19–26.

Osborn, C. (1997). Does disease matter? Incorporating solution-focused brief therapy in alcoholism treatment. *Journal of Alcohol and Drug Education, 43*(1), 18–30.

Peterson, P. L., Dimeff, L. A., Tapert, S. F., Stern, M., & Gorman, M. (1998). Harm reduction and HIV/AIDS prevention. In G. A. Marlatt (Ed.), *Harm reduction: Pragmatic strategies for managing high-risk behaviors* (pp. 218–296). New York: Guilford Press.

Podymow, T., Turnbull, J., Coyle, D., Yetisir, E., & Wells, G. (2006). Shelter based managed alcohol administration to chronically homeless people addicted to alcohol. *Canadian Medical Association Journal, 174*(1), 45–50.

Prochaska, J., & DiClemente, C. (1986). The transtheoretical approach. In J. C. Norcross (Ed.), *Handbook of eclectic psychotherapy* (pp. 163–200). New York: Brunner/Mazel.

Project MATCH Research Group (1997). Matching alcoholism treatments to client heterogeneity: Project MATCH posttreatment drinking outcomes. *Journal of Studies on Alcohol, 58,* 7–29.

Rapp, R. C. (2006). Strengths-based case management: Enhancing treatment for persons with substance abuse problems. In D. Saleebey (Ed.), *The strengths perspective in social work practice* (4th ed., pp. 128–147). Boston: Allyn & Bacon.

Rapp, R. C., Li, L., Siegal, H., & DeLiberty, R. (2003). Demographic and clinical correlates of client motivation among substance abusers. *Health & Social Work, 26*(2), 107–115.

Reamer, F. (1998). *Ethical standards in social work.* Washington, DC: NASW Press.

Riley, D., Sawka, E., Conley, P., Hewitt, D., Mitic, W., Poulin, C., et al. (1999). *Substance use and misuse, 34*(1), 9–24.

Rollnick, S., Butler, C., & Stott, N. (1997). Helping smokers make decisions. *Patient Education and Counseling, 31,* 191–203.

Rollnick, S., & Miller, W. (1995). What is motivational interviewing? *Behavioral and Cognitive Psychotherapy, 23,* 325–334.

Ross, G. (1997). Preventing burnout with solution-focused assessments. *EAP Digest, 17*(2), 26–27.

Saleebey, D. (2006). Introduction: Power in the people. In D. Saleebey (Ed.), *The strengths perspective in social work practice* (4th ed., pp. 1–22). Boston: Allyn & Bacon.

Saunders, B., Wilkinson, C., & Phillips, M. (1995). The impact of a brief motivational intervention with opiate users attending a methadone program. *Addiction, 90,* 415–424.

Silvester, G. (1997). Appreciating indigenous knowledge in groups. In G. Monk, J. Winslade, K. Crocket, & D. Epston (Eds.), *Narrative therapy in practice: The archaeology of hope* (pp. 233–251). San Francisco: Jossey-Bass.

Sobell, L. C., Ellingstad, T. P., & Sobell, M. B. (2000). Natural recovery from alcohol and drug problems: Methodological review of the research with suggestions for future directions. *Addiction, 95,* 749–764.

Stalker, C., Levene, J., Coady, N. (1999). Solution-focused brief therapy—One model fits all? *Families in Society, 80*(5), 468–477.

Substance Abuse and Mental Health Services Administration. (SAMHSA). (2006). *The DASIS Report: Discharges from Intensive Outpatient Treatment, 2000.* Office of Applied Studies. Retrieved October 22, 2006, from http://oas.samhsa.gov/2k3/intensiveOutDischarges/intensiveOutDischarges.cfm.

Tammi, T. (2004). The harm reduction school of thought: Three fractions. *Contemporary Drug Problems, 31*(3), 381–399.

Treasure, J., Katzman, M., Schmidt, U., Troop, N., Todd, G., & deSilva, P. (1999). Engagement and outcome in the treatment of bulimia nervosa: First phase of a sequential design comparing motivation enhancement therapy and cognitive behavioral therapy. *Behavior Research and Therapy, 37,* 405–418.

Trepper, T. S., Dolan, Y., McCollum, E., & Nelson, T. (2006). Steve deShazer and the future of solution-focused therapy. *Journal of Marital and Family Therapy, 32*(2), 133–140.

Twersky, A. J. (2001, March 2). Good deed feels better than fix. *Spokesman Review* (Spokane, WA), p. D8.

U.S. Department of Health and Human Services. (1988). *The health consequences of smoking: Nicotine addiction, a report of the surgeon general.* Washington, DC: U.S. Government Printing Office.

Vaillant, G. (1996). A long-term follow-up of male alcohol abuse. *Archives of General Psychiatry, 53,* 243–249.

Velicer, W. F. (1996). Introduction to special issue. *Addictive Behaviors, 21*(6), 681–682.

Wild, T. C. (1999). Compulsory substance-user treatment and harm reduction: A critical analysis. *Substance Use and Misuse, 34*(1), 83–102.

Wilhelm, S., Flanders Stepans, M., & Hertzog, M. (2006). Motivational interviewing to promote sustained breastfeeding. *Journal of Obstetric, Gynecologic, and Neonatal Nursing, 35*(2), 340–348.

Wilk, A., Jensen, N., & Havighurst, T. (1997). Meta-analysis of randomized control trials addressing brief interventions in heavy alcohol drinkers. *Journal of General Internal Medicine, 12*(5), 274–283.

Winslade, J., & Smith, L. (1997). Countering alcoholic narratives. In G. Monk, J. Winslade, K. Crocket, & D. Epston (Eds.), *Narrative therapy in practice: The archaeology of hope* (pp. 158–192). San Francisco: Jossey-Bass.

THE BIOLOGY
OF ADDICTION

Despite lip service to the biopsychosocial-spiritual model of human behavior, substance abuse counselors often overlook the *bio* piece of the equation. Yet knowledge of the biology of addiction is crucial for an understanding of the hold that certain chemicals or behaviors have on people, the cravings that grip them, and the health problems associated with substance misuse. An awareness of the genetic features in addiction is also important. Thanks to advances in technology—namely, the development of positron emission tomography (PET) and functional magnetic resonance imaging (fMRI)—scientists can capture chemical images of the brain at work; they can also observe not only structures but also actual functions or processes of the living brain. The ability to observe directly the effects of neurological damage caused by long-term substance abuse is a significant accomplishment in itself; the ability to demonstrate the impact of craving itself on the pleasure circuits of the brain is even more remarkable. Due to neuroimaging technology, things can be known today that in previous decades could only be guessed at or only inferred from behavior. To see, as we can today, a slide of the serotonin-depleted brain is to see, in a very real sense, the face, the insanity, of addiction. In providing this glimpse into the inner workings of the mind, modern technology is truly revolutionary. Chapter 4 tackles this awesome task.

Why can one person drink and use drugs moderately over a lifetime while another person gets "hooked" after a short period of time? Why does the alcoholic tend to smoke and have a high tolerance for many depressant drugs? If the answers were simple, this part of the book would be a good deal shorter.

The two chapters that comprise Part II on biology are concerned with the physiological and pharmaceutical aspects of drug misuse and dependence and with related interventions. Chapter 4 provides an overview of the addictive properties of various drugs, the metabolizing process, and the effect of chronic use on the major organs of the body. Major emphasis is placed on the most complex organ of the body—the brain. We will see, through a review of the latest research from neuroscience and with the help of diagnosis, how addicting drugs work *in* the brain and *on* the brain. We conclude Part II with a chapter unique to this book: a presentation of biologically based interventions, the subject of chapter 5. Included under the rubric of biologically based in-terventions are aversion therapy, pharmaceutical remedies, assessment, and early-stage, highly structural group work. More specifically, chapter 5 focuses on interventions that relate directly or indirectly to biology, to interventions introduced very early in treatment, while the individual is apt to still be toxic. The most intriguing part of this chapter is the description of experiments in altering brain chemistry through behavior therapy.

The "strange" behavior of an addicted person—who, despite the disorders that have resulted from the drug use, still sees the drug as the most important thing in life—seems not so strange when we realize the person's brain is really changed.

—Harriette Johnson (1999, p. 50)

SUBSTANCE MISUSE, DEPENDENCE, AND THE BODY

CHAPTER 4

INTRODUCTION

If you down a scotch and soda, take a drag of a cigarette, or snort cocaine, trillions of potent molecules surge through your bloodstream and into your brain. If you inject a drug such as heroin or meth directly into the veins, you get a rush within 30 seconds. Whatever the chosen method of ingestion—swallowing, inhaling, or injecting—psychoactive drugs are absorbed into the bloodstream and carried to the central nervous system. Unlike many other drugs, such as penicillin, these kinds of drugs pass the blood–brain barrier and cause the release of neurotransmitters (feel-good chemicals) in the brain (Abadinsky, 2003). Eventually, drugs are detoxified by metabolic processes or eliminated from the body as waste material (Jung, 2001).

The result of experimentation with drugs ranges from benign to seriously destructive. One purpose of this chapter is to show what happens to the mind and body after drugs enter the system and to present facts concerning the chemical properties of the various drugs—depressants, stimulants, hallucinogens, and cannabis. This knowledge is basic for working with people with problems that are related to urges, compulsions, and cravings, and those urges, compulsions, and cravings often have biochemical roots. Another purpose of this chapter is to explore genetic factors in the etiology of addiction.

Chapter highlights include a study of states of euphoria as registered in the brain and brain changes as pathways to addiction. The concern of the central portion of the chapter is with genetic factors in susceptibility to addiction. Finally, the physiological effects of drugs on the brain, heart, liver, and reproductive system, including the developing fetus, are described. The information

121

of relevant biological processes provided in this chapter should enhance the counseling function regarding the standard tasks of assessment, problem formulation, and intervention as well as contributing to a more comprehensive understanding of the power of addiction.

PROPERTIES OF ALCOHOL AND OTHER DRUGS

A *drug* is any substance, natural or artificial, other than food that by its chemical nature alters structure or function in the living organism (Benshoff & Janikowski, 2000). Psychoactive drugs are mood altering and used for purposes of recreation or self-medication. Such drugs can be categorized in various ways, but the usual division is into depressants (or downers), opiates, stimulants (or uppers), and hallucinogens. These substances all affect the central nervous system and therefore alter the user's mood and even sensory perceptions in some cases. The major drugs of misuse, whether uppers or downers, imitate the structure of neurotransmitters, the chemicals in the brain that give us pleasure.

DEPRESSANTS

This category of drugs includes alcohol, barbiturates, and tranquilizers. Narcotics may be natural (opium derivatives, e.g., morphine and codeine), semi-synthetic, such as heroin, or synthetic, such as morphine and Demerol (Abadinsky, 2003). These drugs depress the central nervous system, reduce anxiety at low dosages, and can induce anesthesia and death at high dosages.

ALCOHOL "Cunning, baffling, powerful!" These are the descriptive words used for alcohol in an oft-cited passage from "The Big Book" (AAWS, 1976/1939, pp. 58–59). Alcohol is a chemical and a drug; the kind that people drink is ethyl alcohol, or ethanol (C_2H_5OH), popularly abbreviated as ETOH. Ethyl alcohol is a colorless, flammable, volatile liquid with a burning taste (Royce & Scratchley, 1996).

Alcohol is widely used as a solvent in industry, where it is denatured by adding a toxin to make it unpalatable (Benshoff & Janikowski, 2000). The kind of alcohol we drink is produced by the fermentation of substances, such as fruit, containing sugar and by enzymes that are produced by a microorganism, yeast (Kinney, 2006). Through the process of distillation, the solution containing the alcohol is heated and the vapors are collected and condensed into liquid form again. This process, as we saw in chapter 2, increases its potency considerably.

Whatever form of alcohol is consumed, when taken to excess, different levels of intoxications are likely to be observed with different individuals and at different time points. Early in the drinking period, as the *DSM–IV–TR* (American Psychiatric Association [APA], 2000) indicates, when blood alcohol levels are rising, symptoms often include talkativeness, a sensation of well-being, and a bright, expansive mood. Later, when blood alcohol levels are falling, the individual is likely to become depressed, less rational, and withdrawn. At the highest level, a nontolerant individual is likely to become sleepy.

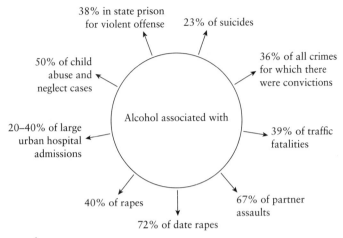

FIGURE 4.1 | ALCOHOL'S TOLL

Source: Statistics are drawn from the Centers for Disease Control and Prevention (CDC) (2005) and the Bureau of Justice Statistics (BJS) (2003).

Individual differences in brain chemistry may explain the observation that excessive alcohol intake consistently may promote aggression in some persons but not in others (Higley, 2001). Father Martin (1972), in his charismatic lecture-film *Chalk Talk,* which is still widely shown in treatment centers, semihumorously depicts four categories of drunks. Each category can represent a progressive stage in the course of an evening, or each can represent the drug-induced behavior of a particular individual. The types are:

- The *jocose* drunk, who is a barrel of laughs
- The *amorose* drunk, who can't keep his hands to himself
- The *bellicose* drunk, "the new man with the new teeth"
- The *lachrymose,* or crying, drunk, full of self-pity

To these, we have a few additions of our own:

- The *somnos,* or sleepy, drunk
- The *clamorose,* or loud, drunk
- The *scientose,* or "know-it-all," drunk

The toll that alcohol takes on U.S. society can be seen most graphically in Figure 4.1. Domestic violence, child abuse, rape, and other crimes (including, of course, driving while intoxicated), serious illness, and accidents requiring hospitalization are all linked to alcohol misuse (only some to alcoholism). The large majority of drunk drivers in fatal car crashes, for example, are casual or binge drinkers rather than chronic alcoholics (Sharman, 2005).

We need to keep in mind that most public health problems related to drinking come from acute intoxication, not dependence. Unfortunately, in many parts of Europe (especially the United Kingdom and Ireland) and North America, binge drinking is the predominant pattern (WHO, 2006).

The highest level of alcohol use is among 21 year olds (Kinney, 2006). Alcohol use is the leading risk factor in three leading causes of deaths among youth: unintentional injuries (including motor vehicle crashes and drownings), suicides, and homicides (Centers for Disease Control, 2005). Among young males, alcohol is a significant factor in about 50% of all drownings (Kinney, 2006).

As Figure 4.1 indicates, a high percentage of hospital admissions involve alcohol use. An analysis of data from the Healthcare Cost and Utilization Project conducted by Russo and Elixhauser (2006) provides some details on such hospitalizations. The first thing we learn from the data is that alcohol abuse disorders are only the stated cause of admission in a small fraction of cases—between 1 and 2%. Those admissions that were specifically for alcohol misuse usually began in the emergency room. Many of these admissions involved chronic conditions such as other substance use, mood disorders, hypertension, or withdrawal symptoms. The typical patient was a young to middle-aged man. The estimated cost of these hospitalizations amounted to about $2 billion during the year of the study. Smothers, Yahr, and Ruhl (2004), based on their examination of extensive hospital data, found that screening for alcohol disorders is rarely done. Yet they found that nearly one fourth of admitted patients who identified themselves as drinkers met the diagnostic criteria for alcohol use disorders.

Another fact we need to bear in mind is, in economic terms, that legal substances (alcohol and tobacco) account for most of the total cost of substance use. In Canada, for example, legal substances (alcohol and tobacco) account for about 80% of the total cost of substance use damage to the economy, and illegal drug use makes up the remaining 20% (Canadian Centre on Substance Abuse, 2006).

Partner violence, also as indicated in Figure 4.1, is commonly associated with alcohol. The most common pattern is drinking by both offender and victim. According to the *Global Status Report on Alcohol* produced by the World Health Organization (2004), the connection between alcohol and domestic partner violence is seen in nations in which drinking is common. A study of police reports in Zurich, Switzerland, for example, found evidence of alcohol use in 40% of investigated situations. In Nigeria, alcohol use was involved in over half of husband–wife knifing incidents. In South Africa, violence was found to rise over fights about the wife's drinking. Even in South India, in a region with an extremely low drinking rate, more than half of spousal abuse was reported to occur during a period of intoxication.

A U.S. investigation of 137 men in domestic violence treatment conducted by Fals-Stewart (2003) gathered daily reports from the batterers. Analysis of the reports revealed that violent episodes often accompanied drinking. Furthermore, individuals in the program who had serious alcohol problems were more likely than others to abuse their partners regardless of their state of sobriety.

According to the new National Institute on Alcohol Abuse and Alcoholism (NIAAA) (2005) weblink on college drinking, drinking by college students aged 18 to 24 contributes to an estimated 1,700 student deaths a year, almost 600,000 injuries, and 97,000 of date rape cases each year. (For more statistics, visit www.collegedrinkingprevention.gov.)

The number of deaths attributed to alcohol by health conditions such as pancreatitis, liver disease, and alcohol poisoning is considerable. In addition to the many adverse health effects that result directly from alcohol misuse, alcohol misuse and addiction often accompany other disorders such as depression, anxiety, as well as other substance use. For example, an estimated 90% of cocaine addicts have alcohol problems, and an estimated 60% of patients treated at mental health centers have problems with alcohol and other drugs (NIAAA, 2006a). Excessive drinking is closely associated with a disregard of safe-sex precautions. Research shows that between 30 and 60% of people with HIV/AIDS also have alcohol use disorders (NIAAA, 2006a).

In Australia, similarly, the toll of alcohol misuse has received considerable attention. The National Alcohol Action Plan 2000–2003, prepared by the Intergovernmental Committee on Drugs, reveals a picture of extensive destruction of human life due to alcohol misuse, with more than 10 deaths a day related to alcohol consumption. More than one third of men and women are consuming alcohol at harmful levels, according to this report ("Alcohol in Australia," 2000).

A Swedish study indicates that 29% of all "unnatural deaths" in Sweden during a 5-year period were associated with alcohol (Sjogren, Erikson, & Ahlm, 2000). *Unnatural deaths* refer to non-disease-related deaths, such as accidents, suicides, falls, traffic injuries, and homicides. The concern of many Swedes, at the time of this article, was that when their very high taxes on alcohol are lowered as required by the European Union by 2004, major changes in consumption and alcohol-related deaths will result. In fact, Sweden has managed to retain high alcohol taxes but has been required to ease restrictions on private imports from Germany and Denmark (Global Information, 2006). Wine sales have rebounded as a result.

Within the European Union, the former Soviet nations of Lithuania, Latvia, and Estonia rank at the bottom of the health categories linked to excessive drinking—liver disease, traffic deaths, suicide, and alcohol poisoning and psychosis. More than 50,000 people die annually from alcohol poisoning in Russia compared to 400 in the United States (Finn, 2005). Throughout Latin America, alcohol intoxication ranks as the number one risk to health, according to an article in the Pan American Health Organization publication *Perspectives* (Sharman 2005).

The secret to prevention, therefore, argues Sharman, is to view alcohol misuse less as an individual malady and more as a problem of public health. Costa Rica is taking such measures today to reduce excessive consumption. These measures include restrictions of advertising, taxes, licensing laws, controls on hours of serving alcohol, and the banning of drinking in parks or on the street. Other measures include tough drinking-and-driving limits and the use of

TABLE 4.1 | INTERNATIONAL CONSUMPTION RATES

Country	Total per Capita Consumption in Liters of Pure Alcohol
Iran	0.00
India	0.82
Cuba	3.65
Mexico	4.62
Norway	5.81
Sweden	6.86
Japan	7.38
United States	8.51
Italy	9.14
Greece	9.30
United Kingdom	10.39
Denmark	11.93
Lithuania	12.32
Germany	12.89
France	13.54
Ireland	14.45

Information from *Global Status Report on Alcohol,* World Health Organization, 2004, pp. 11–12.

screening at health centers and brief interventions with people who manifest problems with alcohol to encourage healthy practices.

We learn from the Global Status Report on Alcohol (WHO, 2004) facts of interest about international levels of consumption. Whereas alcohol consumption in many Muslim nations is close to zero, the level of drinking in the nations of the former Soviet Union is quite high. Table 4.1 gives some examples.

The drinking patterns in the various nations, in terms of preferred beverages, as the Global Status Report further indicates, are very different. Eastern Europeans tend to prefer to take their alcohol as hard liquor or spirits, the British and Irish prefer beer, the French and Italians prefer wine, and the Russians prefer spirits.

As McNeece and DiNitto (2005) suggest, "almost nothing good can be said about the effects of alcohol on the human body, except that moderate drinkers may have slightly lower risk of atherosclerosis and coronary heart disease" (p. 68). True, there are substantial health risks linked to alcohol, as we will see presently when we consider the damage to the various organs of the body through long-term alcohol misuse. Researchers, however, have long reported the health benefits of moderate drinking, namely, in preventing coronary heart disease and stroke. Because they are less prone to coronary artery disease—the leading killer of men and women in the United States—moderate drinkers tend to live longer than abstainers (Raloff, 2003; U.S. Department of Health and Human Services, 2000). (*Moderate* drinking is defined as up to two drinks per day for men and one for women.)

An article in *Science News* (Raloff, 2003) summarizes the research comparing abstainers with moderate drinkers. One problem with such research, she warns, is that surveys are often used. The surveys that ask about weekly consumption patterns compromise data by including people who consume all their alcohol only over the weekend as moderate drinkers. This is why carefully controlled experimental studies are best. In one such study, postmenopausal women drank 15 grams of alcohol each night before bed. Results showed that their insulin values, blood sugar, and cholesterol were healthiest during this two-drink period. Rat experiments show similar results. Other studies show benefits in humans of moderate drinking in terms of reasoning, memory, and decision-making performance. On the whole, moderate drinking effects relate to diseases that emerge in middle age and after; there seems to be little health justification, therefore, for drinking in youth except to develop healthy habits such as learning when to stop. One benefit unrelated to age reported by Shapiro (1996) was the prevention of colds and protection of the stomach from tainted or unsanitary food. And a recent empirically based Mayo Clinic study found, curiously, that moderate drinkers have less tendency toward obesity than do abstainers or binge drinkers (Arif & Rohrer, 2005).

Because of the fear by American public health officials, however, that word of the documented benefits of alcohol would encourage alcohol misuse, public proclamations tend to stress only the negative aspects of alcohol consumption (Peele, 1999). To such negative aspects, we now turn our attention.

One property of alcohol not usually considered is its addictiveness. The mechanisms that promote addiction occur primarily in the brain and relate to the effect of the chemical on the brain over time. Although researchers are only at the threshold of uncovering the mysteries of addiction, it is known that about 7 to 10% of drinkers develop dependence. As Harold Kalant, a former researcher at the Toronto Center for Addiction and Mental Health, speculates, drugs like cocaine and heroin are more addictive than alcohol; about 30% of users becoming addicted to these (Gardner, 2000). Only one drug causes addiction among a majority of its users—nicotine, as Kalant indicates.

The marketers of alcohol, like the marketers of tobacco products, focus their efforts where use is the strongest—on the young to encourage their drinking and on heavy drinkers. Excessive drinkers, according to a report by the National Center on Addiction and Substance Abuse (2003), account for 9% of drinkers but 46% of the total alcohol consumed. A scanning of magazines and TV ads reveals heavy use of images that relate to unquenchable thirst, women as sex object, and sports.

Tolerance, Withdrawal, and Blackouts Most heavy drinkers are proud of their high tolerance for alcohol; they can drink their friends "under the table." Some people have a high tolerance by nature; others develop their ability to handle large quantities of alcohol as the nervous system accommodates to its effects and the liver gets more efficient at metabolizing alcohol. Alcoholics, therefore, because of their behavioral tolerance, may drive fairly well, even though legally intoxicated. *Behavioral tolerance* refers to the process of learning to adapt one's behavior to the presence of the drug. Chronic alcoholics may be only moderately drunk at the blood alcohol level of 0.4, a level at which a normal drinker might be comatose. Many individuals, similarly, smoke a pack of cigarettes a day, a feat that would be highly unlikely for novice smokers, who haven't yet developed that tolerance.

Gmel et al. (2006), in their empirical investigation of emergency room injuries in a Swiss hospital, provide relevant documentation on the paradoxical benefits of tolerance. Chronic heavy drinkers who were admitted to the hospital experienced a lower rate of serious injury than did intoxicated persons who rarely drank heavily. Low-volume drinking women had a high rate of alcohol-related injuries. Prevention efforts, as the researchers recommend, should target heavy drinking occasions.

Low sensitivity to modest amounts of alcohol—as indicated by good performance on a test of coordination and balance—shows a strong link to future alcoholism among the sons of both alcoholic and nonalcoholic fathers, according to longitudinal research undertaken by Schuckit, Smith, Kalmijn, and Danko (2005). Earlier research on the original sample had established a relationship between high tolerance in youth and the later development of alcoholism.

Tolerance levels are subject to alteration following a period of abstinence. Practitioners in Seattle, Washington, working from a harm reduction model, go to great pains to warn their clients immediately on their release from jail, "Don't take your usual level of drugs. Your body won't be able to handle it." Clients have died or nearly died in the past as they rush from jail to take their usual drug dose. (Information obtained in personal communication with Rupert van Wormer, May 12, 2001.)

Tolerance reversal is the phenomenon associated with aging in which the drinker loses his or her ability to handle alcohol. The liver is no longer efficient, and the experienced drinker now gets drunk on the first drink.

Cross-tolerance occurs as the tolerance developed for one drug generalizes to another drug in the same pharmaceutical class. Cross-tolerance also can be understood as tolerance to a substance to which the individual had not previously been exposed (WHO, 1994). Barbiturates, general anesthetics, and alcohol are all sedative-hypnotic drugs, so tolerance for one is tolerance for all.

Withdrawal is defined by the *DSM–IV–TR* (APA, 2000) as "a maladaptive behavioral change, with physiological and cognitive concomitants" of a reduction of intake following prolonged use of a substance. When the depressant effects of a sedative drug such as alcohol are removed, there is a rebound effect, and the central nervous system becomes hyperactive. This is because if the drug causes one effect, the body adapts, and removal of the drug brings the opposite reaction. (For example, opioids may produce constipation, whereas withdrawal produces diarrhea.) Sleeping problems related to alcohol withdrawal may be horrendous. For stimulants such as cocaine and crack, the visible withdrawal reaction is relatively mild (APA, 2000). Depression following the discontinued use of stimulants is common, however, as the person's body crashes from the artificially induced high. The craving for more of the drug can be relentless during this period. There are no withdrawal symptoms with LSD, however.

Withdrawal symptoms usually start within 24 hours and can last up to several days. The typical medical treatment for alcohol withdrawal involves the use of another drug from the same class. The use of newer drugs, such as clonidine, beta-adrenergic blockers, and naltrexone, has been successful (Jung, 2001). In Spain, Israel, and Australia, doctors are using massive injections of naltrexone to speed drug addicts dependent on opioid drugs through the harrowing process of withdrawal. Instead of shaking, sweating, and retching for 10 days, the patients are placed under heavy sedation for a rapid detox. Research in the United States has shown mixed results. One report provided on the substance use research search engine, Join Together (2001), touts the success of the rapid detox technique with 160 patients in Australia. Later research (Join Together, 2005b) reports that the use of anesthesia proved to be dangerous in itself and that few patients successfully completed the program. The use of the anticraving drug naltrexone in detox is discussed in chapter 5.

Black coffee and other favorite remedies do nothing to speed up the brain's recovery from a night or weekend of indulgence. Caffeine plus alcohol creates a wide-awake drunk; reaction time is still impaired. Even the next day after a binge, functions involving coordination and concentration are seriously altered. The most common and least debilitating of the postintoxication withdrawal syndromes is the *hangover*. A hangover simply has to be lived through; the condition is unpleasant but not dangerous. People who don't get hangovers after a hard night of drinking should realize this lack of aftereffects could signal addiction. Advice to prevent a hangover is to drink on a full stomach, avoid darker drinks, such as brandy, red wine, tequila, and whiskey, which have a higher content of congeners (toxic byproducts of alcohol fermentation), and drink lots of liquids, such as water (Lee, 2001). Better yet, drink moderately in the first place.

Withdrawal from alcohol addiction consists of such symptoms as tremor of the hands, tongue, or eyelids; nausea or vomiting; anxiety, depressed mood, or irritability; illusions, headache, and insomnia. Seizures may occur. The patients who have gotten into serious trouble with alcohol may be found in the detoxification wards of local hospitals. Of those who develop withdrawal symptoms, fewer than 10% will develop severe symptoms such as tremors (APA, 2000). Seizures are experienced by up to 15% of alcoholics during withdrawal. Structural brain imaging shows brain shrinkage in the frontal lobes of persons who have had seizures (NIAAA, 2000b). The "DTs," or delirium tremens, which are rare but life threatening, involve visual and auditory hallucinations. The DTs can be avoided by coming off the alcohol gradually or by using a medication such as Valium or Librium.

Different drugs bring different withdrawal symptoms. Withdrawal from heroin or other opiates causes diarrhea, chills, fever, and a runny nose (Benshoff & Janikowski, 2000). Caffeine withdrawal produces frontal headaches, as many coffee drinkers know. Valium withdrawal produces seizures. These may occur 2 or more weeks after cessation of drug use. Since alcoholics are sometimes pill users too, which is a big problem in Norway, clients in inpatient treatment commonly have seizures long after their bodies are clear of the alcohol.

The most powerful portrayal of the throes of withdrawal is given in the classic movie *The Lost Weekend*, produced by Billy Wilder in 1945. Starring Ray Milland and Jane Wyman, this movie marked a milestone in viewing alcoholism as a progressive and chronic disease. The long, lonely weekend contains one unforgettable scene as the hero, locked in a mental ward, suffers extremely gross hallucinations.

Blackouts are perhaps the most intriguing phenomenon associated with alcohol use and the one about which the least is known neurologically. *Blackout* is a term used by both alcoholics and health researchers to describe the total inability to recall events that occurred while the person was drunk, even though the person appeared normal at the time. There is no lapse of consciousness with a blackout. The inability to store knowledge in long-term memory is attributed to a high blood alcohol level, usually over 0.30 blood alcohol concentration (BAC) (Sweeney, 1990). As more alcohol is consumed, larger sections of the brain are turned off, preventing cells from firing and new memories from being laid down (NIAAA, 2004). When blackouts are studied experimentally, they are found to be neither selective nor predictable, nor can they be anticipated by observed behavior. Blackouts are much more common among social drinkers than previously believed. About half of college students report they have experienced blackouts at some point (NIAAA, 2004). Females appear to be especially susceptible to this condition after a bout of heavy drinking. The exact neurological process of this loss of memory is not fully understood. Research shows that college students are at special risks for blackouts as they often drink too much too fast. Fragmentary blackouts are commonly reported by students. Such partial memory blackouts can contribute to greater alcohol misuse in the future as drinkers may fill in the memory gaps with false positive recollections (Bhattacharya, 2003).

The casualness with which a group of recovering alcoholics discuss blackout episodes can be daunting. Often, the blackout is a source of amusement, if not amazement. Women may tell of waking up in bed in a strange place with a strange man; men may speak of having to search endlessly for a "lost" car. One man proposed marriage; this led to an altercation later. Friends later said these people seemed to be acting normally. A typical difficulty encountered by the alcoholic is hiding liquor and then searching high and low for it later, to no avail. Another memorable scene in *The Lost Weekend* graphically depicts the alcoholic hero's utter joy on leaning far back in a chair and spotting his coveted bottle directly overhead in the ceiling lamp.

When experiencing a blackout, it is said, one can remember something for perhaps 15 minutes, long enough to drive a car to a destination. One can think and plan. But nothing is stored in the memory; there is no way to retrieve the memory once lost. This is in contradistinction to repression, in which the memory is buried in the unconscious. The following story provided by Lisa L. (2001) is typical:

> The blackout, as explained to me by an RN, is a chemical amnesia. It won't ever come back. There is stuff I did that I had no awareness of later. Many times I'd wake up and wouldn't know how I got home. Sometimes my car was there and sometimes not; "Where did I leave that damn car?" No matter how much I tried, I couldn't get that memory back.

Legally, the implications of a blackout are significant. Around any courtroom, you will commonly hear the accused say, "I don't remember, I don't remember." In one case that van Wormer attended, the prosecutor told the jury, "Isn't that convenient? He killed his wife and he says he doesn't remember." In fact, even the defense attorney (who thought her client had repressed the memory) did not realize that the defendant, who had consumed a case of beer, had experienced a blackout. Being in a blackout does not exonerate a person from responsibility for crime—the person was thoroughly conscious at the time and probably knew right from wrong—but it does relate to the truthfulness of a witness with a blocked memory.

Because of the memory problem, a major risk in criminal investigation is that the accused will have been "turned in" by the actual culprit for a crime that the accused did not commit. Then, on the assumption of guilt, the accused will sign a confession. Mark Twain (1876) presented a fictional rendition of this happenstance in *Tom Sawyer*. Fortunately, Tom Sawyer and Huckleberry Finn, who were witnesses, were able to save the falsely accused man shortly before he was to be hanged.

In real life, Joe Giarratano was placed on Virginia's death row after confessing to a murder committed by a right-handed person. Giarratano is left-handed. He was also in an alcohol- and drug-induced blackout at the time the crimes were committed. Because of questions raised in the case, Giarratano's sentence was commuted to life in prison (McCarthy, 2000). A team of supporters continues to work for his release. A second case that has come to light is included in a collection by the Northwestern Law Center on Wrongful Convictions (2002). This case involved Gary Gauger who was sentenced to death for the murder of his parents. The police coerced a confession by telling him he was in a blackout when he committed the crimes. Eventually, lawyers got the case overturned, and after that, another man confessed to the double murders.

In a rare TV news special, "Blackout Binge," Connie Chung (1999) of *20/20* explored the connection among college students between binge drinking and blackouts. The program began with a description of a fiery car wreck in which five church elders were killed by a drunken man driving the wrong way on a

New Jersey State parkway. His BAC had been twice the legal limit when the crash occurred. The driver, Kevin Price, is now serving a 21-year prison term for reckless manslaughter. Today, he does volunteer work in prison to teach the dangers of drinking and driving. "Kevin Price," as stated in the broadcast, "now believes his behavior can be explained, at least in part, by a little-understood phenomenon known as alcoholic blackout." The night of the crash, he had 10 beers in less than 2 hours playing a drinking game called Quarters with college friends.

To show how a person having a blackout can appear completely normal to others, the 20/20 broadcast treated viewers to a videotape of a wedding and a soundtrack of the bridesmaid confirming that because of the effects of alcohol, she had no memory of the wedding at all. Two experts interviewed for the program provided the following facts: Youth are the most likely age group to experience a blackout; and blackout is even stronger when alcohol is combined with Valium, sleeping pills, or muscle relaxants. Table 4.2 compares the various commonly used drugs in terms of their modes of administration and addictive qualities. This classification is provided by NIDA.

OPIATES OR NARCOTICS   *Opiates* are naturally occurring chemicals (derived from the opium poppy) and similar synthetic drugs. Afghanistan has emerged as the global source of opium poppy and is associated with 90% of the world's production (Kinney, 2006). These narcotics are commonly prescribed by physicians to supplement endorphins in the brain, which prevent the release of pain neurotransmitters (Benshoff & Janikowski, 2000).

Opium originally was used by early Egyptians, Greek, and Arab cultures for the treatment of diarrhea since there is a constipation effect to this drug (Fisher & Harrison, 2005). Because opium is not easily absorbed in the digestive tract, oral ingestion produces little effect (Jung, 2001). Opiate users, therefore, inject, smoke, or snort the substance for maximum effect. Some mix heroin and cocaine and shoot it; this extremely dangerous practice is called "speedballing" (APA, 2000). The even more dangerous combination of heroin and crack is practiced by some older injectors.

Heroin is cheaper and purer than in the past and is therefore more accessible to young people, who can now smoke or snort it. Opiates produce a powerful rush accompanied by feelings of contentment. The rush results because these drugs bind into endorphin receptor sites located in the pleasure centers of the brain (H. C. Johnson, 2004). Although used for physical pain, their appeal is in alleviating psychological pain. Morphine, an extract of opium, was isolated from opium in the early 1800s and was widely available until the 1900s when its nonmedical use was banned (Fisher & Harrison, 2005). Morphine is a powerful pain reliever and antidiarrhetic agent. It blocks pain signals administered to the spinal cord, effectively blocking pain signals at the spine, a practice that is revolutionizing surgery. Heroin usually appears as a white or brown powder and is a synthetic derivative of morphine. It was originally developed to treat opium and morphine addiction. Demerol is a relatively strong analgesic that has become the drug of choice among addicted medical personnel (Benshoff & Janikowski, 2000).

The short-term effects of heroin use appear soon after a single dose such as by injection. The effect, which is a surge of euphoria, or "rush," is accompanied by a warm flushing of the skin and a sense of heaviness (National Institute of Drug Abuse [NIDA], 2006). Then the user typically nods off.

Associated with older drug addicts, heroin has experienced a resurgence in popularity with young street sellers, who often market heroin and cocaine together. As the drug is increasingly pure today, it can be snorted as well as smoked (chasing the dragon) (Kinney, 2006).

Morphine and heroin are rapidly metabolized by the liver and excreted by the kidneys, and they disappear from the body in 4 to 5 hours. Tolerance is incredibly strong for this drug, with users continually chasing that first high. The user must use more and more of the drug to get high as tolerance develops. Withdrawal in regular users may occur after a few hours; drug craving, muscle pain, restlessness, cold flashes, diarrhea, and vomiting may occur (NIDA, 2006). Withdrawal is painful and characterized by hyperexcitability, but this withdrawal is not dangerous compared to alcohol withdrawal, as Kinney (2006) suggests. The horrible agony of heroin withdrawal was presented in the wrenching bedroom scene in the British film *Trainspotting,* based on Welsh's (1996) novel of the same title.

Heroin overdose takes place due to a reaction to impurities present in this street drug. In Britain, where heroin may be prescribed directly under the close supervision of a registered physician, there are no such dangers accompanying its use. Probably the best-known opioid to treat addicts, methadone, is used in Britain, as in the United States, to block withdrawal symptoms and reduce cravings. Addictive and euphoric for nonaddicts, its euphoric effects are much less than those of heroin (Benshoff & Janikowski, 2000). The effect of orally administered methadone lasts up to 72 hours. Heroin and methadone maintenance treatment are provided in Britain, the United States, and many other countries to reduce contraction of HIV/AIDS, to reduce the patient's temptation to engage in crime to support the habit, and to monitor other drug use. The forms of treatment are a major component in the harm reduction philosophy geared to helping the addict live a stable and normal life.

OxyContin, a morphinelike substance, was introduced as a painkiller for terminally ill cancer patients. The advantage of this drug is that it is time released and effective over a long period (Cohen, 2001). Unfortunately, this drug is in big demand in the underground drug market. Illegal drug prescriptions and pharmacy robberies have escalated. Numerous deaths from overdoses have been reported in Kentucky and Ohio. Drug users crush the tiny white tablets to remove the time-release coating and then snort or boil them to inject the drug to get their high. As new restrictions are being placed on the way this drug is prescribed, it is the cancer patients, unfortunately, who will suffer.

A more recent and frightening development concerns a synthetic narcotic far more powerful than morphine. This is Fentanyl, a drug that has been prescribed in patch form to cancer patients to help them relieve pain by dispensing the medicine

TABLE 4.2 | DRUGS OF MISUSE

Substance: Category and Name	Examples of Commercial and Street Names	DEA Schedule*/ How Administered**	Intoxication Effects/Potential Health Consequences
Cannabis			
hashish	boom, chronic, gangster, hash, hash oil, hemp	I/swallowed, smoked	euphoria, slowed thinking and reaction time, confusion, impaired
marijuana	blunt, dope, ganja, grass, herb, joints, Mary Jane, pot, reefer, sinsemilla, skunk, weed	I/swallowed, smoked	balance and coordination/cough, frequent respiratory infections; impaired memory and learning; increased heart rate, anxiety; panic attacks; tolerance; addiction
Depressants			
barbiturates	Amytal, Nembutal, Seconal, Phenobarbital; barbs, reds, red birds, phennies, tooies, yellows, yellow jackets	II, III, V/injected, swallowed	reduced anxiety; feeling of well-being; lowered inhibitions; slowed pulse and breathing; lowered blood pressure; poor concentration/fatigue; confusion; impaired coordination, memory, judgment; addiction; respiratory depression and arrest, death
benzodiazepines (other than flunitrazepam)	Ativan, Halcion, Librium, Valium, Xanax; candy, downers, sleeping pills, tranks	IV/swallowed, injected	Also, for barbiturates—sedation, drowsiness/depression, unusual excitement, fever, irritability, poor judgment, slurred speech, dizziness, life-threatening withdrawal.
flunitrazepam***	Rohypnol; forget-me pill, Mexican Valium, R2, Roche, roofies, roofinol, rope, rophies	IV/swallowed, snorted	For benzodiazepines—sedation, drowsiness/dizziness
GHB***	gamma-hydroxybutyrate; G; Georgia home boy, grievous bodily harm, liquid ecstasy	I/swallowed	for flunitrazepam—visual and gastrointestinal disturbances, urinary retention, memory loss for the time under the drug's effects
methaqualone	Quaalude, Sopor, Parest; ludes, mandrex, quad, quay	I/injected, swallowed	for GHB—drowsiness, nausea/vomiting, headache, loss of consciousness, loss of reflexes, seizures, coma, death
			for methaqualone—euphoria/depression, poor reflexes, slurred speech, coma
Dissociative Anesthetics			
ketamine	Ketalar SV; cat Valiums, K, Special K, vitamin K	III/injected, snorted, smoked	increased heart rate and blood pressure, impaired motor function/ memory loss; numbness; nausea/vomiting
PCP and analogs	phencyclidine; angel dust, boat, hog, love boat, peace pill	I, II/injected, swallowed, smoked	Also, for ketamine—at high doses, delirium, depression, respiratory depression and arrest
			for PCP and analogs—possible decrease in blood pressure and heart rate, panic, aggression, violence/loss of appetite, depression
Hallucinogens			
LSD	lysergic acid diethylamide; acid, blotter, boomers, cubes, microdot, yellow sunshines	I/swallowed, absorbed through mouth tissues	altered states of perception and feeling; nausea; persisting perception disorder (flashbacks)
mescaline	buttons, cactus, mesc, peyote	I/swallowed, smoked	Also, for LSD and mescaline—increased body temperature, heart rate, blood pressure; loss of appetite, sleeplessness, numbness, weakness, tremors
psilocybin	magic mushroom, purple passion, shrooms	I/swallowed	for LSD—persistent mental disorders
			for psilocybin—nervousness, paranoia
Opioids and Morphine Derivatives			
codeine	Empirin with Codeine, Fiorinal with Codeine, Robitussin A-C, Tylenol with Codeine; Captain Cody, Cody, schoolboy; (with glutethimide) doors & fours, loads, pancakes and syrup	II, III, IV/injected, swallowed	pain relief, euphoria, drowsiness/nausea, constipation, confusion, sedation, respiratory depression and arrest, tolerance, addiction, unconsciousness, coma, death
fentanyl and fentanyl analogs	Actiq, Duragesic, Sublimaze; Apache, China girl,	I, II/injected, smoked,	Also, for codeine—less analgesia, sedation, and respiratory depression than morphine

Substances	Examples of Commercial and Street Names	DEA Schedule/How Administered	Intoxication Effects/Potential Health Consequences
heroin	diacetyl-morphine; brown sugar, dope, H, horse, junk, skag, skunk, smack, white horse	I/injected, smoked, snorted	
morphine	Roxanol, Duramorph; M, Miss Emma, monkey, white stuff	II, III/injected, swallowed, smoked	
opium	laudanum, paregoric; big O, black stuff, block, gum, hop	II, III, V/swallowed, smoked	
oxycodone HCL	OxyContin; Oxy, O.C., killer	II/swallowed, snorted, injected	
hydrocodone bitartrate, acetaminophen	Vicodin; vike, Watson-387	II/swallowed	
Stimulants			increased heart rate, blood pressure, metabolism; feelings of exhilaration, energy, increased mental alertness/rapid or irregular heart beat; reduced appetite, weight loss, heart failure, nervousness, insomnia
amphetamine	Biphetamine, Dexedrine; bennies, black beauties, crosses, hearts, LA turnaround, speed, truck drivers, uppers	II/injected, swallowed, smoked, snorted	Also, for amphetamine—rapid breathing/tremor, loss of coordination; irritability, anxiousness, restlessness, delirium, panic, paranoia, impulsive behavior, aggressiveness, tolerance, addiction, psychosis
cocaine	Cocaine hydrochloride; blow, bump, C, candy, Charlie, coke, crack, flake, rock, snow, toot	II/injected, smoked, snorted	for cocaine—increased temperature/chest pain, respiratory failure, nausea, abdominal pain, strokes, seizures, headaches, malnutrition, panic attacks
MDMA (methylenedioxy-methamphetamine)	Adam, clarity, ecstasy, Eve, lover's speed, peace, STP, X, XTC	I/swallowed	for MDMA—mild hallucinogenic effects, increased tactile sensitivity, empathic feelings/impaired memory and learning, hyperthermia, cardiac toxicity, renal failure, liver toxicity
methamphetamine	Desoxyn; chalk, crank, crystal, fire, glass, go fast, ice, meth, speed	II/injected, swallowed, smoked, snorted	for methamphetamine—aggression, violence, psychotic behavior/memory loss, cardiac and neurological damage; impaired memory and learning, tolerance, addiction
methylphenidate (safe and effective for treatment of ADHD)	Ritalin; JIF, MPH, R-ball, Skippy, the smart drug, vitamin R	II/injected, swallowed, snorted	
nicotine	cigarettes, cigars, smokeless tobacco, snuff, spit tobacco, bidis, chew	not scheduled/smoked, snorted, taken in snuff and spit tobacco	for nicotine—additional effects attributable to tobacco exposure, adverse pregnancy outcomes, chronic lung disease, cardiovascular disease, stroke, cancer, tolerance, addiction
Other Compounds			
anabolic steroids	Anadrol, Oxandrin, Durabolin, Depo-Testosterone, Equipoise; roids; juice	III/injected, swallowed, applied to skin	no intoxication effects/hypertension, blood clotting and cholesterol changes, liver cysts and cancer, kidney cancer, hostility and aggression, acne; in adolescents, premature stoppage of growth; in males, prostate cancer, reduced sperm production, shrunken testicles, breast enlargement; in females, menstrual irregularities, development of beard and other masculine characteristics
inhalants	Solvents (paint thinners, gasoline, glues); gases (butane, propane, aerosol propellants, nitrous oxide), nitrites (isoamyl, isobutyl, cyclohexyl); laughing gas, poppers, snappers, whippets	not scheduled/inhaled through nose or mouth	stimulation, loss of inhibition; headache; nausea or vomiting; slurred speech, loss of motor coordination; wheezing/unconsciousness, cramps, weight loss, muscle weakness, depression, memory impairment, damage to cardiovascular and nervous systems, sudden death

* Schedule I and II drugs have a high potential for abuse. They require greater storage security and have a quota on manufacturing, among other restrictions. Schedule I drugs are available for research only and have no approved medical use. Schedule II drugs are available only by prescription (unrefillable) and require a form for ordering. Schedule III and IV drugs are available by prescription, may have five refills in 6 months, and may be ordered orally. Most Schedule V drugs are available over the counter.

** Taking drugs by injection can increase the risk of infection through needle contamination with staphylococci, HIV, hepatitis, and other organisms.

*** Associated with sexual assaults.

Source: NIDA. Information on Drugs of Abuse—Commonly Abused Drugs Chart. Retrieved from www. drugabuse.gov/DrugPages/DrugsofAbuse.html.

slowly through the skin. Addicts who have gotten hold of this drug, however, have been found to bite and chew the patch and even inject themselves with the gel. Emergency room visits of people who have misused Fentanyl have sky-rocketed; more than 100 deaths have been reported nationwide (Douglas, 2006).

Opioids, including Oxycontin, Darvon, and Vicodin, are the most com-monly abused prescription drugs. Since these drugs are legal, doctor shopping is the means by which people gain access to them. In 2003, Rush Limbaugh, whose earlier tirades against drug users and "femi-Nazis" are well known, was arrested and convicted of illegally obtaining large quantities of painkilling medications, including Oxycontin (Thomas, 2003).

Misuse of pain medication is a growing problem today. More persons initiated use of narcotic pain relievers in 2005 than initiated use of marijuana or cocaine (SAMHSA, 2006). Over half of these persons were female. According to NIDA's (2005) *Research Report*, 9% of 12th graders reported using Vicodin without a prescription. Many elderly persons as well become seriously addicted to pain medication, which, unlike the young pill misusers, they start taking for legitimate reasons. Persons of all ages are ordering such medications over the Internet without a prescription.

INHALANTS   Used almost exclusively by children and teens, inhalants are a group of volatile chemicals or chemicals that easily evaporate and can be inhaled, often directly from their container. These gaseous substances, which were never intended for human consumption, are primarily nervous system depressants (McNeece & DiNitto, 2005). Most of the inhalants ingested today are common household products found in the kitchen or garbage: aerosols, paint, gasoline, glue, and lighter fluid. Users sniff, or "huff," these substances, sometimes by putting their heads in a paper bag to inhale the vapors. The intoxication pro-duced by most inhalants is comparable to that produced by alcohol and includes a light headache. At high levels, permanent damage can be done to the central and peripheral nervous systems (APA, 2000). An overdose can lead to coma. Sniffing highly concentrated amounts of the chemicals can directly induce heart failure or death within minutes of repeated inhalations (NIDA, 2006).

In Toronto, a study of street youth found that 10% had inhaled solvents (e.g., paint thinners or removers, gasoline, or glue) in the past month. A Mani-toba report revealed that half the children who lived on a First Nations reserve had inhaled solvents (Dell, 2005). In the United States, a history of foster care and mental health problems creates a situation of high risks for inhalant dependence (Fred, 2005). Early intervention is important to prevent brain damage.

Proclaiming the dangers of inhalant use, former head of the Office of National Drug Control Policy, General Barry McCaffrey, with funding from the Johnson Institute, produced a free-of-charge video warning parents and teachers of the dangers of "huffing" and "sniffing." In the video, parents mourn the death of their young son; another youth describes his recovery following substance abuse treatment. Because of the association of this drug with chil-dren, many teens sent to group therapy for substance misuse are reluctant to disclose inhalants as their drug of choice. According to Iowa substance abuse counselor Denise Mead (1999), many youth referred for inhalant use claimed to have problems with marijuana instead.

STIMULANTS

Substances in this category stimulate the central nervous system, increasing alertness and relieving fatigue. Stimulants range from mild, such as caffeine and nicotine, to more powerful cocaine and methamphetamines. Stimulants may be sniffed, smoked, injected, or swallowed. Physiological reactions to stimulants include increased pulse and blood pressure rates, dilated pupils, insomnia, and loss of appetite. Usage may be chronic or episodic, with binges punctuated by brief drug-free periods. As with alcohol misuse, aggressive or violent behavior is associated with amphetamine dependence (APA, 2000). As tolerance develops, substantial escalation of the dose is common.

COCAINE   The South American coca plant can be used to provide energy and stave off hunger. When chewed, it rarely creates social or medical problems. When the leaves are soaked and mashed, however, the more potent drug, cocaine, is then extracted as a coca paste (Fisher & Harrison, 2005). Processed from the coca leaf, cocaine is a white powder that is usually snorted. It may also be dissolved in water and injected or smoked as freebase cocaine or crack. Freebasing involves the addition of some dangerously combustible chemicals, which can explode (Gardner, 2000). Today, instead of freebasing, some users convert cocaine into crack (named for the cracking sound heard when the mixture is smoked), which involves cooking cocaine in a mixture of water, ammonia, and baking soda (NIDA, 2006).

Whereas snorted cocaine takes several minutes to reach the brain, the cooked crack delivers the same effect in seconds. Developed in the mid-1980s, crack is more concentrated than other forms of cocaine because the water base is boiled out through the heating process. The product is a crystal, or rock (Jung, 2001). According to the National Survey of Drug Use and Health, 2.3% of Americans surveyed used cocaine in the past month (Office of National Drug Control Policy, 2005). A laboratory study of cocaine's effect on the brain reported in the *Journal of the American Medical Association* ("Medical News," 1998) revealed that the maximal drug effect occurred in women in about 5 minutes on average and in men in 8 minutes. Physiological risks for women from cocaine use should therefore be greater than for men at the same consumption levels. Cocaine's behavioral effects do not differ much with the means by which this drug is delivered, but the effect is much more immediate when it is smoked or injected than when snorted. Feelings of sexual arousal often accompany cocaine use, probably because of an increase in blood flow to the genitals (Stevens & Smith, 2004). Cocaine is associated with violence; today, crack use is down and heroin use is up in the inner city. Some researchers attribute the decreased homicide rate to this switch (Blumstein, 2000).

Cocaine is rapidly metabolized by the brain from the bloodstream and then travels back to the blood. The drug can be found in the urine up to 8 hours after ingestion. The high lasts only about 15 to 20 minutes (Fishbein & Pease, 1996). PET scanners show that cocaine works by blocking dopamine transporter sites, preventing the reuptake of dopamine. Short-acting drugs such as cocaine wear off quickly and leave an unpleasant crash in the wake. The addictive nature of cocaine is revealed in rat studies; addicted rats will continue to press a lever administering cocaine, to the neglect of food and water. Eventually, they die of seizures or dehydration (Fishbein & Pease, 1996). Because it is easy to develop a tolerance for cocaine, the frequency and dosage must be increased to maintain the same effect. In cocaine addicts, dopamine levels are quickly depleted, which leads to severe depression, aggressive behavior, anxiety, and intense craving (Nestler, 2005). Damage to the heart is another major consequence of regular cocaine use. Acting directly on the heart muscle, cocaine causes the heart to beat inefficiently. The most common causes of death from cocaine are heart attacks, strokes, and respiratory failure (NIDA, 2006).

Scientists have found that cocaine misuse coupled with the use of alcohol leads to poorer performance on tests of learning and memory than does the ingestion of either cocaine or alcohol alone. The negative effects on thinking persist for at least a month after the substance use, according to a NIDA (2000a) news release. The mixture of cocaine and alcohol is probably the most lethal of any two-drug combinations known.

AMPHETAMINES AND METHAMPHETAMINES Unlike cocaine, amphetamines are synthetic drugs, yet many of the physiological effects are the same. Amphetamines in nonhyperactive people increase their adrenaline level and suppress the appetite. Hence, they are widely used as diet pills. Tolerance develops quickly, however, so the dosage must be increased. Ritalin is an example of an amphetamine; it is a prescription drug used to treat hyperactivity. This drug helps children and adults focus their attention more strongly. Although generally considered relatively harmless, recent research with gene expression in an animal model suggests that it has the potential for causing long-term changes in brain cell structure and function ("Ritalin May Cause," 2001). Animal research consistently shows that high doses of meth damage neuron cell endings (NIDA, 2006). And in humans, over time, this drug appears to cause reduced levels of dopamine, which can result in uncontrollable shaking, symptoms like those of Parkinson's disease.

Methamphetamines ("meth" or "crank") are usually available in powdered ("crystal meth") form and can be snorted, injected, or smoked to produce a 2- to 4-hour high (Abadinsky, 2003). Smoking is the popular form of ingestion in San Diego, while in Texas most users inject it (NIDA, 2002). When smoked, the meth high can last 8 to 24 hours compared to only a fraction of that time for cocaine (NIDA, 2002).

This drug is hardly new. Nazi troops used methamphetamines to stay awake during World War II battles, and it was later associated with Hell's Angels motorcycle gangs (Stewart & Sitaramiah, 1997). Today, a far more potent formula using common chemicals has been developed; this drug is cheap to make and can be manufactured easily in local laboratories because the ingredients are readily available. Meth is sometimes referred to as the "poor person's cocaine." It is also popularly said that compared to cocaine, meth gives more "bang for the buck."

The active ingredient is either ephedrine or pseudoephedrine, both of which are found in over-the-counter cold medicines. (In 2006, Congress passed a law restricting open sales of cold medicine like Sudafed containing these ingredients.) In meth labs, products such as drain cleaners are used to transform the substance into a powder that can be ingested. Compared to cocaine, meth has a much longer duration, although the rush is not as strong when the drug is snorted. Users stay awake for days, often weeks, at a time. Paranoia, aggression, and a breakdown in the immune system often occur with regular use of this drug (Fishbein & Pease, 1996). Heavy meth users, like cocaine users, are often thin and emaciated.

National surveys show that around 4% of persons aged 12 and older have tried this drug. Because of its energizing properties and relative low cost, meth is highly popular among blue-collar workers in the Midwest, many of whom have more than one job. Its manufacture is extremely hazardous because of the toxic fumes and possible explosions during the cooking process.

The new restrictions on the sale of products containing pseudoephedrine have successfully reduced home production of meth. Meth use has remained fairly constant, however, as supplies continue to be imported from Mexico. A purer form of the drug, called "ice," is smoked today at alarming rates, triggering a rise in meth addiction and treatment admissions (Join Together, 2006).

In Iowa, the prisons are flooded with people who were involved in meth production. Prison dentists report that many of their patients suffer from a problem of "meth mouth" (Associated Press, 2005). Meth use causes severe tooth decay, and the gums turn black from extreme use.

Burn units in Iowa have seen nearly 50 cases of severe burns from 2002 to 2004 caused by explosions in meth labs (Bauer, 2006). These patients typically have no health insurance and are very hard to treat because of drug withdrawal and tolerance to painkiller problems. Thanks to strict laws restricting sales of pseudoephedrine, the numbers of meth lab burns have declined significantly. Still, meth accounts for more emergency room visits than any other illicit drug, according to a survey released by the National Association of Counties (Leinwand, 2006). The toll on local governments in terms of cleanups of toxic waste left by home labs, the care for neglected children of addicts, domestic violence, and criminal justice has been enormous. Associated with rough sex, meth sometimes causes physical injury in the partner of a meth user (NIDA, 2002).

A response to heavy meth use familiar to medical professionals is the sensation of insects creeping under the skin. Users often scratch their skin to the point of bleeding.

Use of methamphetamines is linked to several serious medical complications, such as heart damage, stroke, and psychosis. Long-term neurological damage can result. For recovery, physical withdrawal is not the problem but, rather, anhedonia. *Anhedonia* is an inability to experience pleasure at the normal joys of life. Five percent of former users will have permanent delusional disorders with paranoia (flashbacks) (Salemy, 1998).

Lisa Kuennen (in a talk before a social work class of September 11, 2006) shared how after years on meth, she was unable to experience pleasure in any normal way:

> It took me 3 years to get out of that funk. I was down, unable to enjoy anything. I could go outside and feel the sun but it wouldn't warm me. This last year was the first time I felt the sun—I felt alive for the first time. Sometimes I just enjoy looking at the trees and flowers or the cloud formations in the sky.

NICOTINE   Nicotine, a highly toxic central nervous system stimulant, comes from the dried tobacco plant, which is native to North America. Nicotine is a natural insecticide. Native Americans have known about tobacco for centuries; documented use by the Mayan culture goes back more than 2,000 years (Benshoff & Janikowski, 2000). Dependence on nicotine resembles that of the other drugs discussed in this chapter in that it produces compulsive patterns of use, craving, tolerance, and physical dependence. Smoking is directly responsible for approximately 90% of lung cancer deaths and 80–90% of emphysema and chronic bronchitis deaths (American Lung Association, 2006). Tobacco smoke contains many toxic compounds, including the highly addictive nicotine, tar, and carbon monoxide. Alone or in combination, these compounds are responsible for most smoking-related diseases. A major cause of stroke, tobacco use is the leading cause of preventable death in the United States (NIDA, 2006).

Although far less serious than lung or heart disease, premature wrinkling of the skin has long been associated with smoking. Researchers are learning how smoking causes wrinkling by reducing the skin's elasticity. In a study conducted by London dermatologists, scientists discovered that a gene implicated in wrinkles caused by sunbathing is also highly active in smokers ("Wrinkles Are Traced," 2001).

Cigarette and cigar smoking, pipe smoking, and tobacco chewing are the favorite methods of tobacco use. (The nicotine patch is a modern means of helping wean smokers from their habit.) After inhalation, it takes about 7 seconds for nicotine to reach the brain. One of the effects is to elevate blood and brain levels of serotonin, producing a calming effect. Uniquely, this drug can stimulate or relax the user depending on his or her emotional state and expectations (Dunn, 2000). A major feature of cigarette smoking is its ability to help the smoker lose weight through the release of specific neurotransmitters and the chronic stimulation that increases metabolism (APA, 2000).

Among the facts known about tobacco use from the extensive research on this product and on smokers is that between 80 and 95% of alcoholics smoke cigarettes, approximately 70% of alcoholics are heavy smokers (over a pack a day), and smokers are 10 times more likely to develop alcoholism than nonsmokers (NIAAA, 1998). The reason for the co-occurrence of alcoholism and smoking is not entirely clear but may relate to the generalized tendency for addictive people to be highly susceptible to dependence on whichever drugs are readily available to them.

Studies show that rats bred for alcohol addiction have a high susceptibility for nicotine addiction compared to other rats even before they had ever been exposed to alcohol (Lê, Li, Funk, Li & Shaham, 2006). Interestingly, these highly addictive rats showed little interest in cocaine when it was made available.

Another significant rat study highlights the effects of polydrug interactions. Parnell, West, and Chen (2006) showed that the presence of nicotine decreases BAC levels. This means drinkers would have to consume more alcohol for the same effect as nonsmokers. This in turn would cause more physiological damage. Compounding this innate tendency toward alcohol-nicotine addiction is another factor: cross-tolerance. Drawing on animal studies, the NIAAA (1998) suggests that alcohol's sedating effects may mitigate the aversive effects of nicotine—increased heart rate and so forth—while, conversely, nicotine gives a charge to drinkers who may be in an emotional slump. This cross-tolerance is further revealed in the fact that to achieve the desired effect, smoking alcoholics may require higher doses of nicotine in their nicotine patches than nonalcoholics. Nicotine patches, incidentally, do not cause the health problems related to the smoking itself and to the harmful ingredients that cause lung cancer and respiratory problems (Price, 2000). Nicotine patches should not be used by nonsmokers, however, as they lack the tolerance to nicotine that smokers have acquired.

Taken together, alcohol and tobacco greatly increase one's risk of getting cardiovascular and lung diseases, along with other forms of cancer. The risk involved in both smoking and drinking, according to the NIAAA report, is much higher than the sum of the risks for use of each drug individually. Changes in the liver, coupled with the breakdown of the immune system caused by long-term alcohol misuse, create a heightened susceptibility to the toxic chemicals released in the burning cigarette. A comparison of the brains of chronic alcoholics who smoked had more severe brain damage than occurred with alcoholic drinking or smoking alone (Durazzo, Gazdzinski, Banys, & Meyerhoff, 2004). A related fact is that nicotine dependence is very common among individuals with mental disorders such as schizophrenia; 55 to 90% of individuals with mental disorders smoke (APA, 2000).

Cigarette smoking declined in the United States between 2002 and 2004, according to the National Survey on Drug Use and Health (2006). On average, about 25% of persons age 12 or older smoke. There are pronounced variations in rates among racial and ethnic groups. As indicated in the survey, the rates of smoking in the past month were highest among Native Americans at 34.6% and lowest among Asian Americans at 13.4%. The rate for Whites is 26.6%, Blacks 24.9%, and Latinos 21.9%. As smoking declines among White men, tobacco companies have targeted African Americans, Hispanics, and youth with intensive merchandising (American Lung Association, 2006).

Also, presumably to increase sales, manufacturers increased the level of nicotine that could be inhaled from cigarettes, according to data supplied by tobacco companies (as required by Massachusetts state law) and analyzed by the Harvard School of Public Health for the years 1998 through 2004 (Smith, 2007). The Harvard researchers have called for regulation of tobacco in much the same way that pharmaceutical products are regulated.

Interestingly, Philip Morris issued a report that was used in a lobbying effort to influence politicians in the Czech Republic who had complained that the tobacco industry was saddling the country with huge healthcare expenses

To Die for a Cigarette
Tammy Pearson, MSW

I have quit smoking. Finally. As an adult, I'd think, "I'm not hooked, I can quit any time." Until the day I said, "I need help." I'm a responsible person; everything else I did was in moderation. Everybody smoked. In elevators, in hospitals as employees, the grocery stores. In those days you just stomped it out in the floor. Those were the days when you'd ride in the car with smoking parents, the windows up, the car going 80 m.p.h. and no seatbelts.

Once I witnessed an outstanding example of a man exhibiting the helplessness of a nicotine addiction. I was living in Washington State and was shopping with my mother. We had just come outside to the parking lot when a man drove past, very aggressive in his hurry. When he got to his selected parking space he quickly lit a cigarette, and began an extreme act of deliberate and desperate smoking. We stayed to observe this whole ordeal. The car windows were up and he was dragging on this cigarette so hard and long that I almost expected him to just rumple it up and stuff it in his mouth, eating it. He smoked it down to where it was burning his fingers, then lit another off of the end. Now, I have also chain-smoked, but when this guy finished the first butt he cracked his car window just barely enough to stuff the butt out. He didn't even want the smoke to escape the car. My Mom and I watched the rest of this in disbelief; both of us agreed to never let the other get "that bad" and we went on our way. . . .

I remember when the doctor told me I was pregnant. "Now you're going to quit smoking," he said. I made it one-half hour. My son's father's smoke made me sick. I did everything to stop—threw the car ashtray out of the car. Once I went on crutches to the 7-11 at 2 A.M.! I had to have a cigarette. I busted out the stitches in my foot, undoing the recent surgery.

My parents had smoked for years. My Dad had a cardiac arrest. He woke up from a coma in a hospital where no smoking was allowed. He woke up totally disoriented. We

---

("Philip Morris' Spin," 2001). The report refuted those claims by showing that, inasmuch as smokers die sooner than nonsmokers by over 5 years, smokers saved the government millions of dollars from reduced costs in healthcare, pensions, and housing for the elderly. Not surprisingly, a storm of protest emerged from these findings not only in the Czech Republic but also throughout the world.

Due to nicotine craving, prevention works far better than treatment in curbing tobacco use. No one who smokes, of course, sets out to get addicted. One wonders how many actors, when forced to smoke in the movies, get turned on to nicotine. Malachy McCourt (2000), in his autobiographical *Singing My Him Song,* describes his romance with cigarettes:

> Of the bad habits available, I missed very few. I drank too much, ate too much, philandered too much. I had managed, though, to somehow remain a nonsmoker, a state I remedied at about that time. I really disliked the damn things, but in the course of the commercial (for TV and for Lark cigarettes), I got hooked. I got paid around $300 for the day's work and proceeded to spend thousands of dollars to maintain my new habit, not to mention my damaged health and yellowed teeth and

moved him to the V.A. hospital so he could get a cigarette. He calmed down immediately and came back to himself. There I saw all those veterans—one man had smoked in the navy; he was smoking through his trachea. Later I became Dad's caregiver. Dad had a bubble on his lung that could burst at any time. I would rub his back so he could breathe and it was horrible. 1988 was the last time I performed CPR on him. Mom and I were still smoking all this time.

In Washington State there was an ad on TV—people were throwing dirt on a grave. "Eventually everybody stops smoking," the ad said. Mom developed respiratory problems; she was on oxygen 24 hours a day. She had to go on Prednisone, a drug that causes your bones to break. I got a job at the National Jewish Medical Center in Denver, where she became a patient. I learned so much. Some of my friends there were world-famous scientists. To try to save my mother they even brought in drugs from foreign countries. Mom was deeply loved by everyone. But no one could save her. She suffered so much. I eventually became her primary caregiver. In April of 2000 we lost her to lung cancer.

For myself, I tried patches. I thought I needed a patch over my mouth! Oh God, that's me. Nobody was more addicted than me.

How did I quit? I didn't quit watching my son get sick from secondhand smoke, my mother dying, all the shameful things I did—smelling like smoke, going around feeling dirty like a salamander. I wished someone would just lock me up!

No, there was never a good time to quit. I worked at the number-one respiratory hospital in the world but I was going to have my cigarette! By now I had scar tissue on my lungs; my lungs were so shot. There never was a good time to quit, certainly not when I was happy; quitting would ruin my whole day. Finally, a bad day came. I was so miserable that any more pain wouldn't matter—"kick me while I'm down." Now is a good time. "I'll use this as a marker," I thought. And I did, and I died a thousand deaths but I did it.

Source: Speech given at the University of Northern Iowa, Cedar Falls, February 13, 2001. Printed with permission of Tammy Pearson.

the hundreds of little burn holes I put in various garments (my own and others') over the years. (pp. 33–34)

Quitting smoking, as everyone knows, is immensely difficult; although 80% of smokers desire to quit, only 45% can eventually do so (APA, 2000). Withdrawal effects take place within hours of the last cigarette; one's craving subsides in 3 to 4 weeks. But before then, research shows that the former chronic smokers suffer increased feelings of anger, hostility, and aggression (NIDA, 2006). A serendipitous discovery emerged recently when a stroke victim told his doctor his craving for cigarettes had disappeared. Further investigation revealed that smokers with brain damage involving the insula, a region implicated in conscious urges, were more likely than smokers with brain damage not involving the insula to discontinue smoking immediately with no withdrawal problems (Naqvi, Rudrauf, Damasio, & Bechara, 2007). This finding is likely to point researchers in new directions regarding therapies for addictive craving.

Box 4.1, "To Die for a Cigarette," presents Tammy Pearson's account of nicotine addiction, an account as gripping as that of any alcoholic or heroin addict.

CHEWING TOBACCO Also devastating in its effects on the body is chewing tobacco, or "snuff." When tobacco is chewed, the nicotine is absorbed into the bloodstream and travels to the brain. In 30 minutes of chewing, the individual intakes as much nicotine as from three cigarettes (National Cancer Institute, 2003). A former snuff user and recovering alcoholic shares his experience with chewing tobacco in this passage:

> When I was 18 years old (I refuse to tell how long ago), I saw an advertisement for Skoal chewing tobacco. It featured an ad with Walt Garrison, who was a football star with the Dallas Cowboys and in rodeos. It featured the phrase "Just a pinch between the cheek and gums." If you sent in the ad, you got a free can of tobacco. I thought it looked cool, so I did. We males are attracted to the use of spit tobacco at an early age (I was floored by the average age of 9) because we think it makes us look macho. I thought I was grown up and had a mystique about me when I first used it. I was hooked for the next 17 years of my life. I burnt my lower lip from chewing, so I switched to my upper lip. I finally said, "Enough is enough!" and quit cold-turkey 26 months ago. But as I thought about it, I had a huge urge to chew again that I did not act on. I have so many friends who use chewing tobacco that started when they were kids years ago, I can imagine the oral cancer epidemic that is forthcoming in the near future. What kids don't realize and tobacco companies don't tell you is that the nicotine is absorbed into the bloodstream very quickly through the lip and has a very short trip to begin its effects on the brain. (Larry Cranston, personal communication, 2000)

Major U.S. tobacco companies are rolling out smokeless tobacco products as a less dangerous alternative to smoking. According to the (National Cancer Institute 2003), smokeless tobacco is not a safe alternative to smoking. Its use carries major health risks, including mouth sores, permanent gum recession, and cancers of the mouth and throat.

HALLUCINOGENS

Hallucinogenic plants have been used for centuries as medicines, to cause an altered sense of reality, and for spiritual or religious purposes. *Psychedelic* is a term employed by users of hallucinogenic chemicals. Such substances occur in the natural world and can be produced synthetically. These drugs overwhelm the central nervous system and produce such desired outcomes as "out-of-body" experiences, sensory illusions, strange tactile sensations, an altered sense of time, and hallucinations (Abadinsky, 2003).

LSD AND PCP Perhaps the best-known hallucinogen is LSD (lysergic acid diethylamide). This synthetic drug achieved great popularity during the late 1960s and 1970s as youth sought a different level of reality and conscious-ness and the collective bonding experiences of "taking a trip." Taken orally, this drug is odorless, colorless, and tasteless; it is often squirted onto a small sugar cube. (A unique property of LSD is that it can be absorbed directly through the skin.) Effects take place approximately 1 hour after use and can last up to 8 hours. Heavy users sometimes experience flashbacks, even years after use; the effect is an involuntary return to the drugged state (Fisher & Harrison, 2005). A key danger in the use of LSD is the drug-induced psychosis that can lead users to think they could, for example, fly out the window or walk on water. Such illusions led to many well-publicized deaths in the late 1960s. "Bad trips" were also commonly reported as the drugged state turned nightmarish for some individuals. The long-term effects of LSD use are not known; this drug is not addictive, but tolerance does develop (APA, 2000).

Phencyclidine (PCP, "angel dust"), another synthetic drug, became a street drug in the 1970s because of its ability to produce trancelike states (Jung, 2001). Developed as an anesthetic for humans, it was later used for a while as an animal tranquilizer. It was associated with drug-induced psychosis and violence. PCP can be swallowed, smoked, snorted, or injected for a high that peaks after 30 minutes and can last for 4 to 6 hours (Stevens & Smith, 2004).

PEYOTE AND MESCALINE   The peyote cactus is native to Mexico and the southwestern United States. This psychoactive plant, dried to form a hard button, may be chewed directly or ingested in powder form (Fishbein & Pease, 1996). Native Americans have ritualistically harvested and eaten these plants in ceremonial fashion without ill effects (*Encyclopaedia Britannica*, 2006).

Mescaline, another psychedelic drug, occurs naturally in mushrooms. Less potent than LSD, it was a popular drug during the 1960s. Now, for the first time in 40 years, researchers are assessing the effects of hallucinogenic substances on human subjects in the laboratory (Winslow, 2006). Psilocybin mushrooms, which can be found growing wild throughout the world, produce an intensive religious experience in many people and feelings of fear and paranoia in others. Johns Hopkins medical researchers conducted the study on 36 volunteers under rigorously controlled conditions. Researchers hope this study could revive interest in the effects psychedelic drugs such as "magic" mushrooms have on the human brain. These special mushrooms are associated in some parts of the world with religious experiences. The "sacred mushrooms" of Mexico were called "God's Flesh" by the Aztecs (*Encyclopaedia Britannica*, 2006).

ECSTASY, ROHYPNOL, AND GHB   Developed by a German pharmaceutical firm as an appetite suppressor, MDMA (methylenedioxymethamphetamine), or Ecstasy, which was rediscovered in the 1980s, is sometimes known as a designer drug. Although consumption of drugs like cocaine and marijuana among American teens has stabilized, Ecstasy's popularity has increased exponentially (Klam, 2001). Churned out from underground factories run by international crime syndicates, Ecstasy can produce both stimulant and psychedelic effects (NIDA, 2006). Chemically, MDMA is similar to amphetamines and to the hallucinogen mescaline. MDMA releases the brain chemical serotonin, elevating mood and acting as a short-term antidepressant. In low doses, Ecstasy produces no hallucinogens but, instead, heightens one's sensory experiences and awareness of self. Popular among troops in the military and with youth at "raves" and dance clubs, this drug, in its stimulant effect, enables users to dance for extended periods. The loud music played at raves is thought to intensify the drug's effect. Ecstasy is relatively inexpensive ($10–$20 per pill) and long lasting (Fisher & Harrison, 2005).

Although MDMA is often thought of as a nonaddictive, harmless substance, emerging scientific evidence indicates that long-term use of the drug causes brain damage (Harris, 2004). Use of this drug may also lead to dehydration, hypertension, and heart or kidney failure (NIDA, 2006). In fact, as Harris (2004) reports, there have been deaths by hyponatremia, or low plasma sodium, caused by the consumption of very large quantities of water to offset dehydration.

Klam (2001), a journalist with personal experiences with Ecstasy, describes the visceral effect of this drug as follows:

> The what-ifs, the self-doubts, are knocked flat, and instead a hunger for human connection and a desire to empathize firmly take hold. No other drug produces this kind of feeling. It's also a whopper of an antidepressant. Whereas Prozac-type SSRI antidepressants keep your brain from emptying reservoirs of serotonin too quickly, Ecstasy floods your brain with the stuff. You feel restored, energized. (p. 40)

Although users consistently describe that initial high as one of life's greatest experiences, due no doubt to chemical changes in the brain, replicating that original high is close to impossible, as Klam (2001) informs us. Many of the problems associated with this drug stem from the fact that dangerous chemicals are sometimes added. According to information distributed by the harm reduction network DanceSafe (2006), much of what is sold as Ecstasy on the black market actually contains other drugs, such as PMA, speed, and PCP. Youth who consume Ecstasy tablets are advised to have the tablets chemically tested for foreign substances by DanceSafe representatives. Users are also advised to drink water but not an excessive amount. The deaths associated with Ecstasy use, according to DanceSafe, usually occur as a result of the heat stroke connected with dehydration. Mixing Ecstasy with alcohol or other drugs increases the risk of adverse reactions.

No club drug is benign, as NIDA Director Nora Volkow (2005) notes. Chronic misuse of MDMA appears to produce long-term damage to serotonin-containing neurons in the brain. Damage is most likely associated with depression, sleep abnormalities, and memory disturbances. Despite the damaging aspects, a government-approved study in Spain is using Ecstasy to treat rape victims for which no other treatment has worked (Klam, 2001). This treatment is promoted because of the ability of MDMA to reduce the fear response to stimuli and because of anecdotal reports of success in reducing the impact of past trauma. In the United States, MDMA recently received approval from the Food and Drug Administration to be tested on advanced cancer patients suffering from severe anxiety (Weiss, 2005). These compounds have the uncanny ability to induce spiritual or religious experiences. Promising results have been found in therapy with persons suffering from posttraumatic stress disorder (PTSD) as well. Researchers will administer MDMA to returning U.S. combat veterans who show evidence of combat stress (Join Together, 2005a).

Rohypnol, better known as the "date rape drug" or "roofies," is a sedative manufactured in Europe as a sleeping pill. Although a sedative chemically very similar to Valium, it is included here as a newer drug and a partying drug. Rohypnol is cheap, which makes it popular on college campuses and in gay and lesbian bars. Many of the roofies used in the United States are obtained by prescription in Mexico. Although this drug is reportedly used by date rapists, usually dropped surreptitiously into a woman's drink, women are also known to use this drug purposely for its intoxicating effects. Roofies are often used to moderate the effects of a cocaine binge or to enhance the effects of alcohol or heroin. This drug causes amnesia of events that happened while under its influence. Blackouts can last up to 24 hours (Center for Substance Abuse Research, 2004).

GHB (gamma-hydroxybutyrate) is a substance currently circulating within the dance music scene as an alternative to Ecstasy or speed. An odorless, colorless, and nearly tasteless liquid, GHB is misused for bodybuilding effects and, like Rohypnol, is associated with sexual assaults, especially on university campuses (Hensley, 2002).

CANNABIS (MARIJUANA)

Although cannabis at high doses possesses some of the properties of hallucinogens and at low doses some of the properties of depressants, the *DSM–IV–TR* (APA, 2000) recommends a separate category for this drug due to its unique behavioral effects. The plant *Cannabis sativa* (Latin for "cultivated hemp") grows wild throughout much of the tropical and temperate zones of the world (Abadinsky, 2003). *Cannabis sativa,* grown by George Washington to make rope, is the hemp plant and has varying potency depending on the type of plant grown, the climate, and the soil (Brick & Erikson, 1998). Known variously as Indian hemp, reefer, marijuana, pot, or grass, cannabis can be smoked in pipes or in a cigarette called a joint, eaten (as in brownies), or drunk. As the older generation tells the younger generation, the potency of marijuana has drastically increased in the United States. To what extent the marijuana of today is more potent than yesterday is debatable. Government claims have been made that today's marijuana is 10 to 30 times more potent than that used in the 1960s and 1970s. And while local governments struggle with a seeming meth epidemic, the Office of National Drug Control policy has spent millions on an antimarijuana campaign (*Boston Globe,* 2005). In fact, according to Greenberg (2006) of the Marijuana Policy Project, the higher THC marijuana used today is only somewhat more potent than earlier varieties. More important, as she states, there is no scientific evidence to demonstrate greater risks of health problems from the modern-day marijuana.

Hashish is the resin obtained from the flowering tops of the female plant; it is considerably more potent than marijuana (NIDA, 2006). Tetrahydro-cannabinol (THC), the psychoactive ingredient in marijuana, has been found, in large amounts, in imported products as well. After marijuana is smoked, the THC is absorbed by the lungs; the longer the smoke is held in the lungs, the higher the dose (Benshoff & Janikowski, 2000). Smoking marijuana provides a more immediate high than eating food laced with marijuana. The effect is a state of relaxation, well-being, much gaiety, and laughter. Because THC lowers blood glucose levels, pot smokers often develop voracious appetites. Recent findings confirm that marijuana activates the very receptors in the brain that are involved in the increase of appetite (Evans, 2001). This attribute has a medicinal value in the treatment of cancer and AIDS patients; and marijuana is legally available in some places for this purpose. Regrettably, the U.S. Supreme Court has ruled that the federal government can prosecute medical marijuana users even when state laws allow doctor-prescribed use of the drug (Lee, 2006).

THC is fat soluble and is readily stored in the body's fat cells and organs; its presence can be detected for long periods. No physical tolerance or withdrawal has been clearly documented with marijuana use. The long-term effects on the brain are not well known, and an overdose is not fatal (Benshoff & Janikowski, 2000). Levin (1995) is more negative: "Chronic pot use results in apathy, social withdrawal, and impairment of goal-directed behavior. Impairment of short-term memory also results from chronic use" (p. 27). Lung cancer, as Levin further indicates, has been found to result from heavy marijuana smoking, which leaves a residue in the lungs. The NIDA (2006) report on marijuana is similarly negative and suggests that this drug may be more harmful to the lungs than smoking tobacco. A recent study conducted at the University of California, Los Angeles, that was widely publicized in the media, however, refutes this claim in the largest study of its kind ever conducted (Kaufman, 2006). Over 1,000 persons with lung cancer were interviewed along with a matched sample. The evidence implicated a background of smoking tobacco but not of marijuana in the development of the cancer. The reason cancer-causing ingredients contained in marijuana did not raise cancer risks, as speculated by the article, is that THC may have a protective effect on the body organs in the presence of toxins. Ironically, Donald Tashkin, the scientist who conducted the study, was the very researcher whose previous research was used by the federal government to show that marijuana was a life-threatening drug in the first place.

METABOLISM

Metabolism is the sum total of the chemical processes and energy exchanges that take place within an organism. Metabolic processes, in which complex substances, including food, are broken down into smaller ones for elimination from the body as waste, take place in every cell and tissue of the human body. But the liver is the major organ that metabolizes larger amounts of alcohol and other drugs. When ingested, alcohol passes from the stomach into the small intestine, where it is rapidly absorbed into the bloodstream due to the small size of its molecules. The body reacts to drugs as though they were toxins and attempts to eliminate the drugs by metabolizing and neutralizing them (Benshoff & Janikowski, 2000). If a drug is water soluble, like alcohol, it will mix freely with the blood plasma and travel throughout the entire body, including the brain (Dunn, 2000). A minute amount of alcohol escapes metabolism and is excreted unchanged in the breath and urine (Gordis, 1997). Because alcohol is distributed so quickly and thoroughly, it affects the central nervous system. No digestion is required; alcohol is simply absorbed by the stomach and 80% by the small intestine. The absorption of alcohol from the stomach is very quick, especially when there is little food in the stomach and when the alcohol is at a relatively high concentration. Absorbed alcohol is rapidly carried throughout the body in the blood until an equilibrium is reached such that blood at all points in the system as well as the breath and urine contains approximately the same concentration. Consumed with carbonated beverages, alcohol has an increased intoxicating effect.

Once alcohol enters the bloodstream, it is transported to every cell in the body. Alcohol is diffused in the body in proportion to the water content of the various tissues and organs. Alcohol's small molecule and its solubility in water make it readily transportable across cell membranes, with the effect of harm to many different organs (Levin, 1995).

Since this metabolic activity in the liver takes place at a fixed rate, only part of the alcohol being pumped through the liver is metabolized at a time, while the rest continues to circulate (Royce & Scratchley, 1996). Alcohol is metabolized by enzymes, which are body chemicals that break down other chemicals. In the liver, an enzyme called alcohol dehydrogenose (ADH) mediates the conversion of alcohol to acetaldehyde (Gordis, 1997). The formation of this poison is the first step in the process. The chain of events is as follows:

alcohol > acetaldehyde > acetic acid > carbon dioxide and water

The breakdown of alcohol that occurs in the stomach differs significantly in men and women. In chronic male alcoholics and in all women, the amount of alcohol metabolized by ADH is lower than in nonalcoholic men. For non-alcoholic men, the amount of alcohol that can be metabolized by the stomach may be as great as 30% (Kinney, 2006). Nonalcoholic women metabolize only half that amount in the stomach. More pure alcohol is delivered, therefore, into the bloodstream of women and of chronic alcoholics than of men (Braun, 1996). Women get drunk faster than men not only because they are smaller and their bodies contain less water and more fatty tissue but also because alcohol-destroying enzymes in the stomach work better in men.

Women Under the Influence, a new book produced by the National Center on Addiction and Substance Abuse (CASA) (2006), finds that at lower levels of alcohol use than men, women more rapidly develop alcohol-related diseases like cirrhosis and hypertension, brain damage from drinking and taking Ecstasy, and lung cancer and emphysema from smoking. Additionally, women who use sedatives and antianxiety drugs are almost twice as likely as men to become addicted to these products. Even nicotine dependence proceeds more rapidly in females than in males.

Sometimes, combinations are beneficial however. One recent example is the finding that consumption of large quantities of coffee helps protect heavy drinkers against cirrhosis of the liver (Klatsky, Morton, Udaltsova, & Friedman, 2006).

The toxicity of acetaldehyde is not usually a problem. However, there is a prescription drug, Antabuse (disulfiram), that stops the breakdown of acetaldehyde by blocking ADH. The usefulness of this medication is in the prevention of drinking alcohol. Once Antabuse is ingested, drinking produces a severe physical reaction: nausea, flushing, and shortness of breath. Even if alcohol is placed on the skin, such as with perfume, a strong reaction occurs. Although consumption of alcohol is dangerous to most alcoholics who have ingested Antabuse, some chronic alcoholics will "brag" that they can drink freely with no negative consequences. There is as yet no substantiation of these claims, however, in the literature. For many individuals, Antabuse has a high risk of serious side effects, usually due to a reaction to another medication (Benshoff & Janikowski, 2000).

The flushing response of some Asians and a minority of Caucasians to drinking is thought to derive from a low ADH level, which insulates them from ingesting an excess of alcoholic beverages.

Healthy people metabolize alcohol at a fairly consistent rate, usually eliminating on average 0.25 to 0.5 ounces of alcohol per hour. One-half ounce of pure alcohol can be found in a 12-ounce can of beer, a 6-ounce glass of wine, or a 1-ounce shot of whiskey. The same alcohol is found in beer, wine, and spirits distilled from wine or beer. Most U.S. beer contains between 4 and 5% alcohol; European beer is stronger. Natural wines contain between 8 and 12% alcohol. Fortified wines have had alcohol or brandy added for a higher alcohol content. Spirits, including vodka, gin, whiskeys, and rum, usually contain between 40 and 50% alcohol. The word *proof* in the United States refers to twice the percentage of alcohol: 100-proof liquor is 50% ethanol. In Canada and Britain, 100-proof liquor is 57% ethanol. Beverage alcohol consists of ethanol, various byproducts of fermentation known as congeners, flavoring, coloring, and water. Table 4.3 shows the amount of alcohol in various drinks and facts concerning blood alcohol concentration.

One's blood alcohol concentration (BAC) is of special interest because of the laws regarding drinking and driving. A BAC of 0.1% is a ratio of 1 part alcohol to 1,000 parts blood. All states in the United States now use a 0.08 BAC cutoff point, reinforced by a law passed by Congress in 2000 withholding millions of dollars in federal highway money from states that did not adopt the lower standard by 2004. In Scandinavia, the legal limit ranges from 0.02 to 0.05, in Canada it's 0.08, in Britain 0.08, in Japan 0.05, and in Cuba and Iran, zero. In Russia, although drivers may have no alcohol whatsoever in their bloodstream and police administer roadside tests, arresting officers are highly subject to bribery (see http://en.wikipedia.org/wiki/Blood_alcohol_content).

TABLE 4.3 | KNOW YOUR PERSONAL LIMIT

Number of Drinks Per Hours	100 lbs M/F	120 lbs M/F	140 lbs M/F	160 lbs M/F	180 lbs M/F	200 lbs M/F	220 lbs M/F	240 lbs M/F
1 drink in 1 hour	.02/.03	.02/.02	.01/.02	.01/.01	.00/.01	.00/.01	.00/.00	.00/.00
1 drink in 2 hours	.01/.02	.00/.01	.00/.00	.00/.00	.00/.00	.00/.00	.00/.00	.00/.00
1 drink in 3 hours	.00/.01	.00/.00	.00/.00	.00/.00	.00/.00	.00/.00	.00/.00	.00/.00
2 drinks in 2 hours	.03/.04	.03/.04	.02/.03	.01/.02	.01/.02	.00/.01	.00/.00	.00/.00
2 drinks in 3 hours	.02/.03	.01/.03	.00/.01	.00/.01	.00/.00	.00/.00	.00/.00	.00/.00
2 drinks in 1 hour	.06/.07	.05/.06	.04/.05	.03/.04	.03/.03	.02/.03	.02/.02	.02/.02
3 drinks in 3 hours	.06/.09	.05/.06	.03/.05	.02/.03	.01/.03	.01/.02	.00/.01	.00/.01
3 drinks in 2 hours	.08/.10	.07/.09	.05/.06	.04/.05	.03/.04	.02/.03	.02/.03	.01/.02
4 drinks in 4 hours	.09/.11	.06/.08	.04/.06	.03/.05	.02/.03	.01/.02	.00/.02	.00/.01
4 drinks in 3 hours	.10/.13	.08/.10	.06/.08	.05/.06	.03/.05	.03/.04	.02/.03	.01/.03
5 drinks in 5 hours	.11/.14	.08/.11	.05/.08	.04/.06	.02/.04	.01/.03	.00/.02	.00/.00
3 drinks in 1 hour	.10/.12	.08/.10	.07/.08	.06/.07	.05/.06	.04/.05	.04/.05	.03/.04
5 drinks in 4 hours	.13/.16	.09/.12	.09/.10	.05/.07	.04/.06	.03/.05	.02/.04	.01/.03
4 drinks in 2 hours	.12/.15	.09/.12	.08/.10	.06/.08	.05/.07	.04/.06	.04/.05	.03/.04
5 drinks in 3 hours	.14/.18	.11/.14	.09/.11	.07/.09	.06/.08	.05/.06	.04/.05	.03/.04
5 drinks in 2 hours	.16/.19	.13/.16	.10/.13	.09/.11	.07/.09	.06/.08	.05/.07	.05/.06

One Drink = One bottle of beer (12 oz.)
       = One glass of wine (6 oz.)
       = One "single" drink ($1\frac{1}{4}$ oz. of liquor)

LOW RISK DRINKING GUIDELINES:
Men: 3 drinks per day, *max,* and 14 drinks per week, *max.*
Women: 2 drinks per day, *max,* and 9 drinks per week, *max.*

NO AMOUNT OF ALCOHOL IS SAFE IF YOU ARE DRIVING. YOUR RISK OF CRASHING GOES UP, *EVEN WITH VERY SMALL AMOUNTS.* NO AMOUNT IS SAFE IF YOU ARE PREGNANT OR TRYING TO GET PREGNANT.

Source: National Highway Traffic Safety Administration. Appendix. http://www.nhtsa.dot.gov.

Because of the known dangers of drinking and driving, an effective means of measuring one's blood alcohol level is essential. The most effective is a blood test. However, drawing blood is an invasive and expensive procedure and therefore cannot be required. Urine alcohol testing indicates the presence of alcohol in a person's system but not the current condition (see Breathalyzer, 2007). After $1\frac{1}{2}$ to 2 hours, the alcohol shows up in the urine, so this is a measure of the drinker's condition from several hours before. A dehydrated person, moreover, will have a higher BAC than one with a normal level of fluid in his or her system. This information is crucial in contested driving while intoxicated (DWI) cases. The Breathalyzer is the next most accurate measure.

Most people are quite intoxicated at 0.15% and comatose at 0.4%. Individual differences, however, are striking, with high-tolerance alcoholics functioning well up to levels of 0.3% when others would appear visibly drunk. When alcohol levels are between 0.5 and 1%, the breathing center in the brain or the action of the heart may be anesthetized. If vomiting does not prevent intoxication at this level, death will swiftly follow. Since marijuana prevents nausea and inhibits the vomiting response, the combination of alcohol and marijuana can be lethal.

For a better understanding of what drugs do to the body, let us look more closely at the metabolization process. Alcohol, as we have seen, is metabolized more slowly than it is absorbed. The BAC peaks 30 to 45 minutes after the consumption of one standard drink. After a night of hard drinking, therefore, a person may still be legally intoxicated when driving to work the next morning. At two drinks per hour, a 160-pound man would have a BAC of 0.047% at the end of the first hour. If he had two cans of beer each hour for 6 hours, his BAC would be 0.191%.

Because it is technically a food and because it enters the body by being swallowed, alcohol can be readily metabolized. Other drugs, such as Valium and amphetamines, tend to be swallowed as well. Swallowing drugs, as Jung (2001) indicates, is a relatively slow form of delivery, so the effects are not felt for a few minutes to an hour. Other methods of drug delivery are more direct, such as inhalation, as in the case of cocaine snorting, "snuff" or smokeless tobacco, or glue sniffing. These drugs, like those that are injected, reach the brain quickly and so have a rapid intoxicating effect.

Valium, unlike alcohol, is transformed by the liver's enzymes into various compounds that have greater, rather than fewer, effects on the user (Benshoff & Janikowski, 2000). Whereas Valium is only very gradually eliminated from the body, amphetamines are completely eliminated about 2 days after the last use. Their peak effect occurs about 2 to 3 hours after use. Caffeine is absorbed into the body in about a half-hour, with the maximum impact occurring about 2 hours later. About 90% of this drug is metabolized or absorbed, and about 10% is excreted through the urine (Benshoff & Janikowski, 2000). Unlike alcohol, which is detectable in the blood and urine, cocaine, due to its rapid metabolism, cannot be so readily detected (Jung, 2001).

Fascinating in its implications, research by Chen, Parnell, and West (2001) shows that in laboratory rats, nicotine lowers one's BAC. As a result, more alcohol was consumed to achieve the desired effect. Implications for humans who drink and smoke are that, due to their high tolerance, they will be inclined to consume large quantities of alcohol. Consequently, long-term damage to the body organs associated with long-term alcohol misuse is likely. For pregnant women who drink and smoke, damage to the fetus can be serious for the same reason.

Cannabis, or marijuana, which is fat soluble but not water soluble, is metabolized by the liver and distributed throughout the body much more slowly than alcohol. Cannabis enters readily through cell membranes and is retained in the body for long periods of time (Jung, 2001). Drugs that are fat soluble leave long-lasting traces due to their slow release from fat stores (Price, 2000). For this reason, many persons on parole have been returned to prison for drug use even though tested 1 month after ingesting marijuana.

Drugs tend to be used in combination rather than singly. Many of the deaths caused by drug taking occur because the impact of drugs in combination is far greater than the potency of each drug singly or added together. The chemical reaction of two drugs together often has a multiplying or synergistic effect. Among the elderly, drinking can be especially dangerous because of the interactions of alcohol with medications they are apt to be taking (U.S. Department of Health and Human Services, 2000). The prevalence of polydrug use is often overlooked in research and surveys. The combination of alcohol and tobacco is common, as is the use of illicit drugs and alcohol. Sometimes the user combines drugs to maximize the effect and sometimes to subdue it. For the latter purpose, alcohol is frequently drunk in conjunction with cocaine and amphetamines (Jung, 2001). Valium may be used as well to counter the overstimulating effect of cocaine. This combination apparently was what TV and film actor Robert Downey Jr. was after when he had his much-publicized relapse (four small bags of cocaine and 16 Valium pills were found in his hotel room). He later tested positive for both drugs (France & Horn, 2001). A large proportion of deaths due to heroin overdoses are actually the result of taking alcohol and heroin together (Gardner, 2000). The most dangerous practice is combining two sedatives, such as alcohol and Valium. Many deaths have occurred as well from the liver damage due to the combination of alcohol and Tylenol (U.S. Department of Health and Human Services, 2000). Alcohol impairs the liver's ability to clear toxins from the blood and can easily lead to an overdose. The combination of cold and flu remedies plus Tylenol can lead to liver failure as well. The surprising fact about this popular over-the-counter drug is how unaware the public is of its dangers.

From NIDA's (2006) *Infofacts,* we learn that in the majority of known drug-related deaths, more than one drug was involved. Heroin is the illicit drug most frequently involved in accidental deaths, followed by cocaine.

Denning, Little, and Glickman (2004) describe drug interactions as occurring from the byproducts formed by two dangerous drugs in combination. Alcohol and cocaine in combination, for example, combine to create a new substance that may be especially toxic to the liver. Moreover, alcohol is metabolized by enzymes in the liver. If another drug requires the same enzymes, the removal of both is slowed, with possibly dire consequences. Forty percent of the people who took high doses of Tylenol (eight extra-strength tablets) in a recent experiment showed signs of liver damage (C. Johnson, 2006).

THE BRAIN AND ADDICTION

If we can unravel the secrets of the brain, we can understand the forces that drive humans into paths of destructiveness, their cravings, passions, and dreams. Today, we may not know all the answers, but for the first time, neuroscientists have captured images of the brain of addicts in the throes of craving a drug. And it is this craving that is the root of addiction itself, the craving that sends people back into the dungeon—the gambling den, the bar, the crack house—again and again.

The actions of alcohol and cocaine that cause intoxication, initiate and maintain excessive drug-using behavior, and drive the relentless craving during abstinence occur primarily in the brain. Some basic understanding of the effects of drugs like alcohol and cocaine on the mechanisms underlying brain function is essential to develop and improve addiction prevention and treatment strategies. Contemporary research on the brain and behavior is forthcoming all the time; such research helps clarify the mysteries of addiction. Two aspects of brain research are crucial for our understanding of addiction: First is the adaptation factor—how the brain adapts to and compensates for the abnormal signals generated by the drug. The second aspect, one we know far less about, concerns uniqueness in the brains of potentially addicted persons. Before coming to the innate differences in the way the brains of addicts respond to drugs (i.e., the genetic component), let us summarize what scientists know about the workings of the brain itself with regard to addiction.

THE BRAIN

The brain and the spinal cord together make up the central nervous system (see Figure 4.2). The brain and spinal cord are hollow structures filled with cerebral-spinal fluid. Alcohol, as a drug affecting the central nervous system, belongs in a class with the barbiturates, minor tranquilizers, and general anesthetics—all depressants. Whereas at low levels of alcohol ingestion an excitement phase may set in, including uninhibited and erratic emotional expression, later a gradual dullness and stupor may occur. The effect of the alcohol on motor activity is seen in slurred speech, unsteady gait, and clumsiness. Functioning at the higher level—thinking, remembering, and making judgments—is tangibly impaired by alcohol. Before considering some of the grave neurological consequences of long-term alcohol and other drug misuse, we consider how alcohol affects the brain at the cellular and biochemical levels, which directly affect the emotions.

Each nerve cell of the brain is separated from its neighbor by a narrow gap called a *synapse*. Nerve cells communicate with one another by way of chemical messengers called *neurotransmitters;* most commonly, however, drugs disrupt neurotransmitter functions because they happen to resemble the chemical structure of the brain's own neurotransmitters (Lambert, 2000). Neurotransmitters underlie every thought and emotion as well as memory and learning (Nash, 1997). A good half dozen of some 50 are known to play a role in addiction. Figure 4.3 illustrates the neuron cell membrane.

Cocaine, like alcohol, brings about marked changes in brain chemistry. According to the Harvard Medical School (1993), accumulated evidence indicates that cocaine's chief biological activity is in preventing the reuptake (reabsorption) of the neurochemical transmitter dopamine. Drug-addicted laboratory rats will ignore food and sex and tolerate electric shocks for the opportunity to ingest cocaine. A depletion of dopamine following cocaine use

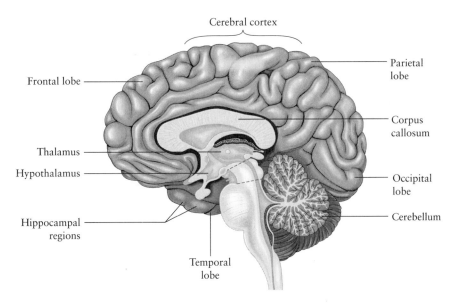

FIGURE 4.2

SCHEMATIC DRAWING OF THE HUMAN BRAIN, SHOWING
REGIONS VULNERABLE TO ALCOHOLISM-RELATED
ABNORMALITIES.

Source: NIAAA. *Alcohol Alert,* October 2004, no. 63, p. 4. Available at www.niaaa.nih.gov/publications.

probably accounts for cocaine binges, tolerance, craving, and the obsessive behavior of cocaine users. The body cuts back on the oversupply, which is why increasing doses of cocaine are needed to keep the user feeling normal (Ginsberg, Nackerud, & Larrison, 2004). And as researchers and the general public are increasingly aware, nicotine behaves remarkably like cocaine, causing a surge of dopamine in addicts' brains. Dopamine is the "feel-good" neurotransmitter; too little dopamine is implicated in the tremors of Parkinson's disease, and too much causes the bizarre thoughts of schizophrenia. This drug-generated surge in dopamine is what triggers a drug user's high (Nash, 1997).

Serotonin is another neurotransmitter highly influenced by alcohol and other drug use. Serotonin is involved in sleep and sensory experiences. It has received a great deal of attention from researchers and the popular press. Decreased levels of this neurotransmitter have been linked to behaviors associated with intoxicated states, depression, anxiety, poor impulse control, aggressiveness, and suicidal behavior. Middle-aged and older men with a combination of alcohol dependence and mood disorders are at particularly high risk of suicide (Sher, 2006).

As Figure 4.4 shows, cocaine blocks the reuptake of certain chemicals by neurons in the brain. It is these nerve cells that release the neurotransmitters. Studies with genetically altered mice suggest that cocaine's effect may involve not only dopamine but possibly dopamine and serotonin in combination

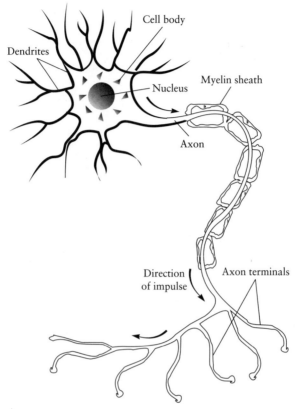

FIGURE 4.3 │ NEURON CELL MEMBRANE

Structural features of a neuron: This drawing depicts the major components of neuronal structure, including the cell body, nucleus, and dendritic trees. At the axon terminal, the synapse links the neuron to another neuron.

Source: NIDA. 2007a. *Mind over Matter: Teacher's Guide.* Available from http://teens.drugabuse.gov/mom/tg_nerves.asp.

(Stocker, 1999). Further research is needed to reveal the exact effect of the multiple neurotransmitters.

The discovery through brain imaging and genetics of the role that serotonin plays in addiction and also in mental disorders, in conjunction with simultaneous discoveries of drugs that reduce drug cravings in rats and monkeys, has opened up a whole world of medical possibilities. We now know that nicotine, for example, sends a rush to the brain's "pleasure center," where cocaine and amphetamines do their work (McFarling, 1998). Continued smoking, like other drug use, actually changes the brain. People with brain receptor types more prone to addiction could be helped with intensive prevention efforts. One antidepressant, Zyban, is commonly prescribed as an aid to stop smoking. For addictive types, breaking the smoking habit is reportedly as difficult as ending heroin addiction.

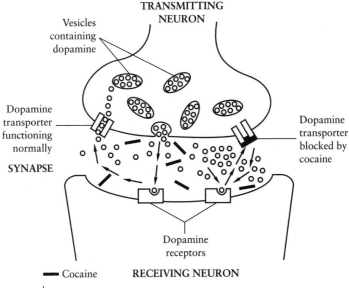

TRANSMITTING NEURON

Vesicles containing dopamine

Dopamine transporter functioning normally

SYNAPSE

Dopamine transporter blocked by cocaine

Dopamine receptors

— Cocaine   RECEIVING NEURON

FIGURE 4.4 | COCAINE IN THE BRAIN

In the normal communication process, dopamine is released by a neuron into the synapse, where it can bind with dopamine receptors on neighboring neurons. Normally, dopamine is then recycled back into the transmitting neuron by a specialized protein called the dopamine transporter. If cocaine is present, it attaches to the dopamine transporter and blocks the normal recycling process, resulting in a build-up of dopamine in the synapse that contributes to the pleasurable effects of cocaine.

When cocaine enters the brain, it blocks the dopamine transporter from pumping dopamine back into the transmitting neuron, flooding the synapse with dopamine. This intensifies and prolongs the stimulation of receiving neurons in the brain's pleasure circuits, causing a cocaine "high."

Source: NIDA. 2007b. *Mind over Matter: Teacher's Guide.* Retrieved from http://www.drugabuse.gov/NIDA_Notes/ NNVol13N2/Brain.html.

Preliminary reports from Europe document that a drug used to treat epilepsy (Topiramate or Topamax) appears to curb cocaine craving in rats and monkeys. Now this drug, which already has a proven record of safety, may legally be used to reduce cravings for all kinds of addictions, including gambling and food addiction (Ehrenfeld, 2005). The drug is thought to work by enhancing the release of the GABA (gamma aminobutyric acid). GABA is an inhibitor that keeps desire from overwhelming us. Preliminary studies with Topamax are very promising. This drug could prove to be a powerful weapon against numerous addictions, including cocaine and nicotine, according to the report.

Alcohol, as Sharon Begley (2001) suggests, opens the neurotransmitter floodgates. Dopamine, serotonin (governing our sense of well-being), and GABA (which, when released, regulates anxiety and has a soporific effect) are all involved in producing a high. Recent research is focusing increasingly on the connection

FIGURE 4.5 | THE REWARD PATHWAY

One pathway important to understanding the effects of drugs on the brain is the reward pathway, which consists of several parts of the brain highlighted in this diagram: the ventral tegmental area (VTA), the nucleus accumbens, and the prefrontal cortex. When the brain is activated by a rewarding stimulus (e.g., food, water, sex), information travels from the VTA to the nucleus accumbens and then up to the prefrontal cortex.

Source: The National Institute on Drug Abuse (NIDA). Retrieved from www.drugabuse.gov/pubs/teaching/ Teaching3.html.

between GABA receptor genes and alcohol, which enhances GABA activity (Hasin, Hatzenbuehler, & Waxman, 2006). The search for a genetic predisposition to alcoholism has led researchers to the finding of a strong relationship between alcoholism and receptor GABA, A2 receptor genes on chromosome 4. We can anticipate much more attention to this neurotransmitter in the future.

Through the use of sophisticated technology such as functional magnetic resonance imaging (fMRI), scientists can observe the dynamic changes that occur in the brain as an individual takes a drug. Researchers are now recording the brain changes that occur as a person experiences the rush, or high, and later, the craving for cocaine (NIDA, 2003). They can even identify parts of the brain, the pleasure circuits, that become active when a cocaine addict sees stimuli such as drug paraphernalia that trigger the craving for the drug. The memories of drug use are so enduring and so powerful that even seeing a bare arm beneath a rolled-up sleeve reawakens the cue-induced craving (NIDA, 2003). The situation is similar to Pavlov's dog salivating when it heard a bell associated with food ring. Relapse occurs, as every AA member knows, from visiting the old haunts from drinking days ("Slips occur in slippery places"). Now there is scientific proof for this folk wisdom about the importance of avoiding people, places, and things associated with past drug use. Figure 4.5 is a diagram of the reward pathway in the brain.

Relapse might also reflect the brain changes described by Leshner (2006). Recall that to produce a high, a drug such as cocaine keeps the transporters of dopamine from clearing the synapse of dopamine following the release

(U.S. Department of Health and Human Services, 2000). Cocaine, for example, blocks the removal of dopamine from the synapse, resulting in an accumulation of dopamine and feelings of euphoria. As Begley (2001) explains, "When all the seats on this so-called transporter molecule are occupied by cocaine, there is no room for dopamine, which therefore hangs around and keeps the pleasure circuit firing" (p. 42). This firing releases dopamine into the synapse. The neurotransmitter in turn must attach itself to receptors on the next cell to fire some more. Repeated activation enhances the high. Repeated activation also leads to cell adaptation over time. Drugs, therefore, don't have the same effect as they did before. This is called tolerance (see NIDA, 2003). With the same dosage, the drug user can't achieve that original high because his or her brain has changed.

An inmate from Oklahoma State Penitentiary describes how, even after years of sobriety, craving can rear its ugly head:

> One thing I observed was the force of psychological addiction. OSP is a maximum security prison, but drugs are as plentiful as blackberries in the spring; however, there are inevitable interruptions, meaning that nobody here can become physically addicted. I lived with one man—the first person I ever saw use a needle—who bought heroin when it was available. He was exceptionally bright and his family was wealthy. He and I would read from dawn to dusk and sometimes not say 20 words to one another, although we were locked in a cell the size of a bathroom for 24 hours a day. He was refined, considerate, gracious, and fairly laid back, the kind of cellmate one does not stumble on often. After 2 months, he received word that some heroin was available. For hours before it arrived, he was a changed man, pacing frantically, jumping up every few minutes to look out the door, noticeably agitated. His anxiety consumed him . . . and amazed me. When it arrived, he was in obvious haste to use it and did not slow down until the needle came out of his arm. I associated all those manifestations with physical addiction. I subsequently saw others who would lie, steal, and risk their life for marijuana. I don't doubt that you know all about this phenomenon, but I had no idea psychological addiction was so intense, especially in sporadic users. I'm addicted to chocolate, and I assumed it was something like that. It's not. (personal communication, November 11, 2003)

Current theories of addiction rely heavily on neurobiological evidence showing connections between addiction-related behaviors and neural structures and functions (Nestler, 2005). Addiction is a brain disease, as Leshner (2006) suggests. These brain changes are neural adaptations to brain functioning under the influence of the drug (Whitten, 2005). When the use is discontinued, the system experiences a breakdown of sorts. Almost all drugs of abuse are believed to induce two kinds of changes in brain structure and function. These are the loss of motivation—to achieve, engage in fun activities, and so forth—and the storing of emotional memories of the high (H. C. Johnson, 2004).

Even though the initial drug taking is a voluntary act, Leshner explains, once neurochemical changes have occurred with prolonged use, the compulsion to return to drug taking or drinking is no longer voluntary. An addict's brain is therefore different from a nonaddict's brain. As some researchers indicate, however, the notion of brain injury is more accurate than the notion of brain disease in describing the course of events involving changes in the brain due to substance misuse. It can be argued, as does Thombs (1999), that the brain of the addict is not so much diseased as injured by exposure to self-administered toxins. As with other injuries, healing can occur when the source of the injury has been eliminated.

The discovery that different parts of the human brain are activated during cocaine *rush* versus cocaine *craving* may be useful in the development of medications for reducing the craving that makes relapse almost a matter of course (Stocker, 1998). Particular regions of the brain can be associated with levels of feeling because cocaine-addicted volunteers can now, with the new technology, rate their rush experiences and their cravings associated with cues. Cues such as the smell of marijuana or cigarette smoke and pictures of drugs such as meth or cocaine trigger this memory. The fact that memory sites are involved in connection with the cues is consistent with drug users' reports of strong feelings associated with drug use and their intense response to what researchers term their "feeling memories" (Whitten, 2005). Such memories of intense pleasure can last a lifetime (H. C. Johnson, 2004). Cues related to the drug evoke the memories and involve serious risk of relapse.

The craving that can preoccupy an addict's mind and very being involves the irresistible urge to get another rush. The memory of past euphoria, coupled with dopamine deficit related to long-term use, means the addict seeks out drugs not to feel low (Nash, 1997). Due to neuronal damage caused by extensive drug use, the individual can no longer feel pleasure normally. Traditionally, it was thought that the reason addicts continue to drink and use was to ward off withdrawal symptoms. As Derrington (2000) indicates, however, the study of various drugs of addiction reveals this is not the case. Cocaine produces no physical withdrawal symptoms, but it is recognizably more addictive than heroin. The drive to return to drug use therefore must be associated with memory as well as with the changes in brain chemistry. Even mere anticipation of receiving cocaine has been shown, in rat studies, to lead to a surge in dopamine in the brain (Phillips, Stuber, Heien, Wrightman, & Carelli, 2003). Hyman (2005) has introduced an "extreme memory" theory to explain the potential of craving. The idea behind this theory is that the human brain for survival purposes evolved to respond to essentials such as food or water or sex. The reward is release of dopamine. Long-term memories are laid down through conditioning. Drugs usurp the system to the extent that the brain overlearns the urge to repeat the experience. Addiction can thus be viewed as a malfunction of the normal human craving for excitement. This new model opens the way to search for medical solutions to breaking the memories of the pleasure of the drug.

What about craving for alcohol? Viewing pictures of alcoholic beverages does activate specific areas of the brain, according to research from the Medical University of South Carolina (*Science Daily,* 2001). The significant finding in this research is that heightened brain activity shows up in problem drinkers only and not in moderate drinkers. This result speaks to biological differences between persons inclined toward addiction and those not so inclined.

Researchers can diminish the euphoric effects of alcohol and other drugs in addicts by giving them drugs that increase the availability of serotonin. Such medications reduce craving because the addiction is to the rush, the euphoria, and not to the substance itself. Later in this chapter and in chapter 5, we will see how medications such as Ondansetron, which acts on serotonin, can help some alcoholics in recovery by reducing their craving for drugs. Following a year or two of recovery, the brain, as far as we know, replenishes itself (Thombs, 1999). Perhaps this is why long-term treatment has been found more successful than the short-term variety. Those who remain in treatment for at least a year, notes Alter (2001), are more than twice as likely as short-termers to remain clean.

What do the brain studies show about male–female differences in neurological damage caused by drug use? Only in recent years have brain studies devoted attention to alcohol-related brain damage in alcoholic women. Results of brain imaging studies show that thinking and memory abilities are markedly affected in female alcoholics compared to females without drinking problems and that brain shrinkage is more pronounced in women than in men with similar drinking histories (*Alcoholism About,* 2003). This research confirms earlier speculation that women alcoholics perform as poorly on memory and special tasks as male alcoholics, even when they haven't been drinking as long as the men.

Research on cocaine's effects on male and female brains, on the other hand, seems to indicate that women process cocaine cues differently from men (Whitten, 2004). As reported by Whitten, an experiment measured the blood flow in the brains of addicts as they listened to a script about cocaine. In both the women and men, the pleasure centers of the brain were activated. During this craving period, however, the brain research showed that part of the emotional response to the craving in women was inhibited. The significance of this difference requires further study; the findings could have important treatment implications, as craving is a key factor in relapse.

Although science is uncovering so many mysteries of the neurobiology of addiction, one question left unanswered is why some people are so highly susceptible to the effects of addictive substances while so many others can just "take it or leave it." These differences in people probably, at least in part, have something to do with genetic makeup.

THE ROLE OF GENES

A widely publicized study of more than 20,000 people in mental hospitals, nursing homes, and prisons found that 53% of those who used chemical substances had a mental disorder such as schizophrenia, anxiety, or major depression (Holloway, 1991). More recently, in testimony before the House Subcommittee on Labor, Health and Human Services, and Education, T. R. Insel (2005), the director of the National Institute on Mental Health, submitted the following information: "Mental and substance abuse disorders are inherently intertwined with co-occurring diagnoses of substance abuse and mental disorders. . . . Substance use disorders are especially prevalent in individuals with schizophrenia (47%), bipolar disorder (45%), anxiety (25%), and major depression (24%)" (p. 2).

Bipolar (manic-depressive) disorder, for example, has a close association with chemical dependence. In their review of the literature, Brady and Sinha (2005) found that estimates ranged between 45 and 86% of men and women with substance use disorders who also had at least one co-occurring psychiatric disorder, and the risk relationship appeared to be reciprocal. This finding of dual disorders in the same individual suggests an underlying biological vulnerability for a number of disabilities. This vulnerability is interactive in that it involves a biological predisposition to overreact to stress in combination with a high-risk, nonprotective, stressful environment (Brady & Sinha, 2005; H. C. Johnson, 2004). Brady and Sinha's model is based in part on animal studies showing that early life trauma and chronic stress result in long-term changes in stress responses. Such changes can alter the dopamine system and can increase susceptibility to stress, leading in turn to the altering substances.

H. C. Johnson (2004) points to the role of serotonin in the addiction process. Decreased levels of this neurotransmitter have been linked to behaviors associated with intoxicated states, depression, anxiety, poor impulse control, aggressiveness, and suicidal behavior. The usual search for whether the mental disorder or the addiction came first may thus be futile. Similarly, a specific vulnerability may not be to alcohol misuse but, rather, to problems with a number of substances. A brain susceptibility to addiction itself may prevail.

Although the *DSM–IV* dichotomizes substance dependence and substance abuse for purposes of classification, more recent genetics research indicates that the tendency toward addiction, like varieties of mental illness, exists along a continuum (Russo, 2007). A gene that relates to risk taking and impulsiveness, for example, is found to vary along a continuum from healthy behavior to extremely high-risk taking, with heroin addicts having the gene for extreme novelty-seeking behavior. The new research gives scientific support to longstanding claims that alcoholism and other addictions are intergenerational.

That there appears to be a genetic tendency for alcoholics and drug addicts to be likely to use an array of different mood-altering substances is revealed in the following description provided by an anonymous wife of an alcoholic:

> At most AA meetings candy, cakes, doughnuts, etc. will be available in large quantities. This appears to be the norm; the addict gives up one substance, but the psychological attribute that allowed addiction to one also carries over to other substances.
>
> My father-in-law, when trying to stop drinking, would become obsessed with ice cream and frozen yogurt. He lived in the country, but would travel to town at least three times a day to eat his ice cream, shakes, sundaes.
>
> My husband has been in recovery for 10 years. His father, grandmother, grandfather, mother, uncles, aunts, all are alcoholics.

Why does alcoholism seem to run in families? Is alcohol behavior learned or inherited? The search for genetic links began in earnest in the early 1970s with adoption studies in Scandinavia. The aim of these studies was to separate environmental from hereditary determinants. Goodwin (1976) sought an answer by interviewing 133 Danish men who'd been adopted as small children and raised by nonalcoholics. Health records were used to substantiate the interviews. The findings are striking: The biological sons of alcoholics were four times as likely to have alcohol problems as the children of nonalcoholics. This result has helped put to rest the popular assumption that alcoholics take up drinking simply because they learned it at home or turned to it because of abuse suffered at the hands of an alcoholic parent. Goodwin's findings are given further credence in a new study from Washington University conducted by Duncan et al. (2006). Using a design that compared hundreds of the offspring of identical twins, researchers determined that there does not appear to be any relationship between exposure to paternal alcoholism during childhood and later development of substance use problems in the children. Genetic influences appear more crucial than modeling the father's behavior as predictors of addiction policies, according to the researchers. In fact, many children who grow up in alcoholic families learn from a negative example of how not to behave, so they are influenced by a heavy drinking father not to follow in his footsteps.

Cloninger et al.'s research in Sweden (1989) helped clarify the role of environment as well as heredity in the development of alcoholism. In the early 1980s, Cloninger joined a team of Swedish researchers and began gathering extensive data on a large group of adopted-away sons of alcoholics. Sweden was chosen, as Denmark before, because of the availability of thorough government records on every citizen.

In Cloninger et al.'s (1989) study of 259 male adoptees with alcoholic biological fathers (of a total of 862 male adoptees), it was found that a somewhat larger proportion of the adoptees with alcoholic fathers were registered with Swedish authorities for alcohol-related problems than were adoptees with nonalcoholic fathers. Alcohol misuse in the adoptive parents, however, was not a determinant of alcohol misuse in the sons. The adopted men were subdivided according to their frequency and severity of registered misuse. Herein lies the major significance of the study: It determined that there is more than one kind of alcoholism.

Cloninger's first group of alcoholics, the Type 1 alcoholics, about 75% of the total, developed the illness gradually over time. It was also known as "milieu-limited alcoholism" because of the environmental influence; low socioeconomic status of the adoptive father seemed to be the key influence. Type 1 alcoholics have personality traits that make them susceptible to anxiety. In response to the antianxiety effects of alcohol, they rapidly become drug tolerant and dependent and have difficulty terminating drinking binges once they have started. The individual prone to this type of alcoholism avoids situations involving harm or risk and seeks approval from others. Guilt feelings are associated with the drinking and with its consequences.

The Type 2 alcoholic, on the other hand, is a risk taker. Type 2 is also called "male-limited alcoholism" because males dominate this category. Personality traits that distinguish this type of drinker are early and sudden development of alcoholism, hyperactivity, antisocial personality traits, and a history of fights while drinking. More recent research conducted by Langbehn, Cadoret, Caspers, Troughton, and Yucuis (2003) reported an increased risk for drug use and dependence among adoptees whose biological parents had a lifetime history of both antisocial personality disorders and substance misuse. Type 2 alcoholism is highly hereditary, passing from father to son, and associated with low levels of serotonin and dopamine in the brain. Cloninger recognizes that Types 1 and 2 are not completely discrete and that there is much overlap between categories.

Brain scans do reveal striking differences among nonviolent alcoholics of the Type 1 variety and among alcoholics with a history of violence (Immen, 1995). A research team in Finland discovered that Type 2 people have a higher than normal number of receptors in the brain and that the substance is absorbed almost immediately for an intense but short-lived rush. Type 1 individuals, in contrast, get to enjoy the substance for a longer period.

A school counselor from Oshkosh, Wisconsin, describes the characteristics of two of her family members:

> Oh my goodness, the Type 1 characteristics personify my father completely. He is prone to severe anxiety and turns to alcohol due to its antianxiety effects. He has never, to my knowledge, attempted to stop drinking. Rather, he turns to alcohol whenever trouble arises. For instance, recently we had to call the ambulance because my mother collapsed. While I turned to prayer, I saw him reach for the bottle, his whole hand shaking. We were both very upset over the situation; however, we turned to different sources for comfort. Further, he avoids situations involving any harm or risk and is very conscious of what others think of him. He is the type of father who doesn't like it when his children do an activity together, such as go on vacation, because his "eggs are all in one basket." He doesn't hunt and has many fears of succumbing to harm. I have not noticed any guilt feelings, but we don't have heart-to-heart conversations, either!
>
> Although I did not know it at the time, my ex-husband was definitely a Type 2 alcoholic. He started drinking at an early age and developed a high tolerance for alcohol. He could be described as hyperactive. He had difficulty sitting still and flitted from one activity to another. He definitely had an antisocial personality, and frequently got into fights while drinking. His pattern was quite predictable; however, I didn't even recognize it as alcoholism at the time. He would get dressed up to go out for the evening. This would consist of visiting several bars. He would *never* just have a couple of drinks. He always drank rapidly and heavily until he achieved intoxication. He would start to act silly and sometimes speak loudly, and would frequently end up fighting with someone. He had a quick temper to begin with, and drinking made it much worse. (personal communication, November 8, 1999)

Similarly, from a prison inmate we learn:

> I don't like to diagnose myself, but under Cloninger's theory I would say that I do tend to fit this category of Type 2 traits. I have taken risks all my life, e.g., drunk

driving, stealing liquor, confrontation with police, indiscreet relationships. I have been hyperactive in my early years. I definitely have to some degree today an antisocial personality: I tend to want to be by myself; I don't like having long conversations with anyone. And I have been in many physical confrontations over the years; in fact, that is why I am in prison now. Also, I believe that I have a low level of serotonin. That is why I believe that I have suffered from depression and suicidal thoughts in the past. After a few years of sobriety, I have just started to come out of the depression and now have a heart to learn about what the heck is wrong with me. The one thing that scares me about Cloninger's study is the fact it can be passed down from father to son. I have two adult sons, and as far as I know neither one of them drinks (their mother never drank). I hope it stays that way. (personal communication, July 1997)

Further scientific validation for the Type 1–Type 2 theory is experimentation with a multiauthored study led by Bankole Johnson, MD, on effects of the medication Ondansetron. Ondansetron, which appears to work by acting on serotonin, was found, in a highly empirical, randomized study, to have little or no effect on the Type 1, or late-onset, variety of alcoholic. It was effective in reducing consumption in patients of the early-onset variety, however. These results led the researchers to conclude that Ondansetron may ameliorate an inherited abnormality in that alcoholic subtype (B. A. Johnson et al., 2000). Personal e-mail correspondence with Bankole Johnson of September 13, 2000, confirms that this drug was effective with the small sample of Type 2 females as well.

Elsewhere, NIAAA (2003) reports a correlation between pain sensitivity and Type 2 alcoholism. According to this study, researchers have shown that all alcoholics perceive stimuli strongly, as do children of alcoholics. Drinking may be one way to adapt to the sensitivity.

Electroencephalographic (EEG) tests of sober alcoholics reveal excessive high-frequency brain waves. Researchers have found that male children of alcoholics also have a lower voltage of EEG activity overall, as do Native Americans, indicating a possible susceptibility to alcoholism (Schuckit, 2000). However, not all EEG studies are in agreement with these findings. A more recent report summarizing brain research based on modern imaging technology provides some indication of a distinctive feature in one brain-wave pattern that can be a marker for later susceptibility to the development of alcoholism (NIAAA, 2006a). Most likely, this finding of subtle brain chemistry differences in children of alcoholics relates to differences in natural opioid activity in the brain that may translate into a difficulty in handling stress.

Rodent studies provide further evidence for genetic factors in alcoholism. As described in the *Tenth Special Report to the U.S. Congress: Alcohol and Health* (U.S. Department of Health and Human Services, 2000), scientists have bred strains of rats with different levels of susceptibility to alcohol effects. Through selective breeding, one strain voluntarily works to acquire large amounts of alcohol. Alcoholic rats get excited when mildly intoxicated; the nonalcoholic strains of rats do not. EEG patterns may vary also. When the drug fluoxetine (Prozac), which raises serotonin levels, is administered to alcoholic rats, alcohol consumption is reduced accordingly.

Twin studies, brain wave studies, and animal studies are other areas of research linking genetics and alcoholism. Studies on twin males suggest that, in men, a strong craving for sweets is linked to a tendency to alcoholism, according to new research from the University of North Carolina. This finding, although on a small sample of 19 sets of twins who were not alcoholic but who had alcohol problems may be significant in leading to a screening test for youth at high risk ("Study Links Cravings," 2000).

Studies of identical twins indicate a likelihood that if one identical twin is alcoholic, the other is likely to be alcoholic also. Twin studies compare behaviors in identical and nonidentical twins or likenesses in twins who were separated at birth. Research shows that about half of alcoholism vulnerability has a genetic basis. When one in a pair of identical twins is alcoholic (or a smoker), the likelihood that the other twin has the same problem is between 40 and 60% (Hasin et al., 2006). Adoption studies reveal a risk in children of alcoholics who were adopted at birth by other parents that is three to four times the risk for other children (APA, 2000). Finding the genes involved in addiction vulnerability is thus a high priority for scientific research. In both animal experiments and research on humans, low sensitivity to alcohol-induced sedation is associated with higher alcohol consumption levels, as the NIAAA (2003) report on hereditary factors indicates. By identifying the proteins these genes encode and the mechanisms that determine the animal's response to alcohol, scientists can pursue the development of pharmaceuticals that short-circuit these genetically defined processes (U.S. Department of Health and Human Services, 2000).

Genetic differences in personality factors may indirectly render some individuals more vulnerable than others to drug dependence. People who compulsively seek novelty, the adventure seekers, also tend to experiment with drugs more than persons who are cautious by nature and prefer routine. The same dopamine system, in fact, is apparently activated both by drugs and by risk-taking adventures such as parachute jumping (Begley, 2001). New research on pathological gambling shows that gambling disorders run in families (Black, Monahan, Temkit, & Shaw, 2006). Relatives of compulsive gamblers disproportionately had substance use problems and personality and mental disorders.

It has long been known that introverts, subject to a strong reaction to stimuli and concomitant anxiety, are inclined to get sleepy under the influence of alcohol, whereas extraverts are inclined to feel more stimulated and ready for action. Variously called introverted, shy, or harm avoidant, individuals who react strongly to stress are prime candidates for misuse of alcohol and tranquilizing drugs. Monkey research offers some evidence that future drinking may be predicted by responses to stress during infancy.

Genetic factors showed that some monkeys separated from their mothers at birth had high cortical concentration in their blood. In adulthood, these more sensitive monkeys drank more alcohol than did other monkeys that had endured the same degree of stress (NIAAA, 2000c). Relevant revelations from a study on children from alcoholic families, presumably highly stressful situations, show that many exhibit extreme play inhibition (Bower, 1999). Together, both studies confirm a nature–nurture interconnectedness.

Now researchers are finding that mice lacking an enzyme (PKCe) are far less likely to consume alcohol than those with this enzyme ("Enzyme Linked," 2000). Mice lacking PKCe react strongly to a limited amount of alcohol and to tranquilizers (benzodiazepines) as well; the absence of this enzyme enhances the effect of alcohol and other depressants on a molecule receptor involved in the transmission of feelings of relaxation and sedation. The findings from this study support the emerging concept that increased sensitivity to intoxication reduces the likelihood that a person will become an alcoholic. If these results are confirmed in humans, they may provide a means to help identify high-risk youth for targeted intervention programs (NIAAA, 2000a).

Genetic differences in people can also inhibit the risk of addiction. Many Asians, for example, suffer rapid metabolism of alcohol to the poison acetaldehyde. This leads to greater buildup of this toxic product in the bloodstream, which produces flushing and palpitations (U.S. Department of Health and Human Services, 2000). Marc Schuckit (2000) includes Israelis and the Maori peoples of New Zealand along with Asians as groups that experience negative reactions to alcohol consumption. All three groups have a lower rate of alcoholism than other ethnic populations, at least in part because of this genetic anomaly.

Another "defective" gene sometimes found in humans prevents nicotine addiction. Men with this genetic mutation are unlikely to become addicted to cigarettes and are likely to be able to quit smoking easily, according to recent research (NIDA, 2000b). It is thought that persons with certain genetic variations can tolerate more nicotine without feeling sick, and therefore, they smoke more and are highly inclined to become addicted (American Psychological Association, 2005). Common genes likely play a part in the strong link between nicotine and ethanol intake in the same individuals.

According to the theory of evolution, members of a species develop traits that are best adapted to their environment, with the result that more of their offspring survive who have those traits. Writing in the best-selling *Genome*, Ridley (2000) provides a striking example of genetic adaptability to the environment by ethnic groups isolated for long periods. The ability to regularly drink alcohol without developing dependence, which most people have in countries where water was unsanitary, resulted from thousands of years of selection of people who could drink. Nomadic peoples in Australia and North America, however, who lived where water was safe, did not require alcohol and developed no resistance to its effects. Such changes that do occur through adaptation, however, have developed through a long evolutionary process (Ginsberg et al., 2004).

Differences in brain chemistry may predispose some people to become users not only of depressants such as alcohol but also of stimulants. In this case, those with lower levels of dopamine D2 receptors in their brains are more inclined than others to like the effect of stimulants (NIDA, 2004). New findings from NIDA demonstrate that cocaine-addicted people have decreased D2 receptors throughout various subdivisions of the brain. Meanwhile, researchers from the National Institutes of Health (2006) are opening many new avenues of research into common factors in genetic vulnerability (differences in the sequence of DNA among individuals) to addiction through their scanning of the human genome to identify genes linked to substance misuse. Studies currently underway are helping to identify how the variations in relevant genes contribute to differences in addiction vulnerability.

Previous research on dopamine receptor genes in smokers, reported in *Science News*, reveals a strong link between a deficiency in this area and severe problems in quitting the habit (Seppa, 1998). Because nicotine is a stimulant and alcohol a depressant, and in light of findings based on twin studies showing a strong correlation between smoking and alcoholism in twins, recent speculation is that smoking may increase the risk of alcoholism by reducing sensitivity to alcohol ("Why Do Some People?" 2000). Although the gateway theory that one drug leads to another has been largely discounted, these research findings give some credence to the notion that the effect of smoking may increase the tolerance for drinking, and tolerance, as we know, is associated with alcohol dependence. For persons wishing to curb their drinking consumption, smoking cessation might be the place to start.

In his book on attention-deficit disorder (ADD) (now called attention-deficit hyperactivity disorder [ADHD] in the 2000 *DSM*), Gabor Maté (1999) comments on the high rate of smoking among persons who have the characteristics of short attention span, often combined with hyperactivity. It is easy to understand, he says, the appeal addictive substances have for such individuals. Nicotine improves mental efficiency, for example. Typically, the individual with hyperactivity is driven to work excessively, to spend money, also excessively, and likely to engage in risk taking such as experimentation with drugs. The self-medication factor is pronounced as well in drug use by people with ADHD in that it improves their level of concentration. An article in the *American Family Physician* (2006) summarizes new research confirming a relationship between smoking and ADHD behaviors. Adolescents who self-report ADHD tend to smoke at an earlier age of onset and to smoke a higher quantity of cigarettes than adolescent smokers who do not have these characteristics.

In conclusion, there is no one genetic marker by which scientists or physicians could determine who will become alcohol dependent. As with other genetic disorders, as Schuckit (2000) cautions, it is likely that a variety of genetic characteristics, in combination with key environmental factors, contribute to the risk of addiction.

MEDICAL CONSEQUENCES OF SUBSTANCE MISUSE

Alcohol misuse costs the United States a staggering $185 billion a year, more than all illegal drugs combined; these costs were attributed to lost productivity, healthcare expenditures, motor vehicle crashes, and so on (NIAAA, 2006a).

American businesses lose an estimated $134 billion a year in lost productivity, on-the-job accidents, compensation claims, and absenteeism from alcohol misuse alone (Brink, 2004). Yet insurance coverage for substance abuse treatment is far from meeting the need.

Because alcohol is water soluble, the body absorbs alcohol directly into the bloodstream. Alcohol's molecules easily travel across the blood–brain barrier and affect brain functioning almost immediately. Alcohol can even cross the placental barrier and affect fetal development in a way that no other drug can. Over the years, medical scientists have documented the effects of alcohol on the body's organs and its role on the development of a variety of psychological problems, including brain structure and functioning, liver cirrhosis, cardiovascular diseases, and fetal alcohol syndrome (McNeece & DiNitto, 2005). In contrast, research on the long-term effects of some of the newer drugs is in its infancy.

Alcohol misuse can be an indirect cause of death such as by a heart attack. The best available estimates have been provided by the *Journal of the American Medical Association* (Mokdad, Marks, Stroup, & Gerberding, 2004); the estimates are inferred from mortality records of alcohol-related conditions and traffic deaths. Their findings of deaths related to indulgence of various sorts for the year 2000 are:

1. tobacco 435,000   18.1%
2. alcohol 85,000   3.5%
3. diet and nutrition 400,000   16.6%
4. illicit drugs 17,000   0.7%

Because many of the estimated deaths associated with alcohol intoxication were due to injuries sustained in accidents, suicides, drownings, and homicides, much of the loss of life is of young people—people in their prime, who would have had many years ahead of them. Note that the numbers of estimated deaths tied to illicit drug use are only about one fifth as many as the alcohol-related deaths. Another interesting fact about mortality statistics, as reported by Sherer (2006) in the *Psychiatric Times,* is that the substance-related fatalities are occurring in an older age group than those in previous decades. In California, for example, the average age of a person who died of a drug overdose was 22 years in 1970, 32 in 1985, and 43 in 2005. Nationwide, people aged 35 to 54 years accounted for more than half of the drug misuse deaths. Reports of emergency room visits nationwide reveal a middle-aged prevalence for every category of illicit drug use, especially of cocaine and heroin.

In this section, we focus on that part of the body uniquely affected by substance (and especially alcohol) misuse—the brain.

BRAIN IMPAIRMENT

Alcohol contributes to brain damage both directly and indirectly. Levin (1995) provides a threefold classification of damage to the nervous system through alcohol misuse: (a) damage in the form of a shrinking of the brain from the toxic effects of the alcohol itself, (b) poisoning of brain cells by toxins circulating in the blood as a result of the failure of a diseased liver to metabolize them, and (c) damage to the nervous system because of nutritional deficits associated with alcoholism. Wernicke's syndrome and Korsakoff's psychosis are thought to derive from a lack of thiamine, or vitamin B_1 (NIAAA, 2004). Some researchers, however, believe the effect of alcohol per se is involved, whether directly or indirectly, from poor general health status or from severe liver disease.

Wernicke's syndrome is characterized by paralysis of normal eye movements, mental confusion, and problems with walking and balance. This syndrome, according to Osher (2000), affects one part of the brain—the midbrain and third and fourth ventricles. Korsakoff's psychosis results from damage to areas of the brain important to memory function. Wernicke's syndrome is often associated with *peripheral neuropathy,* or damage to the peripheral nerves. Numbness in one's lower legs is the consequence. If the numbness does not disappear with vitamin therapy, it indicates that the damage to the nervous system is permanent and irreversible. Approximately 80 to 90% of alcoholics with Wernicke's encephalopathy also develop Korsakoff's (NIAAA, 2004).

Korsakoff's psychosis, sometimes called Wernicke–Korsakoff's syndrome and popularly known as "wet brain," is a long-term result of brain damage. Patients with this disease experience much confusion and severe short-term memory deficits. They may not retain information. *Confabulation* is a unique characteristic that involves fantasizing to fill in the gaps of memory. Although the "tall tales" seem to be ridiculous fabrications or downright lies, there appears to be no "method in this madness" other than an inability to distinguish fact from fiction. Although individuals with this affliction can become paranoid on occasion, they generally have a carefree unconcern about the present or future. Figure 4.6 presents photographs of a normal cross-section of the brain and one that is severely damaged by alcohol misuse.

Research shows that chronic alcoholics have deficits in their sense of smell. A recent study confirmed that alcoholics, even in recovery, have deficiencies in prefrontal cognitive abilities as well and that these abilities are correlated with a defective sense of smell (Rupp et. al., 2006). These findings based on extensive testing of 32 alcohol-dependent patients and 30 healthy comparison subjects provide further support to the hypothesis that the frontal lobes are especially vulnerable to alcohol-related damage.

Oliver Sachs (1985), neurologist and author of *Awakenings* and *The Man Who Mistook His Wife for a Hat,* provides rich case histories of persons with neurological disorders. The second of these books gives portraits of two individuals with Korsakoff's psychosis. Mr. Thompson, an ex-grocer with severe Korsakoff's, was institutionalized for his memory problems. As Sachs describes the working of Mr. Thompson's mind, "Deprived of continuity, of a quiet, continuous, inner narrative, he is driven to a sort of irrational frenzy—hence his ceaseless tales, his confabulations, his mythomania" (p. 111). Lack of feelings is a key characteristic of this condition. This man had become desouled, according to Sachs. Typically, such patients fail to realize the tragedy of the

FIGURE 4.6 | REDUCED BRAIN MASS IN ALCOHOLICS

Images displayed in the coronal orientation from MRI and DTI studies of a 61-year-old healthy man (upper images) and a 60-year-old alcoholic man (lower images). The high-resolution MRI slices are at the same locations as the fractional anisotropy images of the DTI panels. Note on the MRI the thinner corpus callosum displaced upward by enlarged ventricles and, on the DTI, less well-delineated white matter tracts in the alcoholic man compared with the healthy man.

Source: NIAAA, 2004. *Using Magnetic Resonance Imaging and Diffusion Tensor Imaging to Assess Brain Damage in Alcoholics.* Images by Margaret Rosenbloom, Edith V. Sullivan, and Adolf Pfefferbaum. Retrieved from http://pubs.niaaa.nih.gov/publications/arh27-2/146-152.htm.

situation or the distress of their loved ones in dealing with them. (van Wormer's father suffered from Korsakoff's psychosis for the last two decades or so of his life.)

Use of the popular drug Ecstasy also may cause long-term impairment. Brain scans of heavy Ecstasy users provide evidence of neuron damage associated with an inability to use serotonin (Leshner, 1999). Similarly, after heavy methamphetamine use, the impact is seen in memory and motor coordination ("Studies Say," 2001). A review of all the brain research on marijuana users with regard to the long-term impact of use on neurocognitive abilities revealed that although marijuana carries short-term memory and learning problems, the damage is not permanent (Grant, Gonzalez, Carey, Natarajan, & Wolfson, 2003).

LIVER DAMAGE

Because the liver metabolizes alcohol ahead of anything else, the toll to the body through alcohol misuse is enormous. Chronic exposure to alcohol may result in liver damage, with some individuals more highly susceptible than others. The first manifestation of alcohol-related liver problems is the development of a fatty liver. Although the symptoms are not obvious, this condition can easily be detected through blood tests (Doweiko, 2002).

About one in three heavy drinkers eventually develops scars in the liver associated with cirrhosis—a disease in which liver cells are destroyed and the organ no longer is able to process nutrients in food. *Alcoholic hepatitis* (not the same as general hepatitis, which has a different etiology) can be considered the second stage of alcoholic liver disease. This highly dangerous condition is characterized by liver swelling, jaundice, and fever. Many persons with liver disease take on a yellow skin color, which comes from excessive amounts of bile that circulate in the bloodstream. With abstinence, this condition can be reversed. If the condition is not reversed, *cirrhosis* of the liver can occur. About 10% of all people who have been diagnosed as alcoholics develop cirrhosis (Benshoff & Janikowski, 2000). With the progression of this disease, all of the liver's functions are compromised, including, first and foremost, the immune system.

As more and more tissue of the liver is damaged over time, the liver is no longer able to effectively remove toxins from the blood. Blood pressure builds up within the vessels, and increasing pressure is put on the heart (Doweiko, 2002). Alcoholics who smoke more than one pack of cigarettes per day have three times the risk of cirrhosis as nonsmoking alcoholics (NIAAA, 1997). The scarred liver, unable to handle the usual blood flow, moreover, causes the blood to seek alternative routes to the heart. A tremendous pressure builds up in alternative vessels. When bulging veins emerge on the surface of the esophagus, the potentially fatal condition called *esophageal varices* occurs. Spidery veins may appear on the face and chest; hemorrhoids may develop. The patient may die from hemorrhaging. Edema, which is fluid accumulation in other parts of the body, is another serious consequence of cirrhosis. Large amounts of fluid can collect until the abdomen is shockingly distended.

Treatment of alcoholic cirrhosis consists of total abstinence from alcohol and careful attention to diet. For terminally ill patients, a liver transplant provides the only possibility of survival. A summary of empirical research results with liver transplantation for alcoholics reveals a survival rate equal to that of nonalcoholics who get liver transplants (NIAAA, 1993). Scientific policy evaluation, in this case, went against popular opposition to providing replacement for alcoholics who had destroyed their livers through drinking.

Because chronic heavy drinking is the primary cause of cirrhosis, the World Health Organization (2004) presents annual mortality rates by country for death due to cirrhosis. The rates provide researchers with their most reliable estimates of a nation's alcoholism rates. Some interesting examples of the cirrhosis of the liver mortality rates per 100,000 are: Greece 3.8, Ireland 3.94,

Sweden 3.97, United States 7.47, Cuba 7.6, Costa Rica 7.8, Hungary, 45.79. There is speculation that the extremely high cirrhosis of the liver rate in Hungary, as in other European countries, is related to the poor quality of the alcohol consumed (Szcs, Sárváry, McKee, & Ádány, 2005). Interestingly, as a study of these rates will show, high alcohol consumption in a population does not always mean a high rate of disease. A key factor in alcohol-related disease is how much alcohol is consumed at any one time. The reason is illustrated by the case of Wisconsin, where consumption may be spread fairly evenly across the population (Wisconsin ranks as number 1 in overall consumption and 43 among the states in cirrhosis deaths) ("Cirrhosis Mortality," 1999).

Alcoholics, especially those with liver disease, suffer a host of infections. Since alcohol interferes with the function of white blood cells, heavy drinkers are highly susceptible to colds and pneumonia. Skin diseases such as psoriasis may cover the entire body. Alcoholics also are inclined toward malnutrition, itself related to liver dysfunction. Malnutrition in alcoholics is related to poor food intake and poor metabolism of the food taken in. Additionally, digestive abnormalities and chronic diarrhea contribute to the overall susceptibility to disease. Poor nutrition, in itself, influences all aspects of immunity.

The pancreas is another trouble spot for heavy users of alcohol. A major organ of the body, the pancreas secretes digestive enzymes and insulin, which converts blood sugar. Diabetes may result from the cell damage. *Acute pancreatitis*, often caused by alcohol-induced inflammation, is an extremely painful and dangerous condition.

THE HEART

Although moderate drinking generally decreases the risk for cardiovascular disease, heavy drinking over long periods will likely have the opposite effect (WHO, 2004). Chronic alcohol use results in the suppression of normal red blood cell formation and can harm the cardiovascular system. Such heavy drinking can also cause the heart to become enlarged and lose some of its ability to contract ("Medical Consequences," 2000). Damage to heart muscle tissue is a common occurrence over long periods of time.

Nicotine is incontrovertibly implicated in the genesis of cardiovascular disease (Jung, 2001). Nicotine is both water and fat soluble; thus, it accumulates throughout the organs of the body. The effect on the smoker's heart rate is immediate (Doweiko, 2002). While the heart rate is increased, the peripheral blood flow in the body is reduced due to constriction of the blood vessels. The blood pressure rises, and the heart has to work harder. Over 400,000 persons per year die due to tobacco use; the majority of these deaths are from heart disease and stroke, not lung cancer (Fishbein & Pease, 1996). Because of the propensity to continue to smoke during recovery from alcoholism, the leading cause of death for recovering alcoholics is tobacco-related illness (Varner, 1992).

Cocaine is the drug most closely associated in the public mind with heart problems and heart attacks. Cocaine-related deaths may occur on the first use of cocaine, although rarely, and are often a result of cardiac arrest or seizures followed by respiratory arrest. Researchers at the State University of New York at Buffalo now calculate that roughly one fourth of nonfatal heart attacks among people aged 18 to 45 result from use of the drug ("Cocaine Link," 2001). More common is a disturbance in heart rhythm, detected as an irregular heartbeat. The risk comes not in occasional use of small amounts but after tolerance has developed and increased dosage leads to toxicity (Benshoff & Janikowski, 2000). The deaths that do result are commonly due to the synergistic effect of cocaine and alcohol in combination (NIDA, 2006).

THE GENITOURINARY TRACT

In both sexes, problems with urination may result from excessive alcohol use. Indirect interference in the filtration process and the elimination of the waste produced by the kidney seems to be the problem (Kinney, 2006). When *kidney failure* follows, according to Osher (2000), the trouble is not in the kidneys themselves but in a circulating toxic factor resulting from the associated liver disease.

Effects on the *reproductive system* are widely known to accompany heavy alcohol use. The *Tenth Special Report to the U.S. Congress: Alcohol and Health* (U.S. Department of Health and Human Services, 2000) reviewed the most advanced clinical and endocrine studies in the literature. The few clinical studies of alcoholic women suggest ovulation and menstrual difficulties are caused by alcohol-induced hormonal imbalance. In men, impotence, low testosterone levels, low sperm count, and testicular atrophy are widely reported. Breast enlargement has been observed in alcoholic men, as has an absence of body hair accompanied by a lower rate of baldness.

Inasmuch as intoxication lowers inhibitions and caution may be "thrown to the wind," the risks of both AIDS contraction and unwanted pregnancy multiply. Perhaps the most tragic consequences of substance use in one generation are seen in the birth defects of the next generation. *Fetal alcohol syndrome* (FAS) is now recognized as a leading known cause of mental retardation. Medical reports confirm that the fetus takes in alcohol from the mother's blood. Whereas classical fetal alcohol syndrome may be readily identified by physical characteristics in the child—smaller upper lip, flat nose, and small head—milder defects, classified as *fetal alcohol effects* (FAE), are properly diagnosed only rarely. Figure 4.7 shows the discriminating features characteristic of children with FAS.

Although the percentage of hard-drinking mothers who have spontaneous abortions or babies with FAS is not known, it is known that habitual or even occasional drinking by an expectant mother can endanger the health of her fetus. The effect on neurological development is the greatest in the first 3 months of pregnancy (NIAAA, 2006a). By the time a fertile woman confirms her pregnancy, the damage may already be done. In countries such as South Africa, where among certain farm workers high liquor consumption during pregnancy is common, the FAS rate is extremely high.

A large dose of alcohol given to a pregnant mouse experimentally produces severe abnormalities in the developing fetus. The eye damage, stunted brain,

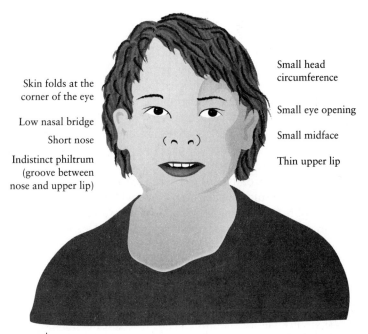

Skin folds at the corner of the eye

Low nasal bridge

Short nose

Indistinct philtrum (groove between nose and upper lip)

Small head circumference

Small eye opening

Small midface

Thin upper lip

FIGURE 4.7 | FETAL ALCOHOL SYNDROME

Facial features characteristic of fetal alcohol syndrome (FAS).

Source: NIAAA. *Alcohol Alert,* October 2004, no. 63, p. 5. http://niaaa.nih.gov/publications/aa63/aa63.htm.

and facial deformities that result are reminiscent of human babies with FAS (Steinmetz, 1992).

The role of intoxication on male sperm and its impact on the conceived child has only recently been studied. Sperm susceptibility to environmental damage, such as pesticides, of course has been known for years; recent studies link male smoking to the birth of underweight infants. Rodent experiments reveal learning difficulties in offspring of morphine-exposed fathers. Data on cocaine's ability to bind to sperm ("Cocaine May Piggyback," 1991; Taleff & Babcock, 2006) indicate the need for further studies on the long-unrecognized impact of male intoxication on development of the fetus. In a review of studies on the impact of alcohol consumption in male rats on their offspring, the U.S. Department of Health and Human Services (2000) concluded that damaged sperm may indeed have an impact on the development of the unborn child.

Longitudinal studies indicate that FAS and FAE exist on a continuum of cognitive-behavioral defects. School-age children born of heavily drinking mothers are found to be highly distractible in their learning operations. Hyperactivity, subnormal intelligence, and mood problems are found to persist over time. Long-term treatment for high-risk pregnant women is one of the greatest unmet needs of alcoholism prevention efforts today. Help for adults who suffer the effects of FAS is also hard to find.

Diagnosis of FAS and FAE has always been difficult. Through magnetic resonance imaging (MRI), we can now compare brain structures in normal adolescents with those exposed in utero to the effects of maternal heavy drinking. Imaging studies have demonstrated structural abnormalities in some brain regions but not in others. Although such research is in its infancy, what we do know is that prenatal alcohol exposure can cause specific irreversible damage and that such brain damage may be present even in the absence of identifiable facial characteristics. Although too expensive for regular use, this technology offers much promise for the future detection of fetal alcohol syndrome in children and adults and clarification of which areas are most affected. A recent news report from Canada indicates that a simple test that tracks eye movements can accurately diagnose fetal alcohol syndrome (Ubelacker, 2005).

What is the effect of cocaine use on unborn children? Are "crack babies" the hopeless cases that earlier media reports made them out to be? In fact, as experts inform us, alcohol and nicotine pose greater dangers to unborn babies than does crack cocaine ("Tobacco, Alcohol," 1998). Fortunately, infants exposed to crack often outgrow their health problems, especially when placed in a nurturing environment. The same is not true for alcohol-exposed babies, however. Tobacco use by pregnant women, according to this report, is highly associated with sudden infant deaths and respiratory problems in babies. Oddly, recent research on mother–child pairs seems to indicate that among adolescent girls whose mothers smoked, drug use is common. Boys whose mothers smoked had a high rate of conduct disorder (Varisco, 2000).

Opiates, like alcohol, cross the placental barrier in pregnant women; babies born to heroin addicts thus have withdrawal symptoms, and some die as a result (Benshoff & Janikowski, 2000). In the Midwest, an increasing number of methamphetamine-addicted babies are being delivered in area hospitals. Because meth has more long-lasting effects than cocaine, experts fear the impact of prenatal exposure could be more long lasting (Lippert, 2000).

SUMMARY AND CONCLUSION

For direct practice with alcoholics and other addicts, the helping professional requires advanced knowledge of the physiology of chemical addiction, including the basic characteristics and organic effects of each of the popular sedative and stimulant drugs. To work with clients, a biological understanding of the nature of addiction, and especially of the kind of relentless craving that accompanies drug use, is essential. (Recovering professionals have an experiential knowledge of such urges that puts them on the same wavelength as their clients; all counselors and educators can benefit, however, from an awareness of the brain changes that make addiction what it is.) Brain imaging has brought about unprecedented breakthroughs in our knowledge. Virtually all psychoactive drugs, as we now know, affect a single pathway deep within the brain and activate the limbic reward system in various ways. The new techniques that enable researchers to view these workings within the limbic system also make it possible to observe changes in the brain caused by prolonged use of harmful chemicals. Previously, those alterations could only be inferred. Scientists can now experience addiction secondhand as an image on a screen; in so doing, they have hit upon some elements in human nature that defy logic. In a real sense, they have brought us face to face with some of our most primitive, pleasure-seeking drives, which may or may not spell addiction.

We are all creatures of biology and of our genes. If we succumb to getting hooked on toxic substances, the physiological damage to the brain, liver, heart, or unborn child can be severe. In focusing on the *bio* portion of the biopsychosocial model of addiction, this chapter has described the most commonly used drugs of choice. Divided into four basic categories—depressants, stimulants, hallucinogens, and cannabis—the drugs of choice were discussed in terms of their chemical properties and metabolism. Then we proceeded to move into more uncharted territory by addressing the imponderables: Is addiction a brain disease? How are the brains of addicts different from those of nonaddicts? Why are some individuals more susceptible to becoming hooked on psychoactive substances than others?

The genetic factor was revealed in research on mice bred to prefer alcohol to water and in studies of children of alcoholics, many of whom displayed a high tolerance for alcohol, which paradoxically is correlated with the later development of alcoholism. Since the mid-1990s, research has offered new understandings both as to why addiction runs in families and also about the precise nature of the damage that psychoactive substances do to the body, most interestingly to the brain. The addicted brain, as we now realize, is significantly different from the normally functioning brain. Through long-term drug misuse, the depletion of the brain's natural opiates creates a condition ripe for the kind of relentless craving that is known to all "who have been there." Compounding the problem of molecular alterations in the brain (experienced as a general malaise) is the fact that each time a neurotransmitter such as dopamine floods a synapse through the introduction of a powerful drug like crack or meth into the body, circuits that trigger pleasure are indelibly imprinted in the brain. So when the smells, sights, and sounds associated with the memory are experienced, these feeling memories are aroused as well. So palpable, in fact, are these feeling memories that researchers can now compare the brain of the addict in a state of craving (elicited by these behavior feelings) with the brain of the addict in a stationary state.

Solutions, to be true solutions, must be directed at the source of the problem. First, the rather tired motto "Learn to say no" could perhaps be replaced with the advice "Learn to stay away." Persons at risk of addictive behavior would do well to seek out a health-supportive environment in which to develop to their fullest potential. Second, all of us can benefit by recognizing that replacing unhealthy thoughts with healthy ones can increase our resilience in life. For alcoholics and addicts in recovery, cognitive work shows great promise in repairing much of the brain injury that has been done by heavy substance use. One of the most promising messages to come out of current research is that biochemical abnormalities associated with drug misuse can be reversed through cognitive work. Finally, many persons in recovery are achieving excellent results through use of one of the new medications on the market. Such medications, such as the nicotine patch, have been developed to target the dopamine and serotonin receptors associated with the kind of relentless cravings that drive a person to relapse. We explore both pharmaceutical and cognitive interventions in chapter 5.

REFERENCES

Abadinsky, H. (2003). *Drug abuse: An introduction* (5th ed.). Belmont, CA: Wadsworth.

Alcoholics Anonymous World Services. (1976/orig. 1939). *Alcoholics anonymous.* New York: Author.

Alcohol in Australia: Issues and strategies. (2000). National Alcohol Action Plan 2000–2003. Retrieved August 2002 from www.drinkingchoices.com.

Alcoholism About. (2003, November, 23). Drinking and the female brain. Retrieved January 2007 from http://alcoholism.about.com/cs/women/a/aa010604.htm.

Alter, J. (2001, February 12). The war on addiction. *Newsweek,* pp. 36–39.

American Family Physician. (2006, May 1). Relationship between smoking and ADHD behaviors. *American Family Physician.* Retrieved January 2007 from http://www.aafp.org/afp/20060501/tips/3.html.

American Lung Association. (2006, March). *Smoking 101 Fact Sheet.* Retrieved August 2006 from http://www.lungusa.org/site.

American Psychiatric Association (APA). (2000). *Diagnostic and statistical manual of mental disorders, text revision* (4th ed.). Washington, DC: Author.

American Psychological Association. (2005, March 6). Studies underscore genetic involvement in nicotine addiction and aggressive hostility. *APA Online.* Press Release. Retrieved January 2007 from http://www.apa.org/releases/gene_variations.html.

Arif, A. A., & Rohrer, J. E. (2005). Patterns of alcohol drinking and its association with obesity: Data from the third National Health and Nutrition Examination Survey, 1988–1994. *BMC* (Biomed Central) *Public Health, 5,* 126. Retrieved July 2006 from http://www.jointogether.org.

Associated Press. (2005, May 8). Meth use rots teeth of inmates in prison. *Des Moines Register,* p. 3B.

Bauer, B. (2006, December 6). Wrestling with the aftereffects of meth. *Daily Iowan,* p. 1A.

Begley, S. (2001, February 12). How it all starts in your brain. *Newsweek,* pp. 40–43.

Benshoff, J. J., & Janikowski, T. P. (2000). *The rehabilitation model of substance abuse counseling.* Belmont, CA: Wadsworth.

Bhattacharya, S. (2003). Alcoholic blackouts may lead to heavier drinking. *Alcoholism: Clinical and Experimental Research, 27,* 628.

Black, D. W., Monahan, P. O., Temkit, M. H., & Shaw, M. (2006). A family study of pathological gambling. *Psychiatry Research, 141*(3), 295–303.

Blumstein, A. (2000). Disaggregating the violence trends. In A. Blumstein & J. Wallman (Eds.), *The crime drop in America* (pp. 13–44). New York: Cambridge University Press.

Boston Globe. (2005, July 15). Meth math [Editorial]. *Boston Globe.* Retrieved July 2006 from http://www.boston.com.

Bower, B. (1999, April 10). Social fears may raise alcoholism risk. *Science News,* pp. 155, 230.

Brady, K., & Sinha, R. (2005). Co-occurring mental and substance use disorders: The effects of chronic stress. *American Journal of Psychiatry, 162,* 1483–1493.

Braun, S. (1996). *Buzz: The science and lore of alcohol and caffeine.* New York: Oxford University Press.

Breathalyzer. (2007). *Wikipedia.* Retrieved January 2007 from http://en.wikipedia.org/wiki/Breathalyzer.

Brick, J., & Erickson, C. (1998). *The pharmacology of abuse and dependence.* New York: Haworth.

Brink, S. (2004). The price of booze. *U.S. News & World Report,* pp. 48–50.

Bureau of Justice Statistics. (2003). *Criminal offenders statistics.* U.S. Department of Justice. Retrieved July 2006 from http://www.ojp.usdoj.gov/bjs/crimoff.htm.

Canadian Centre on Substance Abuse. (2006, March). Assessing the high costs of substance abuse. *Acting News, 16*(1), 1, 4.

Center for Substance Abuse Research. (2004). Rohypnol. Retrieved July 2006 from http://www.cesar.umd.edu.

Centers for Disease Control and Prevention (CDC). (2005). General alcohol information. CDC. Atlanta, GA: Department of Health and Human Service. Retrieved October 2006 from http://www.cdc.gov/about.

Chen, W.-J., Parnell, S., & West, J. R. (2001). Nicotine decreases blood alcohol concentration in neonatal rats. *Alcoholism: Clinical and Experimental Research, 25,* 1072–1077.

Chung, C. (1999, October 18). Blackout binge. ABC *20/20* [Television broadcast].

Cirrhosis mortality low in Wisconsin, drinking high. (1999, February 4). *Waterloo Courier,* p. C9.

Cloninger, C. R., Sigvardsson, S., Gilligan, S., van Knorring, A., Reich, T., & Bohman, M. (1989). Genetic heterogeneity and the classification of alcoholism. *Advances in Alcohol and Substance Abuse, 7,* 3–16.

Cocaine link to heart attack bolstered. (2001, January 13). *Science News, 159,* 24.

Cocaine may piggyback on sperm into egg. (1991). *Science News, 140,* 246.

Cohen, G. (2001, February 12). The "poor man's heroin." *U.S. News & World Report,* p. 27.

DanceSafe. (2006). Promoting health and safety within the rave and nightclub community. Retrieved July 2006 from http://www.dancesafe.org.

Dell, C. (2005, November 7–9). What the data tell us about volatile solvent abuse in Canada. Invited paper presentation by the National Institute of Drug Abuse. Retrieved July 2006 from www.drugabuse.gov.

Denning, P., Little, J., & Glickman, A. (2004). *Over the influence: The harm reduction guide for managing drugs and alcohol.* New York: Guilford Press.

Derrington, A. (2000, April 29). Drugs that flip your switches: Toe to toe. *Financial Times,* p. 2.

Douglas, J. (2006, June 16). Abuse of pain drug fentanyl on the rise. *The Plain Dealer.* Retrieved July 2006 from www.cleveland.com.

Doweiko, H. E. (2002). *Concepts of chemical dependency* (5th ed.). Pacific Grove, CA: Brooks/Cole.

Duncan, A., Scherrer, J., Fu, Q., Bucholz, K., Heath, A., True, W., et al. (2006). Exposure to paternal alcoholism does not predict development of alcohol-use disorders in offspring. *Journal of Studies on Alcohol and Drugs, 67*(5), 649–656.

Dunn, P. (2000). Dynamics of drug use and abuse. In A. Abbott (Ed.), *Alcohol, tobacco, and other drugs: Challenging myths, assessing theories, individualizing interventions* (pp. 74–110). Washington, DC: NASW Press.

Durazzo, T. C., Gazdzinski, S., Banys, P., & Meyerhoff, D. J. (December 2004). Cigarette smoking exacerbates chronic alcohol-induced brain damage: A preliminary metabolite imaging study. *Alcoholism: Clinical and Experimental Research, 28*(12), 1849–1860.

Ehrenfeld, T. (2005, June 13). New hope for addicts? *Newsweek,* p. 68.

Encyclopaedia Britannica. (2006). Alcohol and drug consumption. Macropaedia (15th ed., pp. 195–223). Chicago: Encyclopaedia Britannica.

Enzyme linked to alcohol craving. (2000, June 16). *Substance Abuse News.* Retrieved from http://www.jointogether.org.

Evans, M. (2001, April 12). Marijuana-like substances are found to trigger appetite. *Des Moines Register,* p. 7A.

Fals-Stewart, W. (2003). The occurrence of partner physical aggression on days of alcohol consumption: A longitudinal diary study. *Journal of Consulting and Clinical Psychology, 71*(1), 41–52.

Finn, P. (2005). Russia's one-step program: Scaring alcoholics dry. *Washington Post,* p. A23.

Fishbein, D., & Pease, S. (1996). *The dynamics of drug abuse.* Boston: Allyn & Bacon.

Fisher, G., & Harrison, T. C. (2005). *Substance abuse: Information for school counselors, social workers, therapists, and counselors.* Boston: Allyn & Bacon.

France, D., & Horn, J. (2001, February 12). Robert Downey, Jr. takes one day at a time. *Newsweek,* pp. 52–54.

Fred, S. (2005, January 11). Study explores inhalant abuse among teens. *NASW News,* p. 11.

Gardner, D. (2000, September 11). Do our drug laws harm us more than they help? *Ottawa Citizen Online.* Retrieved January 2007 from http://www.mapinc.org/drugnews/v00/n1355/a06.html?152.

Ginsberg, L., Nackerud, L., & Larrison, C. (2004). *Human biology for social workers: Development, ecology, genetics, and health.* Boston: Allyn & Bacon.

Global Information. (2006, May). Alcoholic drinks in Sweden. *Euromonitor International.* Retrieved July 2006 from http://www.theinfoshop.com/study.

Gmel, G., Bissery, A., Gammeter, R., Givel, J., Calmes, J., Yersin, B., et al. (2006, March). Alcohol-attributable injuries in admissions to a Swiss emergency room. *Alcoholism: Clinical and Experimental Research, 30*(3), 501–509.

Goodwin, D. (1976). *Is alcoholism hereditary?* New York: Oxford University Press.

Gordis, E. (1997). Alcohol metabolism. *Alcohol Alert, 35*(371), 1–6.

Grant, I., Gonzalez, R., Carey, C., Natarajan, L., & Wolfson, T. (2003). Non-acute (residual) neurocognitive effects of cannabis use: A meta-analysis study. *Journal of the International Neuropsychological Society, 9,* 679–689.

Greenberg, R. (2006, April 30). Reefer madness redux [Letter to the editor]. *Des Moines Sunday Register,* p. 20P.

Harris, G. (2004). What all social workers should know about MDMA (Ecstasy). *Journal of Social Work Practice in the Addictions, 4*(1), 23–37.

Harvard Medical School. (1993). Update on Cocaine. Part II. *Howard Medical Health Letter, 10*(3), 1–8.

Hasin, D., Hatzenbuehler, M., & Waxman, R. (2006). Genetics of substance use disorders. In W. Miller & K. Carroll (Eds.), *Rethinking substance abuse: What the science shows and what we should do about it* (pp. 61–77). New York: Guilford Press.

Hensley, L. (2002, September). Drug-facilitated sexual assault on campus. *Journal of College Counseling*. Retrieved January 2007 from http://www.findarticles.com.

Higley, J. D. (2001). Individual differences in alcohol-induced aggression. *Alcohol Research and Health, 25*(1), 12–19.

Holloway, M. (1991, March). Treatment for addiction. *Scientific American,* pp. 95–103.

Hyman, S. E. (2005). Addiction: A disease of learning and memory. *American Journal of Psychology, 162,* 1414–1422.

Immen, W. (1995, June 30). Drugs may help overcome alcohol problems, study finds. *Globe and Mail,* p. A4.

Insel, T. R. (2005, April 27). Testimony before the House Subcommittee on Labor-HHS-Education Appropriations. Washington, DC: U.S. Congress.

Johnson, B. A., Roache, J. D., Javors, M. A., DiClemente, C., Cloninger, C., Prihoda, T., et al. (2000). Ondansetron for reduction of drinking among biologically predisposed alcoholic patients: A randomized controlled trial. *Journal of the American Medical Association, 284*(8), 963–971.

Johnson, C. (2006, July 5). High Tylenol doses linked to liver woes. *The Washington Post.* Retrieved July 2006 from http://www.washingtonpost.com/wp-dyn.

Johnson, H. C. (1999). *Psyche, synapse, and substance: The role of neurobiology in emotions, behavior, thinking, and addiction for nonscientists.* Greenfield, MA: Deerfield Valley.

Johnson, H. C. (2004). *Psyche and synapse expanding worlds: The role of neurobiology in emotions, behavior, thinking, and addiction for non-scientists* (2nd ed.). Greenfield, MA: Deerfield Valley.

Join Together. (2001, July 9). Naltrexone effective in treating heroin addiction. *Join Together Online.* Retrieved January 2007 from http://www.jointogether.org.

Join Together. (2005a, March 2). Studies look to Ecstasy to ease stress. *Join Together Online.* Retrieved July 2006 from http://www.jointogether.org.

Join Together. (2005b, August 25). Study faults "rapid detox." *Join Together Online.* Retrieved July 2006 from http://www.jointogether.org.

Join Together. (2006, May 25). Meth crackdown may have triggered rise in addiction. *Join Together Online.* Retrieved July 2006 from http://www.jointogether.org/news/headlines.

Jung, J. (2001). *Psychology of alcohol and other drugs: A research perspective.* Thousand Oaks, CA: Sage.

Kaufman, M. (2006, May 26). Study finds no cancer-marijuana connection. *Washington Post,* p. AO3.

Kinney, J. (2006). *Loosening the grip: A handbook of alcohol information* (8th ed.). Boston: McGraw Hill.

Klam, M. (2001, January 21). Experiencing Ecstasy. *New York Times Magazine,* pp. 38–43, 64–73.

Klatsky, A. L., Morton, C., Udaltsova, N., & Friedman, G. D. (2006). Coffee, cirrhosis, and transaminase enzymes. *Archives of Internal Medicine, 166*(11), 1190–1195.

Lisa, L. (2001, January 25). *Alcoholism—my personal story.* Class presentation, University of Northern Iowa, Cedar Falls.

Lambert, C. (2000, March/April). Deep cravings: New research on the brain and behavior clarifies the mysteries of addiction. *Harvard Magazine*, pp. 60–68.

Langbehn, D. R., Cadoret, R. J., Caspers, K., Troughton, E., & Yucuis, R. (2003). Genetic and environmental risk factors for the onset of drug use and problems in adoptees. *Drug Alcohol Dependency, 64*(2), 151–167.

Lê, A. D., Li, Z., Funk, D., Li, T., & Shaham, Y. (2006). Increased vulnerability to nicotine self-administration and relapse in alcohol-naïve offspring of rats selectively bred for high alcohol intake. *Journal of Neuroscience 26,* 1872–1879.

Lee, D. (2001, January 1). About that hangover. *Courier-Journal* (Louisville, KY), p. 1E.

Lee, Y. (2006). House allows federal prosecution of medical marijuana users. *All Headline News*. Retrieved July 2006 from http://www.allheadlinenews.com/articles.

Leinwand, D. (2006, January 11). Meth cases put strain on ERs. *USA Today*. Retrieved July 2006 from http://usatoday.printthis.clickability.com.

Leshner, A. I. (1999). We can conquer drug addiction. *The Futurist, 33*(9), 22–30.

Leshner, A. I. (2006). The addiction recovery guide: Your Internet guide to drug and alcohol addiction recovery. Retrieved June 2006 from http://www.addictionrecoveryguide.org.

Levin, J. D. (1995). *Introduction to alcoholism counseling: A bio-psycho-social approach*. Washington, DC: Taylor & Francis.

Lippert, J. (2000, June 23). Meth infants called the new "crack babies." *Des Moines Register*. Retrieved from http://www.geocities.com/joanlippert/methinfants.html.

Martin, Fr. J. (1972). *Chalk talk on alcohol* [Revised. video]. Aberdeen, MD: Kelly Productions.

Maté, G. (1999). *Scattered: How attention deficit disorder originates and what you can do about it*. New York: Plume.

McCarthy, C. (2000, July 23). Life sentences, no time off for innocence. *The Sun* (Baltimore), p. 1A.

McCourt, M. (2000). *Singing my him song*. New York: HarperCollins.

McFarling, V. L. (1998, August 4). New nicotine therapy targets brain. Lexington (KY) *Herald-Leader*, pp. A1, 5.

McNeece, C. A., & DiNitto, D. M. (2005). *Chemical dependency: A systems approach* (3rd ed.). Boston: Allyn & Bacon.

Mead, D. (1999, April 8). Guest lecture on youth and drugs. University of Northern Iowa, Cedar Falls.

Medical consequences of alcohol abuse. (2000). *Alcohol, Research and Health, 24*(1), 27–31.

Medical news & perspectives. (1998, July 8). *Journal of the American Medical Association, 280*(2), 122.

Mokdad, A. H., Marks, J. S., Stroup, D. F., & Gerberding, J. L. (2004). Actual causes of death in the United States. *Journal of the American Medical Association, 291,* 1238–1245.

Naqvi, N., Rudrauf, D., Damasio, H., & Bechara, A. (2007, January). Damage to the insula disrupts addiction to cigarette smoking. *Science, 315,* 531–534.

Nash, M. (1997, May 5). Addicted. *Time*, pp. 69–76.

National Cancer Institute. (2003). *Smokeless tobacco: Health and after effects*. Retrieved July 2006 from http://cancercontrol.cancer.gov./

National Center on Addiction and Substance Abuse (CASA). (2003). Underaged drinkers more likely to drink excessively as adults. *CASA White Paper*. Retrieved June 2006 from http://www.casacolumbia.org/absolutenm.

National Center on Addiction and Substance Abuse (CASA). (2006). *Women Under the influence*. Baltimore: Johns Hopkins University Press.

National Highway Traffic Safety Administration. (2007). Appendix. Retrieved March 2007 from http://www.nhtsa.dot.gov.

National Institute on Alcohol Abuse and Alcoholism (NIAAA). (1993, April). Alcohol and nutrition. *Alcohol Alert, 22*, 1–3.

National Institute on Alcohol Abuse and Alcoholism (NIAAA). (1997, October). Alcohol, violence, and aggression. *Alcohol Alert 38*, 1–6.

National Institute on Alcohol Abuse and Alcoholism (NIAAA). (1998, January). Alcohol and tobacco. *Alcohol Alert, 39*, 1–5.

National Institute on Alcohol Abuse and Alcoholism (NIAAA). (2000a, July). From genes to geography: The cutting edge of alcoholism research. *Alcohol Alert, 47*, 1–4.

National Institute on Alcohol Abuse and Alcoholism (NIAAA). (2000b, April). Imaging and alcoholism: A window on the brain. *Alcohol Alert, 48*, 1–6.

National Institute on Alcohol Abuse and Alcoholism (NIAAA). (2000c, May 22). Stress hormone linked to increased alcohol consumption in animal model. *NIH News Advisory*, pp. 1–2.

National Institute on Alcohol Abuse and Alcoholism (NIAAA). (2001). Strategies plan 2001–2005. Retrieved July 2006 from http://pubs.niaaa.nih.gov/publications.

National Institute on Alcohol Abuse and Alcoholism (NIAAA). (2003, July). The genetics of alcoholism. *Alcohol Alert, 60*, 1–3.

National Institute on Alcohol Abuse and Alcoholism (NIAAA). (2004). Alcohol's damaging effects on the brain. *Alcohol Alert, 63*. Retrieved January 2007 from http://pubs.niaaa.nih.gov/publications.

National Institute on Alcohol Abuse and Alcoholism (NIAAA). (2005). *Fall semester—A time for parents to revisit discussions about college drinking*. College Drinking Prevention website. Retrieved October 2006 from http://www.collegedrinkingprevention.gov.

National Institute on Alcohol Abuse and Alcoholism. (NIAAA). (2006a). *NIAAA five year strategic plan: Alcohol across the lifespan*. National Institute of Health. Retrieved July 2006 from http://www.niaaa.nih.gov/publications.

National Institute on Alcohol Abuse and Alcoholism. (NIAAA). (2006b). Why do adolescents drink? *Alcohol Alert, 67*. Retrieved January 2006 from http://pubs.niaaa.nih.gov/publications/AA67/AA67.htm.

National Institute on Drug Abuse (NIDA). (2000a). *Cocaine and alcohol combined. NIDA news release*. Retrieved October 2006 from http://www.drugabuse.gov/MedAdv/00/NR6-26.html.

National Institute on Drug Abuse (NIDA). (2000b). Update on nicotine addiction and tobacco research. *NIDA Notes, 15*(5), 1–2.

National Institute on Drug Abuse (NIDA). (2002). Methamphetamine abuse and addiction. *NIDA Research Report Series*. Retrieved from http://nida.nih.gov.

National Institute on Drug Abuse (NIDA). (2003). *The brain: Understanding neurobiology through the study of addiction*. Retrieved June 2006 from http://www.drugabuse.gov/Curriculum/HSCurriculum.html.

National Institute on Drug Abuse (NIDA). (2004, September 30). PET scans show cocaine addicts have generalized decrease in D2 receptors. *NewsScan: Research*

News. Retrieved July 2006 from http://www.drugabuse.gov/newsroom/04/NS-09.html.

National Institute on Drug Abuse (NIDA), (2005, August). Prescription drugs: abuse and addictions. *NIDA Research Report,* p. 1.

National Institute on Drug Abuse (NIDA). (2006, April). Science-based facts on drug abuse and addiction. *NIDA Infofacts.* Retrieved July 2006 from http://www.nida.nih.gov/Infofacts.

National Institute on Drug Abuse (NIDA). (2007a). Mind over matter: Teacher's guide. Retrieved March 2007 from http://teens.drugabuse.gov/mom/tg_nerves.asp.

National Institute on Drug Abuse (NIDA). (2007b). Mind over matter: Teacher's guide. Retrieved March 2007 from http://www.drugabuse.gov/NIDA_Notes/NNVol13N2/Brain.html.

National Institute on Drug Abuse (NIDA). (2007c). The brain and the actions of cocaine, opiates, and marijuana. Retrieved March 2007 from http://www.drugabuse.gov/pubs/teaching/Teaching3.html.

National Institute on Drug Abuse (NIDA). (2007d). Information on drugs of abuse.

National Institutes of Health (NIH). (2006, August 24). NIH researchers complete unprecedented genetic study that may help identify people most at risk for alcoholism. *NIH News.* Retrieved October 2006 from www.nih.gov/news.

National Survey on Drug Use and Health. (2006). Past month cigarette use among racial and ethnic groups. *The NSDUH Report. Issue 30.* Retrieved July 2006 from http://oas.samhsa.gov.

Nestler, E. (2005). The neurobiology of cocaine addiction. *Science and Practice Perspectives, 3*(1), 4–12.

Northwestern Law Center on Wrongful Convictions. (2002). *The exonerated: Gary Gauger.* Retrieved July 2006 from www.law.com.

Office of National Drug Control Policy. (2005). *Drug facts: Cocaine.* National Survey of Drug Use and Health. Retrieved October 2006 from http://www.whitehousedrugpolicy.gov.

Osher, F. C. (2000). Medical complications. In J. Kinney (Ed.), *Loosening the grip: A handbook of alcohol information* (6th ed., pp. 66–129). Boston: McGraw-Hill.

Parnell, S., West, J., & Chen, W. (2006). Nicotine decreases blood alcohol concentrations in adult rats: A phenomenon potentially related to gastric function. *Alcoholism: Clinical and Experimental Research, 30*(7), 1413.

Peele, S. (1999, October). Bottle battle. *Reason, 31*(5), 52–55.

Philip Morris' spin on dying draws fire. (2001, August 9). *Waterloo–Cedar Falls Courier,* p. A6.

Phillips, P, Stuber, G., Heien, M., Wrightman, R., & Carelli, R. (2003). Subsecond dopamine release promotes cocaine seeking. *Nature, 422*(6932), 614–618.

Price, T. (2000). Alcohol and the body. In J. Kinney (Ed.), *Loosening the grip* (6th ed., pp. 41–65). Boston: McGraw-Hill.

Raloff, J. (2003, March 8). When drinking helps. *Science News,* pp. 155–156.

Ridley, M. (2000). *Genome: Autobiography of a species in 23 chapters.* New York: Harper Perennial.

Ritalin may cause brain change in children. (2001, November 12). *Washington Post,* p. A8.

Royce, J., & Scratchley, D. (1996). *Alcoholism and other drug problems.* New York: Free Press.

Rupp, C. I., Fleischhacker, W., Drexler, A., Hausmann, A., Hinterhuber, H., & Kurz, M. (2006). Olfactory deficits in alcoholism: Association with impaired executive function. *Chemical Senses, 31,* A34.

Russo, C. A., & Elixhauser, A. (2006, May). Hospitalizations for alcohol abuse disorders, 2003. *Statistical Brief #4.* Rockville, MD: Agency for Healthcare Research and Quality.

Russo, F. (2007, January 18). How to change a personality. *Time,* p. 100.

Sachs, O. (1985). *The man who mistook his wife for a hat and other clinical tales.* New York: Harper & Row.

Salemy, S. (1998, November 8). A drug that steals souls. *Des Moines Register,* p. A1.

Schuckit, M. A. (2000). Genetics of the risk for alcoholism. *American Journal on Addictions, 9,* 103–112.

Schuckit, M., Smith, T., Kalmijn, T., & Danko, P. (2005, November). A cross-generational comparison of alcohol challenges at about age 20 in 40 father-offspring pairs. *Alcoholism: Clinical and Experimental Research, 30*(3), 501–509.

Science Daily. (2001, April 16). Neuroimaging identifies brain regions possibly involved in alcohol craving. News report. *Science Daily.* Retrieved January 2007 from http://www.sciencedaily.com.

Seppa, N. (1998, March 7). Exploring a genetic link to smoking. *Science News, 153,* 148.

Shapiro, L. (1996, January 22). To your health? *Newsweek,* pp. 52–54.

Sharman, C., (2005). The problem with drinking. *Perspectives in Health: Pan American Health Organization, 10*(1). Retrieved July 2006 from http://www.paho.org.

Sher, L. (2006). Alcohol consumption and suicide. *QJM: Monthly Journal of the Association of Physicians, 99*(1), 57–62.

Sherer, R. (2006, April). Drug abuse hitting middle-aged more than gen-xers. *Psychiatric Times, 23*(4). Retrieved July 2006 from http://www.psychiatrictimes.com.

Sjogren, H., Erikson, A., & Ahlm, K. (2000). Role of alcohol in unnatural deaths: A story of all deaths in Sweden. *Alcoholism: Clinical and Experimental Research, 24*(7), 1050–1056.

Smith, S. (2007, January 18). Cigarettes packing more nicotine and puffs, researchers say. *International Herald Tribune.* Retrieved January 2007 from http://www.iht.com.

Smothers, B., Yahr, H., & Ruhl, C. (2004). Detection of alcohol use disorders in the United States. *Archives of Internal Medicine, 164*(7), 749–756.

Steinmetz, G. (1992). Fetal alcohol syndrome. *National Geographic, 181*(2), 36–39.

Stevens, P., & Smith, R. L. (2004). *Substance abuse counseling: Theory and practice* (3rd ed.). Upper Saddle River, NJ: Prentice Hall.

Stewart, P., & Sitaramiah, G. (1997, November 13). America's heartland grapples with rise of dangerous drug. *The Christian Science Monitor,* pp. 1, 18.

Stocker, S. (1998). Cocaine activates different brain regions for rush versus craving. *NIDA Notes, 13*(5), 1–4.

Stocker, S. (1999). Cocaine's pleasurable effects may involve multiple chemical sites. *NIDA Notes, 14*(2), 1–5.

Studies say meth damages brain. (2001, March 2). Retrieved from http://www.jointogether.org.

Study links cravings for sweets, alcohol. (2000, November 8). *USA Today,* Life section, p. 2.

Substance Abuse and Mental Health Services Administration (SAMHSA). (2006, June 19). *2.4 million started using pain relievers in past year.* Retrieved July 2006 from http://oas.samhsa.gov/2k6/raceCigs/raceCigs.htm.

Sweeney, D. (1990). Alcoholic blackouts: Legal implications. *Journal of Substance Abuse Treatment, 7*, 155–159.

Szcs, S., Sárváry, A., McKee, M., & Ádány, R. (2005). Could the high level of cirrhosis in Central and Eastern Europe be due partly to the quality of alcohol consumed? An exploratory investigation *Addiction, 100*(4), 536–542.

Taleff, M., & Babcock, M. (2006, June). What about Dad? *Counselor, The Magazine for Addiction Professionals, 7*(3), 72–73.

Thomas, E. (2003, October 20). "I am addicted to prescription pain medication." *Newsweek*, pp. 42–46.

Thombs, D. L. (1999). *Introduction to addictive behavior* (2nd ed.). New York: Guilford Press.

Tobacco, alcohol more harmful than cocaine during pregnancy. (1998, November 17). Retrieved from http://www.jointogether.org.

Twain, M. (1876). *Adventures of Tom Sawyer*. New York: Harper.

Ubelacker, S. (2005, November 12). New eye test can identify fetal alcohol syndrome. *Globe and Mail*, A6.

U.S. Department of Health and Human Services. (2000). *Tenth special report to the U.S. Congress: Alcohol and health*. Washington, DC: U.S. Government Printing Office.

Varisco, R. (2000). Drug abuse and conduct disorder linked to maternal smoking during pregnancy. *NIDA Notes, 15*(6), 1–2.

Varner, S. (1992, October). Preventing relapse from going up in smoke. *Professional Counselor*, pp. 31–32.

Volkow, N. D. (2005). MDMA (Ecstasy) abuse. From the director. *NIDA Research Reports*. Retrieved January 2007 from http://www.drugabuse.gov/ResearchReports/MDMA/.

Weiss, R. (2005, January 3–9). Easing fear of the greatest unknown. *Washington Post, National Weekly Edition*, p. 35.

Welsh, I. (1996). *Trainspotting*. Scranton, PA: Norton.

Whitten, L. (2004). Men and women process cocaine cues differently. National Institute on Drug Abuse (NIDA). *NIDA Notes, 19*(4). Retrieved from http://www.niaaa.nih.gov.

Whitten, L. (2005). A single cocaine "binge" can establish long-term cue-induced drug seeking in rats. *NIDA Notes, 19*(6). Retrieved June 2006 from http://www.drugabuse.gov?NIDA.

Why do some people drink too much? (2000). *Alcohol Research and Health, 24*(1), 17–26.

Winslow, R. (2006, July 11). Go ask Alice: Mushroom drug is studied anew. *Wall Street Journal*, p. B1.

World Health Organization (WHO). (1994). *Lexicon of alcohol and drug terms*. Retrieved July 2006 from http://www.who.int/substance_abuse/terminology.

World Health Organization (WHO). (2004). *Global status report on alcohol 2004*. Geneva, Switzerland: WHO. Retrieved July http://www.who.int/substance_abuse.

World Health Organization (WHO). (2006, September 20). WHO draws up measures to reduce alcohol-related harm. *World Health Organization: Press release*. Retrieved January 2007 from http://www.wpro.who.int/rcm/en/rc57/press_releases/pr_20060920.htm.

Wrinkles are traced to tobacco. (2001, March 23). *Des Moines Register*, p. 4A.

Drugs to get us off drugs? Just imagine—a generation of Americans trading in martinis for meds!

—Caroline Knapp (1999, p. 19)

INTERVENTIONS RELATED TO BIOLOGY

CHAPTER **5**

INTRODUCTION

In chapter 4, we saw how, through prolonged drug exposure, ongoing damage to the brain creates a situation of high drug tolerance and relentless craving. A major emphasis of neurobiological research today is on finding ways to restore normal brain functioning and treat what Leshner (2006) argues is a brain disease. Just as individuals with schizophrenia require medical treatments to normalize their behavior, we need to contemplate similar treatment for persons whose brain states have been altered artificially through drugs. Far from being a threat to traditional therapy, medical interventions should help clients shape up sooner and, accordingly, be more amenable to treatment.

In this chapter, we again focus on the first segment of the biopsychosocial whole—biologically based strategies applied to reduce the relentless cravings that make relapse all but inevitable. Although the psychological and social components of the illness must be attended to, as long as the "brain is screaming for booze," as Knapp (1996) puts it, "no number of revelations about underlying causes is going to counter that call" (p. 129).

In recent years, the development of medications to treat substance dependence has ushered in a new era of treatment and attitudes toward treatment. Until 1995, when naltrexone obtained government approval, the only medical treatment approved for alcoholism in the United States was Antabuse (or disulfiram). Antabuse simply kept people from drinking because, when combined with alcohol, this drug would provoke intense vomiting. The bulk of the early research in the field of substance abuse treatment focused on reducing withdrawal pain and risk. Today, pharmacological researchers are conducting clinical trials with medications, singly and in combination, designed to help alcoholics and addicts manage drug cravings and avoid a return to alcohol and often drug misuse. The search is on for new and more effective medications appropriate for populations not previously included in clinical trials: adolescents, women, and older adults with various addictions and mental disorders. One of the most promising recent research developments related to the biology of the brain comes ironically from the cognitive school. According to this research, which is still preliminary, behavioral therapies geared toward helping individuals who have problems stemming from low levels of serotonin or dopamine available in the brain can actually alter these levels of the brain's natural opiates through deliberate changes in thought processes.

This chapter looks at interventions that are derived from pharmaceutical, cognitive-behavioral, and motivational approaches. We start with a description of a highly controversial medical treatment that is founded on the principles of behavioral-conditional theory—aversion therapy. Other approaches highlighted in this chapter are methadone maintenance and other harm reduction interventions with a strong medical component, such as needle exchange and DanceSafe programming. Alternative therapies such as nutritional and herbal remedies, yoga, and acupuncture are briefly described as well. Because most of the items on assessment scales relate to the physiological dimension of alcohol and other drug use—ingestion of the substance, how much, how often, and effects on the body such as vomiting and sleeping problems—we include them in this chapter on interventions related to biology. A discussion of group interventions for clients in a very early stage of recovery concludes the chapter. The link among these seemingly diverse interventions is that they are all directed toward the biological side of addiction. For example, the group techniques chosen are those with special relevance to helping clients in the throes of early-stage recovery, when much of their thinking is still drug affected.

BEHAVIORAL THERAPIES

CHEMICAL AVERSION THERAPY

The controversial treatment intervention known as aversion treatment is based on Pavlov's classical conditioning in the form of noxious drugs that produce nausea when paired with alcohol (Burman, 2001). After four sessions of intense vomiting, patients begin to gag at the mere sight of alcohol. This form of treatment became familiar to van Wormer while she was working in Washington State counseling graduates of that program. Schick Shadel Hospital, described on its website in a testimonial as "the only place where you can turn your life around in 10 days" (2006), is a licensed medical facility that qualifies for insurance reimbursement by the major insurance companies. The website at www.schickshadel.com includes the smiling faces of ex-clients and current staff.

The oldest behavioral conditioning approach to alcoholism, aversion therapy was popular before the advent of AA. In fact, as Nan Robertson (1988, p. 184) informs us, Bill Wilson, before he cofounded AA, was treated unsuccessfully in a "purge and puke" program. This type of therapy is based on Skinner's operant conditioning principles: If drinking alcohol leads to rewarding consequences, it is likely to continue; if it leads to punishment, it is likely to be discontinued. For effective results, the punishment must be closely connected to the act. A hangover the day after or bankruptcy a year later is too far removed from the stimulus to yield to aversion therapy.

Treatment relies on nausea-inducing drugs (apomorphine, or Emetine) given in conjunction with alcohol. When this is repeated over time, the alcohol itself, ideally, will elicit nausea. The pairing of the alcohol with the emetic causes the nausea to create the desired association of the experience of vomiting with the drinking. Although there have been a number of unlicensed treatment centers that have used various forms of aversion therapy, only one licensed treatment facility survives, and that is the Schick Shadel Hospital in Seattle, Washington. Schick Shadel is a reputable treatment center, purportedly with a high success rate. Serious precautions are taken at this clinic to screen clients with health problems that could put them at risk from painful procedures. For clients with heart conditions or high blood pressure or for bulimic patients (with their damaged vomiting reflexes), shock treatments are substituted for the Emetine. Pregnant women are excluded from these treatments. As might be expected, there is a high dropout rate from these programs (Fisher & Harrison, 2005).

A full description of Schick Shadel treatment and its philosophy can be obtained on its website. Treatment today, as compared with 10 or so years ago, is no longer only for alcoholism but for problems concerning crystal meth, cocaine, and nicotine addiction. The basic underlying philosophy, according to the website (accessed July 2006), is that addiction is a physiological problem affecting the brain. Addiction messages to the brain are embedded in memory. Treatment must therefore target the signals for those memories with aversive responses. An interview with James Smith, MD, by K. van Wormer (August 7, 2006) provided the following information:

KvW: *Is any therapy or counseling provided?*

JS: Yes, we have a counseling department at our hospital (required by the state). We have certified addiction counselors who develop the continuing care aspect (what they do when they go home). AA (and the many other abstinent support groups) are described in one of the counseling groups. The continuing care program often (but not always) contains a support group.

KvW: *Is it true that "truth serum" is given to patients? What is the purpose?*

JS: The "truth serum" is used to help get the psychiatric diagnosis in a short time. We have a nurse give the substance slowly and have the counselor ask the questions which we put together with bits and pieces we pick up in counseling and elsewhere.

KvW: *What kind of aversion treatment do you have for drugs other than alcohol?*

JS: The Faradic aversion (shock) works very well for cocaine, methamphetamine, marijuana, etc. We do not treat heroin (we found that most of the heroin addicts did not stay for the full treatment). We have developed artificial cocaine and other drugs (not the real drugs). The smoking treatment works (52% at 1 year).

KvW: *What is your opinion of the harm reduction housing program in Seattle that houses persons with mental disorders, most of whom are active alcoholics?*

JS: I do not think much of the "drinking hotels." They were supposed to cut the cost of multiple hospital ER room visits and cut down on the police activity. I don't see that it has cut down much and, of course, the physical damage is still going on from the drinking!

KvW: *Thank you so much for providing this information.*

JS: Thank you very much for the interview. Good luck on your book!

Reports in the late 1970s of high death rates among elderly clients caused several of these types of treatment centers to close their doors. Although the treatment is more carefully provided today, the infliction of pain, nausea, sickness, and electric shock to condition aversion to alcohol raises some ethical concerns. Moreover, it is aesthetically unappealing.

COVERT SENSITIZATION

Another variety of aversion therapy, which according to Burman (2001) has been shown effective, involves instructing clients to imagine physical discomfort in association with drinking. Imagining the sensation of throwing up while drinking can bring positive results. The advantages over aversive conditioning are obvious: Since the client does not actually experience nausea or shock, there are no medical dangers (Fisher & Harrison, 2005). Covert sensitization and imagining are easy for clients to learn and apply when they think they might be using again; these techniques can be tailored for individual use (Stevens & Smith, 2004).

Because of the intense craving associated with cocaine use, which is a key factor in relapse, aversion therapies were used by an inpatient unit with a sample of 70 crack cocaine abusing veterans (Bordnick, 1996). Results showed a complete reduction in craving following eight sessions. Both chemical aversion treatment (inducing vomiting with Emetine hydrochloride) and the use of covert sensitization were effective in reducing craving by session 8. Chemical aversion treatment, however, achieved remarkable results and, as Bordnick argues, offers a highly efficacious method for eliminating craving. Chemical aversion therapy, the tastelessness and cruelty of this procedure notwithstanding, consistently has been shown to be highly effective for alcoholism treatment (Hester & Miller, 2003).

CHANGING BRAIN CHEMISTRY

The bad news about heavy intoxicants, as we learned in chapter 4, is the neurological brain injury that can result. The good news, as Fulton Crews (2001), director of the Center for Alcohol Studies at the University of North Carolina, assures us, is that some of the brain degeneration can be reversed through therapy. Clinical studies, as Crews indicates, suggest that exercising the brain likely brings about regrowth in the frontal cortex. Improvement in this part of the brain enhances one's chances of recovery. Additionally, thiamine therapy seems to increase treatment effects (depletion of this vitamin is thought to be implicated in brain dysfunction associated with alcoholism).

Begley (2007) reveals how modern science has refuted earlier dogma—the doctrine of the unchanging human brain. In place of this dogma has come the realization that the adult brain retains impressive powers of *neuroplasticity*, or "the ability to change its structure and function in response to experience" (p. 74). Jeffrey Schwartz (1997), the author of *Brain Lock* and the coauthor of *The Mind and the Brain* (Schwartz & Begley, 2003), revealed this phenomenon earlier, namely, that psychological counseling can alter brain chemistry and possibly restore more normal functioning. In an experiment described by Schwartz, clients suffering from obsessive-compulsive disorder were guided to substitute healthy for unhealthy thoughts every time an obsessive urge came over them. After 10 weeks of behavioral instruction, neuroimaging revealed observable changes in brain chemistry; these changes were observed in the part of the brain thought to be affected by this disorder. More recently, interviewed by Begley (2007), Schwartz called his cognitive-behavioral therapy a form of "self-directed neuroplasticity" and concluded that "the mind can change the brain" (p. 77).

The implications of these findings are profound. Just as mental and physical practice of the piano paves the way for mastery as the brain strengthens connections among neurons for this function, so the individual can learn cognitive techniques in therapy with results that are physiological as well as psychological. Given the knowledge that the brain has the ability to rewire itself through cognitive exercises, counselors can feel confident that their teaching of exercises geared toward changing the client's unhealthy "self-talk" (see chapter 7) are empirically valid. And lest we be skeptical of these claims, we can contemplate the more familiar phenomenon of brain recovery as revealed in experimentation with stroke victims who learn to redirect activities to undamaged areas of the brain and in people with obsessive-compulsive disorder who learn thinking exercises to get their compulsions under control.

Further support is lent to the notion that brain structure and function can be altered by cognitions in studies of the impact of trauma on the brain. Particular hormones secreted in times of severe stress can alter neurochemistry sufficiently to effect long-term changes in neurons and brain systems. PET scans of eight children reared in Romanian orphanages until their adoption showed such abnormalities, as Harriette Johnson (2004) indicates.

The technological revolution in neurological research is providing documentation for theories that previously were based only on behavioral observation. Although more has been learned in the past few years than in several previous decades, we are just on the brink of understanding addiction and the roots of addiction in the brain.

PHARMACEUTICAL INTERVENTIONS

If drug dependence is considered less a matter of will than of brain chemistry, then the development of medications to prevent the lows or block the highs is inevitable. The growing awareness of serotonin's central role in mood and compulsive behavior has been paralleled by a boom in the introduction of drugs that target serotonin levels. Selective serotonin reuptake inhibitors (SSRIs), such as Prozac, Zoloft, and Paxil, are prescribed to treat a wide range of disorders, such as binge drinking and eating, obsessive-compulsive disorder, as well as autism, panic attacks, schizophrenia, and uncontrolled aggression. This class of antidepressants has become the first line of treatment to combat depression (Mueser, Noordsy, Drake, & Fox, 2003). These drugs are relatively safe even when taken in combination with alcohol or when taken in overdose. Major side effects are sexual dysfunction and difficulty getting off the drug. SSRIs adequately treat only about 60% of patients, however (Jackson, 2003).

Biochemical problems call for biochemical solutions. The findings from brain research have laid the groundwork for a series of more than 50 clinical trials of various prescriptions to be funded by the two major research funding organizations: NIAAA and NIDA (Thayer, 2006). Even many of the leading treatment centers, such as Hazelden in Minnesota, are conducting research on the effectiveness of medications that act on the brain as an aid in recovery.

The concept of taking a pill to curb excessive appetite is hardly new. Still, resistance to the use of any mood-altering substances such as Prozac persists in substance abuse treatment circles (Challender, 1999). Recovering addicts quoted in a *Newsweek* article, for example, assert that there are no shortcuts to staying sober (Kalb, 2001).

But maybe there are. Already, as we will see, medications that target the brain are being prescribed for alcoholics, smokers, cocaine and methamphetamine users, persons with eating disorders, compulsive shoppers, and pathological gamblers. For alcoholism, the new pharmaceutical drugs designed to reduce the cravings for drink have been especially promising. Although healthcare providers, in this time of tight fiscal constraints, are in search of effective but brief interventions, pharmaceutical companies have a strong economic stake in producing and marketing products to meet the growing medical demand.

The identification of genes that encode subunits of receptors for neurotransmitters such as GABA, serotonin, and others paves the way for the identification of people at risk for both depression and alcoholism because both conditions often co-occur in the same individual. Such identification of risk-associated genes also paves the way for specialized medication development (Li, 2004).

ALCOHOLISM

Several types of medications are used to help alcoholics avoid relapse. Saleebey (2001) explains this best. Psychoactive drugs, as he tells us, act upon certain neurotransmitters. Some drugs, such as morphine, bind the receptor site and enhance the effect of the neurotransmitter, whereas certain antipsychotic drugs block the effect of dopamine. Other drugs, such as the SSRI antidepressants (e.g., Zoloft and Prozac), block the neurotransmitters from reuptake, thus allowing the chemical more time and influence at the receptor site. People who are depressed, as all counselors know, lose their incentive to stay sober. Keeping their spirits up, especially early in treatment, is vital.

Naltrexone, the drug approved by the Federal Drug Administration in 1995 to reduce craving in heroin addicts, is in a separate class from the antidepressants or from the addictive antianxiety drugs such as Valium and Librium. Naltrexone works by blocking alcohol–brain interactions that produce a high. In studies with rats on naltrexone that were later given alcohol, this medication was shown to decrease the amount of alcohol-induced dopamine (U.S. Department of Health and Human Services, 2000). Naltrexone is an abstinence-enhancing drug. Basically, the fun is removed from the drinking, so patients taking these drugs lose their desire to partake. Remember the brain studies that showed how visual cues associated with drugs of choice produced conditioned responses in the brain? Well, naltrexone has been shown to block the chemical changes in the brain elicited by the environmental cues (smell of alcohol, sight of foaming beer, etc.). Usually taken several times a week in pill form, naltrexone is now available in a dosage form good for 30 days or more (Office of National Drug Control Policy, 2001). Patients found to derive the most benefits from these drugs are those with poor cognitive skills coupled with an intense urge to keep drinking. Of 300 patients at a facility for homeless persons treated with this drug, 80% were found to be abstinent at the end of 6 months (*Addiction Treatment Forum,* 2000). This once-a-month injectable medication will help ensure that alcoholics in outpatient treatment do not drink.

The aim of the researchers and the pharmaceutical companies, no doubt, is to come up with a menu of medications for alcoholism similar to the variety of depression treatments available. As yet, however, these discoveries, like genetic research, are in their infancy, and most doctors consider alcoholism largely a behavioral problem (Thayer, 2006).

Results from an NIAAA funded study found that naltrexone and up to 20 sessions of behavioral counseling are equally effective treatments for alcohol dependence when delivered with medical management (monitoring to encourage drug compliance). This 3-year COMBINE (Combining Medications and Behavioral Interventions for Alcoholism) study provided 16 weeks of treatment for 1,300 recently abstinent patients and then assessed the patients for clinical outcome. In the carefully controlled study, patients received naltrexone, acamprosate, both of these medications together, or placebo pills. Another four groups received counseling of various sorts in addition to the medications. The results, as reported in the *Journal of the American Medical Association* by Anton, O'Malley, and 17 colleagues (2006), brought surprising results in that acamprosate showed no significant effect on drinking and naltrexone was effective in its own right even in the absence of counseling. A major problem with naltrexone is that most alcoholics and addicts simply stop taking it (*Harvard Mental Health Letter,* 2005). A new option that may help with this problem, and that has been found to be effective with binge drinkers, is the extended release, injectable form of naltrexone, called Vivitrol (Wasserman, 2006). Vivitrol suppresses alcohol dependence by binding to opioid receptors in the brain. This drug blocks the neurotransmitters associated with alcohol dependence. Recent research confirms the effectiveness of this medication in preventing relapse. Garbutt et al. (2005) conducted a placebo-controlled trial with alcoholics at 24 clinics across the United States and found a reduction in heavy drinking among the subjects.

One serious drawback with these types of drugs, however, is the low motivation of addicts to use them. After all, these antagonist drugs block the pleasure of drug taking, something many addicts may have no interest in doing. To keep addicts off the streets, they need to have a choice: Would they like to be treated with harm reduction strategies that help alcoholics and other drug users cut down? Or would they prefer an addiction substitute such as methadone? Or would they prefer to be rendered immune to the drug's euphoric properties with a blocker medication such as naltrexone?

Some very exciting earlier research findings published in the *Journal of the American Medical Association* by Bankole Johnson and eight associates also provide evidence that points research in the direction of tailoring medications for individual alcoholics/addicts. These experiments are with ondansetron, a medication currently prescribed to curb nausea in chemotherapy patients ("Ondansetron Effective," 2000). Among alcoholics in the study, this drug increased abstinence by 40% and cut down consumption by 39% compared with those given a placebo. The study found ondansetron to have few side effects, and it can be given to alcoholics who are still drinking, which precludes the need for detoxification. Oddly, ondansetron significantly reduced alcohol use among patients with biological or early-onset, not late-onset, alcoholism. This drug appears to block serotonin receptors in the brain, thus decreasing the craving for alcohol. Interestingly, as we saw in chapter 4, only men and women who had developed alcoholism early—by age 25—benefited from the drug, presumably because there was something abnormal about their brain chemistry in the first place.

It is often said that seriously addicted alcoholics can never learn to drink moderately. Indeed, without the help of a medication that apparently normalizes their brain, they probably cannot handle alcohol. The alcohol handles them. Other drugs, such as Prozac, had failed to help such clients, although, as Kranzler (2000) indicates in his commentary on this report, a selective serotonin reuptake inhibitor (e.g., Prozac) might be used in patients with low-severity, late-onset alcoholism. As it turns out, though, according to an *Alcohol Alert* newsletter ("New Advances," 2000), the antidepressant Zoloft (but not Prozac) appears to reduce drinking in late-onset, but not early-onset, alcoholics. As this report indicates, a great deal more research is needed to match the appropriate medications to different client types.

One direction for future clinical trials involves the mixing of two prescribed medications, such as ondansetron and naltrexone. The implications of the discovery of the differing effects of medication on different types of alcoholism are dramatic, not only for the future treatment of addiction but for what it says about the biological basis of alcohol dependence in general. Successful medication trials such as the ondansetron study targeting subtypes of alcoholics, mark the dawn of a new day in the substance use treatment field. Recent research with ondansetron has proven its effectiveness with cocaine addicts in research also conducted by Bankole Johnson (Gore, 2006).

One more medication discovery that provides hope for alcoholics and, in fact, all addicts, is a GABA-enhancing drug. (Recall from chapter 4 that the neurotransmitter, GABA, is an inhibitor that keeps our highs from overwhelming us.) The drug, topiramate, known commercially as Topamax, is used to control epilepsy. For years, patients with epilepsy have reported that it helped them fight food cravings and lose weight. Now it is showing promise in early studies with alcoholics, gamblers, smokers, and overeaters (Ehrenfeld, 2005). Applying one drug to different addictions makes sense because the same pleasure centers and pathways in the brain are activated by many different substances and behaviors (Hobson, 2006). This finding is consistent with a major contention of this book, as stated in chapter 1, that the disease is not alcoholism or an eating disorder but rather the tendency toward addiction itself.

Nicotine Treatment

Nicotine takes a terrible toll on American health, greater than does any other drug; more than 400,000 people die per year from smoking-related causes. For women, tobacco-related illness is now the deadliest malignancy (Rubin, 2001). The fact that women continue to smoke in large numbers is attributed to tobacco advertising, which long has linked smoking with values that women care about—independence, sophistication, sex appeal, and above all, slimness (Healton, 2001). Yet, as the title of an article by Bavley (1999) tells us, "Kicking the Habit [Is] a Tough Row to Hoe for Hard-Core Smokers." In fact, the urge to light up a cigarette is practically irresistible for the 50 million or so who are still puffing. Those who would or could quit more easily have already done so. (Whereas in 1965, 52% of men and 34% of women smoked, in 2000, those percentages had changed to 26% of men and 22% of women, according to Rubin, 2001.)

Recent research confirms that secondhand smoke is deadly as well. According to the American Lung Association (2006), 3,000 nonsmokers die each year from lung cancer caused by exposure to secondhand smoke. About ten times that number die from heart disease for the same reason, according to estimates. Children are especially susceptible to respiratory damage as a result of smoke exposure. Thanks to publicizing facts such as these, smoke-free legislation has been passed across the states and in many countries. As of 2006, the states have only just begun to pass really strong smoke-free air laws. New York City has banned smoking from all restaurants. The tobacco industry can be expected to consistently fight all these efforts.

In recent years, nicotine chewing gum, skin patches, inhalers, nasal sprays, and antidepressant medications such as Zyban have helped to quell cravings for tobacco's addictive ingredient. Smoking-cessation classes that draw on mild aversion exercises such as requiring participants to chew the cigarette are waning in popularity now that medications are of proven effectiveness. Zyban is the brand name for buproprion, an antidepressant that is thought to work through blocking dopamine reuptake and targeting the nicotine receptor (O'Malley & Kosten, 2006). Zyban works differently from nicotine-replacement therapies, which help the smoker maintain his or her level of nicotine while breaking the habit. This medication is taken 1 or 2 weeks prior to the quit date as well as after to reduce the urge to smoke. The effectiveness of this antidepressant was discovered by accident when a doctor noticed that many depressed patients on buproprion gave up smoking (Bavley, 1999). Wellbutrin is another brand name for the same drug (Hobson, 2006).

Chantix is another promising medication. It works by making the patient produce more dopamine, which is supposed to lower the cravings. Gonzales et al. (2006) reported a success rate that was about one and a half times that of Zyban in keeping people off cigarettes for 1 year. One problem with the study, published in the *Journal of the American Medical Association,* was that it was funded by Pfizer, the makers of Chantix. This fact was not disclosed until after the study was published. In any case, the Food and Drug Administration has approved this drug so it can now be prescribed.

A yearlong study of pack-a-day smokers who wanted to stop found that of 615 smokers, 23% of the group that got the highest level of the medications had quit 1 year later compared to 12% of the control group ("Antidepressants Help Smokers," 1997). One of the most significant and surprising findings of the study was that while on Zyban, subjects gained only a few pounds compared to quitters who stopped cold turkey. After 6 months, however, all those who quit smoking gained an average of almost 12 pounds.

An insurance agent who quit smoking with the help of Zyban explains what the craving is like without the drug: "You get virtually uncontrollable urges. You're going to go nuts if you don't have a cigarette. Even with the (nicotine) patch, you get these tremendous cravings" ("Antidepressant Proves Beneficial," 1998, p. A8). Zyban is designed for limited use to help smokers get past those first weeks or months of intense craving. It can be used along with the nicotine patch for maximum effect.

Naltrexone, commonly used to reduce addictive behavior in alcoholics and heroin addicts, also helps with smoking cessation, even in moderate smokers, according to the results of an empirical study reported in *Journal Watch Psychiatry* (Roy-Byrne, 1999). Unlike Zyban, naltrexone blocks the reward circuits in the brain. Although naltrexone users did not fully abstain in a related study of 22 smokers, they did significantly cut down (Ritter, 1997). Turning chain smokers into moderate smokers carries significant health benefits and can make quitting ultimately easier. Animal studies using vaccines to produce drug-specific antibodies to reduce nicotine's distribution in the brain are under investigation for possible use in insulating people from nicotine dependence (O'Malley & Kosten, 2006).

A benefit of Zyban and nicotine gum or the patch is that weight gain is significantly less when smokers use these products compared to a placebo group. The drug Accomplia has been found especially effective in preventing weight gain in obese smokers who have quit (Filozof, Fernandez, & Fernandez-Cruz, 2004).

Nicotine maintenance products, such as gum, skin patches, and nasal sprays, help smokers wean themselves from cigarettes. Nicotine elevates mood and sharpens concentration, which explains why people with a history of depression, attention-deficit disorder, or schizophrenia are likely to smoke and get seriously hooked (Schultz, 2000). Although nicotine gum is intended to be used only for several months, researchers are finding that in a small minority of ex-smokers, nicotine gum is chewed for years and years as the only way they can stop themselves from inhaling nicotine ("Downside of Nicotine Gum," 2000). However, the unpleasant taste probably prevents this from happening to many others. An innovative tobacco control program in New York State found that when free coupons for nicotine gum and patches were sent to over 40,000 smokers identified from Smokers' Quitline, about twice as many of them as the others were able to quit (21–35% vs. 12%) (Cummings et al., 2006). The differing figures corresponded to the quantity of supplies sent.

Because continued smoking, like drinking, changes the brain, quitting brings about depression and irritability (McFarling, 1998). Of the 50 million smokers, at least 20 million try to quit each year, but fewer than 6% succeed. Treating nicotine addiction as the medical problem is essential if any headway is to be made in helping people break their life-threatening habit.

NIDA-supported research has played a major role in providing crucial insights into the neurobiological aspects of nicotine addiction; these understandings in turn have paved the way for pharmaceutical advances in treatment. Treating nicotine addiction as a medical problem helps remove the stigma attached to a person's difficulty in giving up smoking. In short, a medical understanding takes some of the blame off smokers and places it on the tobacco companies. This recognition of the similarity of nicotine addiction to other forms of chronic addiction, moreover, has brought about a major shift in thinking for the chemical dependence treatment field. The shift has evolved from clients smoking with staff in their therapy sessions, to smoking only in special areas, to having their smoking addiction treated as a drug dependence like any other.

Although inpatient treatment has been available for some time for alcoholics and other addicts with severe problems, chronic smokers, whose habits may be just as life threatening, have been denied this privilege. According to a study at the Mayo Clinic (Join Together, 2001), hospitalizing smokers who cannot quit through traditional methods significantly increases the chances of turning an addicted smoker into a long-term ex-smoker. Although the source of this study raises questions about bias in that the Mayo Clinic offers inpatient treatment, it makes sense intuitively that the removal of smokers from temptation would be all to the good. Treatment at the Mayo Nicotine Dependence Center consists of the use of medications to relieve withdrawal, individual and group counseling, stress management, exercise sessions, and family work. According to their website, more than 900 people have been treated in the program (Mayo Foundation for Medical Education and Research, 2006). The cost is $5,000, part of which increasingly is covered by insurance (Plutowski, 2005). Health insurers would do well to provide coverage for this intensive but cost-effective form of treatment.

For alcoholic smokers, it is better to quit both addictions at once, according to research on rats done at the Indiana University School of Medicine ("Nicotine Increases Alcohol Craving," 2000). Both nicotine and alcohol lead to the release of dopamine; repeated smoking is thought to enhance the pleasurable effects of alcohol. Just as some addiction treatment centers are pushing clients to stop smoking and drinking simultaneously, guidelines for stopping smoking should emphasize curbing alcohol intake as well.

This research has been confirmed in continuing experiments with humans such as that conducted at the University of California at San Francisco (Meyerhoff et al., 2006). Using MRIs to scan the brains of 25 alcoholics, including 14 smokers, researchers found that brain function and health improved for the alcoholics but not so for the smoking recovering alcoholics. Both chronic alcoholism and smoking are associated with cortical gray matter loss, which is a risk factor in cognitive decline. These findings point to the importance of smoking cessation early in treatment to enhance sobriety (including sober thinking.)

ANTIDOTES FOR COCAINE AND METHAMPHETAMINE

A pharmaceutical strategy to medical treatment for cocaine addiction is to develop a drug that blocks production of dopamine produced in conjunction with cocaine use. Gamma vinyl-GABA, or GVG, a drug used for years in Europe and Canada to treat epilepsy, has shown its effectiveness in a clinical trial conducted in Mexico (National Institute on Drug Abuse [NIDA], 2003). GVG, which blocks the addiction-related effects of cocaine, was administered to 20 subjects. Only eight completed the trial, but all eight were able to remain drug free after treatment; they reported their craving for cocaine had subsided. Brodie, Figueroa, Laska, and Dewey (2005) conducted a larger study with 30 meth and/or cocaine addicts in New York. About half dropped out of the study, but the others had no ill effects from GVG and successfully discontinued their drug use. Excellent results have been obtained in experiments at the University of Virginia with the cancer nausea-reducing drug ondansetron (Gore, 2006). Patients in treatment who were given this drug had lower dropout rates compared to a control group.

MEDICATION FOR HEROIN USERS

When Hurricane Katrina struck, a story that got largely overlooked in the news was the suffering of drug addicts who had been treated at the methadone clinic. Methadone is a synthetic form of heroin that is legally provided for heroin addicts to keep them stabilized and from having withdrawal symptoms. Methadone is a highly addictive medication, however, so without it, the New Orleans heroin addicts faced a harrowing withdrawal (Keilman, 2005). Those who were lucky found their way to the Baton Rouge Treatment Center where there were long lines of people waiting for the medication. There were reports of other desperate addicts looting pharmacies of morphine and other prescription painkillers or buying them on the street.

For the nation's 1 million heroin addicts, the primary remedy is methadone (McCaffrey, cited in *Addiction Treatment Forum*, 2006). Sadly, however, as former drug czar General McCaffrey asserts, only about one in eight heroin addicts participate in methadone programs. Long waiting lists are common; in Seattle, for example, drug users may wait 1 year for treatment. In rural areas, methadone clinics are practically nonexistent. The state of Iowa, for example, has only three such clinics to serve the whole state. Policymakers and even many substance abuse providers reject methadone maintenance in the belief that use of methadone substitutes one addiction for another. Physicians, moreover, have been severely restricted in their authority to dispense this medication.

In Europe, methadone maintenance (and in Britain, heroin maintenance) is the preferred treatment for heroin addicts, where it has been used with some success, especially in reducing the number of AIDS cases. Methadone works by occupying the opiate receptors of the brain that are involved in heroin craving. Given orally, and requiring daily visits to a clinic, methadone gives users a mild high that does not interfere with their ability to work or function. Because tolerance to this drug remains steady, patients can be maintained indefinitely on a fixed amount. Because methadone reduces the harm (risk of heroin overdose, criminal activity to support the habit, contracting AIDS through use of dirty needles), methadone therapy is a mainstay of harm reduction treatment. Still, methadone maintenance is not a panacea. Only about half of heroin patients who attend methadone maintenance clinics are able to stay off heroin. And if they quit methadone, about 80% will relapse over the next few years (Marion, 2005).

Although methadone maintenance is considered an overall success in its lifesaving and crime-reducing aspects, many heroin addicts seem resistant to methadone treatment. Researchers in one study, as reported on the Join Together (2000) website, discovered that the addicts who failed the program were likely to have a genetic variation making them highly addictive and less amenable than other addicts to standardized forms of treatment. Interestingly, this gene—DRD2 (dopamine D2 receptor gene)—has been implicated in more virulent forms of alcoholism, smoking, and compulsive eating as well. A more recent British study from the University of Bristol also found that the dopamine receptor gene was strongly associated with alcohol consumption and the high that some people derive from drugs such as alcohol (*Science Daily*, 2005).

Another reason for treatment failure no doubt relates to the failure of many methadone maintenance treatment programs to prescribe adequate daily doses of methadone. Persons unresponsive to treatment in an experimental study in Switzerland, for example, all did well when levels of the drug were raised well above the usual 100-mg level ("MMT & Beyond," 2001). Over the years, street heroin has gotten purer in quality and lower in price. Consequently, there is a greater need for higher doses of methadone today than are currently considered adequate by previous standards.

A development that may seem somewhat surprising is the use of methadone in the criminal justice system. New York, Baltimore, and Seattle are a few of the cities that provide access to methadone (or another synthetic opioid) for heroin addicts in their jails.

Rachel Baldino (2000), writing in *Welcome to Methadonia*, provides a candid account of working (until she burned out) at a methadone clinic. This book chronicles the authoritarian rules, humiliating urinalysis tests (to see if clients were taking other drugs), and the emotional wear and tear of working with heroin addicts around the clock. Here are her recommendations: Counselors should not be required to play a disciplinary role, such as monitoring urinalysis results; counselors should not have more than a few heroin addicts at a time in their caseload; treatment should be decentralized so that clients can be treated at various doctors' offices and to avoid the drug-ridden atmosphere of the clinics.

Marion (2005) compares methadone treatment of the 1970s with the situation 35 years later. For a start, today's patients are much different from former patients: They tend to be polydrug users, not just addicted to heroin, and there are both a higher percentage of young addicts and elderly addicts than before. The HIV and hepatitis C epidemics have taken their toll in recent years. Regarding treatment, methadone maintenance, as Marion observes, is far more pragmatic today than formerly; in fact, the treatment is going mainstream. Treatment needs are tailored to each individual, and it is no longer assumed that methadone use is only short-term or that patients must be pushed into being drug free within a certain time frame. Today, the methadone dosage is individualized to take into account differences in metabolism and the effects of interaction with other concurrent medications. No longer must every patient report every day for treatment; those in good standing can fill prescriptions at the pharmacy. In short, unless another better drug comes to take its place, methadone is here to stay.

Advocates and policymakers need to know what the costs and benefits are of particular drug treatment programming. A report in *Health Economics* (Zarkin, Dunlap, Hicks, & Mamo, 2005) looked at the lifetime costs and benefits of methadone maintenance for heroin users. Their study included such variables as heroin use, criminal behavior, employment, and healthcare utilization and showed that every dollar spent on methadone treatment yielded $38 in related economic benefits (see *The Addiction Treatment Forum,* a quarterly newsletter devoted to methadone maintenance at http://www.atforum.com).

One drug possibly better than the synthetic methadone for controlled treatment is heroin itself. The Canadian cities of Vancouver, Toronto, and Montreal have adopted a prescription heroin trial of around 500 hard-core addicts, half of whom will get daily doses of heroin and half of whom will get methadone

(Armstrong, 2005). Although similar treatment programs have been set up in Europe, this experiment is unique in North America. Results are expected to be positive consistent with previous research such as that published in the *British Medical Journal,* which has shown heroin maintenance to have more than doubled the success rate of standard methadone maintenance (van den Brink et al., 2003). This research itself was conducted in the Netherlands with a population of over 500 patients who were seen as highly resistant to treatment.

The antiopiate medications, such as buprenorphine and naltrexone, discussed earlier, are now widely used in treatment for heroin addiction. Waismann terms this preferred form of treatment "opioid receptor management" (2000, p. 32). In contrast to methadone, which, as he argues, only masks the problem, neurological regulation can be achieved through the use of medications allowing the patient to get through withdrawal while unconscious (Costello, 2002). Injected with large doses of naltrexone, the patient writhes unconsciously for hours until the withdrawal process is complete. Before we become too sanguine about this expensive treatment, however, we should take into account what happened in one experiment at Columbia University. This experiment, which used general anesthesia for rapid detox, was widely cited in the press as having negative results (Raskin, 2005). The relapse rate was almost 90%, and three patients almost died under the general anesthesia.

At Waismann's clinic (now in Tel Aviv, Israel), patients, upon discharge, are prescribed a regimen of naltrexone, a non-mood-altering medication that successfully reduces the craving for opiates. Such treatment also can be applied in the care of "heroin babies" to replace the long, painful, and damaging current approaches of getting addicted infants through withdrawal. Opiate addiction, as Waismann (2000) further argues, should be viewed as a disorder of the central nervous system that can be reversed with appropriate medical treatment.

Buprenorphine was approved in 2002 for the treatment of opiate addiction. Its advantage over methadone is that it is safer on measures of overdose risks such as respiratory depression (O'Malley & Kosten, 2006). Buprenorphine is the first of a new generation of prescription drugs that is changing the landscape of addiction treatment. The new treatments parallel discoveries about the neurobiological nature of addiction and allow for drug dependence and relapse to be treated like diabetes, hypertension, or any other chronic disease. A new law passed by Congress and signed by the president greatly expands access to this medication; physicians recently restricted to group practice of 30 patients can now prescribe this medication to 100 patients (Curley, 2007).

The drug buprenorphine acts like extra mild methadone at low doses (Cowley, 2001). Unlike other opioids, including heroin, other narcotic painkillers, and methadone, buprenorphine has a "ceiling effect" that substantially reduces the likelihood of death through overdose (Kayman, Rosenblum, & Joseph, 2004). Buprenorphine, moreover, is less addictive than the other opioids. This drug, which can be prescribed directly by doctors once federal approval is granted and which can be taken in lozenge form, should significantly increase the number of heroin addicts receiving treatment.

Unlike naltrexone, buprenorphine is a narcotic, the only controlled sub-stance approved by the Food and Drug Administration for the treatment of opioid addiction that can be prescribed in a doctor's office. Casadonte (2004), a physician who treats heroin-addicted veterans at the New York Harbor Healthcare System medical center, describes how use of buprenorphine has totally changed his treatment program. Previously, methadone was provided; patients took this in a liquid form so they could be watched swallowing the drug. Buprenorphine, in contrast, is taken in pill or lozenge form and weekly rather than daily. Patients not using other drugs can get a prescription for home use. To keep this opiate from being diverted onto the streets, the amount of the drug prescribed is carefully monitored.

New laws have been introduced to allow physicians who take qualifying training classes to prescribe antiopiate medications from their offices (Sub-stance Abuse and Mental Health Services Administration [SAMHSA], 2004). Buprenorphine, sold under the brand name Suboxone, allows opioid-dependent patients to bypass specialized methadone clinics and receive treatment in the privacy of a nonstigmatized setting.

The advantages of office treatment are many; a new clientele is already developing as patients who became addicted to prescription medication feel more comfortable receiving treatment from their doctor than from a clinic frequented by heroin addicts. Lest we get too complacent about these advan-tages, however, we should note the counterarguments of Schilling, Dornig, and Lungren (2006) in favor of standard methadone treatment. Treatment in such a specialized setting provides for tracking over time with relative ease, random drug testing, the collection of data on the large numbers of clients enrolled that is available to investigators, counseling of individual clients, and referral to other needed services. As with any other services, however, the advantages of methadone maintenance must be weighed against the disadvantages.

MEDICATION FOR EATING DISORDERS

Why do compulsive eaters feel such intense cravings for chocolates and other sweets (or potato chips)? Perhaps they have some of the same abnormal brain chemistry seen in drug addicts (Boyce, 2001). Researchers at the University of Pittsburgh Medical Center (2005), building on genetic studies showing gene alterations in some individuals with anorexia nervosa, examined PET scans of 10 women in recovery from anorexia and 12 normal subjects. They found significant differences in the activity of brain dopamine receptors in the two groups of women. The difference was in increased receptor binding; this relates to harm avoidance and reward seeking and may help explain why women with anorexia exhibit exaggerated worry and concern. Significantly, as the medical center's report points out, people who are obese and substance users exhibit reduced binding of these dopamine receptors.

Eating is a survival behavior that must be pleasurable to sustain the species. The same primitive reward system in the brain is central to the development of both excessive eating and chemical addiction. The high rate of comorbidity between eating and other disorders, as discussed in chapter 7, bears out the interconnectedness in these addictive/compulsive tendencies.

Chemical addiction and eating disorders share many clinical features. The commonalties are not limited to behavioral observations but involve an array of neurotransmitter abnormalities. Dopamine is involved in both. Thus, it stands to reason that teasing out dopamine's effects could lead to new drugs for the millions of obese Americans (Boyce, 2001). Researchers are excited about a pill called Accomplia that has been shown in animal studies to fight relapse in drug users. In humans, it helps in weight loss as well as smoking cessation (Join Together, 2006).

Eating disorders characterized by compulsive binge eating and purge behaviors (bulimia) are highly correlated with alcohol and other drug misuse (Halmi, 1998). Whereas bulimics suffer more from depression, anorexics suffer more from anxiety. Because of the extreme rigidity and ritualism found in anorexics, a disturbance in serotonin functioning is probably responsible, as Halmi theorizes.

Luvox (fluvoxamine), a drug similar to Prozac (fluoxetine) and Paxil, have been found to produce significantly better outcomes in binge-eating outpatients than those given a placebo (Figgitt & McClellan, 2000). Although Prozac is considered an antidepressant, it is effective in persons with or without depression. Study results summarized by Brewerton (2004) indicate that cognitive therapy focusing on challenging rigid thought patterns and healthy expression of feelings in combination with medication is more effective than the use of medication alone. What is not known at this point is whether a deficit in receptors in the brain cells of obese people is a cause or a result of the obesity. Future studies should make the connection clear.

Results in the use of pharmacological agents for anorexia in producing weight gain have been disappointing. Only when patients are on the mend do SSRIs such as Prozac help with weight recovery. The reason, as Brewerton (2004) suggests, is because in a body depleted of amino acids due to starvation, the serotonin enhancing drugs cannot take effect. Zypresa, an antipsychotic medication, however, is being given to adolescents with promising results.

HELP FOR BEHAVIORAL ADDICTIONS

Very little is written about the use of prescription medication for the behavioral addictions, such as compulsive gambling and shopping. Given the interrelatedness of these addictions and drug addictions, however, it stands to reason that similar medication would work for both drug-seeking or money-related behavior.

Dr. Donald Black and his colleagues at the University of Iowa Medical School have had some success in prescribing Luvox for compulsive shoppers. The medication, according to preliminary findings, makes it possible for sufferers to walk through a store and spend what they intended. Interestingly, as the research on 55 compulsive buyers showed, close relatives of these subjects suffered disproportionately more from depression and drug use than did persons in the comparison sample (Black, Repertinger, Gaffney, & Gabel, 1998). In subsequent research from the University of Iowa, Kuzma and Black (2006) cautioned against reliance on medication to control their behavior and recommended a cognitive approach. Such an approach would be directed at faulty thinking patterns, such as an overemphasis on clothes or fashion, and the development of self-protective behaviors, such as canceling credit cards and shopping only with an understanding friend or relative.

For compulsive gamblers and kleptomaniacs (persons who compulsively steal), naltrexone has been used successfully in experiments to curb their destructive behavior. The focus at the Brown Medical School is on using drugs to block the receptors in the brain that register the pleasurable high (Grant, 2005). A Mayo Clinic report (2006) confirms this finding. The clinic's recommendation is for an SSRI for compulsive gamblers with bipolar disorder and naltrexone for others. More research is needed, however. Other techniques used to help kleptomaniacs are antidepression drugs, shock treatments, and therapy in which the patient is instructed to hold his or her breath or think of vomiting when experiencing the urge to steal.

Can medication that enhances the neurotransmitters actually cause addiction to a behavior? Although it seems unlikely, recent reports seem to indicate that dopamine-enhancing drugs prescribed for Parkinson's disease possibly lead some people into compulsive gambling and overwhelming sexual urges. According to Vedantan (2006) of the *Washington Post,* anecdotal reports of case after case of strange obsessive behavior associated with these drugs have led some pharmaceutical companies to issue warnings about these possible side effects.

HOLISTIC APPROACHES

Other remedies directed toward the physical side of drug use are more natural, holistic approaches. These include various herbal remedies, acupuncture, massage, hypnosis, and biofeedback. Herbal medicines are regulated as dietary supplements rather than as drugs, so they can make no specific claims to treat a disease. Since plants cannot be patented, there is little financial incentive for private companies to fund clinical trials for research on treatment effectiveness. Sometimes, studies are funded by drug companies such as Pfizer, the makers of Zoloft and others, with vested interests in proving a rival herbal remedy has no benefits (Spinella, 2005). This happened in research on St. John's wort, a popular herbal remedy for depression.

A quick look at the popular literature on herbal remedies reveals that one day's wonder drug is the next day's despair. Until scientific testing is conducted, the truth is hard to ascertain. For example, an article in *Nature* (Aldous, 2005) describes a Vietnamese concoction, Heantos, containing a mixture of 13 herbs that reportedly makes drug cravings disappear. Used for opium addicts in Vietnam, the drug is consumed for 4 days in half-quart doses. The United Nations Development Program and the Norwegian government are funding a scientific study into its effectiveness.

Kudzu, the plant imported from Korea to Alabama and grown out of control to the distress of farmers and foresters, has been found to help heavy drinkers cut down on their consumption (Lukas et al., 2005). A compound extracted from the kudzu weed has been used in China for treatment of alcoholics. Animal studies in the United States were promising. An experiment on men and women who were heavy drinkers by Lukas et al. (2005) showed that when under the influence of this substance, they consumed less because they apparently were feeling the effects of the alcohol more readily. The exact mechanism for how this plant works is unknown.

Ibogaine is a drug derived from a West African shrub. This drug has potent, long-lasting hallucinogenic effects that typically last from 24 to 36 hours (Spinella, 2005). The antiaddictive effects of ibogaine were originally reported by heroin users who, after experimenting with this hallucinogen, find they no longer craved heroin. Animal research, according to Spinella, has shown that the drug reduces cocaine use in mice. "Tales of ibogaine's effectiveness are legion among addicts, but data are in short supply," according to an article in *U.S. News & World Report* (Koerner, 1999). Troubled by reports of seizures in monkeys and dogs under its influence or out of fear because of its hallucinogenic properties, Congress has made this drug illegal in the United States. Although more than 100 academic papers have been written on ibogaine, what is missing, according to a report from the Associated Press ("Attacking Addiction," 2000), are comprehensive studies to convince government authorities that the drug is safe. In the Netherlands, the drug is readily available to suppress withdrawal symptoms and reduce drug cravings. Experiments continue today on the Caribbean island of St. Kitts, where ibogaine reportedly has been highly effective not only in blocking withdrawal from opiates but also in counteracting the "crash" from stimulants like cocaine. Neurobiologist Deborah Mash conducted studies several years ago on the island of St. Kitts and found the results striking. Ibogaine appears to reset the chemical structures in the brain of a heroin addict so that the opiate withdrawal is blocked and the desire to use again is diminished (Hunter, 2005). Finally, Mash has obtained U.S. approval to authorize further testing on this remarkable drug.

St. John's wort, considered nature's own Prozac, is widely prescribed in Germany for depression and sleeping problems (Miller, 1997). The German emphasis is on the natural healing powers of the body, so their preference is for herbal and homeopathic remedies (Payer, 1996). St. John's wort has been shown in multiple clinical studies to alleviate depression in human subjects. Like pharmaceutical products, it takes about 2 weeks to work (Spinella, 2005). It does not seem to have any major side effects. Prozac is rarely prescribed in Germany. American health food stores are now carrying this herb as well as the kava root, which has mildly calming properties, according to Miller.

Kava assumes a social importance in many Pacific island societies similar to that of wine in southern Europe: a sacred drug, a social drink, and a cash crop (Lebot, Merlin, & Lindstrom, 1992; Spinella, 2005). Taken in high doses, kava can cause liver damage. Animal studies on kava confirm that it reduces pain, improves sleep, and has antiseizure effects. As used by the aboriginal people of Australia, however, as Lebot et al. (1992) indicate, this drug from the kava plant species is dangerous in the way that "alien poisons" often are to people who have no history with the drug. Heavy kava drinkers in Australia appear to be substituting kava for alcohol. It is destroying their health in the same way that alcohol has done; the medically harmful effects have been pronounced.

The goal of holistic therapies is to restore the body to its naturally healthy state. Holistic philosophy, as Apostolides (1996) suggests, overlaps with the harm reduction approach to addiction in its focus on treating the entire person, often with psychotherapy as well as medical remedies. In the major U.S. cities, a number of harm reduction centers now offer programs that include acupuncture, massage therapy, yoga, and substance misuse counseling.

Acupuncture consists of stimulating certain points on or near the surface of the body by inserting needles. Practiced in China for more than 5,000 years, its use in the treatment of narcotic addiction goes back only several decades (Reuben et al., 2005). In a clinical trial of 82 dually addicted participants (cocaine and some other drug), individuals in a methadone program were assigned to a control group—needles inserted in the wrong parts of the ear—to a group with correct ear placement, or to a relaxation group. More than 50% of the acupuncture patients later tested free of cocaine compared to 23.5% of the control acupuncture group and 9.1% of the relaxation group (NIDA, 2000). Other studies indicate a reduction in craving for alcohol and heroin (Reuben et al., 2005; Smith et al., 1997).

Acupuncture appears especially valuable during early-stage treatment. According to Smith et al. (1997), acupuncture patients report more calmness and reduced cravings for cocaine even after the first treatment. For methamphetamine use, similarly, studies show a high rate in early treatment when acupuncture is used. Even extremely antisocial people benefit from this treatment (Smith et al., 1997). The relatively small number of studies and methodological difficulties in conducting studies on acupuncture make it difficult to draw conclusions about its effectiveness (McNeece & DiNitto, 2005).

Massage therapy has achieved impressive results in tests on people dealing with anorexia, bulimia, smoking, and other addictions (Apostolides, 1996). The neurological response to body contact and to the loosening of tight muscles releases tension and helps clients "reconnect physically and center themselves emotionally" (p. 37). Similarly, yoga helps people get in tune with their physical processes, including muscular exertion—holding certain positions—and breathing.

Simple exercise is effective in reducing tension and in elevating mood because, with continuous activity, the body produces endorphins the natural way. Exercise has been found to decrease symptoms of depression. Animal studies of exercise show that such physical activity stimulates the secretion of the natural opiates and serotonin in the brain (Haga, 2004). In humans, exercise probably also works by distracting people from their worries and having a calming effect. Unfortunately, treatment centers often overlook the curative powers of activities such as swimming, hiking, and biking.

Heavy drinking and other drug misuse can cause hypoglycemia, or low blood sugar, as well; the craving for sugar by alcoholics is a consequence. Vitamin C sometimes is used by nutrition therapists to modify the withdrawal symptoms of detoxification (Apostolides, 1996). To replenish the body's nutrients that have been depleted through chemical misuse and faulty diets, accordingly, is an important component of recovery. Drinking large quantities of alcohol, for example, depletes the body of thiamine and other vitamins (Volpicelli & Szalavitz, 2000). Nutrients such as niacin, amino acids, and magnesium are given to alleviate problems caused by low levels of glucose in the brain. In early recovery, sleeping in a nondrugged state can present major problems. Drinking a glass of milk or one of the herbal teas, such as Sleepy Bear, can be immensely helpful. Melatonin is an over-the-counter drug that induces a natural sleep and has few side effects.

Pet therapy is recommended by Haga (2004) for stress reduction, providing touch, and building self-esteem, especially for children. Clients suffering from PTSD often bond with animals for valuable companionship. The physical act of taking care of an animal helps pull people out of depression.

Hypnosis is another remedy that helps people gain control over their urges to use, in this case through the use of suggestion. While in a trance, patients may be told to view their drug of choice with distaste (Murphy, 2004). Treatments usually last for 30 minutes, and only a few sessions are required. From a more positive stance, people can rehearse coping with urges to use until they develop the capacity to do so while in a non-trancelike state. Like hypnosis and acupuncture, biofeedback is administered by persons with specialized training.

The aim of biofeedback is brainwave training to reduce stress. And like hypnosis, biofeedback (also called brainwave training) is a "mind over matter" phenomenon in which the individual, through training, learns to attain a deep level of relaxation for the purpose of helping maintain sobriety. Levin (1995) describes the way this method works: Electroencephalograph (EEG) measures of anxiety levels are obtained so that the individual can monitor his or her response in conjunction with the feedback. After pretraining, individuals receive alpha-theta brainwave training. While in the alpha, or deeply relaxed, state, the substance user might be instructed in refusing drinks or drugs. Although this method has shown some success, there are two basic drawbacks noted by Levin: The equipment is expensive, and there are unexpected effects, such as the return of repressed traumatic memories that may lead to emotional distress.

ASSESSMENT OF ALCOHOL AND OTHER DRUG USE

The purpose of assessment is to determine the level of addiction and if there is alcohol or other drug addiction at all, as after an arrest for a drunk driving offense; to find out the drug or drugs to which the individual is addicted; and to determine the kind of program that would be most beneficial to the client. Ideally, the assessment should be done by an independent evaluation agency with no affiliation or commitment to a particular approach or program (Hester

& Miller, 2003). The evaluator can then provide the individual with options and reliable guidelines to help in decision making. For example, outgoing talkers might thrive in a group-based program that requires attendance at self-help groups; more withdrawn, anxiety-prone persons might prefer individual therapy. Motivational enhancement therapy is well suited to the needs of adolescents and resistant clients as well as early-stage alcoholics for whom learning to drink moderately might be a realistic goal. From a harm reduction perspective, assessment is about choice. Realistically, however, the options are only as varied as the third-party payers allow.

Because assessment usually precedes treatment, this process to determine the level and effect of drug and alcohol use comes early, while the mind is often still clouded with the effect of drug taking and alcohol use. The cessation of accustomed drug use leads to all kinds of physiological responses as well. In the final analysis, as we will see in later chapters, however difficult the road to physical recovery is, the psychological aspects are even more profound.

For assessment of substance use problems, cultural awareness is a must. Among Native Americans, for example, peyote use is considered a ritualized experience, not a destructive practice associated with loss of control. In mountain areas of Colombia, similarly, chewing the coca plant (a key ingredient in cocaine) is associated with good health and protection against the stresses of the high altitude. Questions on assessment forms concerning hallucinations need to take into account Native American practices in some tribes where participants go to great lengths to induce hallucinations for spiritual purposes.

When clients and therapists speak different first languages, translation problems and misunderstandings are rampant, whether through written forms or with personal translators. As an example, the English word *craving* is not easily translated into Spanish, nor is the concept easily understood (Blume, Morera, & de la Cruz, 2005). In Norway, in van Wormer's experience, the term *powerless* (as in "powerless over alcohol") was most commonly translated with the word *hjelpeløs* or "helpless" in English.

Alcohol screening questionnaires, invariably designed for male populations, need to be sensitive to female physiological and psychological drinking experiences. A review of alcohol screening questionnaires in the *Journal of the American Medical Association* (Bradley, Boyd-Wickizer, Powell, & Burman, 1998) examined screening devices for effectiveness in detecting alcohol dependence in White women and Black women. Since women suffer adverse consequences at lower levels of drinking and experience fewer economic and employment consequences perhaps than men, yet are more stigmatized by heavy drinking, questionnaires validated for male populations may fail to measure alcoholism in women. The computer search of questionnaire evaluations conducted by Bradley et al. (1998) revealed that CAGE and TWEAK were the optimal tests for identification of alcohol dependence in women (Table 5.1). However, effectiveness varied by ethnicity. For Black obstetric patients and for White women, questionnaires that asked about tolerance for alcohol

TABLE 5.1	CAGE AND TWEAK TESTS FOR ALCOHOL DEPENDENCE
C	Have you ever felt you ought to Cut down on your drinking?
A	Have people Annoyed you by criticizing your drinking?
G	Have you felt bad or Guilty about your drinking?
E	Have you ever had a drink in the morning (Eye opener) to steady your nerves or get rid of a hangover?

Scoring: 1 point for each "yes" response; sum all points; total, 0–4 points. An answer of "yes" to two of these items is considered problematic.

T	Tolerance: How many drinks can you hold ("hold" version: 6 or more drinks indicates tolerance), or how many drinks does it take before you begin to feel the first effect of the alcohol? ("high" version: 3 or more indicates tolerance)
W	Worried: Have close friends or relatives worried or complained about your drinking in the past year?
E	Eye openers: Do you sometimes take a drink in the morning when your first get up?
A	Amnesia: Has a friend or family member ever told you about things you said or did while you were drinking that you could not remember?
K	Kut down: Do you sometimes feel the need to cut down on your drinking?

(e.g., TWEAK) were more sensitive. For use with mixed populations, therefore, the researchers recommend TWEAK. The advantage of these questionnaires is that they are so brief that they can easily be carried around in the counselor's head.

People who drink can do a self-assessment of the risks in their alcohol use at http://www.alcoholscreening.org. This questionnaire is based on AUDIT (Alcohol Use Disorders Identification Test), which was developed by the World Health Organization as a brief, cross-cultural screening tool. An advantage over CAGE is that it assesses current drinking habits.

Campus health professionals and college students will find a useful self-guided questionnaire at www.e-chug.com with a focus on alcohol consumption and www.e-toke.com with a focus on marijuana use. Based on motivational interviewing principles, these questionnaires are designed to lead the heavy drinker toward a realization of the need to adopt healthier attitudes and behaviors.

A lengthier instrument for assessing adverse consequences of alcohol misuse is offered by the National Institute on Alcohol Abuse and Alcoholism (NIH Publication No. 95-3911). This 50-item instrument, the Inventory of Drug Use Consequences, is presented in a manual of the much publicized Project MATCH Monograph Series, Vol. 4 (Project MATCH Research Group, 1997). It is in the public domain and therefore can be reproduced without permission or expense. It is available online at http://pubs.niaaa.nih.gov/publications/niaaa-guide/index.htm.

The World Health Organization of the United Nations has delineated seven major life areas for determining whether or not a substance misuse problem exists. Consistent with harm reduction, the word *harm* is used throughout the report. The major life areas, which have been chosen because of their universal qualities for cross-national research, are physical health, family and relationships, leisure, emotional health, finances, the law, and social life/employment.

URINALYSIS TESTING

Urine analysis, better known as UA or urinalysis, is widely used as a check on client claims regarding substance use. Drug courts conduct random screenings that require the client to urinate in a cup, while the probation officer observes to make sure there is no cheating (substitution of another's urine). Then the urine is sent to a lab for testing. (Test strips may be used by the counselor to give immediate results.) Counselors at most substance abuse treatment centers also conduct such testing—male counselors with male clients and female with female. Such practices clearly are incompatible with the precepts of the strengths perspective because they violate the key principles of trust, listening, and collaboration. In addition, these practices also defy principles of harm reduction, which emphasize reducing the harm such as by cutting down or switching from a more dangerous to a less dangerous drug. Moreover, the invasion of privacy raises issues of ethics and human rights, including rights to privacy.

If there must be testing (often mandated by the court), an alternative technique that is less intrusive is the drug or sweat patch. This device consists of a piece of adhesive that collects sweat over weeks or months. The test is inexpensive; sweat patches can detect the presence of the major drugs of abuse. A more expensive device, the Macroduct, can generate sweat on the spot and has been found to be more sensitive than urinalysis in detecting opiates and cocaine (National Institute of Justice, 2004). Social workers who object to the degrading practice of collecting UAs might advocate for the use of one of these more palatable if not thoroughly acceptable alternatives.

STRENGTHS-BASED ASSESSMENT

Assessment does not only entail substance use but also such matters as readiness to change or motivation, problem-solving skills, and potentially high-risk situations for relapse. From a strengths-based perspective, assessment of individual and family strengths is important as well. The strengths perspective does not ignore or minimize diagnoses but does assert that these diagnoses must be seen as contextual and as part of a larger process (Graybeal, 2001). The therapist needs to ensure that diagnosis is not identity (Saleebey, 2006, Sullivan & Rapp, 2006). Nor is the assessment an end in itself. The intent is to use the assessment, which is viewed as an ongoing process, to decipher a range of possible life goals that can be the focus of the helping relationship (Sullivan & Rapp, 2006).

Graybeal, in his article on strengths-based assessment, contrasts traditional and strengths-based considerations. The focus in the traditional assessment forms is on patterns of use, frequency, and negative consequences. Additional information that can be sought to shift the focus from the negative to the positive, as listed by Graybeal (2001, p. 238), is

"How does using help?" _____

Note periods of using less (difference) _____

Periods of abstinence (exceptions to using) _____

Personal and family rituals _____

What has endured despite use/abuse? _____

Because most agencies use traditional assessment forms (as required by third-party funding sources), and because the collection of information concerning drinking and drug use by clients can be useful, the strengths-based practitioner can do two things: (a) solicit additional information of a positive sort to add to the assessment process and/or (b) provide feedback in a manner consistent with the principles of harm reduction and motivational interviewing. Here, from a strengths-based perspective, the emphasis is on client choice: Whether or not to accept the diagnosis as provided by the instrument used is up to the client. Feedback based on the information obtained from the official instrument is provided in a manner consistent with the principles of motivational interviewing. The counselor, for example, might begin by saying something like, "Let's see if this assessment tells us anything we need to know" or "Let's see if these results are accurate or not and if we should pay any attention to them . . ." Above all, the counselor should ask the client what he or she thinks of the standardized results. Miller and Rollnick's (2002) caution to avoid the expert, labeling, and argumentation traps is relevant here.

It is important to keep in mind that treatment is successful to the extent to which it motivates clients to change in a health-fulfilling direction. Two useful readiness-to-change instruments are available from www.ndri.org. For problem drinkers, The Readiness to Change Questionnaire from the United Kingdom Centre for Alcohol and Drug Studies (fax: 44 [0] 191219 5649) can serve to assess motivational factors. Data provided from this brief questionnaire can be helpful in later bringing the client's attention to the discrepancy between behaviors (e.g., to sleep in half the day) and goals (e.g., to get a rewarding job) that have been set. If the client can make the connection between the failure to achieve a goal and substance misuse, this can be a powerful source of motivation to change.

Further information that is useful is obtaining an objective measure of the level of the client's motivation to change—precontemplation, contemplation, and so on—so that interventions can be shaped accordingly. Various assessment forms can be introduced spontaneously when the timing is right. Assessment, after all, is an ongoing process. (Useful forms are available here: SAMHSA's, 2005, TIP 42, *Substance Abuse Treatment for Persons with Co-occurring Disorders* at http://www.ncbi.nlm.nih.gov/books. Most of the assessment forms in TIP 42 are in the public domain and can be downloaded and used free of charge.)

ASSESSMENT OF PERSONS WITH CO-OCCURRING DISORDERS

Integrated assessment is critical to understanding the interactions between mental illness and substance misuse. Substance misuse worsens the outcome of severe mental illness, and vice versa. Because individuals with two or more disorders typically have a wide range of needs, Mueser et al. (2003) delineate seven types of services that need to be considered for an appropriate treatment plan. These are residential services, case management needs for severe mental illness, supported employment, family psychoeducation, social skills training, training of clients for illness management, and pharmacological treatment.

Homelessness, as Mueser et al. (2003) further indicate, is a crucial area of concern and one that sometimes accompanies either mental illness or substance use alone but even more often when these two disorders coexist. Traditionally, help in obtaining permanent housing was only provided after the client has been treated and is in recovery from substance addiction. Recent evidence, however, would have us turn this practice around and provide the housing immediately. Padgett, Gulcur, and Tsemberis (2006) examined the longitudinal effects of a Housing First program for over 100 homeless, mentally ill individuals. In this program, integrated treatment was provided for persons with both mental and substance-related disorders. Another 100 or so homeless individuals were assigned to receive housing only contingent on their sobriety. Interviews were conducted several times over a 2-year period. Findings were of no difference between the groups in substance use or psychiatric symptoms. "Sober housing," in short, did not produce the desired results in terms of abstinence. Since ending homelessness is a high value in itself both to individuals and society, these findings can be interpreted from a harm reduction perspective as evidence in favor of providing stable, supportive housing for people regardless of their personal habits. That is, policies requiring abstinence for subsidized housing for persons with mental illness and substance use problems should be reconsidered. (See chapter 8, Box 8.1, for details on innovative programming for homeless persons with co-occurring disorders.)

Motivational strategies have been found especially helpful in working with persons who have serious mental disorders. As stated by Padgett et al. (2006), "The one-size-fits-all assumption that mental disorders and homelessness cannot be addressed until a client is clean and sober, is no longer valid" (p. 81). A harm reduction orientation is a must with a population whose risk for relapse is extremely high and whose suitability for total-abstinence-oriented treatment is doubtful. (See SAMHSA, 2005, *Substance Abuse Treatment for Persons with Co-occurring Disorders*: TIP 42.)

Diagnosis for mental disorders is often done by a psychologist or psychiatrist before the social worker sees the client or in collaboration with other mental health practitioners. Knowledge of the *DSM* criteria used by the psychiatric team and insurance agencies is essential for shared understandings among professionals in this field. The social worker then can seek evidence of diagnosis indirectly by checking on the client's medications. (An easy-to-use mental health screening form to assess emotional disturbance in persons with co-occurring disorders is contained in Appendix H of TIP 45. It is available at www.ncbi.nlm.nih.gov/books/bv.fcgi?rid=hstat5.section.77099.)

GROUP WORK FOR EARLY-PHASE TREATMENT

Substance abuse counselors need to shape their interventions to match the biological readiness of the client to participate. A brain damaged by alcohol and other drugs can take in only so much. A client with 6 months of physical recovery and 6 months of practice in social skills and motivational work is clearly in better shape to work on deep emotional issues than a man or woman sober for only 10 days. Long-term outpatient programs using a stages-of-change model are desirable, especially for polyaddicted clients whose bodies require long periods of time to get clean of any substance.

For simplicity, we will describe a treatment modality designed for a group of clients all presumed to be at the initial stage of recovery. In reality, most actual working groups contain clients at various stages of recovery, and those with longer periods of sobriety and group participation ideally serve as models for newcomers. Drawing upon the stages-of-change model proposed by Prochaska, DiClemente, and Norcross (1992), we are providing guidelines for work at the very first stages of thinking about change. These stages are termed "precontemplation" and "contemplation." What we have added to this model is an allowance for the kind of thinking impairment related to brain dysfunction that is characteristic of a history of substance misuse. An awareness of the brain's regenerative powers is an important consideration as well. This focus on healing parallels the strengths perspective's emphasis on the human potential for growth and recovery and the belief that it is never too soon to start the process of tapping into people's inner resources.

Treatment strategies, in short, cannot exceed the mind's ability to absorb them. Interventions, therefore, must correspond to the client's biological state of recovery. Immediately following detoxification, for example, the stress is on the biological aspect of recovery and on clinical interventions geared to healing the mind and body. This first period of treatment ideally lasts for several months. Psychologically based therapy (as described in chapter 7) is only effective at a later stage, when the mind is free of chemicals and alternative ways of dealing with stress have been mastered. In the phase approach, the progression is from supportive, highly structured individual sessions or groups to work in the later period on deeper, more psychologically disturbing issues with long-term ramifications (e.g., career planning, relationships). The following guidelines are geared toward group facilitation; with a few modifications, however, they can serve to inform individual therapy as well.

GROUP PROCESS IN EARLY-STAGE TREATMENT

Will clients be required to abstain totally from use of all mood-altering (non-prescription) medications, or will they be able to attend group sessions while they make up their minds what to do about their drug intake? In reality, the choice very rarely is in the hands of the group facilitator and not always the agency. In the United States, clients are often under court-ordered sanctions. Total abstinence generally is required for the duration of treatment. The focus during the first part of treatment is on the *biological* side of alcoholism and recovery. The question "How do you feel?" is apt to be answered at this time in terms of how the members slept last night, what they are eating, and what kind of mood they are in. Today, one day at a time, keeping things simple and learning how to reduce stress are the guiding principles of an early-recovery group. Typically, an individual in early recovery is very literal and concrete in his or her thinking and may have great difficulty in handling ambiguity (Wallen, 1993). As Patt Denning (2000) indicates, heavy alcohol intake or excessive use of tranquilizers is associated with diminished abstract reasoning ability; paranoid thinking may be evident in long-term stimulant users.

The basic function of initial treatment is to provide basic education on the addictive process and to impart a sense of hope that the alcoholic can somehow overcome and prevail against this addiction that has created so much havoc. Group structure is tight; the group leader lectures, uses diagrams, and generally fulfills the information-giving function of early treatment. Information must be provided on particulars of the total program and the legal requirements, if any. Finally, general and not terribly complicated information concerning the physical illness of addiction is given. Slides of the "brain on drugs" can be immensely helpful in eliciting self-understanding and preparing clients for the down feelings that accompany the early period of sobriety. As a supplement to lecture material, educational films are often shown. Such films teach the effects of substance misuse on the mind, the body, and relationships. Because of the newness of the material, it is often advisable to show each film more than once and to repeat important points periodically.

In the early phase of treatment, the primary focus of intervention is to establish a favorable client–therapist relationship as a springboard for building trust and motivation (SAMHSA, 2005). Once trust is established, the group facilitator is in a position to give advice and, better yet, in a skillful drawing out of helpful comments from group members, to reinforce their insights, which are often quite astute. Group feedback is far more powerful than individual feedback. Group members who may not be ready to assess their own behavior realistically often do quite well in assessing others' behaviors accurately. In van Wormer's women's therapy group in Washington State, for example, group members, many of whom were involved in destructive, often battering relationships, were quick to realize when another woman was being exploited by her boyfriend.

The group norms that develop early can "make or break" the evolving alcoholism therapy group. The leader's role in developing therapeutic group norms is essential. The norms desired are those that promote sharing in the group, sobriety, and individual change efforts. Norms *not* desired are those that sanction complaining about the courts, the police, the program, or those that reinforce externalization and fatalism.

As clients begin to trust the leader and the group, they will begin to self-disclose. As they take more and more risks and get supportive feedback, they come to trust the group more. In working with male alcoholics on gender-based issues, the group leader might first model the desired behavior and then encourage sharing. This process assists members in realizing that they are not alone in their anxieties and inhibitions.

GETTING STARTED

The group leader can help members set their own rules; then he or she can help the group enforce these rules. First, the leader lists the agency rules, such as:

- No smoking or drinking soft drinks in the group
- No admission of intoxicated members into the group

Then group members are asked to suggest rules they would like to set for their group. Invariably, the following suggestions are made and approved:

- What is said in the group stays in the group
- No put-downs or attacks on individuals
- No interruptions when someone is speaking; don't all talk at once
- No name-calling; no shouting

When the leader must remind the group that rules *they* have set are being violated, group members are often relieved to have this form of external protection. They make the rules, and they can rely on the leader to help enforce them.

What is the addiction counselor's role in promoting appropriate group norms? The trained leader makes use of effective group interventions at key points in the group process. Early in the group's life, skillful intervention serves as a model for group members, who are thereby being groomed to assume responsibility for this function at some later stage of the group process. Significantly, well-timed interventions help keep members working on their goals and give everyone a sense of security and structure.

GROUPS FOR PERSONS WITH CO-OCCURRING DISORDERS

Handmaker, Packard, and Conforti (2002) describe a group design for persons with co-occurring disorders who are at the precontemplation to contemplation stage of change. "Talking About Change" is the name of the group; the goal for individuals is simply to attend the group to consider the prospect of making a behavioral change. Structural motivational exercises, such as working through a pros-and-cons list on a flipchart, are conducted. Another exercise is to engage the group in a discussion of the stages of change through use of an illustration of a wheel of change. Group members are asked to place themselves on the wheel and consider what it would take to get them to move forward.

The group facilitator tries to elicit self-motivational statements in the members to help them progress toward the preparation stage of change. Throughout the sessions, the leader helps clients with their cognitive skills, as, for example, to combat depression.

Substance abuse counselor Angela Woods provided the following description of a specialized program at her Iowa treatment center:

> **Dual Diagnosis Program**: addresses the issues of the dual diagnosis (chemical dependency and mental illness). Patients learn that much of the recovery work for chemical dependency is helpful for recovery regarding mental illness. Patients learn about medications, their particular mental illness and symptoms, relapse signs and symptoms. This group is freeing for many as patients speak openly about mental illness in an aura of acceptance. Day to day stressors are addressed as well as many living tasks such as organization, exercise, nutrition, etc. Patients learn how chemical usage impacts mental illness and its symptoms. This group of patients also meets long term, and hence tends to form a very tight bond. This program has a tendency to lean more toward motivational interviewing and harm reduction (than programs for clients without mental disorders) as relapses are viewed here as something that happens and are renamed as an opportunity for growth. (personal communication, July 18, 2006)

SKILLS OF GROUP WORK

Experts in the field recommend a highly structured approach in the initial sessions (Yalom, 1995). Group leaders have to contend with denial, defensiveness, and ingenious avoidance tactics (avoidance of emotionally painful areas). Under the circumstances, leaders have to closely monitor the discussion and continually be prepared to shift the focus back to the therapeutic goals. A helpful strategy in lengthy group sessions is to vary group size. Many individuals who are uncommunicative in large groups will work well in groups of two, three, four, or five. To maintain a sense of unity in the large group, the small groups may choose a spokesperson to report on what they accomplished in their discussion.

A useful way to begin the process in individual or small-group sessions has been proposed by Denning (2000). The therapist divides a sheet of black paper into two halves. The top half is entitled "Change my drinking/drug use," and the bottom half is called "Continue the way I am now." On the left side under each heading is the space to list the pros, and on the right side is an area to list the cons. The purpose of the exercise is to promote decision making and help motivate clients in the direction of change. Ideally, the negative side of drug use will emerge in a compelling fashion through this activity.

According to Kenneth Reid (2002), the group facilitator

- encourages members to actively participate.
- links interrelated issues, ideas, feelings, and thoughts.
- blocks the expression of inappropriate behaviors by members or by the group as a whole.
- limits behaviors and actions by holding to boundaries and structure.
- partializes problems or concerns into manageable units.
- reframes problems and situations.

WHEN INTERVENTION IS CALLED FOR

The group counselor can expect to "step in" with an appropriate question or comment when

1. A group member monopolizes the group and other members either seem uncomfortable or too comfortable with this role (common in groups of involuntary clients).
2. A group member focuses on external events (court, parents, spouse, loss) in ascribing blame and fails to take any personal responsibility.
3. A group member falls into the widely recognized "all-or-nothing" thinking fallacy. Typically heard "all-or-nothing" statements are these: "There are two types of people—the weak and the strong"; "If you don't get an A in a course, why bother?"; "If you can't be the best, then why bother at all?"
4. The recovering member expresses an abnormally high degree of guilt or self-blame over the drug abuse and its consequences.
5. Members fail to confront someone or indicate their concern for one who is "setting him- or herself up" for personal tragedy.
6. Group members are sidetracked and turn the session into a "gripe session."
7. A member fails to see any *positive* thread in his or her attempt to grow and needs appropriate reinforcement for the small steps taken.
8. A client arrives at a group intoxicated or expresses views conducive to harmful behavior.
9. The mood of the group is too heavy and should be lightened. Or conversely, the mood is too light and thoughts should be moved in a more serious direction.
10. Effective individual and group maneuvers are observed; these should be positively reinforced as a model to all participants.
11. When group members make eye contact with the leader but not with each other. Say, "Tell the group, don't tell me."

GROUP EXERCISES

Group exercises during the beginning of treatment focus on getting acquainted, building trust among members who will be sharing parts of their lives with each other, and setting the stage for deeper, more intensive work to follow.

1. Communication

Purposes: To get acquainted; to explore levels of communication.

Clients divide into groups of four. They are told to communicate for the first 3 minutes at a superficial level: talk about the weather, food, clothes. The second 3 minutes, they talk of a recent event—a movie or sports. The third 3 minutes, they express opinions on controversial topics. The next 3 minutes they fill out cards that say:

I feel scared when _____
I feel happy when _____
I feel jealous when _____
I feel rejected when _____

Clients take turns filling in with their responses. The fifth period of time is focused on "the peak experience." Each member describes a peak moment of great revelations in his or her life.

While the interaction is taking place, the leader visits among the various groups. He or she announces the end of each time period and beckons members to move on to the next level. Following the last exchange, the groups rejoin each other. The leader may engage the participants in discussion by introducing such questions as: *At which level did you feel the least (or the most) comfortable? Did you learn something meaningful about each other? What surprised you about this exercise? At which level do you usually communicate throughout the day?* Discussion ensues.

2. Use of Cards

Purposes: To get acquainted; to learn to feel safe; to begin to learn to express feelings in the group.

Group members fill out cards on which questions or statements are written. Some sample statements and questions are:

Say something positive about yourself.
My favorite childhood memory is _____
Something I value highly is _____
Name a famous alcoholic/addict and tell this person's story: _____
_____
If I could have three wishes, I would wish _____
My advice to a young person is _____
My understanding of alcoholism is _____

3. Positive Feedback

Purpose: To boost self-esteem.

Sometimes a group member who is relating well to others puts himself or herself down. Group members are asked to say positive things about the member. The person records the messages. In later sessions, the person is asked to repeat these positive comments. This exercise helps provide substance for improved "self-talk" and to replace negative with positive thoughts.

4. Values Card Sorting

Purpose: To boost commitment to values.

Group members are each given a stack of cards with values about life on them. They are asked to stack the cards in order of the values that they hold dear. In getting clients to argue for the importance of these values, their commitment to them ideally will be reinforced through public expression of the values. The information gathered in this exercise can be used throughout the sessions to enhance motivation for change.

We have considered basic elements of the group during the early stages, not only in the group treatment process but also in the addict's sobriety. In many ways, the early period of therapy is the most difficult; individual resistance is at a maximum, relapse is common, and defensiveness is a characteristic. Principles of motivational interviewing come into play in the group setting as in the individual setting. The individuals are not pushed into decision making but encouraged through compassionate listening to move in a health-seeking direction. As the group leader models this client-centered approach, the members follow. Then two major aims of the first months of treatment are accomplished: Group bonding is developed, and the group members function as a supportive, working group.

SUMMARY AND CONCLUSION

Understanding addiction as largely a biologically based phenomenon may help explain an individual's difficulty in achieving and maintaining abstinence without appropriate treatment. The tendency to relapse is now (thanks to neurological imaging of the brain) known to be as much a biological as a psychological phenomenon. The use of medications to quell the biological urges to relapse is today revolutionizing the field of addiction treatment. The shibboleths of the profession are changing; this includes absolutes such as "Abstain from all mood-altering substances." The pharmaceutical advances should hasten clients' progress in treatment indirectly through improving their mental states. Since one of the leading causes of relapse is depression, medications that help replenish the brain of the natural opiates (e.g., Prozac) are an effective adjunct to relapse prevention. Naltrexone and buprenorphine, drugs in a different category from the serotonin-boosting medications, function by blocking cravings for substances like alcohol and heroin. Because alcoholics and addicts seem to have an underlying vulnerability to a number of compulsive behaviors, including compulsive gambling and eating disorders, medication geared toward normalizing brain functioning should reap benefits in these related areas as well.

The pharmaceutical treatment of addictive behaviors is in its infancy. The next few years should see remarkable progress in this area as new and more effective therapies are developed. As is always the case with new technologies, there is a cultural lag between discovery and treatment. This lag is reflected in public policies predicated on threats of punishment to the neglect of sound biomedical and psychological research. Social workers should follow developments in pharmacology carefully so that they can help educate clients with addiction problems and tell concerned family members about the treatments available. Sadly, the child welfare system, as indicated by social workers Lundgren, Schilling, and Peloquin (2005), has been remiss in its failure to offer methadone as a treatment alternative for drug-dependent parents. Such an option helps keep many families intact by keeping the parents in compliance with the law. Happily, a few states are moving in the direction of integrating child welfare services with harm reduction strategies, so there are hopeful prospects for the future.

A second major development is the realization that cognitive therapies can help reverse irregularities in the brain. Such cognitively based therapy can be provided in individual or group settings. Moreover, behavioral strategies that can be learned in a group can help people during that crucial early stage of recovery to cope with their drug cravings and to avoid drug-related cues. (Such high-risk situations, in all probability, are due to euphoric memories that were imprinted in the mind, which readily can trigger a return to drug-using behavior.)

This chapter focused on therapies aimed at work with clients during their period of maximum craving for chemical relief and vulnerability to relapse. Guidelines were provided for group treatment that uses a phase approach, where interventions are matched to the biological and psychological stages of recovery. Focusing on the mechanics of setting up a nonthreatening therapeutic experience, we provided a framework that is adaptable for use in a variety of settings and with a variety of philosophical approaches. Having completed Part II of this book—the study of the biology of addiction—we proceed to a look at the equally compelling psychological aspects.

REFERENCES

Addiction Treatment Forum. (2000, Winter). Clinical concepts—naltrexone in action against alcoholism. *AT Forum*. Retrieved February 2007 from http://www.atforum .com/SiteRoot/pages/current_pastissues/winter2000.shtml#anchor1221360/current _pastissues/winter2000.html.

Addiction Treatment Forum. (2006, Spring). Atlanta conference focuses on criminal justice system. *AT Forum, 15*(2), 2–4.

Aldous, P. (2005, February 10). Drug rehabilitation: Cold turkey, Vietnamese style. *Nature, 433,* 568–569.

American Lung Association. (2006, June 27). The facts about secondhand smoke. *Lung Association News*. Retrieved February 2007 from http://blog01.kintera.com/ lungusa/archives/2006/07/index.html.

Antidepressant proves beneficial in helping smokers kick the habit. (1998, January 21). *Waterloo–Cedar Falls Courier,* p. A8.

Antidepressants help smokers to quit. (1997, November 15). *Science News,* p. 152.

Anton, R. F., O'Malley, S., Ciraulo, D., Cisler, R., Couper, D. Donovan, D., et al. (2006, May 3). Combined pharmacotherapies and behavioral interventions for alcohol dependence. *Journal of the American Medical Association, 295*(17), 2003–2018.

Apostolides, M. (1996, September/October). How to quit the holistic way. *Psychology Today,* pp. 35–43, 68–70.

Armstrong, J. (2005, January 31). Is free heroin just a quick fix? *Globe and Mail,* p. A1.

Baldino, R. (2000). *Welcome to methadonia: A social worker's candid account of life in a methadone clinic.* Harrisburg, PA: White Hat Communications.

Bavley, A. (1999, May 2). Kicking the habit a tough row to hoe for hard-core smokers. *Waterloo–Cedar Falls Courier,* p. A8.

Begley, S. (2007). How the brain rewires itself. *Time,* pp. 72–79.

Black, D. W., Repertinger, S., Gaffney, G., & Gabel, J. (1998, July). Family history and psychiatric comorbidity in persons with compulsive buying: Preliminary findings. *American Journal of Psychiatry, 155*(7), 960–964.

Blume, A., Morera, O., & de la Cruz, B. (2005). Assessment of addictive behaviors in ethnic-minority cultures. In D. Donovan & G. A. Marlatt (Eds.), *Assessment of addictive behaviors* (2nd ed., pp. 49–70). New York: Guilford Press.

Bordnick, P. S. (1996). Evaluating the relative effectiveness of three aversion therapies designed to reduce craving among male cocaine abusers. *Dissertation Abstracts International, 56*(10-A), 4145.

Boyce, N. (2001, February 12). The debt to pleasure. *U.S. News & World Report,* p. 59.

Bradley, K. A., Boyd-Wickizer, J., Powell, S. H., & Burman, M. L. (1998, July 8). Alcohol screening questionnaires in women: A critical review. *Journal of the American Medical Association, 280*(2), 166–171.

Brewerton, T. D. (2004, May). Pharmacotherapy for patients with eating disorders. *Psychiatric Times, 21*(6). Retrieved August 2006 from http://psychiatrictimes .com/p040559.html.

Brodie, J., Figueroa, E., Laska, E., & Dewey, S. (2005). Safety and efficacy of g-Vinyl GABA (GVG) for the treatment of methamphetamine and/or cocaine addiction. *Synapse, 55,* 122–125.

Burman, S. (2001). Strategies for intervention with individuals. In A. Abbott (Ed.), *Alcohol, tobacco, & other drugs: Challenging myths, assessing theories, individualizing interventions* (pp. 204–246). Washington, DC: NASW Press.

Casadonte, P. (2004, August). Community treatment programs take up buprenorphine. *Science and Practice Perspectives,* pp. 24–29.

Challender, M. (1999, April 18). They thirst for sobriety. *Des Moines Register,* pp. 1E, 2E.

Costello, D. (2002, October 28). Clean and sober in 48 hours? *Los Angeles Times.* Retrieved February 2007 from http://www.opiates.com/media/rapid-detox-latimes .html.

Cowley, G. (2001, February 12). New ways to stay clean. *Newsweek,* pp. 45–47.

Crews, F. T. (2001, March). Cited in How sensitive is your brain to alcohol-induced damage? *Addiction Science.* Retrieved from February 2007 from http:// www.scienceblog.com/community/older/2001/A/200110264.html.

Cummings, K., Fix, B., Celestino, P., Carlin-Menter, S., O'Connor, R., & Hyland, A. (2006). Reach, efficacy, and cost-effectiveness of free nicotine medication giveaway programs. *Journal of Public Health Management & Practice, 12*(1), 37–43.

Curley, B. (2007, January 5). New law expands access to buprenorphine. *Join Together Online.* Retrieved February 2007 from http://www.jointogether.org.

Denning, P. (2000). *Practicing harm reduction psychotherapy: An alternative approach to addictions.* New York: Guilford Press.

Downside of nicotine gum examined. (2000, November 30). Retrieved from http:// www.jointogether.org.

Ehrenfeld, T. (2005, June 13). New hope for addicts? *Newsweek.* Retrieved February 2007 from http://www.msnbc.msn.com/id/8100267/site/newsweek.

Figgitt, D. P., & McClellan, K. J. (2000). An updated review of its use in the management of adults with anxiety disorders. *Drugs, 60*(4), 925–954.

Filozof, C., Fernandez, P., Fernandez-Cruz, A. (2004). Smoking cessation and weight gain. *Obesity Review, 5*(2), 95–103.

Fisher, G. L., & Harrison, T. C. (2005). *Substance abuse: Information for school counselors, social workers, therapists, and counselors.* Boston: Allyn & Bacon.

Garbutt, J., Kranzler, H., O'Malley, S., Gastfriend, D., Pettinati, H., & Silverman, B. (2005, April 6). Efficacy and tolerability of long-acting injectable naltrexone for alcohol dependence. *Journal of the American Medical Association, 293*(13), 1617.

Gonzales, D., Rennard, S. I., Nides, M., Oncken, C., Azoulay, S., Billing, C., et al. (2006). Varenicline, an a4 b2 nicotine acetycholine receptor partial agonist. *Journal of the American Medical Association, 296,* 47–55.

Gore, M. J. (2006, June 16). Kicking the habit: Research yields effective therapy for battling cocaine addiction. *Inside UVA (University of Virginia) Online.* Retrieved February 2007 from http://www.virginia.edu/insideuva/cocaine.html.

Grant, J. E. (2005, January/February). Outcome study of kleptomania patients treated with naltrexone. *Clinical Neuropharmacology, 28*(1), 11–14.

Graybeal, C. (2001). Strengths-based social work assessment: Transforming the dominant paradigm. *Families in Society, 82*(3), 233–242.

Haga, J. (2004). Multiple routes to quality of life. In H. Johnson, *Psyche and synapse behavior, thinking, and addiction for non-scientists* (pp. 299–315). Greenfield, MA: Deerfield Valley.

Halmi, K. A. (1998). A 24-year-old woman with anorexia nervosa. *Journal of the American Medical Association, 279*(24), 1992–1999.

Handmaker, N., Packard, M., & Conforti, K. (2002). Motivational interviewing in the treatment of dual disorders. In W. R. Miller & S. Rollnick (Eds.), *Motivational interviewing: Preparing people for change* (2nd ed., pp. 362–376). New York: Guilford Press.

Harvard Mental Health Letter. (2005, January). Treating opiate addiction, Part II: Alternatives to maintenance. Retrieved February 2007 from http://www .accessmylibrary.com/coms2/summary_0286-18273952_ITM.

Healton, C. (2001, March 26). Smoking clouds women's futures. *USA Today,* p. 19A.

Hester, R. K., & Miller, W. R. (2003). *Handbook of alcoholism treatment approaches: Effective alternatives* (3rd ed.). Boston: Allyn & Bacon.

Hobson, K. (2006, October 23). A wave of new drugs targeting addiction offers hope to people battling the habit. *U.S. News & World Report,* pp. 64–66.

Hunter, A. (2005, February 18). The drug to end all drugs. *Village Voice.* Retrieved August 2006 from http://www.villagevoice.com/news/0508,hunter1,61311,6.html.

Jackson, K. (2003, August). Better living through chemistry. *Social Work Today,* pp. 10–13.

Johnson, H. C. (2004). *Psyche, synapse, & substance: The role of neurobiology in emotions, behavior, thinking, & addiction for nonscientists* (2nd ed.). Greenfield, MA: Deerfield Valley.

Join Together. (2000, April 17). Heroin addiction's genetic component. *Join Together Online.* Retrieved December 1, 2006, from http://www.jointogether.org.

Join Together. (2001, April 6). Checking smokers into treatment. *Join Together Online.* Retrieved December 1, 2006, from http://www.jointogether.org.

Join Together. (2006). Accomplia shows promise as anti-craving drug. *Join Together Online.* Retrieved August 2006 from http://www.jointogether.org/news/headlines.

Kalb, C. (2001, February 21). Alcoholism: Can this pill stop you from hitting the bottle? *Newsweek,* pp. 48–54.

Kayman, D., Rosenblum, A., & Joseph, H. (2004, Summer). Buprenorphine: A promising option for the treatment of opioid dependence. *Alcohol, Tobacco, and Other Drugs,* pp. 7–11.

Keilman, J. (2005, September 9). Storm chaos cuts help for addicts. *Chicago Tribune,* pp. 1, 4.

Knapp, C. (1996). *Drinking: A love story.* New York: Delta.

Knapp, C. (1999, May 9). The glass half empty. *New York Times Magazine,* pp. 19–20.

Koerner, B. (1999, December 6). For heroin addicts, a bizarre remedy. *U.S. News & World Report,* p. 82.

Kranzler, H. R. (2000, August 23–30). Medications for alcohol dependence—new vistas. *Journal of the American Medical Association, 284*(8), 1016–1017.

Kuzma, J., & Black, D. W. (2006). Compulsive shopping: When spending begins to consume the consumer. *Current Psychiatry Online, 5*(7). Retrieved August 2006 from http://www.currentpsychiatry.com.

Lebot, V., Merlin, M., & Lindstrom, L. (1992). *Kava: The Pacific drug.* New Haven, CT: Yale University Press.

Leshner, A. I. (2006). The addiction recovery guide: Your Internet guide to drug and alcohol addiction recovery. Retrieved June 2006 from http://www.addictionrecoveryguide.org.

Levin, D. L. (1995). *Introduction to alcoholism counseling: A bio-psycho-social approach.* New York: Taylor & Davis.

Li, T.-K. (2004, April). Neuroscience research and therapeutic targets. National Institute on Alcohol Abuse and Alcoholism. *Alcohol Alert,* no. 61, 1–4.

Lukas, S., Penetar, D., Berko, J., Vicens, L., Palmer, C., Mallya, G., et al. (2005). An extract of the Chinese herbal root kudzu reduces alcohol drinking by heavy drinkers in a naturalistic setting. *Alcoholism: Clinical and Epidemiological Research, 29*(5), 756–762.

Lundgren, L. M., Schilling, R. F., & Peloquin, S. D. (2005). Evidence-based drug treatment practice and the child welfare system: The example of methadone. *Social Work, 50*(1), 53–64.

Marion, I. J. (2005). Methadone treatment at forty. *Science and Practice Perspective, 3*(1), 25–33.

Mayo Clinic. (2006, April 6). Compulsive gambling. *Health Library.* Special to CNN. Retrieved August 2006 from http://www.cnn.com/health/library.

Mayo Foundation for Medical Education and Research. (2006). Residential treatment program. Retrieved August 2006 from http://www.mayoclinic.org/stop-smoking.

McFarling, V. L. (1998, August 4). New nicotine therapy targets the brain. *Lexington Herald-Leader,* pp. A1, A5.

McNeece, C. A., & DiNitto, D. M. (2005). *Chemical dependency: A systems approach* (3rd ed.). Boston: Allyn & Bacon.

Meyerhoff, D. J., Tizabi, Y., Staley, J. K., Durazzo, T. C., Glass, J. M., & Nixon, S. J. (2006). Smoking comorbidity in alcoholism. *Alcohol Clinical Experimental Research, 30*(2), 253–264.

Miller, S. (1997, May 3). A national mood booster. *Newsweek,* p. 74.

Miller, W. R., & Rollnick, S. (2002). *Motivational interviewing: Preparing people for change* (2nd ed.). New York: Guilford Press.

MMT & beyond—redefining "adequate" methadone dose. (2001, Winter). *Addiction Treatment Forum.* Retrieved from http://www.atforum.com.

Mueser, K. T., Noordsy, D., Drake, R., & Fox, L. (2003). *Integrated treatment for dual disorders: A guide to effective practice.* New York: Guilford Press.

Murphy, K. (2004, February 2). There's entrancing news about hypnosis. *Business Week,* p. 88.

National Institute on Drug Abuse (NIDA). (2000, August 13). Study finds acupuncture shows promise for treating cocaine addiction. *NIDA News Release,* pp. 1–2.

National Institute on Drug Abuse (NIDA). (2003, September 22). Small study suggests anticonvulsant drug holds promise as therapy for cocaine abuse. Press Release. National Institutes of Health. Retrieved February 2007 from http://www.nih.gov/news/pr/sep2003/nida-22.htm.

National Institute of Justice. (2004). Drug users sweat it out. *Technology Update.* Retrieved February 2007 from http://www.ncjrs.gov/pdffiles1/nij/06_04.pdf.

New advances in alcoholism treatment. (2000, October). *Alcohol Alert,* pp. 1–4.

Nicotine increases alcohol craving. (2000, February 2). Retrieved from http://alcoholism.about.com/library/weekly/a.

Office of National Drug Control Policy. (2001). *National Drug Control Strategy: Annual Report.* Washington, DC: U.S. Government Printing Office.

O'Malley, S. S., & Kosten, T. (2006). Pharmacotherapy of addictive disorders. In W. R. Miller & K. M. Carroll (Eds.), *Rethinking substance abuse: What the science shows and what we should do about it* (pp. 240–256). New York: Guilford Press.

Ondansetron effective for treating early-onset alcoholism. (2000, November 17). Retrieved from http://www.jointogether.org.

Padgett, D. K., Gulcur, L., & Tsemberis, S. (2006). Housing first service for people who are homeless with co-occurring serious mental illness and substance abuse. *Research on Social Work Practice,* 16(1), 74–83.

Payer, L. (1996). *Medicine and culture.* New York: Holt.

Plutowski, S. (2005, March). A journey to stop smoking. *NWA* (Northwest Airlines) *World Traveler,* p. 54.

Prochaska, J. D., DiClemente, C. C., & Norcross, J. C. (1992). In search of how people change: Applications to addictive behaviors. *American Psychologist, 47,* 1102–1114.

Project MATCH Research Group. (1997). Matching alcoholism treatments to client heterogeneity. *Journal of Studies on Alcohol, 58,* 7–27.

Raskin, A. (2005, August 24). Heroin detox using anesthesia limited and risky, study says. *Los Angeles Times.* Retrieved August 2006 from http://www.nrapinc.org/newscsdp.

Reid, K. (2002). Clinical social work with groups. In A. Roberts & G. Greene (Eds.), *Social workers' desk reference* (pp. 432–436). New York: Oxford University Press.

Reuben, C., Chen, T. J., Blum, S. H., Braverman, E., Miller, J., Waite, R., et al. (2005, December). Acupuncture and auriculotherapy: Valuable treatment modalities for addiction. *Townsend Letter for Doctors and Patients, 1269,* 81–85.

Ritter, M. (1997, May 21). One last puff: Drug used to treat alcoholism may help smokers quit. *Daily News* (Bowling Green, KY), p. B1.

Robertson, N. (1988). *Getting better: Inside Alcoholics Anonymous.* New York: William Morrow.

Roy-Byrne, P. (1999). Naltrexone for smoking cessation? *Journal Watch Psychiatry,* 5(3), 27.

Rubin, R. (2001, March 28). Women total 40% of smoking deaths. *Des Moines Register,* p. 1A.

Saleebey, D. (2001). *Human behavior and social environments*. New York: Columbia University Press.

Saleebey, D. (2006). Introduction: Power in the people. In D. Saleebey (Ed.), *The strengths perspective in social work practice* (4th ed., pp. 1–24). Boston: Allyn & Bacon.

Schick Shadel web site. (2006). Schick Shadel hospital's effective treatment program. Retrieved from http://www.schick-shadel.com/treatment.html.

Schilling, R., Dornig, K., & Lungren, L. (2006, January). Treatment of heroin dependence: Effectiveness, costs, and benefits of methadone maintenance. *Research on Social Work Practice, 16*(1), 48–56.

Schultz, S. (2000, May 29). Would-be quitters get help winning against nicotine. *U.S. News & World Report*, pp. 58–60.

Schwartz, J. (1997). *Brain lock: Free yourself from obsessive compulsive behavior*. New York: HarperCollins.

Schwartz, J. M., & Begley, S. (2003). *The mind and the brain: Neuroplasticity and the power of mental force*. New York: Regan Books.

Science Daily. (2005, April 4). Genes for alcohol consumption identified. University of Bristol. Retrieved August 2006 from http://www.sciencedaily.com/releases/2005.

Smith, M. O., Brewington, V., Culliton, P., Ng, L., Hsiang-lai, W., & Lowinson, J. H. (1997). Acupuncture. In J. H. Lowinson, P. Ruiz, & R. Millman (Eds.), *Substance abuse: A comprehensive textbook* (pp. 484–492). New Haven, CT: Yale University Press.

Spinella, M. (2005). *Concise handbook of psychoactive herbs*. New York: Haworth Herbal Press.

Stevens, P., & Smith, R. L. (2004). *Substance abuse counseling: Theory and practice* (3rd ed.) Upper Saddle River, NJ: Prentice Hall.

Substance Abuse and Mental Health Services Administration (SAMHSA). (2004, March/April). SAMHSA brings buprenorphine to the field. *SAMHSA News, 12*(2), 1–9.

Substance Abuse and Mental Health Services Administration (SAMHSA). (2005). *Substance abuse treatment for persons with co-occurring disorders*. Treatment Improvement Protocol (TIP) Series, No. 42. Washington, DC: U.S. Department of Health and Human Services.

Sullivan, W. P., & Rapp, C. A. (2006). Honoring philosophical traditions: The strengths model and the social environment. In D. Saleebey (Ed.), *The strengths perspective in social work practice* (4th ed., pp 261–278). Boston: Allyn & Bacon.

Thayer, A. (2006, September 25). Drugs to fight addictions. *Chemical and Engineering News, 84*(39), 21–44.

University of Pittsburgh Medical Center. (2005, July 7). Specific regions of brain implicated in anorexia nervosa. Retrieved August 2006 from http://www.upmc.com/Communications/NewsBureau/.

U.S. Department of Health and Human Services. (2000). *10th special report to the U.S. Congress on alcohol and health*. Washington, DC: U.S. Government Printing Office.

Van den Brink, W., Hendriks, V., Blanken, P., Koeter, M., van Zweiten, B., & van Ree, J. (2003). Medical prescription of heroin to treatment resistant heroin addicts. *British Medical Journal, 327*(7410), 310.

Vedantan, S. (2006, March 19). Lawsuits claim dopamine drugs cause obsessive behavior. *Washington Post*, p. A01.

Volpicelli, J., & Szalavitz, M. (2000). *Recovery options: The complete guide*. New York: Wiley.

Waismann, A. (2000, September). Hope beyond heroin. *USA Today* (magazine), pp. 32–33.

Wallen, J. (1993). *Addiction in human development: Developmental perspectives on addiction and recovery*. New York: Haworth.

Wasserman, B. (2006, April 16). FDA approves Vivitrol for alcoholism. *Drug News*. Retrieved from http://www.foodconsumer.org/777/8.

Yalom, I. (1995). *The theory and practice of group psychotherapy* (4th ed.). New York: Basic Books.

Zarkin, G. A., Dunlap, L. N., Hicks, K., & Mamo, D. (2005). Benefits and costs of methadone treatment: Results from a lifetime simulation model. *Health Economics, 14*(11), 1133–1150.

THE PSYCHOLOGY
OF ADDICTION

PART | 3

The three chapters that make up this part of the book take us into the heart of therapy itself, which gets at the thinking side of addiction and concomitantly at the feelings that emerge during the working stage of substance abuse treatment.

Chapter 6, Addiction Across the Life Span, was placed in the psychological part of the book because it draws on the developmental stages of life and relates the role of drugs to these life stages. For this discussion, we draw on the work of ego psychologist Erik Erikson and family development theorist Jacqueline Wallen.

Chapter 7, Eating Disorders, Gambling, Shopping, and Other Behavioral Addictions, is at the intersection of biology and psychology; biological aspects of the various disorders are discussed—for example, in the etiology of anorexia—and a cognitive focus is adapted from psychology as the intervention of choice.

Mental disorders, the subject of chapter 8, also links biology with psychology. We have included mental disorders in this book on addictions because of the frequent overlap between these dual disorders. Harm reduction therapists and other substance abuse counselors need to be alert to psychological problems, especially those of a serious nature, that can interfere with treatment and recovery. In the past, clients who had a combination of substance misuse and mental health problems were often treated for one diagnosis to the neglect of the other. Alternatively, persons with dual and multiple diagnoses were shuttled back and forth between systems of care. Today, mental health agencies are apt to have substance abuse specialists on the staff, and chemical dependence treatment centers are anxiously recruiting counselors with expertise in mental illness. There is no easy way to assess the relative impact of drug misuse on mental conditions. Another major difficulty is the drug interaction between psychotropic medication and the so-called recreational drugs. Chapter 8 delves into this complex area of so-called dual-diagnosis treatment, or treatment of persons with co-occurring disorders. The central argument of this chapter is the call for integrated treatment of persons suffering from several disorders simultaneously instead of shuffling clients back and forth between specialists for mental and addiction problems.

All the world's a stage,
And all the men and women merely players:
They have their exits and their entrances;
And one man in his time plays many parts,
His acts being seven ages.

—**William Shakespeare,** *As You Like It,* I (139)

ADDICTION ACROSS THE LIFE SPAN

CHAPTER 6

INTRODUCTION

Most of this textbook is concerned with middle adulthood, and because most adults in treatment are in this age category, this chapter focuses on people at either end of the life span—teens and young adults at one end and the elderly at the other. Because society and the media are much more concerned with the habits and destructive behavior of the young than of the old, the literature is extremely lopsided on this subject. Policies to curb substance misuse, similarly, focus almost entirely on social control of the young. Since the beginning of time, the older generation has been preoccupied with ways to control the sexual and other pleasure-driven appetites of the young.

THE STAGES OF GROWTH AND DEVELOPMENT

The behavioral problems associated with alcohol and other drugs emerge, in most people, during late adolescence and early adulthood (Rose, 1998). Identifying and understanding the course of those problems, accordingly, require a developmental perspective. Many of the risk factors, as Rose indicates, can already be spotted in early childhood by children's parents, teachers, and counselors, even as early as preschool.

Erik Erikson (1963) proposed a theory of psychosocial development consisting of eight stages. His model, like other models of growth and development across the life span, focused on how an individual's personality interacts with biological and social systems to affect behavior. From birth to old age, in this conceptualization, life consists of a chronological series of age-related developmental stages and tasks that need to be completed. For the practitioner, knowledge of psychological milestones normally negotiated, such as during adolescence and young adulthood, is important for the overall assessment of behavior and functioning (Zastrow & Kirst-Ashman, 2006).

In Erikson's terminology, at each critical juncture of life, an individual must resolve a crisis relevant to that developmental stage before moving to the next one. Often, as Jacqueline Wallen (1993), the author of *Addiction in Human Development,* contends, behaviors that seem "symptomatic" are in fact coping strategies that enable the individual to survive hardships during childhood.

Three stages that concern us in this chapter are Stage 5: identity versus role diffusion (12–17 years); Stage 6: intimacy versus isolation (young adulthood); and Stage 8: ego integrity versus despair (older adulthood). As substance abuse counselors are aware, when life crises are resolved through consistent use of chemicals, the resolution of crises is put on hold, and the level of maturity does not match the chronological age. In conjunction with the damage done to the drug-exposed brain, the individual addict/alcoholic experiences regression rather than progression.

A formal intervention, according to Wallen, is a technique for persuading an alcoholic or addict to accept treatment. In this process, family members and friends express their concern and caring for an individual in need of help. Following developmental theory, as Wallen indicates, interventions with older persons must proceed differently from interventions with youth. In particular, they must be conducted much more slowly. Awareness of the special needs of older adults and of their difficulty in making changes is important for the therapist. Sensitivity to age-stage differences in recovery also enhances the treatment effort.

The transition between childhood and adulthood is associated with a variety of challenges as youth struggle to acquire the behavioral skills necessary for later independent living (Spear, 2000). Certain features of the adolescent brain may predispose a youngster to behave in ways that place him or her at particular risk for trying alcohol or other drugs. Many teenagers engage in foolish, high-risk behavior that seems incongruous with their values and their physical maturity. But the brain lags behind. We now know this thanks to the powerful new imaging technology. Scientists can actually "see" what changes happen in the brain with age, and they are finding that a spectacular growth of synaptic connections between brain cells occurs in late adolescence. This process is not complete until the mid-twenties (Park, 2003). Adults used to explain teens' impulsive behavior in terms of raging hormones; but once scientists were able to map where and when the brain changes were happening, our understanding about teenage behavior and why teens often don't seem to be able to just say "no" has advanced significantly. The function of the growth spurt is thought to be the enhancement of the learning capacity of the brain as excess synapses that are not stimulated by experience (e.g., by learning to play an instrument or speak a foreign language) are pruned and others strengthened.

We could say that the very plasticity of the adolescent brain that facilitates learning also renders it particularly vulnerable to the temptation of substance use and related brain damage (Monti et al., 2005). Significantly, a number of adult mental disorders, such as schizophrenia and bipolar disorders, have their onset in adolescence and are probably related to the brain changes. Prevention of heavy alcohol and other substance use during this vulnerable period is then paramount.

Because the prefrontal cortex, the part of the brain linked to judgment, novelty seeking, and self-awareness, does not reach full maturity until well after age 20, this is probably why many teens lack the skills to resist peer pressure and why many engage in "daredevil" activity. When hormone changes, peer pressure, and the need for autonomy are added to the equation, the end result can be volatile.

TEENAGE DRINKING AND USING

IDENTITY VERSUS ROLE DIFFUSION

During adolescence, the childhood imitation of adult roles (e.g., playing house) is replaced by experimentation and struggle for a meaningful identity. The risk during this period, every parent's nightmare, is that the adolescent will experiment with drugs and drunkenness and hang around with antisocial peers. The individual who is able to resolve the demands of this period will have a sense of who he or she is and which adult roles to value (Wallen, 1993).

Identity comes as we internalize others' responses to our person and come to see ourselves as others see us. During the turbulence of adolescence, when the growing child pursues his or her identity independently of parents, peer group influence is at its strongest. According to a national survey by the Substance Abuse and Mental Health Services Administration (SAMHSA) (2001), peer drug use and peer attitude are two of the strongest predictors of marijuana use. The odds of youth aged 12 to 17 using marijuana were found to be 39 times higher for those whose close friends used marijuana than for those who did not. At the same time, when the peer group held strong antidrug attitudes, drug use by the youth was uncommon. Parental attitudes were also influential but less so than peer group attitudes. Use of tobacco and alcohol were other risk factors for marijuana use.

As Carol Gilligan (1982, 2002) notes, Erikson's conceptualization for young life stages was male oriented and showed a lack of sensitivity or concern for the developmental issues of girls. Moral development in girls, as Gilligan (1982) pointed out, is about self-sacrifice and accepting responsibility. In her more recent work, *The Birth of Pleasure,* Gilligan likens the gender conformity pressures on masculinity that intensify for the boy around the age of 5, with the pressures placed on girls to be attractive and so forth as they enter adolescence. The loss of freedom is the same in both instances. As we consider drinking and drug use patterns of adolescents, let us be cognizant of sex-role differences; we can also see how the stress on a willingness for the girl to merge her identity with others, such as a peer group or boyfriend, can be problematic in many instances.

EXTENT OF DRUG USE

Providing an international perspective on alcohol and other drug use, the World Health Organization conducted classroom surveys of teenagers in the United States and Europe, from the United Kingdom to the Ukraine (Associated Press, 2001). The study found that 41% of U.S. teens questioned said they had tried marijuana, 16% had used amphetamines, and 10% had used LSD compared with 16% of the European youth who had used marijuana and 6% who had tried another illicit drug. A separate study of drug use conducted by the European Public Health Alliance (2005) indicates that illicit drug use in the age range of 15 to 34 was 22% in the United States and less than half that amount in European Union countries. Only the Czech Republic had more persons in the age group using illicit drugs than in the United States. Alcohol use and binge drinking, however, are far more prevalent in Europe than the United States, and twice as many children smoke at age 13 (around 10% smoke in Europe compared to 4% in the United States) (Hibell et al., 2004). The prevalence of drunkenness among 15-year-olds is highest in the Western countries of Denmark, Ireland, and the United Kingdom and lowest in the Mediterranean countries of Cyprus, Greece, Portugal, Romania, and Turkey.

In American surveys, alcohol is the drug of choice, as always, for American teens and youth. The rate of children 12 to 17 years old who reported any illicit drug use in the past month was 9.9% in 2005. This represented a slight decline since 2002. Data are from the National Survey on Drug Use and Health, a household survey, conducted by the U.S. Department of Health and Human Services and reported by SAMHSA (2006a). In the 18 to 25 age group, 19.4% currently use illicit drugs. The breakdown for current use of these young adults is:

16.6% marijuana

6.3% prescription drugs (e.g., Vicodin) for nonmedical use

3.4% Ecstasy

2.6% cocaine

1.5% hallucinogens

Cigarette use, according to the national survey (SAMHSA, 2006a) was 10.8% in the 12- to 17-year age group. Almost 20% of persons aged 16 and 17 years reported that they engaged in binge drinking at least once in the past month. Binge drinking is defined as five or more drinks on one occasion. White youth topped the list, and the male rate was somewhat higher than the female rate. Such drinking to get drunk is most common in the Midwest and West. The rate peaks for all youth at age 21, when almost half reported regular binge drinking.

The rates of current illicit drug use for major racial/ethnic groups in the 12–17 age range in 2005 in the household survey was 8.1% for Whites, 7.6% for Hispanics, and 9.7% for African Americans. The rate was highest among the American Indian/Alaska Native population (12.8%) and among persons reporting multiple races (12.2%). Asian Americans had the lowest rate, 3.1%.

In school surveys, African Americans reported the lowest rates of drinking and getting drunk, and Hispanic rates were lower than those of Whites in the higher grades (Johnston, O'Malley, Bachman, & Schulenberg, 2006). This discrepancy between the household and school surveys reflects the fact that African and Latino Americans have significantly higher dropout rates than Whites. What about the drug use rates in a younger age group? Among 8th graders, according to Johnston et al. (2006), Hispanics and Blacks have significantly higher drug use rates than Whites; a complete reversal occurs by 12th grade.

The finding of a significantly high rate of substance use for adolescents of mixed races deserves further investigation. Choi, Harachi, Gilmore, and Catalano (2006) studied 2,000 middle school students in Seattle. The multiracial adolescents had extremely high rates of smoking and drinking as well as high rates of fighting and carrying a gun. Researchers explained the findings in terms of lack of positive ethnic identity for these teens. As they indicate, however, the majority of multiracial youth did not have behavioral problems.

According to the 2006 annual survey of high school students, which was conducted by researchers from the University of Michigan, the use of most illicit drugs including cigarettes (illegal for those under age 18) has decreased significantly. Use of alcohol, however, which is the most life-threatening drug in relation to car crashes, accidental deaths, and violence, is widespread. Almost one third of high school seniors report that they have been drunk in the past 30 days, so intoxication among youth is hardly a rare occurrence. (Similarly, for Canada, more than 35% aged 15 to 17 and 51.8% aged 18 to 19 report heavy drinking at least once a month, and almost half of students aged 15 to 19 have tried marijuana; Health Canada, 2005.)

A new report from SAMHSA's Drug Abuse Warning Network (SAMHSA, 2006b) estimates that 142,701 alcohol-related emergency room visits were made to U.S. hospitals by individuals aged 12 to 20. Most of these patients were 18 to 20; many of the visits (19%) involved alcohol and other drugs. About one third of the hospital visits required intensive care.

Emergency rooms today are reporting that almost one quarter of their drug-related admissions are for overdoses of prescription and over-the-counter drugs. The use of OxyContin, a pain reliever prescribed to cancer patients, has become especially popular in recent years; such misuse of prescription medication by teens marks an exception to the trend of reduced drug use. About 4% in the recent annual high school survey reported use of this highly addictive drug or another narcotic prescription medication illegally. Adolescent girls surpass boys in misuse of prescription drugs. For 12th graders, 5.5% have used OxyContin and 9.5% have used another painkiller, Vicodin. According to articles in the *Washington Post* (Flaherty, 2005) and *USA Today* (Leinwand, 2006), abuse of prescription drugs is "epidemic," with teenagers the fastest growing group of new abusers. Teenagers arrange "pharm parties" where they swap drugs they have taken from their home medicine cabinets or purchased off the Internet. The teens, according to experts quoted in the *USA Today* article, are unlikely to equate prescription-drug use with the use of illicit drugs such as heroin or cocaine. Prescription drugs such as Ritalin are familiar mood-altering substances for a generation that grew accustomed to seeing people take a pill to act "normal" or to control their feelings.

The total cost of alcohol use by youth—including traffic crashes, violent crime, burns, drownings, suicide attempts, fetal alcohol syndrome, and treatment—is more than $58 billion per year (National Council on Alcoholism and Drug Dependence, 2000). Children and adolescents who begin drinking before age 15 are four times more likely to develop alcoholism than those who begin at age 21. Similarly, those who begin smoking before age 13 are more likely than later smokers and nonsmokers to have problems with alcohol and other drugs. People who developed their addiction problems at an early age are more likely than others to have psychiatric problems as well (C. S. Martin & Winters, 1998).

Other intriguing facts revealed by the National Council on Alcoholism and Drug Development include:

- 40% of college students have binged on alcohol during the past 2 weeks.
- 31.9% of youth under age 18 in juvenile institutions were under the influence of alcohol at the time of the arrest.
- 30% of children in grades four through six report that they have received a lot of pressure from their classmates to drink beer; 31% to try marijuana, and 34% to try cigarettes.
- A survey of high school students found that 18% of females and 39% of males say it is acceptable for a boy to force sex if the girl is stoned or drunk.

Data from reports such as these reveal a strong relationship between emotional state, risks to health and life, and alcohol use. Furthermore, teens who misuse alcohol at a young age are at high risk for further drinking problems, other substance abuse, depression, and personality disorders as they get older ("Teens Who Abuse Alcohol," 2001).

A study of 14,000 young adults identified a set of risk factors for smoking, including having friends who smoke, parents who smoke, trying cigarettes at a young age, and dropping out of school (Hu, Davies, & Kandel, 2005). Depression, having a risk-taking personality, and liking cigarettes right away are additional risk factors. White youth are more apt to get addicted than are minority youth.

What are the implications of using alcohol and cigarettes together? This question was posed by researchers at the University of Buffalo's Research Institute on Addictions (Weaver, 2001). Analysis revealed a synergistic effect in a combination of drinking and smoking that increased one's likelihood for illicit drug use. In each survey examined in the study, about one third of regular teen drinkers smoked, and almost all current smokers also drank alcohol.

Although media attention focuses on drugs such as Ecstasy and the government spends billions on the controversial war on drugs, little attention is directed toward misuse of the teen drug of choice—alcohol. During the 1980s, the drinking age was raised to 21 in every state. Fewer kids drank after that, but those who do drink today consume huge amounts at one time (Rivera, 2000).

"The booze business is big business," according to a TV news special on *Rivera Live*. Based on alcohol consumption statistics, youth under 21 consume $10 billion worth of alcohol; advertisers beam the message that it's cool to drink. Anheuser-Busch, the largest beer company in America, spends $30 million a year on advertising. Because this and other beer and liquor companies are the most aggressive and well-funded lobbies in Washington, D.C., the government's political focus has been on the kind of drugs that can't be legally marketed. According to commentators on *Rivera Live*, money was put into antidrug ads—a $1 billion White House advertising campaign to educate children about drugs. Proposals to include alcohol in these ads, with announcements such as "2.6 million teenagers don't know a person can die from an alcohol overdose," limits on prime-time alcohol ads, and higher taxes on alcohol all died in Congress. Earlier, according to Anna Quindlen (2001), when members of Congress tried to pass legislation that would make alcohol part of the purview of the nation's drug czar, the measure failed.

At this time of writing, however, thanks to extensive lobbying by youth advocacy and prevention groups, a landmark bill directed at youth alcohol misuse has passed both houses of Congress and been signed into law by President Bush (University of New Mexico Institute of Public Law, 2007). This is the first national legislation to focus exclusively on drinking prevention of youth (Curley, 2006). The new act, the Sober Truth on Prevention (STOP) Underage Drinking Act, promotes a media campaign similar to the antidrug campaign and provides grant funding for communities to set up prevention programming. The STOP Act was sponsored by a large number of influential groups such as the Mothers Against Drunk Driving, the American Medical Association, and the Center for Alcohol Marketing to Youth. According to testimony provided in favor of the bill, alcohol kills six times more young people than all other illegal drugs combined, yet the government spends 25 times more annually to combat illegal drug use than to curb alcohol misuse.

Another problem that has been pushed to the background because of governmental (in this case, the states') vested interest is gambling. Legalized gambling is now a source of revenue that is deeply embedded in state politics. Children are exposed to gambling on the Internet, and many (as revealed in surveys) have played video poker, slot machines, and the lottery (Schouten, 2000). More alarming to researchers is new evidence showing that children get addicted to gambling at a much higher rate than adults; perhaps this is related to the immaturity of the brain at a younger age. Studies indicate that 4 to 8% of teens in the United States and Canada show signs of serious gambling problems. Kids who gamble often steal money from family members, shoplift, and consider suicide. This is the first generation of children to be saturated with gambling possibilities and to grow up surrounded by casinos and other forms of legalized gambling (Schouten, 2000).

Extensive research is being conducted at McGill University at the International Centre for Youth Gambling Problems in Montreal. Hardoon, Gupta, and Derevensky (2004) of the center surveyed over 2,000 students in grades 7 to 13 and found that 4.9% of the adolescents met the criteria for pathological gambling. An additional 8% were at risk. Psychosocial difficulties associated with problem gambling include poor family and social support, heavy substance use, parental gambling, and being male. Another study from the McGill Centre found that escapism and impulsivity were predictive of gambling problems in adolescents (Nower, Derevensky, & Gupta, 2004).

Big money is, of course, involved in cigarette sales. Given the fact that 80% of adult smokers in the United States began lighting up before age 18, tobacco companies have a vested interest in maintaining the smoking rate of youth (Lavelle, 2000). In the wake of the unprecedented tobacco industry settlement with the states, tobacco companies are now targeting young adults, who can legally smoke. But as Lavelle argues, this ploy merely enhances the appeal of cigarettes by introducing flavored varieties and financing prevention programs while simply telling kids they're too young to smoke, which is unlikely to curb their desire to smoke. Meanwhile, smoking figures prominently in Hollywood productions. Millions are spent each year by tobacco companies just to have their product placed in a 1-second or longer shot in a movie (Join Together, 2006b).

Van Wormer had her students collect examples of magazine ads for tobacco products. One student submitted the following description:

> Before beginning this assignment, I asked my boys for suggestions on which magazines I should look through for alcohol and tobacco advertisements. To my surprise, they guided me to their *Field and Stream* magazines. I looked through their latest issue. To my surprise, the magazine was loaded with ads. I had let the boys order this magazine when their school was doing their latest fundraiser. I thought this would be a good educational subscription that the boys would enjoy. I had never looked through them and was shocked at how many ads were included for tobacco products.
>
> The tobacco ads were all for smokeless tobacco. Red Seal said, "25% more tobacco got my attention. Quality won me over. Get more of a good thing. Red Seal—The real deal." It included a picture of two fishermen on their boat holding up the can of chew. Timber Wolf's motto was "Leader of the pack." Copenhagen pictured a handsome cowboy, impressing a pretty cowgirl . . . Other ads were for Jack Daniel's Whiskey and Miller Light Beer. (personal communication, September 2004)

A clever, roundabout way to get youth to quit smoking is to involve them in strenuous exercise programs. According to an article in the *Washington Post* health section (Krucoff, 1999), a study of male runners showed that 70% of those who smoked quit subsequently. Almost half of the women in an exercise group quit smoking as well.

PSYCHOLOGICAL RISK FACTORS

Rose (1998) presents an overview of longitudinal studies conducted in several countries to ascertain whether behavioral assessments made by teachers and classmates could distinguish which children were likely to abuse alcohol by middle or late adolescence. Findings from Sweden were that evaluations done at ages 10 and 27 showed that high novelty seeking and low harm avoidance (daredevil behavior) predicted early-onset alcoholism. Similar results were obtained in Canadian and Danish research studies. Data from Finland differentiated the pathway to alcoholism in males and females. Aggression at age 8 predicted alcoholism 18 to 20 years later in males. For females, children who cried easily when teased or who were anxious and shy were most apt to develop problems later. For both sexes, poor school success was a predictor of later drinking problems.

In his assessment of twin studies in Europe and North America, Rose (2005) concluded that although hereditary factors are important, the age of initiation, which is environmentally determined, is equally influential in the development of alcoholism. Such influences are family drinking patterns, the availability of alcohol, and peer group habits. Although further research is needed, it seems reasonable to assume, as Rose suggests, that children at elevated risk for alcoholism may decrease that risk by remaining abstinent throughout adolescence.

Parents are primary role models for their children; their drinking and drug-using behavior are positively associated with adolescent patterns of substance use (National Institute on Drug Abuse [NIDA], 2005). A survey of nearly 600 teens in drug treatment in New York, Texas, Florida, and California indicated that 20% had shared illicit drugs with their parents—usually marijuana (Leinwand, 2000). On the positive side, parental support and communication about proper and improper drinking behaviors correlate with fewer problems among adolescents.

The teen–father relationship has been found, in a survey of 2,000 youth and 1,000 parents undertaken by the Center on Addiction and Substance Abuse (Associated Press, 1999), to be crucial in affecting youth substance abuse. Teenagers who don't get along with their fathers are more likely to smoke, drink, and use other drugs than those raised by single mothers. Moreover, teens who reported their fathers have more than two drinks a day have a high risk of substance abuse themselves.

Child abuse and other traumas are serious risk factors for later adolescence and adulthood drinking. In their review of the research, Ryan, Marsh, Testa, and Louderman (2006) report that between 70 to 78% of foster home placements result from parental alcohol and drug misuse. Tragically, according to this report, most parents who need treatment don't receive it, and much of the treatment is not appropriate for these, predominately female, parents. Ryan et al. describe an exemplary Illinois child welfare program that integrates substance abuse and child welfare services. Family reunification was more successfully achieved in the integrated model than in a comparison group of families.

Adolescents in treatment for alcohol problems report higher rates of physical abuse, violent victimization, witnessing violence, and other traumas compared with controls ("Youth Drinking," 1997). According to an article in the *Canadian Medical Association Journal,* in a population health survey, it was found that children who are spanked and slapped are twice as likely to develop alcohol and other drug abuse problems as children who were never so treated (Gray, 2002).

Regarding trauma among adults in treatment, the literature consistently reports a strong link between childhood abuse and the later development of alcoholism and other drug problems (Downs, Capshew, & Rindels, 2004; National Center on Addiction and Substance Abuse at Columbia University [CASA], 2006). Girls who are sexually abused are three times more likely to develop drinking problems later than are girls not so abused, according to a national study conducted by Wilsnack (reported by Elias, 1998). The interpersonal interviews in the study revealed that those molested as children have more than double the depression rate of other women. Abuse is the single strongest predictor of alcohol dependence in girls, even stronger than a family history of alcoholism, as the conductor of this research noted. Smoking in women, similarly, has been found in a new Mayo Clinic study to be strongly related to a history of child sexual abuse (Join Together, 2005b).

In a sample of 938 adolescents in residential therapeutic communities, Hawke, Jainchill, and DeLeon (2000) found prevalence rates of sexual abuse were 64% for girls and 24% for boys. The sexual abuse was correlated with earlier onset of alcohol and illicit drug use. Interestingly, sexually abused boys were more likely to be diagnosed with conduct disorder, dysthymia (mild depression), and ADHD, while girls were likely to be diagnosed with post-traumatic stress disorder and major depression.

How do we explain the early sexual abuse/later alcoholism link? We cannot conclude the relationship is necessarily causal because other variables, such as parental substance use, may have an influence. Yet to identify youth at risk for substance abuse, we need to help them deal with life events that may be of a traumatic nature. The explanation given by Hawke et al. (2000)—the self-medication hypothesis—is the one provided throughout the literature: The drug use functions to ameliorate feelings of depression and poor self-esteem that accompany childhood abuse. Based on her work with alcoholic women in the United States and Norway, van Wormer (1995) provided a somewhat more complicated explanation of the sexual trauma/alcoholism link:

> What is the meaning of all this? If childhood sexual abuse can be considered a factor in the later development of alcoholism, there must be some intervening variable resulting from the abuse and leading to the drinking later in life. My hunch is that the combination of a general sense of shame and self-disgust prevails but that specific events (and feelings associated with them) may be repressed to make survival possible. The child survives, but the adult may appear emotionally stunted; there is little resilience for ordinary life crisis. There is no "talking things out" or "laughing it off." The discovery of alcohol, often in the teenager years, may seem to offer relief.
>
> A client I once had (I'll call her Mary) seemed as cold as ice. Her mother, also in treatment as a result of a court-ordered referral, told me that Mary had once been a sweet and affectionate little girl. But at age 11, "when her father started messing with her," she began to change. When Mary initially told about her father's activities, her mother did not believe her. For years Mary was thought to be a liar. Then one day the mother discovered the truth. By then, the daughter, overwhelmed by the original feelings, plus the anger at her mother and, perhaps, at her own

helplessness, had built up her own wall of defenses. Now a mother herself, Mary was verbally abusive and suspicious. Although Mary learned to control her drinking as a practical matter (her mother did not), she never learned to trust or to love. Unable to love herself, she could not reach out to others. Her extremely low self-esteem is characteristic of both alcoholic women and incest survivors; perhaps this connection occurs because of the overlap between these two categories. (pp. 169–170)

This theory linking early trauma and a later inability to cope with psychological stress is entirely consistent with recent neurological evidence of brain chemistry changes that result from early trauma. Because of these changes, the former victim's stress response is weakened; this fact sets the stage for future psychological problems, especially under conditions of repeated stress (Basham & Miehls, 2004). Adults who have been traumatized as children retain their immature responses (fight-or-flight reactions) to stress. This memory becomes a "body memory," as Basham and Miehls explain. When childhood trauma occurs with the accompanying brain chemistry, the stage is set for future psychological problems, especially under repeated conditions of stress. In a controlled laboratory study, survivors of childhood trauma have been shown to react very strongly to deliberately stress-inducing situations compared to a control group who did not suffer trauma in childhood (Heim et al., 2000).

The mechanisms responsible for the relationship between childhood trauma and adolescent alcohol use disorders are relatively unexplored. Probable explanations are the use of alcohol for emotional pain relief, dulling bad feelings about the self, and anxiety related to the abuse through heavy alcohol consumption. We know from animal studies that stress and alcohol consumption levels are highly correlated (Spear, 2000). Presumably, the physiological response to stress—increased heart and pulse rates, for example—is being subdued through self-medication with alcohol.

As Albert Ellis said long ago, it is not the event itself but our perception of the event that is important (1965). There is evidence that sensitivity (defined as an exaggerated response to stimuli, which is perceived as stress) is an inborn trait (Aron, 1996) and that it is correlated with alcoholism (see chapter 4). Researchers have postulated that the presumed increase in anxiety and stress during adolescence contributes to the frequent initiation into drug use observed at this time. Experiments have shown that juvenile mice exhibit a greater overall hormonal response to stress than both younger and older animals (Spear, 2000). Compared to mature rodents, those of adolescent age exhibit a heightened response to alcohol and to other drugs as well. Spear (2000) cites research findings that the adolescent's perception of the events as stressful was a more important predictor of alcoholism than the absolute number of such events. The need for further research into the effects of stress on the development of alcohol problems in humans is clearly indicated.

The link between trauma and stress is further confirmed in a remarkable study on child abuse presented in the *Journal of the American Medical Association,* as reported by Sternberg (2000). It is touted as the first human study to find persistent changes in stress reactivity in adult survivors of early trauma. A comparative study of 49 healthy women revealed detectable biochemical abnormalities in those who had been severely abused in childhood. In a laboratory situation, women survivors were four times more likely than other women to develop excessive stress responses to mild stimuli. Those who were abused and now have anxiety disorder or depression are six times more likely than other women to suffer an abnormal stress response.

Psychiatric Disorders

Boys with attention-deficit hyperactivity disorder (ADHD) have been found to have significantly higher rates of substance misuse than boys without ADHD (Childress, 2006). Studies of adult cocaine abusers have found that many of them had undiagnosed ADHD as children (Stocker, 2000). NIDA-supported researchers have been trying to explain the connection between ADHD and later substance abuse. In a Massachusetts study, 56 boys with ADHD who were medically treated with stimulants, 19 untreated boys with ADHD, and 137 boys without ADHD were studied over 4 years. Stocker (2000) reported that only 25% of boys treated for ADHD, 18% of boys without ADHD, and 75% of the unmedicated ADHD boys had started to show drug and alcohol problems. More research is needed, however, as there could have been extenuating factors accounting for these results. (For a positive description of ADHD as a personality characteristic rather than a disorder, see van Wormer, 2007.)

A study of hundreds of ADHD youth of both sexes found that significantly more ADHD youth who smoked later developed alcohol and drug abuse and dependence than youth who did not smoke. Nicotine use thus emerged as the key intervening variable. Together, this research has important implications for treatment of children with attention-deficit hyperactivity disorder.

Other psychiatric disorders, such as anxiety and depression, correlate highly with substance misuse among youth. Depression, a key risk factor for substance abuse, tends to be higher in girls than in boys (Office of National Drug Control Policy, 2006). Suicidal behavior correlates highly with alcohol misuse in teens as well (CASA, 2006).

Special Risks for Girls

More girls are being arrested and jailed for drug abuse, assault, and loitering than ever before, according to a study by the American Bar Association (Join Together, 2003). One reason for the increase in arrests is an expansion of the definition of domestic violence to include girls' assaulting their parents. A lack of services aimed at helping troubled girls is another reason cited in the report for the fact that girls are the fastest growing segment of the juvenile justice population.

Girls who have been sexually assaulted (as indicated earlier), physically abused, or neglected are twice as likely to be arrested as juveniles and twice as likely to be arrested for violent crimes as girls who were not similarly victimized (Widom, 2000). Victimization may lead girls into delinquency indirectly through their alcohol and other drug involvement or through causing them to run away from home. As runaways, girls may engage in panhandling, petty theft, prostitution, and drug use. Early intervention in the lives of victimized children is crucial to protect them from a path of self-destructiveness.

Related to childhood victimization, self-mutilation or "cutting" is a common problem known to practitioners who work with troubled teens. Within the peer group or in institutions, this behavior has a contagious element. Research on this problem is scarce. Ross and Heath (2002), who studied self-mutilation in an urban high school and reviewed clinical files from elsewhere, found that 13.9% of high school students had mutilated themselves at least once. Teens (the ratio of girls to boys is about two to one) engaged in this behavior, according to Ross and Heath, to relieve anger in conjunction with anxiety by turning it inward. The most popular forms of self-mutilation were cutting the skin, hitting oneself, and pinching. Some researchers look to neurological factors, such as endorphins released by the body that reinforce self-mutilations (Kluger, 2005).

Here are some of the facts revealed in a special report from the National Clearinghouse for Alcohol and Drug Information ("Alcohol Use Among Girls," 1999):

- Adolescent girls who are heavy drinkers (drunk five or more drinks in a row on at least five different days in the past month) are more likely than boys to say that they drink to escape problems or because of frustration or anger.
- Friends have a big influence on teenagers overall, but girls are particularly susceptible to peer pressure when it comes to drinking. Adolescent girls are more likely than boys to drink to fit in with their friends, while boys drink largely for other reasons and then join a group that also drinks.
- Girls often are introduced to alcohol by their boyfriends, who may be older and more likely to drink.
- Early-onset drinking is a major risk factor for developing alcohol abuse or dependence.
- Teenage girls who are heavy drinkers are five times more likely to engage in sexual intercourse and a third less likely to use condoms, which can result in pregnancy and in the contraction of sexually transmitted diseases, including HIV/AIDS. Women make up the fastest-growing segment of the population infected with HIV in the United States, and adolescents and young women are at particularly high risk.
- Alcohol is involved in up to two-thirds of all sexual assaults and date rapes among adolescents and college students.
- Among 8th grade girls who drink heavily, 37% report attempting suicide— compared to 11% who do not drink.
- Daughters of alcoholics are at increased risk for alcoholism. They are also more likely to marry men who are alcoholics. (pp. 1, 2)

A more recent status report on teen drinking in the United States released by the Center on Alcohol Marketing and Youth (CAMY) (2006) at Georgetown University provides this additional information:

- According to all three federal surveys, girls are binge drinking more, while boys are bingeing less or increasing their bingeing at a slower rate than their female peers.
- Twelfth-grade female drinkers and binge drinkers are now more likely to drink distilled spirits than beer. The new "alcopops" are particularly attractive to girls and most popular with the youngest drinkers.

And a special report from the Office of National Drug Control Policy (2006) entitled "Girls and Drugs" reminds us that girls are closing the gap with boys in usage of marijuana, alcohol, and cigarettes, and they exceed boys' misuse of prescription medications. Use of alcohol and other drugs places girls at high risk of having unprotected sex, sometimes with multiple partners. It is estimated that girls who binge drink are up to 63% more likely than others to become teen mothers.

Prevention efforts are vitally needed to help young women cope with the stresses of adolescence, much of which is related to dating pressures, sexuality, concerns over weight, and issues of self-esteem and body image. Unlike boys, who often use illegal substances for a sense of excitement, teenage girls use alcohol and other drugs as an escape or as a result of peer pressure.

For girls, dissatisfaction with and attempts to control body weight play an important role in promoting eating disorders and substance use (CASA, 2006). Media-generated weight obsession is a major problem among girls of European American ethnicity. Not only does this obsession lead to major problems with eating, such as anorexia and bulimia (as discussed in chapter 7), but many Whites are resorting to another high-risk behavior—cigarette smoking—for the purpose of weight control. Teenage girls who diet frequently also seem more likely to smoke. In one study, over a third of the smoking initiation by girls was attributable to dieting (Join Together, 2001). The statistics on cigarette smoking reveal that 23.4% of females smoke, and among adolescents aged 12–17, the numbers of girls who smoke (10.8%) is about the same as the number as boys (10.7%) who do so (SAMHSA, 2006a).

About one third as many Black female adolescents as White female adolescents smoke, according to a national household survey of teens aged 12–17 (Centers for Disease Control and Prevention [CDC], 2006). So striking are the racial differences in female smoking that some years ago the Centers for Disease Control and Prevention commissioned a study that involved talking with 1,000 adolescents in 150 focus groups ("Black Teens More Likely Than Whites to Reject Cigarettes," 1996). Findings were that some White women equated smoking with empowerment and sexual equality; White girls appeared to buy into advertising images of smokers as attractive and competent. Weight consciousness among Whites is thought to be a key contributing factor in starting to smoke. Among female teens, Native Americans have the highest smoking rates and Asian Americans have the lowest (CDC, 2006).

SPECIAL RISKS FOR BOYS

The biggest threat to life and health for adolescent boys is alcohol-related accidents. Surveys show that males 12 to 20 years old often engage in binge drinking. Such heavy drinking by males is highly associated with car crashes, sexual assaults, and other violence (Dizon, 2000).

The male counterpart to anorexia in females is muscle dysmorphia, a newly identified psychiatric disorder. A male with this condition, which is characterized by a body obsession, could be so preoccupied with his body that he might spend all day in the gym or weigh himself throughout the day. Although studies are filling the psychiatric literature, the *DSM–IV–TR* (American Psychiatric Association [APA], 2000) discusses body dysmorphic disorder only briefly and in a gender-neutral manner. (This is in sharp contrast to its extensive treatment of anorexia.)

According to a recent report by the National Association of School Psychologists, steroids that are used are smuggled in from other countries or diverted from pharmacies (Gober, Klein, Berger, Vindigni, & McCabe, 2006). The extent to which obsessive bodybuilding is a major problem for young males is revealed in the popularity of anabolic steroids, which are human-made substances related to male sex hormones. When used in combination with exercise, training, and high protein diets, anabolic steroids can promote muscle building, improve endurance, and decrease recovery time between workouts (Gober et al., 2006). "Anabolic" refers to muscle building. These drugs are available only by prescription to treat conditions related to testosterone deficiencies. According to a nationwide survey, 2.6% of all male high school seniors reported using steroids compared to only 0.4% of girls (Johnston et al., 2006). The good news from this survey is that in the younger age groups, steroid use has tapered off.

Pressures from coaches, parents, and peers to gain muscle weight and strength are attributed as factors in enticing athletes and weightlifters to take this drug. Media images of the ideal physique for a man and articles on strengthening muscles are appealing to adolescent boys whose bodies are rapidly changing. According to a nationwide survey (U.S. Department of Health and Human Services, 2000):

- More than two thirds of the heavy users began steroid use before age 16.
- About 44% said they shot or ingested several types of steroids at the same time.
- And 38% used injectable steroid packages—putting themselves at risk for contracting a disease such as AIDS.

Here are the words of a former steroid user:

Any bodybuilder would be on steroids. Ventura (governor of Minnesota) in his wrestling days took that. . . . The drugs are transported to this university from a big guy who brings them in from Mexico. . . . I was lifting weights and hit a plateau. I'm goal oriented. Some guys said, "You should get on the juice. One time won't hurt; the results are great. I take an injectable steroid from Mexico."

I'm 6 feet tall, had a 48-inch coat size. Taking eight shots once a week, after 2 months I took a 56-inch coat size. I had to buy all new clothes. I never was comfortable. I could feel my kidneys hurt; my blood pressure rose; I couldn't breathe. A lot of my friends stacked—took a lot all in a row. I was really in a bad mood for 2 months straight. The drug is not physically addictive but psychologically addictive. Here we were sticking needles in each others' butts. You have to switch cheeks, and it hurts. All the things I thought wouldn't happen to me did happen: balding (see, my hair never grew back), weight gain, water retention, sleeping problems. I blew a disc in my back from the weight. My chin got big. Before, I was a happy-go-lucky guy. But steroids change you; you get aggressive and people back off. On juice you start to like that. I remember a guy who hit a kid who hit on his girlfriend. He left him lying unconscious in the snow. (personal communication, February 20, 2001)

Health hazards of misusing anabolic steroids include risk for heart attacks and strokes, liver problems if taken orally, and undesirable body changes, such as breast development and shrinking testicles, stunted growth, and acne (U.S. Department of Health and Human Services, 2000). Personality changes associated with the use of this drug are frightening. Rapid mood swing, irritability, and aggression are listed as side effects (Gober et al., 2006). During withdrawal, antidepressants may be required to alleviate depression. That steroids may be physically addictive is indicated by experiments that show for the first time that rats will self-administer drinks laced with testosterone ("Rats Get Hooked," 1999). Like other addictive drugs, testosterone and its synthetic counterparts may activate pleasure pathways in the brain, according to the scientists who conducted this study.

Binge Drinking in Young Adults

Talk of "underage" drinking laws swept across the United States after President Bush's college student daughters, "the Bush daughters," as they are now known, received citations. One was cited for using a false identification card, and the other for possession of alcohol (Kenworthy, 2001). Because of laws restricting public drinking in the United States to persons over age 21, a debate of sorts about the laws has ensued. As drinking surveys reveal and everybody knows, these laws are not obeyed. "Party till you puke" is a sign occasionally posted in University of Northern Iowa dorms to announce a pending raucous event. On this midwestern campus, one's 21st birthday is celebrated by being taken by friends from bar to bar for unlimited free drinks. This initiation into adulthood has led to hospital trips for some individuals with low tolerance.

Wyoming, Montana, and the Dakotas are states that emerged in a nationwide survey as the top regions in the U.S. for under-21 binge drinking (Egan, 2006). Regions with the lowest rates are the urban areas of Washington, D.C., Detroit, and Los Angeles. Binge drinking predominates among rural White youth and in the West and Midwest and occurs the least in the Northeast and South. The *New York Times* article indicates that parents and others should crack down on kids for underage drinking. Elsewhere, such as in certain municipalities in California and New York, ordinances are being passed to punish adult hosts of parties in which there is underage drinking (Associated Press, 2006). Missing from these media reports is any analysis of the unintended consequences of laws that keep the parents away from the drinking scene altogether.

According to the National Survey on Drug Uses and Health (SAMHSA, 2006a), 44.8% of college students compared to 38.3% of noncollege students aged 18 to 22 engage in binge drinking one to four times per month. Cigarette smoking, however, is less among college students (30.6%) than among others of the same age (42.7%). Of these binge drinkers, very frequent bingeing was engaged in by 19.5% and 13%, respectively. The illicit drug use rate was slightly lower at 20.2% for college students.

"Binge Drinking and Teetotaling Spread at U.S. Colleges" is the title of an article that reveals the growing divide between youth who drink to the point of intoxication and those who abstain from all alcoholic beverages (Clayton, 2000). Evidence for the article is drawn from the Harvard School of Public Health, which conducted a widely cited survey of 14,000 students nationwide. As revealed in the study, in fraternity and sorority houses, 80% are binge drinkers, and among male athletes, 61% reported binge drinking in the previous 2 weeks compared to 22.3% for others of the same age. Among college students, about half of all alcohol consumed is consumed by those under age 21 (Center on Alcohol Marketing and Youth, 2006). Awareness of student alcohol-related deaths, vandalism, and sexual assault has contributed to a certain revulsion against drinking excesses that have been widely publicized. Many fraternities are working hard to clean up their reputation for uninhibited revelry.

The conservative British magazine *The Economist* describes the American fraternity scene as follows:

> Although it is illegal in America to serve alcohol to people under 21 (an absurdly high age limit by European standards), teenagers get booze with ease in fraternity houses. And this is not a matter of a few cocktails before dinner. American students—all the more defiant, perhaps, for being deprived of it for so long—prefer determined binge drinking on Friday and Saturday nights. A 1995 Harvard study suggested that half of American students are binge drinkers. In an attempt to improve matters, some fraternities have followed the sororities in banning alcohol. ("Raise a Fond Last Glass," 1997, p. 37)

In light of the magnitude of the campus binge drinking problem, the National Institute on Alcohol Abuse and Alcoholism (NIAAA) (2005) recently developed a website on this subject at www.collegedrinkingprevention.gov. On this website, under the heading "Snapshot of Drinking Consequences," the following fact sheet is provided:

THE HIGH TOLL OF ALCOHOL & DRUG ABUSE

Death: 1,700 college students between ages 18 and 24 die each year from alcohol-related unintentional injuries, including motor vehicle crashes.

Injury: 599,000 students between 18 and 24 are unintentionally injured under the influence of alcohol.

Academic Problems: About 25 percent of college students report academic consequences of their drinking including missing class, falling behind, doing poorly on exams or papers, and receiving lower grades overall.

Suicide: Between 1.2 and 1.5 percent of college students indicate that they tried to commit suicide within the past year due to drinking or drug use.

Drunk Driving: 2.1 million students age 18 to 24 drove under the influence of alcohol last year.

NIAAA obtained much of the data from the NIAAA Task Force on College Drinking led by Ralph Hinson (Hinson, Heeren, Winter, & Wechsler, 2005). The research concluded with the following recommendations to reduce college drinking and its associated harm: provide greater enforcement of the legal drinking age of 21 and zero tolerance laws, increase alcohol taxes, implement more exclusive college screening and counseling program, and offer comprehensive community interventions.

From a harm reduction perspective, likely recommended strategies would be to work toward a lowering of the drinking age to 18 (or even 16 as it is in many European countries), to impose tight restrictions on the marketing of alcoholic products in college newspapers and at sports events, and to forbid policies that encourage heavy drinking such as "happy hours." The key is to teach students to drink in a responsible way and thereby change the culture of campus drinking. Unfortunately, the heavy episodic drinking that occurs on many college campuses has evolved into a rite of passage, and this culture will perhaps take a whole new generation to change.

In the 1980s, in an overzealous attempt to curtail drunken driving by youth, the U.S. government imposed (through funding directives) a nationwide minimum drinking age of 21. Thus, we had prohibition on the basis of age. Harsh total abstinence campaigns were conducted on college campuses, with some unintended negative consequences. Michael Clay Smith, a professor of criminal justice, argues for a repeal of such laws (Smith & Smith, 1999). Legal adulthood occurs at age 18 in the United States, which is the first point. Other arguments are: The drinking age of 21 has driven students to partying underground and away from faculty supervision, students are getting police records for sharing alcohol with underage friends, and it has soured relations between students and police. Finally, the policy of prohibition is leading to binge drinking and probably other drug use, just as it did in the 1920s.

As Barrett Seaman (2005), author of *Binge,* argues, tighter enforcement of the minimum drinking age of 21 is not the solution; it's part of the problem. Seaman notes that a sea change in campus culture began with the new laws. This change was marked by a shift in drinking from beer to hard liquor, "consumed not in large social settings, since that is now illegal, but furtively and dangerously in students' residences" (p. 80). In his interviews with college officials around the country, Seaman learned that they thought the law impeded their efforts to monitor students' drinking.

American students who have lived in another country, as on a student exchange, have discovered a different drinking culture altogether. Melissa Hoekstra, a school counselor, describes her experience as a 16-year-old exchange student in Argentina:

> It was a wonderful experience, and one thing I learned was the United States is going about handling the alcohol situation the wrong way. In Argentina there was no drinking age. We did not have milk for supper; we had wine or beer. I believe that the norm in Argentina is to drink to be social, not to get drunk. I believe that there should be no drinking age law and that, instead, we should emphasize teaching moderation. (personal communication, April 5, 2000)

P. L. shares his memories of growing up in the United States, where he got such a rush from secretly drinking to get drunk with friends, and in Greece:

> The Greek guys that I went to school with would go out with me to eat, and normally they would have a drink or two and stop because that was the social norm for their culture, and I would have to have at least a six pack or my friends from Iowa would, too. The social norm I believe for the United States is that we don't drink on a daily basis unless you are an alcoholic, whereas the Europeans do drink on a more regular basis so they can control better the amount of liquor they ingest. As Americans we drink fewer times than the Europeans, but it is a norm for us to go out when we get the chance to drink and just get drunk; then normally, we feel that we are okay to drive ourselves home. When I would sit at the bar when I drank heavily, you would see maybe a handful of people who were sober to drive home, and everyone else would be drunk. My Greek friends knew that they either limited their intake or they would have a designated driver to accompany them. Americans who don't drink every day but who binge drink when they get the chance are at a greater risk to become alcoholics as they move from an Epsilon to Gamma. They start to think that they need to have alcohol around to have fun, and they, like myself, progressed to the Gamma where I got my body thinking I needed it to survive. (personal communication, August 8, 2005)

In recognition of these facts and in light of high-profile cases in the media of campus rioting and students dying of overdoses, a number of U.S. colleges are changing their approach to on-campus drinking (Join Together, 2005a). Messages of moderation are replacing messages of "don't drink." In fact, Anheuser-Busch has committed hundreds of thousands of dollars to six colleges for social norms campaigns. An example of such a message—displayed on T-shirts and posters—is: " 'A' students average no more than three drinks when they party, while 'C' students average five."

Another new strategy is to notify parents when their underage children get into trouble because of their drinking. A more controversial measure, which affects recovering drug addicts, is Congress's decision to deny financial aid to college students who have been convicted of drug offenses. Students from underprivileged and minority backgrounds have been hit especially hard by this law ("Attack on Campus Drug Use," 2000).

Colleges have been slower to restrict enticing beer ads from campus newspapers and "happy hour" traditions at bars (two drinks for the price of one). Restrictions of this sort would be consistent with harm reduction. In fact, colleges accept millions from the beer industry, especially in their sport sponsorships (Brogan, 2004). The industry invests around $58 million annually on commercials televised during college sports programs. Despite their claims to the contrary, the alcohol industry makes an estimated $22.5 billion by selling to underage drinkers and somewhat more from sales to alcoholics and binge drinkers (Foster, Vaughan, Foster, & Califano, 2006). A first-time study released by the White House Office of National Drug Control Policy portrays the degree of alcohol, tobacco, and illicit drug use in popular movies and music (Weber, 1999). Findings reveal that 98% of movies and 27% of the songs studied depicted substance use. The entertainment media clearly have an enormous impact on young people, who are inundated with these messages favorable to substance use.

Movies celebrating binge drinking such as *Beerfest,* released in 2006, portray as a lot of fun beer drinking competitions that get contestants falling-down drunk. They are hardly conducive to healthy attitudes. Anheuser-Busch's latest scheme is the opening of a TV and film division designed to getting their products featured in humorous short films and sitcoms to be distributed online and through cell phones (Join Together, 2006a).

Brief Alcohol Screening and Intervention for College Students: A Harm Reduction Approach (Dimeff, Baer, Kivlahan, & Marlatt, 1999) is an instructive manual designed to assist colleges in helping students reduce their alcohol consumption and decrease the behavioral and health risks associated with heavy drinking. Useful reproducible handouts and assessment forms are included in this book. Recent research has confirmed these findings. Grossberg, Brown, and Fleming (2004) found that even 4 years later, brief interventions of young adults by physicians had a significant effect in reducing incidents of alcohol-related accidents compared to a control group that did not receive the intervention.

The DrinkWise program was developed in Canada and especially designed for students with moderate alcohol problems. The focus is on choice. Students are directed to conduct a self-evaluation (available to the public at Carleton University at http://notes.camh.net/efeed.nsf/feedback) to assess their likelihood of developing alcohol problems.

Other countries, such as New Zealand and the United Kingdom, have looked toward harm reduction strategies. The New Zealand Parliament voted to lower the drinking age from 20 to 18 because the old law was not enforceable. Later, despite a strong move to reverse this law, Parliament voted to retain the lower drinking age because raising it would lead to more unsupervised drinking, according to arguments (P. Wilson, 2006). In the United Kingdom, where binge drinking is the highest in all of Western Europe (two fifths of young men drink heavily on a regular basis), a surprising harm reduction strategy was to remove requirements that bars close at any particular time. The aim was to stagger the exit of intoxicated youth from the bars. So far, there has not been any increase in drinking problems (Carvel, 2006).

Long-term studies concerning alcohol and other drug use offer encouraging news. Most individuals mature out of the kind of wild drinking days of early adulthood. Bachman, O'Malley, Johnston, and Schulenberg's (2002) analysis of data gathered annually on more than 33,000 young adults reveals how they change over time. Drinking is heaviest among singles and the divorced. College students who live in dorms or share apartments have the highest binge rates. Yet they typically have settled down to moderate drinking a few years later. The one exception to the trend toward moderation, as these researchers point out, concerns cigarettes. The majority of men and women who smoked a half a pack or more daily in high school are still smoking by age 32. Because of the well-recognized addictiveness of nicotine, prevention efforts are far more effective than treatment long after the addiction has set in.

PREVENTION OF SUBSTANCE MISUSE IN TEENS

A new view of addiction holds that for children and youth it is a "developmental disease" (Addiction Technology Transfer Center [ATTC], 2004). This view recognizes the significance of timing—at what stage of development the use of addictive substances began. The beginning of drug and alcohol use in childhood and youth has a significant impact because of the brain changes that occur in adolescence. This fact probably explains why the rate of drug and alcohol dependence in adulthood is significantly higher among those who started using at an early age compared to late starters. Animal studies confirm the significance of early-life drug experience. Researchers using rats have shown that juvenile rats exposed to amphetamines were more sensitized to the drug when it was reintroduced in maturity, opening the door to addiction (Avital & Richter-Levin, 2005). This rat study also revealed that exposure to extreme stress early in life is associated with a reduced ability to handle stress at a later stage. Other studies have shown that subjects low in self-esteem are more vulnerable to stress (Gorman, 2007). In fact, brain differences have been found on brain scans of people who test low on measures of self-esteem, in the memory area of the brain; these findings suggest that it is harder for such individuals to turn off the stress response. Some people have extreme over-reactions to stress, and others get so overwhelmed they fail to seek rational ways to reduce the stress. Experiments with mice bear this out; if the escape route is blocked while a mouse is given an electrical shock accompanied by the sound of a bell, and later the escape path is open, the animals simply freeze at the sound of the tone, even when they earlier knew how to avoid the shock. Behavioral scientists use the term *learned helplessness* for the same phenomenon. One could speculate from these findings that youth who experience extreme and chronic stress might be highly vulnerable to later behaviors that are self-destructive as well as depression.

Adolescent alcohol misuse is more likely to kill young people than all illegal drugs combined (NIAAA, 2003). Yet the federal government spends 25 times more on preventing illicit drugs than on preventing misuse of alcohol (Vedantam, 2003). Recently, a Government Accountability Office probe of the White House's antidrug media campaign found that the $1 billion-plus spent so far has not been effective in reducing teen drug use (Melillo, 2006). Random drug testing is another strategy that has been generously funded by the government and that has been criticized for its failure to achieve its objectives. As described by Rosenbaum (2004), who has written a book on the subject:

> Random drug testing alienates students. Students must be observed (by a teacher or other adult) as they urinate to be sure the sample is their own. The collection of a specimen is a humiliating violation of privacy, especially embarrassing for an adolescent. Testing can have the unanticipated effect of keeping students from participating in after-school, extracurricular programs—activities that would fill their time during the peak teenage drug-using hours of 3–6 P.M.
>
> A student in Tulia, Texas, summed it up: "I know lots of kids who don't want to get into sports . . . because they don't want to get drug tested. That's one of the reasons I'm not into any [activity]. I'm on medication, so I would always test positive, and then they would have to ask me about my medication, and I would be embarrassed. And what if I'm on my period? I would be too embarrassed." (p. 1)

Yet, early intervention is essential to stem the tide of high-risk experimentation with alcohol, tobacco, and other drugs. Because zero-tolerance policies of officials, teachers, and parents drive the drinking underground and encourage other high-risk behaviors, realistic and proven-effective measures may make the difference between life and death. Harm reduction strategies start where young people are at on a personal level, working with them rather than against them. At the societal level, strategies for youth include strict drinking and driving laws, high taxes on alcoholic beverages, and restrictions on marketing practices.

Harm reduction principles apply at various levels, ranging from community-based educational programs to individual guidance. Some methods of reducing harm are indirect—for example, reducing the size of schools and classes to create a more personal learning environment. Unlike law enforcement strategies that focus on reducing the supply side of drugs, harm reduction strategies are geared to reducing the demand for drugs in the first place. This form of prevention, sometimes termed *primary* prevention, includes interventions to reduce primary risk factors, such as child abuse, as well as early prevention education and treatment programs. The aims of all these efforts are to help children get through adolescence relatively unscathed and to prevent experimentation with substances whose use carries the potential for personal destructiveness down the road. Many of the developmental changes that are necessary prerequisites for healthy adulthood increase an adolescent's risk of smoking, drinking heavily, or using drugs. Due to adolescents' unique developmental issues, differences in priorities, and susceptibility to peer influence, they must be approached differently from adults.

The public health approach to preventing harm is multidimensional and ideally operates across systems. Knowledge of the developmental progression of substance use is important for the focus and timing of preventive interventions. Knowledge of the typical pathways that lead to the reckless use of substances is also instrumental in alleviating or treating underlying psychological problems that can increase the risks for harmful experimentation. Prevention of early-childhood abuse and trauma is key to prevention of the development of the kind of substance misuse that relates to affect—use of chemicals to counteract low feelings resulting from early-childhood trauma. Social policy initiatives must include a coordination of services to protect children from the earliest age onward. Parenting courses, periodic public health nurse visits to all homes where there are babies, a well-funded child welfare system to ensure the safety of children as the first priority are among the initiatives sorely needed. In the United Kingdom, the Labour government introduced strategies based on a coordination of efforts across national and local bodies, including education, health, and prevention services to reduce the demand for drugs (Howard, 1998). The message to the British "drug tsar," according to this report, is that treatment is a cornerstone to reducing demand; harm reduction gets the seal of approval.

For our purposes, primary prevention efforts can be divided into eight general strategies:

1. Child protection aimed at the cycle of violence and substance misuse
2. School-based prevention programs directed toward social influences prompting youth to smoke
3. Information dissemination approaches focusing on the immediate consequences of smoking (bad breath, breathing problems)
4. Mass media campaigns showing the negative side of alcohol, tobacco, and other drug misuse
5. Social resistance and personal competence skills approaches (e.g., anxiety management skills, assertiveness training)
6. Campaigns to reduce or eliminate TV beer ads, student newspaper local bar ads, and national beer ads
7. Advocacy for hiring more school counselors and social workers to work with high-risk students (bullies, victims, children who suffer from mental disorders, children of alcoholics/addicts)
8. The creation of small schools to reduce the sense of alienation and provide a personalized learning environment

An underlying assumption of this prevention model is that an all-out effort should be made to keep youth from ever starting to smoke; this effort should be bolstered by community and media support. (Research from the National Center on Addiction and Substance Abuse at Columbia University [CASA] reveals that teens who smoke cigarettes are 14 times likelier than nonsmokers to try marijuana and have friends who smoke marijuana.) Because many families can enjoy moderate drinking while condemning intoxication and because cultural traditions come into play here, our second major assumption is this: Moderate drinking and abstinence should be presented by health education classes as equally acceptable choices. Since practically all youth will at least sample alcohol, a focus on safe and unsafe practices associated with its use is the only practical course.

The marketers of alcoholic products are having a field day in enticing youth to buy their products, given that the young are highly exposed to media and they are potentially a huge market. Well over one third of sales are linked to young adult drinking, so the alcohol industry, as mentioned earlier, is directing its focus here (Foster et al., 2006). To appeal to women and teens, the whiskey industry has created lighter and sweeter versions of its products (Join Together, 2004). Latino youth are a special target; in fact, they are exposed to the most advertising per capita of any ethnic group (Center on Alcohol Marketing and Youth, 2005).

Are such marketing efforts effective? A recent investigation into the effectiveness of alcohol advertising exposure found that such exposure led to increased drinking levels well into the late 20s (Snyder, Milici, Slater, Sun, & Strizhakova, 2006).

Expecting youngsters not to drink until they reach 21 and then suddenly to become responsible drinkers is unrealistic. Information based on ideology rather than fact, furthermore, will be given little credibility by teens. The whole strategy of demonizing alcohol for youth and reserving its pleasures for adults over a certain age merely increases its attractiveness.

A behavior disorders teacher from rural Iowa draws a link between the words "prohibit" and "defiance":

> When another person tells me what to do and leaves no room for alternative or choice, I become offended. The same applies to our youth and consumption. Choices provide my students with a sense of integrity and responsibility for their actions. When I present my behaviorally challenged students with alternatives, defiant behavior decreases. Part of the reason we have such a high rate of illegal consumption during adolescence is because no choice is allowed. If we taught our youth to drink moderately and allowed them to think for themselves, defiant behavior would decrease. Currently, the right to consume is celebrated on an individual's 21st birthday. Is this the positive alternative we want to provide our youth for the abstinent use of alcohol: a drunken celebration? Why not teach our youth to drink moderately, if at all? After all, our society seems to welcome moderate consumption in the social arena. In my behavior disorder classroom, I am constantly providing choices of socially appropriate behavior. Isn't the moderate consumption of alcohol socially appropriate? If not, then maybe we as adults are living a double standard! It's my belief that the Prohibition movement has caused us to become negligent in imparting healthy social values. Our youth deserve better! (personal communication, March 5, 2000)

Special mention should be made of the advantage of small schools over larger ones. The results of a national longitudinal study of 72,000 junior high and high school students found that when the number of students exceeded 1,000, students become isolated (Fletcher, 2002). The sense of connectedness that a child feels to the small school community means that he or she is less likely to engage in high-risk behavior. Some large urban school systems are developing learning communities within the megaschools in hopes of creating a more intimate learning environment. A positive development that is benefiting children in some of the urban areas is stemming from a decision by The Bill and Melinda Gates Foundation to contribute millions of dollars to finance the creation of small schools across the United States. Such a policy can be considered a form of harm reduction.

Given the high rates of pregnancy, sexually transmitted diseases, growing rates of HIV infection, and risk of lethal overdose among teens, especially among marginalized teens, harm reduction holds the maximum potential of protection. Leshner (1999) describes two paths to drug use. The first path involves the group of kids who are seeking novelty or excitement and striving to be "cool." These kids are most likely to be responsive to prevention education about the harmful effects of drugs on their bodies. The second path to substance use involves dynamics of another sort. Using drugs to escape emotional pain, youth in this category are bent on self-medication. Their problem is getting through today; therefore, messages about long-term damage are apt to have little impact. Fear-arousing messages, paradoxically, are apt to attract the risk takers among them. Leshner recommends professional help for these youth. Unfortunately, however, only one in five of all adolescents in need of treatment services actually receives treatment (U.S. Department of Health and Human Services, 2001).

One very helpful resource relevant to prevention and available in most communities free of charge is the self-help group for children of alcoholics, Alateen, the children's equivalent of Al-Anon, which addresses the needs of families and friends of alcoholics. Supervised by an adult, often a recovering adult, Alateen is a support group where the children of alcoholics can learn that they are not alone and not at fault. The attention given to expressing one's feelings can do much to stem the intergenerational cycle of addiction.

Research on prevention effectiveness surveyed by Botvin and Botvin (1997) points to social life skills training, either alone or in combination with other approaches, as having the most effective impact on substance use behavior. These approaches, as Botvin and Botvin indicate, utilize well-tested behavioral intervention techniques; they also provide preparation for dealing with strong feelings without resorting to the use of alcohol and other drugs. The coping mechanisms acquired here should be invaluable in later life as well.

The war on drugs is exacting a double toll on children. First, it takes their parents away and subjects them to the tragedy of premature separation. Second, the stigma of having a parent incarcerated weighs heavily upon a growing child. Half the 1.5 million children with a parent in jail or prison will commit a crime before they turn 18 (Drummond, 2000).

Youth who get into trouble with drugs and who are sent to juvenile facilities have high rates of recidivism (Noble & Reed, 2000). Yet more and more youth are being dealt with harshly in juvenile court for minor crimes and tried as adults for major crimes. The drug court movement—an innovative and carefully orchestrated development—provides mandatory alcohol and drug treatment and a continuum of community services to ensure compliance with its 2-year program. Education, vocational experiences, and life skills training are provided.

Today, there are more than 300 juvenile drug courts that provide intensive case management to youth who would otherwise reside in training schools (Butts & Roman, 2004). Treatment strategies are geared to a person's maturity level—that is, to his or her readiness to address the substance use problem. Another innovative approach is the recovery school. As of 2006, there are around 20 recovery schools, which high school students can attend straight from chemical dependence treatment (ATTC, 2004). Helping students in recovery make the transition back into student life is the underlying purpose of the program. The most unique and student centered of these schools is the PEASE Academy (Peers Enjoying Sober Education) in Minneapolis (Riestenberg, 2005). Communication and learning are done through restorative circles in which students share their feelings, progress in maintaining sobriety, and concern for each other. The circles make use of a talking stick passed from speaker to speaker. Staff are trained in the principles of restorative justice in which the focus is on truth telling, relationships, and healing.

MOTIVATIONAL ENHANCEMENT STRATEGIES

Ideally suited for work with troubled and rebellious substance misusers, the harm reduction model meets the youth where the youth is and is disarmingly nonthreatening. There is no moralizing tone here and no forcing teens to sit in a circle and label themselves as alcoholics or addicts. A certain amount of ambivalence is expected and deemed healthy in fact. In every stage of the stages-of-change model, originally formulated by Prochaska and DiClemente (1992)—precontemplation through maintenance or relapse—resolving ambivalence is a central theme of focus. Helping people make decisions that will benefit their lives is the overriding good of motivational enhancement therapy. Table 6.1 presents typical client statements at each stage of the stages-of-change continuum.

Through a close therapeutic relationship, the counselor can help a person develop a commitment to change. Motivational theory maintains that if the therapist can get the client to do something, *anything,* to get better, this client will have a chance at success. This is a basic principle of social psychology. Such tasks that William Miller (1998) pinpoints as predictors of recovery are going

TABLE 6.1 | STAGE-SPECIFIC MOTIVATIONAL STATEMENTS

Stages of Change	Adolescent Comments
Precontemplation	My parents can't tell me what to do; I still use and I don't see the harm in it—do you?
Contemplation	I'm on top of the world when I'm high, but then when I come down, I'm really down. It was better before I got started on these things.
Preparation	I'm feeling good about setting a date to quit, but who knows?
Action	Staying clean may be healthy, but it sure makes for a dull life. Maybe I'll check out one of these groups.
Maintenance	It's been a few months; I'm not there yet but I'm hanging out with some new friends.

to AA meetings, coming to sessions, completing homework assignments, and taking medication (even a placebo pill). The question, according to Miller, then becomes: How can I help my clients do something to take action on their own behalf? A related principle of social psychology is that in defending a position aloud, as in a debate, we become committed to it. One would predict, according to motivational enhancement theory, that if the therapist elicits defensive statements from the client, the client would become more committed to the status quo and less willing to change. For this reason, explains Miller, confrontational approaches have a poor track record. Research has shown that people are more likely to grow and change in a positive direction on their own than if they get caught up in a battle of wills.

The effectiveness of motivational strategies in eliciting change in even the most recalcitrant of people (see chapter 1) is worthy of closer analysis. Actually, the effectiveness of this model of person-centered counseling should come as no surprise because each of the basic principles is derived from strategies that have been shown effective in social psychology laboratory situations. The overall technique of eliciting self-motivating statements by the client is perhaps the most basic of these scientific insights. We have filtered from one of the most popular books on social psychology—*The Social Animal* by Elliot Aronson (2003)—the basic principles of persuasion. The ones that most closely parallel the principles of motivational enhancement are these:

- If we're encouraged to state a position, we become motivated to defend that position (p. 85).
- When individuals commit themselves in a small way, the likelihood that they will commit themselves further is increased. The behavior needs to be justified so attitudes are changed (p. 158).
- People with high self-esteem are more likely to resist the temptation to commit immoral acts (p. 186).
- A person can become committed to a situation by making a decision, working hard to attain a goal (p. 186).
- Dissonance theory predicts that people will change their attitudes to bring them in line with the evidence (p. 189).
- Changing one's attitudes in order to justify one's behavior can initiate the processes that are persistent over time (p. 193).
- People desire dissonance-reducing behavior (p. 198).

Keep these teachings in mind in your study of motivational strategies and compare them with less scientific attempts to get people to break their bad habits and self-destructive behavior.

In their seven-part professional training videotape series, W. R. Miller and Rollnick (1998) provide guidance in the art and science of motivational enhancement. In this series, the don'ts are as revealing as the do's. According to this therapy team, the don'ts, or traps for therapists to avoid, are:

- A premature focus, such as on one's addictive behavior
- The confrontational/denial round between therapist and client

- The labeling trap—forcing the individual to accept a label such as alcoholic or addict
- The blaming trap, a fallacy that is especially pronounced in couples counseling
- The question/answer habit, which is characterized by asking several questions in a row and reliance on closed yes-or-no responses, which exchange paves the way for the expert trap
- The expert trap, whereby the client is put down (the opposite of a collaborative exchange of information)

These precautions relate exceptionally well to work with teens, as does the motivational theorists' handling of client resistance. As he states in the videotape on motivational enhancement, Miller is uncomfortable with the concept of *resistance;* his preference is to think of clients as simply cautious in trusting the therapist. To establish this trust and enable the client to elicit the desired self-motivated or insightful statements, such as "I think I do have a problem," the skilled therapist relies on open and multifaceted questions, reflective listening, and purposeful summarizing of the client's story. Key to this process is the reframing of the client's story in the direction of decision making. A format such as "I sense that you are saying, on the one hand, that smoking means a lot to you and, on the other hand, that you are beginning to have some health concerns about the damage that the smoking is causing you or may cause you in the future" provides helpful feedback to the reluctant client by reflecting back to him or her what is heard.

Following the formulation set forth by W. R. Miller and Rollnick (2002) and Wallen (1993), major tasks for the adolescent's counselor at each stage of decision making directly parallel the client's state of mind. At the *precontemplation* stage, goals are to establish rapport, to ask rather than to tell, and to build trust. Eliciting the young person's definition of the situation, the counselor reinforces discrepancies between the client's and others' perceptions of the problem. During the *contemplation* stage, while helping to tip the decision toward reduced drug/alcohol use, the counselor emphasizes the client's freedom of choice. "No one can make this decision for you" is a typical way to phrase this sentiment. Information is presented in a neutral, "take-it-or-leave-it" manner. Typical questions are: "What do you get out of drinking?" "What is the down side?" and (to elicit strengths) "What makes your sister believe in your ability to do this?" At the *preparation* for change and *action* stages, questions like "What do you think will work for you?" help guide the youth forward without pushing too far or too fast. When there is resistance, as there inevitably will be with young substance misusers, Miller and Rollnick advise rolling with the resistance instead of fighting it. Use of reflective summarizing statements is helpful; for example, "Let's see if I've got this right. You have a concern that I'm trying to get you to give up smoking and drinking all at once. We do seem to be moving along too fast. Why don't we look at some things people have done in this situation, some of the options you might want to consider?" Central to this whole treatment strategy is the belief that clients are amenable to change and that timing is crucial in persuading clients to take the steps that will free them from harm.

On the college campus, the most promising type of intervention to address high-risk alcohol use (and ultimately reduce harm) appears to be a brief intervention with motivational interviewing. In Britain, New Zealand, and Canada, such brief sessions that promoted reflection on substance use and the personal consequences have been shown in randomized controlled trials of high-risk students to reduce drinking and drug use significantly (Poulin, 2006).

GENDER-SPECIFIC PROGRAMMING FOR GIRLS

Equality does not mean sameness; recognition of male–female developmental differences is important in shaping approaches that will tap into the interests and strengths of each gender. As Belknap and Holsinger (2006) inform us, programs for boys are more successful when they offer ways to advance within a structured environment, whereas programs for girls do better when they focus on relationships and assertiveness within relationships. Gender-responsive policy provides effective interventions that address intersecting issues of substance use, trauma, mental health, and economic oppression (Bloom, Owen, & Covington, 2004).

Special attention to girls' unique biology and body image concerns is essential as well, for these are major female concerns. In view of the recognition of girls' special needs, so often ignored in male-oriented treatment programs, the *Juvenile Female Offenders* report (Office of Juvenile Justice and Delinquency Prevention, 1998) recommends the establishment of girls' group treatment homes. Such homes would provide gender-specific programming focused on healthy relationships, a female-centered school curriculum, caring mentors to provide encouragement in setting realistic educational goals, and special services for pregnant and parenting young women. Individual and group counseling for survivors of sexual abuse trauma would be provided as well; these matters cannot be properly addressed in mixed settings or in gender-neutral programs.

Rudolph Alexander (2000) describes a pilot treatment program at the Santa Monica Hospital Medical Center developed for girls who have been sexually abused. After engaging in friendly warmup exercises, the girls played the "Hat Game," in which they all get to answer a question pulled out of a hat. The questions relate to how they feel their bodies have changed since they were molested and whether they would say to a girl who had been molested that they thought it was her fault. The girls later write their own questions: "Have you felt like killing yourself?" and "Have you ever felt real crazy?" are examples (p. 208).

In Waterloo, Iowa, group homes that were once co-ed now specialize in the care of teenage girls, many of whom are already mothers. A system of nurturant foster care has been established in Waterloo, Iowa, in conjunction with Quakerdale, one of the few youth residential facilities in the state that accepts pregnant teens. "Patterning with families . . . restoring hope" is the theme of this program that places pregnant teens in trouble with the law in the residential facility. Following their release date, teens have the option of moving into foster care with their babies (Hemenway-Forbes, 2001). Central to all these program innovations is the theme of personal empowerment. In a program that is empowering, the client is aided to build a positive self-identity and find strength in her own voice and pride in her cultural heritage.

The learning of life skills and the importance of family can flow naturally and spontaneously through involvement in mutual-aid or support groups focused on a common, all-absorbing task. From a strengths perspective, the hallmark of the effective group leader is enthusiasm and unshakable confidence in the young women's latent talents and abilities. The leader's or social worker's role, as Gutiérrez and Suarez (1999) state, should be that of consultant and facilitator rather than instructor, so as not to reinforce the sense of powerlessness that these victimized and addicted girls need to overcome. Small groups, according to these authors, have special relevance for empowerment practice with Latinas because it is in keeping with the Latinas' history of working with one another to provide mutual aid. African American culture is similarly oriented more toward family and community systems than toward individual achievement.

The importance of such group work for all the participants is that gaining competence in one area—writing poetry, drawing, parenting—can lead to skills in performing other adult roles valued by society. The socially empowering group, even within the confines of the stark juvenile justice setting, can be individually transformative, the more so among women who have been removed from and punished by society, estranged from loved ones, and forced into lockstep with institutional demands. The actively working, fun-loving group can thus represent a strange and powerful anomaly, given where it is and the personal history of its members. Such a group can serve as a bridge to the cultural and social milieu of the larger society (Wilson & Anderson, 1997). And above all, reintegration of the juvenile offender into society is the one thing the present correctional apparatus is the most tragically, shamefully, ill prepared to do. The negative labeling and punitive response to girls in trouble with the law put them at more risk of further drug misuse in the future, often by way of self-destructive relationships. The widespread use of a model geared to break convicts of criminal thought patterns is consistent with the present politically conservative climate and entirely inappropriate for work with girls and women (Pollack, 2004). We concur with Carol Lee Pepi's (1997) call for a paradigm shift from society's current retributive justice response to the healing model of gender-based restorative justice. In restorative justice, the focus is on restoring individual family networks: Healing, not punishment, is emphasized (see van Wormer, Besthorn & Keefe, 2007).

ADDICTION PROBLEMS AMONG THE ELDERLY

Moving to the other end of the spectrum, we come to the final stage of life. The challenge at this stage, according to Erikson (1963), is to achieve ego integrity rather than despair. Ego integrity is defined as the ultimate form of identity integration; people who attain this attribute, suggests Erikson, enjoy a sense of peace and pride in their contribution and accomplishments. Others fail to cope satisfactorily, however; retirement, widowhood, and the accumulation of losses can lead to loneliness and depression.

Persons aged 65 and older constitute about 13% of the U.S. population; they are the fastest growing age cohort (U.S. Census Bureau, 2005). Few realize the true extent of substance abuse by the elderly because the elderly are more likely to drink and use drugs (prescription medication) at home than in public. Alcohol-related consequences of heavy drinking, moreover, are often confused by health professionals and family members with medical or psychiatric conditions among the aged. The diagnosis and treatment of alcohol problems are likely to become increasingly important as this segment of the population grows.

ALCOHOL MISUSE

In contrast to young alcohol abusers, the elderly drink smaller amounts at one time, use drugs prescribed by doctors (licit as opposed to illicit drugs), experience a hidden alcohol problem, and drink in connection with a number of late-life stresses, including bereavement from the loss of family and friends and loss of occupational roles through retirement. The rate of smoking is 9.3% by older men and 7.3% by older women (U.S. Census Bureau, 2005). Around 29% over age 65 are regular consumers of alcohol, about half as many as among those in the younger age group. Whites are more likely to drink than members of minority groups. Unlike young adults, who seek out drugs for recreational use, the elderly may be seeking a therapeutic effect, such as pain relief.

Surveys of various age groups in the community suggest that the elderly consume less alcohol and have fewer alcohol-related problems than younger persons. As might be expected, this segment of the population consumes 25 to 30% of all prescription medications (Benshoff, Harrawood, & Darwin, 2003). Of great concern to health and mental health professionals is the large number of elderly using a variety of prescription medications without proper physician supervision. Prescription drug misuse is estimated to affect as many as 17% of older adults (U.S. Department of Health and Human Services, 1998). Addiction to the benzodiazepines, such as Valium and Xanax, is quite common in this age group.

In contrast to studies of the general population, surveys conducted in healthcare settings have found a substantial prevalence of signs of alcohol problems—6 to 11% of those admitted to hospitals, 20% in psychiatric wards, 14% in emergency rooms, and curiously, 49% of those admitted to nursing homes (U.S. Census Bureau, 2005). The extremely high prevalence of alcohol problems in nursing home admissions may reflect a trend toward using nursing homes for short-term alcoholism rehabilitation stays. To gauge the extent of the problem in a local Iowa nursing home, Marcia Walker, at the request of van Wormer, interviewed a social worker who worked there. In the words of the social worker:

> The rule in the retirement community is that anything that says, "Keep out of reach of children" has to be locked up in their med room. That includes medicines,

scissors, cigarettes, alcohol, some soaps, some deodorants, etc. If residents are smokers, they must go outside independently without the help of staff to smoke. The nursing home tries to put these people on medication to stop smoking. Of course, they must have a doctor's order for this.

The retirement center uses the patch and a prescription to Wellbutrin for the purpose of helping a resident stop smoking. Staff are not allowed to provide cigarettes or alcohol to residents. Residents can use alcohol anywhere in the facility; but those that do must have a doctor's order to use it. The doctor usually gives the order of one drink per day or one beer every two days. The alcohol must be locked up in the med room. The retirement center doesn't have a big problem with this. With residents who have been alcoholics all their lives, usually when they enter a retirement home, they don't have much family support. Those family relationships have been broken by the time the alcoholic gets to the nursing home. (interview conducted June 2006)

And as Walker later commented:

So, how widespread is the problem? The social worker says there is no problem now; but as the younger generation gets older and enters the retirement community, she thinks there will be a bigger problem with drug usage since the younger people experiment with it and make it now.

Investigators have distinguished two types of elderly alcoholics: early onset and late onset. The early-onset alcoholics are those who began to have drinking problems early in life and have carried them into old age. Persons who have been drinking heavily their whole lives are more apt than others to be dually or multiply diagnosed and to have a family history of alcoholism (Ruffin & Kaye, 2004). Early-onset alcoholics are more likely to be men; late-onset are more likely to be women (U.S. Department of Health and Human Services, 1998). Approximately two thirds of the elderly alcoholics are of the early-onset variety (Kinney, 2006). In an empirically based comparative study, Schonfeld and Dupree (1991) matched 23 early-onset alcoholic abusers admitted for treatment with 23 late-onset abusers in treatment. Early-onset subjects were likely to have changed residence, to have been intoxicated more often, and to have experienced more severe levels of depression and anxiety. A large group of early-onset but now abstinent male alcoholics reside in nursing homes and suffer from Korsakoff's syndrome and other alcohol-related neurological problems (Benshoff & Janikowski, 2000). For both groups, depression, loneliness, and lack of social support were the most frequently reported antecedents to readmission drinking behavior. In contrast to the long-term drinkers, late-onset subjects were more likely to remain in treatment.

In van Wormer's experience, the late-onset group had close family ties; initially, these clients were overcome with the stigma of the alcoholism diagnosis: After a life of sobriety, a tainted self-image in old age (such as following a DWI arrest) was an unexpected blow. For these well-motivated but sensitive clients, an empathic therapeutic environment is essential.

One reason for finding a lower rate of alcoholism among the general population of older adults undoubtedly is related to the high mortality rate among heavy alcohol consumers and smokers. The statistics also reflect the fact that a disproportionate number of the elderly are women. And elderly women, due to sex-role expectations from their youth, are apt to drink little if at all (Benshoff et al., 2003). If they do drink to any great extent, they are careful to keep this fact hidden.

Other Drug Misuse

Older Americans comprise fewer than 13% of the population but receive between 25 and 30% of all prescriptions and account for more than half of the hospitalizations resulting from drug reactions. About 17% of older adults experience problems with abuse of alcohol or misuse of prescription drugs, and 20% of the mental health problems experienced by those over 55 are not part of the normal aging process, according to *SAMHSA News* (2006). With these facts in mind, SAMHSA and the Food and Drug Administration (FDA) have launched an information campaign for older adults called "Do the Right Dose." To counter the upward trend in misuse of opiates, the SAMHSA and the FDA are embarking on a joint advertising campaign to caution elderly persons about the risks associated with taking pain medication.

National data provided in the *SAMHSA News* report indicate that the proportion of persons aged 55 and older admitted to substance abuse treatment with alcohol as their primary problem decreased between 1995 and 2002, but the rate of drug admissions doubled for both men and women within this age group. Nine percent of the adults admitted to substance abuse treatment were aged 50 or older (Office of Applied Studies, 2006). About half of the admissions were for alcohol only. Persons with alcohol problems were more likely than those with other substance use problems to be in treatment for the first time. The remaining half of the admissions included 15% who reported misuse of alcohol plus an illicit drug and 37% who reported a heroin or pain medication problem.

Significantly, the government survey showed that 4.4% of baby boomers aged 50 to 59 indicated use of illicit drugs in the past month. What we are seeing is the carry-over of habits from the 1970s when drug use among the young was at its peak. Much media attention has recently been devoted to what the *AARP Bulletin* (Karaim, 2005) terms "a hidden epidemic" (p. 26) of older drug addicts. A *Time* magazine article titled "Balding, Wrinkled and Stoned" (Kluger, 2006) notes that the impact of the baby boom generation's recreational use of drugs is now being evidenced in health problems.

In spite of the increased recognition in recent years that elderly substance misuse is a growing problem, many researchers believe that the numbers are grossly underestimated. Few of the older alcoholics are getting the help they need. Reasons contributing to their neglect as singled out by Beechem (2002) are:

- The elderly tend to avoid substance abuse services.
- They are rarely referred from court services for drug-induced criminal activity.
- The problem of misdiagnosis mentioned previously exists.

- Friends and relatives can be indulgent or neglectful.
- Established criteria for classifying alcohol problems among the aged are inadequate or irrelevant.
- So much of their time is spent alone.

BIOLOGICAL CONSIDERATIONS

One reason drinking inventories are inadequate as diagnostic tools for people over a certain age is that their bodies metabolize alcohol differently. Any psychoactive drug is likely to have a more pronounced effect on an elderly person than on someone younger. A decline in body fluid and an increase in the proportion of body fat make for a decreased volume of distribution for alcohol. The slower metabolism, lower body mass, and decrease in an enzyme called alcohol dehydrogenase that accompany aging drive down the tolerance of older adults (Hauser, 2005). The high tolerance that younger alcoholics so seem to enjoy gives way with long-term use and age, and tolerance reversal is characteristic. As Father Martin (1972) once phrased it in his memorable videotape *Chalk Talks on Alcohol*, "You get drunk quicker and it ain't worth it." (Virtually all the standard drinking inventories include high tolerance as a criterion of alcohol dependence.)

The inability to handle alcohol with advancing age is also related to slowed rates of metabolism and excretion and the fact that elderly persons are apt to have other drugs in their system already that exacerbate the effect of alcohol, often with serious consequences. Alcohol use among the elderly is most often a case of polydrug (not single-drug) use with all the problems that may ensue from this eventuality.

Compared to younger persons, elderly drinkers are more prone to addiction due to their more frequent use of medications, especially of depressants, blood pressure medication, and painkillers, and due as well to the high prevalence of depression and anxiety disorders in this age group. Death due to the synergistic effect of drug interactions is higher among the elderly than among any other group, including adolescents (Beechem, 2002).

Other medical complications associated with long-term alcohol misuse include:

- Problems in the gastrointestinal system—ulcers, pancreatitis, cirrhosis of the liver
- Hip fractures related to decrease in bone density and falls while intoxicated
- Injuries in car crashes
- Alcohol–medication interactions that decrease the effectiveness of prescription medications
- A likelihood of suicide associated with depressive disorders
- Brain damage in the cerebellum affecting balance and in the frontal lobes affecting functioning
- The incidence of pneumonia, pulmonary disease, heart disease, and lung cancer is extremely high because the majority of elderly alcoholics smoke.

SOCIAL RISK FACTORS

Aging in our society is equated with obsolescence and physical decay—witness all the magazine and TV ads highlighting products to disguise the aging process. In a future-oriented society, those with a claim on the past may find themselves considered passé. Stresses in old age are related to the accumulation of losses— loss of family members and friends, loss of meaningful activities (including work), of identity as a teacher, truck driver, construction worker, and so forth, and loss of health. In Erikson's terms, in the absence of integrity, there is despair.

Psychological factors related to loss and unresolved grief contribute to drug and alcohol problems among the elderly. The isolation and withdrawal associated with substance misuse reduce one's inclination to socialize and lead an active life. Family members may avoid or reject heavy-drinking individuals out of embarrassment and/or accumulated anger over previous episodes. In the belief that the elderly are unlikely to change, relatives rarely bring them in or commit them to treatment. They often come to treatment because of arrests for drinking and driving. Once in treatment, their recovery prospects, especially for late-onset drinkers, are very good (Benshoff et al., 2003).

ASSESSMENT

Healthcare providers are advised to include questions about drinking and smoking habits on their health inventory forms, and most of them do. Very brief interventions at the doctor's office—advice to quit or cut down—have proven effective. Advice to older patients should include warnings about medical conditions, such as high blood pressure and ulcers, that can be worsened by drinking and the risks of taking over-the-counter and prescription drugs in combination with alcohol (NIAAA, 1998).

When clients appear at a treatment center, a thorough assessment of their drinking and drug-using habits is undertaken. As mentioned previously, the standard forms, like diagnoses from the *DSM–IV–TR*, contain several items that are inappropriate for clients of advanced age (e.g., items concerning tolerance and legal and occupational consequences of substance misuse).

Because of the expanded availability of gambling establishments, many older persons gamble for excitement and escape from boredom. Binge drinking has been found to be one of the strongest predictors of at-risk gambling behavior (Levens, Dyer, Zurbitsky, Knott, & Oslin, 2005). This study assessed the prevalence of gambling problems in a sample of over 800 elderly patients with scheduled primary-care clinic appointments. Just under 70% of the patients reported that they gambled at least once a year, around 11% of whom were identified as at-risk gamblers. Other risk factors of which counselors should be aware are the presence of current posttraumatic stress disorder symptoms, minority race/ethnicity, and being a Veterans Administration patient. These findings indicate that substance abuse clinics would do well to assess for gambling problems by including a few simple questions about gambling activities, winnings, and losses in assessment forms.

Two well-known alcohol-screening devices that have been validated for use with older adults are CAGE and the Geriatric MAST (NIAAA, 1998). CAGE consists of four simple questions (see chapter 5). The MAST-G (Michigan Alcoholism Screening Test—Geriatric Version) consists of 24 questions with special relevance to the elderly. Samples are: "Does having a drink help you sleep?" "Did you find your drinking increased after someone close to you died?" "When you feel lonely, does having a drink help?" (Center for Substance Abuse Treatment [CSAT], 1998, pp. 7–8). (The Geriatric MAST can be downloaded at http://kap.samhsa.gov/products/tools/keys/pdfs/KK_26.pdf.)

TREATMENT INTERVENTIONS

Whether to treat older patients in age-segregated settings or with the regular substance abuse treatment population is an unanswered question in the research literature. Kathleen Farkas (2006) convincingly makes the case for senior programs. Based on her experience, Farkas has found that older adults bond with each other because, like the young, they share similar problems. In mixed groups, the issues of the young may be horrifying to elderly clients; prostitution among heroin addicts is one such example and the use of strong language is another. In age-specific programs, which are slower paced and use treatment techniques adapted for older clients, such clients feel more comfortable and will remain in treatment longer. Many treatment centers do not have the luxury of separate programming. Van Wormer, in her personal experience, found that many clients thoroughly enjoyed the mix of ages in her therapy groups: Older clients seemed to benefit from giving advice and sharing their stories with younger group members. They also seemed to like getting personally involved in hearing of the intrigues and relationship crises of others in the group. One drawback was the general lack of patience toward those occasional group members who were hard of hearing. The chiding of participants to speak up had a dampening effect on group interaction.

Excellent results are reported from the Elder Care Program at Odyssey House, a residential program in New York City for those over age 55 (Jones, 2005). The clients in this treatment center sit in circles and share stories of heroin and other drug use. Residents speak of spending quality time with their grandchildren and wanting to now take care of their health. Fewer than 20% of licensed substance abuse treatment centers offer such programs specifically for the elderly.

Panelists who prepared a *Substance Abuse Among Older Adults* treatment improvement protocol (U.S. Department of Health and Human Services, 1998, p. xxi) recommended incorporating six features into treatment of older alcohol misusers:

1. Age-specific group treatment that is supportive and nonconfrontational and aims to build or rebuild the patient's self-esteem
2. A focus on coping with depression, loneliness, and loss (e.g., death of a spouse, retirement)

3. A focus on rebuilding the client's social support network
4. A pace and content of treatment appropriate for the older person
5. Staff members who are interested and experienced in working with older adults
6. Linkages with medical services, services for the aging, and institutional settings for referral into and out of treatment, as well as case management

Additional tips provided by this government source are to provide a clear statement of the goal and purpose of each session; to make use of simultaneous visual and audible presentation of material, enlarged print, nonglaring light, reduction of background noise; to keep group sessions short (55 minutes maximum); and to begin each session with a review of previous material.

In her work with elderly females, van Wormer found them remarkably receptive to treatment, grateful for the opportunity to come to group, and as often as not, seeing the crisis that brought them through the treatment doors as a blessing. When two elderly graduates of the program requested diplomas to put on their walls, the receptionist obligingly rushed out to have some made up. (Such a request had never been made before.) In working with older women, one can expect that feelings of guilt and shame about drinking will emerge. Cohen (2000) recommends approaching an older woman about her drinking in an atmosphere of privacy and respect for her personal history. In addition, there should be an understanding of the stigma that the words "alcoholism" and "alcoholic" might hold for her. Terms like "drinking" and "drinking problems" can be used instead. A focus on health and a healthy lifestyle is usually well received.

Hanson and Gutheil (2004) detail the use of motivational strategies with older adults who have drinking and other drug problems. These strategies are especially useful in healthcare centers, social service agencies, nursing homes, and other establishments that are likely places of first contact with elderly alcoholics and addicts. Brief interventions can be provided while using the client's concerns as a focal point to facilitate discussion. To build motivation for sustained change, feedback must be personalized but also raise the client's awareness of the extent of the problem. Involving the client's family can help increase the success of motivational counseling. Because many elderly individuals are sensitive to the stigma of alcohol misuse, motivation strategies provided in nonstigmatized agencies such as healthcare facilities work best (American Association for Geriatric Psychiatry, 2003).

Beechem (2002, chap. 8) delineates common pitfalls for the counselor who provides substance abuse treatment to an elderly clientele: (a) *ageism* and stereotyping of which the counselor may be unaware (use of derogatory off-the-cuff remarks such as "this dates me" sends a message that old is bad); (b) *countertransference,* the unconscious process in which elderly persons trigger feelings in the helper about his or her parents and grandparents that interfere with therapy; (c) *avoidance and denial* of the addiction problems in assessing elderly clients; and (d) *expressing sympathy* rather than empathy, which compounds the clients' self-pity and helplessness.

Contemporary barriers to healthcare stemming from managed healthcare restrictions and federal and state cutbacks take a heavy toll on elderly alcoholics in need of treatment. Whereas Medicare, the healthcare provision for the elderly, traditionally covered 12 days of inpatient alcohol treatment, many states, under pressure from managed care companies, are eliminating this coverage. In view of the large number of physical and cognitive problems among polydrug-using older adults, including lengthy withdrawals, coverage of at least 12 days of inpatient treatment is an extremely important option (U.S. Department of Health and Human Services, 1998).

One exemplary program described by Graham and Brett (1994) utilized a harm reduction approach to treating older adults with substance dependence problems. Funded by a grant from the city of Ottawa, the project, Lifestyle Enrichment for Senior Adults, was designed to reach senior apartment residents suspected of having problems with alcohol and psychoactive medication. Participants learned of the project through news stories, hospital referrals, or friends. This client-centered program was conducted in the tradition of Carl Rogers, a tradition high on empathy and warmth and low on confrontation. Unique to this program was the acceptance given to persons who had little or no desire to quit drinking or drug using and would have been excluded from conventional, abstinence-based programs. By focusing on the harm associated with substance use rather than solely on the use itself, both counselor and client could consider a broad range of solutions (e.g., delaying drinking until the evening). To reduce the stigma of slips and relapses, the focal point was on personal issues rather than substance use. For example, a person who had begun using drugs or alcohol following the death of a spouse might, in developing a rapport with the counselor or group, find solace through dealing with repressed feelings related to unresolved grief and/or in joining a local bereavement support group.

In their in-depth interviews with participants and graduates of the Lifestyle Enrichment for Senior Adults program, Graham and Brett (1994) found the clients' dependence problems were of two varieties. Either these problems were related to a mental disorder and were longstanding in nature, or more often, the addiction problems had evolved out of loneliness and isolation. Program participants improved their health-seeking behaviors considerably as a result of the treatment interventions and personal attention received. Social events were an active and popular component of this program; group meetings served as aftercare insurance against relapse.

Although based on a small sample, Graham and Brett's findings are consistent with research demonstrating that in working with older people with alcohol or drug problems, a nonconfrontational approach achieves considerable objective success (U.S. Department of Health and Human Services, 1998). As recorded in their interviews, clients gave evidence that they understood the health goal of the program and were actively working toward minimizing drinking as a part of this goal. Personal empowerment came from a focus on client successes rather than failures. "Perhaps it's time for the addictions field to adopt a less dogmatic and more pragmatic approach to addressing alcohol and drug abuse," as Graham and Brett (1994) thoughtfully concluded (p. 19).

Many elderly problem drinkers in harm reduction and conventional programs decide abstinence is their best course. Some of the most active members of Alcoholics Anonymous are retired individuals who derive great personal satisfaction in helping newly sober younger alcoholics. AA's use of storytelling is attractive to older people, who often have spellbinding stories from years past. Most cities have meetings specifically for older AA members. Attendees often derive great satisfaction from the camaraderie and interactive ritualism of such mutual-support groups.

PREVENTION OF RELAPSE

Relapse, or a "lapse" as it is commonly called by harm reduction model proponents, does not mean, in AA parlance, "one drink, one drunk." Nor does it refer to a failed drug test that shows one is "dirty" if one smokes a single marijuana cigarette over a month's time. A relapse is not a one-time slip or setback but rather a process. A client's return to harmful use can be interpreted as a temporary lapse in the path to changing addictive behavior. At the thinking level, relapse is seen as leading back from the action stage to the contemplation or precontemplation level (Daisy, Thomas, & Worley, 2002). By helping clients appreciate that changing addictive behavior is a learning process, lapses can be reframed as valuable learning opportunities rather than indications of personal failure (Witkiewitz, 2005). This reframing is crucial to keep the lapses from leading to a full relapse. Once a client is overwhelmed with guilt and conflict, his or her sense of failure can easily become a self-fulfilling prophecy. Specific strategies to prevent a lapse from turning into a full-blown relapse, offered by Weingardt and Marlatt (1999), are:

- Stop, look, and listen. Clients can be taught in advance that a lapse is a warning signal that they are in danger and need to retire to a quiet place to review these strategies as summarized on their reminder card.
- Stay calm; avoid feelings of guilt and self-blame; a lapse is a mistake, not a failure.
- Renew your commitment; think back over the reasons you decided to change in the first place.
- Review the situation leading up to the lapse.
- Make an immediate plan for recovery, such as getting rid of the pills or alcohol or leaving the high-risk situation.
- Draw on your support network for help.

Broadly speaking, interventions for relapse management can be thought of as efforts to minimize the harm associated with a return to unhealthy practices following a period of abstinence or controlled use.

The return to addictive patterns following treatment more often than not is associated with negative emotions, such as anger, anxiety, depression, and boredom, and a desire to suppress those strong emotions. Clients can be taught to avoid or to prepare themselves to handle unrealistic expectations, environmental cues, or triggers such as the smell of alcohol; both positive and negative emotional states; and sexual triggers. Achieving a balanced satisfying lifestyle is an essential part of reducing the potential for relapse (Washton & Zweben, 2006). A favorite saying in substance abuse treatment is HALT! Don't get too

Hungry

Angry

Lonely

Tired

"Triggers" such as peer pressure and work-related problems are common among younger alcoholics, but elderly alcoholics are more apt to be influenced by late-life situations (Beechem, 2002). Depression, loneliness, and unresolved loss-grief issues are negative emotions that may be associated with the use of a chemical to dull the senses, if not to get high. In extreme cases, such low feelings combined with drug use can be a precursor to suicide.

Especially for young people, the setting of an unrealistic goal, such as never drinking again, can be counterproductive. If the treatment goal is total abstinence, then any transgressions may be viewed negatively, which may actually lead to an increase in the problematic behavior (Witkiewitz, 2005).

The learning of critical thinking skills is a key factor in maintaining recovery following treatment. Valtonen, Sogren, and Cameron-Padmore (2006) conducted research in rehabilitation facilities in Trinidad. Their focus was on coping styles in handling stress. They found that only a minority of the clients had acquired mature problem-solving skills or knew how to draw strength from social support systems to deal with grief and loss, for example. As research such as that of Valtonen et al. indicates, one focus of therapy practice must be directed to counterproductive responses learned early in life that would have to be unlearned to help insulate the person from relapse.

Beechem offers a cognitively based three-stage approach to relapse prevention geared toward high-risk situations for the elderly. In stage one, high-risk situations are spelled out. Although a standardized checklist of typical risks may be provided, the client's personal list is derived through collaboration and discussion. Typical risks that may be listed are watching old family movies, returning home from a family reunion or funeral, suffering sleep loss, harping on one's regrets in life ("if only I had . . . "), and hanging around bars.

In stage two, clients are helped to monitor the antecedents of drinking urges. Together with the counselor, a plan for continuous self-monitoring of negative thoughts and deeds is drawn up. Evolving from homework assignments is a clear sense of the client's strengths, support systems, and capabilities. Through prompting, as the elderly client reviews his or her life crises and blessings, the counselor can help the client appreciate his or her coping style, strengths, and purpose in life (professional and/or personal triumphs). Stage three stresses the self-management and self-efficacy that are keys to sober living.

Central to this three-stage approach of high-risk prevention is the notion that clients are consumers and that their concerns and needs are paramount. Forcing them to conform their thinking to standard belief systems that have worked for some (e.g., to have to say, "My sobriety comes first") is less effective than helping an individual elicit his or her own insights. Many clients have a spiritual life or did at one time. Helping the client tap into his or her spirituality can provide a source of strength and comfort. Other persons with substance misuse problems might be of a more secular bent; a group such as Rational Recovery or Women for Sobriety might suit their particular needs. In Patt Denning's words, "We as workers have the responsibility of developing a needs hierarchy for the people under our care that is based on *their* assessment of their needs more often than *our* assessment of their needs" (1997, p. 15).

Loss and Grief

Death of their loved ones is a constant fact of life for persons who survive into old age; loss and grief are therefore inevitable at this stage of life. Most people grieve and go on. Unresolved grief and depression, however, sometimes are associated with excessive drinking and pill use.

As alcoholics share their life histories in treatment, the link between grief and loss and other feelings such as guilt and anger becomes apparent. In long-term alcoholics, an early loss that was deeply troubling and even traumatizing may have played a role in the later use of chemicals as a form of relief. Guilt feelings connected to the early childhood loss would now be compounded by the addictive behavior.

In elderly widows and widowers, too, many of whom never had a drinking problem, unhealthy guilt feelings may arise in connection with a dying family member. Three types of guilt typically found in family members of the terminally ill are survivor guilt, a sense of helplessness, and ambivalence guilt. Interestingly, these same unhealthy responses are often seen in the families of alcoholics, torn as they are by feelings of helplessness and responsibility.

Survivor guilt occurs when one person is spared death or a calamity while another or others are not. The one who is spared may go into a depression marked by obsessive thoughts. The "why me?" syndrome of the victim has its counterpart in the "why not me?" reaction of the survivor. The survivor, such as the person who lived through Hiroshima or a plane crash, may feel a need to justify his or her own survival. Underneath, there may be a feeling of unworthiness.

Parents who have lost children, children who have lost parents, and surviving spouses and partners all can experience their own version of survivor guilt. For parents who survive their children, their failure to carry out the most fundamental task of protection arouses a special overwhelming despair. Sometimes, the very elderly have outlived a middle-aged son or daughter.

When a family member is terminally ill, the partner or spouse invariably will feel a sense of personal failure, for the caregiver is unable to do what should be done—namely, to heal the one who is suffering and make the pain go away. This is the second type of guilt—*guilt due to helplessness*. The dying person's dependence on drugs for relief may further contribute to the survivor's sense of helplessness and frustration, especially when the drugs fail to bring the relief desired. Futile attempts to get the dying patient to eat can also be problematic.

Ambivalence guilt is present as the caregiver begins to resent this role. Loss of a partially loved spouse is sometimes more difficult than loss of a beloved spouse. As one elderly woman in this situation once said to van Wormer, "Sometimes I wish this whole thing would end. Do you think I'm terrible?" Loss due to suicide compounds the guilt, which is often accompanied by a sense of shame (Jackson, 2004).

Some individuals grieving over suicide are so overcome that they themselves are at risk for suicide and/or substance misuse. Jackson likens a woman who had been addicted to heroin, was homeless, and had died in the street of an overdose to suicide in the feelings of shame brought out in the family members. People blame each other in an event of this sort.

Persons who work with elderly clients with addiction problems would do well to explore the dynamics of grieving and the relationship between negative feelings and the use of substances to quell them. Therapy groups for older clients can delve into bereavement issues as they arise. In helping group members understand the emotional impact of death and dying and to accept any alien feelings for what they are—an integral part of the grieving process—the practitioner can help them cope better.

A poem, such as the following, written by William Faulkner for his epitaph, can be read and shared with the group:

> If there be grief, then let it be but rain,
> And this but silver grief for grieving's sake
> If these green woods be dreaming here to wake
> Within my heart, if I should rouse again.
> But I shall sleep, for where is any death
> While in these blue hills slumbrous overhead
> I'm rooted like a tree? Though I be dead,
> This earth that holds me fast will find me breath.
>
> (*This Earth, A Poem*, 1932)

The ability to come to terms with loss and grief, and thereby to transcend them, is a major factor in the alcoholic's successful recovery.

SPIRITUAL HEALING

Many early psychologists, Jung (1933) and Maslow (1950/1971) the most renowned among them, have written of the essence of experience that goes beyond the "natural" realm into a higher level of consciousness. Today, however, spirituality is a resource that is often overlooked in the literature, especially in the literature on empowerment practice and harm reduction. And yet, if they seek to draw on the strengths of clients and of their community, how can practitioners disregard a force that traditionally has offered marginalized people the greatest support of all?

"In a crisis or occasion of grief and loss, there is often a shaking of the foundation of one's sense of meaning," suggests social work professor Edward Canda (interviewed by D. Miller, 2001), "who one is, what life is about, and what reality is about. We cannot escape these questions." Thanks to lobbying by Canda and others, religion was added by the Council on Social Work Education in 1994 to key characteristics of diversity and, more recently, spiritual development as a central aspect of human behavior. The American Psychological Association, however, according to Wallen (1993), has not given official acknowledgment to an explicit focus on spiritual development. "Spirituality is a force that needs to be understood, enhanced, and utilized because it is quintessentially starting where the client is" (Ortiz & Smith, 1999, p. 318).

Michael Sheridan (2004) describes the healing power of nature that her students discovered in their work with women in residential treatment. Her goal, paralleling that of Besthorn (2003), is to enable clients to become more aware of the spiritual dimension of their experience with the natural world. Van Wormer learned in Norway from her alcoholic clients of the Higher-Power-As-Nature—that the sense of oneness with nature can have a marvelous unifying effect on people and provide a sense of meaning and comfort. The cultural ethos of Norwegians is reminiscent of that of North America's First Nations Peoples (see van Wormer, Besthorn, & Keefe, 2007).

Attention not only to the biopsychosocial but also to the spiritual dimension has special relevance to the field of substance abuse treatment because of the strong spirituality component of AA. The Twelfth Step (which begins, "Having had a spiritual awakening as the result of these steps . . .") sums up this focus, which entails a move away from a self-centered view of the world to one that places the individual in relation to a larger universe. Spirituality is of special relevance to addictions treatment not only because of AA's stress but also in its own right. The heavy load of guilt feelings that recovering people often carry explains the desire that many persons in recovery have for reconciliation and renewal, even forgiveness. Some who once derived great satisfaction from membership in a religious organization may seek a return to that type of involvement. Elderly clients in treatment for alcohol or other drug problems very often have spiritual needs related to their stage of life, perhaps to their growing familiarity with the prospect of death. In the face of despair associated with earthly losses, spirituality can bolster one's courage in taking risks to pursue personal change and maybe get involved in a formal association or reading group.

Based on observation from the 1980s, Father James Royce (1989) noted that an overwhelming majority of alcoholism treatment clients complained that their spiritual needs were not met in standard treatment programs. *Spirituality* is a word not generally associated with harm reduction enthusiasts. Today, happily, as Orzech (2006) indicates, there is a keen recognition of how spiritual and religious factors affect the quality of one's recovery. People who attend Twelve-Step groups are more likely than others to get in tune with their spiritual side. Early results of research funded by NIAAA single out spirituality as a boon to sustained recovery (Orzech, 2006).

What about harm reduction advocates? An earlier view was voiced by Patt Denning (2000) who boldly stated in the introduction to her book on practicing harm reduction psychotherapy that her increasing resistance to Twelve-Step-based interventions, "particularly the emphasis on powerlessness and spirituality," led her to seek out an alternative model (p. xvi).

More recently, one of the best known of the harm reduction researchers, Alan Marlatt, took a step in the other direction. He introduced a treatment approach for prison inmates in Washington State that is rooted in Buddhist meditation. Clients meditate for long hours for 10 days in a row. When compared to a control group, the inmates used significantly less tobacco and heroin upon release (reported by Orzech, 2004).

If we conceptualize recovery as a kind of journey, we can see it as a path leading from isolation to meaning, as the achievement, in the final analysis, of serenity and spiritual health. Grief work can help people who want to pursue it to move beyond self-blame into a realm of higher consciousness. Recovery itself can be conceptualized as a grieving process. Letting go and grieving, as Maria Carroll (1999) suggests, are integral to the human and spiritual journey.

Carroll (1987, 1999) conceptualizes the spiritual journey in terms of breaking the bonds to earthly attachments and achieving a mastery of oneself through strengthened virtues. For the recovering alcoholic, one earthly attachment is to the substance alcohol. Only when the bond to their addiction is broken can alcoholics move to higher things and embark on "a journey home." To Carroll, the journey home entails constructing a personal reality, becoming disillusioned with this reality, letting the ego-self disintegrate, surrendering, reframing the old reality, and then allowing a new reality to develop as the transformed state. Through *surrendering* to the reality of the present, the recovering alcoholic moves through a spiritual awakening process toward wholeness and a larger humanity. Drawing on her exploratory and in-depth research on spirituality and recovering alcoholics, Carroll (1993) suggests that the Twelve Steps can offer a guide toward increasing self-knowledge, giving to others, and reaching a higher state of consciousness. Other ways of achieving spiritual well-being and belongingness include religious faith and a sense of harmony with nature and the universe.

Writers on spirituality contributed to the alcoholism literature in their conceptualization of alcoholism as a spiritual illness, a condition seen as resulting from a spiritual void in one's life and from a search for a connectedness. As Royce (1989) suggests, alcoholics may be unconsciously seeking to fulfill their spiritual needs with alcohol. This is an important issue in need of further research.

For the alcoholic, merely being well does not provide enough protection to withstand future temptations of alcohol and/or some other addiction. Mantell (1983) believes that to ensure sobriety, alcoholics must achieve a level that is "weller than well." Spiritual well-being is considered by Cowley (1993) to be the epitome of health. It may come from a sense of unity with the cosmos or from a personal closeness to God or to nature. The experience of wholeness and integration is not dependent on religious belief or affiliation. Fulfillment of the spiritual dimension is important in providing a sense of meaning in life.

Studies on addiction recovery indicate that approaches to heightened spiritual awareness markedly increase a sense of purpose in life (O'Connell, 1999). A growing body of research indicates, moreover, as O'Connell reports, that spiritual practices such as prayer, contemplation, yoga, Zen, and transcendental meditation have a measurable effect on physiological processes in the brain. The fact that spiritual contemplation can be registered in terms of brain activity (actually inactivity in one region of the brain) gives the experience a neuroscientific reality. Recent advances in neuroscience help explain why some people experience ineffable, transcendent events to be as real as their normal range of sensory impressions (Begley, 2001). O'Connell's recommendation is that the client's attitude toward and sense of spirituality be routinely assessed in the recovery process. There is a growing recognition among providers of culturally specific programs such as those for African Americans and North American Native populations that spiritual beliefs offer a great resource. Clients from other ethnic groups as well can benefit from tapping into this often overlooked resource. This resource has special meaning to persons who have reached the time of life when they are inclined to review the past—look back over the years and reflect on the turning points. Wrestling with issues of mortality and immortality, people in late adulthood are prone to ponder the meaning of their lives and of life itself.

In the words of theologian Karen Armstrong (1993), "Human beings cannot endure emptiness and desolation; they will fill the vacuum by creating a new focus of meaning" (p. 399). Without imposing their own religious and spiritual beliefs on their clients, professionals in this field should help clients in their search for spiritual truth. All clients should have access to spiritual literature and the possibility of consultation with a spiritual mentor.

SUMMARY AND CONCLUSION

The first and the last, the new and the old—this chapter has focused on the major psychological growth tasks and pitfalls confronting youth and the elderly. Although problems with drinking and drug use occur across the life span, we have chosen to focus on these two stages of life because of the special vulnerabilities accruing to these transitional stages. If we were following the lives of particular clients in treatment for one of the substance use disorders, we could see that unresolved crises and bad habits from the earlier period of life have come to a head at a later stage. Adolescent addicts require intensive treatment stays because of attitude, whereas the elderly require a lengthy recovery period because of biology. Although the young have little or no sense of their mortality, the old may be much too absorbed with this same issue.

Two prevalent myths in society are that the young will not listen and the old will not learn. According to this logic, there would be little point in treatment for either of these groups. In fact, cost-effectiveness research reveals just the opposite: Prevention and treatment at each level of maturity can be highly effective when geared toward the special concerns of the clients in that age group. Each stage of life carries its own reward for sobriety and its own treatment needs. As a basic principle of effective leadership and counseling states: Lead a person only as far as he or she is likely to follow. The focus is set by the client, not the counselor, and so is the rhythm of therapy.

REFERENCES

Addiction Technology Transfer Center (ATTC). (2004). Adolescents. *ATTC Networker, 6*(2), 1–2.

Alcohol use among girls. (1999). The National Clearinghouse for Alcohol and Drug Information. Retrieved February 2007 from http://ncadi.samhsa.gov/govpubs/rpo993/.

Alexander, R. (2000). *Counseling, treatment, and intervention methods with juvenile and adult offenders.* Belmont, CA: Wadsworth.

American Association for Geriatric Psychiatry. (2003). Alcohol misuse in late life: Treatment issues. *Annual Meeting—Symposia highlights.* Retrieved February 2007 from http://www.cmecorner.com/macmcm/AAGP/aagp2003_08.htm.

American Psychiatric Association (APA). (2000). *Diagnostic and statistical manual of mental disorders, text revision* (4th ed.). Washington, DC: Author.

Armstrong, K. (1993). *A history of God: The 4,000-year quest of Judaism, Christianity, and Islam.* New York: Ballantine Books.

Aron, E. (1996). *The highly sensitive person: How to thrive when the world overwhelms you.* New York: Broadway Books.

Aronson, E. (2003). *The social animal.* New York: Worth Publishers.

Associated Press. (1999, August 29). Teen–father relationship called substance abuse key. *Waterloo–Cedar Falls Courier,* p. A1.

Associated Press. (2001, February 22). U.S. teens use drugs more than Europeans. *Des Moines Register,* p. 6A.

Associated Press. (2006, September 2). More laws seek to punish parents to deter underage drinking. *Insurance Journal.* Retrieved September 2006 from http://www.insurancejournal.com/news/national.

Attack on campus drug use ends up teaching kids to lie. (2000, June 13). *USA Today,* p. 16A.

Avital, A., & Richter-Levin, G. (2005). Exposure to juvenile stress exacerbates the behavioural consequences of exposure to stress in the adult rat. *International Journal of Neuropsychopharmacology, 8*(2), 163–173.

Bachman, J. G., O'Malley, P. M., Johnston, L., & Schulenberg, J. E. (2002). *The decline of substance use in young adulthood: Changes in social activities, roles, and beliefs.* Mahwah, NJ: Erlbaum.

Basham, K., & Miehls, D. (2004). *Transforming the legacy: Couple therapy with survivors of childhood trauma.* New York: Columbia University Press.

Beechem, M. (2002). *Elderly alcoholism: Intervention strategies.* Springfield, IL: Charles C Thomas.

Begley, S. (2001, May 7). Religion and the brain. *Newsweek,* pp. 52–57.

Belknap, J., & Holsinger, K. (2006). The gendered nature of risk factors for delinquency. *Feminist Criminology, 1*(1), 48–71.

Benshoff, J. J., Harrawood, L., & Darwin, S. (2003). Substance abuse and the elderly: Unique issues and concerns. *Journal of Rehabilitation, 69*(9), 43–48.

Benshoff, J. J., & Janikowski, T. P. (2000). *The rehabilitation model of substance abuse counseling.* Belmont, CA: Wadsworth.

Besthorn, F. H. (2003, February). *Eco-spiritual helping and group process: Earth-based perspectives for social work practice.* Presentation at the annual meeting of the Council on Social Work Education, Atlanta, GA.

Biederman, J., Monuteaux, M., Mick, E., Wilens, T., Fontanella, J., Poetzl, K., et al. (2006). Is cigarette smoking a gateway to alcohol and illicit drug use disorders? A study of youths with and without attention deficit hyperactivity disorder. *Biological Psychiatry, 59*(3), 258–264.

Black teens more likely than Whites to reject cigarettes. (1996, November 22). *Waterloo–Cedar Falls Courier,* p. A11.

Bloom, B., Owen, B., & Covington, S. (2004). Women offenders and the gendered effects of public policy. *Review of Policy Research, 21*(1), 31–48.

Botvin, G., & Botvin, E. (1997). School-based programs. In J. H. Lowinson, P. Ruiz, R. Mulliman, & J. G. Langrod (Eds.), *Substance abuse: A comprehensive textbook* (pp. 764–775). Baltimore: Williams & Wilkins.

Brogan, P. (2004, March 14). Scrap TV ads for alcohol, campaign urges colleges. *Des Moines Register,* p. 6A.

Butts, J., & Roman, J. (2004). *Juvenile drug courts and teen substance abuse.* Washington, DC: Urban Institute Press.

Carroll, M. M. (1987). Alcoholism as an attachment and a gift on a spiritual journey. *Journal of Consciousness and Change, 10*(2), 45–48.

Carroll, M. M. (1993). *Spiritual growth of recovering alcoholic adult children of alcoholics.* Unpublished doctoral dissertation, University of Maryland, Baltimore.

Carroll, M. M. (1999). Spirituality and alcoholism: Self-actualization and faith stage. *Journal of Ministry in Addiction & Recovery, 6*(1), 67–84.

Carvel, J. (2006, November 29). Britain's binge drinkers begin to sober up. *The Guardian.* Retrieved December 1, 2006, from http://society.guardian.co.uk.

Center on Alcohol Marketing and Youth (CAMY). (2005, November 26). Alcohol industry's marketing overexposes Hispanic teens. *Join Together Online.* Retrieved September 2006 from http://www.jointogether.org/sa/news.

Center on Alcohol Marketing and Youth (CAMY). (2006, March 27). Underage drinking 2005: Girls bingeing more. *CAMY.* Retrieved August 2006 from http:// camy.org/press.

Centers for Disease Control and Prevention (CDC). (2006). Racial/ethnic differences among youths in cigarette smoking. *Mortality and Morbidity Weekly, 55*(47), 1275–1277.

Center for Substance Abuse Treatment (CSAT). (1998). KAP (Knowledge Application Program) keys for clinicians. *CSAT.* Retrieved February 2007 from http:// kap.samhsa.gov/products/tools/keys/pdfs/KK_26.pdf.

Childress, A. R. (2006). What can human brain imaging tell us about vulnerability to addiction and to relapse? In W. R. Miller & K. M. Carroll (Eds.), *Rethinking substance abuse: What the science shows, and what we should do about it* (pp. 46–60). New York: Guilford Press.

Choi, Y., Harachi, T. W., Gilmore, M. R., Catalano, R. F. (2006). Are multiracial adolescents at greater risk? Comparisons of rates, patterns, and correlates of substance use and violence between monoracial and multiracial adolescents. *American Journal of Orthopsychiatry, 76*(1), 86–97.

Clayton, M. (2000, March 15). Binge drinking and teetotaling spread at U.S. colleges. *Christian Science Monitor*, p. 2.

Cohen, M. (2000). *Counseling addicted women: A practical guide.* Thousand Oaks, CA: Sage.

Cowley, A. D. (1993). Transpersonal social work: A theory for the 1990s. *Social Work, 38*, 527–534.

Curley, B. (2006, November 17). House passes underage-drinking prevention bill. *Join Together Online.* Retrieved November 20, 2006, from http://www.jointogether .org/news/features.

Daisy, F., Thomas, L. R., & Worley, C. (2002). Alcohol use and harm reduction within the Native community. In G. A. Marlatt (Ed.), *Harm reduction: Pragmatic strategies for managing high-risk behaviors* (pp. 327–352). New York: Guilford Press.

Denning, P. (1997, Spring). Clinical psychology and substance use management. *Harm Reduction Communications, 4*, 13–15.

Denning, P. (2000). *Practicing harm reduction psychotherapy.* New York: Guilford Press.

Dimeff, L. A., Baer, J. S., Kivlahan, D. R., & Marlatt, G. A. (1999). *Brief alcohol screening and intervention for college students: A harm reduction approach.* New York: Guilford Press.

Dizon, N. Z. (2000, June 4). Campus arrests soar for alcohol abuses. *Washington Post*, p. A10.

Downs, W. R., Capshew, T., & Rindels, B. (2004). Relationships between adult men's alcohol problems and their childhood experiences of parental violence and psychological aggression. *Journal of Studies on Alcohol, 65*(3), 336–345.

Drummond, T. (2000, November 6). Mothers in prison. *Time*, pp. 105–107.

Egan, T. (2006, September 2). Boredom in the West fuels binge drinking. *New York Times.* Retrieved September 2006 from http://www.nytimes.com/2006/09/02/us/ozbinge.html.

Elias, M. (1998, January 5). Study links sexual abuse, alcoholism among women. *USA Today*, p. 1A.

Ellis, A. (1965). Commentary in *Three approaches to psychotherapy.* Montreal, Canada: Peerless Film Processing.

Erikson, E. (1963). *Children and society.* New York: Norton.

European Public Health Alliance. (2005). European Monitoring Centre for Drugs and Drug Addiction. Retrieved from http://ar2005.emcdda.europa.eu.

Farkas, K. J. (2006). Alcohol abuse in later life. In S. L. Straussner (Ed.), *Clinical work with substance abusers* (pp. 330–346). New York: Guilford Press.

Faulkner, W. (1932). If there be grief. In W. Faulkner, *This earth, a poem* (pp. 1–4). New York: Equinox.

Flaherty, M. (2005, July 7). Study cites drug abuse "epidemic" among teens. *Washington Post.* Retrieved August 2006 from http://www.washingtonpost.com/wpdyn/content/article/2005/07/07/AR2005070701180.html.

Fletcher, M. (2002, April 12). Connectedness called key to student behavior. *Washington Post*, p. A03.

Foster, S., Vaughn, R., Foster, W., & Califano, J., Jr. (2006). Estimate of the commercial value of underage drinking and adult abusive and dependent drinking to the alcohol industry. *Archives of Pediatric and Adolescent Medicine, 160*(5), 473–478.

Gilligan, C. (1982). *In a different voice: Psychological theory and women's development.* Cambridge, MA: Harvard University Press.

Gilligan, C. (2002). *The birth of pleasure.* New York: Knopf.

Gober, S., Klein, M., Berger, T., Vindigni, C., & McCabe, P. (2006). Steroids in adolescence: The cost of achieving a physical ideal. *National Association of School Psychologists (NASP) Communiqué, 34*(7). Retrieved August 2006 from http://www.nasponline.org.

Gorman, C. (2007, January 29). Lessons for handling stress. *Time*, pp. 84–85.

Graham, K., & Brett, P. J. (1994, March 7–10). *A harm reduction approach to treating older adults. The clients speak.* Paper presented at the fifth International Conference on the Reduction of Drug-Related Harm. Toronto, Canada.

Gray, C. (2002, March). Pediatricians taking a new look at corporal punishment issue. *Canadian Medical Association Journal, 166,* 793.

Grossberg, P. M., Brown D. D., & Fleming, M. F. (2004). Brief physician advice for high-risk drinking among young adults. *Annals of Family Medicine, 2*(5), 474–480.

Gutiérrez, L., & Suarez, Z. (1999). Empowerment with Latinas. In L. Gutiérrez & E. A. Lewis (Eds.), *Empowerment of women of color* (pp. 167–186). New York: Columbia University Press.

Hanson, M., & Gutheil, I. (2004). Motivational strategies with alcohol-involved older adults: Implications for social work practice. *Social Work, 49*(3), 364–372.

Hardoon, K. K., Gupta, R., & Derevensky, J. (2004). Psychosocial variables associated with adolescent gambling: A model for problem gambling. *Psychology of Addictive Behaviors, 18*(2), 170–179.

Hauser, C. (2005, December 16). As baby boomers approach 60, experts see upsurge in aging addicts. *New York Times*, p. C14.

Hawke, J. M., Jainchill, N., & DeLeon, G. (2000). The prevalence of sexual abuse and its impact on the onset of drug use among adolescents in therapeutic community drug treatment. *Journal of Child & Adolescent Substance Abuse, 9*(3), 35–49.

Health Canada. (2005, March). Canadian Centre on Substance Abuse. Retrieved August 2006 from http://www.ccsa.ca/CCSA/EN/Statistics/2004Canadian AddictionSurvey.htm.

Heim, C., Newport, J., Heit, S., Graham, Y., Wilcox, M., et al. (2000). Pituitary-adrenal and autonomic responses to stress in women after sexual and physical abuse in childhood. *Journal of the American Medical Association, 284,* 592–597.

Hemenway-Forbes, M. (2001, April 30). Comfort in love. *Waterloo–Cedar Falls Courier*, p. B4.

Hibell, B., Andersson, B., Bjarrason, T., Ahlström, S., Balakireva, O., Kokkevi, A., et al. (2004). *The Espad Report 2003: Alcohol and other drug use among students in 35 European countries.* Monitoring the Future. Retrieved August 2006 from http://www.monitoringthefuture.org.

Hinson, R., Heeren, T., Winter, M., & Wechsler, H. (2005). Magnitude of alcohol-related mortality and morbidity among U.S. college students ages 18–24: Changes from 1998 to 2001. *Annual Review of Public Health, 26,* 259–279.

Howard, R. (1998, October 8–14). Labour in power. *Community Care*, pp. 17–29.

Hu, M., Davies, M., & Kandel, D. B. (2005). Epidemiology and correlates of daily smoking and nicotine dependence among young adults in the United States. *American Journal of Public Health, 96*(2), 299–308.

Jackson, K. (2004, May/June). In the shadow of suicide. *Social Work Today,* pp. 38–40.

Johnston, L. D., O'Malley, P. M., Bachman, J. G., & Schulenberg, J. E. (2006). *Demographic subgroup trends for various licit and illicit drugs, 1975–2005* (Monitoring for the Occasional Paper No. 63). Retrieved August 2006 from http://monitoringthefuture.org/.

Join Together. (2001, March 2). Smoking, dieting linked among teen girls. *Join Together Online.* Retrieved December 1, 2006, from http://www.jointogether.org.

Join Together. (2003). Juvenile-justice system getting tough on girls. *Join Together Online.* Retrieved December 1, 2006, from http://www.jointogether.org.

Join Together. (2004, November 16). Whiskey industry goes sweet to grab youth market. *Join Together Online.* Retrieved September 2006 from http://www.jointogether.org/sa/news.

Join Together. (2005a). Colleges curtail campus alcohol marketing. *Join Together Online.* Retrieved December 1, 2006, from http://www.jointogether.org.

Join Together. (2005b, January 1). Sexual abuse, smoking related, study says. *Join Together Online.* Retrieved March 2005 from http://www.jointogether.org.

Join Together. (2006a). Anheuser-Busch opens TV, film division. *Join Together Online.* Retrieved September 2006 from http://www.jointogether.org.

Join Together. (2006b, May 16). Study tracks alcohol, other drug use in movies. *Join Together Online.* Retrieved August 2006 from http://www.jointogether.org.

Jones, C. (2005, January 21). Senior drug addicts increasing. *USA Today,* p. 3A.

Jung, C. G. (1933). *Modern man in search of a soul.* New York: Harcourt Brace & World.

Karaim, R. (2005, March). Calling it quits. *AARP Bulletin,* pp. 26–27.

Kenworthy, T. (2001, June 1). Bush daughters cited in Texas. *USA Today,* p. 3A.

Kinney, J. (2006). *Loosening the grip: A handbook of alcohol information* (8th ed.). Boston: McGraw Hill.

Kluger, J. (2005, May 16). The cruelest cut. *Time,* pp. 48–50.

Kluger, J. (2006, January 23). Balding, wrinkled, and stoned. *Time,* pp. 54–56.

Krucoff, C. (1999, March 23). Smoke and mirrors. *Washington Post,* p. 20.

Lavelle, M. (2000, February 7). Teen tobacco wars. *U.S. News & World Report,* pp. 14–16.

Leinwand, D. (2000, August 24). 20% say they used drugs with mom or dad. *USA Today,* pp. 1A, 2A.

Leinwand, D. (2006, June 13). Prescription drugs find place in teen culture. *USA Today,* pp. 1A, 2A.

Leshner, A. I. (1999). Science-based views of drug addiction and its treatment. *Journal of the American Medical Association, 282*(14), 1314–1316.

Levens, S., Deyer, A., Zurbitsky, C., Knott, K., & Oslin, D. (2005, January). Gambling among older, primary-care patients. *American Journal of Geriatric Psychiatry, 13,* 69–76.

Mantell, M. (1983). Student and employee assistance programs: A model for secondary prevention. *Labor–Management Alcoholism Journal, 12,* 113–124.

Martin, C. S., & Winters, K. C. (1998). Diagnosis and assessment of alcohol use disorders among adolescents. *Alcohol Health & Research World, 22*(2), 95–105.

Martin, Fr. J. (1972). *Chalk talks on alcohol,* revised. Video. Aberdeen, MD: Kelly Productions.

Maslow, A. (1971). *The farther reaches of human nature.* New York: Viking Press. (Original work published 1950)

Melillo, W. (2006, August 25). GAO: $1.8 billion + anti-drug effort ineffective. *Ad Week*. Retrieved September 2006 from http://adweek.printthis.clickability.com.

Miller, D. W. (2001, May 18). Programs in social work embrace the teaching of spirituality. *Chronicle of Higher Education*, p. 36.

Miller, W. R. (1998). Enhancing motivation for change. In W. R. Miller & N. Hester (Eds.), *Treating addictive behaviors* (2nd ed., pp. 121–132). New York: Plenum Press.

Miller, W. R., & Rollnick, S. (1998). *Motivational interviewing: Professional training videotape series*. Directed by Theresa Moyers. Albuquerque: University of New Mexico.

Miller, W. R., & Rollnick, S. (2002). *Motivational interviewing: Preparing people to change addictive behavior* (2nd ed.). New York: Guilford Press.

Monti, P. M., Miranda, R., Jr., Nixon, K., Sher, K. J., Swartzwelder, H. S., Tapert, S. F., et al. (February 2005). Adolescence: Booze brains and behavior. Proceedings of symposium at the 2004 RSA meeting. *Alcoholism: Clinical and Experimental Research, 29*(2), 207–220.

National Center on Addiction and Substance Abuse at Columbia University (CASA). (2006, August). National survey of American attitudes on substance abuse XI: Teens and parents. Retrieved at http://www.casacolumbia.org.

National Council on Alcoholism and Drug Dependence. (2000). *Youth, alcohol and other drugs*. Retrieved from http://www.ncadd.org/facts/youthalc.html.

National Institute on Alcohol Abuse and Alcoholism (NIAAA). (1998, April). Alcohol and aging. *Alcohol Alert, 40*, 1–4.

National Institute on Alcohol Abuse and Alcoholism (NIAAA). (2003, April). Underage drinking: A major public health challenge. *Alcohol Alert, 59*, 1–4.

National Institute on Alcohol Abuse and Alcoholism (NIAAA). (2005, September 23). Snapshot. Retrieved August 2006 at http://www.collegedrinkingprevention.gov.

National Institute on Drug Abuse (NIDA). (2005). The Monitoring the Future Study: The University of Michigan. Retrieved May 2006 from http://www.drugabuse .gov/Newsroom.

Noble, M. C., & Reed, C. (2000, January). Kentucky drug courts. *Bench & Bar, 64*(1), 6–10.

Nower, L., Derevensky, J., & Gupta, R. (2004). The relationship of impulsivity, sensation seeking, coping and substance use in youth gamblers. *Psychology of Addictive Behaviors, 18*(1), 49–55.

O'Connell, D. F. (1999, December 13). Spirituality's importance in recovery cannot be denied. *Alcoholism & Drug Abuse Weekly, 11*(47), 5.

Office of Applied Studies. (2006). *The DASIS (Drug and Alcohol Services Information System) Report*. Substance Abuse and Mental Health Services Administration (SAMHSA). Retrieved August 2006 from http://www.oas.samhsa.gov.

Office of Juvenile Justice and Delinquency Prevention. (1998). *Juvenile female offenders*. Washington, DC: Office of Justice Programs.

Office of National Drug Control Policy. (2006, February 9). *Girls and drugs*. Retrieved August 2006 from http://www.mediacampaign.org/pdf/girls_and_drugs .pdf.

Ortiz, L., & Smith, G. (1999). The role of spirituality in empowerment practice. In W. Shera & L. M. Wells (Eds.), *Empowerment practice in social work: Developing richer conceptual foundations* (pp. 307–319). Toronto: Canadian Scholars Press.

Orzech, D. (2004, May/June). Meditation: The less traveled road to recovery. *Social Work Today*, pp. 32–35.

Orzech, D. (2006, March/April). Soul survivors. *Social Work Today,* pp. 36–39.

Park, A. (2003, January 20). Postcards from the brain. *Time,* pp. 94–97.

Pepi, C. L. (1997). Children without childhoods: A feminist intervention strategy. *Women & Therapy, 20*(4), 85–101.

Pollack, S. (2004). Anti-oppressive social work practice with women in prison: Discursive reconstructions and alternative practices. *British Journal of Social Work, 34,* 693–707.

Poulin, C. (2006, August). Harm reduction policies and programs for youth. *Canadian Centre on Substance Abuse.* Retrieved August 2006 from http://www.ccsa.ca.

Prochaska, J., & DiClemente, C. (1992). In search of how people change: Applications to addictive behaviors. *American Psychologist, 47,* 1102–1114.

Quindlen, A. (2001). The drug that pretends it isn't. In H. T. Wilson (Ed.), *Drugs, society, and behavior* (pp. 79–80). Guilford, CT: McGraw-Hill/Dushkin.

Raise a fond last glass to Dionysus. (1997, October 4). *The Economist,* pp. 36–37.

Rats get hooked on testosterone. (1999, November 13). *Science News, 156,* 319.

Riestenberg, W. (2005, July 19). PEASE Academy: The restorative recovery school. International Institute for Restorative Practices. *E Forum.* Retrieved June 2006 from http://www.iirp.org.

Rivera, G. (2000, July 14). Smashed: Kids and alcohol. *Geraldo Rivera Reports,* NBC TV. Retrieved February 2007 from http://tvnews.vanderbilt.edu/tvn-openweb-request.pl.

Rose, R. J. (1998). A developmental behavior-genetic perspective on alcoholism risk. *Alcohol Health & Research World, 22*(2), 131–143.

Rose, R. J. (2005). Prenatal programming of behavior: A twin-study perspective. *Neuroscience and Biobehavioral Reviews, 29,* 321–327.

Rosenbaum, M. (2004, March 18). Con: Merits, pitfalls of student drug testing. *The Fresno Bee* (California). Retrieved May 2004 from http://www.fresnobee.com.

Ross, S., & Heath, N. (2002). A study in the frequency of self-mutilation in a community sample of adolescents. *Journal of Youth and Adolescence, 31*(1), 67–78.

Royce, J. E. (1989). *Alcohol problems and alcoholism: A comprehensive survey* (Rev. ed.). New York: Free Press.

Ruffin, L., & Kaye, L. W. (2004, May/June). Alcohol and aging. *Social Work Today,* pp. 24–27.

Ryan, J. P., Marsh, L., Testa, M., & Louderman, R. (2006). Integrating substance abuse and treatment and child welfare services. *Social Work Research, 30*(2), 95–108.

Schonfeld, L., & Dupree, L. (1991). Antecedents of drinking for early- and late-onset elderly alcohol abusers. *Journal of Studies on Alcohol, 52,* 587–592.

Schouten, F. (2000, March 12). Gambling takes toll on teens. *Des Moines Register,* p. AA.

Seaman, B. (2005, August 29). How bingeing became the new college sport. *Time,* p. 80.

Sheridan, M. (2004). Earth as source of spirit. *Spirituality and Social Work Forum, 10,* 14–15.

Smith, M. C., & Smith, M. (1999, March 12). Treat students as adults: Set the drinking age at 18, not 21. *Chronicle of Higher Education,* p. B8.

Snyder, L., Milici, F., Slater, M., Sun, H., & Strizhakova, Y. (2006, January). Effects of alcohol advertising exposure on drinking among youth. *Archives of Pediatrics and Adolescent Medicine, 160*(1), 18–24.

Spear, L. (2000). Modeling adolescent development and alcohol use in animals. *Alcohol Research & Health, 24*(2), 115–123.

Sternberg, S. (2000, August 2). Abuse can damage girls' brain chemistry. *USA Today,* p. 10D.

Stocker, S. (2000). Medications reduce incidence of substance abuse among ADHD patients. *NIDA Notes, 14*(4), 1–4.

Substance Abuse and Mental Health Services Administration (SAMHSA). (2001, March 7). Key influences on youth drug use identified. *SAMHSA New Release,* pp. 1–2.

Substance Abuse and Mental Health Services Administration (SAMHSA). (2006a). National survey on drug use and health. Retrieved September 2006 from http://www.samhsa.gov.

Substance Abuse and Mental Health Services Administration (SAMHSA). (2006b, January/February). Underage drinkers seek help in emergency rooms. *SAMHSA News,* p. 14.

Substance Abuse and Mental Health Services Administration (SAMHSA) News. (2006, May/June). SAMHSA, FDA launch campaign for older adults. *SAMHSA News, 13*(3), 7.

Teens who abuse alcohol face lifelong problems. (2001, January 3). Retrieved from http://www.jointogether.org.

University of New Mexico Institute of Public Law. (2007, January). STOP (Sober Truth on Prevention) Act becomes law. *Traffic Safety News,* p. 3.

U.S. Census Bureau. (2005). *65+ in the U.S.* U.S. Department of Health and Human Services. Retrieved September 2006 from http://www.census.gov/prod/2006pubs.

U.S. Department of Health and Human Services. (1998). *Substance abuse among older adults.* Treatment protocol series 26. Rockville, MD: U.S. Government Printing Office.

U.S. Department of Health and Human Services. (2000). *Anabolic steroid abuse. Research report* (pp. 1–8). Washington, DC: National Institutes of Health.

U.S. Department of Health and Human Services. (2001). *National drug control strategy: 2001 annual report.* Washington, DC: Office of the National Drug Control Policy.

Valtonen, K., Sogren, M., & Cameron-Padmore, L. (2006). Coping styles in persons recovering from substance abuse. *British Journal of Social Work, 36*(1), 57–73.

van Wormer, K. (1995). *Alcoholism treatment: A social work perspective.* Belmont, CA: Wadsworth.

van Wormer, K. (2007). *Human behavior and the social environment, micro level: Individuals and families.* New York: Oxford University Press.

van Wormer, K., Besthorn, F. H., & Keefe, T. (2007). *Human behavior and the social environment, macro level: Groups, communities, and organizations.* New York: Oxford University Press.

Vedantam, S. (2003, September 10). Severe steps to curb teen drinking urged. *Washington Post,* p. A01.

Wallen, J. (1993). *Addiction in human development: Developmental perspective on addiction and recovery.* New York: Haworth.

Washton, A., & Zweben, J. (2006). *Treating alcohol and drug problems in psychotherapy practice: Doing what works.* New York: Guilford Press.

Weaver, K. (2001, February 22). Adolescent cigarette, alcohol use examined. *University of Buffalo Reporter, 32*(21). Retrieved February 2007 from http://www.buffalo.edu/reporter/vol32/vol32n21/n5.html.

Weber, M. (1999, April 28). *New study first to quantify illicit drug and substance use in movies and music popular among youth*. Press release from SAMHSA. Retrieved from http://www.mediacampaign.org/newsroom/press99/mediascope.html.

Weingardt, K. R., & Marlatt, G. A. (1999). Sustaining change: Helping those who are still using. In W. R. Miller & N. Heather (Eds.), *Treating addictive behaviors* (2nd ed., pp. 337–351). New York: Plenum Press.

Widom, C. S. (2000). Childhood victimization and the derailment of girls and women to the criminal justice system. In *Research on women and girls in the justice system* (pp. 27–36). Washington, DC: U.S. Department of Justice.

Wilson, M. K., & Anderson, S. C. (1997). Empowering female offenders: Removing barriers to community-based practice. *Affilia, 12*(3), 342–359.

Wilson, P. (2006, November 8). Strong vote against bill to raise drinking age. *Weekend Herald* (New Zealand). Retrieved December 1, 2006, from http://www.nzherald.co.nz/section/1/story.cfm?c_id=1&objectid=104098.

Witkiewitz, K. (2005). Defining relapse from a harm reduction perspective. *Journal of Evidence-Based Social Work, 2*(1/2), 191–206.

Youth drinking: Risk factors and consequences. (1997, July). *Alcohol Alert, 37*, 1–4.

Zastrow, C., & Kirst-Ashman, K. (2006). *Understanding human behavior and the social environment* (7th ed.). Belmont, CA: Wadsworth.

All addictions are anesthetics. They separate us from the distress in our consciousness.

—Gabor Maté (1999, p. 297)

EATING DISORDERS, GAMBLING, SHOPPING, AND OTHER BEHAVIORAL ADDICTIONS

CHAPTER 7

INTRODUCTION

The addictions we discuss in this chapter, rarely covered in books on substance misuse, are not your ordinary addictions, and only one involves a substance—food. What these addictions share is that they all involve everyday legal activities: eating, shopping, sexual activity, gambling, and surfing the Internet. What these behavioral or pleasure-related addictions have in common with the substance dependencies is that they are compulsive and obsessive and involve euphoria that is not induced artificially by a drug. Like all addictions, the ones we discuss in this chapter have strong biological, psychological, and social components.

Nora Volkow, the director of the National Institute of Drug Abuse and one of the country's leading addiction researchers, believes that low levels of dopamine receptors in the brain, whether caused by a high degree of stress or due to genetic susceptibility, may explain why some can drink or use a drug without getting addicted while others apparently cannot (Wingert, 2006). And although we may think that being addicted to food is not as bad as being addicted to heroin, researchers are learning that all addictions are more alike than different.

For helping professionals working in the substance abuse treatment field, an understanding of these other addictive behaviors commonly found in clients receiving treatment for another disorder is essential. For example, an alcoholic may suffer from bulimia; the meth addict may be a pathological gambler. In recovery from drug misuse, the client may become a workaholic or, worse, a shopping addict. "Everything we learn about one type of addiction," notes Volkow (2006), "has the potential to teach us something about the others" (p. 77).

"I get addicted to everything I touch." How often this comment is heard in substance abuse treatment circles! Yet the dynamics of this phenomenon, the tendency of some individuals to take everything to extremes, have not been properly understood or even acknowledged by scientists until now. Today, there is mounting evidence that all addiction—chemical or otherwise—arises from the same neurobiological processes located deep inside the brain and not in the cerebral cortex, which is the rational, thinking part of the brain. Recent research shows, for example, that compulsive gambling may hijack the reward and pleasure pathways of the brain in somewhat the same way that psychoactive drugs do (Preuschoff, Bossaerts, & Quartz, 2006). Recently, reports of tanning addiction have hit the news. The out-of-control drives of people to constantly sunbathe or to visit tanning booths have been shown to meet the same criteria for addiction or dependence as does drug dependence and to have a neurological basis (*Medical News Today,* 2006b). Van Wormer had earlier observed unhealthy tanning booth patterns among alcoholic clients at a treatment center in Norway that had its own tanning room. (The effects of excessive tanning could be easily observed in the fair-complected Norwegians.)

In his book on attention-deficit disorder, *Scattered,* Gabor Maté (1999) anticipated what we now know about the nature of addiction from science:

> Less obvious (than alcoholic lurches) but no less physiological are the effects on the brain of self-stimulating behaviors. The gambler and the sexaholic, the compulsive shopper, and the man or woman who insists on skiing uncharted glaciers are all looking for the same hit of dopamine and endorphins that the ingestion of substances gives the drug addict. Whatever gets you through the night. (p. 298)

Some individuals, because of a genetic predisposition or trauma early in life, are especially vulnerable neurologically to the disorganizing effects of substance misuse. They have what Watkins, Lewellen, and Barrett (2001) term "fragile brain chemistry" (p. 3); they tend to get "hooked." The source of the addiction may be a mood-altering substance or a love relationship or a thrilling pastime, such as betting on horses, or all three. Based on our theory of vulnerability, we would predict that medication for any one of these "maladies" should alleviate the other problems as well. This, in fact, is the case. Drugs that reduce the craving to drink, for example, might make an individual more "laid back" in other areas.

One way to study the effects of genetic and personality characteristics on the later development of addiction problems is to study children across the life span. Slutske, Caspi, Moffitt, and Poulton (2005) designed such a study that included about 1,000 children born in the 1970s. One purpose of the study was to determine which kind of temperaments were most likely to lead to addictions. The results showed that the children who later became compulsive gamblers, alcoholics, and other addicts had personalities characterized by negativity, nervousness, anger, and a tendency to worry and feel victimized. Another significant trait—impulsiveness combined with thrill seeking—was also part of the mix. Add to that the availability of drugs or casinos and we could say that "nature takes its course."

Keeping in mind that the biology and psychology of addiction are so often inseparable, we can see further that the particular form the addiction takes may be a matter of chance or availability; that is, whether the addiction is to a substance such as heroin or to a behavior such as gambling, the pattern is more or less the same. Psychologically, this pattern entails all the mind games that the addict engages in to continue the mad pursuit (e.g., inappropriate sex or betting on cards). Socially—the impact on family, peers, and colleagues—the consequences are relatively comparable as well. Could anyone argue that the parents of a child with anorexia don't suffer as much as the parents of a child using drugs?

In this chapter, we consider both the commonalities and uniquenesses of numerous varieties of addiction: eating disorders, gambling addiction, shopping addiction, sex addiction, as well as Internet addiction, the newest "kid on the block." Consistent with the psychology-of-addiction focus of this section of the book—Part III—our concern is with cognition. The fundamentals of cognitive therapy, including the thinking and feeling work and the use of positive self-talk that are described in the final portion of this chapter, are principles as relevant to working with alcoholics and drug addicts as with individuals out of control with eating, gambling, or sex. The cognitive interventions presented in this chapter are not viewed as a separate treatment modality but rather as strategies that transcend all the basic modalities. All therapy and counseling are about helping people take control of their lives, learning how to cope, and learning how to survive. All therapy is psychological in this sense. Here, what we do is single it out and define the tools therapists need to help clients modify, and thereby moderate, unhealthy thought patterns (e.g., "I'm going to fast for a week"; "I'm going to gamble for big stakes to get back what I lost."). Management of anger and stress, reframing of one's definition of self, and the therapeutic use of humor are among the other topics covered. In contrast to much of the cognitive work that counselors are engaged in today, especially in working with offenders and addicts, our approach is consistent with the strengths/empowerment perspective.

EATING DISORDERS

"Eating Disorders Start in Brain" (2001)

"Scientists Hot on Trail of Bulimia Genes" (DeNoon, 2005)

So state the headlines in *USA Today* and *MedicineNet.com*, respectively. Although researchers have known for several years that a person's chances of developing an eating disorder depend partly on genetics, this is the first time, according to the *USA Today* article, that an anorexia-related gene has been identified. Twice as many subjects in the European study had a variant form of a gene that stimulates appetite as did subjects without anorexia. Many other genes are involved in this compulsive behavior.

Research findings from two recent studies identified several core traits that appeared to be linked to genes associated with anorexia and bulimia. The first study (Bulik et al., 2005) filtered out from the literature concern over mistakes (perfectionism), early age of menstruation, and food-related obsessions that were linked to bulimia. Anxiety and obsessiveness were more closely linked to anorexia. The second of the two articles (Bacanu et al., 2005) linked behavioral characteristics to genetic information. The bulimia cohort showed more linkage with their identified characteristics and certain chromosomes than did the anorexic cohort. One of the chromosomes is also linked to obesity. Anorexia was linked as predicted with the obsessiveness trait. The significance of these papers is in revealing genetic differences between these two eating disorders.

The National Center on Addiction and Substance Abuse (CASA) at Columbia University (2003), in its comprehensive report, *Food for Thought,* examined the link between substance abuse and eating. Researchers found that about one half of individuals with eating disorders misuse alcohol or other drugs compared to 9% of the general population. At the same time, up to 35% of substance misusers have eating disorders compared to 3% of the population. The risk factors for substance misuse and eating disorders are relatively the same and include common brain chemistry, the impact of stress and trauma, and susceptibility to messages from advertising and entertainment media. Girls and women are especially influenced by advertisements, according to the report. Women's magazines contain more than 10 times the ads and articles related to losing weight than do men's magazines. The average female model appearing in these magazines is 5 feet, 11 inches tall and weighs 117 pounds, which is far thinner than the average woman.

Other findings of interest from the CASA report are:

- Middle school girls (10–14 year olds) who diet more than once a week are nearly four times likelier than other girls to become smokers
- Girls with eating disorder symptoms are almost four times likelier to use inhalants and cocaine
- Hispanic girls are slightly more likely than Caucasian girls and significantly more likely than African-American girls to report having fasted for 24 hours or more and having vomited or taken laxatives to lose weight
- As many as one million men and boys suffer from an eating disorder; gay and bisexual males are at increased risk of such disorders (p. 2).

Anorexia nervosa is characterized by a refusal to maintain a minimally normal body weight, even to the extent of self-starvation. One of the most perplexing aspects of anorexia is that its victims continue to think they are fat despite the ribs and other bones showing through. Bulimia, in contrast, is characterized by repeated episodes of binge eating followed by vomiting, abusing laxatives or diuretics, taking enemas, or exercising obsessively to get rid of the food or burn the calories (National Institute of Mental Health [NIMH], 2006). Some anorexics binge and then purge to maintain their low weight. Family, friends, and physicians have difficulty detecting bulimia in someone they know because the person's body weight may be normal. Dentists may detect telltale tooth enamel damage in vomiters.

As with anorexia, bulimia typically begins in adolescence. More than 90% of cases of these two eating disorders occur in females. The lifetime prevalence of anorexia among girls and women is 0.5%, and that for bulimia is approximately 1 to 3% (American Psychiatric Association [APA], 2000). A surprise finding with regard to bulimia in men is that when it does exist, its medical consequences are severe and its occurrence is related to low levels of the male hormone testosterone ("Anorexia, Bulimia Found More Dangerous in Men," 2000). A recent study, for the first time using nationally representative data (extracted from national mental health survey data) on eating disorders, found that 0.9% of women and 0.3% of men said they had had or were still suffering from anorexia nervosa, whereas for bulimia, the figures were 1.5% of women and 0.5% of men (Hudson, Hiripi, Pope, & Kessler, 2007).

ANOREXIA NERVOSA

The *DSM–IV–TR* (APA, 2000) includes in its diagnostic criteria for anorexia that weight be less than 85% of normal body weight; intense fear of weight gain; and amenorrhea in young women (the absence of at least three consecutive menstrual cycles). Many of the physical signs and symptoms are attributable to starvation: cold intolerance, lethargy, constipation, and the appearance of lanugo, or fine body hair. Mortality from anorexia is over 10%, with death most commonly resulting from starvation, suicide, or electrolyte imbalance. The average lifetime duration for anorexia is only 1.7 years (Hudson et al., 2007).

People with eating disorders share certain personality traits: low self-esteem, clinical depression (which often runs in their families), and an inability to handle stress (NIMH, 2006). The high anxiety and social phobias associated with anorexia most commonly begin in early childhood before the onset of an eating disorder. This was the conclusion of an extensive study of more than 500 persons with eating disorders conducted by Kaye, Bulik, Thornton, Barbarich, and Masters (2004). Perfectionism is pronounced among people with anorexia, as is a likelihood of athletic involvement (especially gymnastics and ballet). An empirical study by Ringham et al. (2006) based on assessments of dozens of ballet dancers found that 83% had eating disorders. Binge eating and purging were common; their profiles were similar to a comparison group of women with eating disorders. The following description found in *Dancing on My Grave,* by prominent ballerina Gelsey Kirkland (1986), is typical:

> I sat in bed at night and thumbed through fashion magazines, memorizing faces and figures. This began as a game I played to beat insomnia. I wanted to be a gorgeous someone, anyone other than who I was. I clung irrationally to the idea that my body had been the cause of all my problems. I prayed for a perfect body. Please, God, make me into the doll that everyone wants me to be. I stared at pictures of models and imagined that I might wake up in the morning as one of them. I wanted to free myself from the weight of artistic choice. . . . Starvation and poisoning (from cocaine) were not excesses, but measures taken to stay within the norm, both professionally and aesthetically. (pp. 205–209)

A social work major shares this narrative account:

When I got down to 70 pounds, I could not do most of the activities that I did before. I knew that I had a problem. My physical appearance was frightening. I was a human skeleton. The color of my face was gone. My hair was falling out. It took a lot of energy for me to do anything. I knew that I had to eat but I just could not eat. I was afraid to eat. If I ate, I thought something bad might happen to me. I knew if I did not eat something bad might happen. I was stuck and I did not know what to do. I told my friend's mother what I was doing. We had a long talk. I was afraid to go to my mother about my problem. My friend's mother told me if I get any worse she will tell my mother. I began to eat again gradually but I became very nauseous but I still ate because I knew that I had to. I ate small portions and little things at first. I am not cured completely of this disorder. When I become stressed, nervous, or mad, I cannot eat. I try but nothing seems to go down. I can finally talk to my mother about my disorder but not very well. She still does not understand why I did what I did. I do not understand entirely why I did what I did. I know what I did had to do with major emotional and internal problems with people that I have been dealing with from my childhood and adolescence. (personal communication, December 2004)

Similarly, Angie Huisman shares her earlier struggle with an eating disorder, a struggle that led to her hospitalization and treatment:

I knew that I was not healthy. I stopped having my period, was tired all the time, and became very easily agitated. Despite all of this, I kept up my rituals without hesitation. I weighed myself at least three times a day, praying that I had lost at least a pound. If I didn't, I would do anything to get the weight off. By that time, I was too weak to do almost anything, so I did as many sit-ups or jumping jacks as I could until I literally passed out. Then one day I got on the scale and it said 89 pounds. I stared at myself in the mirror and broke down. I was so weak and tired, but still I wanted to lose more weight. (personal communication, October 1997)

Note the theme of compulsive ritualism in these personal descriptions. The connection between anorexia and obsessive-compulsive disorder (OCD) is more than coincidental; it is real. Before reviewing the research findings on this connection, let us examine the psychiatric criteria provided by the APA (2000). Under the heading OCD, obsessions and compulsions are defined separately; the person with OCD may have obsessions, compulsions, or both. *Obsessions* are defined as recurrent and persistent thoughts or impulses that are experienced as intrusive and that cause marked anxiety or distress. *Compulsions* are the repetitive behaviors (compulsive hand washing, checking, etc.) often associated in the public mind with OCD. These rituals may be associated unrealistically with some dreaded event. Scientists, according to Johnson (2004), have found biochemical similarities between people with eating disorders and OCD. The similarities relate to abnormal serotonin levels. NIMH researchers have found that many patients with bulimia have OCD as severe as patients actually diagnosed with OCD. A genetic trait is likely a key factor in the development of eating disorders, according to psychiatric research at the University of Iowa (Segall, 2001). Interestingly, OCD, like anorexia, often begins in adolescence.

In *The Mind and the Brain,* Schwartz and Begley (2003) describe Schwartz's clinical research and treatment approach with obsessive-compulsive, "brain-locked" patients. Such patients are typically overwhelmed by insistent, repetitive urges to wash their hands of feared germs or ward off uncomfortable feelings of danger by persistently checking stoves and lights. As explained by Schwartz and Begley, OCD can be considered "brain lock" because four key structures of the brain become locked together, and messages from the front part of the brain get stuck there. This leads to a maddening repetition of unwanted thoughts. Schwartz's "Relabel, Reattribute, Refocus, Revalue" (4Rs) approach to treating OCD is a cognitive approach that relies on constant self-talk; this method differs dramatically from a sometimes disturbing behavioral exposure approach in which the client is exposed to the source of the fear (e.g., snakes). Central to the 4Rs method is the theme of *neuroplasticity*. This theme asserts that the human brain's neurons have the ability to form new brain connections, stimulate new pathways through the cortex, and assume new roles and functions. Brain scans reveal marked improvement in brain functioning through cognitive exercises that are performed by patients with OCD.

The form that the obsession takes—the relentless intrusiveness—is universal in persons with OCD, according to Schwartz and Begley, but the content of the obsessions varies with the individual and culture. The fact that eating disorders occur primarily in cultures or subcultures that value thinness and in which there is exposure to media images of "Barbie doll"-shaped bodies attests to the significance of culture in determining the expression of a mental disorder. Thus, mothers, concerned about their own weight, typically will transmit the cultural prescription to their daughters. Writing in the journal *Pediatrics,* Davison and Birch (2001), however, reported that girls who were constantly dieting said it was their father's opinion that was goading them on. For men, homosexuality is a risk factor, owing to a stress on slimness in the gay community (National Center on Addiction and Substance Abuse [CASA], 2003). Lesbians, on the other hand, rarely have anorexia (Andersen, 1999).

Sometimes, anorexia as the primary disorder is accompanied by uncontrollable bingeing that follows the period of starvation. Brandi Halverson shares her story:

> I have suffered from both anorexia and bulimia for the last 10 years. It took many forms: limiting calories to about 700–1,000 a day; to bingeing and purging; to bingeing and exercising; to bingeing and restricting. My symptoms have occurred on and off over the last 10 years, but most recently, I have had bulimia to such a degree that I sought inpatient hospitalization for it.
>
> While my eating disorder began in junior high at about age 14, I lived in denial of its gravity until much later and after many years of suffering alone. I, like many who struggle with eating disorders, am very good at hiding it and denying it, not only to others, but to ourselves. I would tell myself I was okay. But no matter what I looked like, or what behavior I chose, I was still suffering. This is an important thing about people with eating disorders—what the person looks like on the outside does not give a clear idea of how much the person is suffering on the inside.

> Over and over again I have thought about what might have caused my eating disorder. I don't know anyone else in my family who has or had an eating disorder, so I couldn't conclude "it ran in the family." I guess to some degree it was a combination of things. I felt pressure from society (primarily in the form of media) to be thin. I lacked self-esteem, didn't know how to handle stress or express my emotions and feelings, had a terrible drive for perfection, and desperately feared failure. (personal communication, May 1, 2006)

The form of anorexia to which the writer is referring is sometimes called the binge-purge anorexia. In contrast to bulimia, this disorder is characterized by severe underweight.

A frightening development is occurring on the Internet where some 500 websites that deal with anorexia are often "pro-ana" (ana is short for anorexia) and "pro-mia" (for bulimia). Girls share tips for losing weight on these sites and provide a positive image of these disorders that is very enticing (Song, 2005).

BULIMIA NERVOSA

NIMH (2006) lists the following symptoms of bulimia nervosa:

> Recurrent episodes of binge eating, characterized by eating an excessive amount of food within a discrete period of time and by a sense of lack of control over eating during the episode

> Recurrent inappropriate compensatory behavior in order to prevent weight gain, such as self-induced vomiting or misuse of laxatives, diuretics, enemas, or other medications (purging); fasting; or excessive exercise.

> The binge eating and inappropriate compensatory behaviors both occur, on average, at least twice a week for 3 months (p. 2)

Unlike anorexics, bulimics may have a history of weight gain or come from a family in which overweight is a problem. In terms of personality, bulimics usually are extraverted, have voracious appetites, and experience episodes of binge eating. Unlike anorexia, which is not necessarily a chronic illness, the average lifetime duration for bulimia and binge-eating disorder is more than 8 years (Hudson et al., 2007). In her fascinating book *Wasted: A Memoir of Anorexia and Bulimia,* Hornbacher (1998), who suffered from both problems, differentiates bulimia from anorexia:

> Bulimia, of course, gives in to the temptations of the flesh, while anorexia is anointed, is a complete removal of the bearer from the material realm. Bulimia hearkens back to the hedonistic Roman days of pleasure and feast, anorexia to the medieval age of bodily mortification and voluntary famine. (p. 153)

A key characteristic of bulimia is its common association with alcohol and other drug misuse; the National Center on Addiction and Substance Abuse (CASA, 2003) found that up to one half of individuals with eating disorders misuse alcohol or other drugs compared to 9% of the general population. Eating disorders, similarly, are commonly found in cocaine addicts and alcoholics in substance abuse treatment (CASA, 2003). Whether it's cutting a line of cocaine or a slab of cake, the symptomology of eating disorders and substance misuse is the same. Both disorders are long term, chronically relapsing, and life threatening.

Women with bulimia are three times more likely to have been sexually abused as children than women who do not suffer from this disorder, according to data from an Ontario Health Survey ("Many Bulimic Women," 1995). Thirty-five percent of women with severe bulimia reported childhood sexual abuse; many were also likely to have lived in foster homes, often because of their parents' alcoholism, according to this survey. Perhaps because compulsive eating stimulates a rise in the levels of mood enhancers in the brain, food can serve as a drug to curb the feelings of shame, self-disgust, and depression that often accompany compulsive eating problems. This urge to binge may explain why sexual abuse is more predictive of bulimic than of anorexic symptoms and related to the severity of symptoms. Gerke, Mazzio, and Kliewer (2006) found that depression was a mediating factor in the incidence of bulimia in girls who had been emotionally abused in childhood.

COMPULSIVE OVEREATERS

And what about those individuals who binge eat but don't throw up? Compulsive overeating, in the absence of bulimia, is a grave health risk because persons with this disorder sometimes put on hundreds of pounds. Yet compulsive overeating, sadly, is an area of scant research in the United States and is included in the *DSM–IV–TR* only under the category "criteria sets and axes provided for further study." Hudson et al. (2007), who have gathered the first national data ever on the prevalence of binge eating, found binge eating to be the most prevalent eating disorder. They therefore suggest that this illness be included in the next edition of the *DSM* as a psychiatric illness in its own right. Substance abuse treatment centers, meanwhile, have been slow to screen for eating disorders, which is probably related to the lack of insurance coverage for persons with eating disorders. NIDA also has been slow to finance the research needed on compulsive eating and drug dependence as interlocking illnesses (Vastag, 2001). This may all be changing, however, under leadership provided by the new NIDA director, Nora Volkow, a neuroscientist who has personally participated in obesity research (Wingert, 2006). A recent study directed by Gene-Jack Wang that was funded in part by NIDA, for example, provides evidence of the link between a certain region of the brain and overeating (*Medical News Today,* 2006a). An implanted device that stimulates a part of the brain linked to emotional eating and other addictions was shown in this study to reduce this excessive eating in seven experimental subjects. Predictably, more such research will be forthcoming.

Binge-eating disorder is characterized by NIMH (2006) in terms of binge-eating episodes as follows:

> The binge-eating episodes are associated with at least 3 of the following: eating much more rapidly than normal; eating until feeling uncomfortably full; eating

large amounts of food when not feeling physically hungry; eating alone because of being embarrassed by how much one is eating; feeling disgusted with oneself, depressed, or very guilty after overeating. (p. 3)

From the British medical journal *Lancet* ("Scientists Find Link," 2001) comes a groundbreaking study on the neurological characteristics of morbidly obese people. A lack of dopamine receptors in the brains of morbidly obese people has been documented through the use of PET scans. The greater the weight of the person, the lower his or her level of receptors. Later brain research has confirmed this finding (Wang, Volkow, Thanos, & Fowler, 2004).

Related research focusing on male twins found that a strong craving for sweets may be linked with a tendency toward alcoholism and that the cause may be genetic (*Science Daily*, 2000). As reported by the subjects in the study, cravings were worse when they were nervous or depressed. If verified in future studies, this link is further evidence that cravings for drink and cravings for food are closely related phenomena.

An interesting case history is provided by Spencer (2006) in an article in the *Wall Street Journal*. The case is of Patty Worrells, a compulsive overeater who would binge on cookies and ice cream at 3 A.M. Her weight shot up to 265 pounds. She found her solution in gastric-bypass surgery as her weight dropped 134 pounds. A new craving consumed her, however, drinking 15 to 20 shots of tequila at a time. "I drank the way I ate," she said (p. 3). Part of the reason she took to alcohol so quickly is that bypass surgery enables the alcohol to pass more rapidly into the patient's system. Alcoholism also ran in her family, so the tendency was there. Paradoxically, Worrells worked as a director of a substance abuse clinic. Finally, she got help through attending Twelve-Step meetings. What this case history shows, according to the article, is the probability of a neurological and psychological basis for compulsive eating that is similar to other addictions. At the Betty Ford Center, around 25% of alcoholics switch to a new addictive drug or behavior after treatment. And it is also known that roughly 20% of gastric-bypass surgery patients acquire new addictive behaviors.

Because it is directly linked with severe obesity and other damaging health problems, compulsive overeating is a major public health concern. As Hudson and his colleagues (2007) have shown from their analysis of national health statistics, binge-eating disorder is more prevalent than other forms of disordered eating. This finding is a wake-up call for the federal government to do more in terms of data gathering and the funding of treatment and prevention efforts.

TREATMENT INTERVENTIONS

A combination of pharmaceutical and cognitive interventions is the preferred treatment for disordered eating. Selective serotonin-enhancing antidepressants have been found helpful for bulimia (Vastag, 2001). Ondansetron, a drug normally given to cancer patients to prevent nausea and vomiting, also works for bulimia. (Ondansetron has also been found effective with alcoholism of the highly hereditary variety.) In a study comparing 14 bulimic patients given

Ondansetron with 12 others given a placebo, the patients on the real drug showed a marked decline in the number of bingeing and vomiting episodes. This drug not only helped bulimics know when to stop eating, but it also acted to make more serotonin available in the brain.

In severe cases of anorexia, where clients have lost 25% of their expected body weight, inpatient treatment is necessary. The sole focus in the initial period is weight restoration. Once weight is restored to a level that is no longer life threatening, much of the depression lifts and thinking becomes more rational.

Vastag (2001) pointed to the lack of effectiveness of medication in ameliorating anorexia. It stands to reason, however, because of the close connection between OCD and anorexia, that the same drug would be effective for both. Anorexia, unlike the addictions, is not about getting high or dulling the senses. Anorexia has more in common with compulsive, ritualistic behavior based on a delusion; it is related more to avoidance of pain than to pleasure. Probably for this reason, Johnson (2004) recommends medical management as a useful adjunct to cognitive-behavioral treatment of anorexia. And researchers are now finding that antidepressant medication such as Prozac can help if the patient's weight has returned to normal (De Angelis, 2002). The favored treatment for eating disorders is multimodal intervention; this includes, in addition to medication to reduce the obsessiveness, education on the basics of good nutrition, consciousness raising concerning media images and unhealthy thinking, and intensive psychotherapy in cases of a history of early childhood sexual abuse. Promising results have come from a large-scale experiment in which therapists targeted the obsessive anorexic mindset as the villain rather than the patient or the family. Instead of blaming family members, they can be coached to work as a supportive treatment team to help restore the anorexic's weight to normal (De Angelis, 2002).

Research indicates the efficacy of various types of group work with eating-disordered individuals (NIMH, 2006). The effectiveness of group treatment for women troubled with eating problems stems from the tremendous sharing and support that derive from a positive collective experience. Women's relationships become more open through the process of mutual decision making and feedback. Women can develop a sense of self in relation to others in a group setting. When a woman begins to build trust and empathy with others, she also may begin to look at herself differently as she learns to value herself for who she is rather than to judge herself in terms of her body size.

The primary challenge in eating disorders treatment compared to other substance abuse treatment is that, because food, unlike alcohol and cocaine, is required for life, treatment protocols that involve a commitment to abstinence (successful with alcohol and cocaine) do not apply. Moderation must be learned by those with eating problems. As many cigarette smokers are aware, it is often easier to give up a substance altogether than to practice moderation. A second factor affecting recovery evaluation and outcomes is the difficulty in defining or detecting a relapse of abnormal eating patterns. The binge–purge cycle, in fact, can go on for years undetected by family members as well as practitioners. Third, as every adolescent girl or woman knows, society rewards slimness far more than it rewards moderation.

| Box 7.1 | In Treatment for Bulimia: Two Contrasting Programs |

The first of the two programs we will be discussing is Iowa City's Eating Disorder Program. This program is a very cognitive-behavioral-based program, which has been proven to be among the top ways in treating an eating disorder. It was very structured in that every single day was the same, with every hour from 7 A.M. to 10 P.M. filled. The patients had no knowledge or control of what they ate, or how much. Diet was taken care of by a nutritionist based on what the patient weighed.

Group sessions were cognitively based, providing education on the patients' core beliefs, schemas, cognitive distortions, how the distortions might have been acquired, and rational ways to perceive disturbing situations. The patient met with the doctor every day, discussing any concerns or effects of medication that might have been pre-scribed. The patient was required to keep a daily journal, to map out the day including downtime, and to report events that were anxiety provoking. The program was built on a level system; one could progress upward based on behavior, improvement, and weight. The eating disorder track was on the same wing as the mood disorder track. This created some conflict and uncomfortable situations.

Iowa City's program was entirely focused only on the eating disorder and "fixing" the coping mechanisms. These counselors did not address the issues that may have provoked needing the coping mechanisms in the first place. In fact, when the doctors were con-fronted with a patient who had already done work in the area of sexual abuse treatment and wanted to do more within the context of eating disorder treatment, they told her to focus only on the eating disorder and not to talk about the other issues, even in a group

---

Cognitive-behavioral therapy is the treatment of choice in addressing the complex interplay of irrational thoughts that plague persons with eating disorders (NIMH, 2006). The focus here is on the beliefs that power the distorted thoughts and the behavior based on those thoughts. Women's pursuit of the cultural ste-reotype of feminine beauty is characterized by thoughts such as "If I am fat, then I am ugly, and if I am ugly, I am unlovable," and "Since I have eaten three cookies, I might as well eat the whole box." These self-defeating thoughts and the resultant actions serve to sabotage women's lives and perpetuate the eating disorder.

The skilled cognitive-behavioral therapist will selectively address issues of weight phobia, distorted perceptions of the body, fear of loss of control about eating and weight, and negative self-perceptions. Cognitive-behavioral treat-ment is generally focused on the present, serving to identify the immediate behavioral consequences of irrational beliefs (Fossati et al., 2004).

Affective (feeling) work is critical in the treatment of persons with eating disorders. Inability to cope with early painful experiences such as rape, incest, an alcoholic family, and transitions from childhood to adolescence or from adolescence to adulthood are common underlying dynamics.

Because these persons may lack experience in identifying and expressing a broad range of feelings, counseling sessions initially may be oriented toward the examination of affective states, with counselors modeling appropriate affect for given situations and practicing healthy modes of expression.

setting. This was like saying that the patient needed to forget about what caused the disorder in the first place, or at least heavily contributed. The approach was strictly cognitive, in a limited sense of the term.

The second program that I attended was at Two Rivers Psychiatric Hospital in Kansas City, Missouri, but specifically their trauma-based program. Eating disorders there were classified as a trauma disorder, as childhood sexual abuse, rape, and domestic violence are highly correlated to eating disorders and the development of other addictive problems. This program's primary focus was to stabilize behavior teaching different healthy coping tools, providing a safe environment for healing and growth, with the eating disorder program promoting improvements in balanced living. The eating disorders track functioned separately, but the two were not mutually exclusive.

This program also provided groups, including anger management, body awareness, cognitive therapy, crafts, contours drawing, psychodrama, etc. This program, like that of Iowa City, provided a psychiatrist who came every day to discuss individual concerns and medication. Each individual patient also had a therapist that he/she met with daily for an hour. This time provided opportunity to discuss any personal questions or issues with group counselors on the unit, and go a little more in depth with the complex issues surrounding their childhood or adulthood.

Two Rivers' treatment model is much more effective in the treatment of an individual with a dual diagnosis of an eating disorder and a history of sexual trauma. Iowa City's eating disorders program is nationally acclaimed for their treatment of such disorders, so when I found that they had no support for, or even acknowledgment of such issues with sexual trauma given the high correlation between the two, I was both surprised and upset.

Anonymous (October 14, 2004).

Family therapy, particularly for the adolescent girl, is an important first step in educating the family as a whole to the apparently strange behaviors of eating-disordered individuals. Parents need to be encouraged to set clear boundaries about appropriate behaviors, such as insisting on some financial contribution to the household grocery bill from a daughter who regularly binges on "family" food. Family members also need a forum in which they can express the feelings of frustration, confusion, and mistrust that accompany life with an eating-disordered person, as well as a place to begin to explore the familial issues that encourage the dysfunctional eating.

For clients who are overweight, strict dieting is discouraged because, for many people, food deprivation sets the stage for a starvation–binge-eating cycle. Besides, counting calories reinforces food and eating obsessiveness. Used alone or with other treatments, cognitive-behavioral therapy results in significant reductions in behavior associated with disordered eating (Fossati et al., 2004). Such therapy principally addresses irrational thought patterns, such as distorted body image, low self-esteem, perfectionism, and preoccupation with the body and with gaining weight.

A student in van Wormer's addiction course whose bulimia was out of control went to one treatment center with a strong cognitive base and then was transferred to another clinic for intensive trauma work. In Box 7.1, the student compares and contrasts the two treatment experiences.

A controversial cognitive-based "love-them-back-to-health" approach was taken by Peggy Claude-Pierre (1997), author of *The Secret Language of Eating Disorders*. Claude-Pierre became a celebrity following extensive television coverage of her work in saving the lives of starving anorexics. Little attention was paid to early childhood experiences; the focus was on the "here and now." The girls at her center (since closed down by the British Columbia health authorities after allegations of forced-feeding were made) did attend workshops to learn practical strategies to survive. They kept journals with two columns per page, one for recording the self-talking voice of anorexia or bulimia and the other for the voice that argued against the negative thoughts. Although the television broadcasts focused on miracle cures, this form of treatment in the absence of medical supervision is ill advised.

Nevertheless, training by reputable professionals in the control of rigid thought patterns, including the identification and handling of feelings and assertiveness, can have lifelong benefits. The insights and tools acquired for dealing with an eating disorder can empower a person to overcome any number of challenges and obstacles in day-to-day life. Johnson (2004) recommends dialectical behavior therapy, an approach that is kin to motivational interviewing in starting with acceptance of the client where the client is. This approach can be used in conjunction with medication for maximum results.

Nicole, age 20, described her battle overcoming bulimia:

> I weighed 160 pounds in college, got into exercising so I could wear cute shorts. It was normal dieting at the beginning; I got my weight down to 120. The social pressures were enormous, so many compliments, "What are you doing to look so good?" I ate it up. . . . In reality, I was a mess, addicted to laxatives, surviving on apples and graham crackers. After taking 10 laxatives, I landed in the hospital and from there into counseling. Social workers and a dietician worked with me and my family.
>
> In family counseling we explored family secrets; we were a "perfect" family. Rules were set for us—not talking about food. I learned about underlying factors in my behavior—my feelings, the "voice in my head."
>
> Later I joined a support group. An educator showed us magazine clippings and explained how distorted our images are. We made lists: Ten things to do, instead of bingeing. My list said: "Go for a walk, call a friend, sister, pray." I deal with my problem every single day. (personal communication, February 7, 1997)

Gradually, most adolescents with an eating disorder mature out of it but nobody knows why. Perhaps the recovery is related to the maturity of the brain and the stabilizing of hormones. Still, there is no cure for this disorder. As Hornbacher (1998) describes her state of recovery in her memoir, aptly entitled *Wasted,* "It is not a sudden leap from sick to well. It is a slow, strange meander from sick to mostly well" (p. 284).

Sometimes, however, in middle age, the old imposter returns. In Philadelphia, the Renfrew Center Foundation reported a recent jump in admission of women older than 35 (Newsome, 2005). To meet the need, the center has set up an outpatient recovery group for over-30s. These women deal with issues related to family responsibilities and aging. The health risks of eating disorders to mature women, such as bone fractures, demand specialized attention as well.

Because similar problems in men—obsession over the way their bodies look—have been largely ignored, male-oriented treatments are scarce (Holm, 2006). Although some men with eating disorders have a kind of fat phobia and become emaciated, it is the impetus to have a muscular build that creates for men, according to one newspaper headline, "The 'Flip Side' of Anorexia" (E. Smith, 1997). Bodybuilders seeking physical perfection may watch every ounce of food they eat, gorge on protein, weigh themselves throughout the day, and devote hours per day to lifting weights. *Muscle dysmorphia* is the psychiatric term for this disorder. Sufferers commonly take steroids (see chapter 6). The good news, according to the article, is that antidepressants can control this behavior. The bad news is that only a few will seek help, and for those who do, treatment centers for males are hard to find (Holm, 2006).

Overeaters Anonymous (OA) is the self-help group for individuals who seek group support for a variety of eating problems. The beauty of OA is that it is ubiquitous in the United States, is free, can be attended as needed, and is open to all who desire to stop eating compulsively. Founded in 1960 by three people in southern California and patterned after AA, OA now has approximately 6,500 meeting groups in more than 60 countries throughout the world (*Wikipedia*, 2007). There are also online group meetings. According to *Wikipedia*, OA members do not all have one specific and common substance or attribute that causes cravings. Because individual members have cravings for different kinds of foods or eating behaviors, each member has to develop her or his own plan of eating. OA uses the concept of "abstinence from compulsive eating" rather than "sobriety"; a plan of eating ideally, therefore, would eliminate those foods and/or eating behaviors that cause cravings. (Information available at www.oa.org/index.htm.)

A semihumorous encounter with OA is given by Malachy McCourt (2000). Refusing to deal with his alcoholism problem, McCourt decided to do something about his weight problem. After getting poor results, he tried a number of diets, among them the protein diet and the grapefruit diet. Weight Watchers costs money, so he decided to go to OA:

> I sat with a group made up almost entirely of women, of every age, and heard horrendous stories of anorexia, bulimia, starvation, bingeing, and other stuff I never knew went on in this prosperous society. . . . People talked about "stuffing down feelings with food."
>
> [Following a month of meetings, McCourt came to the realization that his problem was alcohol.] So I stopped drinking, just like that—suddenly, precipitately, and perhaps foolishly, but being a man of extremes, it seemed the right thing to do. (pp. 175–176)

COMPULSIVE GAMBLING

Because some form of gambling has become legal in every state except two (Utah and Hawaii) and nearly 900 casinos are operating in 29 states (Peterson, 2006), and casino or casino-style gambling is available in most states (Kearney,

2005), we can say that gambling clearly has become socially acceptable and accessible for both men and women. According to a recent national poll, two of three Americans gambled in the last 12 months, mostly through state lotteries (Pew Research Center, 2006). Consequently, many men and women suffering the consequences of excessive gambling are surfacing and asking for help. The economic cost of gambling—treatment for addiction, domestic violence, job loss—is estimated by a report to Congress by the National Council on Problem Gambling at $6.7 billion a year (White, 2006).

Pathological gambling (the lay term is "compulsive gambling") is defined by the National Research Council (1999, chap. 2, p. 4) as a "mental disorder characterized by a continuous or periodic loss of control over gambling, a preoccupation with gambling, and with obtaining money with which to gamble, irrational thinking, and a continuation of the behavior despite adverse consequences." A clinical diagnosis is reached when a person meets five or more of the *Diagnostic and Statistical Manual–IV–TR* criteria (APA, 2000). Among the criteria are a preoccupation with gambling, a need to gamble with increasing amounts of money, making repeated efforts to quit, gambling from stress, lying to conceal activities, and borrowing money to pay debts (see chap. 1 of *DSM–IV–TR*). Pathological gambling is listed under "impulse control disorders not otherwise classified" along with kleptomania and pyromania. Yet the symptoms of this addiction, as certified gambling counselor Patricia Sweeting (2000) indicates, are interwoven with those of all mood-altering substance disorders. The loss of control, the family disintegration, increased tolerance— the features, tragedies, of one addiction are the features, tragedies, of the other. In its power to captivate and hook the player, video poker is said to be the "crack cocaine of gambling." A large majority of people in treatment for gambling disorders are heavy video poker players (Robb, 2005).

Researchers have begun focusing on the biology of gambling addiction and how a situation of risk punctuated by occasional rewards can have such a powerful attraction to many individuals, dulling, in effect, the rational portion of the mind. A scientific study led by Maria Roca showed that pathological gamblers exhibit complex impairments in decision making associated with the prefrontal cortex of the brain (*Science Daily*, 2005). Another study using fMRI to map brain activity in men and women as they performed a risk versus reward task pinpointed specific regions of the brain that responded to risk and to receiving reward (Preuschoff et al., 2006). Such research helps us understand what clinical evidence shows—that "pathological gamblers engage in destructive behaviors: they commit crimes, they run up large debts, they damage relationships with family and friends, and they kill themselves" (National Research Council, 1999, p. Exec. 2).

Consider the following headlines, all obtained from the recent news category of Google news stories on the topic of gambling:

"College class president blames gambling addiction for robbery conviction" (Granju, 2006).

"Lawyer sentenced for embezzling 3.1 million from Nevada casino" (Associated Press, 2006).

"Mother embezzled millions to fund lottery addiction, authorities say." (Weir & Goldiner, 2006).

"Problem gambling" is a category generally used in research studies to indicate that the person has developed some family, work, or financial problems because of gambling but hasn't met at least five of the *DSM–IV* criteria. It is also applied to adolescents, regardless of their scores on various assessment instruments, because of a reluctance to label them "pathological" while in the midst of fluctuating/experimental behavior patterns. Many times, the general term "problem gamblers" is used inclusively to indicate both pathological and problem gamblers (Pavalko, 1999).

How big is the problem? Owing to the widespread expansion of casinos, the cost of pathological and problem gambling has soared to nearly half the annual cost of drug abuse in the United States, according to economist Earl Grinols (2004), the author of *Gambling in America: Costs and Benefits*. The social costs of gambling, such as increased crime, lost work time, bankruptcies, and financial hardships faced by the families of gambling addicts, have reached epidemic proportions and cost the economy as much as $54 billion annually. Most experienced no negative consequences; approximately 7.5 million were either problem or pathological gamblers. The Pew Research Center (2006) found in their nationwide survey that 70% of Americans say that legalized gambling encourages people to gamble more than they can afford and also leads to a sharp increase in participation in casino gambling and the use of slot machines. Some 7% of respondents in the survey and 9% of those who gamble say they sometimes have gambled more than they can afford, and 6% say gambling has been a source of problems within their own families. The National Research Council (1999) estimates that between 3 and 7% of those who gambled in the past year reported some symptoms of problem or pathological gambling. Prevalence breakdowns by race are rare; however, a 1993 study for the North Dakota Department of Human Services found that 14.5% of Native Americans in the sample were probable pathological gamblers compared to 3.5% in the general population (Volberg, 1993).

Westermeyer (2005) compared American Indian and Latino veterans in the Southwest and found the rate of pathological gambling of American Indian veterans at 9 to 10% was more than double that of Latino veterans. His explanation was that where gambling is widely available, a higher percentage of the population will develop problems. Female veterans had the same rate as male veterans, an unexpected finding.

In a random sample of 2,630 U.S. residents, Welte, Barnes, Wieczorek, Tidwell, and Parker (2002) came up with the following breakdown:

- Men and women gambled in equal numbers, but male gamblers risked larger sums of money.
- African Americans were less likely than Whites to have gambled in the past year, but those who did gambled more heavily.
- Blacks and Latinos were more likely than average to be pathological gamblers.

- New Englanders gambled more than other Americans.
- Compared to women, men were more likely to participate in games of skill.

A look at the prevalence studies of the upcoming generation, the first generation brought up with sanctioned gaming, indicates that adolescents are at particular risk of developing problems with gambling. About 1 in 20 youth is considered to be a pathological Internet gambler (*Christian Science Monitor,* 2006). The National Research Council's (1999) survey of the research literature revealed estimates of the "past year" rate of adolescent problem and pathological gambling combined range from 11.3 to 27.7%, with a median of 20%.

Internet gambling is the fastest growing segment of the gambling market (Pew Research Center, 2006). In 2004 alone, Internet gamblers spent $8 billion on an estimated 1,800 websites nationwide (Robb, 2005). Despite the fact that Internet gambling has skyrocketed in the United States, Congress has been slow to act to enhance the ability of prosecutors to go after the online gaming industry. Congress, however, did finally pass the Unlawful Internet Gambling Enforcement Act, which was signed into law in October 2006. This law prohibits the use of credit cards and bank transfers by U.S. citizens in transactions. The passage of the law was surprising because, as argued in an earlier editorial in the *Christian Science Monitor* (2006), a reluctance to crack down on illegal Internet gambling could be attributed to the over $7 million paid in campaign donations to political candidates for federal office by the casino and gambling industry. Despite the new law, the lure of lottery and other gambling industry revenues for state governments, as stated in the article, has led to laxity in enforcement of laws against youth gambling at all levels of law enforcement.

The new forms of gambling such as video lottery terminals in community settings, Internet gambling, and community casinos are associated with high societal cost. A Canadian national survey found the prevalence of gambling problems, which average 2% nationally, was considered higher in regions of the country with video lottery terminals (Cox, Yu, Afifi, & Ladouceur, 2005). These findings show that studies of the impact of gambling need to take into account the various forms of gambling and draw comparisons in impacts on communities with gambling establishments versus comparable communities without them. Chhabra, Lutz, and Gonnerman (2005) conducted such a study for the Iowa legislative council. Their research showed that crime rates were higher in casino than control counties. There was also an association between gambling availability and rate of bankruptcy.

Perhaps even more than with other addictions, gambling strikes at families, places of employment, and friends (Davis, 2002). As compulsive gamblers begin to lose and lose big, forever chasing that original high of an early win, they sell or pawn possessions, plead for loans from all around them, and steal the rest. Embezzlement is a big problem among addicted gamblers (Beaucar, 1999). Where gambling is widely available, gambling problems are often experienced by elderly community members. A New Jersey poll, for example, found that 23% of older persons who gambled had gambling disorders (Fairleigh Dickinson University, 2006).

Writing about the wives of compulsive gamblers, LairRobinson (1997) reports that they are not only constantly harassed by bill collectors but very often physically abused by their husbands. These wives have a high rate of suicide attempts as well. Children of such gamblers have double the rate of suicide attempts as their peers; they are also more likely than their peers to develop a gambling problem themselves. Muelleman, DenOtter, Wadman, Tran, and Anderson (2002) interviewed 61 women who were treated in an Omaha emergency room for partner violence. Disproportionately high numbers of these women compared to other female patients in the emergency room reported gambling problems in their partners. Drinking plus gambling was even more closely associated with problem gambling.

Gender Differences

Epidemiological surveys consistently report that men are much more likely to be pathological or problem gamblers than are women (Petry, Stinson, & Grant, 2005). Approximately one third of pathological gamblers are female. In treatment programs, females are underrepresented; they are only 2 to 4% of the population of GA (APA, 2000).

Most of the state problem gambling helplines, however, report that the percentage of women seeking help with gambling problems has been increasing. As early as 1993, an Alberta, Canada, study concluded that women are the gender group now most likely to experience gambling problems. In New Jersey, calls about women problem gamblers have doubled since 1990. In Texas, calls about women have increased from 34% in 1992 to 40% in 1999 (Texas Council on Problem and Compulsive Gambling, 2000).

In contrast to women, who are inclined to gamble as an escape mechanism, even to the point of feeling "hypnotized" or in a "trance" (personal communication, September 2000), men are more likely to be characterized as "action" gamblers; that is, gambling for men began early in life, has been a long-term problem for 10 to 30 years, focuses on "skill" games, such as poker, horses, and sports, and provides action as well as escape (Arizona Council on Compulsive Gambling, 2000). Another motivation for women to gamble compulsively may be the social stereotypes and economic limitations that are still imposed on many of them. Female gamblers coming into treatment after "losing it all" on slot machines had taken up gambling as an escape from very unhappy lives (Beaucar, 1999). Results from an online survey of over 250 women in recovery from compulsive gambling reveal that many women reported getting started with gambling because of a sense of boredom. The majority of respondents to the survey reported severe family problems in their backgrounds or emptiness in their lives (Davis & Avery, 2004).

In a poster session at the conference of the American Society of Addiction Medicine, Silvia Martins reported the results of her comparative study of 78 men and 78 women in treatment in Brazil for gambling problems. She found that men more often than women had substance-related problems, an earlier onset of gambling, and involvement in Gamblers Anonymous. Significantly more women had made a suicide attempt and were seriously depressed than were the men (Evans, 2004).

A special attraction to women, according to an article in *Time* magazine, is betting in Cyberspace. On the Internet, women who are new to gambling can find online teaching tools (Russo, 2005). They also can disguise their gender and take notes on plays. At Empire Poker.com, women have gone from 3% of players 3 years ago to 20% today. In addition, many women are now playing on all-female sites.

An innovative program to counsel women with gambling problems is conducted at the Coffee Creek Correctional Facility in Oregon. An earlier survey found that 20 to 30% of the female inmates have such problems and that 86% of the problem gamblers admitted to crimes, including prostitution, to pay off debts. Before their release, the women with gambling problems are provided with an intervention by a team of certified problem gambling counselors. Treatment includes weekly 90-minute group sessions (Oregon Department of Corrections, 2004).

CO-OCCURRENCE OF OTHER PROBLEMS

According to the National Research Council (1999), substance use disorders (nongender specific) are associated with both progression to problem gambling and subsequent pathological gambling. A more recent national sample found that three fourths of persons who suffered from a pathological gambling disorder also had problems with alcohol, and over one third had a problem with drugs. Around 60% reported nicotine dependence. Pietrzak and Petry (2005) evaluated 237 pathological gamblers in an outpatient treatment program. They found that over 16% met the diagnosable criteria for antisocial personality disorder. They also found that within this subgroup, the clients were predominantly male and had severe gambling and drug problems disproportionate to the other clients. Similarly, a study of over 2,000 Canadian high school students found that youth with gambling problems reported more negative life events than other students and had less mature coping styles in dealing with problems (Bergevin, Gupta, Derevensky, & Kaufman, 2006).

According to the National Council on Problem Gambling, the suicide rate for pathological gamblers is higher than for any other addictive disorder (National Gambling Impact Study Commission, 1999). At a minimum, shame, guilt, and remorse are constant companions related to huge losses, making it even more difficult for a problem gambler to seek help (see Davis, 2002).

TREATMENT PROVISIONS

Because most health insurers and managed care providers do not reimburse for pathological gambling treatment, and because persons with gambling problems are in no position to "self-pay," treatment provisions are sparse (Robb, 2005). State helplines now operate in only 35 of the 48 states that have some form of legalized gambling. About half of these states support some type of treatment with public funding, but the level of funding is miniscule compared to the amount of income the states receive from gambling enterprises. As of 2006, less than $36 million a year are spent by the government and gambling industry for education and treatment of gambling problems (Peterson, 2006). This is out of the $20 billion or so in tax revenues states collected from gambling in the same year. Given this current state of affairs and the reluctance of compulsive gamblers to seek out specialized help for the gambling problem, it is important that helping professionals become knowledgeable about compulsive gambling and screen for this as well as other addictions in their clientele.

The addiction/disease model is the conceptual basis for using treatment methods established in substance abuse treatment centers and slightly modifying them for pathological gamblers. Since many of the *DSM* criteria are indicative of physiological dependence, treatment professionals are relying on the strategies of other addictive disorders, including the prescription for abstinence. Treatment centers for persons with gambling problems commonly refer the clients to the Twelve-Step group Gamblers Anonymous (GA) for additional help. Of the GA Twenty Questions (based on the *DSM* criteria), most compulsive gamblers will answer yes to at least seven (Gamblers Anonymous, 1999). As is customary in Twelve-Step groups, the final "diagnosis" is left up to the person to decide for himself or herself. The state of being powerless over one's urges is all that is required. When one has reached that point, abstinence from all gambling is deemed a necessary goal.

The GA program acknowledges Alcoholics Anonymous (AA) as a guide and foundation and utilizes the same Twelve Steps of recovery and the same organizational principles. The only requirement for membership is "a desire to stop gambling" (Gamblers Anonymous, 2000, p. 2). GA is run entirely by recovering compulsive gamblers, who volunteer their time to be sponsors, chair meetings, arrange for meeting places, secure GA literature, and respond to requests for help day and night. GA meetings can be found by calling the state problem gambling helpline, looking in the yellow pages of the phone book for a local contact number, or accessing the Gamblers Anonymous International Service Office online site at http://gamblersanonymous.org/. For family members, Gam-Anon can be extremely helpful; information and listings are available at this same site.

Even normal people register increased blood flow to the same region of the brain affected by cocaine use, according to a widely publicized study from Massachusetts General Hospital (Wen, 2001). What differentiates these normal euphoric states from those in compulsive gamblers is probably a matter of intensity or the contrast between this high and the person's normal state of mind. The anticipation of winning triggers a dopamine rush (Johnson, 2004). The impulsive part of the brain then drives the behaviors as judgment is put to sleep. Curiously, as widely reported in the media, elderly patients with Parkinson's disease who were medicated with dopamine-boosting drugs developed all sorts of addictions, including to food, sex, and gambling (Ubelacker, 2005). The reason for this unexpected reaction that occurs in a minority of patients is attributed to a mania-like state that is sometimes induced by this drug. Mania is

| BOX 7.2 | REFLECTIONS OF A MALE COMPULSIVE GAMBLER |

Gambling is a source of entertainment for many people in the world today. With the increase in casino outlets, as well as the influx of offshore gambling available through the Internet, Americans can bet on practically anything imaginable. For many of these people, gambling does not present a serious problem (to borrow a phrase from the Iowa lottery advertisements). However, for a small percentage statistically, gambling can become a serious addiction. I, myself, fall into this category. For nearly 5 years, I was addicted to sports betting. Although I have not related this story to anyone previous to now, I hope that it will shed some light on the subject of compulsive gambling.

In Omaha, I worked with behaviorally impaired adolescent boys. In this field, the support staff is dominated by males who usually have a background that includes, at some level, participation in competitive sports. Such men are supposedly more equipped to deal with the rough nature of the clients involved. It was in this environment that I was first introduced to the world of sports gambling. The circumstances were that a colleague would pick up a bookie sheet (a form containing a list of all of the available games that could be bet on during a particular day) and bring it to work. Initially, I only looked at college and professional football games that were played on the weekends. This, however, did not produce the winnings I imagined. My gambling eventually became daily, if not twice daily. I went from betting on weekend games to daily gambling on basketball, baseball, and hockey contests, and as this happened over the period of 5 years, I lost thousands and thousands of dollars and numerous other possessions. Before it was over, I nearly lost my family.

In the beginning, my wife had participated in the "fun" of gambling. The very occasional wins were encouraging and euphoric. As I began to delve deeper into the gambling, however, she bored of the losses and began to see less pleasure in the hobby. In fact, she encouraged me to get out of the practice. But by then the compulsion for me was too great.

As I began to spend a large portion of my salary on gambling, this created a strain on the marriage. My wife is a certified teacher and makes a considerable amount of money working with students who are emotionally and behaviorally impaired in a private educational setting. In one year, according to our tax returns, we earned nearly $50,000, and yet we had to file bankruptcy not once, but twice! The bank account just could not keep up with the mounting losses.

My ambition in life became the same as other compulsive gamblers, to get my money back. I was always going to win big. Be persistent—that's the thought pattern of a compulsive gambler.

Located in the heart of the Black neighborhood, these bookie joints are packed with people; one would be hard pressed to find a larger crowd at any of the local churches in the area. There is a distinct culture among the gamblers who socialize while discussing the

---

associated with high risk-taking behavior. Problems with gambling and spending have also developed with Requip, the widely advertised medicine prescribed for people with restless legs syndrome.

The addiction/disease model is bolstered by research indicating that dopamine and serotonin brain functions are altered in pathological gamblers (APA, 2000). Consistent with the disease model, experiments with medications such as serotonin-reuptake inhibitors to treat compulsive gamblers are currently under way. A promising area of research involves the use of naltrexone, an opioid antagonist that has been used to block the excitement of addictive drugs such as odds. What's the hot pick of the day? Who's guaranteed to lose? And so forth. There isn't a Caucasian in sight. If one does appear, there is hushed silence until the stranger is identified as a regular or knows someone present. The staff of about six or seven (two who remain behind a counter while the others mingle in the crowd) write tickets and collect the money. In the particular neighborhood I frequented, there is no credit issued when you place a bet. The fee is paid up front; this eliminates the need for henchmen to go collecting on outstanding bets. After placing the bet, my favorite thing to do would be to watch the game.

For the casual gambler, the win or loss would put an end to the matter for the day. However, for the compulsive gambler, this is just the beginning. As soon as the outcome was determined—win or lose—I would be racing out of the door to place my afternoon bet. If I lost, I was going to get it back. If I won, I was going to make more money to make up for past losses. It was an endless cycle. The excitement of the game was my driving force. Often after losing in the afternoon games on the weekend, I would rush off to the bookie joint with the intention of betting on the night games. If the place was closed, I would be extremely upset that I had arrived late. Dejected, I would return home to consider my losses and to plot for the next day's picks. It was very difficult to suppress my emotional roller coaster from my wife and children. My mood swings were apparent. As things began to collapse around me, I sought help from the local Gamblers Anonymous group. After a short period of sobriety though, I returned to gambling. Gambling had simply become a part of my life that I couldn't avoid. It was entrenched in my social contacts and easily accessible, making it very difficult for me to stop. For me, a geographical relocation was the answer.

Living in Omaha had become increasingly difficult. The embarrassment that accompanies the life of a compulsive gambler, although at times nonexistent to the gambler, is always apparent to their family. Evictions, repossessions, cut-off utilities, collection agencies, and the daily concern of paying the bills are real to the family. My wife was advocating for a "new life," one she believed could exist without gambling. She was also at a point in her career that she needed a change, and she began to explore graduate programs. I, myself, had not completed a bachelor's degree, earning only 40 credits in my many attempts at college, and I began to contemplate seriously a return to school.

It is frequently said in Alcoholics Anonymous that a geographical relocation is not a cure. As one adolescent treatment counselor once said, "A drunk in South Dakota can as easily be a drunk in Iowa." This is probably true for all addictions. However, in my case, the geographical relocation was my answer for a cure. I have not gambled in 4 years, have completed my BA in History, and am one semester away from my MA in sports psychology. My relationship with my wife has improved dramatically, and I now have time to spend with my kids. I can watch sports without feeling the need to bet on who will win—with the exception of an occasional $1 bet with my 11-year-old son.

Personal story presented to van Wormer on July 27, 2000, for use in this book. The author, due to the nature of his work, wishes to remain anonymous.

alcohol, cocaine, and heroin. In tightly controlled studies, naltrexone has been found to mitigate the frequent and intense cravings experienced by compulsive gamblers who are receiving treatment (Grant & Kim, 2002). Drugs such as lithium, used to treat concurrent bipolar disorder, have also been found to decrease compulsive gambling (Rogers & Goodwin, 2005). Box 7.2 presents the portrait of a compulsive gambler, the tale of a highly respected African American youth worker who ended up getting "hooked."

MOTIVATIONAL AND COGNITIVE THERAPY

It is important to remember that with gambling, the main source of information about the behavior is self-reporting by the gamblers themselves. There is no urine drug screen or even the typical patterns of withdrawal symptoms that might confirm recent use or severity of the problem. Many sources in the literature focus on the gambler's "uncanny ability to deceive relatives and clinicians, at least in the short run" (Blanco, Ibanez, Saiz-Ruiz, Blanco-Jerez, & Nunes, 2000, p. 401). In the alcohol/drug field as practiced in the addiction/ medical model in the United States, this behavior is commonly interpreted as "resistance and denial." Gathering collateral information from friends, spouses, partners, and relatives is recommended to confront the person with his or her behavior and "break down" the denial. The therapist in this framework is allied with the forces (legal, familial, societal) that aim to stop the person from further gambling and further damage.

A perspective based on strengths, in contrast, is less concerned with breaking down defenses, which are coping mechanisms, after all, and more concerned with building trust. Motivational interviewing is especially relevant to work with clients such as compulsive gamblers who, typically, are plagued with guilt feelings, having thrown so much of their and others' earnings away. If they do not feel backed into a corner by a confrontational therapist, they likely will welcome the opportunity to "open up." To the extent that there is "resistance," a motivational interviewing model or a solution-focused therapy model interprets this as a natural product of a confrontational environment (Berg & Miller, 1992; W. R. Miller & Rollnick, 2002). Interviewing strategies that would engage the person in formulating his or her own goals for change and be congruent with the client's process of change are preferred. The strengths-oriented therapist is allied with the client in working on goals, even if these goals don't initially include giving up gambling (Berg & Miller, 1992).

Programs for youth founded on a harm reduction approach inform youth of the risks associated with gambling and help them develop the critical thinking skills to remain in control of the situation. Harm reduction programs need to identify and work with at-risk youth, including communities and/or schools where gambling problems proliferate (Messerlian, Derevensky, & Gupta, 2005). Given that age of onset is a significant risk factor, the availability of gambling activities needs to be drastically restricted. Parents must be educated into marketing ploys that are used to appeal to youth, and they must monitor their children's Internet activity.

WORK IN THE COGNITIVE AREA

"I'm wondering how gambling activities or the gambling of someone in your family may play into what we've been discussing. Could I ask you a few questions?" This is one of the exploratory-type questions that might be asked in a typical counseling session. Drawing on principles from a solution-focused rather than problem-focused approach, the therapist would assist the client in defining his or her own conception of the problem and goals for change. Specific techniques to find out what is important to the client might involve asking for exceptions to the problem and about how he or she coped with earlier difficulties in life. Strengths and past successes in dealing with problems of living would be highlighted instead of deficits or "pathology." The strengths-based therapist will strive to reinforce the client in the direction of positive thinking ("I think I can") while helping the client to eliminate counterproductive and superstitious beliefs. Here are the words of one gambler, for example:

> The lady on the other side of me swears, and I glance at her machine just in time to see that she'd "missed" the white 7's by one. "They look like they're ready to come," I say. "Just teasing me," she replies. (anonymous contribution, GA website, 2000)

This excerpt illustrates two cognitive distortions common among compulsive gamblers: giving the slot machine human qualities and misunderstanding the nature of randomness.

In fact, problem gamblers, as sociologist Bo Bernhard tells us, "have unique cognitive distortions" whereby the cause of their problems is also the cure of their problems. Unlike substance misusers, gamblers are notorious for "chasing their losses" or doubling their bets from one day to the next. "By asking the right questions, clinicians can strengthen their safety nets and start catching problem gamblers" (quoted by Robb, 2005, p. 22).

The cognitive model is based on the premises that thoughts influence emotions and behaviors and that distorted and maladaptive thoughts can be brought to awareness and changed, resulting in behavior change. Especially relevant to gambling, cognitive therapies emphasize the development of irrational cognitive schemas in response to early and repeated wins. These include illusions of control, biased thinking, the attribution of human qualities to gambling devices, and erroneous beliefs about the nature of randomness (Blaszczynski, 2000; Turner, 2000).

The most common errors include a false belief concerning the phenomenon of randomness and the extent to which outcomes could be predicted ("I've put so much money into this machine, it's bound to hit!") and the personification of the gambling machines or dice (giving them human qualities, as in "Come on baby!"). Gender comparisons in one small study ($n = 20$) revealed that women were more likely than men to personify slot machines (Delfabbro & Winefield, 2000). Other common distortions include (a) "the illusion of control," such as believing that conditions such as the choice of a dealer or a certain table, choosing a favorite slot machine, and walking into a casino through a certain entrance will enhance success; (b) "flexible attributions," such as transforming losses into "near wins," predicting a loss after it has happened by identifying "fluke" events that contribute to the loss; (c) the "availability bias," where a person judges an event's probability based on the sounds of winning around him or memories of highly publicized winners; and (d) the "fixation on absolute frequency," where the gambler measures the absolute frequency of wins (they win a lot because they gamble a lot), not the relative frequency (they lose more than they win) (Griffiths, 1994).

The role of the therapist in cognitive therapy is to help clients identify the irrational thoughts that influence them to continue to gamble, bring those thoughts to conscious awareness, monitor them, and replace them with rational and more adaptive thoughts (Davis, 2002).

Here are several questions that can serve to aid professional counselors in identifying gambling problems once clients are willing to proceed (derived from the criteria for diagnosis of pathological gambling from the *DSM–TR–IV*) (APA, 2000).

1. Have you ever borrowed money to gamble or cover lost money?
2. Have you ever thought you might have a gambling problem or been told that you might?
3. Have you ever been untruthful about the extent of your gambling or hidden it from others?
4. Have you ever tried to stop or cut back on how much or how often you gamble?

Answering yes to any one of these questions suggests a problem and indicates that further exploration would be useful.

Here are several practical suggestions that may help the individual with gambling problems avoid further problems:

1. Carry the minimum amount of money needed for that day.
2. Turn personal checks and credit cards over to the care of someone else.
3. Require an additional signature to withdraw money from a bank.
4. Voluntarily request a "ban" from frequented casinos and card rooms.
5. Avoid the company of other gamblers.
6. Avoid going to places where gambling is allowed.

As noted by Blanco et al. (2000), "After more than 10,000 years of the existence of the disorder, the field of pathological gambling research and treatment is still in its infancy" (p. 406). The bulk of the research has been done on male, not female, problem gamblers. Nevertheless, women with gambling problems (sometimes reported in the news in cases of embezzlement) are becoming more visible to the general public, and research studies have begun to focus on women and report gender differences that should be of interest to practitioners.

Policies of harm reduction for the community would minimize accessibility, disallow drinking at casinos, produce ads on TV about the risks of gambling addiction, and provide for treatment at little or no cost. All levels of government have a responsibility to develop policies and regulations to restrict the most addictive forms of gambling—those that carry high social costs, such as video gambling machines.

The opposite of harm reduction is seen in strategies used by gambling establishments to get people to fork over their money. Since casinos depend on enticing new gamblers to spend large sums of money, and approximately 30 to 40% of their revenues come from pathological gamblers, casino executives use marketing techniques based on principles of psychology. As described in an article in the *U.S. News & World Report,* slot machines are designed so players push buttons; this speeds up the process and leaves little time to think. To manipulate bettors, casino owners offer free drinks, use fake money such as chips so there's little reluctance to bet, use artificial lighting to mask the passage of time, have an absence of clocks, and even crowd slot machines to make it seem like there is a multitude of winners (Clark, 2005). A more subtle strategy is to design the slot machine so gamblers think they have suffered near misses. Another favorite technique is to inflate the patron's win ratio during the free introduction games. It is well known that if a first-time player loses, he or she probably won't come back. But if the player wins some money, the thrill is fantastic, and he or she might forever after be "chasing that first high." As with any addiction, the cues set off the brain's juices and the craving intensifies. The casino industry hires psychologists as consultants to help them boost their winnings while keeping customers coming back.

Some researchers have noted that casinos have jingling bells and whining sirens associated with the high of gambling. People get conditioned to the sound of bells, smell of cigarette smoke, and the glamour and glitz of the casino (Robb, 2005). People fast become addicted to the sensations of gambling just as the state becomes addicted to the enormous revenues generated.

To determine scientifically the proportion of revenue derived from problem as opposed to recreational gamblers, Canadian social scientists Williams and Wood (2004) paid a random sample of gamblers to fill out a diary of their gambling practices—wins, losses and which gambling devices they used. These researchers found that, on average, 35% of Ontario gambling revenue came from mild and severe problem gamblers and that males, Native populations, low-income persons, and single people were disproportionately represented. With gaming machines, the addiction rate is much higher; 62% of the revenue from this fast-paced equipment is derived from problem gamblers. Citing research that shows that casinos breed crime in the areas surrounding their location, Williams and Wood concluded that the social costs well outweighed the benefits.

SHOPPING ADDICTION

Shopping addiction and spending addiction derive from the same urge to get something for nothing, to drive a hard bargain, and the "urge to splurge." They are both examples of impulsive buying. The consequences in unpaid bills and wrecked families are the same as well. The problem isn't the shopping, of course; it's the buying of merchandise that one doesn't need or even later want that causes a momentary euphoria or high. Estimates are that between 2 and 8% of people in the United States are prone to shop compulsively (Stanford School of Medicine, 2003).

Compulsive shopping is a disorder of impulse control. Although compulsive shoppers may obsess about material possessions such as clothes, shopping addiction, at its core, is not about materialism or attachment to what consumers buy but rather about a lack of control over buying itself. The following self-description of a shopping addict, who is also "an exercise freak" and compulsive dieter, is typical:

> I also have this disorder in relation to shopping for clothes through mail-order catalogs. I have had it for a good 10 years but it probably started before that. I spend a lot of time every day thinking about, listing, planning for clothes that will go together if I order them and the costs involved and the time spent ordering, looking at the items over and over, etc. I have so many clothes now; I could probably go over a year and never wear the same thing twice. My common sense tells me that I have all I will ever need. My will to say no and not give in doesn't always work. I went 8 months last year without buying a thing. Then after my mom died, I got depressed and gave in and started buying all over again. This is kind of like alcoholics who can be sober for a period of time and something happens in their lives to drive them to drink again or becomes the excuse they use to drink again. It is the same for me as a shopaholic—I even worked with a company to figure out payments for the credit cards I have with mail-order companies to get them all paid off in 2 years. I was able to stick to the schedule for a while but am floundering again. I finally reached a point where I closed accounts as I paid each one off, and I wrote the mail preference service to have my name taken off mail-order lists. I hope I can be successful, but this is how I see obsessive-compulsive disorder. I have it. Thank God I don't drink, because with my family history I would probably be the all-or-nothing type. (personal communication, January 1999)

An assessment done at the University of Iowa on people with obsessive buying urges found that the typical troubled shopper was a 31-year-old female who had overspent for 13 years and was awash in clothing, shoes, and compact discs (Anderson, 1994). Most of those studied had multiple credit cards; many had bounced checks and fought with their spouse over money.

Mental health professionals say compulsive shoppers feel euphoric as they buy and spend. The druglike high following a purchase can lead to kleptomania, particularly if the money has run out (O'Leary, 2000). The index of the *DSM–IV–TR* does not include shopping dependence or any other listing for shopping. It does list *kleptomania,* defined as the stealing of items not needed, an act associated with a buildup of tension beforehand and gratification or relief afterward. Kleptomania, according to this source (APA, 2000), "may be associated with compulsive buying" (p. 667). This is not the usual form of shoplifting and characteristic of only around 5% of the U.S. population. Shopping addiction, or compulsive buying, isn't the usual form of shopping either.

Luvox is the drug prescribed by Dr. Donald Black, professor of psychiatry at the University of Iowa, who initially reported success in turning compulsive buyers into people who can pass through a store without making a purchase while buying only what they need. Later, when a placebo pill was used, success was also reported. Black attributed the success to the behavioral therapy that accompanied the medicine (Frankenfield, 1999). More research is currently under way. Promising results have been found in controlled studies with the antidepressant and serotonin enhancer citalopram (Celexa) (Stanford School of Medicine, 2003). Some credence is given to the neurobiological aspect of this disorder in the effectiveness of medication in its treatment. A further finding that compulsive shoppers are apt to have more than one psychiatric disorder, while their close relatives are likely to suffer from depression and a drug use disorder, is also indicative of a biological component in this disorder (Black, Repertinger, Gaffney, & Gabel, 1998).

In an interesting development, a woman facing up to 18 months in prison for the theft of $250,000 from her employer to finance her shopping addiction was sentenced to probation. The federal judge ruled that the defendant suffered from diminished mental capacity due to her shopping addiction (O'Connor, 2001).

Debtors Anonymous (DA) groups are springing up all over the United States (Lobet, 2000). DA members, like those in AA, first admit they have a problem and then try to fight it by devising a budget they can live with and a realistic repayment plan. According to the DA website, "Today numerous DA members come to us from court programs and counseling services, some arrive voluntarily; others do not. . . . Our primary purpose is to stay solvent ("Information for Professionals," 2006). Practical tips are to have only one or no credit cards, to shop with cash only, to avoid shopping or buying online, and to exercise when there is an urge to shop.

Related to compulsive buying is hoarding, or the refusal to throw anything away. Typically, hoarders have basements and rooms in their houses that look like flea markets or garbage dumps. This bizarre compulsion that makes it almost impossible for its sufferers to move around in their living space is thought to be a form of OCD (Neziroglu, Bubrick, & Yaryura-Tobias, 2004; Schwartz & Begley, 2003).

LOST IN CYBERSPACE

The media today are full of accounts of a new, technology-generated disorder variously called "computer addiction," "pathological Internet use," or "online obsession." There is even a special Web site for people who fear they are "caught in the Net": Netaddiction.com. The Internet's omnipresent offer of escape from reality, its accessibility, and the opportunity for anonymity can lure otherwise ordinary people to compulsive use (Kershaw, 2005). South Korea, which leads the world in per capita high-speed connections, takes Internet addiction and its treatment seriously. The Korean government is currently training psychiatrists all over the nation to help children who are addicted to the Net (Si-Young, 2006).

According to Netaddiction.com and the book *Caught in the Net* (Young, 1998), typical warning signs of this form of addiction are preoccupation with the Internet; spending increasing amounts of time online; failed attempts to control this compulsion; jeopardized relationships; lying behavior; and escape from problems. How do these heavy Internet users spend their time? Clinical research conducted by the psychologists associated with this website reveals that these users spend their time mainly in chat rooms (a practice that often leads to "Cyberaffairs") and in playing multiuser dungeon games. The cure offered on this website is online therapy at their "Virtual Clinic"!

According to recent surveys, approximately 8% of web users develop serious problems with their pastime (Stanford School of Medicine, 2006). Online activity is a fairly acceptable way of shifting consciousness: Some users enter a fantasy world where they "bare their souls" to strangers; often, they use fictitious names. Among employers, a real concern is that workers are using their office computers to enter chat rooms and pornography sites and to trade stocks. Internet activity at the workplace is increasingly being monitored, often with embarrassing results. Around 30% of companies have terminated employees for inappropriate Internet use as reported by the Stanford School of Medicine (2006). Consider, for example, this recent news story:

> **White Plains, New York** (AP)—A man who was fired by IBM for visiting an adult chat room at work is suing the company for $5 million, claiming he is an Internet addict who deserves treatment and sympathy rather than dismissal.
>
> James Pacenza, 58, of Montgomery, says he visits chat rooms to treat traumatic stress incurred in 1969 when he saw his best friend killed during an Army patrol in Vietnam.
>
> In papers filed in federal court in White Plains, Pacenza said the stress caused him to become "a sex addict, and with the development of the Internet, an Internet addict." He claimed protection under the Americans with Disabilities Act. ("Man Sues IBM over Firing," CNN, February 18, 2007)

Here are some harm reduction strategies for people whose Internet use is out of control: Set a kitchen timer and force yourself to log off when it rings; visit only sites needed for work or for information and don't detour; and cut back mailing list memberships.

Drawing on William Miller's motivational enhancement therapy (MET), Maressa Orzack (1999), a psychologist and coordinator of Computer Addiction Services, provides four sessions for compulsive Internet users. Sessions take place over a 3-month period. The MET methods are summarized by the acronym FRAMES (p. 8):

- *Feedback:* The therapist assesses the computer use of patients in great detail and reaffirms their acknowledgment of the need for help.
- *Responsibility:* Patients are told that they are responsible for changing their behavior.
- *Advice:* Patient and therapist together work out the goals, which include learning how to recognize the difference between healthy and addictive computer use.
- *Menu:* A schedule is devised by which the patient monitors computer use and the associated thoughts and feelings.
- *Empathy:* The efforts of patients are constantly reaffirmed, and they are not scolded for slips or failures.
- *Self-efficacy:* Patients learn to use the computer mainly for work, with the help of feedback through telephone contacts with the therapist. In the last session, therapist and patient review progress, renew motivation, and reaffirm the patient's commitment to change.

SEX ADDICTION

When former President Bill Clinton was battling allegations of multiple sexual transgressions, there was speculation that he might be the victim of sex addiction (Hamilton, 2003). Among the arguments put forward were that Clinton was prone to lying, he had an insatiable need to be loved, he grew up in an alcoholic and violent household, he learned to use sex as an escape, and he would risk all for reckless sexual intrigues (Levin, 1998). More recently, in conjunction with Republican Mark Foley's forced resignation for his history of seducing 16-year-old male pages, the topic of sex addiction has figured in the news once again (J. Smith, 2006). As Foley checked himself into a rehab center for alcoholism treatment, his lawyer announced to the public that Foley had been molested as a child by his priest, an accusation that was later oddly confirmed by the now elderly priest.

Despite the press and popular book accounts, there is no consensus that sex addiction is a bona fide disorder at all; sex addiction is not recognized by the American Medical Association or its Canadian counterpart, not even as an impulse disorder. Most clinicians, however, agree there is such a thing as pathological sexuality (G. Miller, 2005). But questions remain about whether this condition should be classified as an impulse-control disorder or as an addictive behavior (Goodman, 1997). The empirical data that could provide a basis for most statements about this subject are not yet available.

Defining elements of this addiction are secrecy and its escalating nature that often result in diminished judgment and self-control (Carnes, 2001). Sex addiction takes many forms. Carnes lists the range from obsessions with pornography and masturbation to the more dangerous forms of voyeurism, Cybersex, affairs, sex with strangers, and incest and rape.

In the minds of members of Sex Addicts Anonymous, there is no doubt that having "out of bounds" sex is an addiction. Sex addicts in this group may request to have sponsors help them monitor their behavior. Sobriety is defined as remaining "in the bounds." There are thousands of adherents to this self-help movement and over 790 Sex Addicts Anonymous meetings worldwide (Sex Addicts Anonymous, 2007).

The gender breakdown of sex addiction is unclear; it is generally conceived as a predominantly male problem. According to an article in the *Journal of Addictions Nursing*, sex addiction in women is increasingly recognized as a problem, although much of it is misconstrued as normal but sexually provocative behavior (Cyndi, 2004). The neurochemistry of addiction in the brain is relevant to this addiction. Women who compulsively act-out sexually in a compulsive manner are at high risk of contracting diseases and suffering violent victimization.

Therapists and other experts say the problem usually has its origins in childhood, often in homes plagued by addiction, violence, and sexual abuse of the child. Sex addicts tend to come from rigid, authoritarian families (Carnes, 2005). High-risk behavior typically progresses into riskier behavior. The addictive act, once it has begun, invariably fuels the problem with guilt, shame, lowered self-esteem, and isolation (G. Miller, 2005). These feelings in turn can lead to seeking a dangerous sexual situation, the thrill of which produces an intense adrenaline rush (Parker, 1998). Who the partner is makes little difference. Treatment consists of psychotherapy, group counseling, prescription medication in some cases, and referral to a self-help group. Therapists need to be cognizant of the use of Cybersex on the Internet, which includes pornographic sites and chat rooms (G. Miller, 2005).

COGNITIVE THERAPY AND THE STRENGTHS PERSPECTIVE

Distortions in thinking are common in all addictions, but they play a special role in the addictions discussed in this chapter. Compulsive gamblers, as we saw earlier, suffer from denial, superstitions, overconfidence when the rush is on, and/or an unrealistic sense of power or fate. Anorexics have the delusion that they are fat in conjunction with a phobia about being fat. Compulsive Internet users retreat into a fantasy world, and sex addicts and compulsive spenders keep having lapses in judgment. Common to all these addictions is the tendency toward extreme and immoderate behavior.

As far as the biological side of addiction is concerned, medication may provide a boost and be immensely helpful during the first stages of sobriety. And as for the social aspects, one's social world certainly plays a role in sustaining (or controlling) high-risk behavior. But in the final analysis, the psychological component is primary. The client, in conjuring up his or her inner resources, can channel biological impulses of a destructive sort into productive directions while controlling the social environment through the selection of friends and activities conducive to health.

Although cognitive-behavioral therapy (CBT) can be considered a specialized modality, such as the CBT strategies used in Project MATCH, a formulation that taught specific social skills and stress management techniques (Project MATCH Research Group, 1997), the *cognitive approach,* as the term is used here, is much broader. The focus of clients' thought patterns is characteristic of all the treatment modalities except for aversion treatment, in fact. The success of AA, OA, GA, and so on is due in part to the help they provide people in clearing up their "stinking thinking," in replacing thoughts conducive to harmful, addictive behavior with healthy, calming slogans, such as "one day at a time" or, as the Norwegians say, "Hurry slowly."

The method known as rational recovery (RR) is built almost exclusively on cognitive work. As Jack Trimpey (personal communication, November 30, 2000) describes it, "Rational recovery is purely a program of planned, permanent abstinence." Trimpey, an alcoholic who disliked AA, originally based RR on rational-emotive behavior therapy but then developed an online course for self-development. RR, therefore, no longer holds meetings but offers a for-profit crash course on its website (Volpicelli & Szalavitz, 2000).

Motivational interviewing (MI) is a strategy designed to mobilize a person's own motivation and resources for change (W. R. Miller & Rollnick, 2002). MI can be differentiated from other cognitive strategies in that its techniques are derived from principles of social psychology about getting people to change their behavior. Argumentation and confrontation are avoided in favor of a focus on "building up" rather than "tearing down." Motivational interviewing is both cognitively based and client centered at once. In contrast to MI, rational-emotive behavior therapy (REBT), formulated by Albert Ellis, is adversarial in tone. (The guidebook *Rational-Emotive Therapy with Alcoholics and Substance Abusers* [Ellis, McInerney, Di Giuseppe, & Yeager, 1989] contains an excellent chapter on unhealthy relationships, however. See also *Overcoming Destructive Beliefs, Feelings, and Behaviors* [Ellis, 2001].) Like CBT, of which it is a part, REBT concentrates on peoples' current beliefs, attitudes, and statements (van Wormer, 2007). Homework assignments are given, following assessment of the individual's thought patterns, to promote client awareness. Compared with harm reduction strategies, the REBT model is more authoritative; the therapist, in the role of educator, teaches the client what is wrong with his or her thinking. There is no "rolling with resistance" here. Much more negative are the cognitive principles presented by Yochelson and Samenow (1976) and Samenow (1984). Unfortunately, these theories and techniques, which are geared toward criminal thinking and manipulations, are commonly used in correctional addictions programming. In such programming, offenders are required to focus on their wrongdoings, with the goal of instilling self-disgust and a desire to reform their errant ways (see van Wormer, 2001).

Collaboration and choice are hallmarks of MI. Cognitive therapy, as Volpicelli and Szalavitz (2000) indicate, is often used in conjunction with motivational enhancement to help people unlearn what their addictive lifestyle has taught them. As with REBT, the focus is on thoughts (cognitions) and the addictive behaviors associated with them. The motivational therapist's style here is demonstrably different from the therapist's style, however. Instead of telling the client what is wrong, the MI therapist gets the client to achieve this insight and tell the therapist what is wrong (e.g., about continuing to gamble). Then therapist and client together collaborate to identify, assess, and plan for situations that may be problematic. These situations include negative emotional states, interpersonal conflict and stress, and social pressures. Having a balanced lifestyle and avoiding excess are emphasized throughout.

HOW TO ELICIT STRENGTHS

Self-defeating thoughts are intertwined with low feelings and a sense of fatalism. The leading cause of relapse is depression of this sort: "Who cares? I might as well go back to what I was doing before."

The starting point for behavior change is a collaborative analysis of the thinking and feeling realm. Developed by Aaron Beck in the 1970s, cognitive therapy is based on the theory that the way a person thinks determines how he or she feels and behaves (see Beck, 1991). Underlying most of the problems for which people seek counseling—depression, addiction, anger, violence—is an intensity of feeling or emotional pain. The challenge for the worker is to help the client separate the feelings from the thoughts and the thoughts from the actions as a first step toward alleviating the pain. The cognitive approach, so often used to break addicts' defenses, such as denial, can be much more effectively directed toward promoting motivation while at the same time building a sense of self-worth and awareness of inner strengths and capabilities.

McQuaide and Ehrenreich (1997) have devised a very useful, 38-item strengths questionnaire that the client can fill out together with the counselor. The complete questionnaire is provided in their article "Assessing Client Strengths" (p. 209). Among the agree–disagree items in this clinical instrument are the following: I am a creative person; I have an accurate view of my strengths and weaknesses; I think about my mistakes and learn from them; I have techniques I use to calm myself down when I'm upset. This thoughtful and positive questionnaire contains a wealth of valuable information.

Cowger, Anderson, and Snively (2006), similarly, provide helpful guidelines to help social workers assess individual strengths and resilient capacities through attentive listening to people's personal narratives. These authors have drawn up sample questions to facilitate the assessment process. Among these are: Is there anything about yourself that you feel you were born with that has helped you in your life? Are there any religious or spiritual activities that helped you in your life? Are you involved in any activities that "give back" or help others? (p. 108). To these we can add: Can you tell about a time when you successfully handled a problem that confronted you? Where did you find the strength to deal with those challenges? How have your family members helped you get through this situation? How have you managed to cope up to this point? What do other people like about you? What have you learned from your situation?

When counselors think from a strengths-based perspective, questions such as these emerge naturally. Building on client strengths may require looking at a client's problems from a different angle. The strengths assessment process itself, as Rapp and Goscha (2006) suggest, is often experienced by clients as a unique experience because they are not used to thinking of their talents and dreams. This exercise is highly motivating as the client recalls past successes long forgotten. Helping clients see the well part of themselves is a way to reinforce their wellness.

W. R. Miller and Rollnick (2002) recommend pretreatment testing such as addictions inventories not only for screening purposes but as a foundation for motivational counseling. Test results can be very helpful in mobilizing the client toward commitment for change. Results can be presented with a prefatory comment, as the authors recommend (p. 150), that emphasizes freedom of choice: "I don't know what you will make of this result but . . . ." Any scare-tactic tone is avoided. Finding the positive in test results gives a boost to an approach centered on uncovering client strengths. A cautionary reminder: The role of "expert" should be underplayed; the client and helper *collaborate* on figuring things out (Saleebey, 2006). Clients are usually the experts on their own situation; *they* are the ones who have been there, after all.

SELF-TALK AND POSITIVE REFRAMING

Through the learning of positive "self-talk" and cognitive restructuring, clients can be actively helped to replace unhealthy thought processes with healthy and productive ones. In leading a client to awareness of his or her own resources and the possibility of utilizing them, the strengths perspective joins the cognitive approach. Self-defeating patterns of behavior, we need to remember, are often associated with criminality as well as addictive behavior. The legal and social problems that result in turn compound the original negativism and even fatalism.

One way out of this maze of destruction is through collaborative work with a therapist to help eliminate illogical and/or self-defeating thought patterns. Positive self-talk is taught by the counselor's juxtaposition of the client's defeatist cognition—"I might as well quit"—with more encouraging pronouncements—"I can do it; I've done it before!" The client can be trained to say "Stop!" when the old ideas appear and then to very deliberately substitute new formulations for them. Often, the client may have been previously unaware of the destructive nature of the thoughts that were going through his or her head as well as of their emotionally draining power. The underlying premise of this approach is the belief that people's cognitions, or the way they view the world, and their motivation to improve their life circumstances are intertwined.

Sometimes, as in the case of a younger woman suffering from bulimia, the self-destructive behavior and low self-esteem are rooted in the past as an outgrowth of early sexual trauma. This abuse often does not end in childhood but continues as a damaging feature of adult experiences as well. Theorists writing about motivational interviewing and cognitive therapy nevertheless focus only on "the here and now." The Twelve-Step program, similarly, and even the emphasis on sharing your "experience, strength, and hope," presents a largely present-oriented focus. That you can't change the past and that what happened in the past is just an excuse for bad behavior are the themes of most modern-day approaches, including many in social work.

The cognitive approach can be reformulated, however, to incorporate the past, to help women and men come to terms with their lives, and to see themselves as survivors rather than victims of their childhood. "Start where the client is"—this is a theme of social work. If the client's problems (and low self-esteem) are rooted in the past, that is the place to begin. The unconscious mind knows neither past nor present; sometimes, to go forward, you have to trace your steps backward and find out where you took a wrong turn. The cognitive techniques of restructuring our view of the past are essential to self-acceptance. The cognitive framework is ideally suited for this task.

The repetitive nature of information provided to clients in the early stage of recovery serves to reinforce learning and memory. New members of Twelve-Step groups are continually restructuring self-defeating beliefs through slogans such as "Easy does it" and "Let go and let God." When the thinking gets a little frantic or the "old tapes" start playing again, the universally known Serenity Prayer may be said: "God grant me the serenity to accept the things I cannot change, the courage to change the things I can, and the wisdom to know the difference."

Feeling Work

Treatment centers often have clients list their losses in connection with their addictive behaviors. Sometimes, they have to add up the costs in dollars as well. Such exercises, however, only reinforce the negative feelings of loss, compounded now with public shame as these "consequences" are shared in a group. Compulsive gamblers and spenders have problems enough with self-flagellation; there is no need to accentuate these kinds of thoughts. It would be better to provide information concerning how slot machine owners bilk their customers or how marketers of products seduce unwitting buyers. Information concerning the brain and addiction can help the client overwhelmed with the consequences of his of her behavior make sense of things. Being with others in a supportive group can bring home the awareness that good people can make foolish choices.

Anger Management   Male gamblers who have "lost it all" may be consumed with anger; they may displace this anger on their family members. Their female counterparts may be unaware of the anger, which has become internalized, and be overcome with depression or guilt. Among addicts in recovery, anger may cause problems both in its suppression and its manifestation (e.g., periodic explosions of rage). Sometimes, anger at one object (e.g., the judicial system) is displaced onto another (e.g., the counselor or correctional officer).

Knowledge of feelings and the thought processes connected with these feelings ("I hate my mother," "I hate myself") help clients work toward change. Sheafor, Horejsi, and Horejsi (1997) describe four guidelines for helping clients get in touch with their feelings. These can be summarized as follows:

1. Identify what you are feeling and thinking right now.
2. Listen to your self-talk. Look for extremes in thinking—avoid the use of words such as *never, can't, always,* and *everybody.*
3. Examine objective reality. Once the facts are identified, relax, take a deep breath, and repeat them *out loud* three times. (For example, "I used drugs to escape from problems. I now have learned solid coping skills and I have been clean for two years. My children are proud of me. My life is not ruined.")
4. Note how your feelings change. (p. 474)

Sometimes, anger that surfaces is a cover for another deeper emotion, such as a feeling of betrayal or even insecurity. An intriguing question to ask the perpetually angry client is, "If you weren't feeling anger, what would you be feeling?" The answer may be a revelation to the client as well as to the therapist.

Some women who have difficulty labeling or expressing anger become compulsive housecleaners, energizing themselves in the endless war on dust and dirt. Such individuals need coaching to help them learn to absorb the angry feeling without fear and to mobilize that energy in a positive direction. Assertiveness training can help people get their needs met. Persons who have difficulty containing their anger should work on the de-escalating techniques of anger management.

Anger management training teaches the origins of anger, what triggers extreme anger and why, and that there is nothing wrong with having stormy feelings. Learning to express anger verbally and calmly—for example, to say, "When you do . . . I feel insulted (or rejected, or annoyed)"—instead of lashing out physically or with cursing is the kind of training that can be offered in groups. Group members enhance their self-esteem as they take more responsibility for themselves and learn to channel the energy that goes into outbursts of anger into more productive and rewarding directions.

One anger management program with a lot of promise is described by Demaree and Harrison (2003) as an outgrowth of ongoing neurological research that examined the link between hostility and brain chemistry. Hostile people might have deficits on the right side of the cerebrum and an inability to control negative emotions or simply a lack of awareness of physiological changes that occur when they are angry. Teaching people to be more self-aware of bodily cues, such as a racing heart, can help them to protect themselves from chronic anger.

Venting anger inappropriately not only might get the client in trouble but also might actually increase his or her level of hostility. This is what psychology research has always shown, in fact (American Psychological Association, 2006). Repression is bad, but the unhealthy release of anger (e.g., beating the dog) is bad as well. A healthier response would be to pet the dog. Bushman (2002) recommends this method of deferring anger. His conclusion is derived from his experimental research on a large sample of students in an anger-inducing situation. Students who vented their anger on a punching bag demonstrated an escalation of aggression compared to a control group who did not vent their anger. Table 7.1 lists healthy ways to deal with anger.

STRESS MANAGEMENT   Stress is considered a major precipitant of relapse in humans (Koob, 2006). This is understandable in that stress hormones interfere with sleep and create a heightened alertness; the heart and breathing rates increase, and blood pressure rises (Johnson, 2004). The perpetual nervousness

TABLE 7.1 | DEALING WITH ANGER

Goal	Means of Achievement
Learn to control angry outbursts	Use "time-outs"
Reduce feelings of anger	Find healthy outlets for feelings of anger—exercise
Lessen periods of angry thoughts	Use healthy self-talk to replace angry thoughts
End violent, angry outbursts	Learn to verbalize the reasons for anger; join an anger management group
When appropriate, feel the anger	Explore the socialization history of your anger suppression; assertiveness training

that plagues many individuals with addiction problems can be readily reduced through cognitive therapy techniques. Worrying, anxiety-provoking self-talk ("My kids will hate me; my parents will never forgive me") can be replaced with new ways of thinking ("I'll do my best to explain things; they'll be happy to see how much healthier I am now that I'm sober").

Some commonly set therapeutic goals pertaining to fear and anxiety are learning to handle fears, managing to face fears calmly, identifying what one is truly afraid of, and being emotionally prepared for likely outcomes. Imagining the worst possible thing that can happen is often helpful. For clients who have phobias, or irrational fears, the origins of the phobias should be traced. Behavioral treatment provides for exposure to the feared source (e.g., a snake) in slow steps until the panic response is extinguished.

Teaching the development of adaptive coping skills to stress is a vital part of relapse prevention (Wallace). Such training is based on the identification of high-risk situations where negative emotions are strong. Skills training is a method that can increase the client's sense of control in a threatening situation. Research has verified the effectiveness of such training that often consists of rehearsal and role-play (Wallace, 2005).

Through cutting down on the use of stimulants, such as coffee and tea, physical anxiety can be reduced greatly. A drink of warm milk at any time can produce a quieting effect. When adrenaline is high, brisk exercise aids in using up the excess energy and enhancing relaxation. The usefulness of physical exercise as a treatment intervention has been verified in empirically conducted studies with animals and humans (Johnson, 2004). For persons with co-occurring disorders, exercise has been shown highly effective, yet it is used too rarely. Results indicate significantly reduced levels of both anxiety and depression by virtue of the physical training provided.

Perfectionism is almost always a part of the compulsiveness found in pathological dieting; it also may play into the relentless drive to strike it rich through gambling or day trading on the Internet. The perfectionism itself is not a side effect of these disorders but a personality trait that puts people at risk for these problems and for substance misuse as well ("Persistent Perfectionists," 1996).

ALL-OR-NOTHING THINKING   An all-or-nothing mode of thinking causes people to get trapped in their destructive behavior. "I can't quit until I hit the jackpot" is typical of this line of thought. An anonymous graduate student describes this phenomenon "to a tee":

> People who are all-or-nothing thinkers need to be the best at things or they are not worth trying. An example of a situation involving several all-or-nothing thinkers could be found within a casino. I have gone with people to the casino who had the attitude that they were either going to win big or lose all of their money. An interesting thing about one such person is, even if he gets $100 ahead in the casino, he still does not stop. This does not seem to be big enough of a win for these people, who end up staying until they lose all that they had just won.

Some people with weight disorders also have all-or-nothing thinking. They may feel that if they cannot have the perfect figure, then why even try to diet or exercise.

Examples of illogical beliefs, in a checklist that can be used very effectively in group sessions, may include the following:

- All-or-nothing thinking.
- Jumping to negative conclusions.
- Overgeneralizing about others.
- Making mountains out of molehills.
- Putting down members of your own group (e.g., other women).
- Self-blaming.
- "I can't live without" a certain person.
- I must be perfect.
- Everyone must like me.
- If things do not go according to plan, it is a catastrophe.
- I never forgive or forget a wrong.
- People are either all good or all bad.
- Victims of crime have themselves to blame.

Sometimes, the simple act of realizing that one's present thinking is irrational brings about a major improvement in this area. In talking to a counselor who is nonjudgmental and enthusiastic about analyzing thought processes we all share, clients will begin to question and challenge many of their long-held assumptions and find they can change the way they feel (depressed, anxious, guilty) by being more accepting of themselves and of others.

USE OF HUMOR   One of the best ways to conquer the kind of catastrophizing and fatalistic thinking that lead to dangerous forms of escape (from indulgence in addictive behavior to suicide) is through the use of humor. Humor provides perspective on the human condition and on one's personality quirks in a healthy way. In many treatment centers, unfortunately, clowning and laughing are pathologized and off limits. The episode in the movie *28 Days* effectively captures this tradition. After Gwen, the young woman sentenced to 28-day rehab, cracks a joke, a counselor asks her, "Do you always use humor to deflect things when you're uncomfortable?"

In recognition of the contribution it makes to group bonding and enjoyment, the typical AA meeting uses humor quite a bit. Here are a few examples collected by van Wormer over the years:

- A man attending an AA meeting said he was like Dr. Jekyll and Mr. Hyde when drunk. "Too bad you sobered up the wrong one," a member called out.
- A good Irish joke is "Last week I drank only twice, once for three days, once for four."
- There is even a group for paranoid people. It's called Paranoids Anonymous—PA. The only problem is if you call the number in the phonebook, they won't tell you where they are.

EXERCISES FOR FEELING WORK IN THE GROUP

Consistent with the principles of strengths-based MI as described in this chapter are the following exercises. Such exercises can be used to provide structure for a therapy group. The focus of these activities is on allowing deep feelings to arise spontaneously in a warm, supportive group setting.

1. Art Therapy
   Purposes: To reveal feelings that may not be expressed. May bring out perfectionism as a secondary function.

   Have clients draw their world during the time before they came to treatment, during treatment, and after treatment. Clients are told they can draw stick-people; there's no need for talent. This exercise, seriously undertaken, gives an indication of future hopes and fears. Those who, because of lack of confidence or anxiety, resist this exercise can have someone else draw what they describe in words.

2. Turning Points
   Purpose: To promote critical thinking about one's life and reinforce change from a life of crime.

   Have participants as a homework assignment write about or prepare to tell about a turning point in their lives. At the next session, they will share their revelations.

3. Faces
   Purpose: To elicit discussion of feelings.

   Use a sheet of faces with diverse expressions on them. Simple cartoon faces, including duck faces, are effective. This exercise works with non-readers and equally well with men and women. Give the following instructions: "Choose the face that shows how you feel today and also one that shows how you felt earlier in the week. Each of you will share your selection with the group."

4. Grief and Loss
   Purpose: To reveal underlying feelings of grief and guilt over loss.

   On a sheet of paper have clients:

   a. Identify a significant loss. (This can be a person, a job, or some other loss.)
   b. Describe the support you have received for the loss and what you have learned from this experience.

5. Quiz Cards
   Purposes: To share in the group; to elicit a wide range of responses. This exercise is a continuation of the card game described in an earlier group exercise in chapter 5. These questions call for deeper level responses.
   Examples:
   When I think of my mother _____
   When I remember my father _____
   Eating, spending money, cocaine, heroin, etc. was for me _____

Sobriety is _____

As a child, I was lucky I had _____

Love is _____

I feel proud of myself for _____

6. Dream Analysis

Purpose: To help clients get in touch with a part of themselves they may have little awareness of.

Give an ongoing homework assignment for participants to record their dreams on paper immediately after they have them. Then have those who can remember them share their dreams in the group as members look for meanings. Themes to look for are fears, anxieties, anger, forgiveness, attempts to communicate with loved ones, sobriety issues, and return of repressed memories. This often-untapped resource of recalling dream content can speak to group members, often in unexpected ways. Dream content can provide counselor and group members with clues about the individual's readiness to make changes. (Native Americans are often very skilled at remembering and learning from their dreams.)

7. Assertiveness

Purpose: Clients in treatment, when asked to set a goal for themselves, often say they would like to be more assertive or to work on assertiveness. Assertiveness training is geared toward persons who come across as aggressive when they do not intend to and persons who need to learn to speak up for themselves to have their interests met. Assertive behavior involves expressing preferences without undue anxiety in a manner that will be well received by others. Alternatives to aggressive reactions include calming self-talk, making polite requests, and reframing situations so that they do not overwhelm the individual (Gambrill, 1997). The University of Texas Counseling and Mental Health Center provides assertiveness workshop guidelines for use by professionals at www.utexas.edu/student/cmhc/clearinghouse/TI007.html. These materials are free of charge.

SUMMARY AND CONCLUSION

In vulnerable individuals, influences by the mass media and corporate marketing create situations ripe for problems with overeating or self-starvation, buying products never used or needed, and games turned into nightmares. In this chapter, as in others, we looked at the biological, psychological, and social factors related to the addictions in question: eating disorders, gambling, shopping, sex, and Internet addiction, among others. Research using new brain imaging techniques indicates that gambling may share the same addictive process and have similar effects as those produced by psychoactive drugs. New medications are currently being developed to target the dopamine and serotonin levels in the brain to quell addictive urges.

We chose this chapter as one to present a focus that is psychologically based—the theory and therapy of cognitions. Cognitively based therapy has been found very effective in helping people cope with their problems and stresses and, somewhat remarkably, if the reports from studies on obsessive-compulsive disorder are accurate, to promote recovery of the brain as well. Although usually geared toward thinking and feeling patterns related to the disorder at hand, cognitive therapy is also suitable for helping clients deal with past issues. From the vantage point of today, clients can begin to view themselves as survivors rather than as victims of their lives. From a strengths perspective, a counselor can help clients reframe their life stories to identify strengths and survival skills that were all but taken for granted until then. In so doing, they might let go of some of the anger they have felt for family members as well.

Speaking of stories, in this chapter, we have heard from a self-starved ballerina, a bulimic student whose desperate practices landed her in the hospital, an overweight Irishman who gave OA and later AA a try, and a youth counselor who unwittingly got in "over his head" with compulsive betting. What these narrators all had in common, apart from their addictive behavior, was that they eventually got the help they needed for a new start in life. Some of the techniques they might have learned in treatment were presented here: stress management, anger management, and ways to deal with powerful feelings and somehow get beyond them. In the next chapter, we will see how many of these same interventions can be adapted to serve the needs of clients with co-occurring disorders—that is, who are mentally ill and have serious substance use problems as well.

REFERENCES

American Psychiatric Association (APA). (2000). *Diagnostic and statistical manual of mental disorders, text revision* (4th ed.). Washington, DC: Author.

American Psychological Association. (2006). Controlling anger before it controls you. Retrieved March 2006 from http://www.apa.org/pubinfo.

Andersen, A. E. (1999). Gender-related aspects of eating disorders: A guide to practice. *Journal of Gender-Specific Medicine, 2*(1), 47–54.

Anderson, J. (1994, July 15). Shop till you drop. *Chicago Tribune*, p. 15.

Anorexia, bulimia, found more dangerous in men. (2000, June 7). *Chicago Tribune*, evening update, p. 7.

Arizona Council on Compulsive Gambling. (2000). Retrieved from http://www.azccg.org.

Associated Press. (2006, August 25). Lawyers sentenced for embezzling $3.1 million from Nevada casino. *Las Vegas Sun*. Retrieved September 2006 from http://www.lasvegassun.com.

Bacanu, S. A., Bulik, C., Klump, K., Fichter, M., Halmi, K., Keel, P., et al. (2005). Linkage analysis of anorexia and bulimia nervosa cohorts using selected behavioral phenotypes as quantitative traits or covariates. *American Journal of Medical Genetics, 139*(1), 61–68.

Beaucar, K. O. (1999, October). When games turn into nightmares. *NASW News*, p. 3.

Beck, A. (1991). Cognitive therapy: A 30-year retrospective. *American Psychologist, 46*(4), 368–375.

Berg, I., & Miller, S. (1992). *Working with the problem drinker: A solution-focused approach*. New York: Norton.

Bergevin, T., Gupta, R., Derevensky, J., & Kaufman, F. (2006). Adolescent gambling: Understanding the role of stress and coping. *Journal of Gambling Studies, 22*(2), 195–208.

Black, D. W., Repertinger, S., Gaffney, G. R., & Gabel, J. (1998). Family history and psychiatric comorbidity in persons with compulsive buying. *American Journal of Psychiatry, 155*, 960–963.

Blanco, C., Ibanez, A., Saiz-Ruiz, J., Blanco-Jerez, C., & Nunes, E. (2000). Epidemiology, pathophysiology and treatment of pathological gambling. *CNS Drugs, 13*(6), 397–407.

Blaszczynski, A. (2000, March). Pathways to pathological gambling: Identifying typologies. *E-Gambling: Electronic Journal of Gambling Issues, 1*. Retrieved from http://www.camh.net/egambling/issue1/feature.

Bulik, C., Bacanu, S. A., Klump, K., Fichter, M., Halmi, K., Keel, P., et al. (2005). Selection of eating disorders phenotypes for linkage analysis. *American Journal of Medical Genetics, 139*(1), 81–87.

Bushman, B. (2002). Does venting anger feed or extinguish the flame? Catharsis, rumination, distraction, anger, and aggressive responding. *Personality and Social Psychological Bulletin, 28*, 724–731.

Carnes, P. (2001). *Out of the shadows: Understanding sexual addiction.* Center City, MN: Hazelden.

Carnes, P. (2005). *Facing the shadow: Starting sexual and relationship recovery.* Carefree, AZ: Gentle Path Press.

Chhabra, D., Lutz, G., & Gonnerman, M. (2005). *Socioeconomic impact of gambling on Iowans: Final report.* Des Moines: Iowa Legislative Council.

Christian Science Monitor. (2006, August 1). Tempting the temptation of Web casinos. *Christian Science Monitor*, p. 8.

Clark, K. (2005, May 23). Against the odds. *U.S. News & World Report*, pp. 47–54.

Claude-Pierre, P. (1997). *The secret language of eating disorders.* New York: Times Books.

Cowger, C. D., Anderson, K., & Snively, C. (2006). Assessing strengths: The political context of individual, family, and community empowerment. In C. Saleebey (Ed.), *The strengths perspective in social work practice* (4th ed., pp. 93–115). Boston: Allyn & Bacon.

Cox, B., Yu, N., Afifi, T., & Ladouceur, R. (2005). A national survey of gambling problems in Canada. *Canadian Journal of Psychiatry, 50*(4), 213–217.

Cyndi, R. (2004). Sex addiction and women: A nursing issue. *Journal of Addictions Nursing, 15*(2), 53–62.

Davis, D. (2002). Queen of diamonds: Women and compulsive gambling. In S. L. Straussner & S. Brown (Eds.), *The handbook of women's addictions treatment: Theory and practice.* New York: Jossey-Bass.

Davis, R. D., & Avery, L. (2004). Women who have taken their lives back from compulsive gambling. Results from an online survey. *Journal of Social Work Practice in the Addictions, 4*(1), 61–80.

Davison, K. K., & Birch, L. L. (2001). Weight status, parent reaction, and self-concept in five-year-old girls. *Pediatrics, 107*(1), 46–53.

De Angelis, T. (2002). Promising treatments for anorexia and bulimia. *Monitor on Psychology, 33*(3). Retrieved February 2007 from http://www.apa.org/monitor/mar02/promising.html.

Delfabbro, P., & Winefield, A. (2000). Predictors of irrational thinking in regular slot machine gamblers. *Journal of Psychology, 134*(2), 117–128.

Demaree, H. A., & Harrison, D. W. (2003). Physiological and neuropsychological correlates of hostility. In P. K. Lehman, C. Dula, & J. Finney (Eds.), *Introductory psychology recitation reader* (pp. 27–37). Boston: McGraw-Hill.

DeNoon, D. (2005, September 20). Scientists not on trail of bulimia genes. *WebMD Medical News*. Retrieved September 2006 from http://www.medicinent.com.

Eating disorders start in brain. (2001, April 9). *USA Today*, p. 4D.

Ellis, A. (2001). *Overcoming destructive beliefs, feelings, and behaviors: New directions for rational emotive behavior therapy*. Essex, UK: Prometheus Books.

Ellis, A., McInerney, J. F., DiGiuseppe, R., & Yeager, R. J. (1989). *Rational-emotive therapy with alcoholics and substance abusers*. New York: Pergamon Press.

Evans, J. (2004, October 1). Pathological gambling differs in females, teens. *Family Practice News, 34*(19), 39–40.

Fairleigh Dickinson University. (2006). New Jersey seniors gamble away. Public mind poll. Retrieved February 2007 from http://publicmind.fdu.edu/gamble.

Fossati, M., Amati, F., Painot, D., Reiner, M., Haenni, C., & Golay, A. (2004). Cognitive-behavioral therapy with simultaneous nutritional and physical activity education in obese patients with binge eating disorder. *Eating and Weight Disorder, 9*(2), 134–138.

Frankenfield, G. (1999, December 21). Could popping a pill help those who shop 'til they drop? *Lycos Health*. WebMD. Retrieved from http://www.WebMD.lycos.com.

Gamblers Anonymous (GA). (1999). *Sharing recovery through Gamblers Anonymous*. Los Angeles: Author.

Gamblers Anonymous (GA). (2000). *Gamblers Anonymous: A new beginning* (4th ed.). Los Angeles: Author.

Gambrill, E. (1997). *Social work practice: A critical thinker's guide*. New York: Oxford University Press.

Gerke, C., Mazzeo, S., & Kliewer, W. (2006, October 30). The role of depression and dissociation in the relationship between childhood trauma and bulimic symptoms among ethnically diverse female undergraduates. *Child Abuse and Neglect, 10*, 1161–1172.

Goodman, A. (1997). Sexual addiction. In J. H. Lowinson, P. Ruiz, R. B. Millman, & J. G. Langrod (Eds.), *Substance abuse: A comprehensive textbook* (3rd ed., pp. 340–354). Baltimore: Williams & Wilkins.

Griffiths, M. (1994). The role of cognitive bias and skill in fruit machine gambling. *British Journal of Psychology, 85*, 351–369.

Grinols, E. (2004). *Gambling in America: Costs and benefits*. Cambridge, England: Cambridge University Press.

Granju, K. (2006, August 17). College class president blames gambling addiction for robbery conviction. Knoxville, TN: WBIR. Retrieved September 2006 from http://www.wbir.com.

Grant, J. E., & Kim, S. W. (2002). Effectiveness of pharmacotherapy for pathological gambling: A chart review. *Annals of Clinical Psychiatry, 14*(3), 155–161.

Hamilton, N. (2003). *Bill Clinton: An American journey: Great expectations*. New York: Random House.

Hershey, R. D. (1999, May 21). Workers ignore jobs to trade stocks on Net. *Lexington Herald-Leader*, p. A11.

Holm, K. (2006, July 30). Dying to be thin. *Courier, Waterloo–Cedar Falls*, pp. A1, A7.

Hornbacher, M. (1998). *Wasted: A memoir of anorexia and bulimia*. New York: Harper Flamingo.

Hudson, J. I., Hiripi, E., Pope, H., & Kessler, R. C. (2007). The prevalence and correlates of eating disorders in the national comorbidity survey replication. *Biological Psychiatry, 61*(3), 348–358.

Information for professionals. (2006). Debtors Anonymous. Retrieved October 2006 from http://www.debtorsanonymous.org/professionals.htm.

Johnson, H. C. (2004). *Psyche and synapse explaining worlds: The role of neurobiology in emotions, behavior, thinking, and addiction for non-scientists* (2nd ed.). Greenfield, MA: Deerfield Valley.

Kaye, W., Bulik, C., Thornton, L., Barbarich, N., & Masters, K. (2004). Comorbidity of anxiety disorders with anorexia and bulimia nervosa. *American Journal of Psychiatry, 161,* 2215–2221.

Kearney, M. (2005). The economic winners and losers of legalized gambling. *National Tax Journal, 58*(2), 281–303.

Kershaw, S. (2005, December 1). Hooked on the web. *New York Times.* Retrieved September 2006 from http://www.nytimes.com/2005/12/01/fashion.

Kirkland, G. (1986). *Dancing on my grave.* New York: Jove Books.

Koob, G. (2006). The neurobiology of addiction. In W. R. Miller & K. Carroll (Eds.), *Rethinking substance abuse* (pp. 25–45), New York: Guilford Press.

LairRobinson, R. (1997). Men and gambling. In S. L. Straussner & E. Zelvin (Eds.), *Gender and addictions: Men and women in treatment* (pp. 471–492). Northvale, NJ: Jason Aronson.

Levin, J. D. (1998). *The Clinton syndrome: The president and the self-destructive nature of sexual addiction.* New York: Random House.

Lobet, I. (2000, September 18). Shopaholics climb on the wagon. *U.S. News & World Report,* p. 60.

Man sues IBM over firing, says he's an Internet addict. (2007, February 18). CNN. Retrieved February 2007 from http://www.cnn.com/2007/LAW.

Many bulimic women were abused as kids, study says. (1995, July 10). *Toronto Globe and Mail,* p. 6.

Maté, G. (1999). *Scattered: How attention deficit disorder originates and what you can do about it.* New York: Plume.

McCourt, M. (2000). *Singing my him song.* New York: HarperCollins.

McQuaide, S., & Ehrenreich, J. H. (1997, March/April). Assessing client strengths. *Families in Society,* pp. 201–212.

Medical News Today. (2006a, November 27). Study offers new clues to brain-stomach interaction in overeating. Retrieved November 27, 2006, from http://www .medicalnewstoday.com.

Medical News Today. (2006b, September 5). Tanning addiction exists, study. Retrieved September 2006 from http://www.medicalnewstoday.com.

Messerlian, C., Derevensky, J., & Gupta, R. (2005). Youth gambling patterns: A public health perspective. *Health Promotion International, 20*(1), 69–79.

Miller, G. (2005). *Learning the language of addiction counseling* (2nd ed.). New York: Wiley.

Miller, W. R., & Rollnick, S. (2002). *Motivating interviewing: Preparing people to change addictive behavior* (2nd ed.). New York: Guilford Press.

Muelleman, R., DenOtter, T., Wadman, M. C., Tran, T. P., & Anderson, J. (2002). Problem gambling in the partner of the emergency department patient. *Journal of Emergency Medicine, 23*(3), 307–312.

National Center on Addiction and Substance Abuse (CASA). (2003). *Food for thought: Substance abuse and eating disorders.* New York: Columbia University. Retrieved September 2006 from http://www.casacolumbia.org/absolutenm/?a=350.

National Gambling Impact Study Commission. (1999, June 18). *Report of the commission*. Washington, DC: U.S. Government Printing Office. Retrieved October 2006 from http://govinfo.library.unt.edu/ngisc/index.html.

National Institute of Mental Health (NIMH). (2006). *Eating disorders*. Retrieved September 2006 from http://www.nimh.nih.gov/publicat/eatingdisorders.cfm.

National Research Council. (1999, April 1). *Report of the commission: Pathological gambling: A critical review*. Washington, DC: National Academy Press.

Newsome, M. (2005, September). Not just for kids. *Time*, p. W12.

Neziroglu, F., Bubrick, J., & Yarura-Tobias, J. (2004). *Overcoming compulsive hoarding: Why you save and how you can stop*. Oakland, CA: New Harbinger.

O'Connor, M. (2001, May 24). Judge buys shopaholic defense in embezzling. Retrieved from http://www.chicagotribune.com.

O'Leary, S. (2000, November 23). *Shopping addiction: Out-of-control spending can ruin lives and families*. Retrieved from http://healthsurfing.com/health/2000/11/23/?p=1.

Oregon Department of Corrections. (2004, June 14). CCCF (Coffee Creek Correctional Facility) helps inmate with gambling problem. Retrieved September 2006 from http://egov.oregon.gov/DOC.

Orzack, M. H. (1999, January). Computer addiction: Is it real or virtual? *Harvard Mental Health Letter, 15*(7), 1–8.

Parker, M. (1998, April 8). Addiction to sex. *Waterloo–Cedar Falls Courier*, p. C5.

Pavalko, R. M. (1999). Problem gambling. *National Forum, 79*(4), pp. 28–34.

Persistent perfectionists. (1996, May/June). *Psychology Today, 29*(3), 11.

Peterson, K. (2006, May 23). 48 states raking in gambling proceeds. Pew Research Center. Retrieved from http://www.stateline.org.

Petry, N., Stinson, F., & Grant, B. (2005). Comorbidity of *DSM–IV* pathological gambling and other psychiatric disorders: Results from the national epidemiologic survey on alcohol and related conditions. *Journal of Clinical Psychiatry, 66,* 564–574.

Pew Research Center. (2006). *Gambling: As the take rises, so does public concern*. Washington, DC: Author

Pietrzak, R., & Petry, N. (2005). Antisocial personality disorder is associated with increased severity of gambling, medical, drug, and psychiatric problems. *Addiction, 100*(8), 1183–1193.

Preuschoff, K., Bossaerts, P., & Quartz, S., (2006). Neural differentiation of unexpected rewards and risk in human subcortical structures. *Neuron, 51,* 381–390.

Project MATCH Research Group. (1997). Matching alcoholism treatments to client heterogeneity: Project MATCH post treatment drinking outcomes. *Journal of Studies on Alcohol, 58,* 7–29.

Rapp, C. A., & Goscha, R. (2006). *The strengths model: Case management with people with psychiatric disabilities* (2nd ed.). New York: Oxford University Press.

Ringham, R., Klump, K., Kaye, W., Stone, D., Libman, S., Stowe, S., et al. (2006). Eating disorder symptomatology among ballet dancers. *International Journal of Eating Disorders, 39*(6), 503–508.

Robb, M. (2005, November/December). Gambling USA: What every social worker should know. *Social Work Today*, pp. 18–22.

Rogers, R., & Goodwin, G. (2005). Lithium may reduce gambling severity in pathological gamblers with bipolar disorder. *Evidence Based Mental Health, 8,* 80.

Russo, F. (2005, October 31). Ante up, ladies: As poker mania grips the nation, more women are mastering the game. *Time, 166*(18), W6.

Saleebey, D. (2006). Introduction: Power in the people. In D. Saleebey (Ed.), *The strengths perspective in social work practice* (4th ed., pp. 1–24). Boston: Allyn & Bacon.

Samenow, S. E. (1984). *Inside the criminal mind*. New York: Times Books.

Schwartz, J. M., & Begley, S. (2003). *The mind and the brain: Neuroplasticity and the power of mental force*. New York: Regan Books.

Science Daily. (2000, November 7). Twin study suggests genetic link between craving alcohol, sweets. University of North Carolina, Chapel Hill. Retrieved October 2006 from http://www.sciencedaily.com/releases.

Science Daily. (2005, April 25). Pathological gambling associated with brain impairments. Retrieved September 2006 from http://www.sciencedaily.com.

Scientists find link between dopamine and obesity. (2001). News Release. Retrieved February 2007 from http://www.bnl.gov/bnlweb/pubaf/pr/2001/bnlpr020101.htm.

Segall, R. (2001, March/April). Never too skinny. *Psychology Today*, p. 22.

Sex Addicts Anonymous. (2007). Sex Addicts Anonymous (SAA) home page. Retrieved February 2007 from http://saa-recovery.org/.

Sheafor, B., Horejsi, C., & Horejsi, G. (1997). *Techniques and guidelines for social work practice*. Boston: Allyn & Bacon.

Si-Young, H. (2006, September 15). Korea: Internet addicts to receive counseling. *Korea Herald*. Retrieved September 2006 from http://www.asiamedia.vcla.edu/article.

Slutske, W., Caspi, A., Moffitt, T., & Poulton, R. (2005). Personality and problem gambling. *Archives of General Psychiatry, 62,* 769–775.

Smith, E. (1997, November 24). Bodybuilders' fret "flip side" of anorexia. *USA Today*, p. 1A.

Smith, J. (2006, October 1). Foley built career as protector of children. *Washington Post*, p. A04.

Song, S. (2005, July 18). Starvation on the web. *Time*, p. 57.

Spencer, J. (2006, July 18). The new science of addiction. *Wall Street Journal*, pp. D1, D2.

Stanford School of Medicine. (2003, July 16). Internet addiction: Antidepressant helps alleviate compulsive shopping disorder, Stanford researchers find. News Release. Retrieved February 2007 from http://mednews.stanford.edu/releases/2003/july/shopping.html.

Stanford School of Medicine. (2006, October 17). Internet addiction: Stanford study seeks to define whether it's a problem. News Release. Retrieved February 2007 from http://mednews.stanford.edu/releases/2006/october/internet.html.

Sweeting, P. (2000, July). The invisible addiction. *Issues of Substance, 4,* 10, 11.

Texas Council on Problem and Compulsive Gambling. (2000, July 7). E-update on problem gambling new. *Women and Problem Gambling, 1*(23), 1–3.

Turner, N. (2000, August). Randomness, does it matter? *E-Gambling: Electronic Journal of Gambling Issues, 2*. Centre for Addiction and Mental Health. Retrieved February 2007 from http://www.camh.net/egambling/issue2/research/.

Ubelacker, S. (2005, July 11). Parkinson's medication linked to compulsive gambling, sex. *Globe and Mail*. Retrieved September 2006 from http://www.theglobeandmail.com.

van Wormer, K. (2001). *Counseling female offenders and victims: A strengths-restorative approach*. New York: Springer.

van Wormer, K. (2007). *Human behavior and the social environment, micro level: Individuals and families*. New York: Oxford University Press.

Vastag, B. (2001). What's the connection? No easy answers for people with eating disorders and drug abuse. *Journal of the American Medical Association, 285*(8), 1006–1008.

Volberg, R. (1993, April 23). *Gambling and problem gambling among Native Americans in North Dakota*. Report to the North Dakota Department of Human Services, Division of Mental Health.

Volpicelli, J., & Szalavitz, M. (2000). *Recovery options: The complete guide.* New York: Wiley.

Wallace, B. C. (2005). *Making mandated addictions treatment work.* Lanham, MD: Jason Aronson.

Wang, G.-J., Volkow, N., Thanos, P., & Fowler, J. (2004). Similarity between obesity and drug addiction as assessed by neurofunctional imaging. *Journal of Addictive Diseases, 23*(3), 39–53.

Watkins, T., Lewellen, A., & Barrett, M. C. (2001). *Dual diagnosis: An integrated approach to treatment.* Thousand Oaks, CA: Sage.

Weir, R., & Goldiner, D. (2006, August 24). Mother embezzled millions to fund lottery addiction, authorities say. *New York Daily News.* Retrieved September 2006 from http://www.macon.com/mld/macon/news/nation.

Welte, J., Barnes, G., Wieczorek, W., Tidwell, M.-C., & Parker, J. (2002). Gambling participation in the U.S.: Results from a national survey. *Journal of Gambling Studies, 18*(4), 313–338.

Wen, P. (2001, May 24). An addictive thrill. *Boston Globe,* pp. A1, A21.

Westermeyer, J. (2005). Gambling in American Indian and Hispanic veterans. *American Journal of Public Health, 95*(5), 860–866.

White, K. (2006, April 12). *Statement of the National Council on Problem Gambling regarding current Internet gambling legislation.* Report to U.S. House of Representatives, Committee on the Judiciary.

Wikipedia. (2007, February). Overeaters Anonymous. Retrieved February 2007 from http://en.wikipedia.org/wiki/Overeaters_Anonymous.

Williams, R., & Wood, R. (2004, June 23). *The demographics of Ontario gaming revenue.* Paper prepared for the Ontario Problem Gambling Centre. Retrieved February 2007 from http://www.gamblingresearch.org/contentdetail.sz?cid=198.

Wingert, P. (2006, December 25). Nora Volkow. *Newsweek,* pp. 77–79.

Wooley, S. C. (1994). Sexual abuse and eating disorders: The concealed debate. In P. Fallon, M. A. Katzman, & S. C. Wooley (Eds.), *Feminist perspectives on eating disorders* (pp. 171–211). New York: Guilford Press.

Yochelson, S., & Samenow, S. (1976). *The criminal personality* (Vol. 1) New York: Jason Aronson.

Young, K. S. (1998). *Caught in the Net: How to recognize the signs of Internet addiction.* New York: Wiley.

I was much too far out all my life
And not waving but drowning.
—STEVIE SMITH (1983, p. 303)

CHAPTER 8

SUBSTANCE MISUSE WITH A CO-OCCURRING MENTAL DISORDER OR DISABILITY

INTRODUCTION

Mental illness is terrifying when it spirals out of control. Repeated alcohol or drug misuse often brings misery, regret, and dire consequences. When the two are combined, the result can be a double whammy of troubles for the person experiencing it. This applies to a person who also has a developmental, physical, or cognitive disability or any other major challenge to living life and uses alcohol and drugs in a harmful way. One such person is Eddie, mentally ill with an alcohol or other drug (AOD) disorder, who was interviewed for the Washington, D.C., Dual Diagnosis Project (Quimby, 1995): "All I do is smoke and do drugs. I be drinking and drugging. I hope someone can help me. My family don't help me at all. They don't want to help me when I got problems. And I bother them for help" (p. 266).

Getting help when you have multiple needs, like Eddie, has not been easy. Professional treatment providers and educators in the mental health, disability, and substance misuse field have acted as if a person could be divided up into just one area of trouble at a time. Competition around traditionally separate national and state funding streams, turf battles over which disorder is "primary," different attitudes toward treatment methods, and educational deficits for professionals in each field have contributed to this unhelpful stance. In the

331

recent past (and even today), a person who is diagnosed both bipolar and alcoholic and still drinking could be refused treatment at a mental health facility because she wasn't abstinent. At the same time, she could be refused treatment at a substance abuse treatment center because of her mental health symptoms or unless she gave up her antidepressant medication. As one treatment provider put it, "All of us treat dually diagnosed patients, but few of us provide dual diagnosis treatment" (Shulman, 1995, p. 33). Standard practice by most mental health systems in the United States is not evidence based; the same is true for most substance abuse treatment centers (Biegel et al., 2003).

Similarly, persons with physical disabilities or cognitive impairments have generally not been served well by existing treatment and support systems (Handmaker, Packard, & Conforti, 2002). For example, professionals and families in these fields have tended to overlook substance misuse problems, and treatment facilities and self-help groups are not accessible for those with mobility problems. Written and other visual materials are designed for people who see and don't have brain trauma or learning needs, and interpreters for the deaf are seldom employed.

Overwhelming evidence documented that the "hardening of the categories" between mental health disabilities and substance abuse was not working. Most research studies indicated that parallel or sequential treatment approaches for dual disorders had annual rates of stable remission of less than 5%. Parallel and sequential treatments in which clients are treated by two agencies for each problem separately have been found ineffective because this approach ignores the interactive and cyclical nature of the two types of disorders. For years, different bureaucracies and philosophical approaches at the mental health and substance abuse agencies as well as funding barriers have precluded active collaboration. Traditional approaches protected program boundaries but have been shown ineffective for the care of either psychiatric or substance use disorders (Mueser, Noordsy, Drake, & Fox, 2003).

Something had to give—and did. In the mid-1980s, reforms began developing, catalyzed by 13 federally funded demonstration projects across the country in 1987. By 2004, 35% of the facilities surveyed in the National Survey of Substance Abuse Treatment Services had special programs or groups for clients with co-occurring psychiatric and substance abuse disorders (SAMHSA, 2004). However, in 2005, among the 5.2 million adults with both serious psychological distress and a substance use disorder, 53% received no treatment at all, 34.3% received only treatment for mental health problems, and 4.1% received only specialty substance use treatment. A mere 8.5% received both treatment for mental health problems and specialty substance use treatment (SAMHSA, 2006b). Although the policy surrounding the treatment of persons with both a mental and a substance use disorder is advancing from bifurcation in programming to a "no wrong door" philosophy, we clearly have a way to go to achieve integrated care for all who need it.

However, the implications from these projects, other pilot programs, and recent research findings have stimulated substantial and dramatic changes in traditional treatment practices. In addition, concurrent developments of the consumer and advocacy movement in the mental health field and the independent living movement in the disability field have supported the direction of these changes. Some people refer to this as a movement toward a "nonpunitive helping stance."

Traditionally, the most common approach to treating clients with dual or multiple disorders has been to identify one disorder as "primary" and the other as "secondary" (Mueser et al., 2003). Social workers often were taught that if they got at the underlying problem (e.g., depression) and treated that disorder, the addiction problems would then go away. Meanwhile, substance abuse counselors generally viewed the mental health disorders as symptoms that would disappear once the substance misuse stopped. One of the major ideological conflicts around which problem was "primary" receded from view when more advanced technologies taught us more about diseases of the brain. It then became possible to treat clients simultaneously with an "integrated" approach for all their needs. The introduction of harm reduction techniques and motivational interviewing has been helpful in engaging people who were alienated by traditional assessment and treatment strategies. Abstinence is now considered an appropriate long-term goal for many, instead of a rigid requirement for receiving treatment. Categories variously named *dual diagnosis, coexisting disorders, persons with mental illness and chemical abuse or addiction* (MICAA, indicating an Axis I mental disorder), or *persons with chemical abuse and mental illness* (CAMI, indicating an Axis II personality disorder) are now referred to as *co-occurring disorders* to indicate the presence of both substance abuse/dependence and mental disorders (CSAT, 2005). Funding streams for research and pilot programs are now available. New approaches that emphasize self-determination, client strengths, and harm reduction have shown promising results.

This chapter presents the new body of knowledge that has been developed since the early 1990s to address the needs of persons with coexisting problems. The first part of the chapter presents a brief summary of the prevalence, characteristics, and typical concerns that a person with multiple problems may present. Then, following a description of the basic mental disorders, we discuss treatment practices for persons who have substance misuse and mental health problems. Next we address working with persons who have substance misuse and developmental, cognitive, or physical disabilities. Throughout this chapter, we discuss treatment approaches and programs that show promising results and provide practical tips for working with several types of coexisting disorders.

SUBSTANCE MISUSE AND MENTAL DISORDERS

PREVALENCE AND CHARACTERISTICS

Prevalence rates depend on what is included in the "mental disorders" category. The definition is far from simple. Based on brain imaging and finding new genes, some researchers are speculating that we are all mentally ill to some degree ("Is Everybody Crazy?" 1998). If this were true, all persons with substance misuse would be in the category of co-occurring diagnosis. At least some clinicians in the substance abuse treatment field would agree that it is rare to uncover a normal, well-adjusted, average person hiding under a serious addiction because the substance misuse in and of itself takes a heavy psychological and emotional toll (Denning, 2004). To address the challenge of defining the population with co-occurring disorders, The Quadrants of Care was developed by the National Association of State Alcohol and Drug Abuse Directors (NASADAD) and the National Association of State Mental Health Program Directors (NASMHPD). The four quadrants are: (a) less severe mental disorder/less severe substance disorder, (b) more severe mental disorder/less severe substance disorder, (c) less severe mental disorder/more severe substance disorder, and (d) more severe mental disorder/more severe substance disorder (CSAT, 2005, p. xviii). People with severe mental illness seem to have a heightened sensitivity to the effects of alcohol or psychoactive drugs. Just a small amount can be their undoing and precipitate hospitalization or other major living problems. Very few persons who are severely mentally ill (less than 5%, according to Drake & Wallach, 1993) can even drink alcohol or use drugs at a moderate level without consequences. Consequently, most of these people (about 50%) choose abstinence, and those who do use are unlikely to sustain heavy use (Drake & Mueser, 2000). In the case of severe mental illness, any use at all may be considered enough to put a person in the category of "coexisting disorder."

For persons clinically diagnosed with a severe mental illness, coexisting substance misuse is at least more common than not, especially if they are young, male, single, less educated, and have a history of substance misuse or conduct disorder or if they are homeless, in jail, or present to an emergency room (Drake & Mueser, 2000). In 2005, 5.2 million adults met the criteria for both serious psychological distress and a substance use disorder. Past year illicit drug use was higher among adults with serious mental illness (26.8%) than adults without it (12.7%). The rate of past month cigarette use in 2005 was 42.8% among adults with serious mental illness compared to a 24.5% rate for adults without it. Combining all categories of substance dependence or abuse (including alcohol), 21.3% (5.2 million) of adults with serious mental illness were dependent on or abused illicit drugs or alcohol; the rate among adults without serious mental illness was 7.7% (14.9 million) (Substance Abuse and Mental Health Services Administration [SAMHSA], 2006b).

Alcohol, cannabis, and cocaine, in that order, are the most commonly used substances by persons with severe mental illness (Mueser et al., 2003). In a sample of 497 persons diagnosed with either schizophrenia or schizoaffective disorder, 79% had an alcohol use disorder, 46% a cocaine use disorder, 32% a marijuana use disorder, and 8% an opiate use disorder (Ziedonis & Trudeau, 1997). Persons with coexisting disorders appear to use alcohol and other drugs for the same reasons persons without coexisting disorders use substances— loneliness, anxiety, boredom, and insomnia (Mueser, Drake, & Wallach, 1998; Mueser et al., 2003). This finding, from an extensive review of the research, contradicts the popular notion that persons with mental illness use alcohol and other substances to "self-medicate" their symptoms or the side effects of their medication.

Persons who are dually diagnosed with substance misuse and mental disorders can expect more vulnerability than just plain substance misusers in a variety of ways. They are more likely to experience frequent hospitalizations, relapse, depression and suicide, severe housing and financial problems, homelessness, high rates of sexually transmitted diseases, violence, incarceration, and legal problems. At the same time, they are less likely to comply with their medication regimen (Drake & Mueser, 2000), and medication may be less effective (e.g., nicotine decreases the potency of standard antipsychotic medication; Goff, Henderson, & Amico, 1992).

The problems of mental illness and substance misuse are particularly severe among poor urban individuals. A homeless, dually diagnosed woman interviewed in the Washington, D.C., Dual Diagnosis Project describes her situation as follows: "Sometimes I do think I'm going to get murdered. I was raped and stuck up before.... I was just spending money on drugs.... People—friends, relatives and mental health staff—just did me in. They did enough torture to put a butcher knife to me and throw me off the bridge" (Quimby, 1995, p. 266).

All too frequently, these extremely vulnerable persons are still shuttled back and forth between the mental health system and the alcohol/drug system. They receive neither sequential nor parallel treatment, or they are excluded altogether from one or the other system because of their coexisting disorder or the inadequacy of the system.

THE PERILS OF DIFFERENTIAL DIAGNOSIS

In the best of all worlds, clinicians and treatment providers would be able to determine with some certainty whether the specific mental illness is independent of or is dependent on the substance abuse, and they could plan treatment accordingly (see Case Study 8.1).

What is most important is to continue to evaluate psychiatric symptoms and their relationship to abstinence or ongoing substance abuse over time (CSAT, 2005). Most substance-induced symptoms begin to improve within hours or days after substance use has stopped. For example, anxiety symptoms (worry, apprehensive expectations, tension, sweating, hyperarousal, insomnia, irritability, poor concentration) are the most common psychiatric symptoms manifest by substance misusers (CSAT, 1994). However, most of these anxiety symptoms are gone within a few days or weeks of abstinence, in which case little or no treatment is required. Notable exceptions are psychotic symptoms caused by heavy and long-term amphetamine abuse and the dementia (problems with memory, concentration, and problem solving) caused by using substances directly toxic to the brain, which most commonly include alcohol, inhalants like gasoline, and again amphetamines (CSAT, 2005). If mild to debilitating anxiety continues long after abstinence, it makes sense to assess the

| CASE 8.1 | Diagnosis in a Team Setting |

The following narrative, by Catherine Crisp (2005), who at the time of the writing was a clinical social worker on an inpatient psychiatry unit at a large teaching hospital, expresses some of the challenges of diagnosis in a team setting:

> On several occasions, our team has had lengthy debates about the diagnosis of a particular client. Is he/she depressed because he/she can't get off drugs? Did the depression precede the drug use? If the depression preceded the drug use, at what point did they start to use drugs and how did that affect their depression? What is their diagnosis? Is it substance-induced mood disorder or is it a major depression with a coexisting substance dependence problem? Is the client's irritability due to: (1) a component of their mental illness, (2) the effects of withdrawing from their drug of choice (irritability is particularly common among people who are addicted to crack cocaine), (3) a component of a personality disorder, or (4) just a part of their personality style? Many times, each of the team members has a very different opinion about the diagnosis and the recommended course of treatment. It seems like a miracle when we can all agree. At other times, it is clear that we will not reach a consensus. When this happens, the attending psychiatrist ultimately makes the final call about the diagnosis and treatment that we will provide. Although I am surrounded by people with a clear medical model bias, I feel that my opinions and the bio-psycho-social-spiritual perspective I bring to the team are respected and valued by those I work with. (p. 206)

person for a coexisting anxiety disorder that may require specific medication and treatment intervention.

Unfortunately, many real-world problems interfere with this neat and tidy diagnostic regimen. For example, numerous studies have found that the majority of mentally ill persons do not start out ready and motivated for abstinence-based treatment (Mercer-McFadden, Drake, Brown, & Fox, 1997); consequently, a period of abstinence to tease out whether the anxiety is dependent on or independent of the substance abuse frequently does not occur right away, and sometimes, it never occurs. Taking a detailed history from the person to determine the presence of a mental illness prior to substance misuse may not be an option if the person is confused, depressed, or agitated in some way. Some people start drinking or using drugs at an age earlier than when mental illnesses become apparent. Persons who are homeless are unlikely to have reliable family members available to elaborate on their history. Careful attention to prior inpatient and outpatient records is a good strategy, but it is only viable when those records can be found and made available in a timely manner.

Other problems in diagnosis occur because AOD use can cause symptoms that mimic almost every psychiatric problem, especially during acute intoxication or withdrawal. For example, acute intoxication from a stimulant type of drug can cause highly agitated states or paranoid psychosis. A person withdrawing from stimulants may become seriously depressed, with suicidal thoughts. A further complication is that AOD use can help hide some psychiatric symptoms and disorders.

Sometimes, the historical division between treatment systems contributes to an underdiagnosing of coexisting disorders. For years, psychiatric symptoms were overlooked, unrecognized, or misunderstood as "acting-out behavior" in substance abuse treatment. Similarly, mental health staff explained away substance use or misuse as "self-medication" or as normal behavior. If a mental health or substance abuse problem was diagnosed, it frequently resulted in the ejection of the person from the system.

Because of the problems in making an accurate differential diagnosis in the short run, Denning (2000) advocates working without a diagnosis or with a partial diagnosis "with a general spirit of courage and risk taking on the part of clinicians" (p. 167). She cites the wasted time in arguing about a correct diagnosis, the need for constant reassessment, and the growing knowledge base in pharmacology and treatment strategies as good reasons to carry on working with a person even though a differential diagnosis may not be readily apparent. Assessment in this framework really becomes part of ongoing treatment. Specific strategies will be discussed later in the section on Integrated "No Wrong Door" Treatment Practices.

Prescribing psychiatric medication can be another challenge connected to diagnosis, especially if the medications are psychoactive or potentially addictive. Addiction treatment staff historically avoided the use of any medication. This made sense given the number of patients they saw addicted to prescription drugs and the large number of primary care physicians who were prescribing anti-anxiety medications, many of which (e.g., the benzodiazepines) were psychoactive and could be addictive. However, this prohibition has changed as treatment providers have become trained in the appropriate use of nonaddicting psychiatric medications and come to understand that withholding psychiatric medication can increase relapse. For more information on current medications commonly prescribed in mental health treatment and the effects these drugs may have on the recovery process of an individual who is also misusing alcohol or drugs, see the publication "Psychotherapeutic Medications 2006: What every counselor should know," available from the Mid-America Addiction Technology Transfer Center for free downloading at www.mattc.org. This information is updated annually, and addresses generic and brand-name psychiatric medication names, purpose, usual dose and frequency, potential side effects, emergency conditions, cautions, and common addiction treatment medications. Medication strategies are still in the process of being developed in this complex area; some of these will be discussed in a later section on new treatment practices.

DISORDERS AND DISABILITIES THAT COMMONLY CO-OCCUR WITH SUBSTANCE MISUSE

This section describes mental disorders that coexist with substance misuse in many cases. The diagnostic labels and brief descriptions are from the *DSM–IV–TR* (American Psychiatric Association [APA], 2000). For further description, see the CSAT Treatment Improvement Protocol (TIP 42) on Substance Abuse

Treatment for Persons with Co-occurring Disorders, available on the Internet at www.ncadi.samhsa.gov. It may seem contrary in a text such as this, which focuses on the strengths perspective and harm reduction, to include a section based on the *DSM–IV–TR*. The purpose is to (a) provide for a means of communicating with other mental health professionals trained to use these categories, (b) use the *DSM* for the resource it provides best (i.e., behavioral descriptions of well-accepted categories), and (c) recognize the reality that many providers cannot exist without payments based on utilizing *DSM* diagnoses. Later in the chapter, we will detail how critical the strengths perspective and harm reduction practices are when actually working with individuals with multiple challenges.

ANXIETY

Anxiety symptoms are experienced by everyone at some time in their lives— cold, clammy hands, tremulous voice, the shakes, panic, shortness of breath, increased heart rate, restlessness, or the almost relentless urge to move about. Anxiety is a normal response to danger. The *DSM–IV–TR* includes panic attacks, agoraphobia, phobias, obsessive-compulsive disorders, posttraumatic stress disorders, as well as generalized anxiety disorders within the classification of anxiety disorders. However, in persons with AOD problems, anxiety and mood disorders are the most common psychiatric symptoms encountered. Anxiety is sometimes a direct result of ingesting psychoactive drugs, such as stimulants, marijuana, and hallucinogenic drugs. The *DSM–IV* diagnosis substance-induced anxiety disorder is used to describe anxiety symptoms associated with intoxication or withdrawal states. In recovery, anxiety can be the result of acute or prolonged abstinence syndromes, especially from alcohol, sedative depressant drugs, opiates, and long-term cocaine use. Most anxiety symptoms related to AOD misuse clear within 2 to 4 weeks. Anxiety is frequently combined with depression, and the combination puts the person at high suicide risk. When symptoms persist after 30 days of abstinence, the person should be assessed for an independent coexisting anxiety disorder that might interfere with recovery.

POSTTRAUMATIC STRESS DISORDER (PTSD)

It was not until 1980, in response to Vietnam War veterans and the militancy of the antiwar movement, that the American Psychiatric Association (APA) included the diagnosis of posttraumatic stress disorder (PTSD) in the *DSM* in acknowledgment of the symptoms. The feminist movement was influential in this development as well because women had begun to speak out about the impact of rape for the first time (van Wormer, 2007). The *DSM–IV–TR* (2000) describes PTSD as the reexperiencing of an extremely traumatic event that the person has experienced or witnessed, accompanied by symptoms of increased arousal (e.g., sleep disturbance, irritability, hypervigilance, difficulty concentrating) and by avoidance of stimuli associated with the trauma and numbing.

According to the National Mental Health Association (NMHA, 2006), 25 to 30% of people exposed to severe trauma, and 5 to 10% of people exposed to moderate trauma, will develop substance use problems. Clients with the dual diagnosis of PTSD and substance misuse have worse outcomes than those with either disorder alone and may internalize a sense of failure when they do not succeed in standard treatment programs that work for others (Navits, 2004). A study of 60 women participants in a prison-based substance abuse treatment program, over half of whom were diagnosed with PTSD, found that the dually diagnosed women had a significantly higher rate of drug relapse upon release than did women with a background of substance misuse only (Kubiak, 2004). Typical sources of the trauma were early childhood sexual abuse and/or later battering and rape experiences.

Addiction treatment for clients with PTSD raises several issues. It is important for the counselor to recognize that becoming abstinent from substances does not resolve PTSD, and indeed, some of the symptoms might even become worse at first (CSAT, 2005). Clients may be overwhelmed by a flood of memories that their substance use had kept at bay. Still, integrated treatment is likely to be more successful than substance abuse treatment alone; treatment outcomes for clients with PTSD and substance use disorders typically are worse than for other clients in treatment, even for other clients with other mental disorders (CSAT, 2005). Counselors are recommended to prepare clients with PTSD for this possibility and to consider referral for medications targeting anxiety. If the client is at risk of further harm, developing a plan for increased safety is essential.

PTSD RELATED TO COMBAT   After the war in Vietnam was over, some 30% of Vietnam veterans suffered PTSD; flashbacks were common. A recent study involving 6,200 soldiers who had served in Iraq several months earlier was conducted by a team at the Walter Reed Army Institute of Research (Hoge et al., 2004). Results showed that one in six of the veterans showed symptoms of PTSD, depression, or anxiety; 12% had symptoms of PTSD alone. (These figures are an underestimate as the study was done before the far more brutal urban combat efforts got underway.) The risk of developing trauma rose in proportion to the number of instances of combat in which the soldier had engaged. These figures need to be seen in comparison to the 5% rate of PTSD in a sample of soldiers before deployment.

Some of the veterans of past wars are among the homeless people who congregate on city streets. According to Veterans Administration (VA) studies, 76% of homeless veterans experienced alcohol, drug, or mental disorders over the past month of the survey (CSAT, 2004). PTSD was associated with an increased rate of substance misuse: About one third of men and women who report PTSD during their lifetime also report drug or alcohol misuse at some point in their lives.

An Israeli psychiatrist with extensive relevant experience recommended immediate intervention with a cognitive-behavioral therapy (CBT) and serotonin enhancing drugs. Serotonin enhancing drugs and even tranquilizers (or alcohol) are likely to offset the formation of traumatic memories because they dull the senses and reduce the flow of adrenaline associated with the imprinting of memories. People in Manhattan who experienced the horrors of 9/11 and

Box 8.1	Trauma and Resilience Post-Katrina and Rita
	Diane Rae Davis

The car full of Red Cross volunteers driving into New Orleans a few weeks after Katrina became silent when we crossed the only bridge passable to get into the city. Silence, then soft murmurs of disbelief, then tears. We experienced block after block of no people, no dogs or cats, no noise at all. Only an upside-down world of mud, and cars where they shouldn't be, and broken houses, signs, and telephone poles. Being there helped make sense of what people from Louisiana were telling us when they made it to the Red Cross service center in Mississippi, where we had been volunteering as mental health professionals for the past week.

In Mississippi, Rita, or the "hidden hurricane," directly impacted many of the families we saw from the surrounding region. One of the many unreported results of this hurricane was the lack of electricity for 2 to 3 weeks. In rural Mississippi in 100° weather, this means one thing: The freezer thawed out. Food that had been carefully and thriftily "laid by" for the winter was spoiled. In the rural poverty that exists in Mississippi, this was disaster, and the Red Cross, FEMA, and public assistance such as food stamps were not prepared to deal with it. More obvious traumas, such as houses blown away, made whole counties "eligible" for the aid of these formal support systems.

As mental health workers, we worked with immediate problems one might expect in such circumstances, such as panic, depression, and anxiety, with the disaster victims and sometimes the Red Cross volunteers. What was unexpected for me were the stories that revealed incredible strength and resilience in the midst of tragedy. Some people talked about camping out with their family near their devastated house, reading stories to the kids by candlelight, and becoming close as a family in ways that normal modern life did

---

who were taking psychotropic medications, for example, seemed to cope better in the wake of the attack (Jackson, 2003).

A social work graduate student shared her experience as the third wife of a Vietnam veteran who has a severe case of PTSD. In her words:

> C's drinking was once so bad that his daughter had to go into foster care. My husband was on the front lines in Vietnam; he saw the people he killed eye to eye. C is 100% disabled with PTSD. He keeps reliving a mission in which he didn't bring his men back. When certain anniversary dates come, he binges and can't stop. It affects the children because out of the blue, Dad's gone crazy again.
>
> C's sleep disturbances are so bad he leaves the TV running for distraction. And then there's his hyperalertness—you do not want to approach him straight on. In a restaurant, his back is to the wall. C has flashbacks, is not present for 3 hours, thinks he is in Vietnam; he almost beat me with a pole. Watching news reports of war on TV or visiting a military base brings it all back...
>
> The VA sent out a document of the effects of war trauma. The government is working on this, not like it was during the war in Vietnam. The VA is using Ecstasy to bring down the distrust level. C has gone through the PTSD unit at the VA and has been in and out of the hospital. (personal communication, November 2005)

One can see from this wife's description that PTSD isn't just a problem of the individual; like addiction, it affects the whole family. Also, just as the Vietnam not foster. One woman told me, "I know how to survive this 'cause I grew up poor." Another explained how, while her husband went to find help, she spent one whole day under a bridge up to her knees in water, holding her infant granddaughter, to keep the baby cool enough in the hot, humid weather to survive.

An extraordinary study, funded by NIMH post-Katrina/Rita, attests to the phenomenon of "post-traumatic personal growth" that has been noticed in other disasters (Kessler, Galea, Jones, & Parker, 2006). Over a period of years, the study will track the mental health needs of the 1,034 members of the "Hurricane Katrina Community Advisory Group," a sample of people who lived in Alabama, Mississippi, and Louisiana who were directly affected by Hurricane Katrina. The results of the first baseline survey revealed serious mental health problems among 11.3% of respondents compared with 6.1% in a similar sample before the hurricane. Mild to moderate mental illness also nearly doubled, from 9.7 to 19.9%.

However, according to the authors of the study, there are more sides to trauma than just the negative mental health consequences. Instead of an expected suicide increase, they found that thoughts of suicide among people with mental health problems actually decreased. They also found that 88.5% of respondents said, "Their experience with the hurricane helped them develop a deeper sense of meaning or purpose in life" (Kessler et al., 2006, p. 19). The vast majority of respondents (including persons with mental health problems) also said their experiences made them more spiritual or religious. They were highly optimistic of their ability to rebuild their lives, and the hurricane helped them discover inner strengths they did not know they had.

Although the authors of the study (and this author) caution that these resilient qualities may be temporary, and that the survey will hold more weight over time, the initial results do attest to the assumption held throughout this text. Even in the most dire circumstances, it is possible to find a ray of hope.

---

veteran's wife reported, the Iraq War, with the guerrilla warfare and explosions and the feeling that the enemy is everywhere, is a trigger for flashbacks of horrors experienced long ago by many Vietnam veterans. Figures from the VA show a 36% rise since 2003 in the number of Vietnam veterans seeking help for trauma (St. George, 2006). Women are seeking help due to their exposure to high-risk situations in the danger zones. Other women are seeking counseling for sexual assault, a growing problem for women in the military (Streisand, 2006). The best place for veterans of either sex to get the help they need is at the local Vet Centers, which operate without the delays and bureaucratic restrictions of VA. The centers are small and staffed by veterans who help with practical matters concerning veterans as well as deeper issues.

Trauma from Natural Disasters

National disasters, such as Hurricanes Katrina and Rita in 2006, are examples of extremely traumatic events that can elicit PTSD or other mental health problems. As a result of the hurricanes, an additional 30% of Louisianans are expected to develop symptoms of PTSD, and a need for substance abuse treatment (NMHA, 2006). However, even in disasters like this, there is the phenomenon of "post-traumatic growth" that supports a strengths perspective (see Box 8.1). Some clinicians and persons now in recovery would say that addiction itself can be a trauma because of the extreme stress of living and surviving an "addicted life." Many times, such a life can include homelessness, dangerous and illegal activities, physical assaults, acute illness, and extreme isolation from friends and family. The process of recovery also becomes a process of dealing with what Twelve-Step groups call "the wreckage of the past," the nightmares, and the fragility of surviving.

PATHOLOGICAL (COMPULSIVE) GAMBLING

A clinical diagnosis of pathological gambling is defined in the *DSM–IV–TR* when a person meets five or more of the following criteria: preoccupation with gambling, a need to gamble with increasing amounts of money, making repeated efforts to quit, gambling from stress, lying to conceal activities, and borrowing money to pay debts (APA, 2000).

Prevalence rates for pathological gamblers are higher in populations in treatment for AOD disorders than in the general population, with estimates for pathological gambling at around 10 to 15% and another 10% reporting problem gambling (Blume, 1997). CSAT (2005) estimates that the rate of problem gambling among people with substance use disorders is four to five times the rate found in the general population. According to the National Research Council (1999), substance use disorders are associated with both progression to problem gambling and subsequent pathological gambling. Not surprisingly, persons who are compulsive gamblers have a much higher chance of having coexisting substance use disorders over their lifetime, with estimates ranging from 25 to 63%. In a general population study in St. Louis, problem gamblers were three times more likely to meet criteria for depression, schizophrenia, alcoholism, and antisocial personality disorder than nongamblers.

Attempted suicide and suicide may be real threats. A study of 114 consecutively admitted patients to a gambling program for veterans found that 40% had made a suicide attempt at some point in their lives. Of these suicide attempters, 73% had a history of substance misuse, but so did 62% of the others. Impulsivity was correlated with suicide risk in these gamblers (Kausch, 2003). According to the National Council on Problem Gambling, the suicide rate for pathological gamblers is higher than for any other addictive disorder (National Gambling Impact Study Commission, 1999). A short, user-friendly screen for gambling problems and, if positive, a suicide assessment are highly recommended (Davis, 2002).

EATING DISORDERS

Eating disorders are described in the *DSM–IV–TR* as severe disturbances in eating behavior. This category includes anorexia (refusal to maintain a minimally normal body weight) and bulimia (repeated episodes of binge eating followed by compensatory behaviors such as self-induced vomiting, misuse of laxatives, excessive exercise) (APA, 2000). Stimulant use is widespread to help control weight. Although estimates vary widely, persons with bulimia have more prevalence of substance abuse (between 3 to 49%) than persons with anorexia nervosa (not much different from women in the general population). One study of an inpatient treatment center found that 15% of the women and 1% of the men had an eating disorder (CSAT, 2005). Treatment centers report eating binges and starvation as relapse triggers. Food is also a powerful mood-altering substance on its own and is sometimes used (by bingeing or starving) to enhance the euphoric effect of drugs (see chapter 7).

MOOD DISORDERS

Mood disorders, which include major depression, dysthymia, mania, hypo-mania, bipolar disorders, and cyclothymia, are basically abnormal (patholog-ical) highs and lows in mood. Since all psychoactive substances affect mood, it is not surprising that mood disorders, along with anxiety, are the most common psychiatric diagnoses for persons with an AOD disorder. Among persons with a coexisting AOD disorder, women, Native Americans, patients with HIV, patients on methadone, and the elderly are all at higher risk for depression. Manic symptoms can be induced by a variety of substances, such as stimulants, steroids, hallucinogens, and can also occur during withdrawal from alcohol. Depressive symptoms can result from acute or chronic drug use and can also be triggered by withdrawal. It is critical to assess whether the person is at immi-nent risk for suicide or a danger to themselves or others. Symptoms that persist after 30 days of abstinence or 30 days after acute intoxication should be assessed for an independent coexisting mood disorder that might mildly to severely interfere with the recovery process.

Bipolar disorder (formerly called manic-depressive disorder) is charac-terized by episodes of mania and depression. The mania is extreme; the person is highly talkative and evidencing a flight of ideas and engagement in activities that are highly pleasurable, such as spending sprees (CSAT, 2005). The depres-sion is extreme at the other end of the spectrum. In a study of a prison popula-tion, 90% of persons diagnosed with bipolar disorder also had substance-related problems. Some persons with this disorder use cocaine to lengthen the euphoric mood state or alcohol to help subdue the mania.

PERSONALITY DISORDERS

Personality disorders—such as borderline, dependent, antisocial, or narcissistic personality and passive–aggressive and obsessive-compulsive—are described in the *DSM–IV–TR* as rigid, maladaptive patterns of deeply ingrained behaviors and thoughts that deviate markedly from the expectations of the individual's culture, are pervasive, and cause great personal distress (APA, 2000). Unfortu-nately, the diagnosis of a personality disorder has too often been the result of cultural, ethnic, or personal bias. For example, women are most often diagnosed with dependent, histrionic, or borderline personality disorders, and men are most often diagnosed with antisocial personality disorders. The diagnostic criteria for personality disorder is expected to change in the next revision of the *DSM* because of lack of clarity among categories and a concern about what distinguishes normal behavior from pathological behavior (CSAT, 2005). Many persons with AOD disorders do not meet the criteria for antisocial personality once they become abstinent; the "antisocial" behaviors were part of their strategy for maintaining addiction. The CSAT (1994) says that it is helpful to conceptualize personality disorder behaviors as "survivor behaviors" because they have helped the person survive serious difficulties. Suicidal behavior or threats of other self-harm must be taken seriously and attended to promptly. Counseling strategies for personality disorders often involve working with (not against) the person to reach his or her own stated goals (provided they are legal) in small, concrete, measurable steps.

Psychotic Disorders

Persons who suffer from psychotic disorders (e.g., schizophrenia and schizoaffective and delusional disorders) typically experience periods when they cannot distinguish between information from the outside world and information from the inner world of the mind. There can be some confusion over the term *psychotic,* which historically was used in a vague sense to denote mental illness (CSAT, 2005). The narrowest definition of psychotic as used today is restricted to delusions or prominent hallucinations, with the hallucinations occurring in the absence of insight into their pathological nature. A slightly less restrictive definition also would include prominent hallucinations that the individual realizes are hallucinatory experiences. Broader still is a definition that includes other positive symptoms of schizophrenia (i.e., disorganized speech or grossly disorganized or catatonic behavior). The most commonly diagnosed psychosis is *schizophrenia.* About 1% of people develop schizophrenia during their lifetime; it usually develops between the ages of 16 and 30 (Mueser et al., 2003). According to the American Psychiatric Association (2000), to be diagnosed with schizophrenia, a person must experience a decrease in social functioning for at least 6 months and experience two or more of the following symptoms for at least 1 month: delusions, hallucinations, disorganized speech, grossly disorganized or catatonic behavior. *Paranoid schizophrenia* is a subtype in which the person experiences delusions that he or she is being attacked or about to be attacked. Nobel Prize–winning economist John Nash today is in remission from this form of schizophrenia; his life was portrayed in the award-winning 2001 film, *A Beautiful Mind,* directed by Ron Howard and starring Russell Crowe.

Negative symptoms associated with schizophrenia are flattened affect, apathy and low motivation, loss of pleasure, and limited content of speech. This psychosis may cause problems in concentration or in one's ability to relate to or tolerate others. Drug and alcohol use and misuse are likely. For example, the Epidemiologic Catchment Area study reports a lifetime substance misuse in the general population of 17% compared with 48% for persons with schizophrenia. Amphetamines are commonly used as well (CSAT, 2005). As noted earlier, treatment of persons with coexisting disorders requires a highly supportive, long-term commitment and integration of both substance abuse and mental health treatment strategies.

HOMELESSNESS

Clients with co-occurring disorders are vulnerable to housing instability and homelessness, as their illnesses often lead to erratic, agitated behaviors that result in eviction by landlords or family (Mueser et al., 2003). According to SAMHSA's treatment data set, more than 175,000 admissions to substance abuse treatment in 2004 were homeless at that time; the homeless comprised 13% of all admissions, which is an increase from 10% in 2000. Alcohol was the primary substance of abuse (SAMHSA, 2006a). Although it is generally thought that the addiction causes the homelessness, it is more likely the case that the stress caused by homelessness and availability of alcohol and other drugs on the streets causes people to seek relief in alcohol or drugs.

Traditionally, it has been thought that housing should not be provided until the homeless people got off the drugs and alcohol. According to Padgett, Gulcur, and Tsemberis (2006), however, longitudinal comparative research shows no significant group differences in substance misuse in participants who received the housing first and then got treatment compared to the reverse arrangement.

A promising development is the provision of housing under the supported housing model. This model seeks to provide a permanent place to live (as opposed to transitional housing) and intensive case management for persons with co-occurring disorders (see Box 8.2). Thus, they get help with budgeting, referral to community services, and medication compliance. Donald Linhorst (2006) describes supported housing as empowering in that the residents have some control over their housing and decisions related to their life in that residence. This includes, according to the harm reduction model, a choice of diet, times to sleep and wake up, and the choice of which substances people use in their own homes (Mueser et al., 2003).

INTEGRATED "NO WRONG DOOR" TREATMENT PRACTICES

One of the most important system changes for a person needing help with coexisting disorders is the development of the integrated treatment program, now the preferred model of the Substance Abuse and Mental Health Services Administration (CSAT, 2005). A parallel development is the principle of "no wrong door"—that is, the healthcare delivery system (substance abuse treatment, mental health, and physical health) has a "responsibility to address the range of client needs wherever and whenever a client presents for care" (CSAT, 2005, p. 12). Integrated treatment (in contrast to sequential or parallel treatment) provides simultaneous treatment for the mental illness and the substance use disorder. The person no longer has to travel to two different locations to receive and try to reconcile two different messages. Although this may sound like mere common sense from today's vantage point, it required (and still requires in many parts of the country) massive system changes to become a treatment option.

Although this section focuses on integrated treatment programs, traditional treatment (parallel and sequential) programs can benefit from these as complementary to their programs. Many traditional treatment programs have already become less confrontational, more collaborative with other helping systems, and more likely to use treatment stages—all hallmarks of an integrated approach. Other developments, such as the mental health "consumer" movement that underscores the rights of the individual patient (Minkoff, 1996), the adaptation of some self-help groups to clients with co-occurring disorders, and pharmacological advances with fewer side effects have supported treatment innovation. The emergence of treatment populations with high rates of co-occurring disorders (e.g., people who are homeless, imprisoned, or have HIV/AIDS or PTSD) have also led to new models of service delivery.

CSAT (2005) classifies integrated treatment into four levels: (a) basic (treatment for one disorder, screening and consultation for the other); (b) intermediate (treatment for one disorder, but addresses some of the needs of the other, such as continuing psychiatric medication); (c) advanced (provides services for both disorders); and (d) fully integrated (actively combines treatment for the whole person, including related problems, with fully integrated staff, funding, and policies and procedures). At the crux of a fully integrated treatment program is the designation of one clinician (supported by a treatment team that may include professionals such as physicians, probation officers, AOD and mental health specialists, self-help sponsors, and housing specialists) to provide a seamless and individualized menu of interventions for a specific person over a long period of time. This shift alone requires providers to:

- Acknowledge that their profession doesn't have all the answers.
- Find a home for the integrated program (outpatient mental health programs, separate hospital units, community agencies).
- Change admission criteria to include persons with co-occurring disorders; implement serious cross-training of professional staff.
- Change the target population of the agency.
- Sort out funding streams, state regulations, and legal requirements.
- Create new procedures for confidentiality, data collection, and reimbursement.
- Participate with other providers in developing long-term structural mechanisms (coordinating bodies, letters of agreement, etc.) and planning that will improve the delivery of seamless services to persons with a dual diagnosis (see CSAT, 1994).

Philosophically, professionals from different types of agencies need to find common ground in their understanding of boundary issues. For example, as Mueser et al. (2003) indicate, mental health services attempt to "enable" clients to find and maintain stable housing, benefits, and social networks, whereas in the substance abuse treatment field, such helping behaviors are labeled "enabling" in a very negative sense of the word. Yet, as Orlin, O'Neill, and Davis (2004) point out, if a patient appears at risk of relapse, staff must respond promptly with appropriate interventions, such as accompanying the client to appointments and facilitating negotiations of difficult systems. These differences can be overcome over time, however, through joint training and perhaps requiring more similar professional training for licensing and certification. Motivational interviewing training is now widely provided in the substance abuse field as a new and exciting way to engage clients in treatment. Because this nonconfrontational model is incompatible with the formerly pervasive ethos in substance abuse treatment circles, there will necessarily be some resistance. In contrast, motivational theory, since it is derived from validated principles of basic psychology with which most mental health professionals are familiar, should be highly acceptable to this group. The challenge for them will come in the area of learning to pay more attention to addiction and other substance-related issues, however (DiNitto, Webb, & Rubin, 2002).

Is the transition from separate to integrated treatment worth the effort? Research seems to indicate it is. Mueser, Drake, and Noordsy (1998), for example, found that as the result of integrated treatment practices, stable remission rates went from 5% per year under the traditional system to 10 to 20% per year. Although this may still seem very low, it comes close to the same rate as persons with only substance use disorders. There are also other positive improvements associated with integrated treatment, such as more and better housing, decreased victimization, more satisfaction with life, decreased shame, open expression, and increased socialization, learning, and insight (Drake, Yovetich, Bebout, Harris, & McHugo, 1997; Mueser, Drake, & Noordsy, 1998; Sciacca & Thompson, 1996). More recent research summarized by Mueser et al. (2003) reveals the comprehensive, motivation-based, long-term integrated treatment programs resulted in significantly better substance-related outcomes than those of standard, nonintegrated care. Studies that compared various treatment approaches reported the best outcomes with behavioral skills training and intensive case management compared to a Twelve-Step approach. In general, the effects of short-term programming were not positive; there was insufficient time to engage these clients or to help them organize their lives better. DiNitto et al. (2002), for example, conducted a randomized comparative study of an inpatient population assigned to nine sessions of a group to deal with both disorders simultaneously or a control group with a more traditional approach. No significant differences were found between the groups in terms of treatment effects upon follow up. DiNitto et al. (2002) would like to see practitioners continue to develop and evaluate alternative integrated treatment approaches. Similarly, Mueser et al. (2003) call for more controlled research to reveal which components of the programming are critical.

New screening and assessment practices are readily becoming available. Unfortunately, screening for substance misuse still does not occur routinely in the mental health field, especially with women who present with severe mental illness (Breakey, Calabrese, Rosenblatt, & Crum, 1998). In addition, many traditional screens are confusing, too long, or irrelevant for persons with severe mental illness. However, recent evaluations of traditional screenings for persons with mental disorders have given some guidance to their use, and a new instrument has been created specifically to detect substance misuse in this population.

The 18-item screen, called the Dartmouth Assessment of Lifestyle Instrument (DALI), has been designed by filtering out items from several traditional instruments that are suitable for persons with mental illness (Rosenberg et al., 1998). Sample questions on this brief form are: Do you wear seatbelts when riding in the car? How many cigarettes do you smoke each day? Initial findings suggest that the DALI functioned significantly better than traditional instruments such as the TWEAK, T-ACE, MAST, and CAGE for detecting alcohol, cannabis, and cocaine use (which are the most common substances used among persons with severe mental illness). It is short and easy to use and can be obtained easily (and free) directly from the authors at the New Hampshire–Dartmouth Psychiatric Research Center website: www.dartmouth.edu/dms/psychrc/.

The Alcohol Use Disorders Identification Test (AUDIT) has been tested in Australia for use with people diagnosed with schizophrenia and was found to have high sensitivity (87%) and specificity (90%) in detecting diagnosed alcohol disorders (Dawe, Seinen, & Kavanagh, 1999). The AUDIT is also readily available (Saunders, Aasland, Babor, De La Fuente, & Grant, 1993) and short (10 questions), can be self-administered, requires only a seventh-grade reading level, and the questions do not refer to symptoms that could be confused with symptoms of schizophrenia. Another recent investigation found that the CAGE (see chapter 5) had reasonably high sensitivity (76%) for detecting lifetime prevalence of alcohol use disorder in persons with serious mental illness (Breakey et al., 1998). Either of these instruments will help mental health clinicians identify the possibility of a coexisting disorder.

If the obvious problem is substance misuse, it may be necessary to screen for a mental disorder. A brief mental status exam and the history of psychiatric medications/treatment can be helpful in screening for coexisting disorders. However, this can occur only when the person has been detoxified from the substances he or she was using. Safety is the first concern if the patients appear in a toxic or dangerous withdrawal state or if their behavior is suicidal, violent, impulsive, or psychotic. In this case, a rapid response is required, such as inpatient detoxification or a trip to the nearest emergency room.

Deeper assessment begins after a positive screen and continues throughout the professional relationship. A goal of integrated treatment is that the client becomes adept at assessing changes in mood, the effects of changing circumstances or relationships, and the interactive effects of alcohol or drugs on his or her mental health status and well-being. The integrative model provides for one primary clinician or case manager to work consistently with the individual. This provides many opportunities for both client and clinician to observe how the person's life is developing. A helpful stance to practice is that of a "curious anthropologist" delving into details and finding meanings that matter to the client.

The goal over time is an ongoing multidisciplinary assessment that includes the client's perspective. If other disciplines are represented on the team, their specialty areas would also be included. Basic areas of inquiry that are consistent with harm reduction and motivation enhancement practices (Denning, 2004; Drake & Mueser, 2000) include finding out what stage of change the person is in, how much insight the person has about the harms and benefits of her or his use of alcohol/drugs, and what personal strengths and resources may be helpful (past exceptions to the present troubles, important persons or family that care about the person, survival strategies, and capacities for development).

In addition to finding out the details of the person's use of alcohol and drugs (e.g., type, frequency, amount, patterns, expectancies related to use, positive and negative results), it is just as important to find out the details of any prescribed psychiatric medications, both past and present, and the person's particular patterns in taking the medication. This can lead to a discussion of any other attempts the person has made to help him- or herself or alleviate symptoms, such as professional treatment, self-help group participation, and religious or cultural practices. What helped and what didn't?

Eventually, it will be important to elicit personal goals in the areas of use of alcohol and drugs; types of supports, resources, and treatments desired to attain this goal and personal goals in the areas of social relationships; fun, recreational activities, hobbies, work, and education; financial or legal circumstances; and spiritual, religious, or cultural practices.

The continuous development of these areas of inquiry over time will help the clinician focus on finding meaningful direction for the person with a coexisting disorder, on validating the person's unique experience, and on mutually discovering strengths that can be brought to bear on the situation at hand.

The Center for Substance Abuse Treatment (CSAT) (2005) offers the following summary of the essential knowledge for counselors who plan to work with the combination of substance misuse and psychotic disorders:

- There is no clear pattern of drug choice among clients with schizophrenia. Instead, it is likely that whatever substances happen to be available or in vogue will be the substances used most typically.
- What looks like resistance or denial may in reality be a manifestation of negative symptoms of schizophrenia.
- An accurate understanding of the role of substance use disorders in the client's psychosis requires a multiple-contact, longitudinal assessment.
- Clients with a co-occurring mental disorder involving psychosis have a higher risk for self-destructive and violent behaviors.
- Clients with a co-occurring mental disorder involving psychosis are particularly vulnerable to homelessness, housing instability, victimization, poor nutrition, and inadequate financial resources.
- Both psychotic and substance use disorders tend to be chronic disorders with multiple relapses and remissions, supporting the need for long-term

treatment. For clients with co-occurring disorders involving psychosis, a long-term approach is imperative.

- It is important that the program philosophy be based on a multidisciplinary team approach. Ideally, team members should be cross-trained, and there should be representatives from the medical, mental health, and addiction systems. The overall goals of long-term management should include (1) providing comprehensive and integrated services for both the mental and substance use disorders, and (2) doing so with a long-term focus that addresses biopsychosocial issues in accord with a treatment plan with goals specific to a client's situation. (pp. 231–232)

CASE MANAGEMENT TEAMS

Case management in the integrated treatment model does not mean that a professional expert or team of experts provides services to a "case." Case management in this approach is closer to the independent living model in disability and the consumer movement in mental health, where it is recognized that consumers have the strength and right to manage their own lives (Mackelprang & Salsgiver, 1999). Consequently, although individual team members may be expert in their respective fields, they have also become experts at collaboration with each other and most important, with the person they are trying to help. The purpose of the collaborative case management approach is to offer a menu of supports, services, and opportunities that are in tune with the person's direction rather than prescribing these services for the "case."

The Santa Barbara, California, Regional Health Authority (SBRHA) identified the typical needs of a woman with coexisting disorders on Temporary Assistance for Needy Families (TANF). These include mental health and substance abuse treatment, parenting education, child care, job-skills training, assistance in going back to school, legal aid, help with domestic violence, and transportation to appointments (Bearman, Claydon, Kincheloe, & Lodise, 1997). Although they don't mention it, housing is also a common need. When faced with a list of needs like this, many professionals have been trained to "fill up the hole" with referral after referral. Sometimes, coercion is used to require the person to participate in what the case manager has decided is in the client's best interest, such as withholding income or other financial support. These practices reinforce the oppressive notion that a person with coexisting disorders cannot make decisions in his or her own best interest.

The need for integrated services is described in the tell-it-like-it-is chronicle of five drug addicts in Shavelson's (2002) *Hooked:*

"I don't believe in bouncing clients like Ping-Pong balls between substance abuse and mental health," Kathy tells me. "But mental health *has* to provide her with case management. And substance abuse services—which means me—is just not set up for that. Sure the politics frustrates me. So I keep my focus on the client, not the politics. A mental health case manager can get Darlene on the right medications, help her with food, transportation, disability income. I can't get near those services! But if her case manager works with all that, maybe Darlene will start showing up here again and I can finally help her with a drug program." (p. 119)

A staff member may have intense emotional reactions and disagreements about how to be an effective consultant to the person, particularly when there are a variety of unmet needs in the eyes of the professional. Clinicians who are used to working on an appointment schedule using a specific therapeutic process will find themselves needing to be more flexible in their ways of helping (Denning, 2004). For example, tackling a housing problem is more likely to come before therapy or insight or abstinence. Staff members need time to readjust and redefine their roles in an integrative treatment team. It takes about 1 year of training to solidify a team (Drake & Mueser, 2000), and it may take several years of work to make the necessary system changes. The good news is that it is demonstratively worth the effort. Persons with coexisting disorders can move from being "no one's clients" to becoming "everyone's clients" (Sciacca & Thompson, 1996) and ideally move from being perceived as a "client" to being viewed as an individual, citizen, and/or consumer.

Box 8.2 describes the intensive case management services provided at an innovative Seattle program that is based on principles of harm reduction. This harm reduction program includes housing for 200 "chronic public inebriates" in the Seattle region, who as chronically homeless persons with serious mental disorders had cost the most to the community in medical care, jail lockup, and other emergency services. A recent *New York Times* (Kowal, 2006) article described the program as one for the unsympathetic homeless, which is widely criticized on radio talk shows as "bunks for drunks."

CREATIVE ENGAGEMENT PRACTICES

According to the description of the new SBRHA program for dually diagnosed women on TANF, the designated intensive case manager will be the "single, human point of reference to coordinate care and assure participation" (Bearman et al., 1997, p. 364). In reality, "assuring participation" is a bit like ensuring abstinence—it's a good long-term goal. Because persons with coexisting disorders often present with disorganization, confusion, and a past history of unhelpful professional contacts and may live in an environment oppressed by poverty, violence, and ongoing substance misuse, it is understandably difficult for them to engage and remain active in a treatment process. Research on integrated treatment suggests it can be done. In fact, most persons with a dual diagnosis can be engaged in treatment for extended periods of time (beyond a year) (Mueser, Drake, & Noordsy, 1998). New ideas about stages of treatment and the role of the clinician in the engagement process have been critical in making this possible.

Many of the successful integrated treatment programs embrace a stages-of-treatment (or stage-wise treatment) model that involves matching a person's

Box 8.2	A Day in the Life of a Mental Health Case Manager

Rupert van Wormer, MSW, Seattle, Washington

It is Monday morning, the busiest day of the week at the Downtown Emergency Service Center (DESC) Mental Health Program. After a half hour bus ride, I arrive in downtown Seattle, more specifically to the Pioneer Square district, which is the old part of the downtown area. The agency itself is one block away from Yesler Way, famed for being the original Skid Road (later misnamed Skid Row). Hundreds of homeless people live in this area today. This area is reported as having the highest arrest rates in the entire city: Panhandling, public consumption of alcohol, drug dealing, and prostitution are common sights. The alleyway next to the building that houses the outpatient mental health program is commonly used by people as a place to smoke crack cocaine and inject heroin.

As I approach the front entrance to the clinic, where I work as a mental health case manager, I see a crowd of about 30 people, mostly our clients, waiting for the door to open at 9 o'clock. I unlock the door to let myself in, and am greeted by four or five of my clients simultaneously; some just say hello, while others ask to meet with me immediately. I explain that I will see them after the clinic opens at 9. (In this job, it is important to set limits.) Entering the building, I lock the door behind me.

I have an interesting and unique caseload. Many of my clients are dually diagnosed. Several have either schizophrenia with coexisting chemical dependence or major depression with chemical dependence. Persons with schizophrenia generally are prescribed what are called "atypical antipsychotics," which include Clozaril, Risperdall, Seroquel, and Zyprexa. For depression, Paxil, Prozac, Zoloft, Effexor, and Wellbutrin are commonly prescribed. Drugs most commonly misused by my clients include: heroin, crack cocaine, methamphetamine, marijuana, and alcohol. Many of my clients also have physical health concerns as well, including hepatitis C, TB, HIV/AIDS, and diabetes.

At DESC, we endorse the harm reduction model. We would like to get our clients off drugs; we settle for keeping them alive and helping them stay out of trouble. If someone has a bad liver, for example, I might advise him or her to smoke marijuana rather than take drugs that would hurt the liver. For a man who is breaking antennae off old cars (to use to smoke the crack), I might advise him to buy a glass pipe at the shop.

We run pre-recovery treatment groups at the center; sometimes clients are nodding off in the group from heroin. Still, we'd rather have them come than to lose touch with them. We provide coffee and bagels and plenty of nurturance. The groups are unstructured, the focus on being open and honest about substance use. When our clients go off to AA or NA meetings or traditional treatment programs, though, they get confused. They are told to get off their antidepressants that the doctor here has urged them to take. Because of their emotional instability, these clients can't handle the contradictions. Also, they often can't resist the temptation to use when they are off their antidepressants.

I pour myself a cup of coffee and walk back to my cubicle. I check my voice mail, taking notes of all the messages that require a response. Typically, I have anywhere between 5 and 15 messages on a Monday morning. Often, these messages are from clients or mental health workers reporting an incident, arrest, or hospitalization that occurred during after-hours. A few minutes after 9 A.M., the receptionist at the front desk pages me with a list of my clients who have requested to meet with me and are now waiting in the reception area. I try to be as fair as possible; however, clients with emergency situations are always bumped to the top of the list. I usually reserve the first hour or two of each day for this type of client, the "walk-ins." The rest of the day I meet with the more stable clients who have scheduled appointments.

Fourteen of my 28 clients are money-management clients, which means that my agency is their representative payee. Their SSI (Supplemental Security Income) and SSDI (disability) checks are sent to my agency, and we assist these clients with their finances. For most of our payee clients, this means we pay their bills and disperse cash to them between one and five times per week, depending on their level of need. At the end of each month, I sit down with these clients individually and help them plan the next month's budget. One client I work with comes in daily, Monday through Friday, to pick up $10 a day. He also picks up his daily medications during this time at the nurse station. For many clients, the money-management program encourages treatment involvement. For example, a client I'll call Ben lived a life of instability until recently, when he became a payee client. Before this change, his SSDI check was sent to his mother, who would then send a money order for the full amount ($688) at the beginning of each month. Ben would be flat broke in less than 2 weeks, have nothing to show for it, and would still live at the shelter to get room and board. During this time, Ben had frequent drug binges, taking his psychiatric medications for schizophrenia inconsistently. This resulted in frequent psychiatric hospitalizations. While Ben was "decompensated," he would think he was a pedophile and would turn himself in at police stations. But after DESC became his representative payee, stability returned to his life one step at a time. Ben started coming in regularly for medications. I met with him twice a week, during which time I helped him fill out housing applications and encouraged him to continue taking his medications consistently. I also used our time together to discourage him from using alcohol and other drugs. After a few weeks of this, I worked with coaching him in role-playing for the interview with an apartment manager. He did well at the interview and was able to get "clean and sober" housing that provided daily medication monitoring.

The clients I see first thing in the morning are usually money-management clients. Money is a good engagement tool. While I am giving them their money, I have the opportunity to ask them how they are doing. I often ask questions relating to nutrition, housing, drug use, relationships, personal hygiene, medication compliance, and psychiatric stability. Some of these can be observed without needing to ask questions. A client who is "decompensated," for example, will often have worse-than-usual hygiene, may be responding to hallucinations, and may seem confused. A few things I always need to monitor for are suicidal ideation, homicidal ideation, and grave disability. Any of these could require immediate psychiatric hospitalization.

By the time 11:45 rolls around, I will have met individually with nine clients for money management. Today, their sessions range from 5 minutes to a half hour. Those clients who need additional time with me are given appointment times later in the week.

The afternoon is spent doing the progress notes for each of the client interactions I have had this morning and answering mail. Today, there is a letter from the Social Security Administration telling me that one of my clients is up for "disability review." I fill out the multipage form and drop it in the outgoing mailbox.

Then it is off to the DESC Shelter, home to about 250 people each night, a place to socialize or rest by day. The purpose of my visit is to look for a man in his mid-40s diagnosed with schizophrenia who I have not seen in several weeks. (This part of the job is referred to as "outreach and engagement.") As I walk through the shelter hallway, I am reminded of a 19th-century insane asylum. It is dirty, there is a foul odor, and there are dozens of disheveled-looking people lining the wall. Some are standing or sitting, while

continued

BOX 8.2	A DAY IN THE LIFE OF A MENTAL HEALTH CASE MANAGER *continued*

others are stretched out asleep on the linoleum tile floor. Scanning the faces, looking for my client, I notice one person talking to himself in "word salad." Then I see my client. He is leaning against a wall, staring blankly. I say hello and try to interest him in reconnecting with mental health services and suggest that we meet later to work on housing applications. We set a time and I return to my office.

Back at the office, I check my voice mail: a few new messages but nothing urgent. It is now 2:15 and my 2 o'clock appointment is still not here. I have in my office some possessions that belong to a client who has recently moved into an assisted-living facility. Since this person's new residence is only about 10 blocks away, I decide now would be a good time to bring them to her. Gathering her things, I put them in a bag and start walking to her residence. After getting about a half block from my building, I notice one of my other clients, Joe, walking toward me. He stops in front of me and says, "Guess what?" Since Joe has a big smile on his face, I expect that it will be something positive. To my surprise, however, this is not a positive situation (a case of inappropriate affect). Joe tells me that he has just swallowed all of his medications and injected a gram of heroin, an obvious suicide attempt or suicidal gesture. I get him to come with me back to the clinic so we can get a "med list" from the nurse. After getting the list, we rush to the ER, pushing our way to the front of the line. I explain the situation to the intake nurse and give her the med list. While Joe is getting his stomach pumped, I talk to the hospital social worker and advocate for my client to be admitted into the inpatient psychiatric unit of the hospital after he is medically cleared. Feeling confident that the appropriate follow-up care will be provided, I leave.

It is now almost 5 P.M. A few blocks from the hospital is the assisted-living facility that was my original destination this afternoon. Fortunately, I remembered to bring this other client's bag with me. I make this delivery and call it a day.

One of the toughest things about my job is the difficulty associated with trying to get clients into inpatient chemical dependency programs. Frequently, clients will reach the point when they realize they are in need of inpatient chemical dependency treatment, and they are ready and willing to get the intensive treatment they need. The hard part for me at this moment comes when I have to tell them that I will try to get them on a list somewhere, and it may be 3 months to a year before they will be admitted. This problem stems from the shortage of publicly funded inpatient chemical dependence centers. As a result, the centers that do exist have the option of being selective when it comes to choosing who gets in and who doesn't. Clients with a diagnosis of schizophrenia, bipolar mood disorder, or major depression as well as chemical dependency generally have a harder time getting into treatment than people who are not identified as having mental health issues in addition to chemical dependency issues. One client, a daily crack cocaine user, had his moment of clarity nearly 6 months ago. He completed an application to an appropriate treatment facility, and we are still waiting. Another client from our agency was awaiting an opening at another treatment center. But before she could get the help she needed, she was picked up by the police and was later sentenced to 3 years in prison for providing an undercover agent with crack cocaine.

Printed with the permission of Rupert van Wormer.

current motivational state to a particular stage (Brady et al., 1996; CSAT, 2005; Mercer-McFadden et al., 1997; Mueser et al., 2003). This pragmatic approach builds on the model of five stages of change of Prochaska and DiClemente (1992), which includes precontemplation, contemplation, preparation, action, and maintenance (and sometimes a sixth stage, relapse) and suggests different intervention strategies for each stage (see chapter 3). For example, before a person can jump into active change or treatment, there are usually some steps needed to enhance readiness to change. It is no longer necessary to label people "resistant" or "in denial" because they haven't done what we, the clinicians, want them to do when we want them to do it. Instead, the role of the clinician becomes one of understanding and respecting where people are in the cycle of change and offering appropriate strategies for that stage.

The precontemplation stage (when a person doesn't even recognize the need to change) roughly translates to what is called the "engagement" phase of integrated treatment. The goal of engagement from a clinician's standpoint is to develop a therapeutic alliance with the person that is built on trust, not to attend to substance misuse. Without a trusting relationship, it is difficult to further any change in behavior other than temporary compliance. A key philosophy is to emphasize "respect for the person and empathy with their experience, and contrasts with a tendency of many treatment providers to blame them for a perceived failure to make progress" (Kavanagh et al., 1998, p. 142). Needless to say, it is a stretch for many traditionally trained substance abuse counselors to adopt this approach, but with training, team support, and the experience of more long-term success, substance abuse counselors are doing this all over the country.

The Ohio Substance Abuse and Mental Illness Coordinating Center of Excellence provides an integrated model to address the needs of the whole person in the context of community social supports (Biegel et al., 2003). This model utilizes biopsychosocial treatments and educational intervention in programming and provides training across the state; funding is provided by the Ohio Department of Mental Health. This integrated model requires that team members have a basic awareness of addictions and mental health assessment; training interviewing strategies as well have a solid grounding in the biological aspects of co-occurring disorders.

Creative strategies for promoting engagement typically involve outreach, some kind of concrete practical assistance, crisis intervention services, support in building a wider arena of social networks, and efforts to stabilize the psychiatric symptoms (Mueser et al., 2003). Outreach is especially important with persons who are homeless (see Case Study 8.2).

Other examples of engagement strategies used in integrated programs include:

- Introducing informal drop-in informational groups at the medication clinic to parallel the lack of structure in actively drug using clients (Handmaker et al., 2002).

CASE 8.2	LONG-TERM COMMITMENT

The following story illustrates the long-term commitment necessary to help a person with coexisting disorders.

Ms B is a 35-year-old Caucasian woman with a long history of frequent psychiatric hospitalization beginning at age 17. She has a diagnosis of schizophrenia (paranoid type) and at referral met criteria for binge-pattern alcohol dependence. Her drinking was associated with impulsive outbursts of violence, toward both herself and others. When not drinking, she was childlike and friendly, although persistently paranoid about the efforts of others to "poison her." She had been living in the streets and in the shelter system of a large urban city for 10 years prior to referral to an assertive community treatment (ACT) team that targeted homeless persons with severe mental illnesses.

After a six-month period of outreach and regular meetings at a local diner, she seemed increasingly comfortable with several members of the case management team and agreed to a low dose of antipsychotic medication that she took irregularly. She initially refused to discuss her alcohol use, stating "It's none of your business." Over the six months she acknowledged that she drank but vehemently denied that this alcohol use created any problems for her. At this point, she agreed to live in a transitional shelter that prohibited any substance use and provided on-site AA and NA group meetings. The ACT team was able to convince the shelter staff to waive their program requirement that all residents attend daily self-help meetings for Ms B because of her behavior in groups. The team assured the shelter staff that alcohol abuse would be addressed in individual meetings with Ms B.

She did not drink for almost three months while living at this shelter. During this time, the ACT team assisted her in obtaining Social Security disability benefits; the team was named as the representative payee for this income support. She was assisted in finding her own apartment, and being sober enabled her to gain access to housing subsidies. Although the team ensured that Ms B's rent and bills were paid, she would sometimes use the leftover funds to buy alcohol, which induced bizarre behavior. Whenever her landlord threatened eviction because of a behavioral disturbance, the ACT team would intervene by coming into the apartment to provide crisis counseling. These bingeing episodes became less frequent. Ms B slowly became willing to acknowledge that alcohol use was not in her best interest and agreed to try group educational meetings about alcohol. She became increasingly attached to her apartment and stated that she did not want to do anything that might lead to her becoming homeless again. The team used this information to gently persuade her to examine the likely consequences of ongoing alcohol abuse, and over time her drinking episodes disappeared entirely. Ms B's compliance with medication improved somewhat, but she remains suspicious and slightly paranoid.

From Osher and Dixon (1996).

- Being available in an area populated by people who are homeless and meeting with them at a local diner, not a clinic; providing for basic needs such as clothes, showers, and food (Osher & Dixon, 1996).
- Helping people learn how to shop, clean apartments, and do laundry (Mueser et al., 2003).
- Assigning a substance abuse "consultation-liaison" person to a psychiatric inpatient unit to meet with designated patients with potential coexisting AOD disorders and offer them education and options in a nonconfrontational manner (Greenfield, Weiss, & Tohen, 1995).
- Providing nonverbal stress management training, such as basic yoga, progressive relaxation techniques, and gentle movement exercises (Brady et al., 1996).
- Addressing acute needs through crisis intervention for a housing, medical, or psychiatric emergency (Osher & Dixon, 1996).

If a person becomes acutely ill, actively suicidal, or dangerously psychotic, it may be absolutely necessary to use coercive interventions such as involuntary hospitalization to help the person stabilize. This kind of behavioral control can be seductive to professionals, especially when the clinician and/or the family really wants the person to be abstinent. It's important to keep in mind that coercive interventions are only temporary and are designed to prevent immediate harm, not to further the change process. Abstinence cannot be coerced in the long run. For the person to continue to move forward beyond a coercive intervention, it is still necessary to have a motivation to change.

STRENGTHS-BASED INTERVENTIONS

There are two important assumptions that set integrated treatment apart from historical mental health and substance abuse treatment in the United States. One major premise is that persons with coexisting disorders are capable of making decisions and taking actions that will help them achieve their goals. A second premise is that "motivation for abstinence must reside *in the patient,* not in the clinician or family" (Mueser, Drake, & Noordsy, 1998, p. 135). Together, these assumptions point the way to a variety of interventions that view persons with coexisting disorders through strengths perspective glasses.

Stage-wise treatment is a successful strategy that is built on the premise that people go through (and continue to recycle through) stages of change. The utility of stage-wise treatment was first demonstrated in the evaluation of the 13 Community Support Program federal demonstration projects between 1987 and 1991 (Mercer-McFadden et al., 1997). As discussed in the Creative Engagement Practices section, the menu of intervention strategies is respectfully offered and geared to whatever stage the person is in. Stages can be determined by finding out how much persons with coexisting disorders are aware of the negative consequences of the substance misuse to them, their motivation to change their substance use, and their goals for living and/or treatment. The model developed by Osher and Kofoed (1989), based on Prochaska and DiClemente's cycle of change (1992) and used in many integrated treatment models, divides the stages into four parts:

1. *Engagement* (as described earlier), where there is little or no insight into the consequences of the substance misuse, no plan to change the pattern of use, and no regular contact with treatment staff
2. *Persuasion,* where there is still no motivation to change the substance use but where regular contact is occurring with a case manager or treatment staff, practical assistance and support are accepted, and psychiatric symptoms are stabilizing
3. *Active treatment,* where the person has identified how substance misuse interferes with personal goals, is attempting to reduce or stop use, and is willing to pursue treatment strategies (e.g., self-help and psychoeducational groups, counseling, family therapy, and education) to achieve goals
4. *Relapse prevention,* where the person has been abstinent or has not experienced any negative consequences from substance use for at least 6 months and is willing to work on sustaining a meaningful recovery in all areas of life

Perhaps the most difficult stage for clinicians trained in traditional substance abuse or mental health practices is the persuasion stage. As described by Denning (2004), this is when dominant stereotypes, assumptions (e.g., that addicts routinely lie and deny their problems), and expectations about who is in control may enter the potential therapeutic relationship. "The client expects to be controlled and does not want to be, and the therapist expects the client to want to be helped, to be willing to be controlled in some subtle way. When we view an addict as being a problem, or not motivated, or in denial, we are often speaking of this conflict of expectations" (p. 108). Clients are also likely to have their own expectations that they are mistrusted, even scary to the clinician, and feel protective about disclosing anything that might bring on negative consequences.

To break through these barriers, clinicians need to give up the illusion that they are in control. It is critical to rid ourselves of the idea that people with coexisting disorders will change their habits of drug or alcohol use just because it might be "good for them," *even if this is obvious to the clinician and the family.* When a clinician can embrace the fact that, like it or not, "motivation for abstinence must reside *in the patient,* not in the clinician or family" (Mueser, Drake, & Noordsy, 1998, p. 135), strategies for increasing motivation to formulate goals around substance use can begin. A practical suggestion from Denning (2004) for the beginning stages is to affirm clearly with clients that they have the right to live their own life and that your job as a therapist is to help them find their own goals and make decisions on how to reach them. Then expect to be tested on this assertion.

Motivational interviewing (MI; see chapter 3) is a particularly helpful strengths-based practice with persons who are in the persuasion stage; that is, they haven't yet discovered a relationship between the misery they experience and their use of alcohol or drugs (Carey, 1996; Mueser, Drake, & Noordsy, 1998; Sciacca & Thompson, 1996). By helping clients to clarify goals and decide how their substance use interferes with their goals, it is possible to consistently address the important question that all of us ask at decision points: "What's in it for me?"

Goals that may be meaningful for persons with coexisting disorders include getting or holding a job, finding housing, surviving or improving health, avoiding AIDS or death, getting admitted to detox for room and board when hungry or homeless, allowing medications to work, stopping the consequences of AOD use (e.g., increased anxiety, child protective service involvement), and placating family or significant others. The fact that many of these goals result from the consequences of alcohol or drug use is not relevant in the beginning stages. The therapeutic goal is to establish an environment of trust and to provide concrete assistance, not judgment.

Motivational interviewing can also be used effectively in a brief session prior to psychiatric hospital discharge to enhance outpatient treatment entry into a dual diagnosis program. Daley and Zuckoff (1998) report using the MI principles of (a) accepting clients' ambivalence toward change as normal, (b) avoiding confrontation, (c) identifying current needs, wishes, and goals, (d) exploring the risks associated with continued substance use and the probable impact on these goals of offering a menu of change options that may help clients, (e) supporting clients' self-efficacy that positive change can occur, and (f) inviting clients to consider the benefits of keeping their outpatient appointment as a first step. This process contrasts with the more usual directive to follow through with the outpatient appointment. As a result, the initial outpatient show rate almost doubled, from 35 to 67%, for the clients who received a brief MI session. In a rare ethnographic study of substance abuse among people with severe mental illness, Alverson, Alverson, and Drake (2000) found that attaining four "positive quality-of-life factors" actually preceded and predicted sobriety among the people in the study. Furthermore, reduction of the factors preceded rather than followed a relapse into substance abuse. These important factors are similar to those for any persons recovering from substance abuse: a meaningful activity (job, hobby, social network), decent and stable housing, a meaningful relationship with someone who accepts them, and a positive, regular relationship with a mental health professional. The fact that, for the clients in this study, achieving these factors came before sobriety underscores the importance of focusing on the needs identified by the client, even when these needs do not include abstinence.

Pathways to Housing, Inc. of New York City is an award-winning program that illustrates these findings. Pathways' focus is on clients that no one else wants; they have been homeless for a long time, have a serious mental health problem, most (75%) have a co-occurring substance use disorder, and have usually failed in other programs. The program is based on the principles that consumers can make competent choices, housing is a basic right of every human being, and recovery is possible. Housing is offered immediately, regardless of whether a person has "earned" that right by completing substance abuse treatment or any other preconditions. Harm reduction practices include honoring client choices about the services they want to use and helping to support their choices through Assertive Community Treatment (ACT) teams who provide individually tailored case management, psychiatric and medical treatment, counseling, supported employment, self-help groups, budgeting, obtaining benefits, and classes such as art, photography, and writing (Pathways to Housing, 2005). Research on the program indicates much higher rates of housing stability than standard care programs, and clients can remain stable without increasing their substance use. One longitudinal study of this program found that at the end of 5 years, 88% of the Pathway clients remained housed compared to 47% of the clients who were housed through a linear residential treatment approach (Tsemberis & Eisenberg, 2000). Another study found that after 48 months, there were no significant group differences in alcohol and drug use when the Pathways clients were compared to standard care programs (Padgett, Gulcur, & Tsemberis, 2006).

Harm reduction is an essential correlate of strengths-based practice that is used consistently in integrated treatment programs. Again, harm reduction does not mean "nonabstinence." In integrated treatment, it means that although abstinence may be assumed to be the safest long-term goal for persons with coexisting disorders, any movement toward reducing use or reducing the consequences of use is encouraged. Using less often, using smaller amounts, experimenting with the "consequences" of abstinence for 24 hours, and using clean needles are all examples of attainable initial goals. Harm reduction has the additional advantage of being a "low-threshold" practice in that persons are accepted as they are, with no "high-threshold" requirements, such as abstinence, that can provoke little or no participation in the program. In a harm reduction framework, changes, no matter how small, are examined with curiosity as to what effect the change had on the person's mood, psychiatric symptoms such as depression or anxiety, relationships with others, and identified goals in living. The clinician's role is to support the person through these small changes by tuning into potential fears, by offering concrete help (e.g., medical or hospital admission assistance) when needed, and by raising hope that things can be better (Carey, 1996; Denning, 2004; Phillips & Labrow, 2000).

In the active treatment stage, when the person has identified how substance misuse interferes with his or her own personal goals and is attempting to reduce or stop use, psychoeducational and therapeutic groups may be helpful. A key ingredient found helpful in these groups is the maintenance of a highly supportive environment (Timko & Moos, 1998). This makes it possible to deal with all aspects of substance misuse, mental illness, the interaction of the two, relapse, or "slips," in a caring and nonconfrontational manner. Dealing with emotions and feelings is "very difficult" for the majority of persons with dual diagnoses, according to a recent study (Laudet, Magura, Vogel, & Knight, 2000), so group support is critical in encouraging a person to speak about these sensitive matters. Brady et al. (1996) suggest the following practical guidelines from their experiences working with inner-city, chronically mentally ill persons with substance misuse problems:

- Use stress management techniques (relaxation and breathing exercises) to decrease distress.
- Emphasize links between alcohol and drugs and physical, psychological, and social problems.
- Teach group members an array of techniques to manage mental illness symptoms, including avoidance of alcohol and drugs.
- Maximize client participation.
- In later sessions, move into testimonials, role-playing, peer praise, and peer confrontation to enhance motivation for change. (p. 577)

Research on the effectiveness of specific types of treatment (individual, group, or family) is scarce. There is some evidence that attending a "dual-diagnosis group" correlates with a favorable outcome, especially when combined with intensive case management (Klein, Cnaan, & Whitecraft, 1998), but no particular type of group appears more effective than another (Drake & Mueser, 2000). However, "more is better," according to the findings of Laudet et al. (2000), where higher levels of support from a greater number of people were linked to less substance use. One such group, called "The Good Chemistry Group," is a combination of therapy, psychoeducation, and peer support. Members are encouraged to have "natural highs" and "good chemistry" by getting involved in fun and healthy activities that don't require using alcohol or drugs (DiNitto & Webb, 2005).

Mutual-help groups such as Alcoholics Anonymous (see chapter 12) can provide much needed social support for some persons outside the professional arena. However, research also suggests that many clients with major mental illness, especially schizophrenia, will have difficulties participating in these groups (Noordsy, Schwab, Fox, & Drake, 1996). Members may have trouble understanding severe mental illness and be uncomfortable with some of the behavioral manifestations of the illness. Historically, some AA members have refused to consider psychiatric medication as anything other than "drugs" and have urged people who very much need it to discontinue use. For these reasons, a referral to AA or NA should be accompanied by some help in linking them to a receptive group in the community.

Other suggestions for increasing the likelihood of a good experience in AA include (a) waiting to refer until the person is in the active treatment stage and wants abstinence; (b) affirming that the person has the absolute right to choose whether to attend and participate; (c) suggesting that he or she can be a "visitor" for a few meetings to observe and politely "pass" the invitation to read or talk during the meeting; (d) giving them the AA-approved brochure "The AA Member—Medications and Other Drugs" that welcomes persons who are taking psychiatric medications (Alcoholics Anonymous [AA], 1984);

(e) introducing the person to an AA member who will take that person to his or her first meeting (Powell, Kurtz, Garvin, & Hill, 1996).

Special community support groups with limited professional involvement may also be very helpful. Double Trouble in Recovery (DTR) groups, which are adapted from AA for persons with coexisting mental disorders, have over 100 meeting sites in the United States. A recent study of 310 DTR members who had participated for at least 1 month revealed that 75% of them also attended either AA or NA; those who did not reported feeling judged, uncomfortable, or not accepted because of mental health issues or medication or felt that DTR met their needs. Participation in DTR was positively linked to recovery (Laudet et al., 2000).

Relapse prevention strategies for persons with coexisting disorders have a dual focus on substance abuse and mental health problems (Nigam, Schottenfeld, & Kosten, 1992; Ziedonis & Trudeau, 1997). For example, a social skills training group may be developed to emphasize problem solving, communication skills, management of psychiatric symptoms, medication compliance, and relapse prevention. Relapse and slips are generally handled in a nonjudgmental manner. Group members help bring out the circumstances and results of slips to help the person with a new plan (see Case Study 8.3). Group members learn to identify triggers and early warning signs of substance use and psychiatric symptoms and at the same time support hope and self-efficacy with each other. Depending on the membership, the group process may need to be adapted to fit the attention span and communication skills of the group.

Long-Term Consequences

A person with coexisting disorders is likely to experience problems that touch almost every aspect of life: basic needs such as housing, relationships, employment, medication stabilization, physical problems, and legal troubles. In addition to the many external problems, it takes a long time for the internal work needed to go from zero awareness that one even has a problem to choosing and then maintaining successful solutions to the problem. It could be said that recovery involves building a whole new life, inside and outside. It is no wonder that stability takes months and years, not weeks. Research findings on treatment effectiveness indicate that the course of recovery involves gradual reductions in substance use for most persons with coexisting disorders (see Case Study 8.2 on Ms B). Drake (1996) and other studies suggest that the proportion of clients attaining abstinence increases every 6 months, until at the end of 3 years almost half have attained abstinence.

Integrated Pharmacotherapy

The use of medications for both mental health and substance use disorders is a complex issue because of the interactions between some psychiatric medications and alcohol and drugs and because undermedication for psychiatric

| CASE 8.3 | GROUP TREATMENT STRENGTHS |

The following story is an example of how group members can support a person who has lapsed into drug use.

Sherry binged on IV cocaine nine months after entering the dual-diagnosis group. She reported this to the group at the next meeting and explained that one of her drug-abusing friends visited her and offered her cocaine. She told the group that she was feeling low on that day and was alone in her apartment without anything to do. She felt that she could not resist getting high, although she tried to resist at first. The group listened to her very carefully and sympathetically. They discussed and developed a relapse prevention strategy for this patient, as follows:

1. Don't allow your drug-using friends to visit you, and say "No" boldly.
2. Disconnect yourself completely from drug abusers.
3. Call one of the group therapists or any other member of the group when you are feeling low.

When she encountered the same situation the following week, she was able to say "No" and control herself. In the next session she happily told the group that this strategy worked for her.

From Nigam, Schottenfeld, and Kosten (1992).

symptoms may cause a relapse in substance misuse. Ideally, a physician is part of the treatment team, and medication is integrated and closely monitored as part of the total integrated approach. Denning (2004) advises that the entire team have expertise in pharmacology and the potential drug interactions that may occur, be prepared to provide references to other clinicians, be willing to examine their own biases around medication for substance misusers, and engage in frequent discussions about these issues on behalf of each client. For example, it's important to distinguish "psychoactive" medications (e.g., opioids, stimulants, benzodiazepines, barbiturates, and other sedative-hypnotics), which can cause rapid changes in mood, thought, and behavior, from "nonpsychoactive" medications (e.g., lithium, antipsychotics, beta-blockers, antidepressants, monoamine oxidase inhibitors, antihistamines, anticonvulsants, and anticholinergics), which normalize thinking processes.

Specific pharmacotherapies for persons with coexisting disorders are still in the beginning stage, and there is a lack of research, especially controlled studies, to guide clinicians. However, the Center for Substance Abuse Treatment (CSAT) (2005) offers these guidelines:

- Acute and severe symptoms that occur with such disorders as mania, psychotic depression, and schizophrenia require immediate medication.
- If symptoms are not acute, use a "stepwise" approach of (a) trying no medication for less severe problems, such as anxiety or mild depression, (b) adding nonpsychoactive medication if the symptoms do not lessen after

detoxification and psychosocial approaches, and (c) adding psychoactive medications if the symptoms do not abate or if they get worse (p. 461).

In summary, integrated treatment programs, as developed over the past 15 years, have begun to offer more hope to the person with coexisting disorders. Research affirms that when this type of treatment is provided over several years, clients attain higher rates of stable remission as well as improve their quality of life. The integrated approach embraces many strengths-based practices, such as motivational interviewing, harm reduction, and stages of treatment interventions. Multidisciplinary teams with a variety of training and philosophical backgrounds have, over time, been able to put aside their differences and learn new approaches to helping people in this vulnerable situation.

SUBSTANCE MISUSE AND DEVELOPMENTAL, PHYSICAL, AND COGNITIVE DISABILITIES

Substance misuse can stand in the way of a person's adequately dealing with an adjustment to a disability as well as aggravate the disability itself. However, until recently, substance misusers who have coexisting developmental, physical, or cognitive disabilities have been largely ignored in treatment settings, research, professional training, and public awareness.

The 1990 Americans with Disabilities Act (ADA) helped changes begin by guaranteeing full participation and access to community services and facilities for all people with disabilities. Treatment programs and mental health centers were put on notice that they must adapt their programs to meet the needs of people with coexisting disabilities. The Department of Justice ADA website at www.usdoj.gov/crt/ada/index.htm offers technical assistance, mediation, and current information on all aspects of the act. However, findings from a national study suggest that at least 50% of all persons with a coexisting disability are still not being identified as such by the system that provides them with services (Rehabilitation Research and Training Center on Drugs and Disability, 1995).

This section focuses on a wide range of disabilities, excluding the mental disorders already covered. Using the principle of the independent living movement that persons with disabilities share more commonality than differences in their experience of living, we discuss common themes around traditional barriers to treatment, the development of new assessment tools, and new treatment practices relevant to persons with substance misuse and a coexisting disability. Because many people in the able culture still view people with disabilities in terms of what they cannot do or should not attempt to do and because helping agencies continue to reflect that bias, a strengths-based approach to practice is particularly important and will be emphasized. Space requirements limit detailed discussion of individual types of disability; we attempt to compensate by using examples from a range of different disabilities.

Prevalence and Characteristics

Prevalence studies of substance misusers with coexisting disabilities are scarce. According to the Center for Substance Abuse Treatment (CSAT, 1998), one of the few states to keep comprehensive records on substance use disorder services for persons with disabilities is New York's Office of Alcoholism and Substance Abuse Services. In 1997, they reported that 22.4% of the total clients receiving substance use disorder services had a coexisting physical or mental disability. Of these, over half (58.9%) had a disability not related to mental illness, such as mobility impairment, visual impairment, or deafness. The CSAT suggests that because the reports were generated by treatment staff not trained in assessing specific disabilities, many disabilities may be underreported, such as traumatic brain injury, learning disability, and attention-deficit hyperactivity disorder (ADHD).

DiNitto and Webb's (2005) review of existing research on the prevalence of substance misusers with mental retardation suggests that this population is less likely to use or misuse alcohol and drugs than the general population. However, as they also note, this finding may be the result of such factors as close supervision, reporting bias from institutional settings that prohibit alcohol or drug use, people's unwillingness to report use, or the fact that individuals with mental retardation are a protected class and securing informed consent to participate in research is difficult and time consuming. Findings from McGillicuddy and Blane's (1999) survey of substance use in persons with mental retardation ($n = 122$) living in the community suggest that the rate of alcohol misuse comes close to the rate in the general population. The percentage of use in the past month in this sample was alcohol 39%, nicotine 23%, and illicit drugs 4%. The majority of individuals (61%) did not use alcohol, while 21% were classified as users (no consequences), and 18% were classified as misusers (experienced consequences and met other misuse criteria, such as drinking to intoxication). Other studies report that persons with mental retardation experience the same kind of alcohol- or drug-related problems that persons with only substance misuse experience, such as troubles at work, problems with friends and family, and legal problems.

Several studies indicate that persons with disabilities have a greater risk for alcohol and drug misuse than the general population. For example, spinal cord and head injuries are often related to accidents linked with the use of alcohol or drugs. In a review of the research, Heinemann and Hawkins (1995) found that between 17 and 68% of people with these injuries were intoxicated. Another study found heavy drinking in 55% of the sample 6 months before the spinal cord injury, which decreased to 20% one year following the injury (Heinemann, Schmidt, & Semik, 1994). In their review of the literature on substance misuse, CSAT (2004) concluded that people who qualify for vocational rehabilitation services are two times more likely to use alcohol and other drugs (20%) than the general population (10%). Because of the stress in the lives of people with disabilities and their high risk for victimization and isolation, a heightened rate of substance misuse would be predicted with this population.

When compared to data from the National Household Survey on Drug Abuse (1994), women with disabilities appear to use illicit drugs at a higher rate than women in the general population. A study by Li and Ford (1998) on 900 women with a variety of disabilities found that marijuana was the substance most used in the last month (6.6%), followed by cocaine (0.7%), compared to women in the general population: use of marijuana (4.6%) and cocaine (0.5%). Risk factors associated with illicit drug use include younger age, best friend who uses drugs, an entitlement attitude toward using drugs because of the disability, and being a self-reported victim of substance-abuse-related physical violence. Although chronic pain was reported by 43% of the women, a surprising finding was that chronic pain was not associated with the use of illicit drugs.

Wounded war veterans are another group at high risk for substance-related problems. Because of the large number of wounded veterans who survive explosions, the United States can expect to be paying for the war in Iraq for many years to come. One worrisome fact contained in information again supplied by the Walter Reed Army Medical Center (Okie, 2005) is that more than 60% of soldiers injured in the war in Iraq have potentially life-altering brain injuries.

According to a news report in *USA Today,* traumatic brain injury is the sort that many soldiers in previous wars never lived long enough to suffer (Zoroya, 2005). The body armor used today keeps people alive. But the shock wave from the bomb explosion can damage brain tissue. Behavioral changes, headaches, and a loss of problem-solving abilities are common. Those who survive head injuries often suffer from emotional problems, including difficulty with memory, as well as high rates of depression, alcohol use, and posttraumatic anxieties. Substance abuse counselors can expect to work with the injured victims of the wars in the Middle East, whether their injuries are to the mind or the body, who have sought relief in drinking or other drug misuse.

The Center for Substance Abuse Treatment (1998) estimates that, overall, coexisting disabilities (including psychiatric disorders) may affect up to 40% of all clients who enter substance use disorder treatment. New screening practices are needed to find these "hidden" conditions so that the program can be modified and adapted to meet the needs of such persons. The days of filling established treatment "slots" with a standard treatment program are over.

ASSESSING TREATMENT BARRIERS

In spite of the prevalence of substance misuse among people with disabilities, there is much evidence that they are less likely to enter or complete treatment. Likely reasons include physical, attitudinal, or communication barriers that make treatment unsatisfactory, irrelevant, or limited (CSAT, 1998). A Canadian survey of all the alcohol and drug treatment programs in Ontario found that few agencies offered services tailored especially for persons with disabilities (Tyas & Rush, 1993). At the time of the survey, only 40% of the 219 programs had wheelchair accessibility, and few agencies reported services specifically targeted to people with disabilities.

People with learning differences (mental retardation, borderline intelligence, learning disabilities, hyperactivity, and traumatic brain injury) can experience a number of barriers to effective treatment (Campbell, Essex, & Held, 1994). Insight-oriented approaches and the use of complex audiovisual aids and extensive writing assignments may be confusing. The popular modality of group treatment is likely to be too fast paced or abstract or to demand behaviors that a person with a brain injury may not be able to sustain. Fellow group participants may have negative stereotypes of persons with learning differences. Programs may need to adapt by using picture books, flash cards, and art therapy techniques.

Other barriers result from a lack of knowledge, experience, and understanding among treatment staff. Stereotypical beliefs that may be prevalent in the larger culture can also find a home in treatment staff. A list provided by CSAT (1998, p. 9) of commonly held beliefs that pose barriers to treatment includes:

- People with disabilities do not abuse substances.
- People with disabilities should receive exactly the same treatment protocol as everyone else so that they aren't singled out as different.
- A person is noncompliant when her disability prevents her from responding to treatment.
- A person with a disability will make other clients uncomfortable.
- People with disabilities will sue the program regardless of the services offered.
- People with disabilities deserve pity, so they should be allowed more latitude to indulge in substance use.

Communication barriers are particularly prevalent with people who are deaf and persons with slow or impaired speech, significant respiratory problems, or delays in cognition. Accommodations need to be made by using sign language interpreters, telecommunication devices for the deaf (TDDs), computer terminals and boards, and speech synthesizers.

It is a major premise of the independent living movement that "nonaccess in society resulted from architectural and attitudinal barriers rather than the dysfunction of the individual person with a disability" (Mackelprang & Salsgiver, 1999, p. 51). Architectural barriers include everything from no wheelchair access to a lack of transportation from the bus stop to the program entrance. The critical point is that when the physical, attitudinal, and communication barriers are removed, it becomes possible to establish a productive relationship that has a chance of being helpful to a person with coexisting disabilities.

Arguably, some of the greatest barriers to treatment for disabilities occur in the military, especially as far as troops who are serving on the battlefield are concerned. The goals of treatment, from the military's standpoint, are to provide temporary relief of mental or even physical symptoms to maintain the fighting force. For this purpose, in Iraq, for example, there are more than 200 mental health professionals who counsel soldiers after a tough battle to help them get their emotions under control (Streisand, 2006). Since it is well established that repeated exposure to combat stress is the greatest risk factor for PTSD, this work of the psychiatrists and other mental health experts raises some ethical issues related to their first responsibility, which is to the welfare of the client.

When their term of duty is up, the returning soldiers are assessed for mental health problems, and then again, 3 to 6 months later, they are given a mental health screening. Few of these former soldiers are referred for treatment, however (Streisand, 2006). Yet research has shown that during this time period—several months after departure from a war zone—30% of the former troops will have developed stress-related mental health problems (USA Today, 2005). This barrier to treatment is institutional. A more serious barrier, though, is psychological—the reluctance of traumatized soldiers to admit their problems and to seek help in the belief that any such request will jeopardize their military careers. Acknowledgment of a mental disorder, as well, is often viewed, especially by men, as a sign of weakness. Still, unprecedented numbers of veterans who saw combat in Iraq and Afghanistan are seeking treatment at the VA, and many were pushed to take this step by worried and frightened family members. Recently, the Departments of Defense and Veterans Affairs have stepped up efforts to meet the increasing demand.

Intake and Screening

As with any other person who might be seeking help, the most important task of the intake procedure is to begin to build trust and credibility with that person. This requires a nonconfrontational, supportive environment that will reduce anxiety, not increase it. If it is already known that the person has a particular disability, accommodations should already be made to eliminate functional barriers. For example, for persons in a wheelchair, the table should be at the right height; for persons who are deaf, a sign language interpreter must be available; for people with traumatic brain injury, questions should be concrete and checks for understanding should be made often. For a thorough discussion of potential accommodations needed, see CSAT (1998).

If a person is willing to seek help with stopping his or her substance misuse or in eliminating the consequences of such use, it is important to find out if there are any functional barriers that may get in the way. It is not necessary to diagnose a disability; that role is reserved for a disabilities expert (e.g., specialized medical services or state vocational rehabilitation programs). It is necessary to find out if any functional adjustments are needed that could help the clinician be a more helpful consultant to this person.

An initial screening for disabilities is very practical: It helps identify potential programmatic barriers so they can be modified. It is important to ask everyone involved in the intake process, "Do you need any accommodations to participate fully in this program?" Screening can also help identify areas where it may be beneficial for the person to link with other services. A basic screening instrument for identifying functional limitations that may pose barriers in treatment can be found in CSAT (1998, p. 21).

TREATMENT PRACTICES

There are a number of therapeutic issues that need to be addressed to increase the likelihood of treatment success. Treatment plans may feature different elements and concerns and may require more time depending on the disability. A person with coexisting disabilities may have quite different reasons for wanting to abstain from alcohol or drugs. For example, the fact that alcohol can lower the seizure threshold for persons with traumatic brain injury (TBI) may be a motivation to quit drinking alcohol for such persons.

The CSAT 19 recommends that each task written on a treatment contract be accompanied by a list of specific accommodations needed for that task to be accomplished. For example, for persons with memory problems expected to attend group sessions, "Call and remind them that a session is occurring or assist them in creating memory books that include necessary information on group meetings" (CSAT, 1998, p. 49).

Modifications for counseling sessions could include flexibility with the time and length of the session, sensitivity to what matters may be more readily discussed in individual sessions, preparing for sessions by researching the disability, providing specific examples of behaviors and concepts to persons with cognitive disabilities, preparing accessible written materials, and finding alternative media. Behavioral therapy may be preferable to insight-oriented, psychodynamic approaches because it offers small, concrete steps to long-term goals (DiNitto & Webb, 2005).

Helwig and Holicky (1994) suggest specific therapeutic issues that are common to many persons with physical disabilities and particularly trauma-induced disabilities:

> Learning to live in a world designed for able-bodied people who value normality and who shun difference, demands the ability to face and solve a never-ending string of problems ... These problems include major changes in almost every aspect of life, including a loss of privacy in areas of self-care; devaluing, enabling, or patronizing social attitudes; loss of control or determination; and incredible stress on one's family and support system. (p. 229)

In addition, grief and loss issues around the disability and the addiction may be important therapeutic themes.

Motivational interviewing techniques have been found successful with adults who have traumatic brain injury. By helping the person to assess his or her motivation to use alcohol and other drugs, identify and evaluate goals, resolve conflicts among interfering goals, and develop skills for reaching realistic goals, the person is engaged in immediately gratifying activities. Homework activities are designed to be positive, goal oriented, and immediately measurable on a "goal ladder" that leads to a long-term goal. Results from an evaluation of using this approach with 60 persons with TBI during a 12-week treatment program suggest that motivational interviewing was effective in reducing substance use. At 1-year follow-up, 40% maintained abstinence, 14% became abstinent, 38% continued using, and 8% began using (Heinemann, 1997).

Many authors discuss the need to practice from a strengths perspective when working with persons who have a disability (CSAT, 1998; Mackelprang & Salsgiver, 1999). If a treatment goal is not met, it is important to look first at whether or not accommodations were sufficient to support the process instead of immediately blaming the individual for resistance to treatment.

SUMMARY AND CONCLUSION

In the mid-1980s, clinicians were still arguing about which disorder should be treated first: mental illness or substance dependence. Clients were falling through the categorical cracks. Since then, research has demonstrated that it works best when we treat both problems at once in an integrated team approach that coordinates the treatments of both systems. Within the overall context of harm reduction, strengths-based interventions, such as motivational interviewing and stage-wise treatment, are successful strategies that help the clinician stay focused on the client's goals. Professionals who work with persons who have physical disabilities or cognitive impairments are recognizing that substance misuse problems can no longer be overlooked, and substance abuse treatment programs are making innovative accommodations to better serve these populations. The challenge now is for health maintenance organizations and state and federal funding sources to create reimbursement and policy practices that will enhance these developments.

References

Alcoholics Anonymous (AA). (1984). *The AA member—medications and other drugs.* New York: AA World Services.

Alverson, H., Alverson, M., & Drake, R. E. (2000). An ethnographic study of the longitudinal course of substance abuse among people with severe mental illness. *Community Mental Health Journal, 36*(6), 557–569.

American Psychiatric Association (APA). (2000). *Diagnostic and statistical manual of mental disorders, text revision* (4th ed.) (DSM–IV–TR). Washington, DC: Author.

Bearman, D., Claydon, K., Kincheloe, J., & Lodise, C. (1997). Breaking the cycle of dependency: Dual diagnosis and AFDC families. *Journal of Psychoactive Drugs, 29*(4), 359–367.

Biegel, D., Kola, L. A., Ronis, R. J., Boyle, P. E., Reyes, C., Wieder, B., et al. (2003). The Ohio Substance Abuse and Mental Illness Coordinating Center of Excellence: Implementation support for evidence-based practice. *Research on Social Work Practice, 13*(4), 531–545.

Blume, S. B. (1997). Pathological gambling. In J. Lowinson, P. Ruiz, R. Millman, & J. Langrod (Eds.), *Substance abuse: A comprehensive textbook* (3rd ed., pp. 330–336). Baltimore: Williams & Wilkins.

Brady, S., Hiam, C. M., Saemann, R., Humbert, L., Fleming, M., & Dawkins-Brickhouse, K. (1996). Dual diagnosis: A treatment model for substance abuse and major mental illness. *Community Mental Health Journal, 32*(6), 573–579.

Breakey, W. R., Calabrese, L., Rosenblatt, A., & Crum, R. M. (1998). Detecting alcohol use disorder in the severely mentally ill. *Community Mental Health Journal, 34*(2), 165–174.

Campbell, J. A., Essex, E. L., & Held, G. (1994). Issues in chemical dependency treatment and aftercare for people with learning differences. *Health and Social Work, 19*(1), 63–70.

Carey, K. B. (1996). Substance use reduction in the context of outpatient psychiatric treatment: A collaborative motivational, harm reduction approach. *Community Mental Health Journal, 32,* 291–306.

Center for Substance Abuse Treatment (CSAT). (1994). *Assessment and treatment of patients with coexisting mental illness and alcohol and other drug abuse.* Treatment Improvement Protocol (TIP) Series, No. 9. U.S. Department of Health and Human Services, Public Health Service. Rockville, MD: Author.

Center for Substance Abuse Treatment (CSAT). (1998). *Substance use disorder treatment for people with physical and cognitive disabilities.* Treatment Improvement Protocol (TIP) Series, No. 29. U.S. Department of Health and Human Services, Public Health Service. Rockville, MD: Author.

Center for Substance Abuse Treatment (CSAT). (2004). *Substance abuse treatment and family therapy.* Treatment Improvement Protocol (TIP) Series, No. 39. U.S. Department of Health and Human Services. Rockville, MD: Author.

Center for Substance Abuse Treatment (CSAT). (2005). *Substance abuse treatment for persons with co-occurring disorders.* Treatment Improvement Protocol (TIP) Series, No. 42. DHHS Publication No. (SMA) 05-3922. Rockville, MD: Substance Abuse and Mental Health Services Administration.

Crisp, C. L. (2005). Dual diagnosis: Substance abuse and mental health in an inpatient setting. In L. M. Grobman (Ed.), *Days in the lives of social workers: Forty-one professionals tell "real life" stories from social work practice* (3rd ed., pp. 205–210). Harrisburg, PA: White Hat Community.

Daley, D. C., & Zuckoff, A. (1998). Improving compliance with the initial outpatient session among discharged inpatient dual diagnosis clients. *Social Work, 43*(5), 470–473.

Davis, D. R. (2002). The Queen of hearts: Women and compulsive gambling. In S. L. Straussner & S. Brown (Eds.), *The handbook of women's addictions treatment: Theory and practice* (99–126). San Francisco: Jossey-Bass.

Dawe, S., Seinen, A., & Kavanagh, D. (2000). An examination of the utility of the AUDIT in people with schizophrenia. *Journal of Studies on Alcohol, 61,* 744–750.

Denning, P. (2000). *Practicing harm reduction psychotherapy: An alternative approach to addictions.* New York: Guilford Press.

Denning, P. (2004). *Practicing harm reduction psychotherapy: An alternative approach to addictions.* New York: Guilford Press.

DiNitto, D. M., & Webb, D. K. (2005). Compounding the problem: Substance abuse and other disabilities. In C. A. McNeece & D. M. DiNitto, *Chemical dependency: A systems approach* (2nd ed., pp. 423–483). Boston: Allyn & Bacon.

DiNitto, D. M., Webb, D. K., & Rubin, A. (2002). The effectiveness of an integrated treatment approach for clients with dual diagnoses. *Research on Social Work Practice, 12*(5), 621–641.

Drake, R. E. (1996). Substance use reduction among patients with severe mental illness. *Community Mental Health Journal, 32*(3), 311–314.

Drake, R. E., & Mueser, K. T. (2000). Psychosocial approaches to dual diagnosis. *Schizophrenia Bulletin, 26*(1), 105–118.

Drake, R. E., & Wallach, M. A. (1993). Moderate drinking among people with severe mental illness. *Hospital and Community Psychiatry, 44,* 780–782.

Drake, R. E., Yovetich, N. A., Bebout, R. R., Harris, M., & McHugo, G. J. (1997). Integrated treatment for dually diagnosed homeless adults. *Journal of Nervous and Mental Disease, 185,* 298–305.

Goff, D. C., Henderson, D. C., & Amico, E. (1992). Cigarette smoking in schizophrenia: Relationship to psychopathology and medication side effects. *American Journal of Psychiatry, 149,* 1189–1194.

Greenfield, S. F., Weiss, R. D., & Tohen, M. (1995). Substance abuse and the chronically mentally ill: A description of dual diagnosis treatment services in a psychiatric hospital. *Community Mental Health Journal, 31*(3), 265–277.

Handmaker, N., Packard, M., & Conforti, K. (2002). Motivational interviewing in the treatment of dual disorders. In W. R. Miller & S. Rollnick (Eds.), *Motivational interviewing: Preparing people for change* (pp. 262–276). New York: Guilford Press.

Heinemann, A. W. (1997). Persons with disabilities. In J. Lowinson, P. Ruiz, R. Millman, & J. Langrod (Eds.), *Substance abuse: A comprehensive textbook* (3rd ed., pp. 716–725). Baltimore: Williams & Wilkins.

Heinemann, A. W., & Hawkins, D. (1995). Substance abuse and medical complications following spinal cord injury. *Rehabilitation Psychology, 40*(2), 125–140.

Heinemann, A. W., Schmidt, M. F., & Semik, P. (1994). Drinking patterns, drinking expectancies and coping after spinal cord injury. *Rehabilitation Counseling Bulletin, 38*(2), 134–153.

Helwig, A., & Holicky, R. (1994). Substance abuse in persons with disabilities: Treatment considerations. *Journal of Counseling and Development, 72,* 227–233.

Hoge, C. W., Castro, C. A., Messer, S., McGurk, D., Cotting, D., & Koffman, R. (2004). Combat duty in Iraq and Afghanistan, mental health problems, and barriers to care. *New England Journal of Medicine, 351*(1), 13–22.

Is everybody crazy? (1998, January 26). *Newsweek,* pp. 51–56.

Jackson, K. (2003, June). Trauma and the national psyche. *Social Work Today,* pp. 20–23.

Kausch, O. (2003). Suicide attempts among veterans seeking treatment for pathological gambling. *Journal of Clinical Psychiatry, 64*(9), 1031–1038.

Kavanagh, D. J., Young, R., Boyce, L., Clair, A., Sitharthan, R., Clark, D., et al. (1998). Substance treatment option is psychosis (STOP): A new intervention for dual diagnosis. *Journal of Mental Health, 7*(2), 135–143.

Kessler, R. C., Galea, S., Jones, R., & Parker, H. A. (2006). Mental illness and suicidality after Hurricane Katrina. Retrieved September 23, 2006, from http://www.hurricanekatrina.med.harvard.edu.

Klein, A., Cnaan, R., & Whitecraft, J. (1998). Significance of peer social support with dually diagnosed clients: Findings from a pilot study. *Research on Social Work Practice, 8*(5), 529–551.

Kowal, J. (2006, July 5). Homeless alcoholics receive a permanent place to live, and drink. *The New York Times.* Retrieved September 2006 from http://www.truthout.org/cgi-bin/artman/exec/view.cgi/62/20990.

Kubiak, S. P. (2004). The effects of PTSD on treatment adherence, drug relapse, and criminal recidivism in a sample of incarcerated men and women. *Research on Social Work Practice, 14*(6), 424–433.

Laudet, A. B., Magura, S., Vogel, H. S., & Knight, E. (2000). Addictions services: Support, mutual aid and recovery from dual diagnosis. *Community Mental Health Journal, 36*(5), 457–476.

Li, L., & Ford, J. (1998). Illicit drug use by women with disabilities. *American Journal of Drug and Alcohol Abuse, 24*(3), 405–418.

Linhorst, D. M. (2006). *Empowering people with severe mental illness.* New York: Oxford University Press.

Mackelprang, R., & Salsgiver, R. (1999). *Disability: A diversity model approach in human service practice.* Pacific Grove, CA: Brooks/Cole.

McGillicuddy, N., & Blane, H. (1999). Substance use in individuals with mental retardation. *Addictive Behaviors, 24*(6), 869–878.

Mercer-McFadden, C., Drake, R. E., Brown, N. B., & Fox, R. S. (1997). The community support program demonstrations of services for young adults with severe mental illness and substance use. *Psychiatric Rehabilitation Journal, 20*(3), 13–24.

Minkoff, K. (1996). Discussion of "Substance use reduction in the context of out-patient psychiatric treatment." *Community Mental Health Journal, 32,* 307–310.

Mueser, K. T., Drake, R. E., & Noordsy, D. L. (1998). Integrated mental health and substance abuse disorders. *Journal of Practical Psychiatry and Behavioral Health, 4,* 129–139.

Mueser, K. T., Drake, R. E., & Wallach, M. A. (1998). A review of etiological theories. *Addictive Behaviors, 23,* 717–734.

Mueser, K. T., Noordsy, D. L., Drake, R. E., & Fox, L. (2003). *Integrated treatment for dual disorders: A guide to effective practice.* New York: Guilford Press.

National Gambling Impact Study Commission. (1999, June 18). *Report of the commission.* Washington, DC: U.S. Government Printing Office. Retrieved from http://govinfo.library.unt.edu/ngisc/.

National Mental Health Association (NMHA). (2006) Hurricane Katrina: NMHA responds. Retrieved September 23, 2006, from http://www.nmha.org/katrina/index.cfm.

National Research Council. (1999). *Pathological gambling: A critical review.* Washington, DC: National Academy Press.

Navits, L. M. (2004). Treatment of posttraumatic stress disorder and substance abuse: Clinical guidelines for implementing seeking safety therapy. *Alcoholism Treatment Quarterly, 22,* 43–62.

Nigam, R., Schottenfeld, R., & Kosten, T. (1992). Treatment of dual diagnosis patients: A relapse prevention group approach. *Journal of Substance Abuse Treatment, 9,* 305–309.

Noordsy, D. L., Schwab, B., Fox, L., & Drake, R. E. (1996). The role of self-help programs in the rehabilitation of persons with severe mental illness and substance use disorders. *Community Mental Health Journal, 32,* 71–81.

Office of Applied Studies. (2004). Results from the 2003 National Survey on Drug Use and Health. *National Outcome Measures.* Rockville, MD. Retrieved September 2006 from http://www.oas.samhsa.gov/nhsda.htm.

Okie, S. (2005) Traumatic brain injury in the war zone. *New England Journal of Medicine, 352,* 2043–2047.

Orlin, L., O'Neill, M., & Davis, J. (2004). Assessment and intervention with clients who have coexisting psychiatric and substance-related disorders. In S. L. Straussner (Ed.), *Clinical work with substance-abusing clients* (pp. 103–124). New York: Guilford Press.

Osher, F. C., & Dixon, L. B. (1996). Housing for persons with co-occurring mental and addictive disorders. *New Directions for Mental Health Services, 70,* 53–54.

Osher, F. C., & Kofoed, L. (1989). Treatment of patients with psychiatric and psychoactive substance abuse disorders. *Hospital and Community Psychiatry, 40,* 1025–1030.

Padgett, D. K., Gulcur, L., & Tsemberis, S. (2006). Housing first services for people who are homeless with co-occurring serious mental illness and substance abuse. *Research on Social Work Practice, 16*(1), 74–83.

Pathways to Housing. (2005). 2005 APA gold award: Providing housing first and recovery services for homeless adults with severe mental illness. *Psychiatric Services, 56,* 1303–1305.

Phillips, P., & Labrow, J. (2000). Dual diagnosis—Does harm reduction have a role? *International Journal of Drug Policy, 11,* 279–283.

Powell, T. J., Kurtz, L. F., Garvin, C. D., & Hill, E. M. (1996). A model of AA utilization by persons with a dual diagnosis (the co-occurrence of alcoholism and severe mental illness). *Contemporary Drug Problems, 23,* 139–157.

Prochaska, J., & DiClemente, C. (1992). Stages of change in the modification of problem behaviors. In M. Hersen, R. M. Eisler, & P. M. Miller (Eds.), *Progress in behavior modification* (pp. 184–214). Sycamore, IL: Sycamore Press.

Quimby, E. (1995). Homeless clients' perspectives on recovery in the Washington, D.C., Dual Diagnosis Project. *Contemporary Drug Problems, 22*(2), 265–289.

Rehabilitation Research and Training Center on Drugs and Disability. (1995). *National Needs Assessment Survey results summary.* Dayton, OH: Author.

Rosenberg, S. D., Drake, R. E., Wolford, G. L., Mueser, K. T., Oxman, T. E., Vidaver, R., et al. (1998). Dartmouth assessment of lifestyle instrument (DALI): A substance use disorder screen for people with severe mental illness. *American Journal of Psychiatry, 155*(2), 232–238.

Saunders, J. B., Aasland, O. G., Babor, T. F., De La Fuente, J. R., & Grant, M. (1993). Development of the Alcohol Use Disorders Identification Test (AUDIT): WHO collaborative project on early detection of persons with harmful alcohol consumption: II. *Addiction, 88,* 791–804.

Sciacca, K., & Thompson, C. (1996). Program development and integrated treatment across systems for dual diagnosis: Mental illness, drug addiction, and alcoholism (MIDAA). *Journal of Mental Health Administration, 23*(3), 288–297.

Shavelson, L. (2002). *Hooked: Five addicts challenge our misguided drug rehab system.* New York: New Press.

Shulman, G. (1995, September/October). Reorienting CD treatment for dual diagnosis. *Behavioral Health Management,* pp. 30–33.

Smith, S. (1983). *Collected poems.* New York: New Directions.

St. George, D. (2006, June 20). Iraq war may add stress for past vets. *Washington Post,* p. A01.

Streisand, B. (2006, October 9). Treating war's toll on the mind. *U.S. News & World Report,* pp. 55–62.

Substance Abuse and Mental Health Services Administration (SAMHSA). (2001). New SAMHSA report shows value of integrating state mental health, substance abuse, and Medicaid data. Retrieved from http://www.samhsa.gov/news.

Substance Abuse and Mental Health Services Administration (SAMHSA). (2004). The DASIS Report: Facilities offering special programs or groups for clients with co-occurring disorders, 2004. Office of Applied Studies. Retrieved February 14, 2007, from http://www.oas.samhsa.gov/2k6/DualTX/DualTX.cfm.

Substance Abuse and Mental Health Services Administration (SAMHSA). (2006a). Homeless admissions to substance abuse treatment: 2004. The Drug and Alcohol Services Information System (DASIS). Retrieved October 2006 from http://oas.samhsa .gov.

Substance Abuse and Mental Health Services Administration (SAMHSA). (2006b). Results from the 2005 NSDUH: National Findings. Office of Applied Studies. Retrieved September 22, 2006, from http://www.oas.samhsa.gov/NSDUH/ 2k5NSDUH/2k5results.htm.

Timko, C., & Moos, R. H. (1998). Outcomes of the treatment climate in psychiatric and substance abuse program. *Journal of Clinical Psychology, 54*(8), 1137–1150.

Tsemberis, S., & Eisenberg, R. (2000). Pathways to Housing: Supported housing for street-dwelling homeless individuals with psychiatric disabilities. *Psychiatric Services, 51*, 487–493.

Tyas, S., & Rush, B. (1993). The treatment of disabled persons with alcohol and drug problems: Results of a survey of addiction services. *Journal of Studies on Alcohol, 54*, 275–282.

USA Today. (2005, July 28). Survey: 30% of returning Iraq vets suffer mental ills. *USA Today.* Retrieved September 2006 from http://www.usatoday.com/news/health/ 2005-07-28-iraq-vets-health_x.htm?csp=34.

van Wormer, K. (2007). *Human behavior and the social environment, micro level: Individuals and families.* New York: Oxford University Press.

Ziedonis, D. M., & Trudeau, K. (1997). Motivation to quit using substances among individuals with schizophrenia: Implications for a motivation-based treatment model. *Schizophrenia Bulletin, 23*(2), 229–238.

Zoroya, G. (2005, March 3). Key Iraq wound: Brain trauma. *USA Today.* Retrieved from http://www.usatoday.com/news/nation/2005-03-03-brain-trauma-lede_x.htm.

RECOMMENDED VIDEOS

The following videos have been recommended by the National Association on Alcohol, Drugs and Disability Inc. (NAADD), an organization developed to promote awareness and education about substance abuse among people with coexisting disabilities. More information can be found on their web site at www.naadd.org/index.html.

An American Sign Language Interpretation of the 12-Step Program
    Availability: Minnesota Chemical Dependency Program for Deaf & Hard of Hearing Individuals, 2450 Riverside Avenue, Minneapolis, MN 55454. (800) 282 3323 (TTY).

Dreams of Denial
    Availability: Minnesota Chemical Dependency Program for Deaf & Hard of Hearing Individuals, 2450 Riverside Avenue, Minneapolis, MN 55454. (800) 282 3323 (TTY).

J.R.'s Story: The Disability of Chemical Dependency
    Availability: AIMS Multi-Media. (800) 367 2467. $49.95.
    Follows a young man who is quadriplegic as he struggles with his alcohol and drug addiction (28 minutes).

PRTA: Living Out Loud
    Availability: Progressive Research & Training for Action, 2809 Telegraph Avenue, Ste. 208, Berkeley, CA 94705. (510) 705 8918; (510) 705 8535 (TTY).
    Chronicles a high-risk youth prevention program for teenage girls with disabilities.

Silent Storm: Disability and Coexisting Substance Abuse
    Availability: United Cerebral Palsy Association of New Jersey, 354 South Broad
    Street, Trenton, NJ 08909. (609) 392 4004; (609) 392 7044 (TTY). $40.00.
    A brief overview of the major issues surrounding alcohol and other drug problems
    and people with disabilities. Features interviews with NAADD board members
    and staff (10 minutes).
Understanding a Need ... Alcohol and Other Drug Abuse Prevention for People with
    Disabilities
    Availability: National Clearinghouse on Alcohol and Drug Information, Catalogue
    #VHS091. (800) 729 6686; (800) 487 4889 (TTY).
    An overview of the major issues of people with disabilities and prevention
    (15 minutes).

THE SOCIAL ASPECTS OF ADDICTION

Addiction to substances and behaviors begins and ends in the context of social relationships and therefore must be treated in the larger context of the social network. Unlike traditional treatment, typically focused on the individual in a standardized format, strengths-based therapy looks to family and other support systems as a buffer against addiction and as an essential resource in recovery. Strengths-based therapy, moreover, starts where the client is and stays where the client is: in his or her role in the family and community life. The starting point in treatment therefore should be with the family in terms of both risks and resiliencies. Accordingly, chapter 9, the first chapter in this part, describes family dynamics and strategies for engaging the family in treatment. Chapters 10 and 11 focus on race/ethnicity and gender, respectively. Gender is used in the broad sense here to encompass gender nonconformity as well as conformity in sex-role behavior. Because they do not conform to society's definition of sexuality, gays, lesbians, bisexuals, and transgender persons are highly vulnerable to drug use and misuse.

The task for practitioners who work with these and all other populations is to help people tap into their individual and collective resources. Throughout this part of the book, therefore, attention is paid to family-centered (chapter 9), ethnic-sensitive (chapter 10), and gender-specific and gay-sensitive (chapter 11) interventions. Chapter 12 applies the strengths perspective to an appreciation for the role that mutual-help support groups play in recovery. Consistent with the model that is the guiding theme of this book, the focus is on the appreciation, rather than the depreciation, of strategies that work.

377

Chapter 13, the policy chapter, which stands apart from the others in Part 4, is linked to them by the common thread of a concern with the social side (as opposed to the biological or psychological aspects) of addiction. The chapters that comprise the final portion of this book, in short, relate to social (including cultural and political) factors because these factors relate to treatment. We start with the oldest and most fundamental and enduring of all social institutions—the family.

Mam asks him if he brought any money. He tells her times are hard, jobs are scarce, and she says, Is it coddin' me you are? There's a war on and there's nothing but jobs in England. You drank the money, didn't you? You drank the money, Dad.

—Frank McCourt (1996, p. 270)

FAMILY RISKS AND RESILIENCIES

CHAPTER 9

INTRODUCTION

How we cope, how we see ourselves, how we love—these are the lessons learned at our mother's knee and at our father's. Whether as ghosts or as active participants, our grandparents (often our nurturers) are there as well.

The family is a system composed of members in constant and dynamic interaction with one another. Patterns of interaction get established—who interacts with whom, who talks and who listens, who has the authority, and who is the controlling force behind the scenes. The family has a pattern, a rhythm that is more than the sum of its parts. Any change in the behavior of one of its members affects not only each of the others but the system as a whole. Addiction is often defined as an illness not just of the individual but of the entire family. Sometimes, the misery is so intense that the system barely functions at all; such was the situation immortalized in *Angela's Ashes,* as expressed in the chapter's opening quote. Children growing up in such families fail to get the nurturing and care they need. The anger in such a family is palpable. Because needs are not met, the webs of addiction and impaired parenting perpetuate themselves across generations.

For every alcoholic, compulsive gambler, and cocaine addict, the lives of at least four other people are consistently altered. These other individuals may be in as much pain as the addict; they also may require help in how to deal with the addict or with their own powerful feelings. Family therapy, even in only a few sessions, can be invaluable in reducing the significant others' feelings of guilt or confusion. Family therapy, moreover, can be invaluable in preparing the family for changes that are needed to enhance and maintain the addicted person's recovery. Sometimes, the anger and resentment that significant others harbor need to be addressed before a recovering family member can return to the family setting. Sometimes, of course, the family environment itself is toxic, with all the participants having serious problems with drugs, for example. Here, too, interventions must be directed toward the whole family. To treat the individual in isolation is to ignore the context in which much of that behavior takes place.

From the perspective of this chapter, the family is viewed as a preventive resource—a system of both risk and resilience. Relevant to families in which alcoholic or other addictive behavior is a problem, a determination of both family risks and resiliencies is an important aspect of assessment (Gruber & Taylor, 2006). *Resilience* is more than just the ability of an individual family member to recover; rather, it involves protective factors within the entire family system or the family system dynamics. To know the context within which the addiction operates, an understanding of the systemic and intergenerational nature of addiction is essential.

That addiction is a family disease is a basic assumption of this book. The term *family disease* refers to the fact that the addicted family is malfunctioning. It does not mean that the addiction stems from family dynamics but, rather, that it affects the family dynamics. The chaos that the addict experiences in the abyss of his or her addiction is replicated in the chaos and unpredictability of family life surrounding the addiction. Even more than ordinary illness, addiction is a source of major stress that reverberates across and within the family system and affects the family's interactions with every other system in the community. The emotional and financial resources of the family may be almost entirely depleted by the stress of the addict's illness. Box 9.1 aptly depicts the havoc that methamphetamine addiction wreaks on the parents, the children, and one Iowa community.

That the family is a natural source of interpersonal influence on the individual is a second basic assumption. As William Miller (2006) tells us:

> It is now abundantly clear from research that an individual's motivation for changing substance abuse can be enhanced by unilateral intervention through concerned significant others. . . [U]nilateral family counseling approaches have been successful both in relieving family distress and in engaging a high percentage (usually two-thirds to three-fourths) of substance-abusing loved ones in treatment. Here a professional counselor helps family members to learn strategies for decreasing their loved one's substance use and for initiating treatment. (p. 139)

Because of addiction's stigma, the family therapy field has devoted little effort to addictions-focused treatment and has tended to refer afflicted members to specialized services or self-help groups. And because of the difficulty that substance abuse treatment centers face in working with the whole family, combined with third-party reimbursement disincentives to do so, often little more than lip service is given to family members' needs by these treatment centers. Yet for children and partners in the family system, the need to sort out their feelings and learn more about the nature of the problem that has so consumed them over the years is crucial for the long-term recovery of everyone involved. Too often, also, any family that doesn't match the traditional mold

Box 9.1	CHILDREN OF ADDICTS
	Colleen Krantz

Zoey Montgomery was 8 years old when she got on her hands and knees to look for a missing television remote under her family's couch and found bags of drugs instead. She knew her mother was the reason the marijuana was there in the room where she and her little brother played.

It's the kind of story that Zoey, now 10, knows only her friend Toddy Svoboda—and other children of addicts—could truly understand.

It was those shared stories of methamphetamine-addicted mothers leaving them for long periods, of caring for themselves too often, too young, and of being sent to live with grandparents when things went badly that led the two Fort Dodge girls to start a support group for children of addicts. They started out planning to call it Kids of Meth Heads, but were soon persuaded by other adults in their lives that it might go off better as Kids Supporting Kids of Addicted Parents.

They've hung fliers around Fort Dodge, which begin: "Do your parents spend more time with their 'friends' than with you? Are your parents taking money from you? Do you feel like you are being dumped?"

It's one more sign of how far meth has infiltrated Iowa, where 760 clandestine labs—a setting where meth is "cooked"—were found in the state last year. The numbers are a significant decline from the previous year—with most of the credit recently being given to a new law that makes it more difficult to obtain pseudoephedrine, a meth ingredient—but the highly-addictive drug is a long way from disappearing from the lives of Iowans, including children whose parents are too focused on the drug to pay attention to them.

"It's really become a societal problem," said Dixie Lovain, a child advocate with the Fort Dodge-based Domestic/Sexual Assault Outreach Center. "It's such a problem, but I thought the girls' idea was the neatest thing I'd heard of."

In 2005, more than 1,350 abuse cases involved children who were found to have illegal drugs in their system because of actions of a parent or caregiver, according to the Iowa Department of Human Services. The department found 128 children who were present while a parent or guardian was manufacturing meth.

Statewide data pertaining to the number of children whose parents are addicted to meth is not kept. But last year, nearly half of the 1,605 child-welfare cases in a 16-county area in southwest Iowa involved parental meth use, according to a study done by an Iowa Department of Human Services social work administrator.

Zoey and Toddy are hoping other children who have been neglected by parents addicted to meth or another drug show up at the weekly meetings the two girls have begun holding with Lovain, the child advocate.

"We don't want it to be just kids of meth heads," Toddy, 11, said. "But all things like alcohol, other drugs or even gambling."

Toddy's mother, Stephanie Svoboda, who is now in treatment and has been clean for more than two months, would often leave her daughter home alone during the night at age 8 or 9, said Toddy, who is living temporarily with Zoey's grandparents, who are family friends.

"She'd always threaten she was going to kill herself and then would leave for the night," Toddy said. "I couldn't sleep because I'd be worried."

continued

| Box 9.1 | CHILDREN OF ADDICTS *continued* |

She also remembers having to break up verbal and physical fights between her mother and her mother's boyfriend. "I'd just get in the middle of it and make them stop. I hated it," Toddy remembers. "I'd make them sit down or make one of them leave."

"I was a parent for a long time," Toddy said.

Zoey, who now lives with her father, can relate to Toddy's stories. By the time she was 7, she was not only getting her own breakfast and dinner, but was also often feeding her brother, who is six years younger. She also frequently changed her brother's diapers.

She remembers one morning when her mother hadn't returned home from a night of partying and she couldn't wake her stepfather. She had to get on the school bus and felt terrible because her little brother was essentially "alone in that house."

Stephanie Svoboda, 30, said she has been using illegal drugs since she was 18 or 19 and has known for years that she had to kick the habit for her and her daughter's sake.

"Right now, every day is hard for me" because of the continuing temptation that meth represents even after being clean for more than two months, said Svoboda, who attends a Moms Off Meth support group while the girls meet.

She thinks the group her daughter and Zoey have started is a "good idea."

The challenge, she said, will be that many parents will view taking their children to such a meeting as a threat since it might be seen as admitting use of illegal drugs.

Zoey's mother, Jody Montgomery, 30, said she is "really proud" of her daughter for helping establish the group. "I am ashamed of what I've done. But it is a disease and it's harder for kids if you don't communicate with them about it," said Montgomery, who is undergoing treatment for her addiction. The group may help her daughter and others to do the talking that's so important.

Zoey said she and Toddy don't hate their mothers, they just hate what they've put them through. "I love her, but she still has to earn back my trust," Zoey said.

The girls will continue sharing stories with each other, but hope others will be able to join them. "We talk about our moms a lot and it's better" when someone else understands, Zoey said.

Lovain said: "What impressed me about these girls is not only that they want to do this, but they really, really care."

Source: *Des Moines Register*, April 1, 2006, p. 1A. Reprinted by permission of the *Des Moines Register*. Article by Colleen Krantz.

tends to be invisible while the importance of the extended family as a vital resource goes unrecognized.

Dedicated to the principle that addiction is a family illness, this chapter starts by reviewing the precepts of family systems theory, historical and modern, and then, through drawing on personal testimonials, shows what addiction does to family rules, roles, communication patterns, and above all, to love. As dramatically stated by Linda Leonard (1989): "All addictions are killers; each in its own way kills living in the moment, kills creativity, love, and the trusting faith of the inner child" (p. 196). In contrast to traditional family therapy, the family treatment interventions described in this chapter are designed to elicit resilience and healing in family members rather than focusing on the family's presumed role in perpetuating addiction. We have adapted interventions to parallel the readiness of the family for change—a phase approach. The phase approach views treatment needs in terms of the five basic intervals, stretching from precontemplation through the maintenance period. The stages of family needs may or may not correspond directly to the addict's stage of recovery. The chapter concludes with a listing of exercises geared toward work with families in Family Week programming.

CLASSIC FAMILY SYSTEMS THERAPY

The leading proponents of family systems theory have tended to focus almost exclusively on interpersonal transactions. From the classic systems perspective, a disorder such as mental illness, anorexia, or alcoholism is viewed as stemming from faulty family communication or functioning. In this tradition, the systems therapist does not do individual therapy—that is, try to fix "the identified patient." Rather, the patient is viewed solely within the context of the family, where the symptoms or problems presumably evolved (Galanter, Dermatis, Keller & Trujillo, 2002; Hanson, 1996). Relationships and communication are stressed. The fact that the designated sick person in the family could truly be sick and be the source of the family's stress and malfunctioning is not considered.

Much of what we know as family mental illness patterns, systems theory, and therapy today was developed by Bowen in work with families of schizophrenic children (Lawson, Lawson, & Rivers, 2001). Key concepts concerning the intricacies of family communication, such as double-bind theory and receiving mixed messages, were seen as instrumental in the development of schizophrenia in the child. The presenting problem was seen as serving a function within the family (Thompson, Pomeroy, & Gober, 2005). Following her work with Gregory Bateson, Virginia Satir helped popularize the notion of the role of family interaction in the "development of mental illness in a family member" (Chase-Marshall, 1976). Similarly, alcoholism was conceptualized by Bowen (1978) as a mere symptom of a problem in the larger family or social unit. Alcoholism, like schizophrenia, was not viewed as the problem but as the solution to the problem. Family therapy, divorced from alcoholism treatment, was the sole intervention required; once the family was working as a system, individual problems such as mental illness and alcoholism would evaporate.

The drug addict is viewed by classical family system theorists as "the symptom carrier" of the family dysfunction (Bradshaw, 1988). In his or her aberrant behavior, the addict helps maintain the family balance by deflecting attention away from the real problems (Kaufman & Kaufman, 2002). Common to all these systems thinkers is the belief that the key to changing the drinking behavior lies in strengthening interaction patterns among family members. The significance in addiction is in maintaining equilibrium in the family; remove the addict as scapegoat and another family member will start acting out, goes the thinking.

Family therapy, as Krestan (2000) indicates, too frequently has considered the systems in the interior of family life but neglected the larger social systems in the community. In an extensive ethnographic study of the families of persons with mental illness, Hanson (1994) records the utter frustration of family members whose contributions were continually devalued in the process of family therapy. Missing from traditional family systems models is a grounding in empirical research as well as a confusion of cause and effect—that is, whether unique communication patterns and role-playing in the family were the cause of the disorder (e.g., schizophrenia) or whether dealing with the disorder had affected the communication patterns and role-playing. Accordingly, medical needs were often overlooked, and angry responses or guilt feelings in the family clients were aroused.

The literature on eating disorders, likewise, is rife with what we might term "systemic determinism" or a pathology focus. Minuchin (1974) and Nichols (1984) were only the first of thousands of theorists to place the source of anorexia in the tension within the family. Even in the early 1990s, researchers such as Ellis-Ordway (1992), in his article titled "The Impact of Family Dynamics on Anorexia," echoed the classic formulation. Consistent with this formulation, the parents were targeted and family therapy was the treatment of choice to discover the underlying family problems responsible for the adolescent's symptoms (Woodside & Shekter-Wolfson, 2003). Much criticism came from a feminist perspective, however. Rabinor (1994), for example, decried what amounted to the "mother-blaming" in the eating disorders literature.

Fortunately, attention has shifted today to a recognition of the biochemical component in a number of disorders and behaviors, including disorders related to eating. The role of cultural factors and distorted media images of the "perfect body," in the development of anorexia and bulimia, is also widely recognized. Family researchers view the role of families as caught up in a complex and frightening disorder (Woodside & Shekter-Wolfson, 2003). Increasingly, the focus of family counseling is in teaching family members about the biological and cultural nature of the disorder and in providing support and helping them play a positive role in recovery.

Cultural diversity is another issue that has long been overlooked in family therapy. Only in the past few years, as Krestan indicates, has family therapy as a whole dealt with issues of diversity at all. Family counselors from the helping professions would do well to consult *Ethnicity and Family Therapy*, edited by McGoldrick, Giordano, and Garcia-Petro (2005a) to learn how to best approach members of various ethnic and racial backgrounds. In this comprehensive volume, dozens of chapters, each written by experts on a specific ethnicity—for example, Russian Jewish families, Irish families, Czech and Slovak families—provide helpful guidelines for working with each unique population.

Another excellent resource is provided by the Center for Substance Abuse Treatment (CSAT) (2004), a government office under SAMHSA, which has produced an extensive treatment protocol for family treatment. The CSAT document contrasts the teachings of family therapy and addiction treatment. Family therapists, as the document notes, tend to conceptualize substance misuse as a symptom and dysfunction in the family that serves a purpose within the family unit. Such assumptions as these cannot be empirically verified. Family therapy focuses on the inner dynamics of the family, but substance abuse treatment is geared toward the client and involves the family only for the purpose of helping the client with the addiction problem. Spirituality is addressed in substance abuse treatment but is relatively ignored in family therapy.

Sadly, the legacy of family blaming still persists in some quarters. For example, Saatcioglu, Erim, and Cakmak (2006) state the following: "(Substance) abuse is a family disease, which requires joint treatment of family members. Family is an important part of the diagnosis and treatment chain of alcohol and substance abuse. Abuse of alcohol and substance is a response to fluctuations in the family system. . . A family often needs as much treatment as the family member who is the abuser of alcohol or a substance" (p. 125). (This article, curiously, was published in a prestigious psychiatric journal.) Saatcioglu et al. are correct that joint treatment of family members is highly desirable to ensure recovery of both the alcoholic/addict and family members who have been through their own private hell. Yet the location of the cause of the substance misuse in the family is reminiscent of the flawed deterministic logic of an earlier day. Instead of family blaming, credit is due to many families that, instead of being dysfunctional, have demonstrated remarkable survival skills while encountering multiple levels of oppression (e.g., racism, heterosexism) in the larger social structure.

FOCUS ON THE FAMILY

In addiction treatment, the focus has been on children of alcoholics, adult children of alcoholics, and rules and role-playing in the chemically dependent family. The family's stages of progression into the illness of alcoholism was first noted and graphically described by Joan Jackson (1954), who published an article on the subject in the *Quarterly Journal of Substance Abuse*. During the 1970s, when the family therapy movement began to gain momentum, the concept of viewing the family as a system led to the notion of alcoholism as a family disease (Brooks & Rice, 1997). Sharon Wegscheider's (1981) groundbreaking writing and films on "the family trap" marked a departure from the earlier atomistic and individualistic approaches of addictions specialists. In her depiction of typical roles that members of the chemically dependent's family play, Wegscheider (now Wegscheider-Cruse) conceptualized alcoholism in terms of both its physical and social dimensions. Her approach was highly practical in its implications and one with which family members could easily identify.

Popular author and public speaker Claudia Black was influenced by the writings of fellow social worker and systems theorist Virginia Satir. Black's (1981) thought-provoking book *It Will Never Happen to Me!* applied many of the fundamentals of systems theory concepts to family alcoholism treatment. Her "don't talk, don't trust, don't feel" formulation neatly summed up the dynamics in an alcoholic household. Black (2002) updated her book to include addictions other than alcoholism and issues pertaining to "adult children" as well as children. Dulfano, in her less widely known *Families, Alcoholism, and Recovery* (1982), offered a brief but dynamic ecological interpretation of the alcoholism syndrome.

In 1983, Lawson and Lawson published *Alcoholism and the Family*, which helped integrate family therapy concepts and substance abuse treatment. The view of the family as client was provided in this text. The second edition was published in 1998. Kaufman (1985) similarly provided helpful guidelines for family counseling in his *Substance Abuse and Family Therapy*, and later, Kaufman and Kaufman (2002) further developed the techniques of family therapy in situations of alcohol and other drug use. Wallen's (1993) *Addiction in Human Development* contributed a developmental model to addiction treatment. Because alcoholic families often resist change, as Wallen noted, particular attention must be paid to their life cycle stages as the system adapts to the problem drinking of a family member. Families as well as individuals move through stages of recovery that affect the balance or equilibrium that has evolved through the underfunctioning of one family member. The final stage of recovery, according to Wallen, involves restoring the system to a balance that maintains sobriety.

In addition to family treatment, self-help groups have developed to meet the needs of families torn apart by the ravages of addiction. Al-Anon, founded in the 1950s to serve the families of AA members, today has groups in more than 70 countries. In its early days, Al-Anon was only for wives, who often were seen as somehow responsible for their partners' drinking. Today, male partners of alcoholics, although a minority, are members of Al-Anon as well. The focus is on group support and establishing independence from the sick patterns associated with addiction.

The Twelve Steps used by Al-Anon were modified slightly to pertain to persons who are powerless not over alcohol but over another's use of alcohol. Individual work is directed toward independence and self-awareness. Learning that attempts to shield the alcoholic/addict from the consequences of his or her addiction are futile and counterproductive helps free the family members from the emotionally wearing attempt to control what cannot be controlled. Members are aided in achieving detachment from the active alcoholic/addict. Al-Anon members rave about the close personal bonds that develop from membership in this group. Recognition of one's powerlessness over another's addiction goes a long way toward reducing one's guilt feelings.

One of the most significant referrals the addictions counselor can make to family members of alcoholics is to a local Al-Anon group. Clients should be prepared for a kind of ritualistic openness and friendliness that may at first seem intrusive; they should be encouraged to visit several different meetings before deciding on whether or not to join. Self-help groups such as this are particularly appealing to clients who are outgoing and extraverted.

Alateen is the organization for children of alcoholic parents. Children are helped to achieve understanding of alcoholism and awareness of severe family problems. Nar-Anon is the comparable group for family members of narcotics users, and Gam-Anon is for the families of compulsive gamblers. Adult Children of Alcoholics (ACOA) is a rapidly growing group for those who grew up in alcoholic homes and who may have many unresolved feelings and issues pertaining to their family life. Members are encouraged to give full vent to their repressed feelings. Because emotions may be intense, newly sober alcoholics may be advised to achieve a lengthy sobriety first before joining such an endeavor.

MODERN DEVELOPMENTS

Fortunately, thanks to the influence of the feminist movement and modern biological research concerning the etiology of mental disorders, family systems theory has, to some extent, reconceptualized its teachings. The addiction treatment field, to its credit, never did view the family as the source of pathology; addiction was seen as primary in its own right. It is the cause rather than the symptom of family communication problems. In fact, with the disease model firmly entrenched and the focus on the individual alcoholic, the wonder is that the family was incorporated into treatment programming at all. That the family's needs do get addressed is probably a reflection of the increasingly interdisciplinary nature of the chemically dependent treatment field and the fact that so many practitioners in the field come from alcoholic family backgrounds. Professionals schooled in family counseling techniques, moreover, have brought to addictions work a modified and highly useful understanding of family pain and dynamics. In short, a gradual paradigm shift in thought from family as enemy to family as treatment ally has occurred.

Whereas family therapy as a profession is informed by a systems theory that focuses on internal dynamics of the family, social work draws on systems concepts in a more holistic way, often as part of an ecological perspective. This perspective avoids simplistic explanations about causation and views the person and environment in constant interaction. In its pure form, systems theory and the closely related ecological model view cause and effect as intertwined; relationships are interactive. Causation, like the seasons, is viewed as circular. Combining these basic systems concepts with ecology's model of the person in the environment, an ecosystems perspective provides a useful framework for viewing family dynamics. This approach is especially relevant today because the very concept of what constitutes a family is changing.

In the United States and many industrialized nations, the concept of family has undergone rapid change over the past two generations. During the latter half of the 20th century in the United States, for example, the proportion of married couples with children shrank; such families made up only 24% of all households in 2000. The idea of family has come to signify many familial arrangements, including blended families, divorced single mothers or fathers with children, never-married women with children, cohabiting heterosexual partners, and gay or lesbian families (CSAT, 2004). The family, in other words, is a complex ecosystem.

The ecosystems perspective views people as nested in constant interaction with forces in their environment. Individuals are nested in families; families are nested in communities (Germain, 1991). The substance misuser's ecosystem might consist of the family, peers (those in recovery as well as those still using), treatment providers, nonfamily support sources, the workplace, and the legal system (CSAT, 2004). In severely troubled families, family members often are connected not just to each other but also to any of a number of government agencies, such as social services, criminal justice, or child protective services. From this viewpoint, substance misuse is associated interactively with physical problems, mental health problems, and strains on society's agencies that promote physical and mental health. *Interactionism* is the theme—society's neglect in treatment and prevention and, in the social welfare system in general (e.g., in the lack of affordable housing), individuals finding stress relief in substance use are phenomena that go round and round as society pays a price in regard to the social problems related to widespread substance misuse. The economic toll includes a huge drain on people's employability and other elements of productivity. The social and economic costs are felt in many workplaces and homes.

FAMILY ADAPTATION TO ADDICTION

Adaptation is a useful way to conceptualize the family's response to a member's addictive behavior. Adaptation is defined by Germain (1991) in terms of her ecological framework as an active process of self-change, environmental change, or both, not a mere passive adjustment to circumstances. Adaptation flows from and helps alleviate stress caused in the family system by the drinking, gambling, compulsive sexual behavior, and so on. Paralleling individual adaptation to stress by the addict is the awesome set of demands imposed on family members.

The idea of an ecological framework within which substance abuse occurs is consistent with family therapy's focus on understanding human behavior in terms of other systems in a person's life (CSAT, 2004). Family treatment approaches human behavior in terms of interactions within and among the subsets of a system. In this view, family members inevitably adapt to the behavior of the person with a substance use disorder. They develop patterns of accommodation and ways of coping with the substance use (e.g., keeping children extraordinarily quiet or not bringing friends home).

Each family will have its own peculiar style of adaptation—coping through hiding key resources (money), blaming, covering up for the addictive behavior, joining in the addiction, or becoming extremely touchy with outsiders. The stress of the addictive pattern (e.g., gambling and winning, gambling and entering a losing streak) has a synergistic, or multiplying, effect throughout the family system and related social networks. The family, awkwardly, may come to serve in a mediating role between the addict and other systems—work, school, larger family. But gradually, as the illness progresses, the bridges between the alcoholic and his or her social world will be broken. The family may then adapt to the social isolation and continual stress of the progressing alcoholism, or members may regroup and form a reconstituted family without the addict. A third alternative, of course, is treatment for the addict both separately and within the context of the whole family. Treatment considerations would focus on the development of new, nondestructive communication patterns and adaptation to changes associated with recovery.

A teacher whose husband grew up in an alcoholic home comments on Germain's concept of adaptation by the family to illness in an adult member:

> Perhaps my husband and his younger brother are good examples of Germain's premise. Bill was 16 and his brother, Eric, was 7 when their alcoholic father died. Eric was the younger child. Bill's perception had more years of exposure, while Eric's remained that of a small child's view. Bill grew up to be a man who rarely drinks. Eric not only is an alcoholic, but his behavior when he was an active drinker landed him in prison.
>
> Bill basically hated his father because he saw more abuse and had to shoulder more responsibility because of the alcohol, while Eric did not. Their perceptions influenced the choices they made in living environments. Bill adapted by using the influence as a picture of how not to be. Eric saw that influence as a way to get people to do things for you so you can be "happy." His perception led him to choose similar environments to fill his need for a comfort zone. This environment influenced more abusive drinking and behavior, which ultimately led to his incarceration. (personal communication, May 14, 2001)

As Leo Tolstoy once wrote, "All happy families are alike, but every unhappy family is unhappy in its own way" (1917/1876, p. 1). Individuals within the same family, likewise, adapt differently to the same stress. Next we hear from one adult child of an alcoholic, a high school teacher:

> Communication in my family was much like Claudia Black's rules suggest. "Don't talk, don't trust, and don't feel." We were not allowed to talk about the problems of my dad's drinking and mental illness. If I attempted to talk about it, I was just told, "He's sick and can't help it." Communication was so poor that my mom participated in what I consider an unhealthy game to communicate with my dad. She would call one of my older sisters who lived outside the home and tell her something she wanted my dad to hear within his earshot. For instance, if she wanted to go to a baby shower, she would tell one of my sisters and hope my father would hear. Then he would ask her what she was talking about. Most of the time he didn't allow her to go anyway, but this was her method of trying. My father was guilty of unhealthy communication as well. He would stop talking to my mother for up to four days at a time if she said or did something he didn't like. He would then communicate sarcastically through me. If I would ask him why the television wasn't working right, he would say, "Ask your mother, she thinks she knows everything." He would tell me adult information while she was in the room. Although he was talking to me, he was really talking to her.
>
> I remember coming home and feeling like I was walking on eggshells every day because I never knew what the mood would be. I spent a lot of time being tense. We were not allowed to discuss our problems with outsiders or bring outsiders into the home. We were not allowed to have any feelings except laughter. If we were hurt, we could laugh but not cry. I was told exactly how to feel, so to this day I have a hard time describing how I actually feel. (personal communication, November 2005).

As the addicted person learns to adapt his or her lifestyle to accommodate the tremendous demands of this illness, so the family unit adapts to the stress that has been imposed on its functioning. As various individuals come forward to fill the essential family roles, the integrity of the family is preserved; equilibrium is maintained but at the expense of one or more individual members. If the addict later recovers, the operating family system will be "thrown out of whack," a crisis will occur, and individual and group adaptation will be required.

In summary, according to ecosystems insights, the individual alcoholic/addict is not viewed in isolation but as someone in dynamic interaction with the environment. Attention is paid to the complex ways that individual persons, in terms of the roles they perform, are linked with other roles in the family.

WEGSCHEIDER'S ROLE THEORY

Wegscheider (1981) introduced a small clanging mobile (the same device that hangs over a baby's crib) to represent the family interaction pattern; as one piece of the mobile is moved, the whole apparatus moves. Roles that individual family members play reinforce or clash with roles of other members.

Wegscheider, who, like Claudia Black, was inspired by Virginia Satir's role theory, labeled the following roles played in the chemically dependent family: the chemically dependent person, the chief enabler, the hero, the scapegoat, the lost child, and the mascot. These types are based on her and others' observations and they should be regarded as ideal types only; their existence is not scientifically validated. Associated with upwardly mobile middle-class families, the following purported characteristics may or may not apply to other social classes and ethnic groups. (See Chaput, 2001, and McGoldrick et al., 2005a, for a comparative analysis of styles of family functioning in the presence of substance misuse.) Van Wormer, in her practice in Norway, found that family members readily identified themselves and others in their families with these roles. Many identified with more than one role, saying, for example, "I was a little bit the hero and a little bit the clown growing up." The following descriptions are drawn from van Wormer's Family Week presentation in Norway (see van Wormer, 1995, for more details). Our purpose in presenting these roles is not because we believe they represent reality but because the concept of role-playing has been found helpful in engaging people in family systems work. The use of childhood labels is controversial; even the authors of this text disagree about their usefulness in family group programming. But we do agree that Wegscheider-Cruse's conceptualization has helped popularize the idea of family systems work and that this is a positive development. Please regard the descriptions that follow with appropriate skepticism.

THE CHEMICALLY DEPENDENT PERSON   This member of the family is gripped by contradictions. Sensitive to the point of touchiness, the chemically dependent person is selfishly preoccupied with the sources of addiction. Often charming and talented, this family member tends to see life events and personalities in terms of black and white, all or nothing. There is a tendency to escape the scene when very high expectations (of relationships, work, studies) are not realized. When a man occupies this role, he is often treated with great fondness by his children. The woman alcoholic/addict is inclined to be either divorced or married to a fellow alcoholic/addict. She is subject to strong criticism for her neglect of motherhood responsibilities.

THE FAMILY MANAGER Because Wegscheider's term *chief enabler* has acquired pejorative connotations, in disregard of the survivorship nature of this role, we prefer the term *family manager*. The individual who occupies this position is often the sober partner of an alcoholic/addict. The role that the family manager assumes is to overfunction to compensate for the partner's underfunctioning. As the family sinks along with the alcoholic/addict into near ruin, this individual worries, nags, and struggles to balance the checkbook. His or her denial in the early stages of the partner's addiction may be replaced by a frantic and bitter awareness later on. The person who occupies this position in the family structure suffers from a bad press that relates to the game he or she often ends up playing in conjunction with the games of the alcoholic. Counselors at treatment centers are quick to condemn the sober partner for some of the covering-up devices that make survival as a family possible. If not accorded a great deal of sensitivity, family managers are often plagued by feelings of shame and guilt.

THE HERO Often the firstborn child in the family, this high-achieving and very competent individual is constantly seeking approval. The family labels this child as the star—scholar, athletic hero, or performer. Inclined to suffer from low self-esteem, the child in this position tends to feel loved for what he or she does rather than for who he or she is. Accustomed to baby-sitting and caring for younger siblings, this child often grows up to work in the helping professions. Perfectionism is a key risk. Marrying an alcoholic or addict is a risk, according to Wegscheider (1981) and Black (1981, 2002); such a marriage recapitulates one's caretaking role from the family of origin.

THE SCAPEGOAT This is the child, often the second born, whom everyone loves to blame. The negative label is applied and seems to stick. The irresponsible behavior that accompanies this role often lands the perpetrator in trouble. According to the typology, early pregnancy is a risk for girls and delinquency for boys; school performance is poor, and early experimentation with drugs and alcohol is common.

THE LOST CHILD This child lives in a fantasy world and is said to be little or no trouble. Although he or she may be lonely, this younger child can entertain him- or herself through endless playing with dolls, television, or computer games. When family members fight, the lost child has an excellent escape mechanism. To grow into a responsible, mature adult, the boy or girl in this role requires a tremendous amount of help with self-expression and facing problems realistically.

THE MASCOT Forever clowning, the occupier of this role helps provide comic relief for the family unit. Encouraged to be cute and to joke around, the mascot can attract much positive attention while distracting members from serious matters. Often hyperactive, this child has a short attention span, which may be linked in some way to the needs of the family. The means of escape is laughter.

But don't children in all families play roles? This is a commonly asked question when a counselor presents these role descriptions. The answer is yes. All of us play roles in our families, at work, and in therapy groups. When stress is very high, the roles tend to become rigid and are used as defense mechanisms (i.e., forms of escape). The children's roles, like that of the family manager, are best conceived as normal responses to an abnormal situation.

The strengths inherent in the roles are rarely mentioned. And yet, the family manager typically has excellent organizational skills and flexibility. This person's capabilities and resourcefulness help the family survive. Angela, the mother described by Frank McCourt in *Angela's Ashes,* resorted to all sorts of compromising behavior in her struggle to keep her children from going hungry as the father squandered the family's money through drinking and lost jobs.

Children who grew up in addict/alcoholic homes often develop coping mechanisms that may be useful later. The hero, for example, learns to assume responsibility early and often becomes a leader in adulthood. The scapegoat, who makes friends easily, may become a business success because of his or her willingness to take risks. The lost child has a great imagination and may write poetry or get involved with the arts. The mascot is often popular and, of course, knows how to use humor in creative and original ways. And as Fisher and Harrison (2005) point out, the roles that children play in the alcoholic home are similar to those played in all dysfunctional or disease-ridden families. And most such children play a combination of roles, not just one.

The term *codependence,* originally used to describe the strain of being a partner to a chemically dependent person, has taken on a life far beyond the intent of the original uses of the term. Sometimes, this phenomenon is described as a disease that precedes the relationship with an addict. Despite the lack of scientific evidence for such a conceptualization, the codependence movement has swept the country "in cultlike fashion" (Wetzel, 1991, p. 21). This movement and the associated self-help literature pathologize behaviors associated with female qualities, such as nurturance, as Sandra Anderson (1994) suggests.

Whereas early models blamed wives for their husbands' alcoholism, the most recent theoretical frameworks are more cautious in their formulations. The emphasis in family therapy, according to Simon, McNeil, Franklin, and Cooperman (1991), has shifted away from blaming the family for the etiology of the disease to blaming the family for the perpetuation of the disease. Fisher and Harrison (2005), while acknowledging problems with use of this term, regard codependence as a useful paradigm to depict the impact of substance dependence on the family. And they view the condition of codependence as a potential problem among substance abuse professionals who have experienced the same pain as their client. Taking a cross-cultural perspective, Cable (2000) points out the European American middle-class bias of the codependence movement, with its "one-size-fits-all" prescription for normality. The European American bias is seen in an overemphasis on detachment and taking care of oneself.

As early as 1987, the Hazelden Family Center disassociated themselves from use of this codependence "diagnosis":

> The view we take at the Hazelden Family Center is rooted in health promotion, a systems approach to health problems. We believe that each member of the family has an innate power of self-healing, and we try to awaken that power within our clients. Our practices are based on a combination of Al-Anon principles and the family systems theories developed by Murray Bowen, Ph.D. Both de-emphasize the need for a diagnosable sickness, instead requiring a sincere desire to change.
>
> There are many ways to help families return to health, and we respect the philosophical differences that shape various practices in our growing field. Codependency, both as a clinical and popular term, brings some of these differences into focus. (Hazelden Publishing Company, 1987, p. 2)

Interestingly, the book *Codependent No More*, by Melody Beattie (1980), which has sold over 5 million copies, is published by Hazelden Publishing Company and sold in the treatment center's bookstore. Sum total, nine books with codependent or codependency in the title are listed (as of 2006) in the bookstore catalog at www.hazelden.org/oa-html.

The *DSM–IV* does not include codependence in its manual of mental disorders. This omission was a big issue in the 1980s as chemical dependence professionals sought to have that diagnosis receive official sanction from the medical community and also to open up the possibility for insurance reimbursement for treatment. The notion of codependence as a disease in its own right, characterized by a lack of control, and inevitable progression created a rift between professionals in the mental health field who favor a more evidence-based approach and substance abuse counselors (Fisher & Harrison, 2005).

Instead of using the pejorative term *codependent*, our suggestion is that the more positive term *survivor* be applied to women (and men) who have done whatever is necessary to protect themselves and their families from the consequences of their partners' drinking and drug use. To describe the situation of a family member who is sinking into the abyss of illness along with the addict, the term *coaddict* might be used.

Despite the fact that the partners of alcoholics do not have a disease—only the symptoms of struggling against someone else's disease—individual and family counseling can be extremely beneficial in the healing process for these survivors. Work in the area of self-esteem can do much to help resolve powerful feelings accompanying years of abuse and unshared pain.

SOME MODERN TREATMENT MODELS

Work with the whole family is now recognized, at least theoretically, as a vital component in addiction treatment (van Wormer, 1995). Research shows that family involvement can help mobilize substance users to enter treatment and have a successful recovery (CSAT, 1999; Miller, 2006). In their review of the relevant literature, Waldron and Slesnick (1998) and McCrady (2006) concluded that family-involved treatment is associated with higher rates of treatment compliance and retention than is treatment without family involvement. Having a functioning support system is crucial in preventing a lapse into previous problematic behavior. And since family members often develop problems in response to someone else's drinking or other drug use, including early experimentation with psychoactive substances by children, getting the entire family together for counseling should be a standard of addiction prevention (Velleman, 2000). Family sessions offer an opportunity, moreover, to help children in the family understand some of the stresses their non-problem-drinking parent has been under, as Velleman suggests.

The introduction of network therapy is a disease-based approach to reinforce social networks. This form of treatment, which involves family members and peers in the client's relapse prevention efforts through the promotion of cohesion teamwork among network members, is a welcome addition to the chemical dependence field (CSAT, 2004; Galanter et al., 2002). Research shows that the children in these families benefit from these interventions in preventing their development of substance use problems.

A highly structured approach that trains family members in how best to deal with the addicted client has shown a 64% success rate in getting loved ones into treatment. As Little (2005) points out, this success rate far exceeds the Al-Anon success rate. This approach—the Community Reinforcement and Family Training Approach (CRAFT)—was created by Robert Meyers. The intervention consists of 12 one-hour sessions in which the therapist teaches families how to change their interaction style and a new way of dealing with the drinker or drug user. The training encourages participants to take care of their personal needs and to provide positive feedback when their loved one is sober. Little tested the effectiveness of this approach by randomly assigning 130 significant others to CRAFT, the Johnson Institute Intervention, and Al-Anon Facilitation Therapy. The CRAFT program was found to be several times more effective than the others in helping family members feel empowered and getting the alcoholic/addict into treatment.

Unilateral family counseling, as Miller (2006) indicates, utilizes an approach that is conceptually opposite to Al-Anon in counseling family members that indeed they can have substantial influence on their loved one's substance use and for initiating treatment. In reviewing these statements, we have to keep in mind that the goal of Al-Anon is to help the family member as co-alcoholics/addicts to detach from their chemically dependent spouse or relative for their own peace of mind and personal development. In this regard, attendance at these meetings has been shown to be effective (Miller, 2006).

Family group counseling is a major contribution borrowed from New Zealand child welfare programming, which originally was based on indigenous forms of treatment. The typical format is for social workers to gather all the relatives together who could be helpful in resolving the difficulty (e.g., child neglect due to heavy alcohol use by the parents). The process is empowering for all concerned because the persons with the biggest stake in effecting individual change are the ones looked to for the solutions. Most often, some sort of kinship care is the result.

In child welfare as in some other areas of social work, there has been a paradigm shift in our notion of family. What were once considered alternative family forms—alternative to the stereotypical White middle-class nuclear family—are now considered all-American. Social workers and counselors who have learned to draw on kinship care with African American families are now widening the net for all families in search of resources and strengths. The very concept of family in turn has been expanded as well. As more and more single parents are raising children, relationships involving three or more generations are becoming increasingly important to individuals and families; these relationships are diverse in structure and functions, and for many Americans, multigenerational bonds are important ties for well-being and support over the course of their lives (CSAT, 2004).

McGoldrick et al. (2005b) bring our attention to the role that cultural differences play in worldview and basic values and how these differences impinge on the therapy sessions. Even the definition of family differs greatly from culture to culture, as they suggest:

> The dominant American (Anglo) definition focuses on the intact nuclear family, whereas for Italians there is no such thing as the "nuclear" family. To them, family means a strong, tightly knit three- or four-generational family, which also includes godparents and old friends. African American families focus on an even wider network of kin and community. And Asian families include all ancestors, going all the way back to the beginning of time, and all descendants, or at least male ancestors and descendants, reflecting a sense of time that is almost inconceivable to most other Americans. . . British American families are likely to feel that they have failed if their children do not move away from the family and become independent, whereas Italians generally believe they have failed if their children do move away. (p. 24)

Family interventions, to be effective, need to be geared toward the family's stage of recovery. This stage may or may not parallel the addict's motivation for change or actual changed behavior. The following technique directs the therapist's attention to the needs of the family as they progress into wellness. Consistent with other chapters in this book, we are drawing on Prochaska and DiClemente's (1992) and DiClemente's (2006) stages-of-change model.

STAGES OF CHANGE AND FAMILY TREATMENT

Research on the effectiveness of family counseling based on the motivational enhancement model is sparse. There is no Project MATCH utilizing motivational family treatment techniques. Within Project MATCH, however, the success of treatment outcomes was related to the extent to which the client's social network supported sobriety (U.S. Department of Health and Human Services, 1999). In a review of the motivational literature, the Center for Substance Abuse Treatment (CSAT, 1999) located several studies that involved counseling the spouses of alcoholics from this person-centered perspective that had favorable outcomes. The stages-of-change model has been found helpful for understanding how to enhance families' awareness of the need for help and change in how addictive substances are used in the family.

Thomas and Corcoran's (2001) findings in their review of the empirical literature on family-of-alcoholic interventions are relevant here. Interventions in the studies located were unilateral interventions that involved the family only without the drinker's direct involvement; marital-partner therapy in which the focus is on improvement in communication patterns to promote sobriety; and work with the entire family in which all parties work on the problem in question together. A consistent finding in the literature review was that the unilateral approach, especially when reinforcement training was provided, produced a positive outcome in getting the substance using person to commit to treatment and/or behavioral change.

The following typology of stages relates to the stage of the alcoholic/addict in terms of his or her readiness to change. Individual family members may be at a stage that parallels that of the person with which they are concerned, but more often, at least some of the members are one or two stages ahead. There are many variations on this theme, however; sometimes, especially in cases where a woman is making progress in treatment, her partner is continuing to drink and denying her problem or the fact that he (or with a lesbian, she) has a problem as well.

Precontemplation

Under one scenario, unilateral therapy, the family attends treatment sessions to work on their problems and feelings surrounding an alcoholic/addict who refuses to get help and who is destroying the lives of those around him or her. As mentioned earlier, sometimes the results are surprisingly good as the family members are taught how to help set the stage for the substance user's turn-around. Even if the strategies are not successful, there is some evidence that the sessions help unite the rest of the family and provide benefits in terms of re-duced levels of frustration and depression (Thomas & Corcoran, 2001).

If the family unit is in this stage, it is unlikely the family will approach the treatment center for help. Sometimes, however, their presence is required as a part of the client's treatment plan. They might be encouraged to attend a Family Evening–type program, such as when a family member gets into trouble with the law, such as through a driving while intoxicated conviction and follow-up assessment or through a child welfare referral. Rules for the family at this stage of recovery are likely to be of the "don't talk, don't trust, don't feel" variety (Black, 2002). One 9-year-old child of an alcoholic said to Black when she was encouraged in a counseling session to open up and discuss her father's alcoholism, "When you have a rule in your house for so long, to not talk about Dad's drinking, it's really hard to talk now—even when he is sober" (p. 30). That is the "don't talk" rule. The "don't trust" rule comes about when children lose their sense of safety and when rituals and routines are perpetually broken. "Don't feel" is the end result as children in alcoholic/addict homes get out of touch with feelings they can't communicate and that don't get validated.

A. The *enmeshed family:* Spouses are estranged: one child is enmeshed with
the father, one with the mother.

B. The *isolated family:* Lack of cohesion and social support. Each member is
protected by wall of defenses.

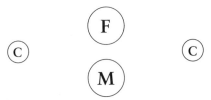

C. The *healthy family:* All are touching, but their boundaries are not
overlapping.

Key: F = father, M = mother, C = child.

FIGURE 9.1 | FAMILY FORMS

Source: van Wormer (1995), p. 207.

   Contact with family members seen at this stage is apt to be short term
and superficial. Sometimes, families attend lectures that present information.
Generally, counselors provide a description of family roles along with a discussion of characteristics of the so-called functional family. And what are the
characteristics of a functional family? Open communication, respect for individual differences and boundaries, stable routines and rituals, and having fun
and a sense of humor are among the qualities generally elicited (from the
grouping of family members). Figure 9.1 depicts various family styles of interaction that can be shared with the group of family members. Participants will
often volunteer to diagram their families of origin and current families in this
manner. A discussion of healthy boundaries often ensues.
   In working with a family in which there are addictive problems, the therapist
might start by helping members identify their family's goals. He or she asks open-
ended questions, such as: "What brings you here?" "What would you like to
happen in our work together?" "If you could change some things, what would
they be?" "Describe a time in the family when things were going well."
   An excellent discussion starter at this point is the miracle question used in
solution-based counseling, "What if a miracle would happen? What would
your family life be like then?" The purpose of this question is to help build

incentives to change the problem as family members contemplate a happier family life than the one they have.

According to O'Farrell and Fals-Stewart (2006), motivational interviewing has a place in counseling partners, both of whom have substance-related problems, because this approach can help them resolve the ambivalence about changing their behavior. Motivational interviewing can be used to help partners discover that their most cherished values are incompatible with the choices they are currently making. It is essential to get both partners to commit to change; otherwise, the relationship is threatened, and the risk of relapse to the partner in recovery is constant.

Typically, assessment of the individual with the addictive problems is done at this initial stage of treatment. As required by the court or insurance company, assessment most often is solely of the individual addict, with family members providing input at a later stage, if at all. In so separating the addict from significant others, however, the opportunity is missed to engage family members in the process. The inclusion of family members from the start offers several advantages. Such inclusion provides a means of observing how family members relate as a unit, a means for discovering strengths in the addict's background, and an opportunity to provide education into the biological and psychosocial aspects of addiction. Besides, it is never too early to begin preparing the family for the changes members will need to make in conjunction with the addict's recovery. The first session may close with the assignment of tasks designed to get family members to take some small steps in areas where change is feasible. One such step might be to attend a relevant support group, such as Al-Anon or Nar-Anon; involvement in such a group can be invaluable in helping members maintain their sanity and receive group support.

One message that family members who attend these Twelve-Step groups receive, however, is that they should give up attempts to influence the addictive person's behavior. (Al-Anon's first step is the same as that of the traditional Twelve Steps: that one is powerless over the alcohol, but here it has an indirect meaning because the powerlessness is through another's addiction to this substance.) The more proactive model that we are describing here, in contrast, is consistent with empirical research. Thomas and Corcoran (2001) hold that caring persons may be able to have an influence in getting the drinker/drug user to seek help. When recommending that clients who are family members attend Al-Anon meetings, the counselor might do well to prepare them for the different messages of the diverse approaches of Al-Anon and the family counseling program.

Barber (2002) combines behavioral theory with the harm reduction model and provides extensive instructions for counselors and family members of behaviors to accompany each of the stages of change. A mistake partners make, he suggests, is to behave the same regardless of whether the other partner drinks or not. "But," he states, "their drinking does matter to you and your behavior should convey this" (p. 71). His recommendations are not to prepare meals or keep them warm or enter into conversations or watch TV with the drunken partner. "If your partner collapses on the floor or gets sick, leave him or her to sort it out when sober" (p. 73). Then he recommends a very loving and nurturing response when the person is not drinking. The message helps the person distinguish acceptable from unacceptable behavior and recognizes that the heavy drinker has good qualities as well.

CONTEMPLATION

During the contemplation stage, the family member acknowledges concerns and is considering the possibility of the need for change—for example, in recognizing that the loved one has a serious addiction problem. Psychologically, the shift is from reluctance to acknowledge a problem to anger caused by the suffering related to the drinking, gambling, or other addiction. Many families are ambivalent, however, and waver between "He can't help it" and "She won't do anything" (CSAT, 2004).

The therapist often gets involved when a client requests counseling for help with a marital problem, child custody situations, or behavioral problems in the children. Then, in assessing the client's needs and goals, the role of addiction in the family's life becomes apparent. Just as he or she does in working with addicts in early-stage treatment, the therapist strives to elicit self-motivational statements of insight and ideas about solutions from the family clients. Reinforcement of clients' capabilities and survival skills are vital to help strengthen these persons to take action toward the desired solution. Possible actions that the family members might be willing to consider are to meet with the therapist for several sessions of family counseling to communicate needs and expectations; to work toward getting the addict to receive help for the addictive behavior, perhaps through attending a self-help group such as AA; and to work on plans for a trial separation. Whether or not the situation improves, family counseling of this sort can be a godsend for the partner and other family members; having a dispassionate but compassionate outsider to talk to can be immensely therapeutic. In their interviews with parents who regained custody of their children after recovering from addiction, Akin and Gregoire (1997) found that parents attributed much credit to social workers who had faith that the parents had the capacity to change, despite their addiction and testing behavior.

Although the participation of significant others in treatment has been found to be one of the best predictors of cocaine abstinence, Laudet, Magura, Furst, Kumar, and Whitney (1999) found the male partners of cocaine-using women to be far more difficult to engage in family treatment than the female partners of users. The men's active drug use and their refusal to focus on this fact are among the reasons hypothesized for this finding.

PREPARATION

The theme for this stage of change can be summarized in the addict's partner or coaddict's attitude of "I can't take it any more. I am at the breaking point." Tasks for the counselor during this period are to help family members clarify their goals and strategies for effecting change, offer a list of options and advice if so desired, and steer the family toward social support networks. Boosting the

Box 9.2	STEPS TO INTERVENE
	Carroll Schuety, Pathways Treatment Center, Waverly, Iowa

It's 2:30 Saturday morning. A car swerves and rolls up over the curb onto the lawn. The driver stumbles out of the car and staggers into the house. Suddenly, there is a shattering of glass as a lamp crashes to the floor and cursing echoes throughout the house. The spouse and children lie silently in their beds, not moving a muscle, fearful of provoking further anger in their spouse or parent. They listen for the sounds of heavy breathing as a sign that he or she is asleep so they can feel safe from verbal and/or physical abuse for a few more hours. Society assumes that alcoholism involves and destroys only the drinker and that the family suffers no devastating effects. Many people also believe that the spouse and children must remain passive and helpless as the drinker sinks deeper into the deadly disease of alcoholism. In fact, nothing is further from the truth. Family members can take constructive action to stop the destruction of the drinker and themselves through the process of an intervention.

What is an intervention? It is a method of confronting the drinker for the purpose of getting him or her into treatment. It is a confrontation that causes a family crisis that will bring the drinker to the painful realization that his drinking has caused problems and he cannot continue as he has been. This can be facilitated by a substance abuse counselor. Although, if a layperson understands the process, a counselor is not necessary.

The first step in organizing an intervention is to gather two or more persons together who have witnessed the destructive drinking behavior. The people could consist of family members, friends, clergy, coworkers, employers, or a physician. It has been my experience that children who have suffered from the behavior of the drinker are often most effective in forcing the drinker to see himself realistically.

In the second step, each person prepares a detailed written list of specific examples involving alcohol misuse that he or she has personally witnessed. These actual events force the drinker to admit that his or her concerns are legitimate. Another important

partner's confidence at this stage is tremendously important. The family members can even be taught the principles of motivational interviewing, which they can use themselves to minimize resistance in their loved one.

Typically, one or more family members in this stage may begin to look for a solution. The motivational therapist will now introduce treatment or other options that have been successful with other clients. This moves the group into the action stage.

ACTION

At this point, let us assume the whole family is involved in counseling except for the addicted individual. All family participants are bent on seeing change happen. Family sessions at this stage are crucial in building solidarity so that the addict will not be able to play one family member off against another. The sessions are crucial also in providing these individuals with the opportunity to ventilate their feelings—grief, rage, despair, and so forth—and to learn about addiction as illness.

aspect of writing the lists and reading them to each other prior to the actual confrontation is that it unites the group. In preparing your list, you should avoid opinions and general statements such as:

"You're always drinking."

"You drink too much."

"You might get fired."

"Your drinking is getting worse."

You should point out instead:

"Last month, I felt scared when you fell down the stairs and broke your foot after you had been drinking."

"Last Thursday, I saw you drinking on the job. I felt concerned because your job performance has been going down in the past few months."

"I'm feeling scared because in the past year, you've been arrested twice for drunk driving offenses."

"When you attended my school conferences, you were drunk and I felt embarrassed."

It is important to talk about your feelings when you share the situation that you are describing with "I feel" or "I felt" statements. Feeling statements will help reduce the defensiveness of the drinker.

You must, as an intervention team, agree on a "what if" clause in case the drinker rejects all your options by declaring, "I can do it myself. I'll just stop drinking." If this happens, you must persuade the drinker to make a commitment to enter treatment if his or her own attempt to quit is unsuccessful. It must also be understood that even one drink constitutes failure on his part. Another action that could be taken is to commit the person to treatment through a legal process. The local prosecutor's office or treatment center can usually provide the details.

Printed with permission of Carroll Schuety.

If the alcoholic/addict is still unwilling to do anything about the problem, professional interventions are often necessary (CSAT, 2004).

If the timing is right, an often effective therapeutic technique that the family members of the addict might want to consider is a formal intervention. Associated with the Johnson Institute in Minneapolis, the ritualized intervention is a process for providing feedback to the person with addiction problems. Key persons in the addict's life are identified; these may include a doctor, a boss (if one's work is in jeopardy), a member of the clergy, and close friends.

In Box 9.2, Carroll Schuety, a counselor who has conducted numerous successful interventions with Iowa farm families, describes the process. This boxed reading is presented with some reservations, however, in light of harm reduction expert and psychologist G. Alan Marlatt's belief (as expressed to Jackson, 2005) that interventions shouldn't be performed under any circumstances. His belief is that interventions are confrontational and punishing and that such strategies increase resistance and denial. Miller (2006) reports that 80% of families find the confrontational meeting unacceptable and refuse to go through with it. Among those who complete an intervention, however, a high percentage of the alcoholic/addicts do enter treatment. The kind of intervention performed by Carroll Schuety uses a softer touch, with excellent results that are well known in her local area. Box 9.2 is presented with a cautionary note in mind: Interventions can place too much psychological pressure on people who may feel ganged up on; sometimes, the reaction is suicide. This happened in the case of the musician Kurt Cobain, whose tragic death, according to Marlatt, came on the heels of an intervention arranged by his wife. Addictions specialist and social work professor Lala Straussner, cited in the same article by Jackson (2005), concurs: She favors a motivational approach and advises social workers to be mindful that there's more potential for harm than good when an intervention is performed by someone without specialized training.

Going from the point of view of counselor to family member, a young woman provides this poignant account of her childhood memory of an intervention with her father:

> When I was around 13, we visited a counselor for a rehearsal. The next week my dad's brothers and sister, close friends who were recovering alcoholics, my mom, my sister, and I gathered at our house on the farm and dad came home. I think he was aware of what was going on and became extremely emotional, crying with his head down at the table. I remember exactly where I was standing, at the end of the table against the wall with my sister, and when it came my turn to read my statement all I could say was "I want you to go because I love you" and began to sob. I remember going up to my mom and dad's room to get his suitcase and dad couldn't say a word; he just cried and hugged us and got in the car to go. It is one of the saddest memories I experienced in childhood. He was gone for 1 month, and about 3 months after he returned we sold our farm and he relapsed, yet to return to treatment about a year later on his own will; he has been sober ever since. I can honestly say I am very proud of him. (personal communication, January 28, 1999)

MAINTENANCE

More important than the role of family in assessment and treatment is the role of family in early recovery. As the addict's progress toward health and wholeness becomes more and more a reality, the family therapist may take on the role of facilitator to aid in the process of reconciliation. Members of the family may want to come to terms with lifelong feelings of rejection; there may or may not be a desire for forgiveness.

Brown and Lewis (1999) delineate the therapeutic tasks and pitfalls involved in the process of recovery. *The Alcoholic Family in Recovery* draws on the experiences of members of four recovering families to describe the ways recovery has challenged and changed their relationships. Much of this process, as Brown and Lewis demonstrate, is painful.

Transition, as Brown and Lewis explain, is characterized by massive change that affects children and adults at every level. The environment feels unsafe; the family structure, after years of chaos, is not strong enough to handle change. In the counseling session, the therapist addresses the family concerns and recovery progress. Individual members may have issues from the past that they want addressed at this time.

Familiar ways of interacting must change if the family is to maintain a healthy emotional balance and support sobriety (CSAT, 2004). As behavioral changes are established in the family, the focus of sessions shifts toward maintenance of change independent of the therapist. Now that the problematic substance use has decreased and other family interactions have improved, other family problems (e.g., suppressed anger and an adolescent's substance misuse) may need to be addressed (Waldron & Slesnick, 1998). Family sessions at this point can help make the difference between sobriety and failure to change and even between keeping the family together and divorce. The therapist can help the family anticipate stressors and support the addict in avoiding triggers and high-risk events.

A complete "what to do if" contingency plan needs to be set in motion in case of backtracking. Clients are given numbers to call and asked to come up with ideas for what to put in a step-by-step plan for getting the help they need. Harm reduction strategies and solutions to sustain the change in behavior should be explored in treatment aftercare counseling. The couple, moreover, often can benefit from receiving information concerning sexual problems that arise in the absence of alcohol and drug use; if the issue is sexual addiction, the posttreatment counseling needs are tremendous.

Together, the family members can benefit greatly with work in the areas of communication, decision making, and discussion of rules and how the rules will be enforced. Now that progress toward recovery is well under way, the stage is set for a shared groping for solutions to problems that may never have been identified without outside help. Ideally, the family therapist is a nonparticipant in the immediate, emotionally charged issues within the family (e.g., who takes responsibility for what and the division of labor). The focus of the therapist is not on the content of the interaction but on the process itself. Through skilled and friendly questioning, the therapist imparts awareness of the form of the interaction: "Have you noticed how whenever the two of you argue, your son leans over backward in his chair until you have to stop him?" "I notice when you cry, Mary, your daughter's eyes start watering up too. Does this suggest a strong closeness of feeling between the two of you?" "Who interrupts whom in this family?"

To handle the all too common situation of the newly sober father's bid to reestablish his role of authority in the family, the therapist (T) might proceed as follows with the father, Bill (B):

T: Bill, I'd like you to stop for a moment and check out what you're doing. You expressed concern that the children don't talk to you more openly. Right?

B: Yes.

T: Let's think about what just happened with Steve. He began to tell you how he felt about those reckless rides in the car and you cut him off with "Not now." Did you notice how he pulled back then? How did you feel, Steve, when your father cut you off in this way?

Instead of excessive emotionalism in family sessions, a calm, intellectual atmosphere should be encouraged. Members are helped to listen to each other. Heavy emotion can be defused. For example, if a mother becomes distraught, other members can be asked what they can do to provide support or how they feel about the outburst. In interviewing with the mother, the focus can be on the thoughts that accompany her feelings.

Emotions may need to be defused when couples shout at each other. A helpful intervention is to interrupt with a loud "Stop!" Each person is then requested to take turns addressing the therapist individually. To reinforce listening, the therapist can ask the nonspeaking partner to reiterate what he or she heard the speaker say.

Conversely, couples who are not connecting emotionally with each other can be asked to look at each other and speak directly to each other, not to the therapist. To encourage engagement in a mutual undertaking or to introduce new forms of communication, homework assignments can be given to strengthen the communication process.

Through the various intervention devices described in this section, the family systems therapist guides a family with a recovering member toward their own process of recovery. As the newly sober member regains responsibility within the family, other members have to adapt accordingly. Acting as a coach or guide, the therapist can help map the course of this adaptation. The entire family must be prepared to accept as a member a sober and somewhat changed person. Every person's role in the family alters in the process of one individual's change.

The following list of rules can be drawn up and passed out to family members. Members read the rules, practice them in sessions, and agree to abide by them at home:

- Attack the behavior, not the person or his or her background. Use a pleasant tone of voice; avoid yelling, hitting, cursing, or name calling. Deal with one issue at a time—don't let your partner counter with, "Well, if you think I'm bad, you ought to see how you come across!" or "When you get a decent job, I'll think about it!"
- No mind reading. Don't say, "You are jealous" or "You're just angry because you. . ."
- Narrow the problem to a manageable size rather than focusing on vague wholes.
- No accusations and putdowns, such as, "You're just like your father!"
- Don't rehash the past.

WORK WITH FAMILIES IN WHICH THERE ARE CO-OCCURRING DISORDERS

Family psychoeducation programs for mental illness teach families in single family and multifamily group formats about the biological nature of the disease, the role of medications, the risks of drug interactions, and how family members can reinforce compliance with regard to prescription medication. A basic principle of family psychoeducation is improving coordination of all elements of treatment (Moore, 2005).

Mueser, Noordsky, Drake, and Fox (2003) describe the role of motivational interviewing strategies in working with families of persons with co-occurring disorders. Early contacts focus on providing support and expressing empathy. Substance use is not given priority at first unless the family members bring it up themselves. When goals are identified, the steps toward achieving them are identified, prompting family members to explore the possible interference by substance abuse to achieving the goal. During the preparation stage, family work involves helping families overcome their ambivalence about change and instilling the hope that change can be achieved even after many years of frustration.

Family members who have experienced so many defeats and disappointments in caring for and maintaining a close relationship with their children and partners with mental disorders need a tremendous amount of affirmation and reinforcement of self-efficacy. In short, as Mueser et al. (2003) suggest, motivational interviewing techniques have wide applicability in working with families in these situations.

IN SITUATIONS OF DOMESTIC VIOLENCE

Intimate partner violence among alcohol and drug misusing couples is alarmingly high (Fals-Stewart & Kennedy, 2005). More often than not, one form of abuse predicts the other form of abuse (Bennett & Williams, 2005). Counselors who work at women's shelters should informally assess women who need their services for substance misuse problems in their families. If the violence is substance related (most often the substance is alcohol, meth, and/or cocaine), treatment should be provided for one or both parties. Any time families are brought in for mental health or relationship counseling, and especially when substance misuse is a factor, it is critical to screen for domestic violence. If there is violence against children or children are endangered, child welfare authorities must be notified. If the wife is being victimized, the husband or partner should be referred to a batterers' group.

Couples in which there is battering should not be referred to conjoint counseling because if the wife reveals secrets about the marriage—for example, some sort of inadequacy in her partner—she is at risk of being beaten when they return home. Even family counseling that includes the children with the mother is a high-risk proposition; an insecure and suspicious husband might question the children to find out what was said at the sessions. Down the line, after the batterer has been successfully treated, some family counseling may be attempted. Safety for all family members, however, must be the first consideration.

Because of the interconnectedness of substance use and violence, close collaboration between substance abuse agencies and women's shelters is essential (van Wormer, 2001). Following screening and assessment of populations that come to the attention of service providers, coordinated programming to reduce the risk of harm to oneself or others is the approach that makes the most sense (Bennett & Williams, 2005). Due to their adherence to different, often conflicting models, however, the two types of treatment settings often operate under completely separate auspices with little or no direct contact. Because women's shelter providers operate from a feminist model and substance abuse counselors from a disease concept, collaboration between agencies has been a source of difficulty. The radical feminist model as applied by the Duluth Domestic Intervention Project focuses on male power and control within a patriarchal society (interview with Michelle Johnson, February 21, 2006); substance use by the perpetrator is regarded as merely an excuse for the battering. By the same token, substance abuse counselors give priority to the alcoholism/addiction factor in physical aggression to the neglect of cultural factors (e.g., a belief in male privilege or coming from a violent family). This bifurcation of treatment resources is much to the detriment of battered women in need of treatment of a substance-related disorder herself or for her partner or of women in counseling for substance misuse who are being victimized in the home.

Harm reduction principles would go far to bridge the conceptual gap between the fields of domestic violence intervention and substance abuse counseling. Safety is the first consideration in both instances. Motivational work and the stages-of-change model are especially applicable to batterer education programs to establish rapport and help him (or her) take steps toward behavioral change. For battered women, the parallels between the stages of deciding to leave a violent relationship and deciding to get help for substance-related problems are striking. Most domestic violence interventions are based on empowerment practice and choice of options, in any case. Frasier, Slatt, Kowlwitz, and Glowa (2001) spell out motivational interventions with battered women to help them at the precontemplation stage develop a safety plan on the road to making a final decision about severing or maintaining the relationship. If the woman reaches the contemplation stage, she is asked to draw up a list of pros and cons regarding her decision to stay or leave. The woman is affirmed in her decision-making powers.

A promising development is the interdisciplinary education being provided across the United States that join staff from substance abuse and domestic violence programming for the purpose of recognizing their common interests. Principles from motivational interviewing are often taught as a mutually relevant model to help men and women in treatment move in new and more productive directions.

CULTURAL CONSIDERATIONS

Chapter 5 of the CSAT protocol Substance Abuse Treatment and Family Therapy provides general guidelines based on the literature for working with multicultural and other specific populations. We draw on much of this information in the following sections. Information contained here is consistent with that provided by McGoldrick et al. (2005a).

Work with African American Families

To work effectively with African American families, family therapists must become familiar with the complex interactions, strengths, and problems of extended families. Many extended African American families incorporate various related people into a network that provides emotional and economic support. Numerous adults and older children participate in raising younger children, often interchanging family functions and roles (CSAT, 2004). Reciprocity is a key theme in the African American community: The practice of exchanging assistance is an essential part of extended family life. Such reciprocity may take the form of caring for another's child and knowing that the favor will be returned when necessary. Many extended families also take in secondary members, such as cousins, siblings of the parents, elders of the parents, or grandchildren. In other cases, families take in children who are not biologically related.

The Center for Substance Abuse Treatment (CSAT, 2004) advises that the personal connection between family and therapist is the single most important element in working with African American families. Without rapport, treatment techniques are worthless and the family will likely terminate therapy early. Techniques shown to be effective with African Americans will be rendered ineffective if the therapist acts in a bureaucratic manner that is naturally alienating to clients.

Work with Latino Families

Keep in mind as we consider establishing a productive working relationship with Latino families that in Latin American countries, the family is generally prioritized above the individual (Tapia, Schwartz, Prado, Lopez, & Pantin, 2006). As a result, family treatment can be very successful, but the quality of the relationship that develops in the first session is crucial to engaging families for return visits. The following guidelines for working with Latino families are adapted from CSAT (2004):

- A businesslike approach to treatment will not appeal to Hispanic/Latino families. A personable tack will yield much more effective results.
- Hispanic/Latino family members will be much more forthcoming when the therapist solicits their feelings through subtle and indirect means. Encouraging clients to speak forcefully and directly may have the unintended effect of inhibiting their participation.
- The establishment of behavioral contracts and homework assignments may be an overly task-oriented approach for this population. Scheduling time ahead to resolve intimate issues may also be unacceptable to these clients.
- Extending the disease model to incorporate the impact of a toxic social environment and the effects of oppression as factors contributing to substance dependence is an effective approach. While still holding people with substance use disorders accountable for their actions, this approach helps to frame substance abuse as a communal problem and spur family members into learning more about the effects of oppression.

- Using fundamental spiritual precepts can inspire hope and patience. The endurance of suffering, the practice of forgiveness, and the importance of repentance may be fertile values to use in working with Latino family members. This strategy should only be used when it is in harmony with the spiritual views of the individual family or family member. (p. 122)

Work with Asian and Asian American Families

CSAT (2004) provides the following considerations for engaging Asian and Asian American families:

- Family therapists should be careful that therapy does not breach proscribed gender roles or boundaries between generations. The first appointment should be made with the decision maker of the family, who will most likely be the father.
- Asian clients respond best to credible experts who provide specific suggestions for alleviating distress.
- Sensitivity to clients' privacy is just as important at a macro level. Because different Asian-American clients may live in the same tight-knit community, therapists should assure them of confidentiality and avoid sharing information regarding one client with another.
- Family therapists should not presume that therapy sessions will move forward on a regular basis. Counselors must choose between making the most of the first or initial sessions and scheduling ongoing regular sessions. Many Asians are unfamiliar with Western treatment models and will adopt a more infrequent, crisis-oriented approach to therapy.
- Clients may feel slighted if the therapist spends limited time with the family without providing a thorough explanation of his or her plan for treatment.
- It may be effective to leverage the family's willingness and arrange a rapid follow-up (sooner than 1 week) to strengthen the budding therapeutic relationship. (p. 126)

Work with Appalachian Families

The following guidelines are drawn from a research article on holistic work with Appalachian families (Denham, Meyer, Toborg, & Mande, 2004). The purpose of the research was to learn how to best increase motivation of the rural Appalachian families to improve their healthcare practices and to reduce risk-taking behaviors within the family such as smoking. Because women in this culture are the family health monitors, messages concerning healthy practices must be directed toward them. Based on extensive focus-group work, observers discovered three levels of motivation among the women that basically ranged from high to low. Messages need to be tailored to each of these groups depending on their readiness for change. Additional guidelines for culturally sensitive disease prevention are these:

- Appalachian women who are motivated and confident only needed to receive the relevant information.

- Women who are motivated but lack self-efficacy require support and encouragement to get the task done.
- Unmotivated women require work in the skills area and then the confidence to help their families get the treatment they need.
- Information must be presented in a factual, nonjudgmental way to allow recipients to draw their own conclusions about those facts.

WORK WITH GAY AND LESBIAN FAMILIES

Family can be a very sensitive issue for gay and lesbian clients. Therapists must be careful to use the client's definition of family rather than rely on a heterosexual-based model. The following guidelines are adapted from the CSAT (2004) discussion of issues relevant to family work with gays and lesbians.

- The therapist should accept whatever identification an individual chooses for him- or herself, usually partner rather than friend or roommate, for example.
- Family therapists must be careful not to pathologize issues of boundaries and fusion as many gay or lesbian couples appear to have more permeable boundaries than are commonly seen among heterosexual couples.
- A lesbian may seek support from an ex-partner to help with difficulties with a current partner more often than would typically be seen in a heterosexual female.
- When violence between partners is a treatment issue, safety must be the therapist's main concern.
- Many lesbian and gay clients may be reluctant to include other members of their families of origin in therapy because they fear rejection and further distancing.
- Gays and lesbians should not be encouraged to come out when they are not ready or when the family is not ready. (p. 131)

HEALING

The family chapter in *Social Work with Lesbians, Gays, and Bisexuals* presented the "rename, reframe, and reclaim" model (van Wormer, Wells, & Boes 2000, pp. 174–175). Because this model is well adapted to the counseling needs of the family in recovery, we have further developed it here to provide a theoretical base for counseling families that contain an alcoholic or other drug addicted member.

RENAME

The particular choices of terminology are up to the family members and relate in part to the treatment model preferred. The addict, for example, may find that terms such as "recovering alcoholic," "recovering grateful alcoholic," and "recovered alcoholic" are positive attributions. The spouse or partner, ideally, will not choose to call himself or herself a "codependent," but ultimately, the choice belongs to the client. If the use of the label brings a good result, the therapist would do well not to argue over the nomenclature. Key questions for the therapist to consider are: Are the new truths and realizations derived from treatment having a positive effect on your life? Are these new concepts consistent with a positive self-concept? In the end, perception is what matters.

The challenge to practitioners in a field whose literature and other teachings are guided by a language of damage and defects is to adopt a language that corresponds to concepts of strengths and resilience. Helping the family members discover how well they have done under trying circumstances, their success in pulling together as a family unit, will go a long way toward reinforcing the strengths that otherwise would go unnoticed. Labels like "survivor" and "family manager" should be used whenever appropriate. Indeed, family members should be encouraged to take pride in their resourcefulness because they have survived (with or without the addict) the turmoil of addiction (and the stress of treatment) and because they have not only endured but prevailed.

Adopting a language of strengths has important ramifications when the substance misuser in the family is an adolescent. Generally, the use of labels like "alcoholic" and "addict" should be avoided. At a stage of life when they haven't yet settled on an identity, the risk in having teens identify themselves as alcoholics and addicts is in creating a self-fulfilling prophecy with negative consequences (Volpicelli & Szalavitz, 2000). Referring youth to AA and NA meetings also may present problems because of the customary use of forced labeling in these groups. Sometimes, on the other hand, the addict or alcoholic label is the more positive alternative, such as when delinquent or criminal behavior can be understood as a part of drug-related addictive behavior. Under these circumstances, a referral to a Twelve-Step program, such as NA, might pave the way toward a more positive self-image and reconciliation with one's family.

From a family systems standpoint, relabeling problem behavior such as compulsive shopping as an addiction as opposed to foolish behavior changes the meaning by casting it in a more compassionate light. Renaming a relapse as a lapse similarly helps it to be seen as a mere setback that is manageable. When dealing with events of the past, the explanation "That was a part of the illness of addiction" helps family members get beyond individual blaming, reduces misunderstandings, and opens the door to more effective communication. These healthier ways of viewing the problematic behavior based on the use of more positive terminology are closely related to reframing.

REFRAME

Positive reframing is a helpful, in fact an essential, technique used by the therapist to instill hope and pride in one's accomplishments. To the seasoned counselor, helping clients reframe their experiences is probably second nature. Take relapse as an example; instead of treating this as a disaster, the counselor typically helps the client see it as a valuable learning experience. Clients can be directed toward a more positive view of a situation through deliberate questioning. Looking over the entire addiction experience in retrospect, clients can be asked, "Can you find anything positive that has come out of this experience?" Somewhat amazingly, clients and family members typically say, for instance, that it makes them understand one another better or that they want to help fellow addicts or families of addicts. Therapists and clients should refrain from looking at children of alcoholics through a deficit framework, such as seems to be the norm in addiction treatment circles.

Instead, as Walker and Lee (1998) rightfully tell us, the search should be for evidence of resilience in the families of origin as well as in the current household. Children of alcoholics, as Walker and Lee further indicate, do not necessarily become substance misusers; nor are they doomed to marry addicted persons. The best insurance against such a happenstance is the development of a strong inner drive to achieve and a strong support system for affirmation. Where other practitioners and theorists seek and find defects in adult children of alcoholics ("guessing at what normal is"), for example, the therapist of the strengths-based school will look for resilience—and will probably find it.

To Maria Carroll (1993), reframing one's reality is integral to the healing process. For recovering persons, only when the bond to addiction is broken can they move to higher things and embark on "a journey home." To Carroll, the journey home entails constructing a personal reality, becoming disillusioned with this reality, letting the ego-self disintegrate, surrendering, reframing the old reality, and then allowing a new reality to develop as the transformed state. Through surrendering to the reality of the present, the recovering addict moves through a spiritual awakening toward wholeness and a sense of oneness with humanity. The process is similar for family members, who are embarking on a journey of their own from isolation to intimacy and from refusing to reach out and seek help to a willingness to ask for help when they need it.

Reclaim

Healing is simply the inner change. It is the sense of peace that may result from therapy work in labeling feelings and controlling them through cognitive techniques, reframing troubling events in one's life, and recognizing how past events influence present feelings, thoughts, and behavior. Reclaiming lost and damaged childhood selves may occur through the joint effort embodied in the treatment relationship.

Healing often involves reclaiming what was lost either through drug addiction or in living in a family consumed with another's addiction. There is so much to reclaim: the fun in life, one's sense of peace and safety, one's spirituality, one's wholeness. Sometimes, to reclaim one's wholeness, the couple bonded by alcohol or other drug use find they have little else in common and can be enabled by the therapist to go their separate ways.

A prominent theme in the literature is that adult children of alcoholics find sources of strength and resilience in the nurturant parts of their cultural community and heritage (Cable, 2000). The emphasis on "we-ness," as Cable

CASE 9.1

The following case study recaptures van Wormer's yearlong, very up-and-down treatment relationship with "Kathy" and "Ed."

The challenge of treating this angry couple was such that I had to conjure up all my training as a sociologist as well as of a social worker. And as is typical with alcoholic clients in treatment, it was not the alcohol that was the focal point of the sessions. No, the focal point was money—fights over money.

This couple is troubled. After 7 stormy years of marriage, they are literally and figuratively tearing each other apart. Ed has spent many nights in jail. "Because of racism," he says. "I never touched her." As I sit facing them both, I notice the racial differences: He is Black; she is White. Physical differences are pronounced also: He is large and muscular; she is small. But as we get into dialogue and emotions run wild, the personality and cultural differences, the seething hatred, are all that count.

Kathy speaks, complains bitterly, and words flow effortlessly while her husband, a laborer, quieter, struggles to get a word in. He is my client; I know and trust him. He has described his wife as a master manipulator, and today, he has brought her in for me to see for myself.

If she hates him so much, how can she love him, I wonder. To help sort out this question, I have each client write on a sheet of paper what is good and what is bad about their marriage. Kathy's negative list is three pages long; on the positive side, she lists only one thing, "great sex." His list is sketchy, but he agrees on the physical attraction.

Money is their biggest source of conflict. I already know Ed is sneaking money for his earlier family. Kathy shouts, "I want every penny accounted for. We have two children to feed! Is he drinking away the money? Where does it go?"

---

indicates, is integral to traditional Native American culture and can be reclaimed through collaboration with natural support systems in treatment.

A communitywide intervention, The Family Circles Program, helped American Indian families reclaim their cultural identity and pride. Described by van Stelle, Allen, and Moberg (1998), this program was designed to reduce alcohol and drug misuse among high-risk youth on a reservation in Wisconsin. The project reportedly was so successful that it had a ripple effect throughout the entire community.

EXERCISES FOR FAMILY GROUPS

1. Family Sculpture
   Purposes: To portray roles in the family; to illustrate how the family works as a system; to help reveal feelings that accompany each role.

   The worker begins by explaining the technique to the family. This is a nonverbal technique that involves physical placement of persons in a symbolic fashion. The "sculptor" moves various family members into particular positions. The exercise begins with everyone standing up.

Earlier in his private session, Ed had told me that Kathy clawed herself on the chest with her own fingernails and then called the police. She claimed physical assault. Upon hearing this story, I talked Ed into getting his own place. He did so, but then, according to him, she called up begging him to return. Because of the risk of violence between them, I do not try to sort out the facts. My aim is to state the obvious: They can't live together and can't seem to stay apart. Yet they need to realize that for the children's sake they are better apart and sane than together and fighting.

After a request for them to work on communication, I bring out my Fighting Fair scheme, which lists the rules of communication. This conflict resolution scheme has rules such as: no name calling, don't rehash the past, and practice exercises that go "I feel _____ when you _____." The purpose of this exercise is to help clients know their feelings and then to make requests of each other. Kathy, it turns out, is tormented with feelings of jealousy and possessiveness. She is putting all her energy into one failing relationship when her need is for other adult support. She is cut off from her family, who disapprove of her interracial marriage and biracial children. The best hope for connection to the wider community for her, therefore, is through active participation in self-help groups. I refer her to a private counselor to help her work on the source of her anger and to realize her need for close personal friends as a support system to help her as a single parent.

Ed, faithfully, sees me once a week for a year; he has had a year of sobriety and is making progress following through on goals. During this time, I explain some of Kathy's behavior in terms of her ethnicity (White Anglo-Saxon Protestant), especially her beliefs about family boundaries and the nuclear family. I reinforce Ed in his strengths and help him arrange visitation with his children.

In the end, Kathy became a local leader in Women for Sobriety, and Ed grew to love his weekly AA support group. Once they developed support systems of their own, they went their separate ways, much healthier apart than they had ever been or would ever be together.

Talking is not allowed. A family member volunteers to be the sculptor. The therapist instructs the sculptor to arrange the family members to show who is close to whom and what people do together. The setting reproduced may be the family at home in the evening or on an outing, such as a picnic. Following the sculpture display, participants discuss the meaning of each sculpture and how each felt about the role he or she played.

Family sculpture can be effectively used in a Family Week program. Volunteers are asked to play the roles they play in their families or, in another variation, to play a very different role. Various roles, such as the addict, the family manager, the mother's helper, the rebel, and the athlete, are given to participants. With the help of the therapist as sculptor, each arranges him- or herself in a way that best represents the role. For instance, the addict may be put high on the chair or seated stooped over the table. The child who fantasizes when things get rough may stand in a corner or watch television. The family manager may extend his or her arm around the addict. All members freeze as for a portrait. Afterward, each person is asked to recapture the feelings of being in the role. The audience and players discuss the meaning of what they saw.

2. Drawing Family Maps

   Purposes: To open discussion about family lines of communication and closeness and to help the family gain insight into where the boundaries are.

   The therapist draws a circle on a chalkboard or flip chart to represent a hypothetical family. For example, an alcoholic mother and daughter could be represented by two circles with boundaries that overlap. Typically, if the mother cries, the daughter cries too. The sober father and the other daughter are also close, but these two, represented by two more circles, are apart from the others. Family members are asked to take turns drawing their families.

3. Family Relapse Prevention Plan

   Purpose: To help the addict and the family identify the warning signs of pending relapse.

   A list of warning signs is written by each participant. Signs must be clearly spelled out. Family members discuss these warning signs, such as extreme and obsessive devotion to work. They discuss what these symptoms meant in the past and reach agreement on what to do if they recur. An action plan is drawn up.

4. Genograms, or Family Tree

   Purposes: To provide information on patterns in families; to reveal possible hereditary and cultural themes that have been passed from generation to generation; to reveal similarities and differences across families joined by marriage.

   See www.samhsa.gov (TIP 39; chap. 3) for an illustration of how diagrams can be constructed through the use of symbols. A marital pair is indicated by a line drawn from a square (male) to a circle (female). Divorce is indicated by two slash marks on the line. Words can be used for events, occupations, dates, and ethnic origins.

5. Showing Videos

   Have the family members arrive early to view a videotape portraying family roles. *Soft Is the Heart of a Child* (1979), though somewhat dated, portrays the family roles memorably. (A Spanish version is available at www.hazelden.org.) Viewers can be asked to discuss the roles and relate the tape to their own lives. A 1996 version, *Reflections from the Heart of a Child,* also includes the roles but adds a theme of domestic violence. Both films are around 20–30 minutes. The earlier one is simpler and more emotionally powerful; the second contains violence.

   Another option is to show *End Broken Promises* (1998) featuring such commentators as Claudia Black in a discussion on the help adults can provide to children in alcohol and drug dependent families. All the videos above are available from the Idaho RADAR Network Center lending library.

   A modern documentary, *Lost Childhood: Growing Up in an Alcoholic Family* (2004), interviews children of alcoholics at a special summer camp and then interviews some of them 15 years later about how the childhood camp experience affected their lives. (Available at a very low price from Young Broadcasting of San Francisco at http://gigcat .midhudson.org.)

Movies can be custom suited to the individual client. An African American survivor of family sex abuse might find a lot of meaning in watching the film adaptation of *I Know Why the Caged Bird Sings*; a southern White survivor might get in touch with her feelings in a viewing of *Bastard Out of Carolina*.

SUMMARY AND CONCLUSION

Family therapy is an exciting dimension of addiction treatment. Family work with alcoholics and other drug misusers is an area especially amenable to the biopsychosocial framework. Systems therapists can utilize a didactic focus to teach biological and physiological factors of substance misuse and the interlinkages among all the addictions. The psychological realm can be addressed through work on the thinking–feeling dyad. The social aspect relates to the systems component. This three-pronged focus can offer a shared assessment of the structure and interaction patterns in the family. Through this multidimensional approach, the therapist can help prepare the family for accepting back a member who, in the words of the old Scottish hymn, "once was lost, but now is found." The therapist can help prepare the family to cope with setbacks and even eventual separation from the addict. Through the use of various communications exercises or listening skills, workers can help family members deal with their own feelings of anger, shame, and guilt that have plagued them for a long, long time.

The family systems approach described in this chapter provides a view of the family as a system of interdependent parts. The commonly used metaphor of a mobile suspended from a ceiling was described: If one part moves, the other parts shift simultaneously. Counselors can use this metaphor as a starting point to educate clients about the boundary concept, the reciprocity of role-playing, and the development and enforcement of rules in the family.

Because addiction did not arise in a social vacuum and the addicts did not suffer the consequences of addiction alone, attention needs to be directed toward the social environment. The growth process for the family often requires a period of chaos that precedes the old state's breaking down before the formation of a new state can occur. The family systems paradigm offers addiction treatment a way of conceptualizing addiction as both an interpersonal and an intergenerational phenomenon. Even if the treatment agency lacks a full-fledged family program, individual counselors can usually invite clients to bring their significant others with them to sessions. The family should be regarded as a potentially valuable resource. Unfortunately, the legacy of blaming the family still persists. This potential can be countered by using the "rename, reframe, reclaim" framework introduced in this chapter.

REFERENCES

Akin, B., & Gregoire, T. (1997, July/August). Parents' views on child welfare's response to addiction. *Families in Society*, pp. 393–404.

Anderson, S. C. (1994). A critical analysis of the concept of codependency. *Social Work, 39*(6), 677–685.

Barber, J. G. (2002). *Social work with addictions* (2nd ed.). Hampshire, England: Palgrave Macmillan.

Beattie, M. (1980). *Codependent no more.* Center City, MN: Hazelden.

Bennett, L., & Williams, O. (2003). Substance abuse and men who batter. *Violence Against Women, 9*(5), 558–575.

Black, C. (1981). *It will never happen to me!* New York: Ballantine Books.

Black, C. (2002). *It will never happen to me: Growing up with addiction as youngsters, adolescents, adults.* Center City, MN: Hazelden.

Bowen, M. (1978). *Family therapy in clinical practice.* New York: Aronson.

Bradshaw, J. (1988). *Bradshaw on the family: A revolutionary way of self-discovery.* Pompano Beach, FL: Health Communications.

Brooks, C. S., & Rice, K. F. (1997). *Families in recovery: Coming full circle.* Baltimore: Paul H. Brookes.

Brown, S., & Lewis, V. (1999). *The alcoholic family in recovery: A developmental model.* New York: Guilford Press.

Cable, L. C. (2000). Kaleidoscope and epic tales: Diverse narratives of adult children of alcoholics. In J. Krestan (Ed.), *Bridges to recovery* (pp. 45–76). New York: Free Press.

Carroll, M. (1993). *Spiritual growth of recovering alcoholic adult children of alcoholics.* Unpublished doctoral dissertation, University of Maryland, Baltimore.

Center for Substance Abuse Treatment (CSAT). (1999). *Enhancing motivation for change in substance abuse treatment.* Treatment Improvement Protocol (TIP) Series, No. 35. Retrieved September 2006 from http://www.ncbi.nlm.nih.gov/books.

Center for Substance Abuse Treatment (CSAT). (2004). *Substance abuse treatment and family therapy.* Treatment Improvement Protocol (TIP) Series, No. 39. Rockville, MD: Substance Abuse and Mental Health Services Administration.

Chaput, L. L. (2001). *Assessment of family functioning in a clinical population of ethnically diverse substance users: Implications for practice.* Unpublished doctoral dissertation, University of Texas, Arlington.

Chase-Marshall, J. (1976, September). Virginia Satir: Everybody's family therapist. *Human Behavior*, pp. 25–31.

Denham, S., Meyer, M., Toborg, M., & Mande, M. (2004). Providing health education to Appalachia populations. *Holistic Nursing Practice, 18*(6), 293–302.

DiClemente, C. C. (2006). *Addiction and change: How addictions develop and addictive people recover.* New York: Guilford Press.

Dulfano, C. (1982). *Families, alcoholism, and recovery.* Center City, MN: Hazelden.

Ellis-Ordway, N. (1992). The impact of family dynamics on anorexia: A transactional view of treatment. In E. Freeman (Ed.), *The addiction process: Effective social work approaches* (pp. 180–191). New York: Longman.

Fals-Stewart, W., & Kennedy, C. (2005). Addressing intimate partner violence in substance abuse treatment. *Journal of Substance Abuse Treatment, 29*(1), 5–17.

Fisher, G. L., & Harrison, T. C. (2005). *Substance abuse: Information for school counselors, social workers, therapists, and counselors* (3rd ed.). Boston: Allyn & Bacon.

Frasier, P., Slatt, L., Kowlwitz, V., & Glowa, P. (2001). Using the stages of change model to counsel victims of intimate partner violence. *Patient Education and Counseling, 43*(2), 211–217.

Galanter, M. D., Dermatis, H., Keller, D., & Trujillo, M. (2002). Network therapy for cocaine abuse: Use of family and peer supports. *American Journal of Addictions,* *11*(2), 161–166.

Germain, C. (1991). *Human behavior in the social environment: An ecological view.* New York: Columbia University Press.

Gruber, K., & Taylor, M. (2006). A family perspective for substance abuse: Implications from the literature. *Journal of Social Work Practice in the Addictions,* *6*(1/2), 1–29.

Hanson, J. (1996). Families' perspectives on the early years of mental illness. *Canadian Social Work Review, 12*(2), 236–247.

Hazelden Publishing Company. (1987). Some thoughts on codependency. *Hazelden Professional Update, 5*(3), 2.

Jackson, J. (1954). The adjustment of the family to the crisis of alcoholism. *Quarterly Journal of Substance Abuse, 15,* 562–586.

Jackson, K. (2005, January/February). Do drug and alcohol interventions really work? *Social Work Today,* pp. 28–31.

Kaufman, E. (1985). *Substance abuse and family therapy.* Orlando, FL: Grune & Stratton.

Kaufman, E., & Kaufman, P. (2002). *Family therapy of drug and alcohol abuse* (2nd ed.). Boston: Allyn & Bacon.

Krestan, J. (2000). Introduction. In J. Krestan (Ed.), *Bridges to recovery: Addiction, family therapy, and multicultural treatment* (pp. 1–12). New York: Free Press.

Laudet, A., Magura, S., Furst, R. T., Kumar, N., & Whitney, S. (1999). Male partners of substance-abusing women in treatment: An exploratory study. *American Journal of Drug and Alcohol Abuse, 25*(4), 607–618.

Lawson, A., & Lawson, G. (1998). *Alcoholism and the family: A guide to treatment and prevention* (2nd ed.). Gaithersburg, MD: Aspen.

Lawson, G., Lawson, A., & Rivers, R. C. (2001). *Essentials of chemical dependency counseling* (3rd ed.). Gaithersburg, MD: Aspen.

Leonard, L. (1989). *Witness to the fire: Creativity and the veil of addiction.* Boston: Shambhala.

Little, L. (2005). Program trains families to address addiction. *Family Practice News,* *35*(22), 43–44.

McCourt, F. (1996). *Angela's ashes: A memoir.* New York: Scribner.

McCrady, B. (2006). Family and other close relationships. In W. R. Miller & K. Carroll (Eds.), *Rethinking substance abuse* (pp. 166–181). New York: Guilford Press.

McGoldrick, M., Giordano, J., & Garcia-Petro, N. (Eds.). (2005a). *Ethnicity and family therapy.* New York: Guilford Press.

McGoldrick, M., Giordano, J., & Garcia-Preto, N. (2005b). Overview: Ethnicity and family therapy. In M. McGoldrick, J. Giordano, & N. Garcia-Preto (Eds.), *Ethnicity and family therapy* (pp. 1–40). New York: Guilford Press.

Miller, W. R. (2006). Motivational factors in addictive behaviors. In W. R. Miller & K. M. Carroll (Eds.), *Rethinking substance abuse: What the science shows* (pp. 134–150). New York: Guilford Press.

Minuchin, S. (1974). *Families and family therapy.* Cambridge, MA: Harvard University Press.

Moore, B. C. (2005). Empirically supported family and peer interventions for dual disorders. *Research on Social Work Practice, 15*(4), 231–245.

Mueser, K., Noordsy, D., Drake, R., & Fox, L. (2003). *Integrated treatment for dual disorders: A guide to effective practice.* New York: Guilford Press.

Nichols, M. (1984). *Family therapy.* New York: Gardner Press.

O'Farrell, T., & Fals-Stewart, W. (2006). *Behavioral couples therapy for alcoholism and drug abuse.* New York: Guilford Press.

Prochaska, J. O., & DiClemente, C. C. (1992). Stages of change in the modification of problem behaviors. In M. Hersen, R. M. Eisler, & P. M. Miller (Eds.), *Progress in behavioral modification* (pp. 184–214). Sycamore, IL: Sycamore Press.

Rabinor, J. R. (1994). Mothers, daughters, and eating disorders: Honoring the mother–daughter relationship. In P. Fallon, M. Katzman, & S. Wooley (Eds.), *Feminist perspectives on eating disorders* (pp. 272–286). New York: Guilford Press.

Saatcioglu, O., Erim, R., & Cakmak, D. (2006). Role of family in alcohol and substance abuse. *Psychiatry and Clinical Neurosciences, 60*(2), 125–133.

Simon, C., McNeil, J., Franklin, C., & Cooperman, A. (1991). The family and schizophrenia: Toward a psychoeducational approach. *Families in Society, 72,* 323–334.

Tapia, M., Schwartz, S., Prado, G., Lopez, B., & Pantin, H. (2006). Parent-centered intervention: A practical approach for preventing drug abuse in Hispanic adolescents. *Research on Social Work Practice, 16*(2), 146–165.

Thomas, C., & Corcoran, J. (2001). Empirically based marital and family interventions for alcohol abuse: A review. *Research on Social Work Practice, 11*(5), 549–575.

Thompson, S., Pomeroy, E., & Gober, K. (2005). Family-based treatment models targeting substance use and high-risk behaviors among adolescents: A review. *Journal of Evidence-Based Social Work, 2*(1/2), 207–233.

Tolstoy, L. (1917). *Anna Karenina.* New York: Collier & Son. (Original work published 1876)

U.S. Department of Health and Human Services. (1999). *Brief interventions and brief therapies for substance abuse.* Treatment Improvement Protocol (TIP) Series, No. 34. Rockville, MD: U.S. Government Printing Office.

van Stelle, K. R., Allen, G. A., & Moberg, D. P. (1998). Alcohol and drug prevention among American Indian families: The Family Circles Program. *Drugs, 12*(1/2), 53–60.

van Wormer, K. (1995). *Alcoholism treatment: A social work perspective.* Belmont, CA: Wadsworth.

van Wormer, K. (2001). *Counseling female offenders and victims: A strengths-restorative approach.* New York: Springer.

van Wormer, K., Wells, J., & Boes, M. (2000). *Social work with lesbians, gays, and bisexuals: A strengths perspective.* Boston: Allyn & Bacon.

Velleman, R. (2000). The importance of family. In D. B. Cooper (Ed.), *Alcohol use* (pp. 63–74). Oxon, England: Radcliffe Medical Press.

Volpicelli, J., & Szalavitz, M. (2000). *Recovery options: The complete guide.* New York: Wiley.

Waldron, H. B., & Slesnick, N. (1998). Treating the family. In W. Miller & N. Heather (Eds.), *Treating addictive behaviors* (pp. 259–270). New York: Plenum Press.

Walker, J. P., & Lee, R. E. (1998). Uncovering strengths of children of alcoholic parents. *Contemporary Family Therapy, 20*(4), 521–538.

Wallen, J. (1993). *Addiction in human development: Developmental perspectives on addiction and recovery.* New York: Haworth.

Wegscheider, S. (1981). *Another chance: Hope and health for the alcoholic family.* Palo Alto, CA: Science and Behavior Books.

Wetzel, J. (1991). Universal mental health classification systems: Reclaiming women's experience. *Affilia, 6*(3), 8–31.

Woodside, D., & Shekter-Wolfson, L. (2003). Families and eating disorders. National Eating Disorder Information Centre, Toronto. Retrieved November 29, 2006, from http://www.nedic.ca.

What sets the world in motion is the interplay of differences,
their attractions and repulsions. Life is a plurality,
death is a uniformity.

—Octavio Paz (Mexican poet, writer, and diplomat, 1914–1998)

RACIAL, ETHNIC, AND CULTURAL ISSUES

CHAPTER **10**

INTRODUCTION

In traditional substance abuse and addiction treatment, an alcoholic is an alcoholic, a compulsive gambler is a compulsive gambler, and nothing else is as important. Regardless of race, ethnicity, culture, age, class, or gender differences, everyone is predicted to go through the same inevitable progressive stages on the U-shaped Jellinek curve, starting with occasional relief drinking (gambling, using drugs) and bottoming out with obsessive drinking (gambling, using drugs). Like the traditional medical paradigm in the United States, the disease is the focus (and the great equalizer), not the holistic person. Research studies in addiction reflect this stance by historically focusing on White males as subjects and rarely reporting separate gender or racial and ethnic groups.

As noted by Gross (1995), a scientific-positivist (medical model) stance from the clinician implies "knowing something 'permanent,' 'true,' 'universal,' and 'essential' about the other, when none of this is true" (p. 212). Rhodes and Johnson (1997) argue that the use of the medical model in addiction trivializes the life experiences of African American women because it ignores the sociopolitical context of racism, sexism, and poverty and instead focuses on individual pathology.

In contrast, a strengths perspective emphasizes a "not knowing" position; that is, it is the counselor's responsibility *not* to have preprogrammed answers but to find out the best way to match prevention and treatment strategies to diverse people from different ethnic communities. The "not knowing" position conveys the message that clients have certain expertise and knowledge about their own life circumstances and how to go about setting realistic goals (Berg & Shafer, 2004). This approach is highly congruent with the desire to honor and work within the client's cultural frame of reference.

Posing as "expert" is particularly detrimental and prejudicial to establishing a working relationship with individuals and families from a culture, class, or ethnicity different from your own. A strengths perspective calls for a more egalitarian balance, where both the clients and the clinician are learning as they go along. In addition, Straussner (2001) notes that "helping them share positive information about their ethnic history, cultural values, traditions, and contributions enhances their self-worth and potential for recovery" (p. 20).

Since the 1970s, with pressure from women and a new consciousness raising regarding civil rights, the term *special population* began to be used in government publications and textbooks about substance misuse to highlight "groups" of people that are underserved by traditional treatment programs, are not included in research studies, or have unique characteristics (both strengths and needs)—that is, people who don't fit neatly into the substance use/treatment paradigm defined by the dominant culture. Treatment plans began to be "individualized" and took into consideration family, religious, ethnic, and community resources that are available to support recovery. Even so, most substance misusers receiving treatment in the United States still receive the same disease-concept AA-facilitated treatment approach regardless of their ethnic group. The national databases still lag behind by aggregating people into huge racial or ethnocultural categories (Black, White, Hispanic, Asian, Native American) and ignoring the many subgroups within each major category (Straussner, 2001).

However, even with these problems, the substance abuse field is ahead of the compulsive gambling field in this effort. Mark and Lesieur (1992) focus on the dramatic exclusion of women and other populations (Asians, Blacks, Hispanics, gays, lesbians) from the existing literature on pathological and problem gambling. They conclude, "it is time for professionals in the field to rethink their conceptualization of problem gambling in terms of the various subgroups within the population at large, and *not* just the dominant culture" (p. 561). Although the authors stop short of contesting the addiction/disease model (which was first included in the DSM in 1980, based largely on the clinical experience of Dr. Robert Custer with White male gamblers), they do note that Custer's chart of the gambler's progression of disease (Custer, 1982) has never been tested on females or any other ethnocultural group. Furthermore, they point out, the classification scheme of gamblers in Custer and Milt's (1985) influential text *When Luck Runs Out* was based principally on the study of White male GA members and White male Veterans' Affairs patients.

Despite the uneven awareness that the use, progression, and recovery process are influenced by ethnocultural norms and values, most clinicians today would agree with Straussner (2001) that "treatment must take into account the client's ethnocultural beliefs, customs, and values, particularly as they relate to alcohol and other drug (AOD) issues, as well as the social conditions that have an impact on the client's ethnocultural group" (p. 12). The crucial question then becomes: How can clinicians learn to be culturally competent and at the same time not stereotype a whole culture or race? The practice of lumping people together by an obvious external trait such as race or ethnic practices is open to criticism because it doesn't take into account other important characteristics (e.g., social class) or the vast differences found within a particular group (McGoldrick, Giordano, & Garcia-Preto, 2005). Collins (1993) calls this practice "ethnic gloss."

To avoid stereotyping or "glossing" a particular ethnocultural group, factors other than race and ethnicity must be taken into consideration. Such factors include the individual's experience of oppression and discrimination, immigration status and experience, degree and effects of acculturation, language and communication skills and patterns, education and socioeconomic status, religion, age, gender, and family structure.

Many authors argue that the effects of group membership cannot be separated from the effects of social class, and in fact many so-called "attributes" of ethnicity or culture are in reality effects of class. For example, close ties and reliance on extended family may be related to the bleak economic future of undereducated and poor individuals on their own. Class, or socioeconomic status, is related to a person's level of education and current employment and income status, but it clearly impacts every aspect of a person's life (see, e.g., McGoldrick et al., 2005). As bell hooks (2000) says:

> Class matters. Race and gender can be used as screens to deflect attention away from the harsh realities class politics exposes. Clearly, just when we should all be paying attention to class, using race and gender to understand and explain its new dimensions, society, even our government, says let's talk about race and racial injustice. It is impossible to talk meaningfully about ending racism without talking about class. (p. 7)

According to the Office of Applied Statistics (OAS) (2006), sociodemographic differences in substance use among and within racial and ethnic subgroups explain, at least in part, the subgroups' different prevalence of substance misuse and differential treatment needs. In their ethnographic study on women and cocaine, for example, Murphy and Rosenbaum (1997) note that race and economic class heavily influence geographic location, access to drugs, and a variety of other factors. In the example they use, Monique is poor and Black; Becky is middle-class and White. Their different status of race and class influences (a) how potent the available drugs are (crack in poor inner cities vs. powdered cocaine in affluent suburbs), (b) the relationship between sex and drugs in the particular social scene (Monique, who had to prostitute for money vs. Becky, who had a well-paying job), (c) the ability of a person to maintain a "nondeviant" identity by being able to conceal drug use, (d) the availability of resources to cushion the consequences of using illegal drugs, and (e) the availability of options to leave the drug "scene" and move on to a different way of life (Monique, who went to a homeless shelter vs. Becky, who went to Hawaii with her dad). Thus, the combination of racial oppression *and* economic class profoundly influences the context of drug initiation, drug use patterns, and the consequences of drug misuse and addiction.

In the case of Native Americans and Alaskan Natives, racial oppression has been taken to a level considered genocidal by some because of the warfare, disease, alcohol, and forcible removal of Native children to English-speaking boarding schools where they were not allowed to practice any aspect of their culture (Weaver, 2001). The subsequent cultural breakdown has been accompanied by years of poverty, unemployment, broken families, substandard living conditions, and meager educational opportunities for many Natives. Some writers explain Native alcohol and drug misuse as a psychological reaction to the loss of tradition and culture (Sutton & Broken Nose, 2005) or, in Lowery's (1998) words, "a crisis of the spirit" (p. 127). Even here, however, prevalence rates vary by tribe and location—rural or urban—and reservation (National Institute on Alcohol Abuse and Alcoholism [NIAAA], 2005).

Some researchers emphasize the effects of recent immigration by various racial and ethnic groups on substance use practices (Center on Substance Abuse Treatment [CSAT], 2004). Asian and Hispanic immigrants may face major stressors, such as crowded, inadequate housing, socioeconomic hardships, not speaking English, and posttraumatic stress resulting from war and life in refugee camps. Additional stressors include separation of families during the immigration process and the inevitable rift between children brought up in the United States and their parents, who may cling to traditional ways. First-generation youth are vulnerable to substance misuse in an attempt to be accepted in the new culture. Many times, as acculturation increases, so do substance use problems. For example, among Hispanics, a higher level of alcohol consumption is linked to a higher level of acculturation, especially among women (Randolph, Stroup-Benham, Black, & Markides, 1998).

Lee and Mock (2005) and Makimoto (1998) point out that the consequences of immigration may be different even for the same ethnic group. For example, the Vietnamese and Cambodians who emigrated shortly after the war in 1975 were mostly well-educated people who had lived in urban areas; however, the second wave, in the 1980s, frequently included farmers and peasants who were illiterate in their own language, had been in refugee camps for a long period, and had experienced violence and starvation before coming to the United States. Although both groups are from Southeast Asia, their acculturation into and adjustment to the United States were markedly different.

Because of the "wildly heterogeneous" (Closser & Blow, 1993) nature of these various groups in terms of acculturation, economic class, and education, among other important variables, many writers pay lip service to the idea that it is not correct to generalize across cultures. As McGoldrick et al. (2005)

indicate, however, without some concept of the cultural norms of a given group, "we would have no compass for our clinical work at all" (p. 13). In the following discussion of Asian/Pacific Islanders, Alaskan/Native Americans, Hispanic Americans, and African Americans, we avoid stereotyping by highlighting the complexity and diversity of each "group" and encouraging the reader to use this information as a launching pad for further investigation of subgroups. We focus on strengths as well as traditional values of the most vulnerable in each group—that is, those who are recent immigrants, are poor, have a history of oppression, and may be undereducated—in an attempt to track influences on the path to drug initiation, drug use patterns, the consequences of drug misuse and addiction, and the resources available for recovery. Although the success of culturally specific treatment programs is a contested area that needs more research, we will describe several programs that have made progress in this area.

Given the great variability and number of factors that influence a person's cultural pattern within his or her group, we go back to the original question: How can counselors learn to be culturally sensitive and at the same time not stereotype a whole culture or race? Amodeo and Jones (1997) suggest a cultural framework for clinical practice that takes several variables into consideration when trying to understand an individual client from a culture different from their own. Elements of a cultural-specific assessment include finding out the cultural attitudes, values, and behaviors of using alcohol and other drugs, how the problem is defined and identified, cultural ways of seeking help (where, when, and what type), the meaning and consequences of relapse, and the support available for recovery. All of these factors are in turn influenced by three other critical variables: the degree of acculturation, subgroup identity, and the context of migration (departure circumstances, trauma experience, and legal status).

For example, according to Bromley and Sip (2001), it is not unusual for traditional Cambodians to use herbs, drugs, and alcohol in moderation, when they were available, to treat suffering and stress in Cambodia. Cambodian immigrants suffered a great deal of stress from war, persecution, torture, refugee camps, and all of the problems of adjusting to a completely different culture and language when they finally got to the United States. Alcohol was suddenly much more available and affordable. The authors theorize that "many Cambodian refugees turned to alcohol to 'medicate' themselves from the impact of these horrifying experiences" (p. 329).

Many intervention approaches that are effective when applied to one ethnic or cultural group fail miserably when transplanted into another (NIAAA, 2005). For example, behaviorally oriented methods may be more effective for some groups than for others. And some mainstream programming has been rejected by certain groups such as Native American populations because it did not take into account the cultural needs of the community (Milbrodt, 2002).

Each one of these variables can shed a whole new light on how to help a particular client or family and the particular strengths of the family experience. Unfortunately, because of time constraints on most clinical practices, this kind of careful, individualized, and culturally specific groundwork is likely to be put aside as something "nice" but impractical. However, we eventually pay the cost in terms of underutilized treatment programs and the failure to meet the needs of many vulnerable groups.

ASIAN AMERICANS AND PACIFIC ISLANDERS

The danger of lumping people into one group is obvious when you consider that this "group" consists of at least 30 Asian and 21 Pacific Islander ethnic groups with different languages, customs, and behaviors (Makimoto, 1998). In the U.S. Census (2000), "Asian" refers to people having origins in the Far East, Southeast Asia, or the Indian subcontinent. It includes people who identified themselves as Asian Indian, Chinese, Filipino, Korean, Japanese, Vietnamese, Burmese, Hmong, Pakistani, or Thai. The term "Native Hawaiian and Other Pacific Islander" refers to people having origins in the original peoples of Hawaii, Guam, Samoa, or other Pacific Islands and includes people who identified themselves as Native Hawaiian, Guamanian or Chamorro, Samoan, Other Pacific Islander, Tahitian, Mariana Islander, or Chuukese. Even with all this variety, there are numerous subgroups within each group that may form a distinct ethnic group with different ways of approaching substance use and addiction.

PREVALENCE PATTERNS

Since both education and economic class influence substance use patterns and the availability of resources to alleviate problems, the variability of these factors within the Asian and Pacific Islander group may help explain some of the variability of substance use patterns. Results from the National Survey on Drug Use and Health indicate that in 2005, the Asian rate of substance dependence or abuse was the lowest (4.5%) compared to all other racial categories (Substance Abuse Mental Health Services Administration [SAMHSA], 2005). However, the rate for Pacific Islanders was 11.0%. A similar result occurred when measuring current illicit drug use. The rate was lowest among Asians (3.1%), while the rate of Native Hawaiians or other Pacific Islanders was 8.7% (SAMHSA, 2006). In 2003, Asian American, Native Hawaiian, or other Pacific Islander comprised 1.1% of admission to publicly funded substance abuse treatment programs (National Institute on Drug Abuse [NIDA], 2006).

The low rate of alcohol/drug misuse for the Asian/Pacific Islander group may be underreported and inaccurate because of several factors: (a) national database surveys have ignored this group and consistently put Asian/Pacific Islanders in the category of "other," (b) the low treatment rate may be the result of the lack of culturally relevant services, (c) methodological weaknesses in the research have resulted in an underestimate of the levels of substance misuse and dependence, and (d) there is a belief that alcoholism is rare in this group because of the absence of the enzyme aldehyde dehydrogenase in widely varying percentages of Asians and Pacific Islanders, which can cause "flushing" and discomfort when alcohol is ingested, although this has proven not to be true uniformly (Ja & Aoki, 1993; NIAAA, 2005).

There is a notable lack of information about alcohol consumption patterns and related problems of Asian Indians, perhaps because they are a relatively small group (Makimoto, 1998). There are some comparisons available within the Asian group indicating that in California and Hawaii, Japanese Americans had the highest rate of lifetime use and heavy drinking, and Chinese Americans had the lowest rate (Makimoto, 1998). Three quarters of methamphetamine users in Hawaii are reported to be Asian/Pacific Islanders, and less than one quarter are Caucasian (Freese, Obert, Dickow, Cohen, & Lord, 2000).

Although female Native Hawaiians comprise less than 10% of the total state population, they constitute 40% of women in prison in Hawaii. Lee Stein (2001) explains this in terms of violent victimization within the family and harsh sentencing practices related to drug use. Discrimination against Native Hawaiians has also played a role. Stein recommends gender-specific and culturally sensitive treatment programming for this group.

SOCIOCULTURAL FACTORS

In addition to ethnic background, this group varies greatly in educational level and economic status. The most recent median income figures (U.S. Census Bureau, 2006c) indicate that Asian households have the highest median income of any racial group (i.e., $61,094). However, the poverty rate for this group is 11.1% (higher than the non-Hispanic White rate of 8.3%), suggesting that some subgroups have a higher than average economic status and other groups are below average.

There are also great differences in education status among this group. Southeast Asians and Pacific Islanders, perhaps because of more recent immigration, tend to have lower educational status than Chinese Americans, Japanese Americans, and Indians (Makimoto, 1998). For example, one in every seven Asians and Pacific Islanders age 25 and older has an advanced degree beyond the bachelor's degree. Unfortunately, the high level of academic achievement for part of this group has led to the myth of Asians as the "model minority." This in turn has contributed to the erroneous belief that addiction is not problematic in this group (Ja & Aoki, 1993).

Although there is great variation because of economic class, education, and level of acculturation as to how traditional values are actualized in individual people, several authors have pointed out consistent traditional cultural themes that may pose barriers to getting help through mainstream treatment programs (Center for Substance Abuse Treatment [CSAT], 2004; Closser & Blow, 1993; Ja & Aoki, 1993; Makimoto, 1998; Mercado, 2000). On the other hand, these same values provide family support, family resources, and a family commitment to the best interests of the family member who may be suffering consequences from addiction. Counselors will want to understand through a "not knowing" and respectful stance whether or not the following traditional immigrant Asian values and practices may apply:

- The theme of filial piety (devotion, obligation, duty) dominates traditional Asian culture. That is, the individual within the family is secondary to the interests of the family as a whole. Communications are indirect and based on roles within the family hierarchy. Emotions are not generally shared because that might emphasize the individual over the interdependent needs of the family.
- The initial response of the family to substance use or mental health problems may be to ignore it. It may not even be considered a problem as long as the individual continues to meet family responsibilities. Among many Southeast Asians, alcohol is viewed as a substance that has healing properties, and it is culturally acceptable for elderly persons to drink alcohol and smoke marijuana.
- If a problem gets identified and family functioning is threatened, the family risks deep shame and "losing face" in the community. To keep from losing face, families may try to isolate the person with the problem from the community, shame or scold the person, and even reject the person. The extended family may be asked to intervene.
- Seeking outside help is equated to failure. When it does occur, families may have "quick-fix" expectations. The person with the problem is likely to be angry because of the family's "betrayal" and resistant when brought to treatment.

Although traditional parents are practicing in ways that mirror their native countries, their sons and daughters may have acculturated to the point of relying more on their peers and popular culture. Consequently, attempts to rein them in using traditional methods of shaming and hierarchical processes may cause a great deal of family conflict.

Ja and Aoki (1993) suggest, from their experience at the Asian American Recovery Services in San Francisco, that it is helpful for counselors to take a structured approach to working with traditional families, using clear intake procedures and outlining rules and procedures. The authors recommend peer group processes that are provided within a framework of positive support. It is particularly helpful if the groups include other Asians. Because families are so critical to a person's well-being, family support should be offered using an educational rather than a confrontational approach (CSAT, 2004).

Treatment Issues

Sakai, Ho, Shore, Risk, and Price (2005) found that Asians with substance dependence are significantly less likely to receive treatment than Caucasians. Although dissatisfaction with standard treatment programs is common and treatment programs appear to be underutilized by this group, there is little outcome research that supports or doesn't support culturally specific treatment approaches (Closser & Blow, 1993). However, advocates of trying to meet the unique treatment needs of Asian/Pacific Islanders are not waiting for research results. In a survey of 294 drug treatment programs in ethnically diverse Los Angeles County, Polinsky, Hser, and Grella (1998) found that services were available in 36 languages, including Vietnamese and Cambodian, and clients speaking languages other than English or Spanish could be served by about one fourth of the programs. The majority of the programs (68%) reported being able to meet the unique needs of Asian/Pacific Islanders.

Closser and Blow (1993) state that "it is futile to search for a single treatment approach for all group members" (p. 205). This may be particularly true for the richly diverse group of Asian/Pacific Islanders. General strategies to become more user friendly to this group involve hiring staff who come from and can speak the language of the primary target group, providing cultural training for all staff, incorporating the use of elders and native healers, using familiar healing strategies such as acupuncture, and incorporating culture-specific beliefs and spiritual practices about healing and recovery.

For example, a culturally based, women-centered residential treatment program in Hawaii uses Küpuna, elders of the Hawaiian Native community who carry wisdom and tradition in extended family, to develop parenting classes, facilitate traditional healing practices, provide child care, and act as counselors and listeners. Ethnographic interviewing of the women who participated in the program revealed positive perceptions about Küpuna involvement (Morelli & Fong, 2000). As one participant commented, "We'd sing and start talking about culture, about how the ancient Hawaiians used to live off the land, and spiritual things. If you had burdens or problems for the day or you weren't feeling right, they'd pray on you" (p. 42).

The "challenge model," a strengths-based intervention developed by the Asian American Recovery Service in San Francisco and San Jose, California, is used as a culturally appropriate treatment model for adolescents. As described by Yuen and Nakano-Matsumoto (1998), features include acknowledgment and support of the strengths of resilient youth, nonconfrontational techniques to avoid "loss of face," home visits to engage families, community outreach and networking to other systems, affirmation of cultural identity and differences, and goal-oriented activities using a psychoeducational approach.

Nav Nirmaan, the only New York City substance abuse treatment program run by and for immigrants from southern Asia, is an inspiring example of culture-specific programming (Box 10.1).

| Box 10.1 | AN IMMIGRANT-RUN TREATMENT PROGRAM |

For years, Mohammed Arif denied he had a drinking problem. He saw himself as an immigrant success story: He had mastered a new language, earned enough to support relatives back in his native Pakistan, and fit right in when his fellow construction workers hit the bars at the end of the day.

"The thing about drinking was this false pride," Mr. Arif said, recalling the dark years when he failed to see how alcohol was corroding his new life. "There was all this finger-pointing in my family, and it would get me so mad. Why is everyone telling me I've got a drinking problem when it's me who's taking care of everybody?"

He eventually sought help, ricocheting from one detoxification program to another. It was not until he landed at Nav Nirmaan, the only New York City substance abuse treatment program run by and for immigrants from southern Asia, that he pulled himself and his family together.

"It made a big difference," said Mr. Arif, who now tells his story as a means of counseling other immigrants at the center, which is in Elmhurst, Queens. "When you're with people from your own background, your own culture, it's like there's no more curtain in front of your eyes."

Nav Nirmaan, which means "new beginning" in the Gujrathi language of western India, is at the vanguard of a growing trend in drug and alcohol treatment programs that not only provide counseling in the native language of immigrants but also consider their particular cultural background and the traumas of the immigrant experience itself.

"In our cultural makeup, the cry for help is the last stage," said Roy V. Tellis, the Indian-born executive director of Nav Nirmaan. "There's a lot of shame involved, and there's the isolation." The typical Nav Nirmaan client, he said, is a man who lives in a cultural cocoon. He drinks as a form of socializing with other men from his home region, reads newspapers and watches television shows in his native language, and feels confusion and rage when his wife and Americanized children try to venture outside the tight circle of southern Asian culture. "It is a male-dominated patriarchal society," Mr. Tellis said. "And the father says: I work hard, I put food on the table. So what if I take a few drinks?"

From: "Tying Drug and Alcohol Programs," 1999.

AMERICAN INDIANS AND ALASKAN NATIVES

Although Asian Americans may be misrepresented by the myth of the "model minority" with few substance use problems, Native Americans and Alaskan Natives have historically been stereotyped in opposite ways. On the one hand, the myth of the "drunken Indian" who is powerless over the White man's "spirits" still colors the popular culture; on the other hand, there is the "politically correct," romantic version of a uniform Indian culture that extols peacefulness, connectedness, and environmental soundness. These contrary beliefs are so widespread that Weaver (2001) cautions that "few people have stopped to critically examine what is actually known and empirically supported" (p. 77).

Prevalence Patterns

In the United States, there are approximately 4.5 million (1.5% of the total population) American Indians and Alaskan Natives, who comprise at least 300 different tribal or language groups (U.S. Newswire, 2006). In Alaska, Natives are around 20% of the total population. In Canada, First Nations People comprise approximately 4% of the population (Graham, Swift, & Delaney, 2000). Many authors agree that it is difficult to make an accurate estimate of alcohol and drug misuse within this group because of the vast differences among Native populations being sampled and a historical distrust of researchers (Weaver, 2001). Differences in drinking patterns among various tribes are influenced by the same factors that influence variation among many ethnic or cultural groups; that is, they may be the result of differing cultural guidelines about tolerating deviant behavior, different socioeconomic conditions, different contexts of highly urban to remote rural areas, differing levels of acculturation to the dominant society, and/or the extent to which traditional values, language, and ways of life are practiced.

In a review of eight studies on drinking prevalence among American Indian adults, May (1996) found a wide variation among "current drinkers," ranging from 30 to 84%, compared to the 64% rate among the general population. Results from the National Survey on Drug Use and Health (SAMHSA, 2005) indicate that among persons aged 12 or older, the rate of substance abuse was highest among American Indians or Alaskan Natives (21.0%) (SAMHSA, 2006). The rate of current illicit drug use for this group (12.8%) was also the highest of all the racial categories. Among youth aged 12 to 17, the rate of current illicit drug use was highest among American Indians or Alaskan Natives (10.2% compared to an overall rate among youth of 9.9%). In 2003, American Indian or Alaskan Natives comprised 2.3% of admissions to publicly funded substance abuse treatment programs, which is about twice their prevalence in the U.S. population (0.9%) (NIDA, 2006).

Whereas American Indians and Alaskan Natives are 1.5% of the U.S. population, they account for 2.1% of all admissions to substance abuse treatment facilities (Office of Applied Statistics, 2005b). They are more likely to report alcohol as their primary substance of misuse; yet they are also the group with the highest rate of illicit drug use. Forty percent were referred from the criminal justice system compared with 36% of all other admissions. American Indians have the highest rate of tobacco use of any group at 53% (Office of Applied Statistics, 2006).

Among Indian youth as well as adolescents in general, drug and alcohol use go together. However, data from school surveys indicate that drug use is higher among Indian youth than among other adolescent groups, and marijuana use is significantly higher (Beauvais, 1998). According to the National Survey on Drug Use and Health (SAMHSA, 2003), the rates of illicit drug use among American Indians and Alaskan Native youth from age 12 to 17 (20.9%) was significantly higher than the rate among all youth (11.6%). Native American youth also have high prevalence rates for use of inhalants, with estimated ranges between 17 and 22% (Herring, 1994). The concern is that inhalant use generally signals a serious level of drug involvement and suggests serious difficulties may lie ahead.

Drinking-related consequences are higher in Native populations compared to other groups. According to the 1996 Indian Health Service report, the age-adjusted alcohol-related death rate was 5.6 times higher within the Indian population than in the general population; chronic liver disease and cirrhosis were 3.9 times as prevalent; alcohol-related fatal automobile accidents were 3 times as prevalent; alcohol-related suicide was 1.4 times as prevalent; and alcohol-related homicide was 2.4 times as prevalent. Native men are twice as likely as women to die from alcohol-related causes between the ages of 45 and 64 (Beauvais, 1998). One Native American woman working in substance abuse treatment in the Northwest described to one of the authors that her reservation was in a state of "perpetual mourning" because of the unremittingly high number of early deaths among people who know each other or are related through extended family. The therapist should be aware of such phenomena as suicide, depression, and alcoholism within the context of ongoing oppression combined with a genocidal history (Sutton & Broken Nose, 2005).

Although there is disagreement about the prevalence of fetal alcohol syndrome (FAS) in the Native population, there is agreement that it is more prevalent among Native Americans than in the U.S. population as a whole. Prevalence rates vary from 6 to 30 times greater and may reflect the variation among different tribes. High rates have been found among some, such as the FAS rate of one in four children on the Pine Ridge and Rosebud Reservations in South Dakota (Weaver, 2001).

SOCIOCULTURAL FACTORS

Socioeconomic and cultural factors are a potent force in the development of alcohol and drug misuse, the ability to get and receive help, and the availability of supports for a recovery process. According to Beauvais (1998), "Many Indian people believe that the loss of their culture is the primary cause of many of their existing social problems, especially those associated with alcohol" (p. 257). The state has invariably been the colonizer of indigenous peoples, leaving a legacy of destruction and despair (Graham et al., 2000).

Historical trauma is the term used by Maria Yellow Horse Brave Heart (2007) to refer to the cumulative emotional and psychological wounding across generations, resulting from a people's collective traumatic experiences. Substance misuse, suicide, depression, anxiety, and difficulty expressing emotions are features most frequently associated with historical trauma. As Brave Heart suggests, this response is prevalent in the American Indian and Alaskan Native population. The legacy of the deliberate breakdown of cultural ties, including spirituality, that began in the 1860s is seen as largely responsible for the loss of cultural pride and stability that characterize much of tribal life today. To regain a sense of cultural mastery and empowerment, Brave Heart has developed the Historical Trauma and Unresolved Grief intervention as a psychoeducational intervention for Native groups. Working through memories and emotions in small and large groups, facilitators use a combination of traditional techniques, including prayer to help participants connect with their Native values.

Another fundamental social problem in the Native community today is poverty. The average poverty rate for American Indians and Alaskan Natives is 25.3% compared to a national rate of 12.6% (U.S. Census Bureau, 2006c). In addition, families have been broken for generations because of the boarding system imposed by the federal government, which had the intent of eliminating Indian culture and replacing it with White culture. Children were separated from their families by hundreds of miles for months from age 6, even for years at a time, and were forbidden to talk in their Native language or participate in any Native practices. More than 100,000 were forced into these Christian schools until the policy ended (Smith, 2006). Members of the Boarding School Healing Project say that the current levels of violence and dysfunction in Native communities are a legacy of human rights abuses perpetrated against past generations.

War, poverty, disease, and displacement have taken a horrendous toll on Native families. For example, in 1900, an influenza epidemic spread throughout Alaska and killed 60% of the Eskimo and Athabascan people, often whole villages. As Lowery (1998) states, "The sense of coherence of an entire people was shattered at the turn of the century. There was no lawfulness, no cultural explanation, no magic, no predictability. The world truly went upside-down" (p. 131).

From this upside-down world, there are some indicators that a remarkable turnaround has begun to occur in some Native American communities, beginning with the civil rights and antipoverty programs of the 1960s and 1970s. Today, 76% of American Indians and Alaskan Natives over age 25 have at least a high school diploma; another 14% have at least a bachelor's degree (U.S. Newswire, 2006). By 1996, 134,000 non-Hispanic American Indians were enrolled in colleges and universities, up from 84,000 in 1980. The number of U.S. businesses owned by American Indians, Eskimos, and Aleuts has increased exponentially since the mid-1990s; by 2002, there were over 200,000 Native-owned businesses (U.S. Newswire, 2006). However, there are still many pockets of poverty, poor health, and "perpetual mourning" that exist in both reservation and urban areas. The poverty rate is approximately 25%.

In cultural areas, treatment and prevention programs have taken a lead in reinforcing, and in some cases teaching for the first time, traditional Native values by incorporating drumming, sweats, beading, medicine wheel philosophy, and other traditional practices into programming. The strong cultural and spiritual component is intended to help invigorate traditional practices as well as give the individual strength in the recovery process (Sutton & Broken Nose, 2005). Community approaches to substance misuse and prevention are reinforcing traditional values of caregiving and responsibility for those who come after them, as, for example, in fetal alcohol syndrome prevention programming. The Native American Church, which uses peyote as a sacramental food and curative for substance misuse, has between 200,000 and 500,000 members in the United States, Mexico, and Canada (Moreno, 2005). This church practices a fusion of Christianity and traditional Indian religions and is the largest indigenous religion in North America.

Spiritual and Cultural Values

It is presumptuous to speak of "Native values" as if they were of one piece, given the differences among individuals and between tribes. However, there are some identifiable cultural beliefs prevalent among many Indian tribes that could impact the path to substance misuse and the path to recovery. Beauvais (1998) points out that social factors, such as viewing drinking as a way of increasing bonding among family and friends and viewing sobriety as carrying a risk of being ostracized, may strongly influence the use of alcohol. Spirituality is often mentioned as a dominant Indian value, manifest in the recognition of the spirit and connectedness in all living things and in the responsibility the Creator gave to Indian people to preserve Mother Earth (Lowery, 1998). However, the idea that the responsibility for one's behavior lies in the hands of spiritual forces is contrary to the Western notion that change is a personal responsibility (Beauvais, 1998). The Indian idea calls for a ceremonial solution to problems and imbalances; the Western idea leads to more confrontational therapeutic practices. Because of the emphasis on spirituality in many Native cultures, addiction is seen as a "crisis of the spirit" and requires "a healing of the spirit, of the mind, and of the body within a larger framework of existence, the extended family network nested within community clan, tribe, and nation" (Lowery, 1998, p. 131).

For example, according to Garrett and Carroll (2000), the concept of the "medicine wheel" in Cherokee and many Plains Indian traditional cultures embraces a holistic framework by including four components of the inner circle: spirit, natural environment, body, and mind. The four directions in the circle represent the four winds: East (belonging), South (mastery), West (independence), and North (generosity). In this conception, disharmony, including substance misuse, results when a person is out of balance or out of harmony with the interaction of mind, body, spirit, and natural environment.

Treatment Issues

Since the mid-1990s, much of the substance abuse treatment provided by the Indian Health Service has shifted to local tribal control. In the process, there has been, as mentioned earlier, an increase in the use of traditional cultural and spiritual practices in treatment, including sweats, medicine wheels, drumming, beading, talking circles, and bringing in elders and medicine men to facilitate healing ceremonies. However, there are no controlled studies to prove the treatment effectiveness of such programming (Beauvais, 1998). As Sutton and Broken Nose (2005) point out, no single approach works for all Indian subgroups; some may benefit from traditional healing practices, and others from mainstream treatment programs. Treatment success for this group involves family involvement, counselor skills in posttraumatic stress and abuse issues, awareness of traumatic history, tolerance of thoughtful periods of silence, and tribal differences. Ethnographic studies and program evaluations have shown positive results of reconnecting people with substance use problems to their culture (Lowery, 1998). According to Kasee (1995), "the availability of traditional religion is a major motivator for recovery for Indian clients, a process so frequent, it is colloquially referred to as 'going back to the blanket'" (p. 84).

Box 10.2	THE RED ROAD TO SOBRIETY
	Raymond Slick

In our world we have a lot of problems with drugs and alcohol. I lost two uncles with cirrhosis and seen some people die.

I want to talk about the Red Road philosophy of life as described in the Indian Film, *The Red Road to Sobriety*. Walking the Red Road is walking with the Creator, seeking visions for guidance. This is an inner journey: There may be dances, deprivation of food, ingestion of substances. Peyote was used on Turtle Island (North America), as sacrament with prayer and ceremonies. The sweat lodge was for purification. Drinking of alcohol was done in a few tribes but only in controlled ceremonies.

When the Europeans came there was suddenly introduced a new form of spirits that was much more potent such as rum. The Chief of the Seneca Nation had a vision leading us back from the Black Road of suffering to the good road.

But we did not have instructions for how to cope with what the white man brought—strong drink. And we were not prepared for the loss of culture, the genocide, the wounded spirits. This was the American Holocaust—100 million Indian people died. War, starvation, and European diseases led to a sense of hopelessness, cultural trauma that passes down the generations.

Today we are trying to find what was lost. Elders are our wisdom keepers and help sustain our culture. Our elders teach us to include the concept of life in a circle—there is the physical part, the mental part, the spiritual part. We need to keep all of these aspects of our selves in balance.

I don't share this very much because I made a commitment to hold most of these experiences sacred but in healing circles that I have had some experiences in, the spiritual bonding is very healing. Sobriety is the traditional way, the Red Road. When people are healed their ancestors are healed.

Raymond Slick, class presentation, University of Northern Iowa, August 28, 2006. Printed with permission of Raymond Slick, Tama, Iowa.

One such program is the Native American Counseling Center in the heart of Seattle, Washington (Shukovsky, 1996). Several counselors on staff are Native Americans, and other staff are trained to be sensitive to cultural differences. A typical day might find people with substance use and alcohol problems sitting in a traditional talking circle, passing an eagle feather around to signal each person's turn to tell his or her story. As one of the counselors, Ruben Peters, commented, "This feather is powerful medicine. Let this feather and their circle represent strength and recovery. This is the circle where the healing begins."(Shukovsky, 1996, p. B1) In addition to standard mental health treatment, the center offers talking circles, the wisdom of elders, sweat lodges, powwows, feasts, and stories. "What we are about here is to help people reconnect with who they are," said Dr. Robin LaDue, the center's clinical supervisor and a member of the Cowlitz tribe of western Washington. "The point is to empower them to define themselves—not be defined by external sources" (Shukovsky, 1996, p. B1).

In Box 10.2, Raymond Slick, a member of the Meskwaki tribe and Wolf clan of central Iowa, describes the role of healing circles in his culture.

Harm reduction philosophy that incorporates the stages-of-change model of Prochaska and DiClemente (see chapter 3) is particularly respectful of the Native view that behavioral change is a circular process that occurs in gradual steps (Daisy, Thomas, & Worley, 1998). Harm reduction methods also support the involvement of the Native substance users and their community in the development of long-term plans that will benefit recovery. The authors point out that the traditional practice of the "talking circle" aligns well with harm reduction philosophy in that it provides an opportunity for community members to express their feelings and opinions on how alcohol, drugs, and gambling have affected the community, how to manage them, and how the community can respond to problems. Such strategies that honor indigenous traditions of consensus building are needed to help heal the effect of colonialism on Native American or Canadian communities.

HISPANICS/LATINOS

Prevalence Patterns

Hispanics/Latinos, who may be of any race, totaled about 14% of the U.S. population in 2005 (U.S. Census Bureau, 2006b). The term "Hispanic" or "Latino" describes a population that includes several subgroups, such as Mexican, Puerto Rican, Cuban, Dominican, Central American, South American, Spaniard, and in the Census Bureau statistics, "other Hispanic." Traditionally, Puerto Ricans identified themselves by class, not race (on a continuum of Black to White), viewing skin color as unimportant. However, because of the racial dichotomy and prejudice experienced by Puerto Ricans who have moved to the United States, whiteness of skin has become more valued (Medina, 2001).

Taken together, the rate of substance dependence or abuse for persons reporting themselves as Hispanic was 9.3% (SAMHSA, 2006). However, an earlier study (SAMHSA, 1998) showed that Hispanic subgroups vary significantly in their prevalence of alcohol and drug use and problems. The rate of illicit drug use (marijuana, cocaine, and other drugs), heavy alcohol use, alcohol dependence, and the need for drug treatment are higher for Mexican Americans and Puerto Rican Americans than for any other Hispanic/Latino subgroup and for the total population surveyed. The lowest rates in these categories are among Caribbean Americans, Central Americans, and Cuban Americans. For example, alcohol dependence varies greatly, from a high rate of 5.6% of Mexican Americans to 3.0% of Puerto Rican Americans, 2.8% of Central Americans, 2.1% of South Americans, and 0.9% of Cuban Americans compared to a total population rate of 3.5% (SAMHSA, 1999).

Cigarette use shows a different pattern, with Hispanics from South America having the highest rate (32.7%), followed by Puerto Rican Americans (31.3%), Mexican Americans (29.1%), Cuban Americans (27.3%), Caribbean Americans (21.2%), and Central American Hispanics (17.9%) compared to the total population rate of 30.9%. Treatment admissions for the United States in 2003 show that Hispanics/Latinos entered treatment at a slightly lower rate (13.3%)

than their incidence in the U.S. population (14%) (NIDA, 2006). Hispanic admissions were more likely to be male and report opiate abuse than non-Hispanic admissions (SAMHSA, 2005). The Drug and Alcohol Services Information System (DASIS) Report provides the following breakdown: The most common primary substance of abuse among Hispanics receiving treatment is reported as alcohol (36%), opiates (28%), and marijuana (15%) (Office of Applied Statistics, 2005a).

Overall, heavy drinking is significantly less prevalent among Latina women than among Latino men; however, the rate of cocaine use is similar to that for non-Hispanic Whites, and crack use is higher than among non-Hispanic White women (Amaro, Nieves, Johannes, & Cabeza, 1998). The effect of acculturation on Latina women is more evident than among men regarding drinking patterns. Traditional sanctions against female drinking break down the more educated, employed, and middle class Mexican American women become. Hispanic youth have a higher rate of cocaine, marijuana, and crack use than any other group, and a concern is developing that Latina girls are becoming a high-risk group, with abstention rates only slightly higher than Latino boys (Alvarez & Ruiz, 2001).

One of the most devastating effects of substance misuse, including injecting drug use in this population, has been the transmission of HIV. AIDS is the second leading cause of death for Latinos in the age group of 25 to 44, and it is the leading cause of death for Hispanic women between 25 and 34 years of age (Centers for Disease Control and Prevention [CDC], 2002). AIDS surveillance data from the CDC indicate that Latino men are more likely to be exposed to HIV through intravenous drug use than White men, and Latina women are more likely to be exposed to HIV by having sex with an HIV positive sexual partner than are White women. Researchers attribute this high risk for HIV infection among Latino and African Americans to factors such as poverty, low educational attainment, poor access to healthcare, and high levels of intravenous drug use (CDC, 2002).

Latina women account for 20% of all injection-related AIDS cases, yet they represent only 10% of the female population in the United States (Straussner, 2001). In addition, Hispanics are overrepresented among alcohol-related deaths; for example, Latino men have a 40% higher risk of death from cirrhosis than White males (Alvarez & Ruiz, 2001).

SOCIOECONOMIC FACTORS

Education and economic status are improving slightly among Latinos/Latinas, but again, there is wide variation among subgroups. Poverty is still a major risk factor. Hispanic families have a 25.6% poverty rate, ranging from 31% for Puerto Ricans and Mexican Americans to 14% for Cuban Americans (U.S. Census Bureau, 2000). As in any culture of poverty, this condition provides few opportunities to buffer the hardships of life, few resources to avoid harmful social and health-related consequences of drinking and using drugs, and greater vulnerability to social sanctions such as jail, prison, and discrimination (Alvarez & Ruiz, 2001).

On the whole, Latinos/Latinas are the most undereducated of all ethnocultural groups in the United States, with high dropout rates (Puerto Ricans have the highest) and a high school graduation rate of only 56% in 1998 (Alvarez & Ruiz, 2001; Medina, 2001; U.S. Census Bureau, 2000). Twelve percent of Hispanics aged 25 and older had a bachelor's degree or higher in 2004, and 58% graduated from high school (U.S. Census Bureau, 2006b). The proportion aged 25 and older with a bachelor's degree in 2006 (12%) represents a small increase from the 10% of a decade and a half earlier (U.S. Census Bureau, 2006b). Cuban Americans are the most educated subgroup, although slightly lower than non-Hispanic Whites, and tend to be more achievement oriented and politically conservative than other Hispanic subgroups (Rothe & Ruiz, 2001). An area of significant success is in the establishment of small businesses; the number of Latino-owned businesses has more than tripled over the past decade; this is three times the average rate of growth (U.S. Census Bureau, 2006b).

CULTURAL FACTORS

Traditional views of family and roles can be protective factors against using alcohol and drugs; at the same time, they make it more difficult to seek help. Protective factors identified in a study of 60 young, low-income, predominantly Mexican American women include a cohesive family of origin, adequate rule-setting by parents, and a strong social support system (Lindenberg et al., 1998). The authors suggest that early identification of both risk *and* resilience factors is important to prevention of substance misuse among high-risk populations.

Latino/Latina traditions sharply differentiate the roles of males and females (Alvarez & Ruiz, 2001; Medina, 2001; Rothe & Ruiz, 2001). Women are expected to be the moral authority of the family and provide family connection and care for children, while men are expected to be the provider for the family as well as the disciplinarian and decision maker in financial matters. Women in traditional families are highly discouraged from using alcohol or drugs because of their critical role in child rearing. Although there is great individual variance, many males relate strongly to the value of *machismo*—that is, being brave, strong, a good provider, and dominant. Identification with these qualities may make it difficult to admit to problems with alcohol or drugs. Kinship (*familismo*) is highly valued, and extended family members commonly participate in child rearing and other activities that support the family. Festive occasions, usually celebrated by the entire extended family, tend to promote excessive drinking among males (CSAT, 2004).

Unfortunately, the stress of immigration, poverty, discrimination, isolation from extended family, and acculturation can cause dramatic effects and strain on the traditional Latino support system. These hardships may contribute to an attitude of fatalism, or the belief that life's problems are inevitable and must be accepted (Alvarez & Ruiz, 2001). Among Hispanic households, 20.2% are female headed compared to 10.4% among the U.S. population as a whole (Pew Hispanic Center, 2006). Higher levels of acculturation are generally associated with higher levels of drug and alcohol use, especially among women (De La Rosa,

Holleran, Rugh, & MacMaster, 2005). Cultural gaps between generations or between the person and the mainstream American culture may lead to acting-out behaviors for young people, which in America means alcohol and substance use.

TREATMENT ISSUES

The extent to which mainstream treatment is actually utilized by Hispanics is not clear. For example, data from a national Veterans' Administration study of hospitalized alcoholics indicate that Latino males were significantly less likely than Caucasian patients to complete treatment or attend detoxification and more likely to be hospitalized for other diagnoses (Booth, Blow, Cook, Bunn, & Fortney, 1992). On the other hand, in 1997, Hispanics were 10.6% of the treatment population, which is only slightly higher than their 10.4% prevalence in the U.S. population (SAMHSA, 1999). In their research on treatment utilization, Arroyo, Westerberg, and Tonigan (1998) found that even though Hispanic and non-Hispanic White clients used somewhat different treatment strategies (Hispanics attended fewer AA meetings and more formal therapy sessions), the posttreatment outcomes were very similar, and the range of treatment services was equally effective for both groups. This led Arroyo et al. (1998) to conclude that "Hispanics do not need culturally specific treatment" (p. 291). One thing is clear in this contested area: There are no published results of clinical trials that might resolve the issue, so more research is needed.

Culturally appropriate treatment continues to be developed, which concentrates on using the strong support system of Hispanic families (CSAT, 2004). Language may be a significant barrier in accessing any mainstream treatment and should be addressed by providing bicultural and bilingual staff as a minimum requirement (Rothe & Ruiz, 2001). The Alcohol Use Disorder and Associated Disabilities Schedule (AUDADIS), which is a structured diagnostic interview developed for the assessment of substance-related disorders and coexisting disorders, has been translated into Spanish and adapted for the Hispanic culture. A recent study found that Spanish AUDADIS demonstrates good to excellent levels of reliability and validity when tested with a sample of low-income Puerto Ricans (Canino et al., 1999). In general, confrontational approaches during assessment should be avoided in order not to offend the person's sense of honor and dignity. Rather, as Alvarez and Ruiz (2001) suggest, the clinician should thoroughly and respectfully review the assessment criteria (particularly, quantity, frequency, and instances of "loss of control") to garner support for change.

Machismo barriers to admitting problems may be reframed by appealing to the Hispanic male's role and responsibility as the head of the family. For example, an Alcoholics Anonymous group in Los Angeles made up primarily of recent immigrants from Central America linked machismo with how AA makes it possible to be a head of family, how "overcoming is manly," and how one needs "to have balls" to stay sober each day (Hoffman, 1994). In a similar fashion, a clinician can reframe a fatalistic attitude toward the problem of substance misuse by commenting, "You are here for a reason. You were meant to be helped" (Alvarez & Ruiz, 2001, p. 124).

Including key figures in the family or extended family in the treatment plan is recommended to bypass potential resistance and maximize the family support system. From a mainstream cultural perspective, a client's dependence on family members may be unusual and even labeled "codependence." However, for many residents of Latin American origin, particularly women, a focus on individualism may be countertherapeutic and actually reduce the potential support available from family members. Medina (2001) recommends working with the family to "support their strengths and needs and to clarify perceptions, feelings, and behaviors that would help them function as a family unit" (p. 153). An example of family involvement she offers is to develop a contract outlining the family goals and behaviors, which the family signs each week for 6 weeks, modifying as needed.

Tapia, Schwartz, Prado, Lopez, and Pantin (2006) describe *Familias Unidas,* an empirically supported, family-based drug use and HIV prevention intervention for Latino immigrant adolescents and their families that has met with some success. Facilitators have all been of Latino origin. The strategy of this program is to first engage the most powerful member of the family, who is usually the father, and to begin with socializing, perhaps by serving coffee. In *Familias Unidas,* parental isolation is addressed by embedding intervention activities within a parent support group format. Therapists will want to keep in mind that the *respeto* (respect) that Latino parents command from children has a different internal meaning and set of expectations from the more egalitarian notion of respect (CSAT, 2004).

The Latino community has strong cultural prohibitions about women drinking (NIAAA, 2005). As Latinas become acculturated to society north of the border, however, these traditions break down and their alcohol consumption significantly increases. Latina women who enter substance abuse treatment, like women in general, may have additional needs beyond just addressing substance use. For example, Latina women entering substance abuse treatment in Massachusetts tend to be Puerto Rican, undereducated, single heads of household, living in unstable housing situations, with few employment skills and with language difficulties (Amaro et al., 1998). The most common coexisting disorder among this group was depression, and 80.3% reported a history of childhood abuse. The authors suggest that poor Latina mothers, like this group, demonstrate the needs to incorporate case management services in substance abuse treatment that will connect them to GED opportunities, English-language classes, and job skills training, as well as to address mental health problems like depression and the effects of abuse. To address these issues, several larger system funding categories and priorities will need to be changed, including the funding of family-centered rather than just one-on-one approaches (see chapter 13).

Interesting findings have come from a qualitative study based on in-depth interviews with 15 Latino clinicians who work with clients of mixed ethnicity (Gelman, 2004). The purpose of the research was to define how these counselors tailored their approach for Latino clients and to discover their practice principles. The interviews revealed that these clinicians modified their techniques to relate them to the clients' cultural values and expectations, so their approach, in this sense, was culturally sensitive. Remarkable consistency was found in the responses. In describing their work, the clinicians singled out their focus on relationship, individuality, reality, and flexibility. The specific modifications they made in working with Latino clients included a willingness to accept gifts, being more active and directive, speaking Spanish, and using more self-disclosure and physical contact.

Latino Culturally Based Services

Because of the strong association between HIV/AIDS and substance use, especially among poor, urban Black and Latino communities, a description of an ethnic-centered program is appropriate. According to Jennifer Herrera, director of prevention services, AIDS Services of Austin, Texas, who was interviewed by Holleran (2005), two significant facts provide the rationale for the prevention services program.

The first is that Latino men who are out of work, undocumented, and under severe stress sometimes turn to injecting heroin or smoking crack. The second is the extreme dependence of Latino women on their husbands. Confronting their partner for his high-risk behavior might mean loss of family income and security.

The Austin program consists of an extensive outreach program of peer educators from the communities with high rates of HIV/AIDS. The educators who are trained in delivering effective health education and safe sex kits stop people walking on the streets, at day labor sites, and at Laundromats. Women are invited to attend a *platica,* or talk, to learn more about the program. The staff members facilitate the workshop in Spanish and provide Mexican food. Following an icebreaker, the women are asked, "Why don't Latinas access HIV prevention services and testing?" A list is written up that includes such reasons as fear of deportation or lack of child care. The women are then informed about the user-friendly services that are provided. As Herrera sums up their approach, "All of our prevention efforts center around a harm reduction model, understanding that people change their behaviors when they are ready, wanting, and able to change, and that our services must address the clients' changing and diverse needs and not our own agendas" (Holleran, 2005, p. 183).

AFRICAN AMERICANS

The U.S. Census Bureau (2006a) reports that Blacks or African Americans now comprise 13.4% of the population. Their ancestral home may be from many different parts of the world, including Africa, Central America, South America, and the Caribbean, or they may be recent immigrants. According to Harris-Hastick (2001), the term *African American* implies a common cultural identification with Africa and mainstream U.S. culture and some kind of response or adaptation to the racism, poverty, and oppression that exist within the

United States. However, English-speaking immigrants from the Caribbean (West Indies, Jamaica, Bahamas, etc.) have a different history of slavery (one associated with their home country, not the United States), tend to maintain close ties to their home country and customs long after immigration, and come from countries where it is common for Blacks to be middle-class, educated professionals in a position of power. Again, one size does not fit all.

Within the United States, there is also much variation in custom and life circumstance, depending on which part of the country is home and whether home is in crowded inner cities, affluent suburbs, or remote rural areas. In spite of these many differences, most people of African ancestry in the United States share a common history of slavery, an ongoing fight for civil rights, and the stress of racial oppression that still exists.

Institutional racism exerts a significant impact on the lives and well-being of African Americans. Their average life expectancy remains substantially lower than that of Whites, and their rate of death due to AIDS and homicide exceeds that of any other major group (Hines & Boyd-Franklin, 2005). The disillusionment and frustration generated by poor living conditions and oppression and the belief in a lack of opportunity have resulted in a high rate of illicit drug use among African Americans.

PREVALENCE PATTERNS

In general, African Americans were lower in the rate of substance dependence or abuse (8.5%) than Native Americans but higher than Asian Americans (SAMHSA, 2006). The rate of current illicit drug use (9.7%) was lower than that of Native Americans but higher than Native Hawaiians or other Pacific Islanders, Whites, and Hispanics. Among youth aged 12 to 17, the rate of current illicit drug use for African Americans was 11.0% compared to an overall rate of 9.9%. According to NIDA (2006), in 2003 African Americans comprised 23.6% of treatment admissions, which is about twice their incidence in the general population. Binge drinking among Blacks is 20.3% compared to 23.7 % among Whites (Office of Applied Statistics, 2006). Tobacco use is also somewhat less at 28.4%.

African American women have a much higher abstention rate (51%) than African American males (35%) or White women (36%) and a slightly higher rate than Hispanic women (48%). The 5% who did drink heavily drank more alcohol than the White women on average (148 vs. 104 drinks a month) (Caetano & Kaskutas, 1995).

The consequences of heavy alcohol use are greater for African Americans, even though their alcohol dependence rate is the same as that of Whites (3.4% for each, according to SAMHSA). African Americans are more likely to die of cirrhosis of the liver, alcohol- or drug-related homicide, and alcohol-related car crashes. The death rate from alcohol-related diseases is 10% greater for African Americans than for the general population (Center on Alcohol Marketing and Youth [CAMI], 2006). In contrast to White Americans, as African Americans age, their rates of binge drinking remain high.

Since the mid-1980s, a major consequence of illicit drug use for African American men and women has been incarceration in numbers far greater than their representation in the population. In 2005, 12% of Black males in their late 20s were in prison or jail (BJS, 2006). Around 80% of imprisoned female crack cocaine offenders are reported to be African American (Henriques & Manatu-Rupert, 2001). A pregnant African American woman who uses drugs or alcohol is much more likely to be reported to child abuse authorities than a White woman (Rhodes & Johnson, 1997). The specter of HIV/AIDS haunts the African American drug-using community (CSAT, 2004). According to the Centers for Disease Control and Prevention (CDC) (2006), African Americans are 50% of all new HIV/AIDS cases and around half of all HIV/AIDS diagnoses overall. AIDS is the number one cause of death for African American women aged 25 to 34 and is among the three causes of death for African American men aged 25 to 54. African American intravenous drug users were the fastest growing group of all new cases (Wright, 2001).

SOCIOECONOMIC FACTORS

Although the African American poverty rate in 2005 was a high 24.9% compared to the nation's poverty rate of 12.6%, this represents a decline from an even higher 1998 rate of 26.1% (U.S. Census Bureau, 2006c). In 2005, African Americans had the lowest median income ($30,858) compared to Hispanics ($35,967), American Indians/Alaskan Natives ($33,627), non-Hispanic Whites ($50,784), and Asian and Pacific Islanders ($61,094). However, according to an article on marketing research, African American married-couple families are doing quite well; their earnings are 17% higher than that of Hispanic married couples. Educational status has steadily been improving. In 1999, about 77% of African Americans 25 years old and older had completed high school. And the number of African Americans enrolled in colleges doubled from 1988 to 1998 (U.S. Census Bureau, 2000). By 2005, more than 80% had completed high school, and 17.6% had a college degree (U.S. Census Bureau, 2005).

Higher social class appears to be a protective factor for African Americans; for example, frequent heavy drinking is associated with older age and low income in African Americans (in Whites it is associated with youth and high income) (Jones-Webb, 1998). However, too many African Americans live in poverty and are subjected to a number of social and environmental risk factors, including violence, racism, deteriorating housing, lack of resources, cutbacks in healthcare, and limited positive role models as more middle-class professionals move from inner cities to more affluent suburbs (Wright, 2001). African American women are victimized at an astounding rate: Homicide is a leading cause of death, and aggravated assault and rape rates are high but also highly underreported by Black women (see West, 2003).

A large segment of the young Black male population is removed from the community in that 12% in this age group are in prison or jail at any one time (BJS, 2006). As a result, many children have no access to their fathers. Within the community, illegal drug activity and the presence of crack houses have had a devastating effect. This kind of unrelentingly negative environment contributes to alienation, powerlessness, and stress. Taylor and Jackson (1990) found in a sample of African American women that stress had a direct and positive effect on alcohol consumption (the more stress, the more alcohol consumed).

In addition, African Americans have been unduly targeted by alcohol advertising in their communities (NIAAA, 2005). In 2004, African American youth saw 34% more alcohol advertising in national magazines than did youth in general; this involved 42% more advertising for distilled spirits (CAMI, 2006). According to Woods (1998), 40% of the entire alcohol advertisement budget is targeted to African Americans. As she sees it, "We are victimized excessively by the day-to-day consequences of too much ethanol and not enough jobs, too much ethanol and no Head Start, too much ethanol and no affirmative action, and too much ethanol and too little compassion" (p. 310).

CULTURAL FACTORS

In spite of the risk factors, there are many strengths and protective factors in the culture of African American families. Traditions have survived from African heritage and been adapted to survive historical conditions like slavery and current conditions like racial oppression in the United States (Wright, 2001). Spirituality, the belief in a power greater than oneself and the importance of spiritual values over material things, is considered a key component of the Afrocentric worldview. It provides a central organizing framework for how African Americans see themselves and the importance of connections to others (Brome, Owens, Allen, & Vevaine, 2000). Several studies have documented the importance of spirituality and religion in the everyday life of African Americans as a way of managing stress and negative events and supporting feelings of self-worth and personal control.

Bowie, Ensminger, and Robertson (2006) examined data from a longitudinal cohort of over 1,000 inner-city African American residents who were studied through interviews of mothers and the children as the children matured from age 6 to 32. Findings from this empirically based study revealed that key factors in the development of alcohol problems were being male, having a major depressive disorder, dropping out of school, and not attending church at least monthly. Brome and her colleagues (2000) examined the relationship between spirituality and African American women in recovery from substance misuse. They found that women who expressed a high level of spirituality had a more positive self-concept, a more active coping style, more positive attitudes toward parenting, more positive relationships with others, and an empowering coping stance. Spirituality appears to be "the cornerstone of hope" for many in the African American community, "enabling them to survive horrendous adversity" (Wright, 2001, p. 34).

A great deal is expected of African American women who are expected to be heavily involved in caregiving and also breadwinning roles. Stress levels can be high. When the mother has a substance use disorder, the family may cover up for her to protect her image in public while judging her harshly (CSAT, 2004).

Communal orientation and family support are also protective factors in the African American community. Individual identity is often defined through relationship to family and extended family and through mutual aid. Family may include people who are not related by blood but are linked with the family through mutual-help arrangements such as child care. *Umoja,* the first of seven principles developed by Maulana Karenga (1977), states that an obligation of every African American is to maintain unity in the family and community. Children should be seen as a gift from God and provided with life-sustaining environments. Elders are to be respected and addressed by their titles to indicate respect, such as Mr., Mrs., Aunt, Reverend. Although many poverty-stricken inner-city environments are currently more hopeless than sustaining, African American Muslims are becoming active in developing community services in these environments (Wright, 2001).

TREATMENT ISSUES

Treatment barriers for African Americans can include culturally biased diagnostic tools, biased and even racist counselors, inadequate opportunities for treatment, program content not relevant to their life experiences, lack of consideration for keeping children in treatment, and for pregnant women, the risk of prosecution or removal of their children by Child Protective Services (Bass & Jackson, 1997; Wright, 2001). The common use of group therapy in treatment programs can also be extremely difficult and confusing for many clients who emigrate from the Caribbean and place a high value on privacy (Harris-Hastick, 2001).

A study that conducted interviews with African American pregnant women who have used crack cocaine and other drugs during pregnancy revealed that all 83 women wanted a program that would not separate them from their children. The second major element in their ideal program would include some treatment program involvement with their significant other. Many had terminated from previous programs because they could not tolerate being away from their children and not being allowed to contact their significant others (Bass & Jackson, 1997).

Transference–countertransference issues related to gender and the reality of the dominance of White culture occur frequently. For example, a Black male immigrant from the Caribbean who is used to having male authority in the family may be more likely to accept a White than an African American female counselor. Black Caribbean women may respond to a male counselor (authority figure) with passivity or anger regardless of race (Harris-Hastick, 2001). In the course of treatment, African Americans may get in touch with repressed rage toward the racism and oppression they have experienced all their lives (Wright, 2001). bell hooks (1993) connects the struggle of people to "recover" from the suffering and woundedness caused by political oppression and exploitation with the effort to break with addictive behavior. David Goodson, a youth shelter worker and himself an ex-convict, speaking before a social work class, says it well (cited in van Wormer, 2001):

> I deal with a lot of cultural pain. The same issues come up again and again, and the issue of race always comes up, the issue of Who I am. Who am I as a black man? In a lecture I heard recently the speaker said the only thing that keeps people clean is the fear of dying of an overdose. But in my work we have to go beyond that and acquire a love for life, a love for yourself, a love for your family, and so on. Sometimes we preach a message of *running from* rather than a message of salvation. My point is we have to go beyond fear to the positive. As African Americans we have to view this [drug use] as self-destructive behavior due to cultural self-hatred. (p. 79)

Because of the devastation from illegal drug activity, drug-related HIV, crack houses, and the co-occurring violence and family dislocation from incarceration, many African American communities are not at all in favor of harm reduction practices, such as needle exchange. As Imani Woods (1998) notes,

> People look at me like I'm crazy when I go to the black community to explain harm reduction. I am accused of supporting a policy that makes peace with genocide. How can one talk about "reducing harm" to a people under siege? Harm reduction is seen as settling, giving up, accepting failure, and bargaining with the devil. (p. 301)

However, according to Woods, harm reduction practices are of value to this community because they encourage a more nonjudgmental attitude toward users instead of vilification and stigmatization. The more that occurs, the better chance the drug user has to build new attitudes that will help him or her diminish or stop drug use, such as looking squarely at his or her drug lifestyle and the consequences, developing a more positive feeling of worth as a Black person, and finding alternative models of living. A change in attitudes and moderation of use can lead to a greater likelihood of employment and access to treatment. For harm reduction to succeed in the African American community, Woods advocates that it be presented, particularly to churchgoers, as a useful step toward eradication and that these efforts incorporate African American characteristics. These may include the use of oral communication, telling stories, a call-and-response type of presentation instead of the expert speaker/passive audience type of presentation, a working knowledge of African American culture and the complexities involved, and a respect for Black priorities.

AFRICAN AMERICAN CULTURALLY BASED SERVICES

"Hi, I'm Michelle; I'm an addict. I always said I'm not grateful. I'm grateful for Mimi [counselor] and the new friends I've met. They clean." It is graduation day at Project Safe, a state-funded program in Rockford, Illinois. These words come from a segment of the unprecedented five-part PBS TV series produced by Bill Moyers (1998).

An outgrowth of a link between the child welfare department and an outpatient substance abuse treatment center, the Project Safe graduation speeches offer moving testimony to the impact on women's lives of a program designed for drug-using mothers. Although the program is more woman centered than culture specific, the clients are largely drug users from inner-city Rockford. As described by an external evaluator, "These women don't hit bottom; they *live* on the bottom. If we wait for them to hit bottom, they will die." The outreach worker, an African American, clean for 7 years, is the chauffeur, counselor, and case manager; she brings women into the program and into the program's heart. "On a typical day, I drive about 100 miles a day, taking women to appointments," she says.

"We are two voices; we are singing; we are two voices; we are singing; we are not alone." This song, which extends to three voices, to four, to five, and so on, expresses the program's philosophy in a stanza. "They step into community of recovery," the outreach worker explains. "Three mornings a week they have a refuge."

In a group session, the women's voices are heard:

"I was here busted for crack cocaine, put on probation, which meant I was to do treatment (or 3–7 years state penitentiary). But once I entered the program I got to listening to others' problems."

"The reason for my relapse is to show me I needed to do more work."

"My babes is suffering. I don't know what to do." ("You're doing the best you can do," replies the worker.)

Moving westward to Waterloo, Iowa, we discover an African American-focused prevention program combined with a gender-specific program that is administered by Pathways Behavioral Services, a substance abuse treatment center. The philosophy is to instill pride in children from high-risk backgrounds and to provide cultural enrichment. Ten children are tracked from the third grade through the end of the fifth grade. This program is described by Felicia Carter, the facilitator of the group:

The Stop and Think program is research based and funded through grants; the goal is to teach children to learn appropriate skills for getting along with others, solving problems, and resolving conflict, so acting out is no longer their only option. This will help children rise above their surroundings and be productive citizens. This is a prevention measure to prevent or offset the age of them experimenting with drugs. We provide programming after school on Tuesdays and Thursdays and expose the children to cultural events they might not, for whatever reason, get to attend. I took them to my church for service once because I wanted them to know that I believe in something that is bigger than me.

All the children are African American. The original group is now in the fifth grade. We go to the theatre, and I want to raise money to take them to Atlanta to visit the Martin Luther King monument and learn more about how slavery begun. We begin teaching them our African history starting from the 1400s to the 1500s about how our ancestors were traded for guns. I want them to take pride in our heritage. The curriculum for girls is "Self-Esteem Through Culture Leads to Academic Excellence" (SETCLAE) facilitated by Jawanza Kunjufu. Another program she facilitates for African American teen girls is the "I'm a Girl Empowered and Strong" (IMAGES). This program is designed to enhance self-esteem and promote awareness of Who am

I? Where am I going? How do I get there? This is a 13-week program that is held during the summer. (personal communication, November 2, 2006)

Felicia Carter describes herself as a highly spiritual person, which provides her with a sense of calling for this work. Washington and Moxley (2003), similarly, discuss the role of spirituality in their counseling of African American women in inpatient treatment for substance misuse problems. In treatment, they found prayer and religious involvement were conducive to increased feelings of self-esteem, to enhanced healing, and to meeting the individuals' spirituality needs. Practitioners who eliminate prayer from the helping process, as Washington and Moxley suggest, may only weaken their efforts to engage in culturally sensitive practice.

On the prevention side, another program, Strengthening Families, focuses on improving family relationships, parenting skills, and increasing the social and life skills of youth from high-risk families (including parents with substance abuse problems). Recognized as a model program by SAMHSA and NIDA and endorsed as effective by the Office of Juvenile Justice and Delinquency Prevention, the program has developed several versions to meet the needs of diverse families (SAMHSA Model Programs, 2006). In Detroit, the original 14-week version of Strengthening Families that was designed for a multicultural audience was modified to reflect more Afrocentric approaches and became the Safe Haven Program (Aktan, 1999). The goal of the revised 12-week program was to reduce risk factors and increase protective factors for families with 6- to 12-year-old children whose parent(s) have been admitted for substance abuse treatment.

Modifications in the Safe Haven Program included the development of an all African American video based on typical situations in the lives of local substance abusers, redesigning all artwork and cartoons to reflect African American heritage, acknowledging if not endorsing, controversially, the historical-cultural use of corporal punishment (spanking), addressing the group in familiar language and terms, and rewriting the manuals accordingly. A process evaluation found that these modifications had a positive effect, or as one staff member explained, "The video stimulated interesting discussion, e.g. the real difficulty of a recovering Black man to find gainful employment after treatment, relapse issues, co-dependency issues and the Black woman who has historically played the role of a caretaker" (Aktan, 1999, p. 237). The outcome evaluation of the program (highly effective in decreasing risk factors and increasing protective factors) was the same for pre- and post-modifications. As Aktan points out, this may be a limitation of the evaluation instruments, which could also explain the fact that outcome research often fails to support culture-specific programs on the whole.

SUMMARY AND CONCLUSION

In this chapter, we support the conclusion that all addicts are not alike by exploring differences among Asian/Pacific Islanders, African Americans, Native American/Alaskan Natives, and Hispanics/Latinos. Although there is great variation because of economic class, education, level of acculturation, and gender as to how traditional values are actualized in individual people, there is considerable agreement that taking into consideration and respecting racial and ethnic values are critical parts of engaging and maintaining people in the recovery process.

Strengths-based practices that focus on assessing what the person wants and the skills, resiliencies, and resources available within the person and the community are well suited to working with clients from different cultures. Instead of defining a medical diagnosis as the problem and a one-size-fits-all intervention as the solution, a strengths-based approach gathers information from the standpoint of the clients' view of their situation and helps plan alternatives within the clients' cultural framework (Rapp, 2006). Harm reduction practices support helping an individual or a family develop an array of choices that fits their unique circumstances.

Developing cultural competence requires a commitment to learn much more about different cultures than could be presented in this chapter. There are numerous resources accessible on the Internet, but a good place to start is the *Substance Abuse Resource Guides* put out by SAMHSA (https://ncadistore .samhsa.gov/catalog/) on Asian and Pacific Islanders, American Indians and Native Alaskans, Hispanic/Latino Americans, and African Americans. For example, the *Asian and Pacific Islander Americans Resource Guide* includes descriptions of videotapes available in English subtitled in various languages, such as Korean, Khmer, and Tagalog, and several that are in Chinese, Vietnamese, Cambodian, and other languages. In addition, the guide features abstracts from a variety of government publications and research journals that deal with cultural competence and ethnic differences; a list of groups, youth councils, and organizations around the United States that deal with specific ethnic groups; and a list of Internet access sites.

Putting cultural competence into practice requires a commitment to slow down and take time to ask a variety of questions from a "not knowing," nonexpert position. It requires acknowledgment that, as counselors, we are just in the margins of the page that represents the richness and complexity of our clients' lives. We may visit, but we do not live there. Even to visit, it is necessary to become aware of our own "biases, racism, internalized oppression, power dynamics, and classism" so that we don't perpetrate these problems on others (Wright, 2001, p. 44).

References

Aktan, G. B. (1999). A cultural consistency evaluation of a substance abuse prevention program with inner city African-American families. *Journal of Primary Prevention, 19*(3), 227–239.

Alvarez, L., & Ruiz, P. (2001). Substance abuse in the Mexican American population. In L. A. Straussner (Ed.), *Ethnocultural factors in substance abuse treatment* (pp. 111–136). New York: Guilford Press.

Amaro, H., Nieves, R., Johannes, S., & Cabeza, N. (1998). Substance abuse treatment: Critical issues and challenges in the treatment of Latina women. *Hispanic Journal of Behavioral Sciences, 21*(3), 266–282.

Amodeo, M., & Jones, L. (1997). Viewing alcohol and other drug use cross-culturally: A cultural framework for clinical practice. *Families in Society: The Journal of Contemporary Human Services,* 240–254.

Arroyo, J., Westerberg, V., & Tonigan, J. (1998). Comparison of treatment utilization and outcome for Hispanics and non-Hispanic Whites. *Journal of Studies on Alcohol, 59*(3), 286–292.

Bass, L., & Jackson, M. (1997). A study of drug abusing African American pregnant women. *Journal of Drug Issues, 27*(3), 659–671.

Beauvais, F. (1998). American Indians and alcohol. *Alcohol Health & Research World,* 22(4), 253–260.

Berg, I. K., & Shafer, K. C. (2004). Working with mandated substance abusers. In S. L. Straussner (Ed.), *Clinical work with substance-abusing clients* (2nd ed., pp. 82–102). New York: Guilford Press.

Booth, B., Blow, F., Cook, C., Bunn, J., & Fortney, J. (1992). Age and ethnicity among hospitalized alcoholics: A nationwide study. *Alcoholism, Clinical and Experimental Research, 16*(6), 1029–1034.

Bowie, J., Ensminger, M., & Robertson, J. (2006). Alcohol-use problems in young Black adults: Effects of religiosity, social resources, and mental health. *Journal of Studies on Alcohol, 67*(1), 44–54.

Brave Heart, M. Y. H. (2007). Historical trauma and substance abuse. *Alcohol, Tobacco and Other Drugs, Section Connection, 2,* 1–5.

Brome, D., Owens, M., Allen, K., & Vevaine, T. (2000). An examination of spirituality among African American women in recovery from substance abuse. *Journal of Black Psychology, 26,* 470–476.

Bromley, M., & Sip, S. (2001). *Substance abuse treatment issues with Cambodian Americans.* In L. A. Straussner (Ed.), *Ethnocultural factors in substance abuse treatment* (pp. 321–344). New York: Guilford Press.

Bureau of Justice Statistics (BJS). (2006, May). *Prison and jail inmates at midyear 2005.* Washington, DC: U.S. Department of Justice. Retrieved from http://www.ojp .usdoj.gov/bjs/pub.

Caetano, R., & Kaskutas, L. (1995). Changes in drinking patterns among Whites, Blacks and Hispanics, 1984–1992. *Journal of Studies on Alcohol, 56,* 558–565.

Canino, G., Bravo, M., Ramirez, R., Febo, V., Rubio-Stipec M., Fernandez, R., et al. (1999). The Spanish Alcohol Use Disorder and Associated Disabilities Interview Schedule (AUDADIS): Reliability and concordance with clinical diagnoses in a Hispanic population. *Journal of Studies on Alcohol, 60*(6), 790–799.

The Center on Alcohol Marketing and Youth (CAMI). (2006, September 26). African-American youth and alcohol advertising. Retrieved September 2006 from http:// camy.org/factsheets.

Center on Substance Abuse Treatment (CSAT). (2004). *Substance abuse treatment and family therapy.* Substance Abuse and Mental Health Services Administration. Treatment Improvement Protocol (TIP) Series, No. 39. Retrieved February 2007 from http://www.ncbi.nlm.nih.gov/books/bv.fcgi?rid=hstat5.chapter.70382.

Centers for Disease Control and Prevention (CDC). (2002). *The state of Latinos in HIV prevention community planning: The HIV/AIDS epidemic in the Latino community.* Atlanta, GA: Author.

Centers for Disease Control and Prevention (CDC). (2006, February). Fact sheet: HIV/ AIDS among African Americans. Atlanta: U.S. Public Health Service. Retrieved October 2006 from http://www.cdc.gov/hiv/topics.

Closser, M., & Blow, F. (1993). Special populations: Ethnic minorities, and the elderly. *Psychiatric Clinics of North America, 16*(1), 199–209.

Collins, L. (1993). Sociocultural aspect of alcohol use and abuse: Ethnicity and gender. *Drugs and Society, 18*(1), 89–116.

Custer, R. L. (1982). Gambling and addiction. In R. Craig & S. Baker (Eds.), *Drug dependent patients: Treatment and research* (pp. 367–381). Springfield, IL: Charles C Thomas.

Custer, R. L., & Milt, H. (1985). *When luck runs out.* New York: Facts on File.

Daisy, F., Thomas, L., & Worley, C. (1998). Alcohol uses and harm reduction within the Native community. In G. A. Marlatt (Ed.), *Harm reduction: Pragmatic strategies for managing high-risk behaviors* (pp. 327–350). New York: Guilford Press.

De La Rosa, M., Holleran, M., Rugh, D., & MacMaster, S. (2005). Substance abuse among U.S. Latinos: A review of the literature. In M. De La Rosa, L. Holleran, & S. L. Straussner (Eds.), *Substance abusing Latinos: Current research on epidemiology, prevention and treatment* (pp. 1–20). Binghamton, NY: Haworth.

Freese, T., Obert, J., Dickow, A., Cohen, J., & Lord, R. (2000). Methamphetamine abuse: Issues for special populations. *Journal of Psychoactive Drugs, 32*(2), 177–182.

Garrett, M., & Carroll, J. (2000). Mending the broken circle: Treatment of substance dependence among Native Americans. *Journal of Counseling and Development, 78*(4), 379–388.

Gelman, C. R. (2004). Empirically-based principles for culturally competent practice with Latinos. *Journal of Ethnic and Cultural Diversity in Social Work, 13*(1), 83–108.

Graham, J. R., Swift, K. J., & Delaney, R. (2000). *Canadian social policy: An introduction.* Scarborough, Ontario: Prentice Hall.

Gross, E. (1995). Deconstructing politically correct practice literature: The American Indian case. *Social Work, 40*(2), 206–213.

Harris-Hastick, E. (2001). Substance abuse issues among English-speaking Caribbean people of African ancestry. In L. A. Straussner (Ed.), *Ethnocultural factors in substance abuse treatment* (pp. 52–74). New York: Guilford Press.

Henriques, Z., & Manatu-Rupert, N. (2001). Living on the outside: African American women before, during, and after imprisonment. *The Prison Journal, 81*(1), 6–19.

Herring, R. (1994). Substance use among Native American Indian youth: A selected review of causality. *Journal of Counseling and Development, 72*(6), 578–588.

Hines, P. M., & Boyd-Franklin, N. (2005). African American families. In M. McGoldrick, J. Giordano, & N. Garcia-Preto (Eds.), *Ethnicity and family therapy* (3rd ed., pp. 87–100). New York: Guilford Press.

Hoffman, F. (1994). Cultural adaptations of Alcoholics Anonymous to serve Hispanic populations. *International Journal of Addictions, 29*(4), 445–460.

Holleran, L. (2005). HIV/AIDS prevention with Latino/a substance abusers: An interview with Jennifer Herrera. *Journal of Social Work Practice in the Addictions, 5*(1/2), 175–183.

hooks, b. (1993). *Sisters of the yam: Black women and self-recovery.* Boston: South End Press.

hooks, b. (2000). *Where we stand: Class matters.* New York: Routledge.

Ja, D., & Aoki, B. (1993). Substance abuse treatment: Cultural barriers in the Asian American community. *Journal of Psychoactive Drugs, 25*(1), 61–71.

Jones-Webb, R. (1998). Drinking patterns and problems among African Americans: Recent findings. *Alcohol Health & Research World, 22*(4), 260–265.

Karenga, M. (1977). *Kwanzaa: Origin, concepts, practice.* Inglewood, CA: Kawaida.

Kasee, C. (1995). Identity, recovery, and religious imperialism: Native American women and the New Age. *Women and Therapy, 16*(2–3), 83–91.

Lee, E., & Mock, M. M. (2005). Asian families: An overview. In M. McGoldrick, J. Giordano, & N. Garcia-Preto (Eds.), *Ethnicity and family therapy* (3rd ed., pp. 269–282). New York: Guilford Press.

Lindenberg, C., Solorzano, R., Krantz, M., Galvis, C., Baroni, G., & Strickland, O. (1998). Risk and resilience: Building protective factors. An intervention for preventing substance abuse and sexual risk-taking and for promoting strength and protection among young, low-income Hispanic women. *American Journal of Maternal Child Nursing, 23*(2), 99–104.

Lowery, C. (1998). American Indian perspectives on addiction and recovery. *Health and Social Work, 23*(2), 127–135.

Makimoto, K. (1998). Drinking patterns and drinking problems among Asian Americans and Pacific Islanders. *Alcohol Health & Research World, 22*(4), 270–276.

Mark, M. E., & Lesieur, H. R. (1992). A feminist critique of problem gambling research. *British Journal of Addiction, 87,* 549–565.

May, P. (1996). Overview of alcohol abuse epidemiology for American Indian populations. In G. Sandefur, R. Rindfuss, & B. Cohen (Eds.), *Changing numbers, changing needs: American Indian demography and public health* (pp. 235–261). Washington, DC: National Academy Press.

McGoldrick, M., Giordano, J., & Garcia-Preto, N. (2005). Overview: Ethnicity and family therapy. In M. McGoldrick, J. Giordano, & N. Garcia-Preto (Eds.), *Ethnicity and family therapy* (3rd ed., pp. 1–40). New York: Guilford Press.

Medina, C. (2001). Toward an understanding of Puerto Rican ethnicity and substance abuse. In L. A. Straussner (Ed.), *Ethnocultural factors in substance abuse treatment* (pp. 137–163). New York: Guilford Press.

Mercado, M. (2000). The invisible family: Counseling Asian American substance abusers and their families. *Family Journal, 8*(3), 267–272.

Milbrodt, T. (2002). Breaking the cycle of alcohol problems among Native Americans: Culturally-sensitive treatment in the Lakota community. *Alcoholism Treatment Quarterly, 20*(1), 19–44.

Morelli, P., & Fong, R. (2000). The role of Hawaiian elders in substance abuse treatment among Asian/Pacific Islander women. *Journal of Family Social Work, 4*(4), 33–44.

Moreno, S. (2005, September 18). A rare and unusual harvest. *Washington Post,* p. A03.

Moyers, B. (1998, March 30). *Moyers on addiction: Close to home.* Part 2. Washington, DC: Public Broadcasting Service.

Murphy, S., & Rosenbaum, M. (1997). Two women who used cocaine too much: Class, race, gender, crack, and coke. In C. Reinarman & H. Levine (Eds.), *Crack in America: Demon drugs and social justice* (pp. 98–112). Berkeley: University of California Press.

National Institute on Alcohol Abuse and Alcoholism (NIAAA). (2005). *Module 10H: Ethnicity, culture and alcohol.* National Institutes of Health. Retrieved September 2006 from http://pubs.niaaa.nih.gov/publications/Social/ContentsList.html.

National Institute on Drug Abuse (NIDA). (2006). NIDA InfoFacts: Treatment trends. Retrieved September 22, 2006, from http://www.nida.nih.gov/Infofacts/treatmenttrends.html.

Office of Applied Statistics. (2005a, August 19). The Drug and Alcohol Services Information System. *The DASIS Report.* Hispanic Substance abuse treatment admissions: 2003. Retrieved February 2007 from http://www.oas.samhsa.gov/2ks/HispanicTX/HispanicTx.htm.

Office of Applied Statistics. (2005b, February 11). The Drug and Alcohol Services Information System. *The DASIS Report.* Substance abuse treatment admissions among American Indians and Alaska Natives: 2002. Retrieved February 2007 from http://www.oas.samhsa.gov/2k5/IndianTX/IndianTX.htm.

Office of Applied Studies. (2006, February 21). *Prevalence of substance use among racial and ethnic subgroups.* Substance Abuse and Mental Health Service Administration. Retrieved February 2007 from http://www.oas.samhsa.gov/NHSDA/Ethnic/httoc .htm.

Pew Hispanic Center. (2006, October 2). A statistical portrait of Hispanics at mid-decade. Retrieved October 2006 from http://pewhispanic.org/reports.

Polinsky, M., Hser, Y., & Grella, C. (1998). Consideration of special populations in the drug treatment system of a large metropolitan area. *Journal of Behavioral Health Services and Research, 25*(1), 7–21.

Randolph, W., Stroup-Benham, C., Black, S., & Markides, K. (1998). Alcohol use among Cuban-Americans, Mexican-Americans, and Puerto Ricans. *Alcohol Health & Research World, 22*(4), 265–270.

Rapp, R. C. (2006). Strengths-based case management: Enhancing treatment for persons with substance abuse problems. In D. Saleebey (Ed.), *The strengths perspective in social work practice* (4th ed., pp. 128–147). Boston: Allyn & Bacon.

Rhodes, R., & Johnson, A. (1997). A feminist approach to treating alcohol and drug-addicted African American women. *Women and Therapy, 20*(3), 23–37.

Rothe, E., & Ruiz, P. (2001). Substance abuse among Cuban Americans. In L. A. Straussner (Ed.), *Ethnocultural factors in substance abuse treatment* (pp. 97–110). New York: Guilford Press.

Sakai, J., Ho, P., Shore, J., Risk, N., & Price, R. (2005). Asians in the United States: Substance dependence and use of substance-dependence treatment. *Journal of Substance Abuse Treatment, 29*(2), 75–84.

Shukovsky, D. (1996, May 6). Healing circle returns Indian heritage: Mental health is attuned to cultural understanding. *Seattle Post-Intelligencer,* p. B1.

Smith, A. (2006). Soul wound: The legacy of Native American schools. *Amnesty Magazine.* Retrieved December 3, 2006, from http://www.amnestyusa.org/amnestynow/soulwound .html.

Stein, L. Y. (2001). The psychosocial needs of Hawaiian women incarcerated for drug-related crimes. *Journal of Social Work in the Addictions, 1*(4), 47–70.

Straussner, S. L. (2001). Ethnocultural issues in substance abuse treatment: An overview. In L. A. Straussner (Ed.), *Ethnocultural factors in substance abuse treatment* (pp. 3–28). New York: Guilford Press.

Substance Abuse and Mental Health Services Administration (SAMHSA). (1998). Prevalence of substance use among racial/ethnic subgroups in the United States, 1991–1993. Retrieved from http://www.health.org/govpubs/bkd262/index.htm.

Substance Abuse and Mental Health Services Administration (SAMHSA). (1999). Treatment Episode Data Set (TEDS) 1992–1997. Drug and Alcohol Services Information System Series: S-7. Retrieved from http://oas.samhsa.gov/teds/ httoc.htm.

Substance Abuse and Mental Health Services Administration (SAMHSA). (2003). Results from the 2002 National Survey on drug use and health. Office of Applied Studies. Retrieved February 2007 from http://www.oas.samhsa.gov/nhsda/2k2nsduh/Overview/ 2k2Overview.htm.

Substance Abuse and Mental Health Services Administration (SAMHSA). (August 19, 2005). The DASIS Report: Hispanic substance abuse treatment admissions: 2003. Office of Applied Studies. Retrieved September 22, 2006, from http://www.oas .samhsa.gov/2k5/HispanicTX/HispanicTx.htm.

Substance Abuse and Mental Health Services Administration (SAMHSA) Model Programs (2006). Strengthening Families Program. Retrieved September 22, 2006, from http://www.modelprograms.samhsa.gov/print.cfm?pkProgramid=14.

Substance Abuse and Mental Health Services Administration (SAMHSA), Office of Applied Studies. (2006). Results from the 2005 National Survey on drug use and health: National findings. Retrieved September 22, 2006, from http://www.oas.samhsa.gov/NSDUH/2k5NSDUH/2k5results.htm.

Sutton, C. E., & Broken Nose, M. A. (2005). American Indian families: An overview. In M. McGoldrick, J. Giordano, & N. Garcia-Preto (Eds.), *Ethnicity and family therapy* (3rd ed., pp. 43–54). New York: Guilford Press.

Tapia, M., Schwartz, S., Prado, G., Lopez, B., & Pantin, H. (2006). Parent-centered intervention: A practical approach for preventing drug abuse in Hispanic adolescents. *Research on Social Work Practice, 16*(2), 146–165.

Taylor, J., & Jackson, B. (1990). Factors affecting alcohol consumption in Black women: Part II. *International Journal of the Addictions, 25*(12), 1415–1427.

Tying drug and alcohol programs to immigrants' backgrounds. (1999, June 16). *New York Times*, pp. 1–2.

U.S. Census Bureau. (2000). *Overview of race and Hispanic origin*. U.S. Department of Commerce, Economics and Statistics Administration. Retrieved October 2006 from http://www.census.gov.

U.S. Census Bureau. (2005, March 28). News: College degree nearly doubles average earnings. U.S. Department of Commerce. Retrieved September 2006 from http://www.census.gov/Press-Release.

U.S. Census Bureau. (2006a, January 25). Facts for features: African American history month. U.S. Department of Commerce. Retrieved September 2006 from http://www.census.gov/Press-Release.

U.S. Census Bureau. (2006b, September 5). Facts for features: Hispanic heritage month. U.S. Department of Commerce. Retrieved September 2006 from http://www.census.gov.

U.S. Census Bureau. (2006c, August 29). Income climbs, poverty stabilizes, uninsured rate increases. News release. U.S. Department of Commerce. Retrieved September 2006 from http://www.census.gov.

U.S. Newswire. (2006, November). Facts for features: American Indian and Alaska Native heritage month. U.S. Census Bureau. Retrieved October 2006 from http://releases.usnewswire.com.

van Wormer, K. (2001). *Counseling female offenders and victims: A strengths-perspective approach*. New York: Springer.

Washington, O. G., & Moxley, D. P. (2003). Group interventions with low-income African American women recovering from chemical dependency. *Health and Social Work, 28*(2), 146–156.

Weaver, H. (2001). Native Americans and substance abuse. In S. L. Straussner (Ed.), *Ethnocultural factors in substance abuse treatment* (pp. 97–110). New York: Guilford Press.

West, C. M. (Ed.). (2003). *Violence in the lives of Black women: Battered black and blue*. Binghamton, NY: Haworth.

Woods, I. (1998). Bringing harm reduction to the Black community. In G. A. Marlatt (Ed.), *Harm reduction: Pragmatic strategies for managing high-risk behaviors* (pp. 301–326). New York: Guilford Press.

Wright, E. (2001). Substance abuse in African American communities. In L. A. Straussner (Ed.), *Ethnocultural factors in substance abuse treatment* (pp. 31–51). New York: Guilford Press.

Yuen, F., & Nakano-Matsumoto, N. (1998). Effective substance abuse treatment for Asian American adolescents. *Early Child Development and Care, 147*, 43–54.

There's a lot of shame attached to being a drunk slut.

—Interview with 43-year-old woman in recovery from alcoholism
(Davis, 1997)

Gender and Sexual Orientation Differences

CHAPTER 11

INTRODUCTION

Since the early 1980s, a great deal of energy, resources, and research, along with many women's voices, have changed the way we look at traditional drug and alcohol treatment programming. In 1984, with the federal requirement that 5% of each block grant to the states be set aside for new or expanded alcohol and drug abuse services for women, a wide array of special services began to appear. Within another 4 years, the war on drugs and the national press obsession with "crack babies" helped inspire Congress to double the federal set-aside to target programs for pregnant women and women with dependent children (see chapter 13). Grants became available to fund demonstration programs for women-only groups and treatment programs, for more supportive and less confrontational approaches, for programs with enhanced services such as parenting, skill development, and prevocational training, and for programs that incorporated prenatal and postnatal care, or at least child care while the woman was in treatment sessions. In 1993, the National Institutes of Health (NIH) mandated that enough women had to be included in clinical trials that gender differences could be tested. By 2004, the Center for Substance Abuse Treatment (CSAT) and the Center for Mental Health Services (2004) had funded over 100 grantees specifically targeting services for women (SAMHSA, 2005).

During this same time frame, the voices of gay men and lesbians also began to be heard. The connection between injected drugs, the gay population, and the AIDS epidemic added pressure for federal funders to pay attention to gay males as a special population. An indication of the change is the National

Institute on Drug Abuse (NIDA) 5-year epidemiological study launched in 1991, which surveyed 1,067 respondents, 53% gay men and 47% lesbians.

Although these legislative and research changes signal an enormous shift in what has been heterosexual male-dominated research and treatment programs, the actual changing of treatment options for women, gay men, and lesbian women is still an ongoing effort. Researchers and practitioners continue to identify gender differences in biology, genetics, paths to dependence, responses to various treatment options, relapse, and social contexts, which suggest different prevention and treatment approaches for men and women. However, these findings are still not widely applied to practice settings; when they have been, the research findings on the outcomes of specialized programs for women have produced mixed results. Very few studies have addressed outcomes in male-only interventions. There is also no consensus as to whether gay men and lesbians should be treated separately from heterosexual clients or separately from each other.

This chapter focuses first on gender differences and then on sexual orientation differences that may affect a person's ability to resist addiction, seek and find treatment, and maintain recovery. Programs designed to enhance the ability of women, gay men, and lesbians to succeed in their recovery are described. Controversies that surround these developments are discussed, and research findings are offered to practitioners.

GENDER DIFFERENCES

All Women Are Not Alike, and Neither Are All Men

Before we lump people into gender categories to illustrate their differences, it's important to remember that all women are not alike, and of course, neither are all men. Scientists and researchers who adhere to a "developmental" approach to addiction stress the interplay of sociocultural, psychological, and neurobiological processes that influence each individual a little bit differently depending on the person's age, gender, and ethnic group and on the cultural influences on each person's age cohort (U.S. Secretary of Health and Human Services, 2000). A European American man in his 20s who grew up in an impoverished inner-city environment in the 1990s (e.g., rap artist Eminem) is likely to have a much different drinking or drug use "trajectory" (a changing pattern over time) than a middle-class triethnic young man who grew up in the affluent suburbs (e.g., golfer Tiger Woods).

Murphy and Rosenbaum (1997) argue that gender, race, and class are more important in shaping how people develop drug problems with illicit drugs than the drug itself. Thus, as described in an earlier chapter, Becky, a typical White, middle-class young woman interviewed in their NIDA-sponsored research project, had more options for controlling her cocaine use than Monique, a young Black woman living in a poor inner-city neighborhood. Becky used cocaine within the protected context that is afforded the middle class. She had a job and resources to buy her own powder cocaine, the privacy to use it without being hassled by police, and thus could maintain a "nondeviant" identity. When her period of heavy use became an unsatisfying experience that threatened other life goals that she had every opportunity to attain, she could rely on the resources of the middle class (school, family, job connections) to help her quit using. On the other hand, Monique was introduced to "crack," a more dangerous form of cocaine that was readily available in her neighborhood, quickly resorted to trading sexual favors for her drug as the only currency available, was frequently arrested on the streets, and became homeless and totally impoverished, with very few resources to deal with her predicament. Becky went to Hawaii with her father to make a break from cocaine use; Monique went to jail.

The protective power of race and class extends only to some women and men, and no one would claim it prevents addiction. However, it can condition and influence how a person uses drugs, alcohol, and gambling and mediate the consequences of that use or misuse. Similarly, cultural differences around the world regarding the acceptance of alcohol for each gender and the extent to which sex roles are strictly defined appear to influence the wide variation in alcoholism. According to the Global Status Report on Alcohol (World Health Organization [WHO], 2004), the male–female ratio of heavy episodic drinking was: Canada, 28:11, France, 27.9:9.7, Germany, 42:13, Italy, 13:12, Mexico, 46:5, Russia, 15:3, United Kingdom, 24:9. One can see by examining these ratios that very heavy drinking is more a male than a female characteristic and that the gender gap in some nations, such as Mexico, is extremely large.

Gender Differences in Prevalence

The Substance Abuse and Mental Health Services Administration (SAMHSA) conducts a yearly survey, called the National Household Survey on Drug Use and Health (NHSDUH), to estimate the use of drugs, alcohol, and tobacco, dependence, and treatment occurring within the United States (SAMHSA, 2006). Data from the 2005 survey indicate that except for adolescents, males were more likely to report current illicit drug use than females (10.2% vs. 6.1%, respectively), twice as likely to use marijuana as females (8.2% vs. 4.0%), and more likely to report current alcohol use (58.1% vs. 45.9%). However, the rates of nonmedical use of prescription-type drugs were similar for both males (2.8%) and females (2.5%). Among youth aged 12 to 17, the rate of current illicit drug use was similar for boys (10.1%) and girls (9.7%), but the rate for current alcohol use was higher in young women (17.2% vs. 15.9%). Figure 11.1 shows the percentages of alcohol and drug use by gender.

In terms of substance dependence or abuse, the rates for males aged 12 or older were about twice as high as for females in 2003 and the years preceding (Figure 11.1). Among youth aged 12 to 17, however, the rate of substance dependence or abuse among males was similar to the rate among females (7.8% vs. 8.3%). As has been noted, this may be "an equality women don't want" (Davis & DiNitto, 2005, p. 503). Some would argue that women have always been drinking and using drugs more than shows up in research studies

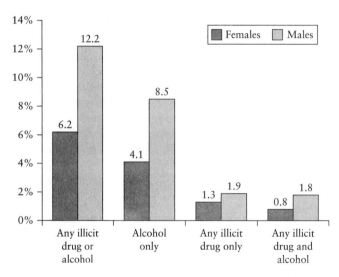

FIGURE II.I

PERCENTAGES OF PAST YEAR DEPENDENCE ON OR ABUSE OF ALCOHOL OR ANY ILLICIT DRUG AMONG PERSONS AGED 12 OR OLDER, BY GENDER: 2003

Source: National Survey on Drug Use and Health, 2004, p. 2.

but that poor methodology, indifference, and sex-role stereotyping have kept the numbers low (Babcock, 1996).

Compulsive gambling surveys consistently report that men are much more likely to be pathological or problem gamblers than are women. The National Research Council (1999) analysis of general population studies (not clinical or institutional) from 18 states conducted since the mid-1990s reveals that the proportion of men among pathological and problem gamblers ranged from 45 to 80%, with a median of 62%; the proportion of women among pathological and problem gamblers ranged from 20 to 55%, with a median of 38%. For youth (ages 14–22), 30% of the females surveyed report gambling in an average month compared to 57% of males (Annenberg Public Policy Center, 2005).

Most of the state problem gambling helplines report that the percentage of women seeking help with gambling problems has been increasing. As early as 1993, an Alberta, Canada, study concluded that women are the gender group now most likely to experience gambling problems. In New Jersey, calls about women problem gamblers have doubled since 1990. In Texas, calls about women have increased from 34% in 1992 to 40% in 1999 (Texas Council on Problem and Compulsive Gambling, 2000). A Manitoba, Canada, study found that 43% of the helpline calls were from women about their own gambling (Heather & Patton, 2006). In Nevada, 44% of the helpline calls were from women concerning their own problems (Nevada Council on Problem Gambling, 2004). Research from Arizona based on a population sample found the male–female ratio of gamblers was about even for persons who gambled in the past month; the frequency of male gambling was more (Volberg, 2005). An interesting finding from this study is that 67.8% of the females with gambling problems were late onset, whereas the majority of the males developed these problems from a young age.

Eating disorders are by far more prevalent in females, with studies reporting a male–female ratio of between 1:6 and 1:20 for anorexia nervosa/bulimia nervosa and a 1:2 ratio for binge-eating disorders. According to Anderson (2000), the diagnosis of eating disorders is gender biased because "most physicians and health care providers view the illness as a female or a homosexual disease" (p. 5). Males may also suffer from "reverse anorexia," a rarer form of eating disorder characterized by a fear of being too thin and a need to add muscle and weight.

Since 1965, men have been smoking less (a drop of 46%), and women have been smoking a little bit less (a drop of 35%). Consequently, the gender gap in smoking rates has narrowed. In 2005, 35.8% of adult males used a tobacco product compared to 23.4% of adult women. Adolescent girls and boys, ages 12–17, are now equally likely to smoke (10.8% for girls vs. 10.7% for boys). The good news is that the rate for teenage girls has declined in the last few years from a high of 13.6% in 2002 (SAMHSA, 2006).

Sociocultural Gender Differences

In the recent past (and even today), women identified as alcoholics, drug addicts, or compulsive gamblers were considered especially deviant and promiscuous. Substance misuse among females is more highly stigmatized than among males and can be a serious barrier to getting help (Brady & Ashley, 2005, SAMHSA, 2005). We can consider alcoholic women a discredited social group who suffer from a "double whammy" because they are both alcoholic and female. It seems reasonable to expect that women addicted to alcohol, drugs, or gambling would internalize these sociocultural forces. In interviews with women recovering from alcoholism, Davis (1997) found that the issue of shame was still alive, even in recovery, and for some women, continued to be a slight barrier in their relationship to nonalcoholics because they felt their alcoholism (and all the behavior that went with it) would not be understood.

To what extent does the "shame factor" affect a woman's path to addiction or her ability to get help and recover? It may be part of the larger environment of women's struggle for economic and political equality. Research into treatment effectiveness has shown that environmental factors may be the most significant variable in determining addiction treatment outcome (Fingarette, 1998). That is, the stability of family ties, the economic and work situation, and the overarching cultural expectations of males and females in society are all vital correlates of recovery.

Women as a group are oppressed in many ways in the dominant culture of the United States. More women than men are poor, and women continue to be paid less than men. Indirect discrimination exists not just with treatment centers but also with employment and educational organizations that don't provide a way for them to meet their child-rearing responsibilities. Cultural stereotypes cast women as illogical, emotionally unstable, and incapable of many tasks that require leadership, math skills, or mechanical skills and as dependent on men (Abramovitz, 1997). Women are far more likely to be subjected to violence and murder by men. These factors affect all women, but a woman who is trying to get help for an addiction may be particularly affected by her lack of money and resources, less tolerance and less support from partner and family, and the lack of treatment available for women with children.

Studies of clients who enter treatment support the reality that women are more dependent on welfare and/or disability payments, while men have more skilled jobs. Women have less education and lower rates of employment than men, and women are more likely to lack employment skills. Women are twice as likely to have children in their households and to report greater concerns about issues related to children, although both men and women were concerned about the effect of drug treatment on the custody of their children (Brady & Ashley, 2005; Wong, Badger, Sigman, & Higgins, 2002). Women problem gamblers are significantly more likely than men to report financial difficulties (even though both groups had many difficulties) and less annual income to deal with these problems, according to a study of callers to a gambling helpline (Potenza et al., 2001).

Using a feminist methodology and analysis to look at environmental factors affecting women gamblers, Sarah Brown and Louise Coventry (1997) launched a community-based research project in Victoria, Australia, called Queen of Hearts. The findings suggest that women compulsive gamblers may be the victims of social stereotypes and the economic and gender limitations imposed on women. Even the definitions of gambling problems that focus on individual "pathology" instead of including a sociocultural framework "have serious stigmatizing effects, such as discouraging gamblers from seeking assistance, inviting moral and legalistic judgments, and invoking the label of 'deviant'" (p. 9).

INVISIBILITY Women are much less likely than men to be encouraged, cajoled, or browbeaten by partners into entering treatment for their addiction (Davis, 1997; Saunders, Wodak, & Williams, 1985). Other than the child welfare arena, women report feeling a sense of "invisibility" about their situation from their partners, their employers, and the professionals from whom they sought help. As a woman interviewed in the Davis study states: "My parents didn't see that I had a drinking problem. Part of it was that they just didn't see a lot. They'd say, 'If your husband would give you some money, you'd be o.k.'" (p. 156).

Some of this invisibility may be because the partner or family member is drinking or using drugs so heavily him- or herself that recognition of a problem might be threatening. Women who are substance abuse dependent are more likely than their male counterpart to have a substance dependent spouse or partner (SAMHSA, 2005). Having a male partner who is drinking or using drugs has consistently been found to be a predisposing factor (some would say the greatest factor) in a woman's addiction (Brady & Ashley, 2005; Westermeyer & Boedicker, 2000). When a woman tries to change her situation by seeking help or treatment, it may create a serious problem for the relationship (SAMHSA, 2005).

Even when a woman finally gets to treatment, she is unlikely to receive the family support available to men. Laudet, Magura, Furst, and Kumar (1999) found that men who were mostly active crack/cocaine users were able to give only passive and inconsistent support to their partners in treatment. Reasons included the men's own active use, their desire to maintain the relationship status quo where the man has the dominant role, their preoccupation working on their own recovery, their disagreement with abstinence as a necessity, and their desire to avoid the stigma attached to their female partner as an "addict." In contrast, men report that they are influenced positively by a spouse or partner to enter treatment or that they enter because of the criminal justice system (Grella & Joshi, 1999).

BEING A MOM   In addition to the lack of familial support and the likelihood their spouse or partner is also abusing substances, women are less likely to enter treatment for many other reasons: (a) the obligation of child rearing, (b) the unavailability of treatment slots for women with children or pregnant women, (c) barriers such as transportation and lack of child care, and (d) treatment programs not designed to meet these and other special needs of women clients. A shocking example of the unavailability of treatment to parents in the U.S. child welfare system is the estimate by The Child Welfare League of America that 67% of parents involved in the system need drug or alcohol treatment, yet services are available to only 31% (Young, Gardner, & Dennis, 1998). It is well recognized in the treatment field that many women do not participate in treatment because they are unable to obtain quality child care or because they fear being required to relinquish their children (National Center on Addiction and Substance Abuse [CASA], 2006).

CRIME AND PUNISHMENT   Addiction and the use of illicit drugs bring women into the criminal and civil justice system in a way unique to their gender. The criminalization of women who use illicit drugs during pregnancy and the termination of their parental rights have no male counterpart. Several states, such as South Carolina, have enacted laws requiring health officials to report women whose newborns test positive for drugs, even if the mother is already in treatment (van Wormer, 2001). Many women have lost custody of their children to child welfare for the same reason. Using substances during pregnancy is considered child abuse in 14 states; in 9 states, healthcare professionals are required to report suspected substance abuse during pregnancy (Figdor & Kaeser, 2005). In Norway, the state may seize custody of the children, who may never be returned even though the mother may later achieve a good recovery.

Since the mid-1990s, more than 240 women in 35 states have been criminally prosecuted for using substances during pregnancy thought to be harmful to their unborn (Rubin, 1998). *Whitner v. State,* a South Carolina Supreme Court decision that allowed a woman to be criminally prosecuted as a child abuser and sentenced to 10 years in jail for using an illicit drug during her pregnancy, is still on the books. Women reported being dragged to jail from the labor room, still bleeding from childbirth. The U.S. Supreme Court declined to hear an appeal of this ruling in 1998. Such groups as the National Association of Social Workers, the American College of Obstetricians and Gynecologists, and the National Association of Alcoholism and Drug Abuse Counselors supported the appeal. A milder approach is carried out in South Dakota, where new statutes force pregnant women with alcohol and drug problems into treatment for up to 9 months (Aamot, 1998).

Consider the impact on pregnant and addicted women of the following ruling by Judge O. H. Eaton of the Seminole County Circuit Court (Florida). Judge Eaton found Jennifer Johnson guilty of delivering cocaine to her baby after the birth during the 60–90 seconds before the umbilical cord was clamped. His finding states:

> The fact that the defendant was addicted to cocaine at the time of these offenses is not a defense. The choice to use or not use cocaine is just that—a choice. . . . [P]regnant addicts have been on notice for years that taking cocaine may be harmful to their children. This verdict puts pregnant addicts on notice that they have a responsibility to seek treatment for their addiction prior to giving birth. Otherwise, the state may very well use criminal prosecution to force future compliance with the law or, in appropriate cases, to punish those who violate it. (*Florida v. Johnson,* Circuit Court, Seminole Co., July 13, 1989; in Siegal, 1997, p. 250)

Although illicit drug use is not limited to any class or race of women, African American and Latina women are much more likely to be targeted for these policies. According to Kershnar and Paltrow (2001), they comprise 80% of those women prosecuted for delivering drug-exposed babies. Further evidence of discrimination can be seen in the fact that alcohol has been extensively documented to cause the most severe birth defects and that cigarette smoking is highly correlated with low birthweight and prematurity. However, the primary targets of prosecution from the legal system and child welfare system are poor women of color using cocaine or crack. The result of such racist and oppressive policies has not been less drug use; rather, it has deterred especially at-risk poor women from sharing important information with their health providers and from seeking prenatal care at all (Lester, Andreozz, & Applah, 2004).

Good news came with the 2001 U.S. Supreme Court ruling that hospital workers cannot constitutionally test maternity patients for illegal drug use for litigation purposes without their consent. Whether any of the 10 plaintiffs who appealed in this case consented to the tests remains to be decided in the lower courts. This ruling is a victory for the individual's right to medical privacy (Greenhouse, 2001).

JAIL AND PRISON Largely because of the impact of the U.S. war on drugs and mandatory sentencing, the female prisoner population in the United States nearly doubled from 1995 to 2005 (Bureau of Justice Statistics [BJS], 2006). Women offenders, especially in the younger age brackets, are arrested at increasingly high rates for drug offenses, and women of color have had the greatest overall increase in criminal justice supervision, including imprisonment. Many of the women

TABLE 11.1 | CORRECTIONAL FACILITIES PROVIDING SUBSTANCE ABUSE
TREATMENT, BY FACILITY TYPE

Response Category	Total	Federal Prisons	State Prisons	Jails	Juvenile Facilities
Total correctional facilities responding to survey	7,243	129	1,069	3,067	2,978
Number of facilities providing treatment	2,731	121	602	1,000	1,008
Percentage of facilities providing treatment	37.7%	93.8%	56.3%	32.6%	33.8%

Source: Findings from Uniform Facility Data Set 1997 Survey of Correctional Facilities (SAMHSA, 2000).

are arrested when their spouses and partners are arrested for drug dealing; unfortunately, the law does not take into account the inequality in most of these male–female relationships (van Wormer, 2001).

Most incarcerated women are serving time and for crimes, especially in the federal prison system, that involved drugs. Around 72% of women confined in the federal prison system were convicted of a drug violation (BJS, 2000). Keep in mind that other crimes for which the women were sentenced, including property crime and public order (DWI—driving while intoxicated), also might have been alcohol/drug related.

Karberg and James (2005) gathered data based on interviews conducted in over 400 jails separately through the Census Bureau. Substance misuse emerged as a primary cause and contributor to crime for both men and women residing in jail at the time of the study. The breakdown by gender for substance dependence and abuse revealed that approximately 68% of female jail inmates met the criteria for substance dependence, a rate that was similar to that of men. Convicted female jail inmates had a higher rate of previous drug use (61%) compared to a male sample (54%). In Iowa, and increasingly in other states, methamphetamine (meth) is listed as the drug of choice among female but not male inmates. Illegal drugs were implicated more than alcohol in women's crimes; for men, the pattern was reversed.

What about treatment for substance abuse problems? A survey from the National Association of Counties showed that over a third of drug and alcohol dependent inmates had received treatment while incarcerated or on probation or parole (Zernike, 2005). Treatment as defined in the survey included attendance at self-help groups such as Alcoholics Anonymous (AA) or Narcotics Anonymous (NA). Female inmates in this category reported more treatment involvement than men, and Whites reported more treatment than persons of other races. Under 10% of drug-involved inmates were receiving specialized treatment since entering jail. Federal prisons offer the highest percentage of substance abuse treatment, and local jails provide the least (van Wormer & Bartollas, 2007). (See Table 11.1.)

The good news is that jail or prison may be the first place anyone has offered treatment or talked to women about the abuse they've experienced.

As told by women in recovery from drug addiction interviewed by Hirsch (1999):

> "I started using alcohol and pills when I was thirteen. I was raped when I was twelve, my father was an alcoholic, my mother was using pills. He used to beat her up all the time—it was pretty crazy. No, no one helped me. The [drug and alcohol treatment program in jail] is the first place anyone talked about it."
>
> "[In jail] they had all different kind of classes—about being raped in the street, about being raped in your family. I needed both those classes."
>
> "This is my first time in treatment. I couldn't get Medical Assistance, so I couldn't get treatment. Now I'm court-stipulated, so I can get treatment." (p. 2)

Violence and Trauma   Violence against women is an area where the influence of sociocultural attitudes has been well documented. Widely cited in the literature is the work of Kantor and Straus (1989), who discovered in an analysis of data from a national family violence survey that the strongest predictor of family violence is cultural approval of violence, and this factor is even more significant than the level of alcohol abuse. In the United States, we "approve" of violence through advertisements featuring malnourished women in stiletto heels and chains, films that show scenes of women being slapped around or raped, ineffective laws and law enforcement, and the lack of a viable well-resourced support system for women seeking help. Yodanis (2004) documented, in a cross-cultural test of feminist theory attributing the extent of violence against women to cultural attitudes, that in nations where women's status is low (as measured in terms of levels of occupational equality), the rate of wife and partner violence is higher than in nations where women have a higher level of equality.

The Centers for Disease Control and Prevention's (CDC) National Center for Injury Prevention and Control estimates that nearly 5.3 million domestic violence incidents happen each year among women 18 years and older resulting in 2 million injuries and 1,300 deaths (CDC, 2006). Women with a history of intimate partner violence are more likely to display behaviors that present further health risks (e.g., substance abuse, alcoholism, suicide attempts). Studies show that the more severe the violence, the stronger its relationship to negative health behaviors by victims, such as engaging in high-risk sexual behavior, having multiple sex partners, and trading sex for food, money, or other items.

The use of alcohol and drugs has consistently been found to be a major factor in intimate-partner violence (BJS, 2003). In several studies, the significant correlation between the use of alcohol and intimate-partner violence against women holds after controlling for sociodemographic variables, hostility, and marital satisfaction. It holds across all ethnic groups and social classes (Kantor, 1993; Leonard, 1993). A descriptive study of the types of violence against women and the associated use of alcohol and illicit drugs by the perpetrator revealed that physical abuse was significantly higher for women with perpetrators who used drugs only compared with perpetrators who used alcohol only (Willson et al., 2000). According to a large data analysis by the National Center on Addiction and Substance Abuse at Columbia University (CASA, 1996), 70% of drug-addicted, low-income pregnant women in methadone maintenance have been beaten—86% by their husbands or partners. Women who use cocaine become high risks for being murdered. In New York City, from 1990 to 1992, the number of fatal injuries following cocaine use was higher than the number of deaths from AIDS, cancer, or heart disease for young Black and Hispanic women ages 15–24. Alcoholic women do not escape either; in one study of spousal abuse, alcoholic women were found to be nine times more likely to be slapped by their husband, five times more likely to be kicked or hit, five times more likely to be beaten, and four times more likely to have their lives threatened than were nonalcoholic women.

In the following, we read the words of a North Carolina woman:

> I married an alcoholic. I married him because I thought he was the only guy who would ever show me any attention. In those seven years, I put up with mental abuse, physical abuse, and somewhat sexual abuse. The way that alcohol and marijuana played a role in my marriage—that was the only way of getting along with him. He was mean as a snake. He run me down onto the ground and start beating me. To relax, I drank, I smoked pot and go into my own little dream world. That's what the marijuana did, was put you in a dream state, where you would forget all the pain and all the anger and all the abuse and get high. Until the next morning, and then it started all over again. (Smith & Chescheir, 1995, p. 32)

In addition to "domestic violence" (which some feminists prefer to call "household terrorism"), women are far more likely than men to be subjected to sexual violence (as children or adults). The National Crime Victimization Survey reports that in 2004, there were 209,880 victims of rape, attempted rape, or sexual assault (BJS, 2004). Since 1993, although the rate of these crimes has fallen by a dramatic 64%, women are still the primary victims (90% compared to 10% males). Most (67%) of these assaults were committed by someone who is known to the victim.

There is a growing body of research that supports the relationship between childhood sexual abuse and subsequent substance abuse in women (Brady & Ashley, 2005; Downs & Miller, 2002; Neumann, Houskamp, Pollock, & Briere, 1996; Wilsnack, Vogeltanz, Klassen, & Harris, 1997). In addition, the experience of childhood sexual and physical abuse is linked to a greater risk of sexually transmitted diseases (STDs) (El-Bassel et al., 1998), unintended pregnancy (Kenney, Reinholtz, & Angelini, 1997), and prostitution in women (Widom, Ireland, & Glynn, 1995). Men who experience sexual abuse are likelier than nonabused men to use drugs and engage in risky sexual behavior (Holmes & Slap, 1998; Pierre, Shrier, Emans, & DuRant, 1998).

An empirically based study that examined the history of abuse and violence in over 1,000 meth users (Cohen et al., 2003) provides validation to media claims that meth leads to violent behavior. In the research on men and women in treatment for meth addiction, the reporting of violence was extensive, with 80% of women reporting partner violence. Experiences of early life violence were commonly recounted as well. Men also experienced violence, more commonly from friends and acquaintances.

Compared to male substance misusers, females have a disproportionately high rate of multiple victimization. Chesney-Lind and Pasko (2004) map out the pathway that would lead a girl, desperate to escape the sexual and physical abuse at home, to run away, seek solace in drugs and the company of drug users, gang members, and the like, and survive on the streets through prostitution. This pattern is highlighted in inner-city females for whom prostitution may serve as a means of survival in circumstances of extreme economic hardship. Belknap (2001) and Enos (2001), similarly, stress the role of poverty and sexual and physical abuse in women who assist men in the commission of crimes.

The use of alcohol and drugs by women is linked to all forms of trauma, not just sexual or physical violence (SAMHSA, 2005). The high rate of co-occurrence of substance use and a history of personal violence has treatment implications. First, for women who have been and are involved in violent relationships, treatment that relies on confrontational approaches, such as that common in therapeutic communities, can trigger the same kind of power-lessness as the original trauma. Also, treatment that is too narrowly specialized and at different agencies—substance abuse treatment here and counseling for victims of domestic violence there—can confuse an individual. The different models underlying the treatment approaches at the various agencies may not be in harmony (Hiebert-Murphy & Woytkiw, 2000).

There is emerging evidence that addressing substance use and trauma in an integrated way may have better results than providing the treatment under specialized umbrellas. For example, in a classic randomized trial, Hien and his colleagues (2004) compared the effectiveness of (a) a cognitive approach that addressed both PTSD and substance abuse and (b) a cognitive relapse pre-vention approach that focused on emotional triggers to standard community care. They found that participants (low-income women from an urban setting) in the two treatment groups significantly reduced their substance use and PTSD symptom severity compared to the standard community care group whose PTSD symptoms actually got worse.

PSYCHOLOGICAL DIFFERENCES BY GENDER

The field of modern psychology focuses primarily on the vulnerabilities and dysfunctions of normal mind processes and only lately is looking at resilience factors and strengths of the mind. The question of precisely how environment and biology affect the mind and addictive processes is still being answered. Maybe men really are from Mars and women from Venus! It seems reasonable that sociocultural gender differences (in economics, victimization, support systems, etc.), as discussed earlier, would be reflected differently in the minds of men and women. For example, researchers on the effects of trauma propose that a lifetime of traumatic abuse, characteristic of many women who are addicted, causes low self-esteem and self-disgust that presses these women into situations of further abuse (Downs & Miller, 2002).

Besides low self-esteem, another indication of psychological distress that is more problematic for women is a higher rate of co-occurring disorders. In 2002, an estimated 2 million adult women had both a serious mental illness and a substance use disorder during the past year (SAMHSA, 2004). A review of recent research indicates that women with a substance use disorder have more major depressions, anxiety disorders, panic disorders, bipolar affective disorders, psychosexual disorders, eating disorders, PTSD, and phobias than men with a substance use disorder (SAMHSA, 2005). In general, these differences are consistent with the differences in psychiatric disorders in the general population. However, there is a unique effect of depression on substance users; that is, depression is associated with relapse, especially in women (Schutte, Seable, & Moos, 1997). Findings from a federal study of services for women found that one third of the sample of women in publicly funded treatment had co-occurring mental health and substance abuse problems (Newmann & Sallmann, 2004). Compared to the other women, 95% of the group with co-occurring problems also reported physical or sexual abuse, over half were separated from their children against their will, and the majority reported incarceration experiences.

Men and women tend to smoke cigarettes to relieve different psychological states. "Males respond more to the nicotine's rewarding effects than do females, especially the dopamine-mediated euphoric effects," according to Dr. Neil Grunberg, professor of medical psychology, clinical psychology, and neuroscience at Uniformed Services University of the Health Sciences, Bethesda, Maryland ("New Study," 2000). Men attempt to relieve boredom and fatigue or increase arousal and concentration by smoking; women attempt to control their weight and to decrease stress, anger, and other negative feelings. Although nicotine helps to decrease appetite and control weight in both genders, it has stronger effects on women. Women also have more difficulty in stopping smoking than men and do not respond well to confrontational approaches in smoking cessation programs.

Gambling as psychological "pain medication" is a common theme in the stories of many women who are compulsive gamblers. In a pioneering study of women in Gamblers Anonymous, Lesieur (1987) found that two major reasons for escape in over half the women interviewed ($n = 50$) were "escape from memories of parental upbringing and escape from troubled husbands and loneliness" (p. 234). In this sample, 40% of the women grew up in homes where one or both parents were addicted to alcohol or gambling. In addition, another 12% had parents with other serious problems, such as bipolar illness and sexual abuse. Having "troubled husbands" was a reality for 60% of the women, who were married to alcoholics (35%), substance users (10%), or compulsive gamblers (15%).

The following story illustrates how using gambling as an escape from trouble worked for "Betty":

> When I first walked into a casino, my personal life was full of stress. Within a couple of months I was "zoning out," running from the stress of my life by feeding a slot machine. Six months after putting my first quarter into a machine I had progressed to losing a thousand dollars of plastic money a night. I can almost laugh now as I think of the stress I added to my life by going to the casino. Physically, I added the stress of no food or drink for hours on end, lack of sleep, and the anxiety of shuffling credit card limits. Emotionally, I left the casino crying all the way home, pounding the steering wheel and telling myself what a rotten, stupid person I was. Guilt consumed me. Spiritually, I was almost dead inside. ("Women Helping Women," 2000)

A common designation of many women like Betty is that they are "escape" gamblers, whereas men are more likely to be "action" gamblers. Escape gamblers tend to become compulsive in their gambling in a span of 6 months to 3 years, play "luck" games such as bingo, slots, and video poker. They start playing as a recreation but quickly move into using gambling to escape from problems (Arizona Council on Compulsive Gambling, 2000; Lesieur & Blume, 1991). The lure of the escape is characterized by changing the feeling of stress or psychological discomfort into feeling "hypnotized," "in a trance," "having tunnel vision where nothing else mattered," or even "out of body."

In contrast, action gamblers tend to begin early in life, have a long-term problem (10–30 years), focus on "skill" games such as poker, horses, and sports, and seek action as well as escape. A gender comparison of a large treatment sample in Australia (Crisp et al., 2000) revealed from the assessment data ($n = 1279$, male $= 696$, female $= 583$) that women were 1.5 times more likely to gamble as a way of escaping from other problems than men. Females reported average debts of less than half what was owed by the male gamblers. Women were far more likely to report using electronic gambling machines than men (91.1% vs. 61.4%) and more likely to play bingo (4.8% vs. 1.0%).

Although the descriptions of action and escape gamblers appear intuitively attractive, one may need to use caution in applying them. There could be a patronizing edge of the dominant culture in designating women as preferring "nonskill" gambling games and consequently not living up to the popular culture's idea of "real" gambling. Discounting out-of-control gambling behavior because it involves games like bingo only adds to the difficulties of these women in recognizing their own problems and getting help. In addition, there is growing evidence that men are participating more and more in what we have called the escape gambler profile. In 1999, 94% of the women and 49% of the men who called the Arizona Council on Compulsive Gambling Hotline identified themselves as an escape gambler. The council makes an interesting point: "The accessibility of casino-type gambling is now affecting men who had no previous history of gambling or compulsive gambling in the same way it affects women. Perhaps the least previously identified and least understood compulsive gambler of all was the male 'escape gambler'" (Arizona Council on Compulsive Gambling, 2000, p. 2).

BIOLOGICAL DIFFERENCES BY GENDER

Earlier research on the pharmacology, genetics, and biological impact of alcohol and drugs was done primarily with males, under the assumption that the findings would apply equally to women. Not true. Beginning in the 1970s and 1980s, we began to realize that women and men differ in their biology and response to alcohol, tobacco, and other drugs in ways that have important treatment implications. The results from the *2005 Alcohol and Drug Services Study* (SAMHSA, 2006) on women in substance abuse treatment make clear that, compared to men, women tend to:

1. Have a much shorter interval between onset of drinking-related problems and entry into treatment. In the past, women started drinking heavily later than men, but today, many high school girls get drunk.
2. Experience a higher rate of physiological impairment earlier in their drinking careers, such as cirrhosis, hepatitis, brain damage, and cardiac problems. The consequences associated with heavy drinking may be accelerated or "telescoped" in women. For example, the female liver appears more vulnerable to the damage from alcohol; consequently, more alcohol-dependent women die from cirrhosis than alcohol-dependent men.
3. Become intoxicated after drinking smaller quantities of alcohol because the alcohol concentration in the blood is higher for women than men after drinking the same amounts of alcohol. Women have more fat and lower body water content than men of comparable size, and because alcohol is diluted through body water, a woman drinking the same as a man of the same size will have a higher blood alcohol level. Also, women may have diminished activity of alcohol dehydrogenase, an enzyme involved in the metabolism of alcohol in the stomach, and a fluctuation in gonadal hormone levels during the menstrual cycle.
4. Have much poorer overall physical health, mental health, overall impairment, and higher mortality rates from alcohol misuse. CASA (2006) found that physical problems (e.g., cirrhosis, hypertension, and brain damage from alcohol; lung cancer, emphysema, and chronic bronchitis from smoking) develop in women more rapidly and at lower rates than men.

Chronic heavy drinking is associated with negative effects on the sexual functions of both men and women. Men report loss of sexual interest, difficulty achieving erections, impotence, and premature ejaculation (National Institute on Alcohol Abuse and Alcoholism [NIAAA], 1993). Although many women and men attest to the disinhibiting qualities of alcohol, in reality alcohol acts as a depressant on physiological arousal. Women alcoholics persist in expecting greater sexual desire and enjoyment after drinking while at the same time reporting a variety of sexual dysfunctions, such as inhibition of ovulation, infertility, and depressed orgasm (Blume, 1997; CASA, 2006). In early sobriety, women have reported avoidance of sex, but another study of recovering alcoholic women who had a regular sexual partner showed significant improvement in sexual desire, arousal, and the ability to achieve orgasm as abstinence continued (Apter-Marsh, 1984).

Smoking affects the reproductive functions of women. In young women, smoking increases the risk of menstrual irregularity and pain (CASA, 2006). Older women smokers are subject to a reduction in estrogen levels and earlier menopause. Because of the link between smoking and cancer and heart disease, women now account for 39% of all smoking-related deaths in the United States. Despite knowing these facts, girls and women often refuse to quit out of fear of weight gain.

The female propensity to weight obsession is also evident in eating disorders. *Feminist Perspectives on Eating Disorders,* edited by Fallon, Katzman, and Wooley (1994), is an invaluable resource for analyzing the role of gender in the etiology and treatment of eating disorders. Overeaters Anonymous (OA), the popular self-help group that has been immensely helpful to some women, is not spared from criticism in this biting and thought-provoking collection (see chapter 7 for a more positive view).

Some effects of illicit drugs vary with gender. Marijuana is reported to enhance the sexual feelings of both men and women, but regular use in men may result in lower testosterone levels, affect sperm production and fertility, and cause erectile difficulties. In women, potential adverse affects include menstrual abnormalities, abnormal ova, and prolonged childbirth (J. R. Hubbard, Franco, & Onaivi, 1999).

In the Drug Abuse Treatment Outcome Study (DATOS) of men and women entering drug treatment (including methadone treatment), women reported greater proportions of health-related issues (Wechsberg, Craddock, & Hubbard, 1998). For women, the rate of respiratory problems was the highest, followed by the rates of gynecological problems and then STDs. For men, respiratory problems also had the highest rate, followed by heart problems and then digestive problems. However, women have higher rates in all three problem areas.

Two of three AIDS cases in American women are associated with drug abuse (CASA, 2006). Because of the strong connection to IV drug use, it's important to note that an HIV-infected woman with half the amount of virus in the bloodstream as an infected man will develop AIDS as quickly. Women are also diagnosed later in the course of AIDS and have poorer access to treatment.

Are there gender differences in the inheritance of alcoholism? Geneticists measure heritability by looking at studies of adoptions, twins, and genetic markers (such as the D2 dopamine receptor). Examining all this evidence to date, McGue and Slutske (1996) conclude that an inherited component of alcoholism exists among men, but there is not unequivocal support for the existence of a heritable component to alcoholism among women. Still, CASA (2006), in its summary of research on women's substance use, brings our attention to research on physical reactions to certain substances. Women with a family history of alcoholism tend to have a higher level of tolerance for alcohol than women without such a history. Other research found that women with such a history tend to produce more saliva when exposed to alcohol than women without such a history. Both reactions are risk factors for alcoholism. Genetics undoubtedly plays a role in the susceptibility to alcohol abuse and dependence in women and men, although there is some evidence that women may be more susceptible to environmental factors.

Treatment Implications

The gender differences in biology, genetics, paths to dependence, responses to various treatment options, relapse triggers, and social contexts suggest different prevention and treatment approaches for men and women. Women-only programs and special programs for pregnant and postpartum women have been developed to provide alternatives to traditional treatment, which is viewed as designed primarily for White males.

During the 1980s and 1990s, federal grants were aimed at developing treatment programs for drug-abusing pregnant women and their children, such as the Pregnant and Postpartum Women and Their Infants (PPWI) initiative that awarded 147 grants in 37 states. SAMHSA, through the Center for Substance Abuse Treatment (CSAT) and the Center for Mental Health Services (CMHS), continues this focus today by funding comprehensive residential substance abuse treatment for pregnant, postpartum, and/or parenting women and their children. More than 100 grantees targeting women have been funded by CSAT as of June 2004, and a 5-year initiative to study women with co-occurring disorders and a history of violence has been launched (SAMHSA, 2005). As the result of these efforts, the National Survey of Substance Abuse Treatment Services found that by 2003, 14% of treatment programs in the United States offered special programs targeted to pregnant or postpartum women, 7.9% offered child care services, more than 33% offered transportation assistance, and 35% offered special programs for women (SAMHSA, 2005).

Typical components of such programs are to (a) address some of the barriers to treatment that many women experience, such as lack of transportation, child care, and treatment availability; (b) change program goals and processes to accommodate "women's needs" for more support, less confrontation, job skill training, and parenting skills; and (c) embrace an "empowerment" model of change rather than the traditional abstinence-only Twelve-Step Minnesota Model, which is perceived as hierarchical, patriarchal, and ineffective. Many of these programs use female staff members so that women clients may feel more comfortable telling their stories. In a comparison of mixed-gender drug treatment programs and women's drug treatment programs in Los Angeles County ($n = 294$), Grella, Polinsky, Hser, and Perry (1999) found that women's drug treatment programs were significantly more likely to provide other services, such as children's activities, assistance in locating housing, transportation, life-skills services, practical and vocational skills, parenting skills, and anger management, client advocacy, and services specific to pregnancy (pediatric, prenatal, and postpartum services).

Particular treatment issues relevant to women include attention to their feelings of shame and stigma and the need to heal from the impact of trauma (SAMHSA, 2005). Substance use recovery and trauma recovery should occur together, and a sense of safety must be ensured so that the woman will feel free to reveal her personal issues.

An example of a program that has many of these attributes is A Woman's Place, established in the mid-1980s to offer substance abuse treatment for women (LaFave & Echols, 1999). Although the program began by using the traditional Twelve-Step Minnesota Model with strict guidelines for compliance, homework, and attendance at AA, program staff became frustrated and disillusioned with their lack of success and the inconsistency between the values of "compliance" and "empowerment" for women. The authors note that compliance is not an attribute of the mutual-help program of Alcoholics Anonymous, which is based on voluntary participation and suggestions only; however, compliance is an element of Twelve-Step-based Minnesota Model programs (see chapter 12). In 1993, the program embraced different change models that emphasize choice, not compliance, such as solution-focused therapy (see Berg & Shafer, 2004) and motivational interviewing (see W. R. Miller & Rollnick, 2002).

All aspects of the program were affected by this change. Women who are court ordered or come voluntarily to treatment are asked at the orientation session to choose which services they think they would like. If a woman is not concerned about her substance use, she is asked whether there are any other goals she would like to address and whether she is choosing to comply with the referral source. The menu of services includes day treatment, substance abuse groups once a week, a women's issues group, individual counseling, couples and family counseling, and case management services, including transportation. In contrast to a traditional Twelve-Step treatment model, the operating premise of this program is that, when offered choices, women will ultimately choose directions that help them function better.

Using the solution-focused approach, any period of sobriety or cutting down on alcohol or other drug use is celebrated, and the woman is questioned closely on how she was able to do this. For clients who are uncertain about the changes they want to make, motivational interviewing techniques help explore the meaning of the problem for them and make a decision about their motivation to change. According to the authors, preliminary quantitative and qualitative evaluations of the program suggest that using these approaches "has a favorable impact on participants' life functioning in a number of domains, and that participants feel that the program has benefited them in a variety of ways" (LaFave & Echols, 1999, p. 350).

As women experience personal growth and consciousness of their need for self-expression through group participation, however, they begin to reexamine their relationship patterns. As we hear from a 34-year-old African American woman, for example:

> He doesn't agree that I can be my own person, he's too controlling and possessive. . . . He didn't like the aftermath of it [drug treatment], he said I changed. He didn't like the way I changed. He said it was a side of me he never thought he'd see. Now I'm into my own independence. I'm not an agreeable person anymore because I'm standing up more for myself today. He doesn't like it. (Laudet et al., 1999, p. 623)

TREATMENT OUTCOMES FOR WOMEN'S PROGRAMS

Early outcome research on specialized women's programs had mixed results (Gerolamo, 2004). Some studies suggested better treatment outcomes in specialized women's programs or women's groups within mixed-gender programs (V. B. Brown, Melchior, Waite-O'Brien, & Hub, 2002; CASA, 2006), and others suggested no difference (Copeland, Hall, Didcott, & Biggs, 1993; Harshman, 2000). Project MATCH, the NIAAA-funded major research study, found no gender-related differences in the outcomes of the three treatment approaches used in individual sessions with a large sample of male and female clients

(Project MATCH Research Group, 1997). Studies that focused on matching patient–therapist gender also found no difference in treatment retention (Sterling, Gottheil, Weinstein, & Serota, 1998) or outcome (Atkinson & Schein, 1996; Corrigan, 1995).

However, several qualitative studies (Davis, 1997; Kauffman, Dore, & Nelson-Zlupko, 1995; Nelson-Zlupko, Dore, Kauffman, & Kaltenback, 1996; Sowers, Ellis, Washington, & Currant, 2002) that have interviewed recovering women participating in all-women's groups or programs told a different story. Kauffman et al. (1995) conclude, from interviews with 34 women participating in two separate addictions programs, that "to treat chemically dependent women successfully, therapeutic interventions must attend to the full complexity of their lives, rather than focusing solely on addiction" (p. 361) and that these needs are better met in women-only treatment groups.

Consider this example of a woman who had participated in both coed and women's therapy groups in substance abuse treatment:

> Guilt puts you at risk of relapsing. You need to talk about it. Take me, for example. Giving up my twins for adoption . . . was the most painful, agonizing experience of my life. No one in either of the coed groups that I've been in knows that I put those babies up for adoption, only the women in this group. The reason being that I felt as if women—whether they agreed or not with my choice—would sympathize with what I had to do. Whereas men—well, I didn't expect a lot of sympathy. They make you feel guilty. . . . In the coed group I don't feel like I could have let it out or cried or that I would have gotten that good of a response. And that was an issue that, when I think about it now, if I wouldn't have been real careful, it could have pushed me over the edge. (Kauffman et al., 1995, p. 361)

In the Nelson-Zlupko et al. study (1996, p. 57), participants "overwhelmingly" felt that their needs were different from those of men, and when they were in mixed-gender groups, these needs were either "silenced or minimized." All of the women in this study had attended at least two other treatment programs, with an average of four treatment experiences per person. These women affirmed previous research that being paired to a female counselor was not important; what they saw as critical to their success was respect from the counselor, no matter the gender.

More recent quantitative research confirms the effectiveness of treatment programming for women. In a review of 37 studies of substance abuse treatment programs for women that occurred between 1980 and 2000, 36 studies reported improved treatment outcomes. In the seven studies that were randomized trials, all showed positive results such as increased birthweight for pregnant, outpatient methadone clinic patients, decreased alcohol use for women in alcohol treatment, reduction of risky injection behaviors, and decreased drug use and increased program retention for cocaine-dependent mothers (SAMHSA, 2005).

Research that has focused on other outcomes, such as service provision and eliminating barriers to treatment, have found that specialized women's programs were more likely to provide services that meet typical women's needs, such as parenting training, empowerment, nutrition, child care, and transportation, and less likely to deny access to women with special needs, such as pregnancy and mental problems (CASA, 2006; Grella et al., 1999; Prendergast, Wellisch, & Falkin, 1995). Through qualitative interviews of women in treatment, Nelson-Zlupko and her colleagues (1996) found another disturbing barrier to mixed-gender patient–therapist treatment: Sexual harassment of female clients by male counselors was spontaneously reported by over half of the study's participants, even though they were never asked about this in the interview.

The National Center on Addiction and Substance Abuse Treatment recommends gender-specific or women-oriented programs to take into account the unique psychosocial and physiological needs of women. Child care and transportation arrangements are vital to ensure the likelihood of successful treatment outcomes. However, these services are not readily available. The success of women-oriented programs in retaining clients may be due in part to their ability to reduce the barriers around entering and remaining in treatment.

Some critics would argue that traditional abstinence-only treatment for both genders produces discouraging results and that a different treatment model for both men and women is needed. Citing studies that indicate poor treatment outcome (e.g., 52 to 75% of men and women in outpatient treatment drop out by the fourth session, [Siegal, Rapp, Fisher, Cole, & Wagner, 1993]; and between 40 and 60% that do complete treatment are not abstinent after 1 year [R. L. Hubbard, 1997]), LaFave and Echols (1999) argue for increasing the flexibility of substance abuse treatment for all populations. Although their article argues for a choice-driven model for women as practiced in A Woman's Place, they join Calamari, Cox, and Roth (1996) in advocating for a treatment model for men "that promotes hope, recognizes incremental changes, such as an increase in number of days of sobriety, and allows men to identify, express, and process their affective experiences" (p. 347).

In her study on the outcome of treatment for Irish alcoholic women, Corrigan (1995) found that at 1-year follow-up, the majority (71%) drank at some point since treatment; however, 43% had not been drinking for 6 or more months. She concludes that "the assumption that treatment programs should insist on total abstinence as the only acceptable treatment goal is particularly questionable in view of the fact that at follow-up only half of the women surveyed are in fact abstinent" (p. 52). At the very least, the research to date has not made clear whether providing specialized women's treatment is sufficient to better help women or whether new approaches different from traditional abstinence-based treatment are needed (Grella et al., 1999).

SUBSTANCE ABUSE COUNSELING AND SEXUAL ORIENTATION

Heterosexism and *homophobia* are words that describe the prejudice against lesbian, gay, bisexual, and transgender people. *Homophobia* refers to fear of homosexuality, often of one's own tendencies in that direction; these tendencies may be displaced onto gays and lesbians. *Heterosexism,* the counterpart to racism and sexism, is prejudice against sexual minorities. It includes stereotyping and a belief in myths. Among the myths pertaining to lesbians are: They hate men, and they turned lesbian after a bad experience with a man; lesbianism can be "corrected" with female hormonal treatment; lesbians would prefer to be heterosexual; in partnerships, one woman plays the part of the man; and lesbians have a high rate of AIDS. In fact, lesbians, like heterosexuals, are a heterogeneous lot; their sex-role behavior ranges from very feminine to very masculine. Some lesbians believe their identity is a preference or choice; others believe it is an innate tendency to be sexually and emotionally attracted to women. Among the categories of gay males, heterosexual males, heterosexual women, and lesbians, lesbians have the lowest rate of AIDS ("Health Care Needs," 1996; National Women's Law Center, 2004).

Pervasive myths pertaining to gay males are: Homosexuality is a choice; gay males are attracted to children and at risk of molesting them; and gay males are effeminate. In fact, the overwhelming number of gay males believe their gayness is an innate characteristic that is often recognized in early to middle childhood (van Wormer, Wells, & Boes, 2000). They prefer the term *sexual orientation* to *sexual preference,* accordingly (Cabaj, 1997). The vast majority of child molesters tend to be heterosexual (Cabaj, 1997; Tully, 2000). In sex-role behavior and mannerisms, gay males range from effeminate to very masculine. Many gay men, however, have traits in common with women. In childhood, for example, their play was often less rough than that of other children, and they were often ridiculed in school for being "sissies" or "different" (Center for Substance Abuse Treatment [CSAT], 2001).

Counselors need to be aware of the numerous myths our society generates so that they can establish rapport with gay and lesbian clients. The best way to build trust is to demonstrate openness about nonnormative living arrangements and sexuality. Use gay-friendly intake forms (including terms such as "partner" and "significant other"), display pamphlets that cater to a variety of ethnically and sexually diverse groups (e.g., gay AA meeting listings), and use inclusive language in interviews and lectures (referring to "spouse or partner" rather than just "spouse").

Despite societal barriers to being gay, lesbian, bisexual, or (most of all) transgendered in our society, there is no reason to assume that such clients need to work on any areas other than the services they came to receive. The focus of their treatment, therefore, should be no different from that of any other client.

LESBIANS AND SUBSTANCE MISUSE

For the most part, lesbians and bisexual women face the same health issues as heterosexual women, but the risks of self-harm and depression may be higher among those who are not open about their sexual orientation and who lack social support (Mravcak, 2006). Although the data are somewhat contradictory, chemical dependence is also a major concern within this group. Because of a serious lack of empirically based national data, however, the exact incidence of substance use among lesbians is unknown. Studies focusing on women's alcohol and other drug use rarely consider sexual orientation as a variable, and studies on lesbian behavior rarely encompass addiction rates. The most commonly cited figure for alcohol-related problems in lesbian women is one of three ("Health Care Needs," 1996; Jackson, 2004; Kus, 1990). A survey of two metropolitan areas revealed that marijuana and tobacco use were approximately double among lesbians compared to heterosexual women (Skinner, 1994). Many of the existing studies, however, are marred by obvious sample flaws, including the recruitment of respondents from gay bars (Senreich & Vairo, 2004). In a comprehensive study by the National Lesbian Health Care Survey of 1987 (described by Bradford, Ryan, & Rothblum, 1994), 14% of the sample expressed worry about their use of alcohol, and strikingly, in sharp contrast with heterosexual behavior, alcohol use increased with age.

A massive research effort that pooled and analyzed data from seven health surveys of lesbian women and covered nearly 12,000 self-identified lesbians overall revealed a concentration of risk factors within this group (Raab, 2001). Relevant to addictive behavior, the collective data showed the following:

- About 55% of lesbians are current or former smokers compared with 36% of women in general.
- Lesbians are slightly more likely to be heavy drinkers—averaging four drinks a day—than women overall.
- About 28% of lesbians are obese, compared to 19% of women in general.

There are several reasons alcohol and tobacco use among lesbians would be high. First is the role of the gay bar and women's bars as a key gathering place for coming-out and closeted lesbians. Second is the heavy drinking and active marijuana use among more mature members of this community, who function as role models. Third is the interactive relationship among stress attached to living what is regarded as a deviant lifestyle, relationship strain in the absence of public role models, and problems related to internalized homophobia, especially among lesbian youth. Fourth, since the mid-1990s, the fact that fewer lesbians than straight women are taking care of children gives them more freedom to party and indulge in substance use than persons tied down by parenting roles (van Wormer et al., 2000). And finally, the intensive marketing of gays and lesbians by tobacco and alcohol companies as reported by the *San Francisco Chronicle* (Allday, 2006) is bound to have had some effect. People who feel good about themselves take care of themselves, as do most lesbians, but people who don't are inclined to jeopardize their health through the use of mood-altering substances.

Due to the unique needs of this special population and the need for lesbians, like other women, to deal with issues related to victimization and sexuality in a safe and understanding environment, a lesbian-affirming treatment atmosphere is essential. Unfortunately, substance abuse providers tend to hold traditional attitudes toward women's sex roles and to lack training in gay–lesbian dynamics (Underhill, 1991). A feminist, nonheterosexist model is appropriate to empower lesbians to make the personal adjustments (in thinking and behavior) necessary for recovery. For lesbian alcoholics in need of inpatient treatment, referral to a lesbian-friendly treatment center, such as the Pride Institute in Eden Prairie, Minnesota, or the Gables Recovery Home in Rochester, Minnesota, is appropriate. The former provides special attention to PTSD issues for gays and lesbians related to the AIDS/HIV crisis, and the latter is a woman-centered treatment center that relies on a Twelve-Step-based philosophy and provides treatment for eating disorders. The expense of residential treatment, however, may be prohibitive for a client who lacks generous insurance coverage for inpatient treatment. A growing trend throughout the United States is the proliferation of healthcare clinics catering to lesbians, such as the Audre Lorde Lesbian Health Clinic of Los Angeles. Some of the clinics offer sperm banks for lesbians wishing to parent children. This positive development has received its impetus from the awareness of the general indifference toward lesbians by medical professionals in traditional practice.

Gay–lesbian self-help groups such as Gay and Lesbian AA are widely available, even in small cities across the United States. Since the 1980s, as VanGelder and Brandt (1996) indicate, heavy alcohol consumption lost ground within the lesbian community. Suddenly, according to these authors, there was a stronger AA crowd than a drinking crowd; lesbians attending the annual October Women's Weekend had a choice of seven Twelve-Step meetings per day.

GAY MALES AND SUBSTANCE MISUSE

Feminine men thrown into a jail cell, cross-dressers, adolescent gays at school: These are examples of males who are prone to be physically attacked and possibly even killed. The scapegoating of gay males, even more pronounced than that of lesbians, creates a major health risk, physically and mentally, for the survivors and victims of this terrifying kind of abuse.

Sometimes, society's hatred is turned within. The highest percentage of teenagers who actually attempt or commit suicide are those struggling with sexual orientation issues (Jackson, 2004). Remafedi, French, Story, Resnick, and Blum (1998), in their research on the relationship between suicide risk and sexual orientation, found evidence of a strong association between suicide risk and bisexuality or homosexuality in young males. A Canadian study conducted through the University of Calgary's center for the study of suicide interviewed young adult men who answered questions on portable computers (King, 1996). Results were startling in that gay and bisexual subjects were found to have the highest rates of attempted suicide. (The rate for celibate males was actually higher, but the sample size for celibate males was extremely small.) The Canadian study is unique in that it is based on a cross-section of young males, not on a sample of persons already known to be gay.

Shernoff (2006), in his study of male barebacking (or anal sex without a condom with strange men), relates this practice to internalized homophobia. Such self-hatred "can contribute to an unconscious sense that a gay man is unimportant and undervalued, thus increasing his sense that he is expendable"

(p. 106). Senreich and Vair (2004) attribute such self-destructive behavior to survivor guilt in gay males who have seen their friends die as they live on. Barebacking also is associated, as Shernoff further suggests, with the widespread use in the gay community of "party drugs" such as Ecstasy and crystal meth. For men who come to the attention of therapists, Shernoff recommends a harm reduction approach to help individuals refrain from self-destructive behaviors and reduce the risks to themselves and others.

Religious fundamentalism was found to be associated with a risk of suicide in gay males, presumably because of their unresolved feelings of guilt. In their work in a psychiatric clinic in the early years of the AIDS epidemic, Flavin, Franklin, and Frances (1986) were disturbed to find that several suicidal gay patients had deliberately tried to contract AIDS as an indirect way of killing themselves. In helping gay men come to terms with their sexuality, a strengths approach is essential. Strategies of gay-positive counseling are described in Crisp (2006) and van Wormer et al. (2000). Use of a gay-affirmative model is crucial to affirm a lesbian, gay, or bisexual identity as positive and to validate same-sex relationships (Crisp, 2006).

Heavy use of alcohol and other drugs has long been noted as a problem in the gay community. Although obtaining a random sample of gay men is extremely difficult, all the research that has been done confirms a high incidence of alcohol and other substance use; estimates range from 20 to 35% (Burroughs, 2003; Warn, 1997). Compared to lesbians, gay males are more likely to have multiple partners; sex and intimacy are more often split off in this group (Cabaj, 1997). Gay bars and clubs are central to the social fabric of gay life; cocaine, methamphetamines, and other dangerous drugs are readily available in after-hours clubs frequented by gay men (Burroughs, 2003). A glance at the ads in gay and lesbian magazines reveals a marketing blitz of hard liquor advertising that is far from subtle in its message.

Approximately 4 to 5% of heterosexual drug injectors are HIV positive. About 40% of men who have sex with men and shoot crystal meth are HIV positive, according to a study by Clay (1997). Clay discovered, in interviews with meth users in Washington State, that crystal meth is used as a powerful sexual facilitator, a means of overcoming sexual fears and reservations. When people are influenced by such strong chemicals, safe-sex practices, needless to say, are thrown to the wayside.

In a sample of 340 gay men from the Cleveland area, Ghindia and Kola (1996) found alcohol to be the drug of choice and cocaine use to be prevalent among those aged 25 through 39. Unique to this population, compared to heterosexual men, is that heavy alcohol consumption and associated problems continue across the life span rather than diminish with age. One possible explanation is that gay men do not "settle down" as readily as heterosexual men, and they are freer to spend more time drinking. Another factor relating to their substance use is the tendency of sexual minorities to use mind-altering chemicals to break down their sexual inhibitions; such inhibitions or hang-ups are related to sexuality that is out of step with societal norms (Warn, 1997). In substance abuse treatment, one of the biggest challenges to sobriety for gays and lesbians entails learning how to initiate same-sex encounters without the aid of alcohol as a "social lubricant."

Transgendered Individuals

A publication from the Center for Substance Abuse Treatment (2001), *A Provider's Introduction to Substance Abuse Treatment for Lesbian, Gay, Bisexual, and Transgender Individuals,* available free of charge from the Substance Abuse and Mental Health Services Administration (SAMHSA), offers a comprehensive discussion of multiple issues related to working with transgender individuals. As defined in this document, *transgendered* individuals are those who conform to the gender-role expectations of the opposite sex or those who may clearly identify their gender as the opposite of their biological sex. In common usage, *transgender* usually refers to people in the transsexual group, which may include people contemplating or preparing for sexual reassignment surgery—called preoperative—or who have undergone sexual reassignment surgery—called postoperative. A transgendered person may be sexually attracted to males, females, or both. *Transvestites* cross-dress—that is, wear clothes usually worn by people of the opposite biological sex. They do not, however, identify themselves as having a gender identity different from their biological sex or gender role (SAMHSA, 2001, p. 5). Table 11.2 presents a list of do's and don'ts related to work with this population.

Of all the sexual minorities, transgendered persons, whether their change is from male to female or female to male, are the most subject to violent assault and employment discrimination. The American Psychiatric Association (APA) (2000) classifies a condition termed "gender identity disorder" as a mental disorder in the *DSM–IV–TR.* This is hardly a positive development.

In contrast to the treatment of transgendered persons in modern society, many American Indian tribes honored them as two-spirited and carved out a special place in society for them. *Berdache,* as this custom was named by outside observers, in effect, constituted a separate gender (CSAT, 2001).

Little research has been done on this population with regard to substance use. As stated by CSAT, one fact that has been revealed in research is an extremely high prevalence of HIV/AIDS in transgendered women who were born with male genitalia.

Bisexuality

Many studies indicate that women tend to be more bisexual by nature (flexible in terms of attraction to either gender) than men, who are more exclusively heterosexual or homosexual (CSAT, 2001; van Wormer et al., 2000). Major points for therapists to know is that a bisexual orientation is a separate identity in itself that is often refuted by both the heterosexual majority and by many gay men and lesbians. A complicating factor is that due to the strident heterosexism within the African American community, many

TABLE 11.2 | DO'S AND DON'TS ABOUT WORKING WITH TRANSGENDER AND TRANSVESTITE CLIENTS

- Use the proper pronouns based on *their self-identity* when talking to/about transgender individuals.

- Get clinical supervision if you have issues or feelings about working with transgender individuals.

- Allow transgender clients to continue the use of hormones when they are prescribed. Advocate that the transgender client using "street" hormones get immediate medical care and legally prescribed hormones.

- Require training on transgender issues for all staff.

- Find out the sexual orientation of all clients.

- Allow transgender clients to use bathrooms and showers based on their gender self-identity and gender role.

- Require all clients and staff to create and maintain a safe environment for all transgender clients. Post a nondiscrimination policy in the waiting room that explicitly includes sexual orientation and gender identity.

- Don't call someone who identifies himself as a female *he* or *him* or call someone who identifies herself as male *she* or *her*.

- Don't project your transphobia onto the transgender client or share transphobic comments with other staff or clients.

- Never make the transgender client choose between hormones and treatment and recovery.

- Don't make the transgender client educate the staff.

- Don't assume transgender women or men are gay.

- Don't make transgender individuals living as females use male facilities or transgender individuals living as males use female facilities.

- Never allow staff or clients to make transphobic comments or put transgender clients at risk for physical or sexual abuse or harassment.

Source: CSAT (2001, p. 119).

people of color define themselves as bisexual even if they focus exclusively on people of the same sex (CSAT, 2001).

TREATMENT ISSUES

Gay and lesbian alcoholics and other substance users most often find themselves in predominantly heterosexual treatment centers. Because of the homophobia present in the typical treatment group, few gays and lesbians want to take the risk of disclosing their sexual orientation. To encourage private sharing in individual sessions, the counselor will find it helpful to display literature about gay–lesbian AA meetings, a Safe Place symbol (placed on a pink triangle), or a rainbow sticker on the office door. Counselors should not post the commonly seen slogan "I'm straight but not narrow," which many gays and lesbians construe as a subtle proclamation of the counselors' heterosexuality. To meet the needs of sexual diversity, every large agency should make a point of having one or more openly gay or lesbian counselors on the staff.

Treatment issues that concern all clients but that have special relevance to sexual minorities include determining the client's comfort level with his or her sexual orientation; respecting gays' and lesbians' heightened need for privacy and confidentiality; recognition of special health risks that pertain to sexual practices among intoxicated gay males; domestic violence issues (note that terms like "wife beating" are inadvertently heterosexist); dealing with child custody issues; and working with the family of origin regarding acceptance of their gay–lesbian children.

The organization Parents, Families, and Friends of Lesbians and Gays (PFLAG) is both a self-help and an advocacy group. Membership is open to gays and lesbians as well as to concerned members of the community. (For an in-depth description of the functioning of this remarkable group, see van Wormer et al., 2000.) Substance abuse treatment centers can call on PFLAG at any time to present a panel, usually of the parents of gays and lesbians, who, in telling their personal stories, help dispel the myths pertaining to homosexuality. Speakers from this group can also enlighten members of the treatment community about the significance of the coming-out process, which substance abuse practitioners might have the opportunity to assist clients in undergoing (information at www.pflag.org).

Most sexual minorities in treatment are in heterosexual-dominated programs. Addiction specialist Philip McCabe (interviewed by Jackson, 2004) states that the programs may range from gay avoidant to gay tolerant to gay sensitive to gay affirming. Pride Institute, a 36-bed facility in Eden Prairie, Minnesota, near Minneapolis, is a gay-specialized treatment center. This treatment center figures prominently in *Dry: A Memoir,* the amusing but informative autobiography of Augusten Burroughs (2003). Burroughs, a gay man who downed a liter of Dewar's scotch each night, was forced into treatment by his advertising company. When given the choice of treatment centers, he chooses what he names in his biography, not very subtly, "Proud Institute . . . the gay rehab center in Minnesota." At the thought of spending a month at this center, Burroughs thinks, "A rehab hospital run by fags will be hip. Plus there's the possibility of good music and sex" (p. 23).

Later, he describes his experience in more down-to-earth terms: "It was like emotion, emotion, emotion half of the day. And facts, facts, facts the other half. It was like *Jerry Springer* meets medical school" (p. 116). *Dry* shows both the uniqueness of the male gay experience, especially in terms of issues related to guilt and grief, and that the treatment, alcohol craving, turbulent journey from denial to acceptance, haunting memories from childhood, and obsessive relationships are the issues faced by every alcoholic who endures treatment.

As described on its website (www.pride-institute.com), we learn that Pride's unique program addresses issues such as internalized homophobia, low self-esteem, coming-out to the family and friends, same-sex sexuality, early-childhood sexual abuse, and safe-sex practices, in addition to addictions education and treatment. Other gay, lesbian, bisexual, transgender specialized treatment centers are Pacifica Treatment Centers, a new residential center in Vancouver, Canada, Alternatives, Inc. in Los Angeles, and the branches of Pride Institute in Florida, New Jersey, and Texas. These gay-affirming programs can be expected to have openly gay staff, a mission statement of gay, lesbian, bisexual, transgender sensitivity, and sensitivity training for the staff. Alternatives, Inc. announces on their website that the clinic specializes in treatment of crystal meth and treatment counseling for grief and loss related to HIV/AIDS.

Most metropolitan communities today have gay-affirming outreach center programs. Harm reduction treatment programs on the West Coast, for example, help clients reduce the harm to themselves in other areas as well as substance misuse.

A FOCUS ON SPIRITUALITY

A source of major comfort to most people—the church—is so often a source of despair to one group of people—sexual minorities. Most of these people, unlike other minority groups, grew up worshiping in religious environments in which the message was hostile to the very essence of what they would become. And sadly, most would have internalized the church's negative teachings on homosexuality. A major cause of suicide among youth dealing with gender issues, as we have seen, is the sense of rejection by fundamentalist churches. A study of 66 lesbians, gay, and bisexual respondents by Schuck and Liddle (2001) found that nearly two thirds had experienced conflict between religion and sexual orientation. Reactions included shame, depression, and suicidal thoughts. The experience of conflict was associated with difficulty in coming-out and establishing a positive gay or lesbian identity.

Resolution may consist of futile attempts to deny one's sexuality while embracing church doctrine, finding a gay-friendly church, synagogue, or mosque or finding spiritual nourishment outside orthodox channels. Achieving a high level of spiritual well-being was found in research on a sample of gays and lesbians to be a significant predictor of their psychological development (Tan, 2005).

Senreich and Vairo (2004) suggest that, when working with gays and lesbians in treatment, a Twelve-Step program can help them get in touch with their spiritual needs. Moreover, spirituality, as distinguished from organized religion, can help people deal with grief issues related to the AIDS pandemic. Referral to a gay AA meeting may be appropriate in this regard. But as Senreich and Vairo warn, such referral should be done with some care because of the sexual cruising that sometimes takes place in these settings. As with heterosexual addicts and alcoholics, the temptation to get romantically involved during the earliest period of recovery can be overwhelming and can elicit emotions for which one is ill prepared. On the other hand, since it's hard for gays and lesbians with substance-related problems to imagine a social life outside the gay bar, a specialized AA or NA meeting or a gay-friendly religious group may provide just the kind of sober support system that is essential to recovery.

SUMMARY AND CONCLUSION

Vulnerability, victimization, and substance misuse are the themes that emerged in this chapter on gender and sex orientation differences. Although there is considerable within-group variability, gender differences in biology, genetics, paths to dependence, responses to various treatment options, relapse triggers, and social contexts continue to be identified by research studies and practitioners. Women entering treatment have lower economic status, less support from their male counterparts, more needs for parenting and vocational skills, quicker and more severe physiological damage, more sexual and physical abuse in their backgrounds, and more needs for transportation and child care than men. Such differences suggest the desirability of gender-specific prevention and treatment approaches for women, and indeed, many new programs have developed since the infusion of female-specific federal funding in the mid-1980s. Research on the outcomes of women who receive treatment programming that includes child care services, prenatal services, women-only treatment, and mental health services is positive. These outcomes are not measured in terms of abstinence only; rather, the focus is on decreased substance use, increased treatment retention, improved birth outcomes, higher self-esteem, lower depression, and HIV risk reduction. Given the consistently poor results when narrowly measuring success as abstinence only, some critics are calling for new models for both men and women that would incorporate more choice and less coercion. Several alternative approaches are discussed in this chapter; refer also to chapter 3, Strengths-Based Helping Strategies.

Lesbians, gays, bisexuals, and transgender people have problems with discrimination and hate crimes that are horrendous. Their invisibility is one difficulty making problematic the pursuit of their rights, including the right to gay-affirmative or at least gay-sensitive treatment. Yet paramount is their need for whole-person counseling that takes into account identities, relationships, and resiliencies. In recognition of this, specialized units are being set up nationwide, albeit only in the major cities.

References

Aamot, G. (1998, May 24). South Dakota laws designed to curb fetal alcohol syndrome. *Courier Journal* (Louisville, KY), p. A8.

Abramovitz, M. (1997). *Regulating the lives of women: Social welfare policy from colonial times to the present* (Rev. ed.). Boston: South End Press.

Allday, E. (2006, August 6). Gay community has higher rate of smoking than other groups. *San Francisco Chronicle*, p. B1.

American Psychiatric Association (APA). (2000). *The diagnostic and statistical manual of mental disorders, text revision (DSM-IV-TR)*. Washington, DC: Author.

Anderson, A. (1999). Gender-related aspects of eating disorders: A guide to practice. *Journal of Gender-Specific Medicine, 2*(1), 47–54.

Annenberg Public Policy Center. (2005). Card playing trend in young people continues. University of Pennsylvania. Retrieved January 2007 from http://www.annenbergpublicpolicycenter.org/07_adolescent_risk/GamblingRelease20050928.pdf.

Apter-Marsh, M. (1984). The sexual behavior of alcoholic women while drinking and during sobriety. *Alcoholism Treatment Quarterly, 1*(3), 35–48.

Arizona Council on Compulsive Gambling. (2000). *Escape vs. action.* Retrieved from http://www.azccg.org.

Atkinson, D. R., & Schein, S. (1986). Similarity in counseling. *Counseling Psychologist, 14,* 319–354.

Babcock, M. (1996). Does feminism drive women to drink? Conflicting themes. *International Journal of Drug Policy, 7*(3), 158–165.

Belknap, J. (2001). *The invisible woman: Gender, crime, and justice.* Belmont, CA: Wadsworth.

Berg, I. K., & Shafer, K. C. (2004). Working with mandated substance abusers: The language of solutions. In S. L. Straussner (Ed.), *Clinical work with substance-abusing clients* (2nd ed., pp. 82–102). New York: Guilford Press.

Blume, S. (1997). Women: Clinical aspects. In J. Lowinson, P. Ruiz, R. B. Millman, & J. G. Langrod (Eds.), *Substance abuse: A comprehensive textbook* (pp. 645–653). Baltimore: Williams & Wilkins.

Bradford, J., Ryan, C., & Rothblum, E. (1994). National lesbian health care survey: Implications for mental health care. *Journal of Consulting and Clinical Psychology, 62*(2), 228–242.

Brady, T. M., & Ashley, O. S. (Eds.). (2005). Women in substance abuse treatment: Results from the alcohol and drug services study (DHHS Publication No. SMA 04-3968). Rockville, MD: Substance Abuse and Mental Health Services Administration.

Brady, K., & Randall, C. (1999). Gender differences in substance use disorders. *Addictive Disorders, 22*(2), 241–252.

Brown, S., & Coventry, L. (1997). *Queen of Hearts.* Victoria, Australia: Financial and Consumer Rights Council.

Brown, V. B., Melchior, L. A., Waite-O'Brien, N., & Huba, G. J. (2002). Effects of women-sensitive long-term residential treatment on psychological function of diverse populations of women. *Journal of Substance Abuse Treatment, 23,* 133–144.

Bureau of Justice Statistics (BJS). (2000). *Women offenders.* Washington, DC: U.S. Department of Justice.

Bureau of Justice Statistics (BJS). (2003). *Intimate partner violence, 1993–2001.* Washington, DC: U.S. Department of Justice.

Bureau of Justice Statistics (BJS). (2004). *National Crime Victimization Survey, Criminal Victimization, 2003* Retrieved October 6, 2006, from http://www.ojp.usdoj.gov/bjs/pub/pdf/cv03.pdf#search=%22National%20Crime%.

Bureau of Justice Statistics (BJS). (2006). *Prison and jail inmates at midyear 2005.* Washington, DC: U.S. Department of Justice.

Burroughs, A. (2003). *Dry: A memoir.* New York: St. Martin's Press.

Cabaj, R. (1997). Gays, lesbians, and bisexuals. In J. H. Lowinson, P. Ruiz, R. Millman, & J. Langrad (Eds.), *Substance abuse: A comprehensive textbook* (3rd ed., pp. 725–732). Baltimore: Williams & Wilkins.

Calamari, J., Cox, W., & Roth, J. (1996). Group treatment for men with alcohol problems. In M. Andronico (Ed.), *Men in groups: Insights, interventions, and psychoeducational work* (pp. 305–321). Washington, DC: American Psychological Association.

Center for Substance Abuse Treatment (CSAT). (2001). *A provider's introduction to substance abuse treatment for lesbian, gay, bisexual, and transgender individuals.* Rockville, MD: SAMHSA.

Centers for Disease Control and Prevention (CDC). (2006). *Intimate partner violence: Fact sheet.* National Center for Injury Prevention and Control. Retrieved October 2006 from http://www.cdc.gov/ncipc.

Chesney-Lind, M., & Pasko, L. (2004). *The female offender: Girls, women, and crime* (2nd ed.). Thousand Oaks, CA: Sage.

Clay, C. (1997, Spring). Bisexual crystal injectors in Seattle. *Harm Reduction,* pp. 18–19.

Cohen, J., Dickow, A., Horner, K., Zweben, J., Balabis, J., Vandersloot, D., et al. (2003). Abuse and violence history of men and women in treatment for methamphetamine dependence. *American Journal on Addictions, 12*(5), 377–385.

Copeland, J., Hall, W., Didcott, P., & Biggs, V. (1993). A comparison of a specialist women's alcohol and other drug treatment service with two traditional mixed-sex services: Client characteristics and treatment outcome. *Drug and Alcohol Dependence, 32,* 81–92.

Corrigan, E. (1995). Outcome of treatment for Irish alcoholic women. *Irish Journal of Psychological Medicine, 12*(2), 48–52.

Crisp, B., Thomas, S., Jackson, A., Thomason, N., Smith, S., Borrell, J., et al. (2000). Sex differences in the treatment needs and outcomes of problem gamblers. *Research on Social Work Practice, 10*(2), 229–242.

Crisp, C. (2006). The Gay Affirmative Practice scale (GAP): A new measure for assessing cultural competence with gay and lesbian clients. *Social Work, 51*(2), 106–113.

Davis, D. (1997). Women healing from alcoholism: A qualitative study. *Contemporary Drug Problems, 24,* 147–177.

Davis, D., & DiNitto, D. (2005). Gender and the use of drugs and alcohol: Fact, fiction, and unanswered questions. In C. A. McNeece & D. DiNitto, *Chemical dependency: A systems approach* (3rd ed., pp. 503–545). Boston: Allyn & Bacon.

Downs, W. R., & Miller, B. B. (2002). Treating dual problems of partner violence and substance abuse. In C. Wekerle & A. Wall (Eds.), *The violence and addiction equation: Theoretical and clinical issues in substance abuse and relationship violence* (pp. 254–274). London: Brunner/Routledge, Hove.

El-Bassel, N., Gilbert, L., Krishnan, S., Schilling, R. F., Gaeta, T., Purpura, S., et al. (1998). Partner violence and sexual HIV-risk behaviors among women in an inner-city emergency department. *Violence and Victims, 13*(4), 1–17.

Enos, S. (2001). *Mothering from the inside: Parenting in a women's prison.* Albany: State University of New York Press.

Fallon, P., Katzman, M. A., & Wooley, S. C. (Eds.). (1994). *Feminist perspectives on eating disorders.* New York: Guilford Press.

Figdor, E., & Kaeser, L. (2005). Concerns mount over punitive approaches to substance abuse among pregnant women. *The Guttmacher Report on Public Policy, 1*(5), 3–5.

Fingarette, H. (1998). *Heavy drinking.* Berkeley: University of California Press.

Flavin, D., Franklin, J., & Frances, R. (1986). The acquired immune deficiency syndrome (AIDS) and suicidal behavior in alcohol-dependent men. *American Journal of Psychiatry, 143*(11), 1441–1442.

Gerolamo, A. (2004). State of the science: Women and the nonpharmacological treatment of substance abuse. *Journal of the American Psychiatric Nurses Association, 10*(4), 181–189.

Ghindia, D., & Kola, L. (1996, November). Gay male substance abuse examined. *Issues of Substance, 8,* 11.

Greenhouse, L. (2001, March 22). Court curbs drug tests during pregnancy. *New York Times,* pp. A1, A16.

Grella, C., & Joshi, V. (1999). Gender differences in drug treatment careers among clients in the National Drug Abuse Treatment Outcome Study. *American Journal of Drug and Alcohol Abuse, 25*(3), 385–406.

Grella, C. E., Polinsky, M. L., Hser, Y., & Perry, S. M. (1999). Characteristics of women-only and mixed-gender drug abuse treatment programs. *Journal of Substance Abuse Treatment, 17*(1–2), 37–44.

Harshman, W. L. (2000). A comparison of a gender-specific and traditional model of substance abuse treatment within the therapeutic community on treatment success (Doctoral dissertation, Wayne State University, 2000). *Dissertation Abstracts International, 61* (1-A), 97.

Health care needs of gay men and lesbians in the United States. (1996). *Journal of the American Medical Association, 257*(17), 1354–1359.

Hiebert-Murphy, D., & Woytkiw, L. (2000). A model for working with women dealing with child sexual abuse and addictions: The Laurel Centre, Winnipeg, Manitoba, Canada. *Journal of Substance Abuse Treatment, 18,* 387–394.

Hien, D., Cohen, L., Miele, G., Litt, L., & Capstick, C. (2004). Promising treatment for women with comorbid PTSD and substance use disorders. *American Journal of Psychiatry, 161*(8), 1426–1433.

Hirsch, A. (1999). Some days are harder than hard: Welfare reform and women with drug conviction in Pennsylvania. *Center for Law and Social Policy.* Retrieved from http://www.clasp.org/publications/some_days_are_harder_than_hard.pdf.

Holmes, W. C., & Slap, G. B. (1998). Sexual abuse of boys: Definition, prevalence, correlates, sequelae, and management. *Journal of the American Medical Association, 280*(21), 1855–1862.

Hubbard, J. R., Franco, S. E., & Onaivi, E. (1999). Marijuana: Medical implications. *American Family Physician.* Retrieved from http://www.findarticles.com/cf_0/m3225/9_60/58252718/print.jhtml.

Hubbard, R. L. (1997). Evaluation and outcome of treatment. In J. H. Lowinson, P. Ruiz, R. B. Millman, & J. G. Langrod (Eds.), *Substance abuse: A comprehensive textbook* (pp. 499–512). Baltimore: Williams & Wilkins.

Jackson, K. (2004, May/June). What's sex got to do with it? Addiction in the GLBT community. *Social Work,* p. 15.

Kantor, G., & Strauss, M. (1989). Substance abuse as a precipitant of wife abuse victimizations. *American Journal of Drug and Alcohol Abuse, 15*(2), 173–189.

Karberg, J., & James, D. (2005). *Substance dependence, abuse, and treatment of jail inmates, 2002.* Bureau of Justice Statistics. Washington, DC: U.S. Department of Justice.

Kauffman, E., Dore, M. M., & Nelson-Zlupko, L. (1995). The role of women's therapy groups in the treatment of chemical dependence. *American Journal of Orthopsychiatry, 65*(3), 355–363.

Kenney, J. W., Reinholtz, C., & Angelini, P. J. (1997). Ethnic differences in childhood pregnancy and adolescent sexual abuse and teenage pregnancy. *Journal of Adolescent Health, 21,* 3–10.

Kershnar, S., & Paltrow, L. (2001, Summer). Pregnancy, parenting and drug use: Which women? Which harms? *Harm Reduction Communication*. Retrieved February 2007 from http://www.harmreduction.org/pubs/news/summer01/kershnar.htm.

King, M. (1996, November 12). Suicide watch. *The Advocate*, pp. 41–44.

Kus, R. (1990). Alcoholism in the gay and lesbian communities. In R. Kus (Ed.), *Keys to caring: Assisting your gay and lesbian clients* (pp. 66–81). Boston: Alyson.

LaFave, L. M., & Echols, L. D. (1999). An argument for choice: An alternative women's treatment program. *Journal of Substance Abuse Treatment, 16*(4), 345–352.

Laudet, A., Magura, S., Furst, R., & Kumar, N. (1999). Male partners of substance-abusing women in treatment: An exploratory study. *American Journal of Drug and Alcohol Abuse, 25*(4), 607–627.

Leonard, K. E. (1993). Drinking patterns and intoxication in marital violence: Review, critique, and future directions for research. In S. E. Martin (Ed.), *Alcohol and interpersonal violence: Fostering multidisciplinary perspectives* (NIH Publication No. 93-3496, NIH Research Monograph 24, pp. 281–290). Washington, DC: National Institutes of Health.

Lesieur, H. (1987). The female pathological gambler. In W. R. Eadington (Ed.), *Gambling research: Proceedings of the seventh international conference on gambling and risk taking* (pp. 230–258). University of Nevada, Reno: Bureau of Business and Economic Research.

Lesieur, H., & Blume, S. (1991). When Lady Luck loses: Women and compulsive gambling. In N. Van Den Bergh (Ed.), *Feminist perspectives on addictions* (pp. 181–197). New York: Springer.

McGue, M., & Slutske, W. (1996). The inheritance of alcoholism in women. In J. M. Howard, S. E. Martin, P. D. Mail, M. E. Hilton, & E. D. Taylor (Eds.), *Women and alcohol: Issues for prevention research* (Research Monograph No. 32, pp. 65–92). Bethesda, MD: National Institutes of Health.

Miller, B., Downs, W., & Gondoli, D. (1989). Spousal violence among alcoholic women as compared to a random household sample of women. *Journal of Studies on Alcohol, 50,* 533–540.

Miller, B. A., Downs, W. R., & Testa, M. (1993). Interrelationships between victimization experiences and women's alcohol use. *Journal of Studies on Alcohol,* Suppl. 2, 109–117.

Miller, W. R., & Rollnick, S. (2002). *Motivational interviewing: Preparing people to change addictive behavior* (2nd ed.). New York: Guilford Press.

Mravcak, S. S. (2006). Primary care for lesbian, bisexual, women. *American Family Physician, 74*(2), 287–288.

Murphy, S., & Rosenbaum, M. (1997). Two women who used cocaine too much. In C. Reinarman & H. Levine (Eds.), *Crack in America: Demon drugs and social justice* (pp. 98–112). Berkeley: University of California Press.

National Center on Addiction and Substance Abuse (CASA). (2006). *Women under the influence*. Baltimore: Johns Hopkins University Press.

National Institute on Alcohol Abuse and Alcoholism (NIAAA). (1993). *Eighth Special Report to the U.S. Congress on Alcohol and Health*. Rockville, MD: Author.

National Research Council. (1999, April 1). *Pathological gambling: A critical review*. Washington, DC: National Academy Press.

National Survey on Drug Use and Health (NSDUH). (2004, October 29). *The NSDUH Report. Gender differences in substance dependence and abuse*. NSDUH. Retrieved October 2006 from http://www.oas.samhsa.gov/2k4/genderDependence/genderDependence.htm.

National Women's Law Center. (2004). *Making the grade on women's health: A national and state-by-state report card.* Washington, DC: Author

Nelson-Zlupko, L., Dore, M. M., Kauffman, E., & Kaltenback, K. (1996). Women in recovery: Their perceptions of treatment effectiveness. *Journal of Substance Abuse Treatment, 13*(1), 51–59.

Neumann, D. A., Houskamp, B. M., Pollock, V. E., & Briere, J. (1996). The long-term sequelae of childhood sexual abuse in women: A meta-analytic review. *Child Maltreatment: Journal of the Professional Society on the Abuse of Children, 1,* 6–16.

Neumann, J. P., & Sallmann, J. (2004). Women, trauma histories, and co-occurring disorders: Assessing the scope of the problem. *Social Service Review, 78*(3), 466–500.

Nevada Council on Problem Gambling. (2004). *Annual Report.* Las Vegas, NV. Retrieved October 2006 from http://www.nevadacouncil.org/2004AnnualReport.pdf.

New study highlights gender's impact on addiction. (2000). *American Medical News, 43*(7), 30.

Pierre, N., Shrier, L. A., Emans, S. J., & DuRant, R. H. (1998). Adolescent males involved in pregnancy: Association of forced sexual contact and risk behaviors. *Journal of Adolescent Health, 23*(6), 364–369.

Potenza, M., Steinberg, M., McLaughlin, S., Wu, R., Rounsaville, B., & O'Malley, S. (2001). Gender-related differences in the characteristics of problem gamblers using a gambling helpline. *American Journal of Psychiatry, 158*(9), 1500–1505.

Prendergast, M. L., Wellisch, J., & Falkin, G. P. (1995). Assessment of services for substance-abusing women offenders in community and correctional settings. *Prison Journal, 75,* 240–256.

Project MATCH Research Group. (1997). Matching alcoholism treatment to client heterogeneity: Project MATCH Posttreatment drinking outcomes. *Journal of Studies on Alcohol, 58,* 7–29.

Raab, B. (2001, April 27). Study: Lesbians have higher risk for some cancers. *Women's E News.* Retrieved from http://www.womensenews.org/article.cfm?aid=528.

Remafedi, G., French, S., Story, M., Resnick, M., & Blum, R. (1998, January). The relationship between suicide risk and sexual orientation: Results of a population-based study. *American Journal of Public Health, 88,* 57–60.

Rubin, R. (1998, August 12). Study: Hands-off pregnant drug users. *USA Today,* p. D1.

Saunders, J., Wodak, A., & Williams, R. (1985). Past experience of advice and treatment for drinking problems of patients with alcoholic liver disease. *British Journal of Addiction, 80,* 51–56.

Schutte, K. K., Seable, J. H., & Moos, R. H. (1997). Gender differences in the relations between depressive symptoms and drinking behavior among problem drinkers: A three-wave study. *Journal of Consulting Clinical Psychology, 65,* 392–404.

Senreich, E., & Vairo, E. (2006). Treatment of gay and lesbian substance abusers. In S. L. Straussner (Ed.), *Clinical work with substance-abusing clients* (pp. 392–423). New York: Guilford Press.

Shernoff, M. (2006). Condomless sex: Gay men, barebacking, and harm reduction. *Social Work, 51*(2), 106–113.

Siegal, H. A., Rapp, R. C., Fisher, J., Cole, C., & Wagner, J. H. (1993). Treatment dropouts and noncompliers: Two persistent problems and a programmatic remedy. In J. A. Inciardi, F. M. Tims, & B. W. Fletcher (Eds.), *Innovative approaches in the treatment of drug abuse: Program models and strategies* (pp. 109–122). Westport, CT: Greenwood Press.

Siegal, L. (1997). The pregnancy police fight the war on drugs. In C. Reinarman & H. Levine (Eds.), *Crack in America: Demon drugs and social justice* (pp. 249–260). Berkeley: University of California Press.

Skinner, W. F. (1994). The prevalence and demographic predictors of illicit and licit drug use among lesbians and gay men. *American Journal of Public Health, 84,* 1307–1310.

Smith, P. H., & Chescheir, N. (1995). *Battered substance-abusing women: A vulnerable and underserved population in North Carolina.* (Final report submitted to North Carolina Governor's Institute for Alcohol and Substance Abuse, Raleigh. North Carolina Governor's Institute for Alcohol and Substance Abuse), as quoted in CASA (1996), p. 32.

Sowers, K. M., Ellis, R. A., Washington, T. S., & Currant, M. (2002). Optimizing treatment effects for substance abusing women with children: An evaluation of the Susan B. Anthony Center. *Research on Social Work Practice, 12*(1), 143–158.

Sterling, R. C., Gottheil, E., Weinstein, S. P., & Serota, R. (1998). Therapist/patient race and sex matching: Treatment retention and 9-month follow-up outcome. *Addiction, 93*(7), 1043–1050.

Substance Abuse and Mental Health Services Administration (SAMHSA). (2005). Substance abuse treatment for persons with co-occurring disorders. Treatment Improvement Protocol (TIP) Series, No. 42 (DHHS Publication No. SMA 05-3992). Rockville, MD: Author.

Substance Abuse and Mental Health Services Administration (SAMHSA). (2005). *Women in substance abuse treatment: Results from the Alcohol and Drug Services Study.* Office of Applied Studies. Retrieved October 7, 2006, from http://oas.samhsa.gov/WomenTX/WomenTX.htm.

Substance Abuse and Mental Health Services Administration (SAMHSA). (2006). *Results from the 2005 National Survey on Drug Use and Health: National Findings.* Retrieved February 2007 from http://oas.samhsa.gov/NSDUH/2K5NSDUH/2K5results.htm.

Tan, P. (2005). The importance of spirituality among gay and lesbian individuals. *Journal of Homosexuality, 49*(2), 135–145.

Texas Council on Problem and Compulsive Gambling. (2000, July 7). E-update on problem gambling news. *Women and Problem Gambling, 1*(23), 1.

Tully, C. T. (2000). *Lesbians, gays, and the empowerment perspective.* New York: Columbia University Press.

Underhill, B. (1991). Recovery needs of lesbian alcoholics in treatment. In N. Van Den Bergh (Ed.), *Feminist perspectives on addictions* (pp. 73–86). New York: Springer.

U.S. Secretary of Health and Human Services. (2000). *Tenth special report to the U.S. Congress on alcohol and health.* Rockville, MD: National Institute on Alcohol Abuse and Alcoholism.

VanGelder, L., & Brandt, P. R. (1996). *The girl next door: Into the heart of lesbian America.* New York: Simon & Schuster.

van Wormer, K. (2001). *Counseling female offenders and victims: A strengths-restorative approach.* New York: Springer.

van Wormer, K., & Bartollas, C. (2007) *Women and the criminal justice system* (2nd ed.). Boston: Allyn & Bacon.

van Wormer, K., Wells, J., & Boes, M. (2000). *Social work with lesbians, gays, and bisexuals: A strengths perspective.* Boston: Allyn & Bacon.

Volberg, R. (2005). *Gambling and problem gambling in Arizona: Report to the Arizona Lottery. Tucson, Arizona.* Retrieved October 2006 from http://www.problemgambling.az.gov.

Warn, D. (1997). Recovering issues of substance-abusing gay men. In S. L. A. Straussner & E. Zelvin (Eds.), *Gender and addictions: Men and women in treatment* (pp. 387–410). Northvale, NJ: Jason Aronson.

Wechsberg, W., Craddock, S., & Hubbard, R. (1998). How are women who enter substance abuse treatment different than men? A gender comparison from the Drug Abuse Treatment Outcome Study. *Drugs and Society, 13*(1/2), 97–115.

Westermeyer, J., & Boedicker, A. (2000). Course, severity and treatment of substance abuse among women versus men. *American Journal of Drug and Alcohol Abuse, 26*(4), 523–535.

Widom, C., Ireland, T., & Glynn, P. (1995). Alcohol abuse in abused and neglected children follow-up: Are they at increased risk? *Journal of Studies on Alcohol, 56,* 207–217.

Willson, P., McFarlane, J., Malecha, A., Watson, K., Lemmey, D., Schultz, P., et al. (2000). Severity of violence against women by intimate partners and associated use of alcohol and/or illicit drugs by the perpetrator. *Journal of Interpersonal Violence, 15*(9), 996–1008.

Wilsnack, S., Vogeltanz, N., Klassen, A., & Harris, R. (1997). Childhood sexual abuse and women's substance abuse: National survey findings. *Journal of Studies on Alcohol, 58,* 264–271.

Women Helping Women. (2000). White-knuckled. Retrieved from http://www .femalegambler.org.

Wong, C. J., Badger, G. J., Sigmon, S. C., & Higgins, S. T. (2002). Examining possible gender differences among cocaine-dependent outpatients. *Experimental and Clinical Psychopharmacology, 10,* 216–323.

World Health Organization (WHO). (2004). *Global status report on alcohol.* WHO. Retrieved October 2006 from http://www.who.int/substance_abuse/publications.

Yodanis, C. (2004). Gender inequality, violence: A cross-national test of the feminist theory of violence against women. *Journal of Interpersonal Violence, 19*(6), 655–675.

Young, N., Gardner, S., & Dennis, K. (1998). *Responding to alcohol and other drug problems in child welfare: Weaving together practice and policy.* Washington, DC: Child Welfare Press.

Zernike, K. (2005, July 6). Officials across U.S. describe drug woes. *New York Times.* Retrieved from http://www.nytimes.com.

You will be able to walk a straight line and pass the balloon test.
You will be able to answer the door without looking through the little hole.
You will realize what a mess you've been and thank God for your Twelve-Step program.

—From "The Twelve Promises for Beginners"; found on www.soberdykes.org/jokes.html

MUTUAL-HELP GROUPS: A STRENGTHS PERSPECTIVE

CHAPTER 12

INTRODUCTION

Although mutual-help groups are typically organized around very serious problems, "The Twelve Promises for Beginners" is a good example of the "strengths" and humor that abound in such organizations. Newcomers and professionals who visit a Twelve-Step group for the first time are often shocked to hear laughter and fun poking when dire situations are described by a fellow member. Later, they understand that the laughter comes from self-recognition and hope. It is a powerful part of the healing process for both listener and speaker. For example, at a recent all-women's meeting of Alcoholics Anonymous with over 50 women attending, a young woman named "Susan," 3 days out of detox at her first Alcoholics Anonymous (AA) meeting, had the following experience:

SUSAN: (very softly) "I just got out of detox . . ."

GROUP: (starts to get very quiet, side-conversations stop)

SUSAN: "I don't know who I am . . ."

GROUP: (very quiet now)

SUSAN: (crying now) "I'm like a stranger in my own body . . . (puts her head down, sobbing) I just want to get fucked-up!"

GROUP: (someone passes her the Kleenex box that has "Crying is healing" written on the outside with purple ink)

SUSAN: "So . . . I guess I'll just take it slow . . ."

GROUP: (laughter all around, cheers, everyone starts clapping)

SUSAN: (smiles shyly)

GROUP: someone shouts, "Keep breathing!!!" and everybody laughs.

There are no easy cures or answers to many of the problems we experience as human beings. With solace, care, and support, we can, as social beings, help each other through difficult experiences that are sometimes excruciatingly painful and can lead to what Gamblers Anonymous members call "incomprehensible demoralization" when faced alone. Since the 1950s, divorce, job relocation, and changing family expectations have undermined the role extended families played in attempting to provide this kind of support. Mutual-help groups (an estimated half-million) have filled in the gap to deal with almost every human problem, including self-care groups for major diseases, recovery groups for addiction and other problems, and advocacy groups for certain circumstances (elderly, mentally ill, etc.). Today, approximately 10 million Americans participate in mutual-help groups each year, and 25 million have done so at some time during their lives (Humphreys, 2003; Kessler, Mickelson, & Zhao, 1997). Online support groups are increasingly common; benefits include accessibility, convenience, and anonymity (Petrucci, Kirk, & Reid, 2004). Information on all these different types of groups is available by a key word search at the American Self-Help Clearinghouse site on the Internet. Another resource guide that is updated monthly and lists groups, Internet resources, and recovery stories can be found at www.facesandvoicesofrecovery.org.

In this chapter, we describe the major mutual-help groups that have been helpful with persons who are oppressed by some addiction, including alcohol, drugs, food, gambling, and smoking. To understand the philosophy, purpose, and meeting behaviors of Twelve-Step programs, we focus in depth on Alcoholics Anonymous, the model for Narcotics Anonymous, Overeaters Anonymous, Gamblers Anonymous, and Nicotine Anonymous. To the extent possible, recent research findings that indicate the effectiveness of these groups are cited, although most research activity has been centered on Alcoholics Anonymous.

"TWELVE-STEP FACILITATION" VERSUS TWELVE-STEP MUTUAL-HELP GROUPS IN THE COMMUNITY

Many harm reductionists and others aligned with strengths perspective practice see AA as the perpetrator of a monolithic disease model that requires abstinence and makes meeting attendance mandatory. This misconception may come from the confusion of "Twelve-Step facilitation" as practiced in professional treatment programs and the mutual-help Twelve-Step programs as they are practiced in the community.

The growth and spread of AA principles in professional treatment began in the United States in 1952 when a psychiatrist and a psychologist created a unique program at Wilmer State Hospital in Minnesota. As the program developed over the next 3 years, it featured the integration of professional staff with trained recovering alcoholics and embraced the disease model and the link to Twelve-Step groups, family involvement, abstinence from all addictive drugs, and client and family education on the effects of addiction, individualized treatment plans, and aftercare (Chappel & DuPont, 1999). This new model of treatment, subsequently known as the Minnesota Model, was adopted by Hazelden in 1961 and spread so rapidly that by 1989, 95% of the treatment programs in the United States were basing their programs on the Twelve-Step AA program.

In actuality, the practice of AA in the community differs in fundamental ways from the Twelve-Step facilitation that is practiced in professional treatment centers. AA in the community is not "treatment." It is a spiritually based fellowship that supports the development and maintenance of abstinence for those who want it and offers "steps" for sobriety and lifelong character development. AA could hardly be more different in its structure than a typical public or private addiction treatment program. As noted by Fisher and Harrison (2005), AA groups in the community are self-supporting, led by fellow alcoholics, and free of charge. There is no federal or state funding, no licensing or monitoring by any regulatory agency, no records of attendance, and no case records. In contrast, Twelve-Step facilitation models implemented in treatment programs have paid professionals teach AA assumptions (powerlessness over alcohol, spirituality, Twelve Steps to recovery), require people to admit they are alcoholics, complete the work on the initial steps in a specific time frame, go to a certain number of AA meetings, charge money for the treatment program, and are monitored by state and federal regulators.

A fundamental difference between the writings of cofounder Bill Wilson, the philosophy of The Big Book of AA, and professional treatment programs that practice Twelve-Step facilitation is around the issue of "compliance." As noted by LaFave and Echols (1999), "Twelve-Step self-help programs stress the voluntary nature of attendance and offer their ideas as suggestions. . . . The highly directive nature of Twelve-Step treatment models is, therefore, a departure from the approach used in Twelve-Step self-help programs" (p. 348).

AA and other Twelve-Step groups do a delicate dance of keeping alive the voluntary nature of the mutual-help program, in spite of pressures from treatment centers and probation/parole officers on clients to bring back attendance slips signed by the chairperson of the particular group. As noted on the official AA website, "proof of attendance at meetings is *not* part of AA's procedure. Each group is autonomous and has the right to choose whether or not to sign court slips. In some areas the attendees report on themselves, at the request of the referring agency, and thus alleviate breaking AA members' anonymity."

TWELVE-STEP PROGRAMS AND HARM REDUCTION

It may surprise some readers that the authors consider Twelve-Step mutual-help organizations such as Alcoholics Anonymous and Narcotics Anonymous to be compatible with a harm reduction philosophy. In addition to the voluntary nature of the program, there are other principles of Twelve-Step programs as practiced in the community that are consistent with harm reduction practices. A fundamental concept of the AA program is the need for self-assessment as to whether or not you "qualify" as a member—that is, "have a desire to stop drinking." This is based on the belief that alcoholics want to stop drinking because eventually their own experience and their failure at numerous experiments to control their drinking tell them they can no longer control it once they start. In other words, they have tried and failed at various harm reduction strategies and consequently have reached the stage of actually having a desire to stop drinking (Zelvin & Davis, 2001). As noted in The Big Book of Alcoholics Anonymous (2001):

> Here are some of the methods we have tried: Drinking beer only, limiting the number of drinks, never drinking alone, never drinking in the morning, drinking only at home, never having it in the house, never drinking during business hours, drinking only at parties, switching from scotch to brandy, drinking only natural wines, agreeing to resign if ever drunk on the job, taking a trip, not taking a trip, etc. (p. 31)

The critical issue is that people finally reach the decision to stop drinking *for themselves,* not because a professional person insisted on it. AA says, "We do not like to pronounce any individual as alcoholic, but you can quickly diagnose yourself. Step over to the nearest barroom and try some controlled drinking" (p. 31).

Other concepts consistent with harm reduction philosophy practiced in Twelve-Step programs in the community are the ideas of limited control; that is, don't drink "one day at a time," rather than "never drink again," and the embracing of human fallibility (the only requirement for membership is "a desire to stop drinking," not "you have to have so much amount of abstinence to stay in this program"). Michael White (2000), codeveloper of the narrative therapy approach (see chapter 3), remarks that

> AA's responses to persons who turn back to the bottle are generally compassionate rather than judging. This is an antidote to the demoralizing sense of personal failure that is so often occasioned by such U-turns, and keeps the door open on options for persons to try again, and yet again. In response to these U-turns, the AA community just goes on reaching out. This is a reaching out by persons who have "been there," and who have a strong appreciation of the desperation that is experienced in this struggle. (p. 32)

ALCOHOLICS ANONYMOUS

Alcoholics Anonymous is the prototype for other mutual-help groups that have adopted the Twelve Steps and traditions. As we explore this organization, it should be understood that the authors do not and cannot speak for Alcoholics Anonymous. (Official AA literature on various topics can be obtained by writing to Alcoholics Anonymous, Box 459, Grand Central

Station, New York, NY 10163, or by accessing the website at http://www
.alcoholics-anonymous.org.)

The meaning of "Alcoholics Anonymous" (AA) varies depending on how
we see ourselves in relation to this increasingly popular mutual-help program
for alcoholics (Davis & Jansen, 1998). Social workers have variously described
AA as a set of principles developed by alcohol-dependent men (Nelson-Zlupko,
Kauffman, & Dore, 1995), "a very successful model for self-help groups"
(Borkman, 1989, p. 63), and disempowering to women (Finfgeld, 2002;
Rhodes & Johnson, 1994). Some see it as not Christian enough (Ryan, 2003).
However, some feminists (Kasl, 1992) dismiss it as another White, middle-class
male organization that enjoins women to depend on "having a Higher Power,
which is usually described as an all-powerful male God" (p. 150) and to follow
one journey to recovery "as defined by privileged males" (p. 147). For other
feminists, the meaning of AA is quite different; Covington (1994) sees it as a
"model for mutual-help programs" within which "women can find the most
powerful resources for healing" (p. 4). Some researchers have concluded that
"without question AA involvement has been associated with vast numbers of
alcohol-dependent individuals becoming abstinent for long periods of time"
(Emrick, 1987, p. 421), but others question whether it is even possible to assess
the effectiveness of this organization in any kind of scientific manner (Harvard
Mental Health Letter, 1996). Perhaps the greatest meaning of Alcoholics
Anonymous, from the vantage point of the individual sober member of AA, is
that "through its program he (she) attained sobriety" (E. Kurtz, 1979, p. 157).

In this section, we address issues about women and other common criticisms regarding AA by reframing the meaning of AA from an alternative
treatment or service delivery model to an understanding based on metaphor
(Davis & Jansen, 1998). Viewing AA in this framework allows us to suggest
meanings of key metaphors, or narratives, of the AA program. We describe
areas of program strength and potential barriers for clinicians (and consequently, for those persons who consult with us) and review the research findings concerning the efficacy of this program.

A Thumbnail Sketch of Alcoholics Anonymous

Alcoholics Anonymous is an approach to recovery from alcoholism developed
by and for alcoholics around 1935, a time when alcoholism was considered
hopeless by the medical profession and a moral failing by most everyone. Bill
Wilson and Dr. Bob Smith, both late-stage alcoholics and desperate for an
alternative, joined together in the creation of anonymous support meetings that
borrowed principles from the Oxford Group (a nondenominational Christian
movement) and created other principles important to the recovery from alcoholism as they experienced it. Their ideas were eventually written in a book on
paper so thick and bulky that the original volume of *Alcoholics Anonymous*
(2001) was called "The Big Book," a title affectionately, and perhaps metaphorically, continued by AA members ever since, even though it is now a
regular-sized book (E. Kurtz, 1979).

| Box 12.1 | THE TWELVE STEPS OF ALCOHOLICS ANONYMOUS |

1. We admitted we were powerless over alcohol—that our lives had become unmanageable.
2. Came to believe that a Power greater than ourselves could restore us to sanity.
3. Made a decision to turn our will and our lives over to the care of God as we understood Him.
4. Made a searching and fearless moral inventory of ourselves.
5. Admitted to God, to ourselves and to another human being the exact nature of our wrongs.
6. Were entirely ready to have God remove all these defects of character.
7. Humbly asked Him to remove our shortcomings.
8. Made a list of all persons we had harmed, and became willing to make amends to them all.
9. Made direct amends to such people wherever possible, except when to do so would injure them or others.
10. Continued to take personal inventory and, when we were wrong, promptly admitted it.
11. Sought through prayer and meditation to improve our conscious contact with God, as we understood Him, praying only for knowledge of His will for us and the power to carry that out.
12. Having had a spiritual awakening as the result of these steps, we tried to carry this message to alcoholics, and to practice these principles in all our affairs.

Source: Alcoholics Anonymous (2001).

At the heart of the AA program is a group of principles "suggested" for recovery called the Twelve Steps (see Box 12.1). These are specific individual actions, spiritual in nature, and "guides to progress . . . not spiritual perfection" (Alcoholics Anonymous, 2001, p. 60). They were painstakingly designed by fellow alcoholics to help a person obtain sobriety and make the spiritual transformation necessary to create a sober life that is worth living. For the developing AA groups to survive and function effectively, a set of principles called the Twelve Traditions evolved to set forth a working philosophy for this mutual-help community. The Foreword to the second edition of *Alcoholics Anonymous (1955)* explains the Twelve Traditions as they apply to community:

> No alcoholic man or woman could be excluded from our Society. . . . Our leaders might serve but never govern. . . . Each group was to be autonomous and there was to be no professional class of therapy. . . . There were to be no fees or dues. . . . There was to be the least possible organization, even in our service centers. . . . Our public relations were to be based upon attraction rather than promotion. . . . All members ought to be anonymous at the level of press, radio, TV, and films, and in no circumstances should we give endorsements, make alliances, or enter public controversies. (p. vii)

These twelve guidelines for a "nonorganization," although not as familiar as the Twelve Steps, have made it possible for AA to avoid the temptations of power, money, and bureaucracy that would have brought about the death of the organization (Borkman, 2006). Instead, more than 105,000 groups of Alcoholics Anonymous meetings in 150 countries have been created and remain stable, with more than 1,867,000 members throughout the world at last count (AA, 2004). According to the Harvard Mental Health Letter (1996), "by 1990, 9% of the entire American population (and 70% of those ever treated for alcoholism) had attended at least one AA meeting" (p. 3). According to the most recent AA member random survey (AA, 2004), of 7,500 AA members in the United States and Canada, the average AA member is male (65% vs. 35% female), White (89.1%), and middle-aged (1.5% under 21, 7.9% age 21–30, 18.2% age 31–40, 33% age 41–50, 23.1% age 51–60, 11.5% age 61–70, and 4.8% over age 70). Before coming to AA, 64% of the members received some kind of professional treatment or counseling.

The program is recognized by many professionals as one of the most effective, user-friendly resources for helping alcoholics (Humphreys, 2003; Riordan & Walsh, 1994). Attributes of the program important to many counselors include a policy of no dues or fees, its availability in small towns and in medium to large cities, its usually offering an array of culturally diverse options for a variety of groups (e.g., women, veterans, elders, Native Americans, Hispanics, gay men, lesbians, newcomers, and even a group for Grateful "Deadheads" called the "Wharf Rats") (Epstein & Sardiello, 1990). Also, transportation for housebound persons or out-of-town visitors is frequently arranged through voluntary help from members who are "on-call" for such circumstances.

RESEARCH ON EFFECTIVENESS

Although beset by methodological problems aggravated by the anonymous, voluntary, self-selection of AA membership, there is evidence to indicate that AA is an extremely useful approach for alcoholics trying to stop drinking. Emrick's (1987) review of surveys and outcome evaluations of AA alone or as an adjunct to professional treatment indicates that about 40 to 50% of alcoholics who maintain long-term, active membership in AA will have several years of total abstinence while involved; and 60 to 68% will improve, drinking less or not at all during AA participation. Numerous studies and reviews of studies have found that participation in AA after treatment is associated with improved outcomes (Bodin, 2006; Tonigan et al., 2003). Involvement or active participation in AA practices (e.g., "working the Twelve Steps"), rather than just attendance at AA meetings, was related to positive outcome in these findings and supported in other studies (Gossop et al., 2003; Montgomery, Miller, & Tonigan, 1995; Snow, Prochaska, & Rossi, 1994). Project MATCH findings confirm that increased engagement in AA-related practices and having subjective spiritual experiences predict positive outcome (Tonigan, Miller, & Connors, 2000).

Other findings suggest that the length of AA attendance correlates with months of abstinence (McBride, 1991; Moos & Moos, 2004). In a 16-year follow-up study, Moos and Moos (2006) found that extended participation in AA throughout the first, second, and third years after treatment was associated with better alcohol-related and self-efficacy outcomes. Other studies support the idea that AA is beneficial as an adjunct to formal treatment and when used as a form of aftercare (Alford, Koehler, & Leonard, 1991; Moos & Moos, 2004; Walsh et al., 1991).

These positive findings are not without their skeptics. Major criticisms include the large percentage of alcoholics who drop out of AA (according to AA's own survey, 50% after 3 months) (Chappel, 1993; Galaif & Sussman, 1995), contradictory studies that indicate AA works no better than other approaches, including no treatment (W. R. Miller & Hester, 1986; Peele, 1992), and findings that indicate no significant relationship between AA attendance and outcomes (McLatchie & Lomp, 1988; W. R. Miller, Leckman, Delaney, & Tinkcorn, 1992). In addition, methodological problems endemic to research on AA lead some researchers to dismiss such attempts as mere exercises in speculation (Harvard Mental Health Letter, 1996). For example, despite years of research, a definitive picture of a person's characteristics that can predict a positive or negative outcome with AA has not emerged (Tonigan & Hiller-Sturmhofel, 1994).

In the meantime, there is adequate (although not perfect) evidence to suggest that many alcoholics who become involved in AA will find something they can use to improve their lives on a long-term basis (Chappel, 1993) and, consequently, that social work professionals will benefit from more knowledge of this potentially valuable resource. L. F. Kurtz and Fisher (2003), in their interviews with 33 individuals actively involved in Twelve-Step fellowships and community activity, demonstrated that through the Twelve-Step fellowship, they developed the skills and confidence to seek out and engage in community service. Emrick (1987), after his extensive review of findings from the empirical literature, concludes that although AA is not for everyone (particularly those who just want to reduce their drinking), "nevertheless, AA has been demonstrated to be associated with abstinence for many alcohol-dependent individuals and thus the professional who comes in contact with alcoholics should become familiar with AA and utilize this self-help resource whenever possible" (p. 421).

MYTHS AND METAPHORS ABOUT ALCOHOLICS ANONYMOUS

Alcoholics Anonymous describes itself as a "simple program" that has only one requirement for membership, "a desire to stop drinking," and one primary purpose, "to carry its message to the alcoholic who still suffers" (AA, 2001, p. 562). The apparent single-mindedness of this nonpolitical, self-supporting program masks a remarkably subtle and, in some ways, counterestablishment worldview that challenges dominant cultural expectations regarding hierarchy, power, and models of helping. Because AA is the language of narrative and metaphor, it is easily misunderstood without the context of lived experience and meaning-making of the membership as a whole.

It is not surprising that AA is miscomprehended and misinterpreted. Flores (1988) notes that many of the critics of AA "fail to understand the subtleties of the AA program and often erroneously attribute qualities and characteristics to the organization that are one-dimensional, misleading, and even border on slanderous" (p. 203). AA has been called everything from a cult to unscientific, totalitarian, and coercive (Flores, 1988). Common criticisms include: AA takes away power from groups that are already disenfranchised (e.g., women); AA adheres to the medical model of disease, not a strength perspective of wellness; the program is just another substitute addiction; AA requires total abstinence; AA is a religion/cult with a suspiciously White, male, dominant-culture, Christian God; AA forces people to constantly degrade themselves by introducing themselves as alcoholic; and AA meetings are undependable because they are run by nonprofessionals.

Because a lack of information and understanding is the most important factor in low referrals to self-help groups (L. F. Kurtz & Chambon, 1987), these criticisms require examination. What follows is an attempt to increase understanding of the AA program, with an aim of avoiding the pitfalls of what John Wallace (1983) calls the unwary translator of AA, who "may find himself banging away at the concrete rather than flowing with the analogy" (p. 301).

FRAMING AA AS A NARRATIVE COMMUNITY

Professional service providers, who live with concepts of treatment, clients, and service models, often understand AA as an alternative treatment model. This understanding, according to Rappaport (1993), is limited for gaining insight into what AA means to those who join. For a different understanding, he proposes to reframe the meaning of AA (and other mutual-help groups) in terms of a narrative perspective:

> In its simplest form, the narrative approach means understanding life to be experienced as a constructed story. The stories that people tell and are told are powerful forms of communication to both others and one's self. Stories order experience, give coherence and meaning to events, and provide a sense of history and of the future. (p. 240)

The stories are told in community, and these communities have powerful narratives about change, about themselves, and about their members. In this sense, AA can be seen as a "normative structure in social experience" (Rappaport, 1993, p. 246). It is a "normative structure" because it is more comparable to other voluntary associations of people "living lives," such as religious organizations, professional organizations, political parties, and even families, than it is to a social service agency setting where clients come to receive services from professional helpers. In the narrative framework, people joining AA are not help-seekers, in search of treatment, but storytellers, who through telling and listening transform their lives. Personal stories become the narratives that define a "caring and sharing community of givers as well as receivers, with hope, and with a sense of their own capacity for positive change" (p. 245).

Consistent with postmodern thought, the narrative perspective embraces the idea that personal reality is itself constructed, as in a life story, and therefore has the capacity to be reconstructed throughout a person's life. In other words, as narrative therapists would say, "people make meaning, meaning is not made for us" (Monk, Winslade, Crocket, & Epston, 1997, p. 33). The AA community provides a safe harbor and a rich tradition of stories useful to reconstruct one's life story from that of a "hopeless alcoholic" to a person with "experience, strength, and hope." Hearing things in the stories of others can offer hope that your own life can change. For example, Smith (1993) cites this woman's experience in her early days in AA:

> A man I met told me that if I didn't think I belonged, I should hang around and I'd hear my story. Then a few weeks later, this girl got up and as she spoke, it started to dawn on me. I was so engrossed . . . every word she said I could relate to where I had come from. Here was this woman with seven or eight years in the program telling my story! (p. 696)

Smith (1993) elaborates on the process of individual integration into the "social world" of AA by describing how each step in the process of affiliation (attending meetings, sharing "experience, strength, and hope" in meetings, getting a sponsor, working the Twelve Steps of recovery, doing service work to help other alcoholics) enhances the person's comfort level in forming new relationships with others. It makes it possible for the individual to take some risks and experience small successes, it enhances self-esteem, and it leads to further commitment to the community. Understanding AA in a narrative framework where people tell stories about their lives within a community implies a conceptual shift from a rational (service delivery) model to a metaphorical (spiritual) understanding.

Michael White (2000), codeveloper of narrative therapy, sees the principal metaphor in AA as a "right of passage" and believes that "the originators of Alcoholics Anonymous had great vision, and a profound understanding of the significance of rites of passage" (p. 31). According to White,

> The center of AA is a ritual event that provides for a formalization of the stages of separation and reincorporation and for a marking of the turning points of persons' lives. This is accompanied by the convening of forums that provide the opportunity for persons to give testimony to the decisions they have made to break from excessive alcohol consumption, to the desires and purposes that motivate these decisions, and to tell and retell the stories of their lives before a group of witnesses, many of whom are veterans of such journeys. (p. 31)

The metaphorical level is the framework for the following interpretations of the meanings of AA.

THE METAPHOR OF POWERLESSNESS: "GIVING IN IS THE GREATEST FORM OF CONTROL" This koan (a mental puzzle used by practicing Buddhists as meditation material to further enlightenment) was created by "solution-focused" therapists to assist a practicing Buddhist client translate the first step of AA to something that utilized her Buddhist beliefs (Berg & Miller, 1992, p. 5). It is also a good example of how the language of AA can be understood as metaphorical. A parallel metaphor more familiar to Christians might be "to gain your life you must first lose it."

Step One of the Twelve Steps of Alcoholics Anonymous, "We admitted we were powerless over alcohol—that our lives had become unmanageable," is the cornerstone of recovery for alcoholics trying to get well through the AA program (AA, 2001; Chappel, 1992; Covington, 1994; E. Kurtz, 1979). However, from a rational purview, it is also the stumbling block for many professionals who are concerned that AA pushes "powerlessness" on persons who are already powerless in the dominant culture. Wetzel (1991) voices these concerns regarding women: "The Twelve-Step program reinforces one's belief in one's powerlessness and the necessity to relinquish the self to a 'higher power' (something most women have been doing all their lives in a secular sense)" (p. 23).

For the nonaddicted to make sense of Step One, it is helpful to try and stand inside the circle of addiction and look around at the miserable state of affairs most women and men face when they first begin the road to recovery. The lived experience of the alcoholic is like the woman who said, "I was on an endless cycle of 'I'll do better tomorrow' and of course I was always drunk again by 9 o'clock that night" (Davis, 1996, p. 152). A study of recovering alcoholics attending AA (DeSoto, O'Donnell, & DeSoto, 1989) revealed an extremely high rate of psychological distress (measured by the SCL-90) in the first 3 months of recovery, comparable to psychiatric inpatients. The authors comment: "With a life situation in disarray, suffering a protracted withdrawal syndrome, and experiencing cognitive deficits, it is a challenge indeed for an alcoholic to abstain from the drug that promises at least temporary relief" (p. 697).

The hard fact of being out of control with the addiction, no matter what you try to do, and having your life in shambles all around you roughly translates to the understanding of "powerlessness" that is the starting point in the AA program. AA invites people who declare themselves eligible to survey their world and to embrace the idea of Step One: "I am powerless *over alcohol*, and my life has become unmanageable" (AA, 2001, p. 59). In other words, Step One says: Face the reality and give up the illusion that you are in control of your use of alcohol. If people have doubts about their status, The Big Book suggests that they figure it out for themselves, experientially:

> Step over to the nearest barroom and try some controlled drinking. Try to drink and stop abruptly. Try it more than once. It will not take long for you to decide, if you are honest about it. It may be worth a bad case of the jitters if you get a full knowledge of your condition. (AA, 2001, pp. 31–32)

The organization invites those who have "lost the power of choice in drink" and have "a desire to stop drinking" to join the fellowship (AA, 2001, pp. 24, 562). Accepting the metaphor of powerlessness, thereby accepting individual limitations, goes against the dominant Western cultural message of "pulling yourself up by the bootstraps," independence, competition, and will power. Bateson (1972) suggests that AA provides a paradoxical metaphor much like the title koan at the beginning of this section in that "the experience of defeat not only serves to convince the alcoholic that change is necessary; it *is* the first step in that change . . . to be defeated by the bottle and to know it is the first 'spiritual' experience" (p. 313). Herndon (2001) puts this paradox in the context of the Buddhist tradition of "having and turning loose" (p. 10).

The AA notion of powerlessness in the context of such group narratives transforms the competitive stance with others (who have tried to force them to stop drinking) into a complementary relationship with other alcoholics who are in the same boat, in the same meeting, and weaving and sharing similar stories of "experience, strength, and hope." Therefore, powerlessness in this context is a metaphor of connectedness, not isolation. It is a good example of the power of the "narrative community" to transform lives by reauthoring one's alcoholic experience. Stephanie Brown (1994) calls this a "power from within model" instead of a "power over" model (p. 26). An alternative understanding is what Riessman (1985) calls "self-help induced empowerment." He states that "when people join together with others who have similar problems to deal with those problems . . . they feel empowered; they are able to control some aspect of their lives. The help is not given to them from the outside, from an expert, a professional, a politician" (p. 2). This is very different from the meanings of powerlessness associated with contemporary social and behavioral sciences, such as alienation, anomie, victimization, oppression, discrimination, and poverty (Borkman, 1989). Understanding this alternative meaning of powerlessness is helpful in resisting the temptation to oversimplify and interpret AA language in terms of social science terminology instead of the language of transformation.

THE METAPHOR OF DISEASE: "ALCOHOLISM IS A THREEFOLD DISEASE—MENTAL, PHYSICAL, AND SPIRITUAL"   AA is often criticized for its support and promulgation of the "disease concept" of alcoholism (Rhodes & Johnson, 1994; Riordan & Walsh, 1994), especially by some clinicians who adhere to the "strengths perspective." These two concepts have been presented as competing metaphors wherein the disease concept is negatively described as emphasizing the pathological, not the healthy, where physicians and clinicians assume the expert role, clients are passive and not responsible for their predicament, and recovery goals are designed and directed by treatment staff. On the other side, the strengths perspective is optimistically portrayed as emphasizing wellness and nonhierarchical and collaborative helping relationships, and recovery goals are co-constructed by facilitators and clients (Rapp & Goscha, 2006; Saleebey, 2006).

Although these comparisons may not do justice to either metaphor, the discourse continues to be fueled by current interest in collaborative models of helping (feminist, narrative, solution-focused, motivational interviewing) and perhaps a desire to set these models apart as different from the medical model of helping. Further complications that obscure the issue of alcoholism as disease include a general inability to agree on just what "alcoholism" is, to have consensus on just what constitutes "disease," or to agree on a single theory that adequately describes the etiology of alcoholism (McNeece & DiNitto, 2005). The disease concept, although still controversial among researchers and treatment professionals, has provided a means of diagnosing and expanding the treatment (and funding of treatment and research) of alcoholism and done a great service in relieving the burden of guilt from both alcoholics and their family members (Burman, 1994).

In theory, the AA program leaves the debate to the professionals; it simply treats the controversy of alcoholism as disease as an "outside issue," following the principle of the Tenth Tradition of AA, which states, "Alcoholics Anonymous has no opinions on outside issues; hence the AA name ought never to be drawn into public controversy" (AA, 2001, p. 562). Although "The Big Book" of Alcoholics Anonymous, the suggested guide to the program, avoids the term "disease," it does use the terms "malady," "illness," and "allergy" to suggest the hopelessness of the condition of active alcoholism. E. Kurtz's (1979) historical analysis states that Bill Wilson (the cofounder of AA) "always remained wary of referring to alcoholism as a 'disease' because he wished to avoid the medical controversy over the existence or nonexistence of a specific 'disease-entity'" (p. 22). It is somewhat ironic that in many current versions of the controversy, AA is linked firmly to the promulgation of the "disease concept" (e.g., Burman, 1994; Rhodes & Johnson, 1994).

However, as E. Kurtz (1979) suggests, "the Alcoholics Anonymous understanding of alcoholism begs for exploration within the insight that disease can also be metaphor" (p. 200). He reminds us that disease as metaphor has been prevalent throughout history, beginning in antiquity with leprosy as "sin," to the Great Plague of decaying Europe, to the "white death" of tuberculosis in the slums of the industrial cities, and to the malignancy of cancer in the postmodern era of uncontrolled growth and greed. "Alcoholism," or any number of "addictions," is perhaps the metaphor for modern-day separation and despair.

Many individual members of AA look upon "alcoholism" as a threefold "disease" involving spiritual, mental, and physical factors. This implies a unity of life, a holistic frame familiar to adherents of Native American traditions, Christian creationist philosophy, and Buddhist meditations, among others. Modern isolation and disconnectedness can be understood as arising from a foolish and doomed attempt to separate these unified parts of the whole person. To be fully human (and in the case of the alcoholic, to want to live sober), the physical, mental, and especially spiritual parts must be integrated. AA members attempt to live out this metaphor on a practical level by working on a spiritual program that attends to the physical, mental, and spiritual needs of the alcoholic who still suffers.

THE METAPHORS OF DEPENDENCE, INDEPENDENCE, AND INTERDEPENDENCE   Another major criticism of AA is that it promotes dependence in the alcoholic by providing a substitute addiction or a "crutch" (Chappel & DuPont, 1999; Wallant, 1995). This is assumed to be bad because it goes against the modern idea that the cure for dependence is absolute and total independence (E. Kurtz, 1979). Inherent in the metaphor of the dominant culture is the notion of "do it yourself," or self-reliance. In contrast, the Alcoholics Anonymous approach to extreme dependence (alcoholism) is to embrace the metaphor of connectedness. That is, we, as humans, are limited and dependent on other humans. Connecting with others through the fellowship of meetings, sponsors, and AA-sponsored events is perceived as a way to help strengthen one's identity, not shrink it. As one woman expressed this feeling, "By the end of the meeting I knew I was at home. I belonged there. Someone told their story and more than anything I felt connected to people again that I hadn't done in so long" (Lundy, 1985, p. 137). According to Van Den Bergh (1991), the possibility of human connection may explain some of the increase in participation in Twelve-Step groups today:

> Patriarchy engenders isolation and anomie; recovery groups provide an antidote to the pain and angst of believing one is alone. Individuals come together to share their "experience, strength, and hope"; through that process a feeling of personal empowerment as well as community affiliation is experienced. (p. 27)

It may be helpful to note that the same criticisms about "creating dependence" are also aimed at psychotherapy, welfare assistance, certain religious communities, mothers, or any other entity that may offer a port in the storm of life. In spite of the dominant cultural suspicion that there is "something undesirable about all dependence" (Riordin & Walsh, 1994, p. 352), levels of dependence usually shift naturally as a person becomes more stable. Chappel and DuPont (1999) suggest that in the early stages of recovery after detox, every alcoholic or drug addict needs a healthy "substitute dependence" and, left to him- or herself, may choose another high-risk behavior, such as gambling, spending, sex, or eating. AA offers a way to begin the development of healthier patterns.

In AA, newcomers may spend entire days in meeting after meeting, and it is routinely suggested that they attend "90 meetings in 90 days." As the length of sobriety and stability increases, participation generally shifts to helping others (making coffee, chairing meetings, sponsoring others). Many "old-timers" with years of sobriety continue participation to provide sponsorship and support for newcomers and because they depend on AA meetings to help them maintain their spiritual program, not just their sobriety. According to the AA 2004 membership survey, members attended an average of two meetings a week. Independence, in the American sense of "doing it alone," is not the goal; instead, the individual (isolated by alcoholism and an array of negative social consequences) is taught in small steps how to depend on others and how to allow others to depend on him or her.

THE REALITIES OF ABSTINENCE: ONE DAY AT A TIME The basic text of *Alcoholics Anonymous (2001)* suggests that "for those who are unable to drink moderately the question is how to stop altogether. . . . We are assuming, of course, that the reader desires to stop" (p. 34). As discussed earlier, the need for self-assessment, and the belief that underneath it all alcoholics want to stop drinking precisely because their own experience and numerous experiments tell them they can no longer control it once they start, is a fundamental concept of the AA program.

However, abstinence (if it means "never drink again") was considered too unrealistic, too absolute, and perhaps too frightening to the alcoholics who created the AA program. Instead, they developed the idea of limited control—that is, not drinking "one day at a time" instead of forever. According to E. Kurtz (1979), this message serves both to "protect against grandiosity and to affirm the sense of individual worthwhileness so especially important to the drinking alcoholic mired in self-hatred over his failure to achieve absolute control over his drinking" (p. 105). The concept of limited control and the embracing of human fallibility are other examples of how the AA program stands apart from our dominant culture's obsessive drive for perfection. Several AA slogans underscore the concept of limited control: "Progress not perfection," "Easy does it," and "One day at a time." Recovery is seen as an ongoing process, more in tune with the feminist principle of emphasizing "process not product" (Van Den Bergh, 1991).

In the addiction field, programs or research that suggest an alcoholic can return to "controlled drinking" are seen as diametrically opposed to the AA premise of stopping drinking (McNeece & DiNitto, 2005; Riordin & Walsh, 1994). On one level of meaning, it is not surprising that the idea of teaching an alcoholic controlled drinking strikes the AA member as absurd because in AA the alcoholic is *self-defined* as a person who cannot control her or his drinking. For those who can control it (through whatever means), the message is, "Our hats are off to him" (AA, 2001, p. 31). On another level of meaning, focusing on controlling drinking misses the point. In AA, the alcoholic who has lost control does not just have a bad habit and does not just need to stop drinking. That is only the first step in eliminating an "alcoholic" lifestyle based on self-centeredness, immaturity, and spiritual bankruptcy (Flores, 1988; E. Kurtz, 1979). As discussed earlier, the alcoholic is viewed as having a threefold problem involving mental, spiritual, and physical suffering. In AA, eliminating drinking is only the first step, although it is both necessary and essential, to begin the process of recovery.

THE METAPHOR OF HIGHER POWER: "IT'S MY SOUL-SELF" Lamb of God, Ancient Thing, Buddha, Yahweh, Love, Truth, Oneness, the Light, Mother God, Mother Nature, God, the Thursday evening "Insanity to Serenity" AA meeting, the Friday at 7 A.M., "Eye-openers" meeting: All of these and many other versions may describe an AA member's Higher Power. The encouragement to choose the nature of this power is a freedom that underlies the spiritual nature of the AA program and distinguishes it from an organized religious program. The emphasis is not on what kind of Higher Power is embraced but that the idea of human limitations and "a power greater than ourselves" is accepted. For atheists, Bill Wilson recommended that the Higher Power be the AA group they were attending: "When they come in, most of their AA group is sober, and they are drunk. Therefore, the group is a 'Higher Power.' That's a good enough start, and most of them do progress from there. I know how they feel because I was once that way myself" (Bill W., 1967, p. 226).

For some, the Higher Power is located *within* the self. For example, in Covington (1994), Maureen describes how important it was to let go of the "ego" on the outside and seek the "bigger self" inside:

> Developing a sense of self is critical to my well-being. . . . There is a power in me that's greater than the small self I've been accustomed to; it's larger than the way I've been trained to think about who I am. It's my soul-self. In cooperating with it, I surrender to a part of me that carries wisdom and truth. It brings me back into harmony and balance with myself—that's what spirituality is for me. (p. 35)

Step Two, "Came to believe that a Power greater than ourselves could restore us to sanity," and Step Three, "Made a decision to turn our will and our lives over to the care of God as we understand Him" (AA, 2001, p. 59), are the spiritual cornerstones of the AA program. These two steps suggest that alcoholics connect with the healing energy (grace, Godness) of the world and/or within themselves and become receptive to spiritual guidance, whether that source be the wisdom of their AA group on staying sober or some other version of a "Power greater than themselves."

A literal reading of the first three steps has been interpreted by some feminists (Kasl, 1992) as sacrificing and martyring oneself for the sake of others, notably males. However, as Clemmons (1991) notes, the Third Step "does not promote this kind of detrimental repression, but it does suggest that we must be willing to let go of people and situations outside of our control. . . . 'Letting go' halts the alcoholic/addict's efforts to control the uncontrollable and focuses on developing and listening to the true self" (p. 104). That is, power is seen not in relational terms with other people but vis-à-vis the addiction. The power of the alcohol, or the "small self" as Maureen put it, is "let go" through the shift of accepting a Higher Power.

AA is fundamentally a spiritual program that promotes the ability of an individual to live a meaningful life (Galanter, 2006). Many clinicians have difficulty with this position; as a counseling profession, we have historically focused rationally on the temporal conditions of our clients and their environment, excluding the spiritual. In addition, Galanter (1999) points out that most psychiatrists (56%) don't believe in God or a Higher Power themselves, in contrast to the 94% of Americans who do. He cites an interesting study on medical students who were treating indigent, hospitalized addicts. The addicts ranked spirituality and belief in God as the most important components of their recovery; the medical students considered these factors the least important. In that mindset, it is easy to construe AA's concept of Higher Power as religion and the metaphor of "letting go" of "those things we cannot change" as passive dependence.

STORYTELLING AS METAPHOR: "HI, MY NAME IS JACKIE AND I'M AN ALCOHOLIC"   Many observers of AA fail to grasp the complex and metaphorical meanings of common terms and practices as they are used by AA members (Davis & Jansen, 1998). Wallace (1983) notes that "the extended meanings that characterize the AA language system will continue to elude external observers who remain at literal, concrete levels of analysis and fail to consider the nature of symbolic communication and the purposes it serves in complex social contexts and transactions" (p. 302). For example, it is common practice (but not required) to introduce oneself in AA meetings with your name, followed by "and I'm an alcoholic." This greeting has been interpreted by some critics as a counter-therapeutic reinforcement of a negative label, but as Smith (1993) points out, "It is understood by AA members that the word takes on a different and positive meaning in the context of AA" (p. 702). Using Wallace's (1983) idea of illustrating how a common AA slogan can have various meanings depending on the context, the meaning of the "I'm Joe and I'm an alcoholic" greeting in the context of an AA meeting could be any or all or none of the following (Davis & Jansen, 1998):

1. I have faced the reality that I am alcohol dependent and I want to quit drinking. Harm reduction strategies have not worked for me and I cannot control my drinking.
2. I have suffered and caused others to suffer, just like you.
3. I don't buy in to the shame attached to this label by the outside world.
4. Even though I am an alcoholic and my natural state would be to be drinking, I'm sober today and participating in this meeting to help my mental, spiritual, and physical recovery.
5. Even though I'm not drinking today, there is a part of me that is immature and self-centered, spiritually bankrupt, egotistical, superficial—that is, an "alcoholic personality" that sometimes operates in the world in a "drunk mode" or "dry drunk." I claim this part, instead of trying to hide my problems in living under a superficial sheen of perfection.
6. I'm grateful to be an alcoholic because having this condition put me on a spiritual path that I never would have found otherwise.
7. I'm not unique, better than, worse off, or any different from any of the rest of you in this meeting. We are here to confront a common problem and to help each other. (p. 178)

These possibilities are extended meanings that can occur within the context of a particular meeting and that are dependent on the circumstances and histories of individuals who are introducing themselves. Central to the meanings of AA phrases and language is a redefinition of the experience of being an alcoholic. A "practicing alcoholic" (one that is currently drinking) may be better understood in AA as practicing a flawed way of life, dominated by self-centeredness, superficiality with others, and spiritual bankruptcy. The personal stories told in AA, "what we used to be like, what happened, and what we are like now" (AA, 2001, p. 58), are vehicles for making sense of the chaos of the typical alcoholic's life by redefining it within this logic. As Marion describes the process in Maracle (1989):

> The more I went to meetings, the more I heard what other people said, I'd come home and think about it. I'd reflect on my own life, far back, up close, when I started drinking, what happened, how much of my life was related to alcohol, drinking. That's how I began to connect the depression and the drinking. I began to connect information, to put pieces together. I'd really *listen* at meetings. *Hear* what people said. And think about it all. And about me. I got real serious about trying to understand. (p. 154)

Thune's (1977) analysis of AA from a phenomenological perspective argues that it is precisely *because* AA members are taught to reinterpret their alcoholic life story as spiritually bankrupt that they can give meaning to a past filled with degradation and chaos and can have hope for the creation of a different future. Thus, the AA approach to recovery, which aims for a trans-formed life based on spiritual principles instead of "alcoholic" strategies, is quite different from approaching alcoholism as merely a disease or a bad habit to be reformed. The deeply individual piece of transformation, within the context of the narrative community, transcends the dichotomies of self–other and exemplifies the embedded interdependence of these communities.

WHOM DOES AA BENEFIT?

Researchers and clinicians would like to know more about who exactly would benefit the most from a Twelve-Step group like AA and who would be least likely to benefit. Unfortunately, there is no definitive answer to this important question. A major goal of Project MATCH was to predict which treatment approach would be more effective, given client characteristics. However, only 4 of 21 possible matches were detected, and one of these matches disappeared after 1 year (Fuller & Hiller-Sturmhofel, 1999). An earlier study by Montgomery et al. (1995) found that AA attendees, when compared with nonattendees, could not be distinguished by pretreatment patient characteristics and that there was no evidence of an "AA personal-ity." However, there continue to be concerns about whether AA is too "culture bound" with American, White, heterosexual, male dominance to be of any help to other groups, such as women, homosexuals, and people from different races and cultures. As one of the authors heard from a woman in an open AA meeting in Scotland, "I never thought I could identify with an American male stockbroker! [i.e., Bill W.]."

Women comprise a steadily increasing membership in Alcoholics Anony-mous. In 2004, women of all ages made up an estimated 35% of members compared with 30% in 1983 and 22% in 1968 (AA, 2004). However, many women in AA continue to react to the predominance of sexist language in the AA Big Book, which remains unchanged since the original edition (1939), "13th stepping" (soliciting more than friendship from vulnerable new members), and the tendency in some groups to be dominated by male chairpersons who call primarily on male members to share their stories. Consequently, in many medium-sized towns and certainly in larger cities, "women-only" groups have developed to alleviate some of this tension. Other women take a more direct approach:

> In my early days, I got white-out and took out all the "Gods" and "he's" in the Big Book. I wrote in the word "hope" for higher power and God. That was an essential change for me. I have told newcomers, if you object to the literature, don't read it. Or fix it. I wish they—AA—would fix it. (Hall, 1996, p. 127)

A Swedish study (Bodin, 2006) suggests that AA does appeal to women and that they participate to a greater degree than men. Women who attended AA reported more affiliation activities, such as calling on an AA member for help, experiencing a spiritual awakening, and reading AA literature.

There are also specialized meetings for a variety of groups, such as veterans, Hispanics, gays, lesbians, elders, and Native Americans. Sometimes, the principles of AA are blended with other cultural traditions to create a more effective approach. For example, the Wellbriety Movement in Native American communities combines the teachings of the medicine wheel with AA's Twelve Steps (Coyhis & Simonelli, 2005). Each step is placed at an appropriate place around the four directions of the medicine wheel: Steps 1 through 3 (honesty, hope, and faith) are grouped in the eastern part of the wheel and so on. However, not all problems can be solved by specialized groups or blending, as demonstrated by the different responses from lesbian women interviewed by Joanne Hall (1996). Some lesbian women felt perfectly comfortable in mainstream AA:

> "It's comforting for me to see people from all walks of life who have the same disease as me. It's not just a bunch of dykes, you know? I just need to see that sometimes." (p. 122)

> "AA is really great. All these people who are not like you are interested in keeping you sober. They call you—and you don't know why they wanna be around you, but they do anyway. I thought it was beautiful that these strangers that I had nothing in common with would call me and cared about me and would sit with me." (p. 123)

Others felt that the inclusion of culturally distinct persons in AA is superficial and that lesbian groups were important for identification:

> "The lesbian AA groups are so much more open-minded. . . . The straight AA groups I find are real traditionally AA. In lesbian meetings other things can come out, like talking about incest, or just about living the life of a lesbian." (p. 123)

Still others rejected lesbian meetings because AA mainstream values lacked prominence in the specialized meetings and because they feared being "engulfed, sexualized, or rejected by women who were 'just like me' when they attended these lesbian meetings" (p. 124).

Some commentators raise concerns that African Americans are less likely to associate with AA because it is culturally bound by middle-class White Americans. A cross-sectional study by Kaskutas, Weisner, Lee, and Humphries (1999) found that African Americans are about twice as likely as Whites to report having attended AA as part of treatment but that Whites are more likely to attend AA on their own. Although both groups are equally likely to actively engage in the program, they participate differently: African Americans were more likely to say they felt like a member of AA (64% vs. 54% of Whites) and had a spiritual awakening as a result of AA (38% vs. 37%), whereas Whites were more likely to have had a sponsor (23% vs. 14%) and to have read program literature (77% vs. 67%).

Project MATCH found no significant differences in the rates of AA attendance among African American, Hispanic, and White clients. Hispanic clients reported a higher level of AA involvement (e.g., working the Steps, having a sponsor, celebrating sobriety birthdays) than White clients (Tonigan, Connors, & Miller, 1998).

The spread of AA to 150 diverse countries and the publication of AA literature in at least eight languages would argue that AA's philosophy is flexible and broad enough that many different kinds of people can find a way to benefit. Because of Tradition Ten, "Alcoholics Anonymous has no opinion on outside issues; hence the AA name ought never be drawn into public controversy" (AA, 2001, p. 562), AA is not involved with any political organizations or social movements that might taint the single purpose of this organization, which is to "carry its message to the alcoholic who still suffers."

GAMBLERS ANONYMOUS

Gamblers Anonymous (GA) is a Twelve-Step mutual-help program of men and women "who share their experience, strength, and hope with each other that they may solve their common problem and help others to recover from a gambling problem" (Gamblers Anonymous, 2000, p. 2). The GA program acknowledges Alcoholics Anonymous (AA) as a guide and foundation and utilizes the same Twelve Steps of recovery and the same organizational principles. The only requirement for membership is "a desire to stop gambling" (p. 2); consequently, abstinence from gambling is a goal.

Like AA, GA is run entirely by recovering individuals, in this case compulsive gamblers, who volunteer their time to be sponsors, chair meetings, arrange for meeting places, secure GA literature, and respond to requests for help day and night. GA meetings are available in all 50 states and are accessible online. GA meetings can be found by calling your state problem gambling 1-800-Helpline, looking in the yellow pages of the phone book for a local contact number, or accessing the Gamblers Anonymous International Service

Office online site (http://gamblersanonymous.org). The number of GA chapters increased from 650 in 1990 to 1,328 in October 1998, which may indicate some impact from the rapid expansion of legalized gambling (National Gambling Impact Study Commission, 1999). There are GA meetings available in many different countries, including the United Kingdom, Japan, Spain, Uganda, Kenya, Israel, and Brazil.

Although GA is "probably the most popular intervention for pathological gambling" (Blanco, Ibanez, Saiz-Ruiz, Blanco-Jerez, & Nunes, 2000, p. 402), like its counterpart AA, it is not without critics. GA, like AA, is perceived by some as a White, male, middle-class organization that is not user friendly to women. Actually, people who do attend GA appear to have different characteristics than those gamblers who present for treatment with no history of GA attendance. Petry (2003) found in her comparative study of 342 pathological gamblers, where 54% had previously attended GA, that the GA attendees were older, less likely to be single, had higher incomes, more debts, more years of gambling, higher scores on the South Oaks Gambling Screen, and more family problems, but fewer drug problems. On an encouraging note, GA attendees were more likely to be abstinent after 2 months of treatment.

The historical dominance of men in GA may still be the case in some areas, but it appears the landscape is changing rapidly as more women seek help for gambling problems. For example, according to the Arizona Council on Compulsive Gambling (2000), even though GA started in that state in 1973,

> for the first 18 years, a few women walked through the doors... and left. By their own admission, the men didn't quite know what to do with them. The women were told they hadn't gambled long enough; they hadn't lost enough to be real gamblers. They didn't play real games. Their tears and their stories were ridiculed. They were "hit" on, "Let's go for coffee... at my place, baby." They didn't stay. The men said, "Women just don't seem to have what it takes to stay in recovery." (Arizona Council on Compulsive Gambling, 2000)

The year 1992 marked a change in Arizona, when one woman (Marilyn L.) started a "women preferred" GA meeting in her home. Although the meeting struggled in the beginning, by 1999 there were three "women preferred" meetings out of the 19 GA meetings in the Phoenix area. The Arizona council estimates that women now make up about 40% of GA meeting attendance.

Responses to an online survey of recovering women (Avery & Davis, in press); support the idea that "times are changing," but a gender barrier can still exist. Some women noted barriers: "When I came into GA in 1991, the men didn't think slot players were real gamblers," and "I'm a woman, so they ignored me the first three months." On the other hand, many of the women responding to the survey felt welcomed: "Although I was the only woman, I felt welcomed," "I did not feel alone," "They understood my problem as no one who is not a compulsive gambler ever will," "When I finally began attending regularly, I felt welcomed in every way... mostly, I felt that I belonged somewhere."

New GA members who have been longstanding members of AA sometimes have a problem adjusting to a different format, as this woman describes:

> When I first came to GA, I felt like they were doing everything wrong! Too much cross-talking, not enough emphasis on a spiritual recovery, way too many details about their gambling exploits, and on and on. Believe it or not, I found these constant criticisms became the perfect excuse for me to keep on gambling. After a while, I learned the hard way that I had to get out of my comfort zone of being "successful" in the AA context and really come to terms with being a very vulnerable new member of a different recovery program. That is, if I wanted to get the help that was offered. It was humbling. (personal communication, January 2007)

How well does GA work? Members of GA will readily admit that "attending GA ruins your gambling," but whether participating in meetings makes a significant impact on long-term abstinence is not known from the small number of research studies available (National Research Council, 1999). Like studies of AA, serious methodological problems arise from the voluntary, anonymous, self-selection of GA membership. One study (Stewart & Brown, 1988) indicates that total abstinence from gambling was reported by only 8% of the GA members studied 1 year after their first attendance and by only 7% after 2 years. On the other hand, Taber, McCormick, Russo, Adkins, and Ramirez (1987) found that attending GA was helpful in maintaining abstinence: 74% of the abstinent gamblers in their sample attended at least three GA meetings in the prior month compared with only 42% of those who continued to gamble. Petry (2005) found there is no evidence to definitively prove the effectiveness of GA because of the lack of rigor in the methodology of the few studies available (no random assignment). However, her review of the research does suggest that persons who attend GA are more likely to become involved in professional treatment, have a higher rate of abstinence after starting professional treatment, and have a higher rate of long-term abstinence. Clearly, more research, and research that is gender specific, is needed in this area.

OTHER TWELVE-STEP GROUPS

As already mentioned, there are numerous other Twelve-Step groups available to help with every possible addiction. Space requirements preclude describing every one of them. The Twelve Steps and Twelve Traditions of Alcoholics Anonymous have been translated to deal with many addictive problems. For example, in Narcotics Anonymous (NA), drug terminology is substituted for alcohol, in Cocaine Anonymous (CA), cocaine is substituted for alcohol, in Nicotine Anonymous (NA), nicotine is substituted for alcohol, and so on.

NA was started in the 1950s when polyaddiction became more common and some "pure alcoholics" in AA were uncomfortable when discussion often included more than just alcohol. Similarly, Cocaine Anonymous emerged with the increased use of this drug and the differences in lifestyle, drug-seeking behaviors, and consequences of this drug. For more information on various

Twelve-Step groups that deal with specific types of addiction, the Internet is a bountiful resource.

OTHER MUTUAL-SUPPORT GROUPS

There are also a variety of other types of mutual-help groups that offer support for addictive behavior that are fundamentally different in philosophy and purpose from Twelve-Step groups. For example, the three groups we briefly describe as examples do not emphasize reliance on a "Higher Power" for recovery, do not offer sponsorship for new members, and do not expect members to attend for life. However, like AA, substantial empirical support for their effectiveness is lacking, they are self-supporting, and they offer meetings at no charge.

WOMEN FOR SOBRIETY (WFS)

Women for Sobriety (2000; see website at www.womenforsobriety.org) was founded by Jean Kirkpatrick, PhD, in 1976 to address the unique issues for women that might be barriers to their recovery, such as lack of self-esteem, depression, and overwhelming feelings of guilt. WFS sees alcoholism as a physical disorder, like diabetes. Kirkpatrick sees spirituality as a goal for recovery but stresses that WFS is not a "God-oriented program." She asks, "Do diabetics go to God-oriented meetings for their diabetes?"(Kirkpatrick, 2001, p. 2). Instead, the WFS meetings stress the "New Life" Program of Acceptance, which is based on Thirteen Statements. These include positive self-statements such as "Negative thoughts destroy only myself" and "The past is gone forever." (For a complete list, see www.womenforsobriety.org.) WFS recommends that women review these statements each morning, use one of them consciously all day, and review its effects at the end of the day.

Meetings are led by a certified moderator, a person with at least 1 year of sobriety and certified knowledge about WFS principles. Meetings are open to all women alcoholics and to those with prescription drug problems. According to Horvath (1997), in 1996 WFS had at least 300 meetings in 40 states and 50 meetings in other countries (primarily Canada, Australia, New Zealand, Ireland, and Finland). He cites two studies by Kaskutas (1994, 1995) that support the idea that women attending WFS find support, nurturance, and a safe environment for discussions of women's issues. However, another study of 115 women in AA or WFS (Talan, 1982) found no differences between groups on reaction to the groups, length of time attending, or treatment outcome.

SMART RECOVERY

SMART, which stands for Self Management and Recovery Training, is another alternative mutual-help group, started in 1992 as an offshoot of Rational Recovery (see website at www.smartrecovery.org). This approach is drawn from the principles of cognitive-behavioral therapy and particularly from rational emotive behavior therapy, as developed by Albert Ellis, PhD. Addiction is viewed more as a maladaptive behavior than a disease and could arise from both substance use (e.g., alcohol, nicotine, caffeine, food, illicit drugs, and prescribed medications) and involvement in activities (e.g., gambling, sexual behavior, eating, spending, relationships, and exercise). As stated on their website "Purposes and Methods," "We assume that there are degrees of addictive behavior, and that all individuals to some degree experience it."

SMART Recovery attempts to fill in the gap posed by the following questions, raised by Nick Rajacic, coordinator of the Keweenaw Area SMART Recovery Program (www.smartrecovery.org):

> Why can't people be encouraged and motivated to creatively seek their own solutions instead of looking for answers outside of themselves in the form of groups and Higher Powers? Why can't people just be taught effective skills to cope with the problems of living sober in a drug-using culture? Why can't they just be taught the cognitive-behavioral skills of emotional self-management? Why can't they develop new and rewarding lifestyles around interests other than recovery alone?

The program has two primary goals: (a) to help individuals gain independence from addictive behavior (through abstinence) and (b) to teach people how to enhance and maintain motivation to abstain, cope with urges, manage thoughts, feelings, and behavior, and balance momentary and enduring satisfactions. To accomplish this, cognitive-behavioral techniques, communication skills, anger management skills, and stress management techniques are incorporated into the meetings.

Meetings typically include discussions of the primary goals, activating events (urges, life happenings, or any other experiences that might lead to negative consequences), and analysis of the events using a cognitive approach. Personal homework projects are usually assigned to put ideas from the meetings into practice. Current meeting locations are listed, by states and contacts, on their website. There are approximately 260 different meetings in the United States and meetings in Canada, Australia, Scotland, and Sweden.

SMART meeting coordinators are volunteers, trained from literature available at the website, recommended readings, and regular consultation with a volunteer professional advisor who is typically a licensed professional with addiction training and experience. To date, no research studies of SMART have been published, but there is a clinical trial in progress.

Moderation Management (MM)

Moderation Management, as the name implies, is a mutual-help group dedicated to supporting individuals who have a desire to drink alcohol moderately (Kosok, 2006). Drinking problems are viewed as bad habits rather than a disease. MM is not intended for "those who experience significant withdrawal symptoms when they stop drinking, or those with any physical or mental condition, including pregnancy, that could be adversely affected by alcohol, even in moderate amounts. Also this association is not intended for former dependent drinkers who are now abstaining" (www.moderation.org). Rather, MM may be viewed as a prevention measure or a harm reduction strategy for persons who wish to drink moderately. Moderation is defined for males as no more than four drinks per day, no more than four drinking days per week, and no more than fourteen standard drinks per week; for females moderation is considered to be no more than three standard drinks per day, no more than four drinking days per week, and no more than nine drinks per week.

MM strategies include a voluntary abstention from alcohol for 30 days, during which the person is asked to examine how drinking has affected his or her life, write down priorities, and take a look at how much, how often, and under what circumstances drinking occurs. Moderate drinking levels are set using the MM guidelines, and the person is encouraged to try cognitive-behavioral techniques found in several recommended texts. MM recommends 6–18 months of weekly meetings, which are devoted to discussion of MM goals and activities since the last meeting.

MM was under fire in the press and from the National Council on Alcoholism and Drug Dependence (NCADD) because of the tragic experience of MM founder, Audrey Kishline (Verhovek, 2000). Mrs. Kishline pleaded guilty to two counts of vehicular homicide after a binge-drinking episode in March 2000 in which she drove in the wrong lane and caused a collision that killed two people.

Although Mrs. Kishline had resigned from MM the previous January, stating she had shifted her drinking goal to abstinence and attending AA, many who are abstinence-only proponents took the opportunity to hold up her experience as an example of "denial in action" and "the delusion behind the idea that alcoholics can be taught to drink without harm" (Verhovek, 2000, p. 1). The board of directors of MM counters this by reminding people that Mrs. Kishline adhered to the basic tenets of MM by shifting her goal to abstinence when she could not maintain moderate drinking. Like many members of AA and other support groups, she relapsed, which should not be blamed on AA or MM but should be seen as a personal tragedy (Moderation Management, 2000).

Current face-to-face meetings and chat rooms can be found on the MM website. To date, no empirically based studies of MM effectiveness have been published. Research has been conducted on the demographic characteristics of members, however. Kosok (2006) examined questionnaire responses from 272 MM members and determined that the growth of the organization was solely through the Internet. The majority of members are women, middle class, and highly educated, who do not have severe drinking problems. Since only a small minority of members were found in the survey to have received treatment previously, Kosok concludes that MM offers a viable treatment option that can reach an unserved population who otherwise would not have entered any program.

HOW TO SUPPORT CLIENT INVOLVEMENT IN MUTUAL-HELP GROUPS

In spite of the positive findings that mutual-help groups do help many people, some clinicians are reluctant to refer clients. To facilitate mutual-help participation, Caldwell (1999) recommends a strengths-based approach, in which clinicians focus on areas where clients feel comfortable with mutual-help groups or have needs, such as loneliness or isolation, that could be satisfied by mutual-help attendance. To accomplish that, clinicians need to find their own areas of comfort with mutual-help approaches.

However, as noted in Davis and Jansen (1998), the habits, practices, and context of professional counselors are likely to be very different from those in the mutual-help community. Getting comfortable with mutual-help groups may be more difficult because of professional adherence to a practice model of "regarding people as recipients of services" and the thought that "the alternatives available to them are viewed as treatments or programs" (Rappaport, 1993, p. 241). A recent study exploring the attitudes of substance abuse treatment staff in England found that fewer than half (46%) were likely to refer their clients to a self-help group (Day, Gaston, Furlong, Murali, & Copello, 2005). Further complications include the reality "always there and typically ignored," according to Riessman (1985, p. 2), that the help given by our professional practice is embedded in the context of paid services, whereas the help provided by mutual-aid groups such as AA is free of charge.

However, there appears to be some common ground on a metaphorical level. Both systems embrace empowerment, connectedness, interdependence, and most important, the principle that people can change, regardless of how oppressed they may find themselves in their circumstances. Readers are encouraged to discover their own meanings of the similarities and differences between their professional social work practice and the help offered by mutual-help groups by putting themselves in a position to experience firsthand the mutual-help community and the hope that it offers to many persons.

For many clinicians, it is helpful to attend at least one meeting of the mutual-help groups in your area. However, attending one "open" AA meeting may not be sufficient. Montgomery and colleagues (1995) found a wide variation in AA groups in terms of their social structure and characteristics, such as cohesiveness, aggressiveness, and expressiveness. If you are in a medium-sized or large city, you may find an array of options or types of meetings that appeal to groups such as men, women, gay men, lesbians, veterans, elders, smokers, and nonsmokers. As a visitor, you are invited to attend any meeting identified as "open." "Closed" meetings are reserved for those who have a desire to stop drinking.

For information regarding meeting times and schedules (which change frequently), consult the yellow pages of the phone book under "Alcoholism," the classified ads in the local newspaper, or the Alcoholics Anonymous website (www.alcoholics-anonymous.org). In larger towns, call the AA central office in your area (run by volunteers, not paid staff) to get the meeting schedule. In

Twelve-Step groups, visitors and newcomers may be asked to identify themselves by their first names only when they attend an open meeting. As members talk, they identify themselves by their first name only, not their profession, not their family name, and not where they live. The practice of anonymity is considered by many Twelve-Step members to be a spiritual foundation of recovery (AA, 2001). As a respectful visitor, it is critical to honor this tradition.

Suggestions from Chappel and DuPont (1999) for how psychiatrists can support clients in mutual-help programs include facilitating a meeting between the client and a temporary contact from the mutual-help group, working with the natural resistance and ambivalence that clients may have about attending meetings, helping dual-diagnosis clients understand AA's and NA's singleness of purpose, and getting comfortable with the spiritual dimensions of healing.

SUMMARY AND CONCLUSION

Much more could be said to describe the various methods and purposes of mutual help, but the purpose of this chapter was limited to introducing counselors to a way of understanding some of the primary features of several main mutual-help organizations. Alcoholics Anonymous, as practiced in the community, is the prototype of Twelve-Step mutual-help organizations, such as Narcotics Anonymous, Nicotine Anonymous, and Gamblers Anonymous. This organization is seen as a narrative community where identity transformation takes place through the telling of stories and the identification of personal meanings of metaphors. Spirituality is central to the healing process in Twelve-Step communities.

In contrast, Women for Sobriety, SMART Recovery, and Moderation Management do not require a spiritual orientation. WFS and SMART are both abstinence-based programs; MM is designed to help problem drinkers drink moderately. All of these programs and many more can be accessed through the Internet, and most have online meetings and chat rooms.

At a minimum, the members of these mutual-help programs can offer acceptance on a deep level to persons who have been isolated and shamed by their circumstances and can affirm the hope that one can recover. For these reasons alone, a referral, with some preparation as to how the meetings are conducted, how to find the meetings, and a brief summary of the meeting format, should be considered.

REFERENCES

Alcoholics Anonymous. (1955). *Alcoholics Anonymous: The story of how many thousands of men and women have recovered from alcoholism* (2nd ed.). New York: Alcoholics Anonymous World Services.

Alcoholics Anonymous. (2001). *Alcoholics Anonymous: The story of how many thousands of men and women have recovered from alcoholism* (4th ed.). New York: Alcoholics Anonymous World Services.

Alcoholics Anonymous. (2004). *Alcoholics Anonymous membership survey*. New York: Alcoholics Anonymous World Services.

Alcoholics Anonymous website. (2006). Retrieved from http://www.alcoholics-anonymous.org.

Alford, G. S., Koehler, R. A., & Leonard, J. (1991). Alcoholics Anonymous–Narcotics Anonymous model in patient treatment of chemically dependent adolescents: A 2-year outcome study. *Journal of Studies on Alcohol, 52*(2), 118–126.

Arizona Council on Compulsive Gambling. (2000). Women and recovery in Arizona: A brief history. Retrieved from http://www.azccg.org.

Avery, L., & Davis, D. (in press). Women's recovery from compulsive gambling: Results of an online survey. *Journal of Social Work Practice in the Addictions.*

Bateson, G. (1972). *Steps to an ecology of mind*. New York: Ballantine Books.

Berg, I., & Miller, S. (1992). *Working with the problem drinker: A solution-focused approach*. New York: Norton.

Bill W. (1967). *As Bill sees it*. New York: Alcoholics Anonymous World Services.

Blackman, S., Simone, R., & Thoms, D. (1989). The Gamblers Treatment Clinic of St. Vincent's North Richmond Community Mental Health Center: Characteristics of the clients and outcome of treatment. *International Journal of Addictions, 24*, 29–37.

Blanco, C., Ibanez, A., Saiz-Ruiz, J., Blanco-Jerez, C., & Nunes, E. (2000). Epidemiology, pathophysiology and treatment of pathological gambling. *CNS Drugs, 13*(6), 397–407.

Bodin, M. (2006). Gender aspects of affiliation with Alcoholics Anonymous after treatment. *Contemporary Drug Problems, 33*(1), 123–141.

Borkman, T. (1989, Spring). Alcoholics Anonymous: The stories. *Social Policy*, pp. 58–63.

Borkman, R. (2006). Sharing experience, conveying hope: Egalitarian relations as the essential method of Alcoholics Anonymous. *Nonprofit Management and Leadership, 17*(2), 145–152.

Brown, S. (1994). Alcoholics Anonymous: An interpretation of its spiritual foundation. *Behavioral Health Management, 14*(1), 25–27.

Burman, S. (1994). The disease concept of alcoholism: Its impact on women's treatment. *Journal of Substance Abuse Treatment, 11*(2), 121–126.

Chappel, J. N. (1993). Long-term recovery from alcoholism. *Recent Advances in Addictive Disorders, 16*(1), 177–187.

Chappel, J. N., & DuPont, R. L. (1999). Twelve-Step and mutual-help programs for addictive disorders. *Addictive Disorders, 22*(2), 425–447.

Clemmons, P. (1991). Feminists, spirituality, and the Twelve Steps of Alcoholics Anonymous. *Women and Therapy, 11*(2), 97–109.

Covington, S. S. (1994). *A woman's way through the Twelve Steps*. Center City, MN: Hazelden.

Coyhis, D., & Simonelli, R. (2005). Rebuilding Native American communities. *Child Welfare, 84*(2), 323–337.

Davis, D. (1996). Women healing from alcoholism: A qualitative study. *Contemporary Drug Problems, 24*, 147–177.

Davis, D., & Jansen, G. (1998). Making meaning of Alcoholics Anonymous for social workers: Myths, metaphors and realities. *Social Work, 43*(2), 169–182.

Day, E., Gaston, R., Furlong, E., Murali, V., & Copello, A. (2005). United Kingdom substance misuse treatment workers' attitudes toward 12-Step self-help groups. *Journal of Substance Abuse Treatment, 29*(4), 321–327.

DeSoto, C. B., O'Donnel, W. E., & DeSoto, J. L. (1989). Long-term recovery in alcoholics. *Alcoholism: Clinical & Experimental Research, 13*(5), 693–697.

Emrick, C. D. (1987). Alcoholics Anonymous: Affiliation processes and effectiveness as treatment. *Alcoholism: Clinical & Experimental Research, 11*(5), 416–423.

Epstein, J., & Sardiello, R. (1990). The Wharf Rats: A preliminary examination of Alcoholics Anonymous and the Grateful Deadhead phenomena. *Deviant Behavior, 11,* 245–257.

Finfgeld, D. (2002). Feminist spirituality and alcohol treatment. *Journal of Holistic Nursing, 20*(2), 113–127.

Fisher, G. L., & Harrison, T. C. (2005). *Substance abuse: Information for school counselors, social workers, therapists, and counselors* (3rd ed.). Boston: Allyn & Bacon.

Flores, F. J. (1988). *Group therapy with addicted populations.* New York: Haworth.

Fuller, R., & Hiller-Sturmhofel, S. (1999). Alcoholism treatment in the United States: An overview. *Alcohol, Research, and Health, 23*(2), 69–77.

Galaif, E. R., & Sussman, S. (1995). For whom does Alcoholics Anonymous work? *International Journal of the Addictions, 30*(2), 161–184.

Galanter, M. (1999). Research on spirituality and Alcoholics Anonymous. *Alcoholism: Clinical & Experimental Research, 23,* 716–719.

Galanter, M. (2006). Spirituality in Alcoholics Anonymous: A valuable adjunct to psychiatric services. *Psychiatric Services, 57*(3), 307–314.

Gamblers Anonymous. (2000). *Gamblers Anonymous: A new beginning* (4th ed.). Los Angeles: Author.

Gossop, M., Harris, J., Best, D., Man, L., Manning, V., Marshall, J., et al. (2003). Is attendance at Alcoholics Anonymous meetings after inpatient treatment related to improved outcomes? A 6 month follow-up study. *Alcohol and Alcoholism: International Journal of the Medical Council on Alcoholism, 38*(5), 421–426.

Hall, J. (1996). Lesbians' participation in Alcoholics Anonymous: Experiences of social, personal, and political tensions. *Contemporary Drug Problems, 23,* 113–139.

Harvard Mental Health Letter. (1996). *Treatment of alcoholism, Part II, 13*(3), 1–5.

Herndon, S. (2001). The paradox of powerlessness: Gender, sex, and power in 12-Step groups. *Women and Language, 24*(2), 7–13.

Horvath, A. (1997). Alternative support groups. In J. Lowinson, P. Ruiz, R. Millman, & J. Langrod (Eds.), *Substance abuse: A comprehensive textbook* (pp. 390–396). Baltimore: Williams & Wilkins.

Humphreys, K. (2003). *Circles of recovery: Self-help organizations for addictions.* Cambridge, England: Cambridge University Press.

Kaskutas, L. (1994). What do women get out of self-help? Their reasons for attending Women for Sobriety and Alcoholics Anonymous. *Journal of Substance Abuse Treatment, 11,* 185–195.

Kaskutas, L. (1995). *An analysis of "Women for Sobriety."* Unpublished doctoral dissertation, University of California, Berkeley.

Kaskutas, L., Weisner, C., Lee, M., & Humphries, K. (1999). Alcoholics Anonymous affiliation at treatment intake among White and Black Americans. *Journal of Studies on Alcohol, 60*(6), 810–817.

Kasl, C. D. (1992). *Many roads, one journey: Moving beyond the Twelve Steps.* New York: Harper Perennial.

Kessler, R., Mickelson, K., & Zhao, S. (1997). Patterns and correlates of self-help group membership in the United States. *Social Policy, 27,* 27–46.

Kirkpatrick, J. (2001). *Spirituality.* Retrieved from http://www.womenforsobriety.org/articles.

Kosok, A. (2006). The moderation management programme in 2004: What type of drinker seeks controlled drinking? *International Journal of Drug Policy, 17*(4), 295–303.

Kurtz, E. (1979). *Not-God: A history of Alcoholic Anonymous.* Center City, MN: Hazelden.

Kurtz, E. (1982). Why AA works. The intellectual significance of Alcoholics Anonymous. *Journal of Studies on Alcohol, 43,* 38–80.

Kurtz, L. F., & Chambon, A. (1987). Comparison of self-help groups for mental health. *Health and Social Work, 12,* 275–283.

Kurtz, L. F., & Fisher, M. (2003). Participation in community life by AA and NA members. *Contemporary Drug Problems, 30,* 875–904.

LaFave, L., & Echols, L. (1999). An argument for choice: Meeting the needs of chemically dependent women. *Journal of Substance Abuse Treatment, 16*(4), 345–352.

Lundy, C. (1985). *Social role enactment and the onset, maintenance and cessation of alcohol dependence in women.* Unpublished doctoral dissertation, Florida State University, Tallahassee.

Maracle, M. F. (1989). *Beyond abstinence: A study of recovery among women in Alcoholics Anonymous.* Unpublished doctoral dissertation, Washington University, St. Louis, MO.

McBride, J. L. (1991). Abstinence among members of Alcoholics Anonymous. *Alcoholism Treatment Quarterly, 8*(1), 113–121.

McLatchie, B. H., & Lomp, K. G. E. (1988). Alcoholics Anonymous affiliation and treatment outcome among a clinical sample of problem drinkers. *American Journal of Drug and Alcohol Abuse, 14,* 309–324.

McNeece, C., & DiNitto, D. (2005). *Chemical dependency: A systems approach* (3rd ed.). Boston: Allyn & Bacon.

Miller, W. R., & Hester, R. K. (1986). Matching problem drinkers with optimal treatments. In W. R. Miller & N. Heather (Eds.), *Treating addictive behaviors: Processes of change* (pp. 175–203). New York: Plenum Press.

Miller, W. R., Leckman, A. L., Delaney, H. D., & Tinkcorn, M. (1992). Long-term follow-up of behavioral self-control training. *Journal of Studies on Alcohol, 53,* 249–261.

Monk, G., Winslade, J., Crocket, K., & Epston, D. (1997). *Narrative therapy in practice: The archaeology of hope.* San Francisco: Jossey-Bass.

Montgomery, H. A., Miller, W. R., & Tonigan, J. S. (1995). Does Alcoholics Anonymous involvement predict treatment outcome? *Journal of Substance Abuse Treatment, 12*(4), 241–246.

Moos, R. H., & Moos, B. S. (2004). Long-term influence of duration and frequency of participation in Alcoholics Anonymous on individuals with alcohol use disorders. *Journal of Consulting and Clinical Psychology, 72*(1), 81–90.

Moos, R. H., & Moos, B. S. (2006). Participation in treatment and Alcoholics Anonymous: A 16 year follow-up of initially untreated individuals. *Journal of Clinical Psychology, 62*(6), 735–750.

National Gambling Impact Study Commission. (1999, June 18). *Report of the commission.* Washington, DC: U.S. Government Printing Office. Retrieved from http://govinfo.library.unt.edu/ngisc/reports/finrpt.html.

National Research Council. (1999, April 1). *Pathological gambling: A critical review.* Retrieved from http://www.nap.edu/books/0309065712/html/index.html.

Nelson-Zlupko, L., Kauffman, E., & Dore, M. (1995). Gender differences in drug addiction and treatment: Implications for social work intervention with substance-abusing women. *Social Work, 40*(1), 45–54.

Peele, S. (1992). Alcoholism, politics, and bureaucracy: The consensus against controlled-drinking therapy in America. *Addictive Behaviors, 17,* 49–62.

Petrucci, C., Kirk, S., & Reid, W. (2004). Computer technology and social work. In A. R. Roberts & K. R. Yeager (Eds.), *Evidence-based practice manual: Research and outcome measures in health and human services* (pp. 85–94). New York: Oxford University Press.

Petry, N. (2003). Patterns and correlates of Gamblers Anonymous attendance in pathological gamblers seeking treatment. *Addictive Behaviors, 28*(6), 1049–1062.

Petry, N. (2005). Gamblers Anonymous and cognitive-behavioral therapies for pathological gamblers. *Journal of Gambling Studies, 21*(1), 27–33.

Rapp, C. A., & Goscha, R. (2006). *The strengths model: Case management with people with psychiatric disabilities* (2nd ed.). New York: Oxford University Press.

Rappaport, J. (1993). Narrative studies, personal stories, and identity transformation in the mutual-help context. *Journal of Applied Behavioral Science, 29*(2), 239–256.

Rhodes, R., & Johnson, A. (1994). Women and alcoholism: A psychosocial approach. *Affilia, 9*, 145–156.

Riessman, F. (1985, Winter). New dimensions in self-help. *Social Policy*, pp. 2–4.

Riordan, R., & Walsh, L. (1994). Guidelines for professional referral to Alcoholics Anonymous and other Twelve Step Groups. *Journal of Counseling and Development, 72*, 351–355.

Ryan, D. (2003). The Christian recovery movement: A brief introduction. Retrieved February 2007 from http://www.nacroline.com/dox/library/daler/survey.shtml.

Saleebey, D. (Ed.). (2006). *The strengths perspective in social work practice* (4th ed.). Boston: Allyn & Bacon.

Smith, A. R. (1993). The social construction of group dependency in Alcoholics Anonymous. *Journal of Drug Issues, 23*(4), 689–704.

Snow, M. G., Prochaska, J. O., & Rossi, J. S. (1994). Processes of change in Alcoholics Anonymous: Maintenance factors in long-term sobriety. *Journal of Studies on Alcohol, 55*, 362–371.

Stewart, R., & Brown, R. (1988). An outcome study of Gamblers Anonymous. *British Journal of Psychiatry, 152*, 284–288.

Taber, J., McCormick, R., Russo, A., Adkins, B., & Ramirez, L. (1987). Follow-up of pathological gamblers after treatment. *American Journal of Psychiatry, 144*, 757–761.

Talan, B. (1982). *Power and control: Predictors for the alcoholic woman's choice and effectiveness of treatment.* Unpublished doctoral dissertation, University of Detroit, MI.

Thune, C. (1977). Alcoholism and the archetypal past: A phenomenological perspective on Alcoholics Anonymous. *Journal of Studies on Alcohol, 38*, 75–88.

Tonigan, J. S., Connors, G., & Miller, W. (1998). Special populations in Alcoholics Anonymous. *Alcohol, Health, & Research World, 22*(4), 281–285.

Tonigan, J. S., Connors, G. J., & Miller, W. R. (2003). Participation and involvement in Alcoholics Anonymous. In T. F. Babor & F. K. Del Boca (Eds.), *Treatment matching in alcoholism* (pp. 184–204). Cambridge, England: Cambridge University Press.

Tonigan, J. S., & Hiller-Sturmhofel, S. (1994). Alcoholics Anonymous: Who benefits? *Alcohol, Health, & Research World, 18*(4), 308–310.

Tonigan, J. S., Miller, W., & Connors, G. (2000). Project MATCH client impressions about Alcoholics Anonymous: Measurement issues and relationship to treatment outcome. *Alcoholism Treatment Quarterly, 18*(1), 25–41.

Van Den Bergh, N. (1991). *Feminist perspectives on addictions.* New York: Springer.

Verhovek, S. (2000, July 9). Advocate of moderation for heavy drinkers learns sobering lesson. *New York Times*, pp. 1, 10.

Wallace, J. (1983). Ideology, belief and behavior: Alcoholics Anonymous as a social movement. In E. Gottheil, K. Draley, T. Skolada, & H. Waxman (Eds.), *Etiologic aspects of alcohol and drug abuse* (pp. 285–305). Springfield, IL: Charles C Thomas.

Wallant, K. B. (1995). *Creating the capacity for attachment: Treating addictions and the alienated self.* Northvale, NJ: Jason Aronson.

Walsh, D. C., Hingson, R. W., Merrigan, D. M., Levenson, S. M., Cupples, L. A., Herren, T., et al. (1991). A randomized trial of treatment options for alcohol-abusing workers. *New England Journal of Medicine, 325*(11), 775–782.

Wetzel, J. W. (1991). Universal mental health classification systems: Reclaiming women's experience. *Affilia, 6*(3), 8–31.

White, M. (2000). *Reflections on narrative practice: Essays and interviews.* Adelaide, South Australia: Dulwich Centre.

Zelvin, E., & Davis, D. (2001). Harm reduction and abstinence-based recovery: A dialogue. *Journal of Social Work Practice in the Addictions, 1*(1), 121–135.

For over a hundred years, U.S. drug policy has been forged by symbolic politics and special interests, by moral entrepreneurs and media magnification, and by efforts of dominant groups to control "threatening" others from different races and lower classes.

—Craig Reinarman and Harry G. Levine (1997, p. 8)

PUBLIC POLICY

INTRODUCTION

The impact of public policies on the availability of resources, treatment methods, the extent to which addicts are penalized, jailed, and punished, and the shaping of public opinion has been emphasized throughout this text. In this chapter, we highlight several current social policies that affect one of the most important public health and social issues facing the United States—that is, how to deal effectively and compassionately with persons who are struggling with addiction and the consequences of addiction.

The authors take the position that the social context of drug use has helped create our drug problems. Instead of practicing harm reduction, many U.S. policies have created a context of "harm maximization" that only makes things worse, never better. This may partly be the result of what Reinarman and Levine (1997) call "pharmacological determinism"—that is, the practice in U.S. culture of treating illicit drugs like contagious diseases that are inherently and uniformly dangerous. In contrast, we endorse the more complicated idea that the social and legal setting and the cultural context within which they are used condition the use of alcohol, drugs, gambling, over- and undereating, or any addictive behavior. For example, in Britain, many heroin addicts have been found to function successfully in their work and lead normal lives, whereas in the United States, they would be incarcerated for possession of an illegal substance, would probably not have access to clean needles, and would be reduced to criminal behaviors to support their addiction. Drug policies, the social context of "zero tolerance," and exaggerated public fears have all shaped this outcome.

There are many alternatives to current policies that would be more compassionate, have more support from scientific evidence, and actually address the problems related to addiction. For example, we could simply have more treatment available, like the city of Baltimore. According to the *Washington*

521

Post, the number of drug-overdose deaths in that city is at the lowest level in 10 years because the funding for treatment in publicly supported clinics tripled (D. Brown, 2006). Across the nation, it was a different story. In 2005, the number of persons aged 12 or older needing treatment for an illicit drug or alcohol use problem was 23.2 million (9.5% of the population aged 12 or older). Of these, 2.3 million (10% of those who needed treatment) received treatment at a specialty facility. Thus, there were 20.9 million persons in the United States who needed treatment for an illicit drug or alcohol use problem but did not receive treatment at a specialty substance abuse facility in the past year (National Survey on Drug Use and Health, 2005).

In this chapter, we discuss many other alternatives to the current state of affairs, starting with the need to disengage from the polarized debate of "legalization versus criminalization," and find a middle way to move forward. In addition, we review recent welfare reforms that impact people with alcohol or drug problems, the results of the war on drugs policies, and briefly address the current lack of social policy and research funding in the area of compulsive gambling.

WELFARE REFORM

Recent welfare reforms are having direct and indirect effects on poor people who have alcohol or drug problems. Federal guidelines for Temporary Assistance for Needy Families (TANF) encourage states to deny cash assistance or food stamps to women with recent drug felony convictions. So far, 32 states have sought an exemption from this requirement or modified the requirements (Drug Policy Alliance, 2004). This legislation applies to males and females, but single mothers and women in public assistance prenatal clinics, who predominate in the welfare system, carry the brunt. The Bureau of Justice Statistics (BJS) estimates that approximately 61,000 women were convicted of felony drug offenses in state and federal courts in the United States during 1996 alone. Every decade between 1995 and 2005, the total number in custody of the federal system expanded by 7.4%; the rate for the entire decade was 72% (BJS, 2006). Of those women, 43% were convicted of drug possession, not sales. Hirsch's study (1999) in Pennsylvania of women with drug convictions who are affected by this provision found that the overwhelming majority of the women had no prior drug convictions and that their felony convictions are for very small quantities of drugs (often only $5 or $10 worth).

Other TANF regulations promote routine drug testing, and some states require abstinence contracts. This has resulted in a dramatic change from the old Aid to Families with Dependent Children (AFDC) system, where only 14% of the states even routinely asked applicants about their drug or alcohol use. Now welfare departments are forging stronger links to substance abuse treatment as a strategy to move recipients into the work force (Schmidt & McCarty, 2000). Since the 1996 welfare reform law, it has become clear that the time limit of benefits and the work requirement may reduce the number of low-income Americans with substance use problems who will receive even temporary financial aid. The prevalence of substance use among women who are TANF recipients is estimated at 8 to 20%; however, because of additional co-occurring problems such as mental health, housing, legal, and domestic violence, these women have consistently poorer employment outcomes (Morgenstern & Blanchard, 2006). A promising demonstration project, CASAWORKS for Families, found that intensive wraparound services in housing assistance, mental health treatment, medical treatment, and specialized substance abuse treatment for women led to significant decreases in substance use and increases in employment (Morgenstern et al., 2003).

Changes in other welfare programs that affect women and men equally include the 1997 removal of all disabilities that were due exclusively to alcohol or drug addiction from eligibility for federal Supplemental Security Income (SSI). General Assistance (GA) programs, which are considered by many the "last resort" for single men and women, have closed down on the local level across the United States, and nearly half of the recipients were single women (Schmidt & McCarty, 2000). Clearly, access to treatment services will be even less because of these new economic barriers.

New policies are needed to counteract the effects of diminished coverage for general health and treatment. Gresenz, Watkins, and Podus (1998) suggest that extending Medicaid eligibility to former SSI recipients would improve treatment access. They also encourage state and local governments to make public treatment available without extensive waiting periods and to assist dually diagnosed individuals in making new applications to SSI on the basis of their mental impairment.

POLICIES PERTAINING TO THE TREATMENT PROFESSION

MANAGED CARE

The substance abuse counseling profession, like any of the helping professions, is largely defined in terms of national laws, local and national fiscal reimbursement policies, and the availability of adequate healthcare resources. Specific laws protecting consumers' rights (e.g., the right to privacy) also have a bearing on how a profession operates. For addictions providers, legislative mandates provide treatment for certain populations (e.g., offenders on suspended prison sentences) but not for others. Such mandates shape the nature of addictions work in terms of the clientele served as well as the types of services rendered (e.g., total abstinence from alcohol and other drugs may be required for probationers).

Historically, addiction treatment has been marginalized rather than integrated with the rest of the healthcare system. Today, due to rapidly rising costs of general healthcare in the United States—costs related to the demand for expensive new technologies and the aging of the population—there is a strong impetus to cut costs in other directions. Working Americans who typically get their healthcare coverage from their place of work are being moved over from traditional health insurance to managed care plans. The purpose of managed care is not to manage care but to manage costs. Severe limits have been placed on mental health services and substance abuse treatment under these plans.

In its emphasis on cost containment, managed care has tended to place increasingly restrictive policies on inpatient detoxification treatment, limiting financial coverage for psychotherapeutic addiction treatment to only brief outpatient visits, and an emphasis on psychiatric medication instead of, rather than in addition to, individual therapy ("Managed Care Takes Toll," 1999). Managed care is not only a phenomenon in the private sector but a major force in Medicaid health reform proposals as well. Yet as data from national statewide studies show, every $1 of treatment saves at least $7 in other medical and social costs (Califano, 2001c).

Although many private, for-profit treatment centers, especially residential units, are closing their doors, there is a tremendous demand for services for the polydrug-addicted, often mentally ill, clients for whom treatment is mandated by the courts. New treatment programming models emphasize case management as well as networking with vocational rehabilitation services, family services, and probation and parole departments. One promising development, similar to the drug court movement, is the mental health court movement. This approach is designed to help mentally ill persons in trouble with the law stay out of jail by diverting them into treatment. The mental health court in Seattle is helping mentally ill clients (the term *defendant* is avoided) receive treatment for substance misuse problems as well as their mental disorders. Preliminary results are excellent (Parker, 2001).

The days of independent alcoholism treatment centers staffed by licensed alcoholism counselors are over. The "new" addictions therapist must be highly versatile and knowledgeable concerning the major mental disorders as well as the currently popular drugs of misuse and the treatment of persons with dual diagnoses. A strong background in psychology, mental health counseling, or clinical social work is recommended.

Federal funding for addiction treatment has fallen well below the need; the bulk of the money is diverted into the war on drugs, with billions put into military operations in Latin America alone. Across the states, however, the trends are more rational and cost saving; state after state is moving to fund community-based programs for youth and other prevention services. California has passed legislation sending all first-time drug offenders into intensive treatment. Some of the money, as in Iowa and Nebraska, comes from the national tobacco settlement funds and is appropriately being funneled into treatment.

THE LAW AND ETHICAL CODES

Respect for client confidence is not only an important aspect of the practitioners' code of ethics but also strictly regulated under federal law pertaining specifically to "alcohol and drug abuse patient records." The law pertaining to alcohol and drug abuse treatment is unique. Rules set forth in federal regulations, entitled "Confidentiality of Alcohol and Drug Abuse Patient Records" (2004), apply to all agencies that provide alcoholism and drug abuse treatment or prevention. The rules are far more stringent than for any other category of treatment. The general rule is no disclosure without the patient's consent. Even with consent, information that is harmful to the patient may not be released. A court subpoena can be honored only with the client's or former client's consent. Violation of the federal law and regulations by a practice or program is a crime. Exceptions to confidentiality restrictions are suspected child abuse or neglect, medical emergencies, information about a crime committed by a patient or about any threat to commit such a crime, and life-threatening situations.

Involuntary commitment proceedings are fraught with ethical and legal dilemmas. The purpose of the proceedings is to send an individual, for his or her "own good," to a jail-like facility for "treatment." This is usually a life-and-death situation, with the individual in question at risk of harm to himself, herself, or others. The first step for the counselor involved in such proceedings is to obtain the facts. Providing information to those outside the treatment program or requests for information from other sources generally require the client's written permission (McNeece & DiNitto, 2005). Such an authorization states the name of the agency, type of information requested, how the information will be used, the agency requesting the information, the date of the request, and the date on which the release expires (usually 6 months later). Requests should be obtained, ordinarily, from lawyers, all family members who may be involved with the client, and relevant agencies with which the client is in communication. Legal complications occur when the client, under proper legal advice, refuses to sign the Consent-for-Release-of-Information form. It becomes impossible under these circumstances to contact family members as witnesses or for input. Should the patient be committed based on medical evidence alone, further restrictions apply regarding communication with the state treatment facility. Treatment and hospital records may not be released to the treatment center, nor may the name of the patient be revealed before his or her arrival.

One legal issue of particular concern to addictions practitioners working with offenders was the ruling in the Seventh Circuit Court of Appeals in Wisconsin (*Kerr v. Farrey*, 1996). A prisoner's (Kerr's) First Amendment rights were violated, according to this ruling, because he was coerced into attending an NA program. Had Kerr not attended, he would have been transferred to a medium-security prison. Because the NA program was ruled to be religious, not secular, Kerr had a right to refuse treatment. Other court rulings at the U.S. district court level have enforced the same principle of separation of church and state. Significantly, as Alexander (2000) indicates, the lack of availability of treatment options is the key factor. If a prison offers options such as SMART recovery and Women for Sobriety, in addition to AA or NA attendance, the prisoners' rights are not violated.

Related to the legal constraints on a profession are ethical considerations. Most professions have a code of ethics to protect clients' rights and to discipline members of the profession if they violate those rights. For substance abuse counselors, each state has its own code of ethics. Typical provisions are non-discriminatory behavior with clients on the basis of race, color, gender, sexual orientation, age, disability, and so on; continuing professional and educational growth; not exploiting clients sexually or financially; and agreement to report professional misconduct of colleagues, such as violations of client confi-dentiality. The Association for Addiction Professionals (NAADAC) includes these principles and also directs professionals to present treatment options to clients and inform them of research about the effectiveness of various treat-ments. This latter requirement is consistent with the position advocated in this book that different approaches work better with different people and the belief in client self-determination.

Laura Kaplan (2005) brings our attention to the issue of dual or multiple relationships in a field like addictions in which the employment of consumers as providers is commonplace. Dual relationships occur with the multiple roles consumer-providers take when the provider and client share relationships outside the professional arena. In the substance abuse field, a personal rela-tionship might precede a previous nonprofessional relationship. This may occur among former "drinking buddies" or, less threateningly, fellow AA members. In both cases, the sharing of intimacies in meetings can be problematic for both parties in outside-of-meeting professional roles. Dual relationships may be further problematic because of concerns with risks of, or actual exploitation of, the client and because the professional's judgment may be impaired. Central to these issues is the perception of power differentials in the professional–client relationship in light of the client's inherent vulnerability. Kaplan's recommen-dation is for open discourse at the agencies on these matters and greater stan-dardization among professional codes of ethics. Counselors should be alert to potential and actual conflicts of interest, inform clients of this, and consult col-leagues and supervisors when questions about boundaries between client and professional arise.

THE WAR ON DRUGS

In 1999, significantly, the then "drug czar" General Barry McCaffrey admitted, "We have a failed social policy and it has to be reevaluated" (Egan, 1999, p. 1.1). In a nationwide telephone poll conducted by Princeton Survey Research Associates, three of four Americans said we are losing the war on drugs (Pew Research Center, 2001). A more recent national poll found that a large majority favor government-funded rehabilitation services, whether in or out of prison, over punishment (Krisberg & Marchionna, 2006).

The failures of the present punitive government policies include social and legal injustice on a wide scale, racial oppression, wasted resources spent in a futile attempt to reduce the availability of drugs, and the relentless spread of misinformation and propaganda to the American public. In spite of the nega-tive assessments, the "war" goes on. The budget for 2007 is expected to be around $12.7 billion, with 65% spent on interdiction (supply control) and 35% on treatment and prevention. Since 2001, there has been a 136.7% increase in U.S. spending abroad and a 20.9% decrease in spending on domestic prevention programs (Teslik, 2006).

Led by our current drug czar, John P. Walters, who supports international control efforts at the expense of treatment, and former Attorney General John Ashcroft, who said, "I want to escalate the war on drugs. . . . I want to renew it. . . . I want to refresh it, relaunch it, if you will," the war keeps going (Nadelman, 2001, p. 1). There is hope for some middle ground here between the side that pushes for legalization and the side that pushes for continuation and even escalation of the war on drugs. For example, in spite of his appointments of Walters and Ashcroft, President George W. Bush said in January of 2001 that "I think a lot of people are coming to the realization that maybe long minimum sentences for first-time users may not be the best way to occupy jail space and/or heal people from their disease" (Nadelman, 2001, p. 1). At the 2000 Republican National Convention, Colin Powell condemned the incarceration of "2 million Americans who, while paying for their crimes, are not paying taxes, are not there for their children, and are not raising families" (Nadelman, 2001, p. 1). The middle ground being developed and proposed by several groups will be presented in more detail at the end of this chapter.

What is the war on drugs? The essential features of the war were developed about two decades ago under the leadership of President Bush (Sr.) and have changed very little to date in spite of growing pressure from numerous constituencies (especially judges who have to carry out the mandatory minimum sentences required by Congress and state legislatures). These features include (a) mandatory minimum sentences and the criminalization of everything that has to do with marijuana, cocaine, heroin, methamphetamines, or other drugs that have been designated illegal; (b) the presumption that abstinence is the only right relationship to those drugs; (c) support for the strategy of international interdiction practices, such as eradicating poppy fields in South America and increasing border surveillance to diminish the supply of drugs in the United States; and (d) using various practices of enforcement such as drug testing, wiretapping, and forfeiture of property. Despite a significant drop in crime over past decades, the prison industry has ballooned into a $40-billion-a-year industry as a concomitant of the punitive and costly war on drugs (Spencer, 2006).

MANDATORY SENTENCING

The Bureau of Justice Statistics (2000) report on women offenders provides evidence of racism and classism ingrained in the system. While nearly two thirds of women under probation supervision are White, nearly two thirds of those confined in local jails and prisons are minority. And the overwhelming majority of the women sentenced to prison for drug law violations are poor. Women of color have been disproportionately affected by the mandatory minimum sentencing laws. These laws were passed by Congress in 1986 and signed by the president in the urgent rush to capitalize on the much publicized death of college basketball star Len Bias, who died from an overdose of cocaine (powder form) (Sterling & Stewart, 2006). Federal judges were now required to sentence drug offenders to a certain number of years in prison without parole, often a minimum of 5 years and up to life imprisonment. The harshest sentences were reserved for crimes related to crack cocaine, the drug associated with inner-city drug use and violence. These laws were geared toward dealers, but they also apply to anyone involved in a "drug conspiracy." In 2005, the U.S. Supreme Court ruled that mandatory sentences are no longer required but may be used as recommendations or guidelines (Doran, 2005). This appropriately places sentencing discretion in the hands of the federal judge.

This seemingly landmark ruling, however, according to the U.S. Sentencing Commission (2006), has not led to a reduction in sentences meted out for drug violations in the federal system. Federal judges are still following the old guidelines, and the federal prisons are filling to capacity.

The gendered nature of drug conspiracy laws is a fact given surprisingly little attention in legal scholarship, yet the enforcement of such laws is highly discriminatory and a clear example of a failed and unjust war on drugs (Gaskins, 2004). As a result of these laws, women are experiencing a significantly faster prison growth rate than men. Between 1995 and 2005, the rate of incarceration for women was 4.7% compared to 3% for the men's growth rate (BJS, 2006).

To get the big picture of the effect of mandatory minimum sentences, it is helpful to review current figures. According to the U.S. Department of Justice (2006), over 56% of inmates in the federal prison are serving time for drug-related crime. The demographic breakdown is given as 92% male, 53.9% Black, 33% Hispanic, and 25.9% noncitizens.

The growth of the prison industry since the federal mandatory guidelines have been in effect has been explosive and dramatic. In 1986, when federal mandatory minimum sentences were enacted, the Bureau of Prisons budget was $0.7 billion. President Bush's fiscal year budget announced for 2006 was $4.7 billion, with another $85 million for more prison construction, including a secure women's prison (Office of Management and Budget, 2006).

According to a report, "Hard Hit: The Growth in the Imprisonment of Women, 1977–2004" (Frost, Greene, & Pranis, 2006), women are the fastest growing population in prison, surpassing the growth rate of the male population in every state. Between the years 1977 and 2004, the women's rate of increase was twice the male rate. Drug offenses account for around one third of women confined in state prisons and a majority in federal prisons.

Since 1987, the number of women in federal prison on drug charges has quadrupled. More than 70% of all women inmates are caring for minor children, and many are pregnant when they enter prison, but judges are not allowed to take this into consideration when sentencing (Frost et al., 2006). The harsh impact on the children is not considered either. Research shows that the children whose mothers are incarcerated typically suffer a host of behavioral problems (Gaskins, 2004). Gender-neutral policies prevent judges from looking

| Box 13.1 | SUZAN'S STORY |

Suzan Penkwitz, the San Diego mother of a two-year-old son, had never even seen heroin until she was arrested when returning to the United States from Mexico. Her friend Jenny had asked her to go along on a drive south of the border, avowedly to help Jenny get her mind off a recent break-up with her boyfriend. Suzan did what she thought a good friend should do. She had no idea that Jenny was really going to Mexico to pick up 43 pounds of heroin. "I never imagined myself going to prison. Never ever!" says Suzan, who is serving a six-and-a-half-year sentence at the Federal Prison Camp for women in Dublin, California. Because of the way the system works, Jenny, who admitted her involvement and agreed to testify against Suzan, got out after serving only six months.

"Out of the 300 women here, I'd say 80% have stories similar to mine." Suzan says. "First-time, nonviolent, low-level drug offenders. I've met women who got five years for what the feds call 'improper use of the telephone': answering the phone for what later turned out to be a drug sale. Not being involved, mind you, but just answering [their own] phone. And of course, the snitches that helped put them here all get off with little or no time. I don't think I've met any high-level drug dealers here. All these women had boyfriends, or husbands, or acquaintances that used them and then let them hang. It's amazing. My roommates are 48, 50, and 58 years old. Sweet, talented ladies, grandmas, doing 14 years for 'drug conspiracy.' It all seems so pointless and tragic."

Source: Szalavitz (1998).

at either the context of the crime or the consequences in their sentencing of women in trouble with the law. Therefore, as stated by Minneapolis Judge James Rosenbaum, "Absolute gender equity in sentencing has turned out to be a war on children" (Thevenot, 1999, p. 3).

To put a human face on these statistics, we turn to what happened to Suzan Penkwitz, a San Diego mother of a 2-year-old son, who is presently incarcerated at the Federal Prison Camp for women in Dublin, California. Maia Szalavitz (1998), who earlier served as series researcher for the Bill Moyers special *On Addiction: Close to Home,* a five-part PBS TV series, wrote the portion of Suzan's story shown in Box 13.1.

The case of Suzan Penkwitz illustrates another feature of the mandatory minimum sentence laws that has caused the incarceration of low-level, first-time, or even innocent people. The only way a federal drug defendant can avoid a mandatory minimum sentence is to provide "substantial assistance" to prosecutors by testifying against other drug defendants. Unfortunately, providing substantial assistance may allow major drug traffickers who have more information to "buy" their way into substantially reduced sentences by testifying against the people who work under them or against people who are merely accidentally involved, like Suzan. The November Coalition, a national coalition of families and people whose lives have been seriously affected by the government's present drug policy, is one organization that has taken on the mission of bringing these stories to the public and lobbying for changes in the mandatory minimum sentence laws (see website www.november.org).

A further serious problem of current sentencing policies is the disproportionate effect on African Americans and Hispanics. Because of the Sentencing Project report in 1995, it became well known throughout the country that one in three Black men between the ages of 20 and 29 was under correctional supervision or control (Mauer & Huling, 1995). Although African Americans make up approximately 12% of the population and had a 9.7% rate of current illicit drug use (Office of Applied Statistics [OAS], 2005), Black males accounted for 60% of state and federal prisoners at year-end 2004, and their drug conviction rate is double that for White and Hispanic inmates in the state prison system (BJS, 2005).

CIVIL ASSET FORFEITURES

A little-known feature of the war on drugs is the practice of law enforcement's taking the money and property of persons "involved" in a drug crime without the owners' being convicted, indicted, or even arrested for a particular crime. According to Blumenson and Nilsen (1998), 80% of people who have property forfeited are not charged with a crime.

The Civil Asset Forfeiture Reform Act of 2000 (HR 1658), which was designed to restrict the law and give protections, actually made things worse. The new law expanded government forfeiture laws to include approximately 200 felonies and violations, making more property subject to government forfeiture, even after the statute of limitations has passed for criminal prosecution (Striker, 2003). As before, only a "mere preponderance of evidence" is needed for federal agencies and police to seize property, not the higher standard of "clear and convincing evidence." Under this law, informants are awarded 25 to 50% of the value of the seized property. The Patriot Act, passed in 2001 and renewed in 2006, has drawn on the 2000 expanded forfeiture act to extend the seizure of property associated in any way with suspected crime from suspected terrorists.

Although it seems incredible in America that a person's money and property can be seized on the presumption of guilt instead of innocence, federal and state law enforcement agencies are doing just that and keeping most of the proceeds. Because of the abuses that have occurred with this kind of police power, several states have initiated reforms that toughen legal standards for forfeiture, require a criminal conviction before seizure, and send the forfeited property to other budget categories, such as education rather than law enforcement. In 2002, for example, the New Mexico Drug Policy Project supported successful reform legislation that requires a criminal conviction and proof that the property was used in or is the fruit of criminal activity before it can be seized and forfeited. Oregon recently enacted legislation that requires a conviction before forfeiture and prevents law enforcement from using the proceeds.

Box 13.2	JUDITH'S STORY

When 55-year-old tax consultant Judith Roderick returned from a long-awaited birthday cruise four years ago, police were waiting. She was searched, questioned, arrested, and led in handcuffs to a waiting van, which took her on an hour-long ride to jail.

Sheriff's deputies seized the Lacey, WA, grandmother's computers, tax software, client records, and two motorcycles. They cleaned out four bank accounts, leaving a slew of checks to bounce. The reason: Roderick had done $500 worth of routine work on a land trust for a tax client whom police suspected of drug dealing. Thurston County sheriff's investigators, who made the arrest, suspected her of laundering the man's money.

Her business was devastated. Her scared employees quit. Roderick had to buy a new computer and software. She borrowed the money. Roderick was never convicted of a crime. All charges were dismissed. Yet it still took two years to win back the seized property. The raids left her reputation and business with a black eye.

"I'm in debt up to my ears," she said.

Source: Roesler (2001).

When assets of suspected drug dealers are seized, the whole family and other uninvolved persons may suffer grievous loss. Even when the charges are dismissed, the results can be devastating. Judith Roderick's story is an example of what can happen to anyone (Box 13.2).

DRUG-FREE ZONES

Drug-free zones were originally designed to protect children from drug trafficking by creating safe harbors in places they might gather. Penalties for drug offenses that occur within designated areas increased dramatically. In 1984, an amended version of the 1970 Comprehensive Drug Abuse, Prevention and Control Act provided federal penalties of twice the maximum punishment for drug offenses committed within 1,000 feet of a school, college, or playground or within 100 feet of a youth center, swimming pool, or video arcade. By 2000, every state had adopted some version of a drug-free zone law. Although no state had done an evaluation of the effectiveness or impact of this policy, the increase of harsh sentences on Black and Hispanic citizens began to spark debate about the fairness of such laws and whether drug-free zones actually protected children.

In March 2006, the Justice Policy Institute issued a stunning report called "Disparity by Design: How Drug-Free Zone Laws Impact Racial Disparity—and Fail to Protect Youth" (Greene, Pranis, & Ziedenberg, 2006). The report found no evidence that drug-free zone laws protect children (in Massachusetts, fewer than 1% of the drug-free zone cases involved drug sales to youth; in New Jersey, students were involved in only 2%). The laws have primarily been applied to adult-to-adult transactions, and instead of declining, drug arrests in the zones have risen steadily.

A major concern is the disproportionate sentences to Blacks and Latinos, who are more likely to live within the zones in urban areas. In New Jersey, 96% of inmates serving harsher zone sentences are either Black or Latino (Fears, 2006). Sometimes, the zones are so large and overlapping that they cover the entire city, and the idea of special protection loses meaning. Although it may be impossible to know whether one is in a drug-free zone (e.g., the Washington State defendant who did not know he was within 1,000 feet of a general education equivalency program with no actual school grounds), the state does not have to prove the defendant knowingly and intentionally violated the drug-free zone prohibition. The Justice Policy Institute report also raises the question of whether the drug-free zones are now used primarily to pressure defendants to plead guilty and accept a plea-bargain rather than risk the higher sentence of a drug-free-zone law if the case goes to trial.

The good news is that policymakers have taken these concerns seriously, and bills have been proposed in New Jersey, Connecticut, and Washington State to sharply reduce the size of the zones and give judges more discretion in sentencing (Crary, 2006). Ideally, other states will follow their lead to eliminate the unintended consequences of this policy of "good intentions."

THE PUNISHMENT OF PREGNANT DRUG ADDICTS

The prosecution of women who are pregnant and addicted and the removal of their children from their care and custody are other repressive side effects of the war on drugs. The interplay of race, class, and gender is also at its most pronounced in the prosecution of drug-addicted mothers. Under the rationale of protecting the fetus, poor Black, drug-addicted mothers are being hauled into court. This is part of an alarming trend toward greater state intervention into the lives of pregnant women. Poor women of color are the primary targets of government control; they are the least likely to obtain adequate prenatal care, yet the most vulnerable to government monitoring, and the least able to conform to the White middle-class standard of motherhood.

Since the mid-1980s, more than 240 women in 35 states have been criminally prosecuted for using substances thought to be harmful to their unborn during pregnancy (Paltrow, 2004). A well-publicized study by Chasnoff, Burns, Schnoll, and Burns (1985) of cocaine-exposed infants made dire predictions about long-term negative effects on the children's developmental progress. At the same time, the media's publicizing of information about "crack houses," the degradation of women who resorted to sex in exchange for crack, and the so-called "crack babies" encouraged judgmental attitudes against mothers who used drugs by the general public (Kandall, 1998). Women described as "junkie broads," "junkie chicks," or "bag brides" led to the public perception that the only way to deal with the problem was to lock the mothers away. Extremely punitive laws were passed to punish women for their addictive behavior.

Several years later, in a not-so-well-publicized study, Chasnoff, Griffith, Freier, and Murray (1992) found that most of the cocaine-exposed babies appear normal by age 2, with no detectable behavioral or learning difficulties. A later review of 36 research studies with comparison groups (Frank, Augustyn, Knight, Pell, & Zuckerman, 2001) concluded that "there is no convincing evidence that prenatal cocaine exposure is associated with developmental toxic effects that are different in severity, scope, or kind from the sequelae of multiple other risk factors" (p. 1614). Harris and Paltrow (2007) explain to physicians in the *Journal of the American Medical Association* that "poverty and its concomitants—poor nutrition and inadequate health care—are now known to overshadow many of the effects popularly attributed to cocaine exposure" (p. 1698). "Crack babies" are more accurately described as "poverty babies," who suffer from the mother's risk factors of substandard environmental conditions and poor healthcare as well as other factors, including prenatal exposure to tobacco, marijuana, or alcohol.

Despite the fact that the earlier media hype over crack babies was found scientifically untenable, it got embodied into law due to a landmark case, *Whitner v. South Carolina,* which became law in 1997 (Sagatun-Edwards, 2003). The case upheld the prosecution of an African American woman who had ingested crack cocaine during the third trimester of her pregnancy. After the baby was found to have cocaine in his bloodstream, the mother was prosecuted under child abuse and endangerment statutes. In a later case, *Ferguson v. City of Charleston,* the Supreme Court decided that performing a diagnostic test (urine drug screen) on a pregnant mother for the purpose of criminal investigation without her consent is an unreasonable search and unconstitutional (Harris & Paltrow, 2007). However, South Carolina remains the only state where using drugs or being addicted to drugs during pregnancy is still criminalized. Although women were charged in other states for child endangerment/abuse, illegal drug delivery to a minor, or fetal murder/manslaughter for using drugs while pregnant, the courts so far have declined to expand existing state laws to punish pregnant women. However, civil commitment laws and civil child welfare laws that are intended to protect the children confuse the status of pregnant and addicted women. For example, three states allow detention of pregnant women using drugs, and in some states, drug use during pregnancy is considered child neglect and can result in the removal of the child when born (Harris & Paltrow, 2007).

Consequently, many women have lost custody of their children, because some states now consider "child neglect" to include prenatal exposure to controlled substances. Since drug testing occurs only in publicly funded healthcare facilities, such laws, needless to say, fall chiefly on poor and minority women. There has been no comparable effort to use a newborn's toxicology screen to check for the role of sperm (damaged by drug use) in causing birth defects (van Wormer & Bartollas, 2007).

Attorney Lynn Paltrow (2004), who specializes in laws that punish pregnant women for potential harm to the fetus, brings our attention to the significance of a law passed and signed by President Bush in 2004—the Unborn Victims of Violence Act. This law, which was aimed at abortion, makes it a crime to cause harm to a "child in utero." More than 30 states have similar laws on the books. Paradoxically, as Paltrow indicates, this federal law does not make it a federal crime to physically attack pregnant women, yet homicide is the number one killer of pregnant women.

The media hyperbole that played into the crackdown on mothers who used crack while pregnant is now being directed toward meth and the mothers associated with this illicit drug. In response to the barrage of stories that appeared in the media concerning an epidemic of birth defects caused by meth use in pregnant women, over 90 leading doctors, scientists, and treatment specialists released a public letter calling on the media to stop the use of terms such as "meth babies" (Lewis, 2005). The use of such terms, they said, harms the children to which they are applied, lowers expectations for their academic success, and is without scientific basis. The suggestion that treatment will not work for people dependent on meth, particularly mothers, also lacks any scientific basis. The scientists also fault news reports and policymakers for not consulting experts to obtain information about the effects of prenatal exposure and about the efficacy of treatment. They cite their experience with almost 20 years of research on the chemically related drug cocaine that "has not identified a recognizable condition, syndrome disorder that should be termed 'crack baby' nor found the degree of harm reported in the media and then used to justify numerous punitive legislative proposals" (Lewis, 2005, p. 2).

Both pregnancy and drug "epidemics" are issues ripe for government exploitation and a way of diverting the people's attention away from the major, structural problems onto issues of individual "morality." Drug wars (whether inner-city Blacks and Latinos associated with crack cocaine or poor rural Whites involved in meth production) today make excellent scapegoats, and the international war on drugs can be justified on the basis of images of people strung out on drugs. The increase in the prison population and huge expenditures on the prison industrial complex take billions of dollars that otherwise could be spent on housing, healthcare, and substance abuse treatment on demand.

In summary, women continue to be singled out for blame for using drugs during pregnancy, as they were in the late 19th and early 20th centuries. It appears easier to blame individual women than to acknowledge that the problem of substance use for women has been aggravated by the increase in poverty, homelessness, substandard education, and lack of healthcare and treatment options since the 1980s. In spite of the NIDA research and demonstration studies on drug use among pregnant women, drug treatment for poor, pregnant women is harder to find than prenatal care (Siegal, 1997).

The unfortunate consequence of legal threats to pregnant women has been to deter some women from seeking prenatal care at all. In addition, policies intended to respond to the concerns about drug use during pregnancy do not work to protect the health of women or the babies they are carrying (Paltrow, 2006). In 1992, the Department of Health and Human Services committed to a strong emphasis on prevention, intervention, and treatment, with monies to states for prevention and treatment services for pregnant and parenting drug-using women. However, long waiting lists, lack of specific treatment services, not enough money, the fear of health professionals, and legal threats still dominate the healthcare system for pregnant drug-using women (Kandall, 1998). (In Norway, compulsory but compassionate drug treatment of pregnant substance using mothers is provided until the time of delivery in homelike facilities; [Helsedepartementet, 2004]). Perhaps the key issue here is not about punishing drug use in pregnant women but about addressing women's basic social and health needs, which exist with or without pregnancy and do not end with delivery.

SYSTEMS OF PAYMENT AND INSURANCE COVERAGE

As indicated previously, most of the women incarcerated in the United States are serving time for drug-related crimes, and most of them have histories of serious long-term substance abuse problems in conjunction with mental health concerns. The latter is related to the fact that prisons have become the dumping grounds for persons with mental illness. Not surprisingly, a review of the literature suggests that most women who are released from jail or prison are likely to return to the same difficult conditions that played into their legal problems in the first place (Richie, 2004). When unaccustomed child care responsibilities of children who have their own serious problems and resentments are thrust upon them and with few financial resources to provide proper care, the challenges can be tremendous.

The relapse and recidivism risks are major public health problems that echo the original risks that were the cause of grief to the women and their families in the first place. We are referring to the lack of treatment availability for women (and the men in their lives) due to the lack of nationalized healthcare in this country. The majority of the women arrestees with drug abuse violations studied in the government's Arrestee Drug Abuse Monitoring (ADAM) annual report (Taylor, Newton, & Brownstein, 2003) did not have healthcare coverage.

As noted in chapter 11, on gender differences, women entering treatment, especially women from highly family-oriented cultures, do better with treatment that is comprehensive, involves children, is family focused, and lasts long enough to engage the participant in skills or language training when appropriate. The system of payment and reimbursement from state and federal funding sources does not support any of these goals. Cutbacks in funding for health and social services have been dismantling the minimal infrastructure that existed to care for people with drug problems or, better yet, to prevent them in the first place (Miller & Carroll, 2006). Major funding obstacles include reimbursement rates that do not cover costs of care or of effective co-ordination of funding streams, especially between mental health and substance abuse services. Reimbursement schedules, moreover, are geared to individuals, not families. And federal drug policy, as we know, continues to emphasize costly law enforcement and incarceration. The government's reluctance to fund needle exchange programming, despite its proven success in addressing the spread of HIV/AIDS and hepatitis B and C, is a policy in desperate need of change (Abbott, 2003).

Harm reduction policies could be far more effectively instituted in one-stop health and social service settings such as exist in Western Europe rather than in the type of specialized treatment clinics set up in the United States, each with different and competing funding sources. A serious consequence of such specialized services, as Miller and Carroll (2006) suggest, has been "continued stigmatization and an unwarranted mystique that has overemphasized the importance of acute treatment" (p. 303). The diseases of addiction can be managed as other chronic health problems with a focus on prevention rather than treatment when people are seriously impaired.

HARM REDUCTION

Although harm reduction continues to be one of the more controversial issues in the substance abuse treatment arena, it is widely recognized in general areas of public health—in the reliance on designated drivers, the mandating of labels issuing warnings on tobacco and all kinds of other potentially harmful products, in immunizations, nicotine replacement therapy, and safe havens (anonymous drop-off places for unwanted infants)—the list is endless. Harm reduction exemplifies the social work value base and our professional commitment to social justice and human rights (Abbott, 2003). As advocated by Brocato and Wagner (2003), this approach is built around social work's values of respect for human dignity, social justice, and client self-determination. It also relates to commitments by all the helping professions to identify the best empirically based practices at the micro- and macrolevels and advocates for these rather than traditional punitive approaches that have been shown ineffective or downright harmful (Miller & Carroll, 2006). The need, as expressed by Ann Abbott (2003), is for a multifaceted approach that encompasses primary, secondary, and tertiary care, a coupling of research and practice, and a marriage of prevention and intervention.

Syringe exchange programs to prevent the spread of HIV/AIDS infection are one of the best-known tertiary prevention programs in the United States. Estimates of 20 to 34% of people with HIV infections and most hepatitis C infections in the United States were caused through sharing contaminated syringes and other drug injection equipment (Center for Disease Control, 2005a; Drug Policy Alliance, 2007). Among women and children, 75% of new AIDS cases can be directly or indirectly attributed to injection drug use. Women who become infected with HIV can transmit the virus to their babies before or during birth or through breastfeeding. African Americans are disproportionately impacted; although they make up only 13% of the U.S.

population, in 2004 they accounted for 43% of the U.S. population living with AIDS.

According to the Center for Disease Control (CDC), one of the most effective strategies for reducing the transmission of HIV and other blood-borne infections is ensuring that injection drug users have access to sterile syringes. A 1997 report from the National Institutes of Health (NIH) to Congress had previously reached the same conclusion: that syringe exchange programs (SEPs) "show a reduction in risk behaviors as high as 80% in injecting drug users, with estimates of a 30% or greater reduction of HIV" (Health and Human Services, 1998). Economic studies have also concluded that syringe exchange programs are cost effective: The cost of preventing one HIV infection by SEPs is $4,000 to $12,000 compared to an estimated $190,000 in medical costs for a person infected with HIV (CDC, 2005a).

In spite of the advocacy of the CDC, the NIH, and an informed Congress, 47 states have drug paraphernalia laws that establish criminal penalties for the distribution and possession of syringes (CDC, 2005a). Our own government still refuses to fund SEPs, although we are one of the largest funders of AIDS prevention in the world. Congress has prohibited the use of federal funds for needle exchange programs since 1989, even though the Secretary of Health and Human Services (Donna Shalala in 1997) made the necessary determination— for releasing federal funding—that such programs reduce the transmission of HIV and do not encourage the use of illegal drugs. Needle exchange programs remain illegal in many jurisdictions throughout the country. For example, in New Jersey, 45% of all HIV infections were caused by contaminated needles, yet New Jersey does not allow any form of sterile syringe access for injection drug users (Drug Policy Alliance, 2007). Public health officials in the communities of the 185 syringe exchange programs that do exist in 36 states have various strategies for legally maintaining their programs, including declaring public health emergencies. The situation is so dire that there are reports that some drug dealers have started providing clean syringes to their customers (Nadelman, 1997).

In contrast, other countries, such as Switzerland, Australia, England, the Netherlands, Scotland, and Thailand, have responded to the spread of HIV by removing restrictions on purchasing syringes and have developed free, accessible syringe exchange programs. Some, such as England and Switzerland, have established heroin prescription programs where users can stabilize or decrease the use of heroin, hold legitimate employment, and live normal lives without the threat of contracting a disease such as AIDS. There is hope that access to clean syringes is improving in the United States. In 2004, California joined the states of Connecticut, Maine, Minnesota, and New York to allow up to 10 nonprescription over-the-counter syringe sales in counties that elect to participate. Five other states (Hawaii, Maryland, Massachusetts, New York, and Rhode Island) and the District of Columbia have given their health departments the power to establish SEPs, and three other states (Connecticut, Massachusetts, and Rhode Island) have exempted the SEPs from their state drug paraphernalia laws (CDC, 2005b). Clearly, help from social workers and helping professionals is needed to continue to educate and inform the public, members of Congress, public officials, and law enforcement about the importance of access to sterile syringes.

METHADONE AND BUPRENORPHINE MAINTENANCE

Methadone maintenance programs represent the other major harm reduction strategy that has been used successfully in the United States since the mid-1970s. Methadone, administered in a daily dose, blocks heroin's narcotic effects while preventing withdrawal symptoms. The extensive research literature on methadone maintenance reveals dramatic reductions not only in heroin use but also in HIV-related needle sharing (Schilling, Dornig, & Lungren, 2006).

However, in spite of their success, programs in the United States are so tightly regulated that they serve less than one in five of those who might be helped (Addiction Treatment Forum, 2006). The most restrictive requirement is that methadone can be prescribed only by "comprehensive treatment programs," which leaves out physicians in private offices, hospital clinics, community health centers, and so on. Most of the clinics receive clients as referrals from the criminal justice system or directly from persons released from prison.

Another issue in the United States is the low dosage level of methadone administered in many clinics as a matter of policy. According to research, the majority of methadone clients receive a suboptimal dose (Addiction Treatment Forum, 2005). Many clinics do not adjust dosages according to the needs of the clients but rely on fixed dosages. These dosages can vary widely, from 25 mg per day for all clients to 60 mg. In an investigation of the effectiveness of a higher dose, Strain, Bigelow, Liebson, and Stitzer (1999) found that a higher dose of 80 to 100 mg per day is more effective in reducing heroin use than a dose of 40 to 50 mg. Given the current increase in heroin use in many cities and the HIV/AIDS epidemic among IV drug users, it simply seems reasonable to remove the restrictions on access and dosage to maximize the benefit of this program to all who can use it.

A promising move in this direction is the Drug Addiction Treatment Act of 2000 (DATA). Through a program of waivers, DATA makes it possible for qualified physicians (in their office) to prescribe schedule III, IV, and V narcotic drugs approved by the Food and Drug Administration (FDA) for the maintenance or detoxification treatment of addiction to opiates (Substance Abuse and Mental Health Services Administration [SAMHSA], 2006). Essentially, the DATA waiver allows persons abusing opiates (including pain medications) to be treated outside the restricted settings of methadone maintenance programs. Because access to treatment will be increased to clients all across the nation (particularly smaller cities and rural areas), the program could potentially revolutionize treatment. The first medication approved by the FDA for use under the act was buprenorphine in October 2002. Qualified physicians are limited to 30 patients.

A recent evaluation of the Buprenorphine Waiver Program by the American Society of Addiction Medicine (ASAM) (2006) found that buprenorphine treatment under the DATA waiver is clinically effective and well accepted by patients. It has increased the availability of medication-assisted treatment for opioid addiction and was effective in supporting positive treatment outcomes. Six-month outcomes revealed that 59% of the patients were abstinent from all drugs, and 81% were abstinent from opioids (except buprenorphine). The 30-patient limit was considered an unnecessary limiting factor by some of the participating physicians. As one put it, "it is akin to placing limits on cardiac or diabetic patients" (ASAM, 2006, p. 48).

Nevertheless, Washton and Zweben (2006) see the need for greater flexibility in such programming. Some of the insurance-funded treatment programs are endorsing buprenorphine but forbidding methadone. Yet the switch from methadone to buprenorphine must be done with great care because of withdrawal symptoms. And some patients, as Washton and Zweben suggest, will not improve on buprenorphine because the dose ceiling is too low to accommodate their needs. The restriction on physicians to treat no more than 30 patients on this drug is also limiting until more physicians and healthcare professionals receive the 8-hour training required to administer this drug. Social workers and substance abuse counselors have an important role to play in alerting clients with opiate addiction (whether from heroin use or prescription pain medication) to the option of obtaining relief from addiction problems or chronic pain through medical treatment with one of the opiate-agonist drugs such as buprenorphine or methadone. In such cases, referral to a knowledgeable physician, familiar with the extensive evidence of treatment effectiveness of these drugs and not influenced by stigma of opiate addiction, is in order. The extent to which social workers appropriately refer and advocate for clients who can benefit from such treatment can be seen as a bellwether of how the profession will perform in the emerging era of cost effectiveness and reliance on evidence-based treatments (Schilling, Dornig, & Lungren, 2006).

METH: THE "UNNECESSARY EPIDEMIC"

The impact of international and national policy on the everyday street life of an American drug addict was perhaps made clearest in the PBS *Frontline* documentary "The Meth Addict" (*Frontline*, 2006), which was based on *The Oregonian*'s award-winning investigation in 2004. This investigation revealed that the rise and fall of the purity of methamphetamine available on the streets were directly correlated to the rise and fall of treatment admissions for meth addicts. That is, if it was possible to control the purity of the product, it would be possible to control and/or reduce the number of addicts. Since meth requires the chemicals ephedrine or pseudoephedrine, which are primarily manufactured in nine factories in the world, it is possible for Congress and federal authorities such as the DEA to control the meth "epidemic" by tightening the control over the supply of these basic chemicals. Although sporadic attempts at control since the mid-1980s had a positive effect of lowering the purity of meth, the regulations continued to have loopholes that suited the pharmaceutical companies that make cold and cough medicines and, ultimately, made it possible for meth suppliers to continue to receive these chemicals.

Although it would still be possible to control the source of the chemicals, and thus contain the addiction, Congress has taken a different course that is more acceptable to the pharmaceutical industry. The Combat Methamphetamine Epidemic Act of 2005 requires that drugs containing pseudoephedrine, ephedrine, and phenylpropanolamine (e.g., Sudafed) be stored behind pharmacy counters and only be sold to buyers who show identification and sign a logbook. The amount a person could purchase daily would be limited. The act also funded drug courts, money for investigating and cleaning up meth labs, and $20 million annually to help children exposed to meth at home (Seper, 2005). According to the DEA, one result of the act has been the decline of meth lab seizures from 17,000 in 2003 to 12,000 in 2005. Unfortunately, the crackdown on "homegrown" meth labs and the new limits on the sale of cold remedies have had another unintended consequence: The international drug cartels are moving in to distribute a purer form of meth known as "ice" to fill the gap (Huus, 2006). According to *Frontline* (2006), the purity of meth is estimated to be as high as it's ever been, around 70%, and is cheaper than ever on the streets.

DRUG COURTS: A PROMISING DEVELOPMENT

One of the most promising developments in recent years is the drug court, an alternative to prison that was first launched in Florida in the late 1980s. The success of these new courts, which divert nonviolent drug offenders from the prison system into treatment, is not like your ordinary adversarial courts. Intensive case management services are provided, mental health disorders are treated simultaneously with drug treatment, and medication is prescribed when appropriate (Huddleston, 2005). The results have been very favorable both for the offender and the community. A team of professionals from the court— county attorney, public defender, and judge—and from probation services, substance abuse treatment, and the police meets weekly to discuss the small number of persons in their charge. Intensive counseling is provided not only for the individual, but attention is also paid to family members in the individual's life. Sobriety and cooperation with treatment are rewarded with all sorts of prizes, such as shopping coupons and the like (information provided in a personal interview with Karen Herkelman, Department of Corrections, Waterloo, Iowa, October 10, 2006).

Today, there are more than 1,621 drug courts across the states. The funding is largely from federal grants. Federally funded drug courts have been set up in Kentucky, Hawaii, and in the midwestern states especially to deal with the meth crisis. Is such an investment in a relatively small number of individuals (the Waterloo court has a caseload of 20) with serious addiction and legal problems worth the effort? The evidence coming in has been encouraging. An extensive review of the literature, conducted by Belenko, Patapis, and French (2005), concluded that the cost savings are substantial. The studies compared the recidivism rates of graduates of drug court with a matched sample of offenders who completed standard probation or jail time. Cost savings went beyond the correctional costs of confinement to include savings through the prevention of criminal activity, unemployment, Medicaid, health and mental health services, re-arrests, reconvictions, criminal victimization of others, and the drug exposure of infants. Significantly, the research, which included data over a 4-year period, showed far higher cost–benefit ratios than did studies limited to 1-year follow-up periods.

The positive results of such close monitoring as provided by the drug court are realized through the close individual attention to persons while reinforcing their positive social networks. As well, these programs are cost effective to the society in allowing people to obtain treatment while maintaining their work and family roles (Springer, McNeece, & Arnold, 2003). For women, the courts' effectiveness is enhanced because of the continuum of services provided and the close partnerships with community-based organizations. From the harm reduction perspective, there is criticism of the drug courts because they are built on the principle of total abstinence and lack of trust. There is extensive urinalysis testing to determine whether or not the individual is taking drugs. Nevertheless, compared to the restrictions of prison life, and within the context of America's war on drugs, we must see this intensive supervision in the community as a welcome improvement over the alternative.

Because many women offenders are mothers, correctional programs delivered in the community are particularly important for women who have young children (BJS, 2000). Community centers that house mothers together with their children are especially valuable, as they can provide counselors who model appropriate parenting skills as issues arise spontaneously in the common living situation. Knowing that jail time awaits them if they begin abusing drugs again can offer women a strong incentive to change. By the same token, without help and the educational and vocational skills necessary to survive on their own, some women continue their patterns of destructive behavior and involvement in destructive relationships.

THE MIDDLE ROAD

There are those who would describe the controversies of the war on drugs as an argument between legalization and criminalization. Legalization proponents see the "zero-tolerance" policies of the United States as incredibly harsh and punitive. As Robin Ellins, a proprietor of a hemp products store in Toronto, Canada, said, "Thank God, I'm in Canada. I just can't believe what's going on down there. . . . That's a war against people" ("Canada Continues Moving," 2001). Canada's movement toward the decriminalization of small amounts of marijuana and expanding its medicinal use is supported by the *Canadian*

Medical Association Journal and is being considered by a new Parliament committee on drug matters ("Canada Continues Moving," 2001).

However, even though Canadian policies are conservative compared to those of the Dutch, where "coffee shops" also sell joints of marijuana, they are unlikely to receive a warm reception anytime soon in the United States. In spite of the unpopularity of the war on drugs and the public's sense of futility that we are "losing it," 66% of Americans in a recent poll still supported interdiction strategies (Pew Research Center, 2001). About as many people (47%) supported mandatory minimum sentences as opposed them (45%). Both White and Black females had a more punitive approach than White or Black males. For example, 53% of men of both races felt that too many people are in jail for drug possession, while only 41% of their women counterparts agreed.

At the same time, a majority of Americans (52%) believed that drug use should be treated as a disease compared to 35% who favored treating it as a crime. The results also indicate that public concern over the problem of illegal drug use has receded since the massive media onslaught of the late 1980s. In 1990, 37% of the public cited alcohol/drugs as the most important national problem; in 2001, only 6% felt that way. However, in a survey conducted for the Drug Strategies and Police Foundation, the majority of police chiefs (63%) say that drug abuse is still the top law enforcement problem (greater than terrorism) and that it is more serious than it was 5 years ago. They also believe (67%) that law enforcement has been unsuccessful dealing with the problem and that it needs to be addressed as both a law enforcement and a public health problem (Hart Research Associates, 2004).

Given both a compassionate and still get-tough American public, it may be an ideal time to act on some middle-ground social policies that could appeal more to the majority than legalization or criminalization. For example, the Federation of American Scientists (1997), a privately funded nonprofit policy organization whose board of sponsors includes 58 of America's Nobel laureates in the sciences, calls for "a third way" that is based on science and evaluated by the results of the policies, not their symbolic value. Robert MacCoun, associate professor of public policy at the University of California at Berkeley, who spoke at the press conference outlining the group's objectives, used the example of harm reduction programs. "You have to do the evaluation program-by-program. . . . Unfortunately, serious discussion of how best to reduce damage has been made difficult by the suspicion that harm reduction is a 'Trojan horse' or 'slippery slope' towards legalization" (p. 2). Another participant, Dr. Charles Schuster, former director of NIDA, stated, "It's time to start passing laws and running programs based on what research has shown us about the problems, not on what public opinion polls say. There is excellent evidence that appropriate treatment reduces drug use. There is no evidence that stiffer prison terms for dealers reduce drug use. At some point our policies ought to start to reflect that" (p. 2).

The Federation of American Scientists published 14 "Principles for Practical Drug Policies" in September 1997 (see the full document at http://fas .org/drugs/Principles.htm). Among the highlights are a recognition that social concern about diminishing self-control through drugs should extend to licit and illicit substances alike; that damage can be reduced by "shrinking the extent of drug abuse as well as by reducing the harm incident to any give level of drug consumption"; that legalizing drugs will not solve the current problems; that the use of "disproportionate punishments to express social norms is neither just nor a prudent use of public funds and scarce prison capacity"; and that treatment that reduces damage but does not produce immediate abstinence should be regarded as "incomplete successes rather than as unredeemed failures."

Joseph Califano (2001c, p. 2), director of the National Center on Addiction and Substance Abuse at Columbia University (CASA) and another voice of the middle road, notes that President Bush's proposed budget increases of 16% for NIDA and 11% for NIAAA are "steps in the right direction" but still fall short of the commitment needed to turn around the disproportionate use of funds on interdiction efforts. An extensive CASA survey (Califano, 2001a, p. 2) of state budgets that considered all the costs of substance use and addiction in 16 budget categories revealed that of every dollar the states spent on dealing with substance use and addiction, 96 cents went to "shoveling up the wreckage" and only 4 cents were used to prevent and treat it. These results add more reason to support the currently proposed Drug Education, Prevention and Treatment Act, which will fund treatment in prisons, drug courts, and diversion programs, provide more treatment in rural areas, and provide funds for drug-free school models and research and evaluation of the effectiveness of treatment and prevention programs (Califano, 2001b).

One encouraging development is that the federal Medicaid program started to pay for screening and brief intervention in January 2007. New codes for treatment reimbursement have been added to Medicaid and Medicare to encourage doctors and public health programs to address alcohol and other drug disorders; private sector facilities, however, are not affected (Curley, 2006).

While social policy change in a progressive direction has been tediously slow at the federal level, there are many exciting initiatives at the state and local levels. Most are geared to the provision of treatment in lieu of incarceration for drug misusers. The introduction of the drug court system is the most conspicuous of these initiatives. It is crucial for practitioners in this field and social workers in this and related fields to engage in policy analysis to influence legislation through lobbying at the state and local levels. For up-to-date facts that should be of interest to policymakers seeking cost-effective alternatives to incarceration, visit "Making Drug Policy at the State Level" at www.drugstrategies.org/criticalchoices.

POLICIES RELATED TO GAMBLING

Between 1976 and 1997, revenues from legal gambling in the United States grew nearly 1,600%, reaching more than $50 billion. And as of 2006, legal gambling in the United States has mushroomed into a $135.9 billion per year business; this figure is based on revenue figures provided by the states (Jewell, 2006). As a result, the gambling industry has quickly become one of the biggest and politically most powerful special interests in the country. In the United States, 48 states have some form of legal gambling, but only 26 appropriate money for treatment, according to an in-depth study by the Community Newspaper Holdings, Inc. (CNHI) news service (Jewell, 2006). Only $35.5 million of the total earnings are spent by government and industry in treatment and educational programming. Usually, the money allocated is a percentage of the state earnings.

Because of the explosive growth of the gambling industry (renamed "gaming" by the industry), Congress created the National Gambling Impact Study Commission (NGISC) in 1996 to study the impact of gambling in the United States and recommend ways to regulate it. According to Common Cause (2000), the gambling industry so feared supervision, regulation, and potential new taxes that it more than doubled its campaign contributions to $5.4 million in PAC and soft money contributions to both parties in 1995–1996. It was also successful in watering down the powers of the commission and stacking it with the appointment of several progambling people. Nevertheless, the NGISC Report (1999) has been instrumental in alerting many to the lack of policies and regulation, which has impact on those people who may become or already are addicted to gambling.

A national helpline is now operating along with state helplines in most of the states that have some type of legalized gambling. About half of these states, as mentioned earlier, support some type of treatment with public funding, but the level of funding is miniscule compared to income the state receives from gambling enterprises. For example, in Minnesota in 2006, 2% of the state's income from gambling went into educational and treatment allocations compared to ½ of 1% in Iowa and 1% in Oregon.

A policy recommendation of the National Gambling Impact Study Commission (1999) was that states mandate private and public insurers and managed care providers to "identify successful treatment programs, educate participants about pathological gambling and treatment options, and cover the appropriate programs under their plans" (p. 34). In addition, the commission urged that state and tribal government use a proportion of their gambling revenue to fund problem gambling-specific research, prevention, education, and treatment programs.

Other important recommendations by the NGISC included restricting all gambling to those who are at least 21 years of age (many states allow lottery tickets to be sold to 18-year-olds), rolling back slot machines in neighborhood outlets, banning betting on collegiate and amateur athletic events, banning aggressive advertising that targets impoverished neighborhoods and youth, prohibiting Internet gambling and passing legislation stating that any credit card debts incurred while gambling on the Internet are unrecoverable, and banning credit card cash advance machines from the immediate area where gambling takes place.

Considerable research is being conducted to assess the socioeconomic costs and benefits of gambling. Most is coming out of the states and Canadian provinces. Only a small portion includes research on women and minorities as separate categories. For a comprehensive summary of available research as of 2006, visit the Canadian website at htpp://gaming.uleth.ca. The findings, as one would suspect, are for high earnings in revenue for the states but at high social cost. In Iowa, for example, social problems occurred in counties adjacent to casinos in comparison with counties farther distant from them (Alberta Gaming Research Institute, 2006).

Three changes in national policy recommended by the NGISC could have an enormous impact on this dismal state of affairs: (a) add gambling to the National Household Survey on Drug Abuse and any other appropriate national surveys on mental health; (b) initiate and fund research by the National Institutes of Health, SAMHSA, or any other appropriate federal agency; and (c) require all state and tribal governments to cooperate fully in any research undertaken by the state to fulfill these recommended policies.

The Queen of Hearts Australian project (S. Brown & Coventry, 1997) elicited suggestions from women for larger system interventions and policies that would help women who are problem gamblers. These include: (a) timely access to other supporting services, such as mental health and especially financial counseling; (b) access to female counselors because of the need to disclose problems such as physical, sexual, and emotional abuse; (c) easily accessible services in downtown areas as well as rural environments where services are co-located with other supportive services to lessen stigmatization and promote referrals; (d) involvement of all the groups associated with gambling (including financial institutions, gaming operators, and government) to work on solutions instead of leaving it up to the "victims" to cope; (e) establishing alternative recreations for women in neighborhoods; and (f) decreasing the accessibility of gaming venues by removing them from shopping centers, strip malls, clubs, and hotels throughout the state.

SUMMARY AND CONCLUSION

At the public policy level, we have looked beyond the problems of the individual person to the bigger picture of how our society cares for its members who may be vulnerable to the consequences of addiction at one time or another in their lives. We ask the questions: What do we do as a society for the poor and addicted? How do we care for women and other minorities who may be quadruple-oppressed by also being poor, addicted, and HIV positive?

Positive policies, such as funding drug courts, spending public money on prevention and treatment, building safety nets of healthcare, job, and educational opportunities, and supporting harm reduction policies like methadone maintenance and syringe exchanges, are under way. However, the impact of criminalization, mandated minimum sentences, civil forfeiture, punishing pregnant and addicted women, and restricting access to harm reduction programs far outweighs these benefits.

We are at a crossroads in this country in terms of public policy. We can go forward with a reasoned compassionate approach that is "user friendly" to those who want to change their relationship to an addiction, or we can continue to punish and shame them in an effort to make them give it up. We can make accurate information available to the public that may prevent addiction to gambling, or we can pretend that gambling has no addictive qualities and merely provides needed money to states in lieu of taxes. In each area of public policy we have discussed, there is a choice to be made. We agree with Kleiman (1998) that a quick fix for better policies is not an option in the near future. We also hope with him that some elected officials and nationally appointed decision makers will risk being called "soft on drugs" and pursue a "slow fix" that will begin the shift to more realistic policies that will reduce the social damage of addiction. As Kleiman (1998) states, "Even when optimism is unjustified, hope remains a virtue" (p. 8).

REFERENCES

Abbott, A. A. (2003). Meeting the challenges of substance misuse: Making inroads one step at a time. *Health and Social Work, 28*(2), 83–88.

Addiction Treatment Forum. (2005, Spring). Straight talk from the editor. *Addiction Treatment Forum, 14*(2), 1, 4.

Addiction Treatment Forum. (2006, Summer). Fates of buprenorphine and MMT intertwined? *Addiction Treatment Forum, 15*(3), 1, 5.

Alberta Gaming Research Institute. (2006, October 5). Gambling literature online database. Retrieved October 2006 from http://gaming.uleth.ca.

Alexander, R. (2000). *Counseling, treatment and intervention: Methods with juvenile and adult offenders.* Belmont, CA: Wadsworth.

American Society of Addiction Medicine. (2006). Expanding treatment of opioid dependence: Initial physician and patient experiences with the adoption of buprenorphine. U.S. Department of Health and Human Services. SAMHSA. Retrieved September 30, 2006, from http://buprenorphine.samhsa.gov/ASAM_06_Final_Results.pdf.

Belenko, S., Patapis, N., & French, M. (2005, February). *Economic benefits of drug treatment: A critical review of the evidence for policy makers.* Philadelphia: Treatment Research Institute at the University of Pennsylvania.

Blumenson, E., & Nilsen, E. (1998). Policing for profit: The drug war's hidden economic agenda. *University of Chicago Law Review, 65,* 35–114.

Brocato, J., & Wagner, E. (2003). Harm reduction: A social work practice model and social justice agenda. *Health and Social Work, 28*(2), 117–125.

Brown, D. (2006, June 9). Drug-related deaths hit 10-year low in Baltimore. *Washington Post,* p. A10.

Brown, S., & Coventry, L. (1997). *Queen of Hearts.* Victoria, Australia: Financial & Consumer Rights Council.

Bureau of Justice Statistics (BJS). (2000). *Women offenders.* Washington, DC: U.S. Department of Justice. Retrieved October 2006 from http://www.ojp.usdoj.gov/bjs/pub/pdf/wo.pdf.

Bureau of Justice Statistics (BJS). (2005). *Substance dependence, abuse, and treatment of jail inmates.* Washington, DC: U.S. Department of Justice. Retrieved October 2006 from http://www.ojp.usdoj.gov/bjs/abstract/sdatji02.htm.

Bureau of Justice Statistics (BJS). (2006, May). *Prison and jail inmates at midyear 2005.* U.S. Department of Justice. Retrieved October 2006 from http://www.ojp.usdoj.gov/bjs/pub/pdf/pjim05.pdf.

Califano, J. (2001a, February 13). *Drug Education, Prevention and Treatment Act of 2001.* National Center on Addiction and Substance Abuse at Columbia University. Newsletter. Retrieved from http://www.casacolumbia.org.

Califano, J. (2001b, May 8). *Learning from Robert Downey, Jr.* National Center on Addiction and Substance Abuse at Columbia University. Newsletter. Retrieved from http://www.casacolumbia.org.

Califano, J. (2001c, January 29). *Shoveling up: The impact of substance abuse on state budgets.* National Center on Addiction and Substance Abuse at Columbia University. Newsletter. Retrieved from http://www.casacolumbia.org.

Canada continues moving toward legalized marijuana. (2001, May 29). *Spokesman Review,* p. 2.

Center for Disease Control. (2005a). Syringe exchange programs. Retrieved February 2007 from http://www.cdc.gov/idu/facts/AED_IDU_SYR.pdf.

Center for Disease Control. (2005b). State and local policies regarding IDUs' access to sterile syringes. Retrieved February 2007 from http://www.cdc.gov/idu/facts/aed_idu_pol.htm.

Chasnoff, I., Burns, W., Schnoll, S., & Burns, K. (1985). Cocaine use in pregnancy. *New England Journal of Medicine, 313,* 666–669.

Chasnoff, I., Griffith, D., Freier, C., & Murray, J. (1992). Cocaine/polydrug use in pregnancy. Two-year follow-up. *Pediatrics, 89,* 284–289.

Common Cause. (2000). *Paying the price: How tobacco, gun, gambling, and alcohol interests block common sense solutions to some of the nation's most urgent problems.* Retrieved from http://www.commoncause.org/publications/campaign_ finance.htm.

Confidentiality of Alcohol and Drug Abuse Patient Records. (2004, June). *Confidentiality of alcohol and drug abuse patient records.* Washington, DC: U.S. Department of Health and Human Services. SAMHSA. Retrieved October 2006 from http://www.samhsa.gov.

Crary, D. (2006, March 23). Drug-free school zone laws questioned. Associated Press, Guardian Unlimited, UK, p. 1

Curley, B. (2006, October 5). Medicaid will pay for addiction screening: Advocates seek AMA action too. *Join Together Online.* Retrieved October 2006 from http://www.jointogether.org.news/features/2006/medicaid-will-pay-for.html.

Doran, A. (2005, June 5). Plea bargains and mandatory sentencing. *Associated Content.* Retrieved October 2006 from http://www.associatedcontent.com.

Drug Policy Alliance. (2004). Denial of public benefits. Retrieved October 1, 2006, from http://www.drugpolicy.org/law/publicbenefi/.

Drug Policy Alliance. (2007). Sterile syringe access. Retrieved February 2007 from http://www.drugpolicy.org/reducingharm/needleexchan/.

Egan, T. (1999, February 28). War on crack retreats, still taking prisoners. *New York Times,* p. 1.1.

Fears, D. (2006, March 23). Drug-free zones off-target. *Washington Post,* p. A05.

Federation of American Scientists. (1997, September 2). *Press conference: Drug experts call for "Third Way"—neither drug war nor legalization.* National Press Club, Washington, DC. Retrieved from http://www.fas.org/drugs/drugspr.htm.

Frank, D., Augustyn, M., Knight, W., Pell, T., & Zuckerman, B. (2001). Growth, development, and behavior in early childhood following prenatal cocaine exposure. *Journal of the American Medical Association, 285,* 1613–1625.

Frontline. (2006). The meth epidemic. PBS. Retrieved October 1, 2006, from http://www.pbs.org/wgbh/pages/frontline/meth.

Frost, N., Greene, J., & Pranis, K. (2006). *Hard hit: The growth in the imprisonment of women, 1977–2004.* Institute on Women and Criminal Justice. Retrieved October 2006 from http://www.wpaonline.org/institute/hardhit.

Gaskins, S. (2004). "Women of circumstance"—The effects of mandatory minimum sentencing on women minimally involved in drug crimes. *American Criminal Law Review, 41*(4), 1533–1554.

Greene, J., Pranis, K., & Ziedenberg, J. (2006). Disparity by design: How drug-free zone laws impact racial disparity—and fail to protect youth. Justice Policy Institute Report. Retrieved September 30, 2006, from http://www.justicepolicy.org/reports/SchoolZonesReport06.pdf.

Gresenz, C., Watkins, K., & Podus, D. (1998). Supplemental Security Income (SSI), Disability Insurance (DI), and substance abusers. *Community Mental Health Journal, 34*(4), 337–350.

Harris, L., & Paltrow, L. (2007). The status of pregnant women and fetuses in US criminal law. *Journal of American Medical Association, 289*(13), 1697–1699.

Hart Research Associates. (2004). Drugs and crime across America: Police chiefs speak out: A national survey among chiefs of police. Drug Strategies and Police Foundation. Retrieved September 30, 2006, from http://www.drugstrategies.org/about.html.

Health and Human Services. (1998). *Needle exchange programs: Part of a comprehensive HIV prevention plan.* Retrieved from http://www.hhs.gov/news/press/1998pres/980420b.html.

Helsedepartementet (Health Department). (2004, July). Bedre behandlingstilbud til rusmiddelmisbrukere [Better treatment offer for substance misusers]. Retrieved October 2006 from http://narkoman.net/doc/russtrategidokument.pdf.

Hirsch, A. (1999). *"Some days are harder than hard": Welfare reform and women with drug convictions in Pennsylvania.* Center for Law and Social Policy. Retrieved from http://www.clasp.org/publications/some_days_are_harder_than_hard.pdf.

Huddleston, C. W., III. (2005, May). Drug courts: An effective strategy for communities facing methamphetamine. *Bureau of Justice Assistance Bulletin.* Washington, DC: U.S. Department of Justice.

Huus, K. (2006). Crystal cartels alter face of U.S. meth epidemic. MSNBC. Retrieved October 1, 2006, from http://www.msnbc.msn.com/id/14817871.

Jewell, D. (2006, May 18). Gambling begets millions of neglected addicts. Community Newspaper Holdings, Inc. (CNHI) News Service. *MacAlester News-Capital* (Southeast Oklahoma). Retrieved October 2006 from http://www.mcalesternews.com/homepage.

Kandall, S. (1998). Women and addiction in the United States—1920 to the present. In C. L. Wetherington & A. B. Roman (Eds.), *Drug addiction research and the health of women* (National Institutes of Drug Abuse, NIH Publication No. 98-4290, pp. 53–80). Retrieved from http://www.nida.nih.gov/WHGD/DARHW Download2.html.

Kaplan, L. E. (2005). Dual relationships: The challenges for social workers in recovery. *Journal of Social Work Practice in the Addictions, 5*(3), 73–90.

Kerr v. Farrey, 95 F. 3rd 472 (7th Cir. 1996).

Kleiman, M. (1998). Drugs and drug policy: The case for a slow fix. *Issues in Science and Technologies, 15*(1). Retrieved from http://fas.org/drugs/slowfix.htm.

Krisberg, B., & Marchionna, S. (2006, April). Focus views from the National Council on Crime and Delinquency: Attitudes of U.S. voters. New Jersey Institute of Social Justice. Retrieved October 2006 from http://www.njisj.org/pubdocs.

Lewis, D. (2005, July 27). Top medical doctors, scientists and specialists urge major media outlets not to create "meth baby" myth. Public letter reprinted by National Advocates for Pregnant Women. Retrieved from http://www.advocatesforpregnantwomen.org.

Managed care takes a toll on substance-abuse treatment. (1999, July 15). Retrieved from http://www.jointogether.org.

Mauer, M., & Huling, T. (1995). Young Black Americans and the criminal justice system: Five years later. Washington, DC: Sentencing Project.

McNeece, C. A., & DiNitto, D. M. (2005). *Chemical dependency: A systems approach* (3rd ed.). Boston: Allyn & Bacon.

Miller, W. R., & Carroll, K. M. (2006). Drawing the science together: Ten principles, ten recommendations. In W. R. Miller & K. M. Carroll (Eds.), *Rethinking substance abuse: What the science shows* (pp. 293–312). New York: Guilford Press.

Morgenstern, J., & Blanchard, K. (2006). Welfare reform and substance abuse treatment for welfare recipients. *Alcohol Research and Health, 28*(1), 63–68.

Morgenstern, J., Nakashian, M., Woolis, D., Gibson, F., Bloom, N., & Kaulback, B. (2003). CASAWORKS for families: A new treatment model for substance-abusing parenting women on welfare. *Evaluation Review, 27,* 583–596.

Nadelman, E. (1997). Drug prohibition in the U.S.: Costs, consequences, and alternatives. In C. Reinarman & H. Levine (Eds.), *Crack in America: Demon drugs and social justice* (pp. 288–316). Berkeley: University of California Press.

Nadelman, E. (2001, May 18). Change of tune on drug policy? *Los Angeles Times.* Retrieved from http://www.drugpolicy.org.

National Gambling Impact Study Commission. (1999, June 18). *Report of the commission.* Washington, DC: U.S. Government Printing Office. Retrieved from http://govinfo.library.unt.edu/ngisc/reports/fullrpt.html.

National Survey on Drug Use and Health. (2005). National findings. SAMHSA, Office of Applied Studies. Retrieved October 1, 2006, from http://www.oas.samhsa.gov/NSDUH/2k5NSDUH/2k5results.htm.

Office of Applied Statistics (OAS). (2005). *Prisoners in 2004.* Washington, DC: Bureau of Justice Statistics. Retrieved October 2006 from http://www.ojp.usdoj.gov/bjs/pub/pdf/p04.pdf.

Office of Management and Budget. (2006). Meeting presidential goals. U.S. Department of Justice. Retrieved October 2006 from http://www.whitehouse.gov/omb/budget.

Paltrow, L. M. (2004, April 5). The pregnancy police. *AlterNet.* Retrieved from http://www.alternet.org.

Paltrow, L. M. (2006, July 17). Blaming pregnant women. Tom Paine, Common Sense, Institute for America's Future. Retrieved October 2006 from http://www.tompaine.com/print.

Parker, L. M. (2001, June 26). Court offers mentally ill an alternative to jail. *USA Today,* p. 1A.

Pew Research Center. (2001). Princeton Survey Research Associates Survey. Retrieved from http://www.people-press.org/drugs01rpt.htm.

Reinarman, C., & Levine, H. (1997). Crack in context: America's latest demon drug. In C. Reinarman & H. Levine (Eds.), *Crack in America: Demon drugs and social justice* (pp. 1–17). Berkeley: University of California Press.

Richie, B. E. (2004). Challenges incarcerated women face as they return to their communities. In M. Chesney-Lind & L. Pasko (Eds.), *Girls, women, and crime: Selected readings* (pp. 231–245). Thousand Oaks, CA: Sage.

Roesler, R. (2001, May 24). Forfeiture standards questioned. *Spokesman-Review,* pp. B1–B4.

Rosenbaum, M., & Irwin, K. (1998). Pregnancy, drugs, and harm reduction. In C. L. Wetherington & A. B. Roman (Eds.), *Drug addiction research and the health of women* (National Institute of Drug Abuse, NIH Publication No. 98-4290, pp. 309–318). Retrieved from http://www.nida.nih.gov/WHGD/DARHW-Download2.html.

Sagatun-Edwards, I. (2003). The legal response to substance abuse during pregnancy. In R. Muraskin (Ed.), *It's a crime: Women and justice* (2nd ed., pp. 129–151). Upper Saddle River, NJ: Prentice Hall.

Schilling, R., Dornig, K., & Lungren, L. (2006). Treatment of heroin dependence: Effectiveness, costs, and benefits of methadone maintenance. *Research on Social Work Practice, 16*(1), 48–56.

Schmidt, L., & McCarty, D. (2000). Welfare reform and the changing landscape of substance abuse services for low-income women. *Alcoholism: Clinical & Experimental Research, 24*(8), 1298–1311.

Seper, J. (2005). Patriot Act report targets meth. *Washington Times.* Retrieved October 1, 2006, from http://www.washtimes.com/national/20051211-110231-2800r.htm.

Siegal, L. (1997). The pregnancy police fight the war on drugs. In C. Reinarman & H. Levine (Eds.), *Crack in America: Demon drugs and social justice* (pp. 249–259). Berkeley: University of California Press.

Spencer, N. (2006, June 5). U.S. prison population continues to soar in 2005. World Socialist website. Retrieved October 2006 from http://www.wsws.org/articles/2006/jun2006/pris_j05_html.

Springer, D. W., McNeece, C. A., & Arnold, A. (2003). *Substance abuse treatment for criminal offenders.* Washington, DC: American Psychological Association.

Sterling, E., & Stewart, J. (2006, June 24). Undo this legacy of Len Bias's death. *Washington Post,* p. A21.

Strain, E., Bigelow, G., Liebson, I., & Stitzer, M. (1999). Moderate- vs. high-dose methadone in the treatment of opioid dependence: A randomized trial. *Journal of the American Medical Association, 281,* 1000–1005.

Striker, R. (2003, September 26). New federal civil forfeiture laws: Creating an army of informants. Friends of Liberty. Retrieved November 30, 2006, from http://www.sianews.com.

Substance Abuse and Mental Health Services Administration (SAMHSA). (2006). Drug Addiction Treatment Act of 2000 (DATA). Retrieved September 30, 2006, from http://buprenorphine.samhsa.gov/fulllaw.html.

Szalavitz, M. (1998, Winter). U.S. war on drugs, war on women. *On the Issues Magazine.* Retrieved from http://www.mapinc.org/drugnews/v99.n001.a06.html.

Taylor, B., Newton, P., & Brownstein, H. (2003). Drug use among adult female arrestees. *ADAM (Arrestee Drug Abuse Monitoring) 2000 Annual Report.* Washington, DC: U.S. Department of Justice.

Teslik, L. H. (2006). The forgotten drug war. Council on Foreign Relations. Retrieved September 30, 2006, from http://www.cfr.org/publication/10373/forgotten_drug_war.html?breadcrumb=%2Fbios%2F12286%2Flee_hudson_teslik.

Thevenot, C. (1999). Crisis of the anti-drug effort, 1999. The Criminal Justice Policy Foundation. Retrieved February 2007 from http://www.cjpf.org.

U.S. Department of Justice. (2006, August). Federal criminal justice trends, 2003. Office of Justice Programs. Retrieved October 2006 from http://www.ojp.usdoj.gov/bjs/abstract/fcjt03.htm.

U.S. Sentencing Commission, (2006, March). Final report on the impact of *U.S. v. Booker* on federal sentencing. Retrieved October 2006 from http://www.ussc.gov/.

van Wormer, K., & Bartollas, C. (2007). *Women and the criminal justice system* (2nd ed.). Boston: Allyn & Bacon.

Washton, A., & Zweben, J. (2006). *Treating alcohol and drug problems in psychotherapy practice: Doing what works.* New York: Guilford Press.

Epilogue:
Providing Options

Writing a book is a journey; there are the things one expects to find all mapped out and researched, and there are the unexpected discoveries along the way. In scholarly terms, there are the truths one plans to include and the truths that seem to emerge on their own accord from the process.

The major task in writing this book was to present an understanding of addiction, one of the most fascinating and baffling of human conditions, and an understanding that would encompass truths from biology, psychology, and sociology. The major challenge, one that never left us, was somehow to make sense of addiction. Addictive behavior (that insatiable thirst for something), by its very nature, of course makes no sense: What sense is there in a woman so hooked on winning at video poker that she won't take a break to use the toilet? What sense does it make when a father in Thailand sells his daughter into prostitution to get money for another fix of heroin or a previous leader of our country risks the presidency for a moment's gratification?

REVELATIONS

A major theme that emerged in this writing was the importance of motivation. How do you get people who have problems caused by chemicals they have learned to use to get a high (or to escape a low) to come in the door and say,

"I'd like to talk about my drug use" or, more generally, "I need someone to talk to." Programs built on abstinence-only models, the use of forced self-labeling, and urinalysis monitoring have their place, but such forms of treatment are hardly inviting. So the questions become not which of the treatments available (forget for the moment that only one may be available) is best, but how far and how fast will people go toward recovery? And how long will they maintain their progress when treatment is done?

Offering a warm, hospitable environment for treatment is critical. Being able to move to the rhythm set by the client/consumer, not by some faraway bureaucrat (from the insurance company or court), is critical as well. Here is where the theory known as motivational enhancement comes in. For each of the populations studied in this book—alcoholics; drug addicts; persons with eating disorders; compulsive gamblers, shoppers, and the like; addicts with mental disorders; the young and the old; African/Latino Americans and European Americans; straight and gay; and even families in need of help—we presented interventions geared toward the group's stages of change. Such interventions were timed, a sort of phase approach, to meet clients where they were rather than where we'd like them to be.

Central to motivationally based treatment, and to the strengths perspective of which it can be considered a part, is the element of choice. In this tradition, practitioners do not encourage clients to rely on the practitioner's expertise. Instead, through dialogue, they help clients discern the pros and cons (for their families and themselves) of any particular course of action. In addiction treatment, choice entails presenting options—for example, trying to find a compatible self-help group such as AA or Al-Anon (GA or OA), giving a Twelve-Step group a chance, linking up with a faith-based group if the client is inclined in a religious direction, attending a moderation management group to control the impulse to binge, or, alternatively, attending no group at all and perhaps choosing individual counseling periodically to work on reducing the harm. Several U.S. District Courts, as mentioned in chapter 13, have confirmed the legal right of criminal justice offenders to have an option to participate in a Twelve-Step group. Other clients should have this privilege as well. There is no "one size fits all" in treatment.

In summary, the imperative of providing options for enhancing client motivation was one of the truths that emerged in writing this book. Other truths emerged as well, some from research (e.g., the impact of craving as seen in brain imaging) and some through the creative process itself, the blending of science and art.

Delving into history, we gained a perspective on the present-day U.S. war on drugs, a "war" so clearly rooted in our puritanical past. We learned from a historical perspective how much the support for the legal prohibition of drugs has been associated with the fear of a given drug's effect on a specific minority group, whether of opium on the Chinese or marijuana on the Chicanos or crack cocaine on African Americans. The combination of wild media reports and politics has resulted in highly punitive legislation in each case. The projection of blame on foreign nations as a source of supply has been another political trend with historical roots.

A further revelation that emerged from our study of the history of treatment was just how formidable an advance was the introduction of the disease model. Within the context of American moralism and the work ethic, the spread of respect for the work of AA ensued, coupled with a belief that alcoholism was a disease. The shift from a label of the "bad" to the "mad," which has so often been belittled, was, on the whole, a positive development. Now treatment replaced punishment as the standard response. (Today, in many cases, the treatment *is* the punishment.) Respect for alcoholics and other drug addicts in recovery, for men and women who so often have assumed leadership roles in their communities, was an outgrowth of the alcoholism as a disease movement. Economic aspects of the movement did not go unnoticed; critics rightly ridiculed the hypocrisy of a society marketing harmful drugs such as tobacco and hard liquor and then marketing the treatment for those who succumbed to the grip of addiction. The *diseasing* of society—women who love too much, men who love too little, the credo that abstinence is the only cure for indulgence—was countered by a resurgence of a new form of *moralism*. The factor behind substance misuse is irresponsibility—so goes the explanation popularized in the 1990s.

Arguably, this opposing dogma reflects the maelstrom within North American society itself concerning the use of alcohol and other drugs. Although alcohol consumption is promoted vigorously by advertisers, it is simultaneously restricted through harsh legislation, especially concerning persons under the age of 21. Lacking is a focus on health and moderation. The criminalization of other drug use has led to a war on drugs, fought both militarily, to wipe out the supply side of drugs, and on the homefront, through mass incarcerations. Each of the two battling ideologies, both influential today, though with different audiences, describes a small part of the whole. Their sole common ground is in their narrowness and in their contempt for proponents of the opposite camp. Both extreme positions promote doctrine to the neglect of the *individual,* the human being described eloquently by Dennis Wrong (1976) as "that plausible creature whose wagging tongue so often hides the despair in his heart" (p. 112). In this case, the forgotten individual is the alcoholic or addict. Somewhere between overdiseasing the society and blaming addicts for their addictive behavior lies a middle way. Somewhere between criminalization and legalization of harmful drug use there is a middle way (as described in chapter 13) as well.

COMMENT

Increasingly, at the start of our new century, there is a realization that a single model of addiction and treatment does not fit all, even for offenders within the criminal justice system. There are varieties in treatment needs among males depending on their personality characteristics and the character of their addiction, and there are the special needs of women of childbearing age, of older men and women, and of gays and lesbians. Culturally specific programs for treatment effectiveness with various racial, religious, and ethnic populations are essential. Common to all these approaches is the realization that instead of trying to eliminate illegal drugs through fighting a war on drugs that is played out as a war on drug users, we can focus on limiting the damage that some people do to themselves and to society through this drug misuse.

Harm reduction services provide individualized treatment and strengthen community action. Harm reduction initiatives, in contrast to the "zero tolerance" approach, include policies such as needle exchange (which has been shown to reduce the spread of AIDS), methadone maintenance to enable addicts to live fairly normal lives, and therapy grounded in motivational enhancement principles to help clients move at their own pace from levels of heavy alcohol and other drug consumption to ever-decreasing levels of drug use. Harm reduction concentrates on achievable goals based on client self-determination; interventions are timed to relate to where the client is in his or her readiness to change. Interventions ideally are also timed to relate to the stages of recovery—biological, psychological, social, and spiritual.

LOOKING BACK

The three opening chapters of the book were conceived as a prologue to the more detailed discussion that followed. Chapter 1, The Nature of Addiction, took us right into the pain and sorrow associated with substance misuse and dependence in contrast to the miracle that is recovery. Chapter 2, Historical Perspectives, could have been subtitled When Will We Ever Learn? Here society's futile attempts to control the flow of drugs and people's bad habits were chronicled. The presentation of the strengths perspective (chapter 3), a conceptualization borrowed from social work, showed how a focus on people's strengths is a viable, indeed essential, element in addiction treatment.

Consistent with the biopsychosocial framework of addiction treatment, the core material of this text is organized into three major parts; each part corresponds to one key component in addiction, with ramifications for treatment. The *biological* component (Part II) focused on exciting new research uncovering the biochemical basis of tolerance, withdrawal, craving, and the memory factor in addiction. As science learns more and more about the key role of the brain in addiction and can demonstrate through magnetic resonance imaging how the addicted brain is different from the nonaddicted brain, there is fresh hope for new treatments. A description of such pharmaceutical remedies was the subject of chapter 5, Interventions Related to Biology. Strategies for group therapy, along with recommended exercises directed toward early-stage recovery, were provided in this chapter.

The *psychology* of addiction is the second major division of this text. Under the rubric of psychology—Part III of the book—first addiction and its treatment across the life span were viewed (chapter 6). Special attention was paid in this chapter to gender-specific treatment, assessment, spiritual healing, and relapse prevention strategies. Cognitive work was the theme of chapter 7 on behavioral addictions; group strategies geared toward the thinking–feeling configuration were described. For work with the dually diagnosed, the case was made in chapter 8 for integrated treatment (as opposed to separate treatment for mental disability and for addiction).

The *social aspects* of addiction made up the concluding portion of this book, Part IV. Chapter 9 explored family risks and resiliencies. The focus was on how addiction affects the lives of the addict's loved ones (sometimes to the point that the love flies out the window). Innovations of this chapter, and of this book, were the adaptation of the stages-of-change model to family recovery and the "rename, reframe, reclaim" framework for strengths-based treatment.

Strengths-based approaches were also directed toward the ethnic-sensitive interventions described in chapter 10 and the gender-specific topics covered in chapter 11. Half of the latter chapter dealt with sexual orientation and substance misuse issues. Chapter 12 examined mutual-help groups, especially Twelve-Step groups, from the strengths approach that is usually directed toward people as individuals. Here the questions considered were: What are the strengths of Twelve-Step treatment? How have Twelve-Step groups helped people? What are their strong points? What are some alternative mutual-help groups?

Addiction Treatment: A Strengths Perspective concluded with a survey of public policy. This time, harm reduction was viewed in policy terms rather than practice terms. Chapter 13 described governmental policies affecting treatment provision and funding as well. Far from a narrow or radical ideology, harm reduction is simply realistic and about saving lives. Broad in focus, harm reduction, as we saw in earlier chapters, helps clients make healthy choices; joining a Twelve-Step total-abstinence group is one such option.

The unique feature of this book, we think, is not the presentation of content in neat biopsychosocial divisions (a challenge in itself) or the inclusion of eating disorders, compulsive gambling, and Internet use along with the chemical addictions. No, the uniqueness is that our application of the principles of the strengths perspective was directed to treatment modalities at all and then that it was directed toward the strong points in various treatments that are often viewed as in opposition to one another. Consistent with this perspective, we extend our appreciation to the vibrant field of addictions and to the many dedicated workers who have passed this way. The large number of recovering alcoholics and other addicts in society, some of whom are professionals in the field themselves, is testimony to the quality of that work. The field is changing rapidly: But what now is, is not necessarily better than what was.

REFERENCE

Wrong, D. (1976). The oversocialized conception of man in modern sociology. In L. Coser & B. Rosenberg (Eds.), *Sociology theory* (pp. 104–113). New York: Macmillan.

Appendix: Resources

ADVOCACY/ASSOCIATIONS/COALITIONS

Addiction Treatment Forum (hundreds of updated websites and journals listed here): http://www.atforum.com

American Association for the Treatment of Opioid Dependence: http://www.aatod.org

American Society of Addiction Medicine: http://www.asam.org

Coalition Against Present Drug Policy: http://www.november.org

Drug Policy Alliance: http://www.drugpolicy.org

Harm Reduction Coalition: http://www.harmreduction.org

Mothers Against Drunk Driving: http://www.madd.org

Motivational Interviewing (resources for clinicians): http://www.motivationalinterviewing.org

National Association of Alcoholism and Drug Abuse Counselors: http://www.naadac.org

National Association of Drug Court Professionals: http://www.nadcp.org

National Association of Social Workers, ATOD section: http://www.naswdc.org (see section on ATOD)

National Drug Court Institute: http://www.ndci.org

Restorative Justice: http://www.restorativejustice.org

CENTERS/INSTITUTES/COUNCILS

American Council for Drug Education: http://www.acde.org

Center for Education and Drug Abuse Research: http://www.pitt.edu/~cedar

Child Welfare League of America: http://www.cwla.org

Drug Strategies, "Making Drug Policy at the State Level": http://www.drugstrategies.org

Hazelden Foundation: http://www.hazelden.org

Johnson Institute: http://johnsoninstitute.org

Moderation Management: http://www.moderation.org

National Center on Addiction and Substance Abuse at Columbia University: http://www.casacolumbia.org

Pride Institute (treatment for gays and lesbians): http://www.pride-institute.com

National Council on Alcoholism and Drug Dependence: http://www.ncadd.org

Rational Recovery: http://www.rational.org

Redfern Clinic: http://www.redfernclinic.com

Self Management and Recovery Training: http://www.smartrecovery.org

FEDERAL GOVERNMENT

Centers for Application of Prevention Technologies: http://captus.samhsa.gov

Drug and Crime Statistics: http://www.ojp.usdoj.gov

National Clearinghouse for Alcohol and Drug Information: http://www.ncadi.samhsa.gov

National Council on Alcohol and Drug Dependence: http://www.ncadd.org

National Institute on Alcohol Abuse and Alcoholism: http://www.niaaa.nih.gov

National Institute on Drug Abuse: http://www.nida.nih.gov

National Institute of Justice: http://www.ojp.usdoj.gov/nij

National Institute of Mental Health: http://www.nimh.nih.gov

National Women's Health Resource Center: http://www.healthywomen.org

Office of National Drug Control Policy: http://www.whitehousedrugpolicy.gov

Substance Abuse and Mental Health Services Administration: http://www.samhsa.gov

Substance Abuse Treatment Facility Locator: http://dasis3.samhsa.gov

INTERNATIONAL

(Canadian) Centre for Addiction and Mental Health: http://www.camh.net

Canadian Centre on Substance Abuse: http://www.ccsa.ca

International Harm Reduction Association: http://www.ihra.net

World Health Organization: www.who.org.int/substance_abuse/en

PREVENTION

Center for Substance Abuse Treatment: http://www.samhsa.gov/centers/csap/csap.html

Drug and Alcohol Treatment and Prevention Global Network: http://www.drugnet.net

Help for smokers: http://www.quitnet.org

Tobacco Information and Prevention Source: http://www.cdc.gov/tobacco

RESEARCH

Addiction Treatment Forum: http://www.atforum.com

American Indian Health Resources: http://www.ldb.org/vl/geo/america/indi_hn.htm

HelpGuide (gambling addiction): http://www.helpguide.org/mental/gambling_addiction.htm

Information for Practice: http://www.nyu.edu/socialwork/ip

Information on eating disorders, teen substance abuse, and gambling: http://www.addictions.net

Internet Addiction and Online Addiction: http://psychcentral.com/netaddiction.

Join Together (provides an e-mail alert service for weekly research): http://www.jointogether.org

Latino Link: http://www.latinolink.com

National Association of Lesbian and Gay Addiction Professionals: http://www.nalgap.org/PDF/Resources/LGBT.pdf

Social Work Curriculum on Alcohol Use Disorders: http://pubs.niaaa.nih.gov/publications/social/main.html

Web of Addictions: http://www.well.com/user/woa

SELF-HELP

Adult Children of Alcoholics World Service Organization: http://www.adultchildren.org

Alcoholics Anonymous: http://www.aa.org

Al-Anon/Alateen: http://www.alanon.org

Children of Alcoholics Foundation: http://www.coaf.org

Cocaine Anonymous: www.ca.org; www.cocaineanonymous.com

Dual diagnosis: http://www.doubletroubleinrecovery.org/; www.dualrecovery.org

Families of compulsive gamblers: http://www.gam-anon.org

Families of drug addicts: http://nar-anon.org/naranongroups.htm

Gamblers Anonymous: http://www.gamblersanonymous.org

Methadone Anonymous: http://www.methadone-anonymous.org

Methamphetamine group: http://www.crystalmeth.org

Narcotics Anonymous: http://www.na.org

National Organization on Fetal Alcohol Syndrome: http://www.nofas.org

SMART Recovery: http://www.smartrecovery.org

Students Against Destructive Decisions (also Students Against Drunk Driving): http://www.saddonline.com

Women for Sobriety: http://www.womenforsobriety.org

INDEX